Social Problems: *A Modern Approach*

Social Problems:
A Modern Approach

Edited by Howard S. Becker
Department of Sociology
Northwestern University

John Wiley & Sons, Inc., New York · London · Sydney

SECOND PRINTING, JUNE, 1967

Copyright © 1966 by John Wiley & Sons, Inc.

All Rights Reserved
This book or any part thereof
must not be reproduced in any form
without the written permission of the publisher.

Library of Congress Catalog Card Number: 66-22835
Printed in the United States of America

Contributors

HOWARD S. BECKER, Professor of Sociology, Northwestern University, Evanston, Illinois

WARNER BLOOMBERG, JR., Professor, Department of Urban Affairs and Extension Division, University of Wisconsin, Milwaukee, Wisconsin

LEONARD J. DUHL, M.D., Consultant, Office of the Secretary, Department of Housing and Urban Development, Washington, D.C.; Associate Clinical Professor of Psychiatry, George Washington University, Washington, D.C.

ARNOLD S. FELDMAN, Professor of Sociology, Northwestern University, Evanston, Illinois

EDGAR Z. FRIEDENBERG, Professor of Sociology, University of California, Davis, California

HERBERT J. GANS, Center for Urban Education, New York, New York; Professor of Sociology, Teachers College, Columbia University, New York, New York

SCOTT GREER, Director, The Center for Metropolitan Studies, Evanston, Illinois; Professor of Political Science and Sociology, Northwestern University, Evanston, Illinois

IRVING LOUIS HOROWITZ, Professor of Sociology, Washington University, St. Louis, Missouri

ROBERT L. LEOPOLD, M.D., Associate Professor of Clinical Psychiatry, University of Pennsylvania, Philadelphia; Senior Psychiatric Consultant, Peace Corps, Washington, D.C.

RAYMOND W. MACK, Professor of Sociology, Northwestern University, Evanston, Illinois

S. M. MILLER, Professor of Education and Sociology, New York University, New York, New York

BERNICE L. NEUGARTEN, Professor of Human Development, University of Chicago, Chicago, Illinois

MARTIN REIN, Associate Professor, Department of Social Work and Social Research, Bryn Mawr College, Bryn Mawr, Pennsylvania

LEO F. SCHNORE, Professor of Sociology, University of Wisconsin, Madison, Wisconsin

MARTIN TROW, Associate Professor of Sociology, University of California, Berkeley, California

STANTON WHEELER, Russell Sage Foundation, New York, New York

HAROLD L. WILENSKY, Professor of Sociology in the Department of Sociology and Research Sociologist in the Institute of Industrial Relations, University of California, Berkeley, California

Contents

Introduction, Howard S. Becker — 1

PART ONE PROBLEMS OF THE LIFE CYCLE

Chapter 1 Adolescence as a Social Problem,
 Edgar Friedenberg — 35
 2 Two Problems in American Public Education,
 Martin Trow — 76
 3 Work as a Social Problem, Harold L. Wilensky — 117
 4 The Aged in American Society,
 Bernice L. Neugarten — 167

PART TWO PROBLEMS OF DEVIANCE

Chapter 5 Delinquency and Crime, Stanton Wheeler — 201
 6 Mental Illness, Leonard J. Duhl, M.D., and
 Robert L. Leopold, M.D. — 277

PART THREE PROBLEMS OF COMMUNITY AND NATION

Chapter	7	Race Relations, RAYMOND W. MACK	317
	8	Community Organization, WARNER BLOOMBERG, JR.	359
	9	Poverty, Inequality, and Policy, S. M. MILLER AND MARTIN REIN	426
	10	Problems of Housing and the Renewal of the City, SCOTT GREER	517
	11	Popular Culture in America: Social Problem in a Mass Society or Social Asset in a Pluralist Society? HERBERT J. GANS	549

PART FOUR WORLD PROBLEMS

Chapter	12	Population Problems in Perspective, LEO F. SCHNORE	625
	13	New Nations: The Problems of Change, ARNOLD S. FELDMAN	655
	14	The Conflict Society: War as a Social Problem, IRVING LOUIS HOROWITZ	695

Name Index 751
Subject Index 763

Illustrations by Lenord Bethel

Social Problems: *A Modern Approach*

Introduction

▼▼▼▼▼▼▼▼▼▼▼▼▼▼▼▼▼▼▼▼▼▼▼▼▼▼▼▼▼▼

Howard S. Becker

Sociology, indeed, social science generally, has a double perspective. Sociology concerns itself with current social ills. At the same time some sociologists are also interested in constructing general theories to explain human behavior. The tension between the drive for a deeper understanding of what is going on in the society we live in, what Robert E. Park called The Big News,[1] and the thrust toward a deeper understanding of the nature of man and society in the abstract characterizes the best of present-day sociology. The scientific study of social problems represents in some ways a merger of the two interests.

Sociologists investigating social problems are not content to make surveys of existing conditions, pointing to wrongs that need to be put right. They concern themselves with how problems come about and are perpetuated and in so doing necessarily attempt to reach conclusions that apply to a broader range of phenomena than the specific problem they study. They study classes of problems and the underlying social conditions that give rise to them.

But the student of social problems still retains an interest in present-day society as an object worthy of study because the problems are those of his own time and place, problems that his knowledge, insight, and skill may help solve.

What Is a Social Problem?

We must first understand clearly what the term *social problem* refers to. At first glance the referent seems obvious—everybody knows

[1] Robert E. Park, *Race and Culture* (Glencoe, Ill.: The Free Press, 1950), p. ix.

what a social problem is. Indeed, the table of contents of this book is a common sense definition of social problems—social problems are problems like crime, poverty, and race relations. For scientific purposes, however, we need more than a list. We need an abstract definition.

Fuller and Myers, a generation ago, presented a definition of social problems that is implicit in much of this book. Though their examples are dated, their conception is as useful now as it was when first presented.

> A social problem is a condition which is defined by a considerable number of persons as a deviation from some social norm which they cherish. Every social problem thus consists of an objective condition and a subjective definition. The objective condition is a verifiable situation which can be checked as to existence and magnitude (proportions) by impartial and trained observers, e.g., the state of our national defense, trends in the birth rate, unemployment, etc. The subjective definition is the awareness of certain individuals that the condition is a threat to certain cherished values.
>
> The objective condition is necessary but not in itself sufficient to constitute a social problem. Although the objective condition may be the same in two different localities, it may be a social problem in only one of these areas, e.g. discrimination against Negroes in the south as contrasted with discrimination in the north; divorce in Reno as contrasted with divorce in a Catholic community. *Social problems are what people think they are* and if conditions are not defined as social problems by the people involved in them, they are not problems to those people, although they may be problems to outsiders or to scientists, e.g., the condition of poor southern sharecroppers is a social problem to the braintrusters of the New Deal but not to many southern landowners.[2]

The central tenet of the Fuller-Myers approach is that a social problem consists of an objective condition in society that is defined by members of the society as a problem about which something ought to be done. There are ambiguities in this view that need to be clarified and implications that need to be explained.

One ambiguity concerns the role of the "objective conditions" in

---

[a] Richard C. Fuller and Richard R. Myers, "The Natural History of a Social Problem," *American Sociological Review*, 6 (June 1941), p. 320. See also Willard Waller, "Social Problems and the Mores," *American Sociological Review*, 1 (December 1936), pp. 922–933. For a less relativistic view of the nature of social problems, see Robert K. Merton, "Social Problems and Sociological Theory," in Robert K. Merton and Robert A. Nisbet, eds., *Contemporary Social Problems* (New York: Harcourt, Brace and World, 1961), pp. 697–737.

INTRODUCTION

the creation of a social problem. Some sociologists argue that the existence of a social problem can be detected objectively whether it is defined as a problem or not. If the members of a society have values and purposes negated by some social condition, then, even when they accept that condition and do not regard it as problematic, it is a social problem. A hypothetical example will help us.

The sex ratio of newborn infants normally runs about 105 to 107 males per 100 females. But women now live longer than men so that in the total population, according to the 1960 Census, there were only 97.8 men for every 100 women. And the proportion of men to women varies at different ages, with the excess of males persisting until age 24 when the excess shifts to one of women. The sex ratio in the population also varies from one time period to the next; in 1910 there were 106 men to every 100 women.[3] But the changes are slow enough that the institutions of our society—kinship, marriage, education, work, housing, and so on—can adapt themselves to the changing number of men and women present in the society.

Suppose that for whatever reason the sex ratio at birth changes suddenly and that the proportion of women surviving increases. In this hypothetical society the new excess of females would have far-reaching consequences for social institutions. The proportion of unmarried women might rise far beyond what it is now, creating grave discontent with our institutions of courtship and marriage. We are inclined to think of some kinds of work as "men's work" and others as "women's work" and, if the sex ratio in the population were to change so radically, there would be too many women for the jobs identified as women's and not enough men to do all the work defined as men's. Problems would arise about the allocation of people to jobs; women would begin to invade men's occupations and the repercussions might be felt in the organization of the family, the appearance of new problems of mental health, and community politics.

In what sense could such a change in the distribution of the sexes be considered a social problem? In what sense would the objective condition in and of itself be problematic? Fuller and Myers suggest that no objective condition is necessarily a social problem. The condition may be troublesome, but members of the society can adapt to it, changing their institutions and practices to cope with the troubles the condition creates. They may change their values and purposes, arriving at a compromise between society as it was and society as it will be.

[3] *Statistical Abstract of the United States* (Washington, D.C.: Government Printing Office, 1963), p. 24.

From this point of view, an objective condition becomes a social problem only if we assume that society must be maintained as it is.[4] Insofar as a sociologist adopts this stance, he can indeed discover objective conditions that will make it difficult to maintain society in a state of equilibrium. But neither social scientists nor laymen agree unanimously that society must be maintained as it is. And, if they did, they might not agree on what in particular was to be maintained without change.

This issue recalls a time when the study of social problems was called "social pathology." The term evokes an analogy to medicine which is appropriate to the view that social problems arise out of objective conditions but which is inaccurate in one significant way. When we speak of pathology in the human body, our knowledge of human physiology allows us to identify the objective conditions that interfere with the normal functions of the organism. A tumor, a blood clot, a broken bone, a derangement of the metabolism all interfere with the way the body normally works.

We cannot, however, describe an analogous "normal state" of human society. It is true that all the data we would need for such a description have not yet been collected and all the research is not yet done. But our knowledge of human physiology is not complete either. In the case of physiology, however, we have reason to believe that all the data, if they are ever gathered, can lead to a useful description of the normal human organism; deviations from the normal state can then be defined as pathological. We have no reason to believe that any amount of research, no matter how much, can produce a description of a "normal society" that deserves to be maintained as it is.

There is little essential disagreement, either among scientists themselves or between scientists and laymen, about what constitutes normal physical functioning, for it is commonly agreed that to be "healthy" is to have no physical difficulty that interferes with carrying out one's daily activities. But there are fundamental disagreements among both scientists and laymen about what constitutes a "healthy" society, for people define the good society in various ways according to their interests and values. And interests and values differ among people placed differently in society. The interests of a rich man are not those of a poor man, and the values of a man from one ethnic or religious group may differ from those of a man from another group. No amount of factual research can resolve these differences, for they do not arise from a disagreement about facts

[4] See C. Wright Mills, "The Professional Ideology of Social Pathologists," *American Journal of Sociology*, 49 (September 1943), pp. 165–180.

but from disagreement about how facts are defined and interpreted.

To return to our hypothetical example, a change in the sex ratio would have consequences that scientific research could uncover. But research could not identify the condition as a social problem, for its problematic character would arise from how people defined its consequences. Social scientists who think society is operating relatively efficiently as it is might view the consequences as upsetting and troublesome and thus see a social problem. Others might think the society was already in bad shape and welcome the changed sex ratio because it made possible changes in institutions that were not functioning well; they would not view the development as a social problem.

In short, as Fuller and Myers argued, no objective condition is necessarily a social problem; social problems are what people think they are. But where does that leave the role of objective conditions? Can people call *anything* a social problem? The question has two parts: can people define *any* condition that exists as a social problem, and can people define a condition that does *not* exist—an illusion—as a social problem? Let us consider the latter question first.

People clearly *can* define nonexistent conditions as social problems. The inhabitants of Salem, Massachusetts believed in witches and imagined that their community was infested with them. They took stern measures to deal with the supposed social problem.[5] Today we know that there are no witches and, consequently, we cannot have that social problem. Many people have believed, in more recent times, that the earth is about to be invaded by flying saucers from other planets and consider this an important problem that needs to be dealt with; so far as we know, their belief is erroneous.[6]

If people can define conditions that do not exist as social problems, it necessarily follows that they can also define any condition that does exist as a social problem. Think of the varied "problems" that have bothered one group or another in the not-so-distant past: dancing on Sunday, dancing at any time, women smoking, anybody smoking, not enough highways, and too many highways in the wrong places. The examples may be frivolous, but they suggest that any set of objective

---

[5] Marion L. Starkey, *The Devil in Massachusetts* (New York: Alfred A. Knopf, 1949), gives an account of the witchcraft trials of colonial Massachusetts. For description of present-day witchcraft, see "Real Witches at Work," *Life*, 57 (November 13, 1964), pp. 55–62.

[6] Leon Festinger, Henry W. Riecken, and Stanley Schachter, *When Prophecy Fails* (Minneapolis: University of Minnesota Press, 1956), describes a contemporary flying saucer cult. Also see J. L. Simmons, "On Maintaining Deviant Belief Systems: A Case Study," *Social Problems*, 11, 3 (Winter 1964), pp. 25–26.

conditions can, from some point of view, be defined as a social problem.

If any set of objective conditions, even nonexistent ones, can be defined as a social problem, it is clear that the conditions themselves do not either produce the problem or constitute a necessary component of it. Why must we include them in our conception of social problems? We include them because the definitions of most social problems refer to an area of social life that objectively and verifiably exists. Most citizens and almost all social scientists in modern society feel the need to buttress their assertions about the existence of a social problem by referring to facts, and they are aware that arguments which can be shown to have no factual foundation can be disposed of easily by opponents.

For this reason, most definitions of social problems have a factual basis. The definitions may be mistaken; they may leave out important elements; they may be open to argument. But they refer to a situation or condition in society that is real enough to be argued about. Thus some scientists and laymen have held that comic books, with their emphasis on violence and sex, constitute an important social problem because reading them leads to juvenile delinquency and sex crimes.[7] Whatever disagreement we have with this view, we cannot argue that there are no comic books, no delinquents, or no sex crimes. But we could argue that there are no witches today, were anyone so foolhardy as to insist that there are and that they constitute a social problem, and most of the country believes that those who await the arrival of the flying saucers from outer space are misinformed.

Objective conditions are an important part of our conception of a social problem, then, because the definition of a social problem by participants in the society is likely to refer to a situation in society which can, as Fuller and Myers say, "be checked as to existence and magnitude (proportions) by impartial and trained observers."[8] The more crucial ambiguity in the Fuller-Myers approach has to do with *subjective* definitions of the problem, and it is to these we now turn.

The difficulty with the Fuller-Myers approach to the subjective aspect of social problems is that it does not specify who the "people" are in the formula "social problems are what people think they are." They seem to suggest that a community will reach a consensus about what does or does not constitute a social problem, and they fail to consider the possibility of differential definitions of the same problem by people differently placed in the society. Since this conception of multiple

[7] See Frederic Wertham, *Seduction of the Innocent* (New York: Rinehart, 1954).
[8] Fuller and Myers, *op. cit.*

points of view on social problems plays an important role in many of the chapters in this book, we shall explore it further.

The chapters of this book do not so much treat "social problems" as they do areas in which various people—citizens, politicians, professional experts, cultural critics, social scientists, and other interested parties—define many kinds of social problems as arising.

A problem is not the same to all interested parties; indeed, there will be as many definitions of the problem as there are interested parties. When we speak of adolescence or race relations, the terms do not define a problem. They only point to phenomena someone defines as a problem; the definitions will not all be alike.

Consider race relations. Although clearly an area of major social concern, it is not clear what the "problem" is. For the Negro and for many white citizens as well, the problem is how to achieve as rapidly as possible the full participation of the Negro in American society. For other whites the problem is different: the possible loss of social advantages they have long enjoyed at the expense of Negroes. For many politicians and for some social scientists the problem is the tension and violence of a situation in which Negroes demand rights that whites are unwilling to grant. For professionals—social workers and educators, among others—the problem is to undo the harm done by generations of segregation and discrimination so that the Negro will be equipped to take advantage of his rights. This does not exhaust the list: parents worry about preserving the neighborhood school, realtors worry about the effect of open housing laws on their business, and diplomats worry about the effect of our racial crises on the leaders of the new African and Asian nations.

Laymen typically define problems in ways dictated by their immediate interests as citizens, interests that develop around the roles they play as community residents, taxpayers, parents and family members, workers, and potential victims of war or depression. In each role they have satisfactions they want to maximize, dissatisfactions they want to avoid. They are likely to define as social problems events or situations that interfere with the satisfactions or make the dissatisfactions more likely to occur.

Many professions, among them education, social work, medicine, law, and politics, have the responsibility of dealing with areas of social life that are likely to be defined as problematic. Professionals do not define problems in these areas the same way laymen do. Each profession has its historically developed and sanctioned theories and techniques, and professions see problems in ways consistent with their theories and amenable to their techniques. Thus social work has traditionally seen the locus of most problems in the individual, in part because the techniques of casework developed over the years are suitable for work with individuals. Since they lack the techniques to deal with problems of social structure (such as segregation), social workers are unlikely to define social problems in ways that take account of the structural context of their clients' problem behavior.

In addition, professionals consider the effect on their income and professional prestige of becoming involved in a given problem area. They may decline to define a problem as meriting their attention because by dealing with it their own income or professional standing may be affected adversely. The laws governing narcotics addiction, as these laws have been interpreted by the Supreme Court, give physicians the right to treat addicts in any way that is consistent with good medical practice. But the Federal Narcotics Bureau has defined outpatient treatment of addicts as illegal (even though the Court has refused to uphold the ruling), and few physicians have been willing to risk their professional standing by challenging the Bureau's ruling. They have accepted a definition of the problem that says compulsory hospital or prison treatment is necessary.[9]

Social scientists, finally, also see social problems differently. They too have favorite theories and methods that affect their conceptions of social problem areas. Specifically, it has been argued that social science theories may have a conservative bias, that the concepts used in analysis of social problems have concealed in them a tendency to regard problems as the "natural" consequences of the operation of society, not amenable to rational plans for change. These theories claim it would be wrong to attempt change in problem areas, for this would disrupt the accommodation or equilibrium that has been reached among opposing forces in the society. Myrdal, the great student of the Negro problem in the United States, criticized a number of common concepts in social science for their do-nothing bias:

> The presence of this same static and fatalistic valuation in the hidden *ethos* of contemporary social science is suggested by some of the terminology found throughout the writings of many sociologists, such as "balance," "harmony," "equilibrium," "adjustment," "maladjustment,"

[9] See Edwin M. Schur, *Narcotic Addiction in Britain and America: The Impact of Public Policy* (Bloomington: Indiana University Press, 1962); *Drug Addiction: Crime or Disease*, Interim and Final Reports of the Joint Committee of the American Bar Association and the American Medical Association on Narcotic Drugs (Bloomington: Indiana University Press, 1962); and Alfred R. Lindesmith, *The Addict and the Law* (Bloomington: Indiana University Press, 1965).

"organization," "disorganization," "accommodation," "function," "social process" and "cultural lag." While they all . . . have been used advantageously to *describe* empirically observable situations, they carry within them the tendency to give a do-nothing (laissez-faire) valuation of those situations. How the slip occurs is easily understandable: When we speak of a social situation being in harmony, or having equilibrium, or its forces organized, accommodated, or adjusted to each other, there is the almost inevitable implication that some sort of ideal has been attained, whether in terms of "individual happiness" or the "common welfare." Such a situation is, therefore, evaluated as "good" and a movement in the direction is "desirable." The negative terms—disharmony, disequilibrium, disorganization—correspondingly describe an undesirable situation, as indicated by the etymological connection of their prefixes to the word "bad." [10]

Though the charge has merit, the difficulties Myrdal describes can be overcome, as he suggests, by being conscious of the biases contained in one's concepts and consciously correcting for them. The social scientist can, for instance, ask how to create "disorganization" that would have constructive results, instead of uncritically accepting the implied suggestion that disorganization is necessarily bad.[11]

The social scientist's approach to social problems, supposing that problems of bias have been adequately dealt with, has an advantage over that of interested laymen and professionals. As he studies and defines problems he makes use of techniques and theories which are unavailable to others and which, however imperfect, give him a more complete understanding of the relevant facts and their interrelations. Techniques of observation, interviewing, and documentation, used by hundreds of investigators and improved over the years by voluminous analysis and criticism, place a greater range of better understood facts at his disposal. Systematic techniques of data analysis, statistical and otherwise, make it more likely that he will not ignore relevant facts and that he will be aware of their probable errors and the limits of their applicability. The theories of society and social organization used by social scientists point out in an abstract and systematic way the multiple connections and causal links between institutions that are often hidden from view by commonsense analyses.

In any event, it is important to realize not only that social problems come into existence by being defined as problems, but also that the

---

[10] Gunnar Myrdal, *An American Dilemma* (New York: Harper and Brothers, 1944), pp. 1055–1056.
[11] Harold Garfinkel, "Some Sociological Concepts and Methods for Psychiatrists," *Psychiatric Research Reports*, 6 (1956), pp. 181–195.

same set of objective conditions may be defined as a problem in many different ways. This realization has both theoretical and practical implications. The theoretical implication is that, in reaching an understanding of the problem area, we must consider not only the objective conditions but also the varying definitions of the problem by the various groups that have an interest in it, because the definitions themselves play a role in giving a problem the form it has in society. To take an obvious case, it has been argued persuasively that the narcotics problem in the United States is created by the reaction to addicts by law enforcement agencies rather than by the characteristic effects of narcotics. Experts argue that addicts steal and engage in other kinds of petty crime primarily because the drugs they need are available to them only on the unlawful market, at a price many times higher than if they were available legally. The drug problem, according to these experts, is created by its *definition* as a problem.[12]

The practical implication of multiple definitions of social problems by various interested groups arises because the definition of a problem usually contains, implicitly or explicitly, suggestions for how it may be solved. Many of the crucial questions in a problem area have to do with possible solutions; given the definition as a problem, the practical question that confronts citizens and experts is what can be done about it. Arguments over measures to be taken are often difficult to resolve precisely because the varying answers to the questions are contained, waiting to be deduced, in the definitions proposed by supporters of different measures.

Alcohol use and alcoholism are considered by many to be among our serious social problems. Prohibitionist groups define the use of alcohol as a moral problem, believing that any consumption of alcoholic beverages is sinful. In line with this definition, they believe that the only effective way to deal with the problem is to prohibit the manufacture and sale of alcoholic beverages.[13] Many experts in the fields of health and welfare, influenced by psychiatric theory, view alcoholism as a disease in which the afflicted person has lost the ability to control his drinking.[14] This point of view allows them to see the solution to the problem in the use of clinics and hospitals, staffed by physicians and other trained personnel, providing psychiatric or quasi-psychiatric

---

[12] See the sources cited in footnote 9 and Alfred R. Lindesmith, *Opiate Addiction* (Bloomington, Ind.: Principia Press, 1947).

[13] See Joseph R. Gusfield, *Symbolic Crusade: Status Politics and the American Temperance Movement* (Urbana: University of Illinois Press, 1963).

[14] For a complete discussion of this view, see E. M. Jellinek, *The Disease Concept of Alcoholism* (New Haven, Conn.: Hillhouse Press, 1960).

treatment to alcoholics. Police, on the other hand, and others are likely to define alcoholism as a problem of public decorum: it is troublesome and aesthetically offensive to have the streets of the city littered with Skid Row drunks. They would solve the problem by gathering up drunks and taking them to a "drunk tank" or county farm or, alternatively, confining them to one area of the city, where easily offended people need not go.

The Development of a Social Problem

If we understand that social problems are what interested parties think they are, we must recognize that they become defined as problems as the result of a lengthy process of development which has identifiable stages. Fuller and Myers called attention to this when they spoke of *the natural history of a social problem:*

> Social problems do not arise full-blown, commanding community attention and evoking adequate policies and machinery for their solution. On the contrary, we believe that social problems exhibit a temporal course of development in which different phases or stages may be distinguished. Each stage anticipates its successor in time and each succeeding stage contains new elements which mark it off from its predecessor. A social problem thus conceived as always being in a dynamic state of "becoming" passes through the natural history stages of awareness, policy determination, and reform.[15]

We need not accept the terms they use, or the stages they posit, to share Fuller and Myers' principal idea: to understand a social problem fully, we must know how it came to be defined as a social problem.

This idea of social problems sees them as the result of a basically "political" process, a process in which opposing views are put forward, argued, and compromised; in which people are motivated by various interests to attempt to persuade others of their views so that public action will be taken to further ends they consider desirable; in which one attempts to have the problem officially recognized so that the power and authority of the state can be engaged on one's side.

Little research has been done on the stages of development of social problems, so we cannot present a commonly accepted scheme of analysis.[16] Instead, we can indicate the kinds of questions that might be

---
[15] Fuller and Myers, *op. cit.*, p. 321.
[16] For theoretical schemes in the related field of collective behavior, see Herbert Blumer, "Collective Behavior," in Alfred M. Lee, ed., *New Outline of the Princi-*

raised in exploring the process in the case of a specific problem.

The first step in the development of a social problem comes when some person or group sees a set of objective conditions as problematic, posing a danger or containing the seeds of future difficulties. To whom does the condition appear troublesome? What brings it to his attention as a potential problem? What kinds of conditions are likely to be problems to what kinds of people? What distinguishes conditions that come to be viewed as potential problems from others (from an objective standpoint equally problematic) which do not provoke that response?

After a problem has come to someone's attention, concern with it must become shared and widespread if it is to achieve the status of a social problem. The person who originally noticed it must point it out to others and convince them the situation is dangerous enough to require public action. We can raise the same kind of questions about the second step in the process as we did about the first. What kinds of people will the original definer of the problem be able to convince that his argument is sound? Who, on the contrary, will think his view foolish or mistaken? What tactics are most successful in winning support for the definition of a condition as a problem? What is the role of the mass media of communication—newspapers, magazines, radio, and television—in promoting widespread concern with a problem, and how does a person who wishes to define a new social problem get access to them?

When widespread concern has been aroused, it must be embodied in an organization or institution if the problem is to achieve lasting existence as a defined social problem. An existing organization may take the responsibility for dealing with the new problem, as the police were more or less forced to do when "juvenile delinquency" was defined as a social problem, or a new organization may be created, as the Narcotics Bureau was created to deal with the newly defined problem of drug addiction. In the first case, the problem will be redefined, so far as possible, by the personnel of the organization to conform with their more general opinion of the character of social problems. If, for instance, a problem like alcoholism is made the responsibility of a mental health agency, its psychiatrically oriented staff will redefine it as a problem of mental health; the police, given the responsibility, will define the situa-

---

ples of Sociology (New York: Barnes and Noble, 1946); Neil J. Smelser, *Theory of Collective Behavior* (New York: The Free Press of Glencoe, 1963); Ralph H. Turner and Lewis M. Killian, *Collective Behavior* (Englewood Cliffs, N.J.: Prentice-Hall, 1957); and Kurt Lang and Gladys Engel-Lang, *Collective Dynamics* (New York: Thomas Y. Crowell, 1961).

tion as a problem of law enforcement. If a new agency is created, it is likely to be staffed by members of one of the established professions, and the same process results.

Once some organization takes charge of a problem, the group of aroused citizens whose collective concern prompted the development is likely to lose interest. They have, after all, turned the problem over to an organization so that they need no longer worry about it.

One of the interesting features of this stage in the development of a social problem is that the personnel of the organization devoted to the problem tend to build their lives and careers around its continued existence. They become attached to "their" problem, and anything that threatens to make it disappear or diminish in importance is a threat. What can be said of "rule enforcers" working in organizations dedicated to controlling deviance may be applied with equal justice to the staff of any organization devoted to dealing with a social problem, even in fields such as race relations, housing, or education:

> In justifying the existence of his position, the rule enforcer faces a double problem. On the one hand, he must demonstrate to others that the problem still exists: the rules he is supposed to enforce have some point, because infractions occur. On the other hand, he must show that his attempts at enforcement are effective and worthwhile, that the evil he is supposed to deal with is in fact being dealt with adequately. Therefore, enforcement organizations, particularly when they are seeking funds, typically oscillate between two kinds of claims. First, they say that by reason of their efforts the problem they deal with is approaching solution. But, in the same breath, they say the problem is perhaps worse than ever (though through no fault of their own) and requires renewed and increased effort to keep it under control. Enforcement officials can be more vehement than anyone else in their insistence that the problem they are supposed to deal with is still with us, in fact is more with us than ever. In making these claims, enforcement officials provide good reason for continuing the existence of the position they occupy.[17]

In summary, every social problem has a history and develops through a series of stages, each stage reflecting a change in who defines the problem, the kind of definition it is given, and the resulting actions taken in an attempt to solve the problem.

The social scientist ordinarily begins his analysis of a social problem by considering the natural history of the problem and the various definitions proposed by interested parties. Each contributor to this book

---

[17] Howard S. Becker, *Outsiders: Studies in the Sociology of Deviance* (New York: The Free Press of Glencoe, 1963), p. 157.

has, in one way or another, attempted this in the beginning of his chapter, confirming the point that no social problem is solely a matter of objective conditions but is instead the product of a process of definition.

The Social Context of Social Problems

Though the social scientist is constantly aware that social problems are the result of definitions made by interested parties, and that there may be no objective condition corresponding to the definitions, he ordinarily assumes that the area of society where the problem is alleged to exist contains some elements, the investigation of which will shed light on the supposed problem. Even though he does not accept the current definition of the problem, he is prepared to investigate the problem area, to see what data he can gather and interpret in the light of accepted theories of society. He may not, for instance, accept the notion, promulgated by police and the press, that the narcotics addict is a dangerous criminal, irrevocably "hooked" on his drug; he may not accept the definition of psychiatrists that addicts are emotionally ill and continue the use of drugs because of their illness. But he supposes that there are people using drugs and that they are involved in a network of relations with the police, their families, non-drug-using associates, and other drug users. He supposes that his investigations will enable him to discover "what is really going on." Most social scientists assume the existence of a reality describable, albeit with some risk of error, by the methods of research at their disposal.

How does the social scientist describe and analyze a social problem area? We can answer briefly by saying that he identifies it as having the qualities of one or more of the kinds of social organization described in his general theory and then proceeds to describe those aspects of reality the theory defines as important. Thus, he does not see the problem as one to be investigated solely or primarily by studying the characteristics of the people involved in it; instead, he looks to the network of social relationships and organizations within which people act for the explanation of why they act as they do and why others think what they are doing is problematic.

C. Wright Mills made the same point, in a slightly different way, when he distinguished between *private troubles* and *public issues*:

> *Troubles* occur within the character of the individual and within the range of his immediate relations with others; they have to do with his self and with those limited areas of social life of which he is directly and

personally aware. Accordingly, the statement and the resolution of troubles properly lie within the individual as a biographical entity and within the scope of his immediate milieu—the social setting that is directly open to his personal experience and to some extent his willful activity. A trouble is a private matter: values cherished by an individual are felt by him to be threatened.

Issues have to do with matters that transcend these local environments of the individual and the range of his inner life. They have to do with the organization of many such milieus into the institutions of an historical society as a whole, with the ways various milieus overlap and interpenetrate to form the larger structure of social and historical life. An issue is a public matter: some value cherished by publics is felt to be threatened. Often there is a debate about what that value really is and about what it is that threatens it. This debate is often unfocused if only because it is the nature of an issue that it cannot be defined by immediate and everyday environments of ordinary men. An issue often involves a crisis in institutional arrangements, and often too it involves what Marxists call "contradictions" or "antagonisms."

Consider unemployment. When, in a city of 100,000, only one man is unemployed, that is his personal trouble, and for its relief we properly look to the character of the man, his skills, and his immediate opportunities. But when in a nation of 50 million employees, 15 million men are unemployed, that is an issue, and we may not hope to find its solution within the range of opportunities open to any one individual. The very structure of opportunities has collapsed. Both the correct statement of the problem and the range of possible solutions require us to consider the economic and political institutions of the society, and not merely the personal situation and character of a scatter of individuals.[18]

The social scientist analyzes a social problem area, to put the matter another way, by locating it in a social context: he sees it as a public issue of social structure to be analyzed as he ordinarily analyzes structural problems. This does not mean, to avoid possible misunderstanding, that in some vague and unspecified way he takes into account the presence of other people; nor does it mean that, sentimentally, he decides that the problem is not the "fault" of the people involved but of society. It means something more specific: he uses the available framework of sociological theory to identify the social relationships and social structures in which people participate, the constraints that such participation places on their behavior, the relation of structures and relationships to one another and to society as a whole, and the way these interrelations affect the actions taken by

---

[18] C. Wright Mills, *The Sociological Imagination* (New York: Oxford University Press, 1959), pp. 8–9.

subgroups and organizations in the society. Having identified all these phenomena and their interrelations, he can then give an account of what is "really" involved in the area defined as a social problem.

A full explanation of what is implied in the preceding paragraph would require a statement about all the available sociological theory for the analysis of social problems—a task that cannot be undertaken here. Sociological theory covers a wide range of phenomena. Some theories are abstract, dealing with the characteristics of any social system; others are restricted to one specific kind of social structure, such as a school, a prison, or an industrial plant; still others are what have been called "theories of the middle range," [19] devoted to explaining a general class of social structures, such as bureaucracies or social class systems. Here we will explore the characteristics of a few of the most important kinds of structural concepts sociologists use; others will be described later in this book in connection with the special topics to which they are relevant.

The most general concept used by sociologists is that of *society* or *social system*. The terms refer to the key element in the sociological perspective—that people everywhere live surrounded by other people and that people living together in groups behave differently than they might if they lived alone. To speak of society implies (1) that human beings are capable of communicating with one another and developing symbols that are commonly understood, on the basis of which they can then develop common understandings and definitions of their environment; (2) that people living in groups typically develop ways of acting together that persist over time so that we may speak of the customs or mores or codes that characterize a given group; (3) that human social groups are typically differentiated, the members recognizing several distinct kinds of person, each of whom is expected to act in ways appropriate to the kind of person he is; (4) that socially defined relationships grow up between the various kinds of people recognized in a group, so that we can speak of the roles that make up any given relationship and the rules that govern interaction between people playing those roles; (5) that the various subgroups and social relationships in a given group affect one another in a variety of ways, so that the society is characterized by an interdependence of its parts, such that what happens in one area of social life affects the whole society.[20]

---

[19] See Robert K. Merton, *Social Theory and Social Structure* (Glencoe, Ill.: The Free Press, revised edition, 1957), pp. 5–10.

[20] The formal definitions of society offered by sociologists often vary greatly; most would accept the postulates given above, though they might add others. For some important definitions, see Robert E. Park and Ernest W. Burgess, *Introduction to*

INTRODUCTION

A conception of society is useful in the study of social problems primarily as a basic framework to which other, more specialized conceptions of specific kinds of social structures can be referred. The most important of these specialized conceptions are the *primary group*, the *organization* or *institution*, the *stratification system*, the *community*, and the *population*. This list by no means exhausts the structural concepts used in this book, but it contains those frequently used as the basis for the analysis of social problem areas and we now consider each briefly.

Shils has provided the following definition of a *primary group:*

> We mean a group characterized by a high degree of solidarity, informality in the code of rules which regulate the behavior of its members, and autonomy in the creation of these rules. The solidarity involves a close identification of the members with one another and with any symbols of the group which might have grown up. (Symbols of the group as a whole are never contrived.) Small size and physical proximity (face-to-face relations) have at times been regarded as elements in the definition of the primary group.[21]

The most familiar examples of the primary group are the family, children's play groups, and friends.

Social scientists do not ordinarily find the locus of social problems in the primary group, although they often consider the effect of larger-scale social processes on the primary group, especially the family. The concept of the primary group does, however, appear in this book, in the analysis of mental health by Duhl and Leopold, who find the core of the problem area in the inability of a person's primary group—be it family or friends—to deal with those moments of crisis in which people can no longer cope adequately with their environment. Although the ultimate causes of the crisis lie outside the primary group, it is the group's inability to provide sufficient support and orientation to reality that leads the person into mental illness.

The term *organization* is now widely used to refer to those kinds of social structures that have one or a few formally stated purposes (even though the informal purposes of both the organization and its partici-

---

the Science of Sociology (Chicago: University of Chicago Press, 1921), pp. 159–162; Kurt Wolff, ed. *The Sociology of Georg Simmel* (Glencoe, Ill.: The Free Press, 1950), pp. 3–25; and Talcott Parsons, *The Social System* (Glencoe, Ill.: The Free Press, 1951), p. 19.

[21] Edward A. Shils, "The Study of the Primary Group," in Harold D. Lasswell and Daniel Lerner, eds., *The Policy Sciences: Recent Developments in Scope and Methods* (Palo Alto, Calif.: Stanford University Press, 1951), p. 44.

pants may be more numerous), a somewhat formal style of organization with official functionaries who have stated duties, and, ordinarily, a permanent location. (Some sociologists use the terms *institution* or *establishment* to refer to this kind of social structure.) The abstract definition should not let us forget that the term refers to concrete organizations: churches, schools, taverns, government agencies, factories, and hospitals.[22]

In the analysis of social problems the concept of an organization is useful in many ways. Sometimes the phenomena that are defined as problematic arise because an organization, following its own rules and procedures in a way that seems sound to its members, produces what others in the society think is bad. A government agency may, by its own lights, be performing in accordance with the law and the bureaucratic rules that govern it, but others in the society may think that it is endangering the public welfare; witness the frequent protests of citizens' groups in California and New York at the operations of dedicated state highway engineers.

At other times, people define as problematic an organization's failure to produce what it is supposed to produce. A mental hospital may, instead of curing mental illness, foster it.[23] Our public schools are often indicted for their failure to educate students adequately. In both cases, an analysis guided by the sociological concept of organization may reveal the structural conditions that produce the unwanted result. In the case of education, for instance, the social scientist may conclude that the school's difficulties come about because it is organized to work well only with children who have been properly prepared and motivated by their families; children from families who do not perform these preparatory tasks prove difficult for the school to work with and the school's staff are inclined to blame the students rather than themselves.[24]

The authors in this text have used the concept of organization in these and a variety of other ways in their analyses of social problem areas. Neugarten, for instance, describes the plight of the aged as a consequence of the inability of social institutions to catch up with the changing needs of older people. Friedenberg and Trow concern themselves with the difficulty the school, considered as an organization, has

---

[22] For a full discussion of formal organizations, see Peter M. Blau and W. Richard Scott, *Formal Organizations* (San Francisco: Chandler Publishing Company, 1962).
[23] See Erving Goffman, *Asylums: Essays on the Social Situation of Mental Patients and Other Inmates* (Garden City, N.Y.: Anchor Books, Doubleday, 1961).
[24] See Howard S. Becker, "Social Class Variations in the Teacher-Pupil Relationship," *Journal of Educational Sociology,* 25 (April 1952), pp. 451–465.

in adjusting to the behavior and aspirations of the many kinds of children who come to it. And Miller locates some of the problems of the poor in the way welfare organizations, as they are presently constituted, operate.

The notation of a *stratification system* or system of social classes is found in almost every chapter. The basic idea of social class is familiar to everyone; it has been defined by Lipset and Bendix as follows:

> In every complex society there is a division of labor and a hierarchy of prestige. Positions of leadership and social responsibility are usually ranked at the top, and positions requiring long training and superior intelligence are ranked just below. The number of leaders and highly educated individuals constitutes everywhere a small minority. On the other hand, the great majority is made up of persons in the lower strata who perform manual and routine work of every sort and who command scant rewards and little prestige. In keeping with this division between "the few" and "the many" the stratification of society has often been pictured as a pyramid or a diamond; in the first analogy, society consists of a series of strata that become larger and more populous as we move down the hierarchy of reward and prestige, and in the second, it has small numbers at the top and bottom, with the mass of the population concentrated between. However it may be depicted, the point is that men grapple with the problems of determining the number of people at each rank in their society, and that through history various methods for doing this have been devised.[25]

Stratification systems ordinarily allow for movement between the classes, or *social mobility:*

> The term "social mobility" refers to the process by which individuals move from one position to another in society—positions which by general consent have been given specific hierarchical values. When we study social mobility we analyze the movements of individuals from positions possessing a certain rank to positions either higher or lower in the social system. It is possible to conceive of the result of this process as a distribution of talent and training such that privileges and perquisites accrue to each position in proportion to its difficulty and responsibility. An ideal ratio between the distribution of talents and the distribution of rewards can obviously never occur in society, but the approximation to this ideal, or the failure to approximate it, lends fascination to the study of social mobility.[26]

Stratification systems, like organizations, form the matrix in which social problems occur in a variety of ways. The differential distribu-

---

[25] Seymour Martin Lipset and Reinhard Bendix, *Social Mobility in Industrial Society* (Berkeley and Los Angeles: University of California Press, 1959), p. 1.
[26] *Ibid.*, pp. 1–2.

tion of rewards may itself become the focus of definition as a problem, as with poverty or the relations among the races. A scientific analysis will show the degree to which rewards are differentially distributed by class or race. More importantly, it can demonstrate the hidden inequities in a class system. For instance, research may show, as Wilensky indicates, that members of the upper-middle class are more likely to find their work satisfying than are members of lower classes. Then one can explore the organizational mechanisms and processes that create the difference.

The social scientist may similarly find, as Greer does, that housing is inequitably distributed, and attempt to uncover the mechanisms by which that inequality is created and maintained. Or the scientist may discover that classes share more than differential rewards, that by virtue of their position in the class system they have developed different class cultures, ways of life, customs and traditions that are adapted to the peculiarities of their class position.[27] The class culture, a result of the unequal distribution of rewards, may produce further inequities; thus lower-class children, already at a disadvantage economically, acquire from their class culture an inability to cope with the discipline and abstract learning tasks of a school oriented to the middle class, which greatly decreases their opportunities for mobility.[28]

Although social class is the most obvious and most ubiquitous kind of stratification in any consideration of social problems, other kinds of hierarchies may prove useful for the analysis of specific social problem areas.[29] Neugarten makes use of the idea of an *age-status system* in discussing the problems of the aged, as do Friedenberg and others (somewhat less explicitly) in analyzing the problems of youth. Gans introduces a new concept in his consideration of mass culture, the idea of a hierarchy of *taste cultures* and *taste publics,* related to but not the same thing as the hierarchy of social classes. Feldman, exploring the newly developing nations of Africa and Asia, finds it useful to consider how stratification systems develop and change under the impact of industrialization and urbanization.

The concept of *community* is of the utmost importance for the un-

[27] See Albert K. Cohen and Harold M. Hodges, Jr., "Characteristics of the Lower-Blue-Collar-Class," *Social Problems,* 10, 4 (Spring 1963), pp. 303–334; Allison Davis, "The Motivation of the Underprivileged Worker," in William F. Whyte, ed., *Industry and Society* (New York: McGraw-Hill, 1946), pp. 84–106; Herbert J. Gans, *The Urban Villagers: Group and Class in the Life of Italian-Americans* (New York: The Free Press of Glencoe, 1962); and Oscar Lewis, *The Children of Sanchez* (New York: Random House, 1961), pp. xxiii–xxvii.
[28] See Becker, "Social-Class Variations in the Teacher-Pupil Relationship," *op. cit.*
[29] For an abstract analysis of hierarchies, see Wolff, *op. cit.,* pp. 181–303.

derstanding of social problem areas. When we speak of "community" we refer to those aspects of human and social interdependence that do not necessarily involve communication and consensus, but arise from the simple fact of men and organizations coexisting in the same geographical location:

> Community, in the broadest sense of that term, has a spatial and a geographical connotation. Every community has a location, and the individuals who compose it have a place of residence within the territory which the community occupies. Otherwise they are transients and are not reckoned as members. They also have an occupation in the local economy. Towns, cities, hamlets, and, under modern conditions, the whole world, with all its differences of race, of culture, and of individual interests—all these are communities. They are all communities in just so far as, through the exchange of goods and services, they may be regarded as cooperating to carry on a common life.[30]

Long has emphasized the way community structure arises from the uncoordinated, though individually rational, strivings of the thousands of participants involved:

> The local community whether viewed as a polity, an economy, or a society presents itself as an order in which expectations are met and functions performed. In some cases, as in a new, company-planned mining town, the order is the willed product of centralized control, but for the most part the order is the product of a history rather than the imposed effect of any central nervous system of the community. For historic reasons we readily conceive the massive task of feeding New York to be achieved through the unplanned, historically developed cooperation of thousands of actors largely unconscious of their collaboration to this individually unsought end. The efficiency of this system is attested to by the extraordinary difficulties of the War Production Board and Service of Supply in accomplishing similar logistical objectives through an explicit system of orders and directives. Insofar as conscious rationality plays a role, it is a function of the parts rather than the whole. Particular structures working for their own ends within the whole may provide their members with goals, strategies, and roles that support rational action. The results of the interaction of the rational strivings after particular ends are in part collectively functional if unplanned. All this is the well-worn doctrine of Adam Smith, though one need accept no more of the doctrine of beneficence than that an unplanned economy can function.[31]

---

[30] Robert E. Park, *Human Communities* (Glencoe, Ill.: The Free Press, 1952), p. 181.
[31] Norton E. Long, "The Local Community as an Ecology of Games," *American Journal of Sociology*, 64 (November 1958), p. 251.

Although, as Park pointed out, we can use the term community to refer to anything from a hamlet to a nation or the entire world, according to the system of interdependence we consider crucial for our analysis, it is most often used to refer to the modern city.

The idea of community can be used to analyze areas that come to be defined as problematic because people, inhabiting a common location, have an effect on one another but have no agreement about how individual behavior should be regulated to prevent the occurrence of unwanted problems. The clearest and most familiar example, perhaps, is the traffic jam, where individual acts of hundreds of drivers, unregulated by anything but the basic traffic laws, create unmanageable congestion.[32]

But the notion of community has a much broader range of application. The social scientist, analyzing a social problem area, may use the concept of community whenever he wishes to take account of the conflicting interests and patterns of action characteristic of the individuals and organizations involved. Bloomberg's analysis of the problem of community organization, of course, relies heavily on such a notion in considering why communities cannot cope more effectively with their problems. Wheeler uses the notion when he examines the differing points of view on how crime should be dealt with and the consequences of different methods of dealing with it. On a larger scale, Horowitz uses similar ideas to explain what is involved, at both the national and international levels, in the problem of thermonuclear war.

Social scientists turn to the concept of a *population* when they wish to consider a social problem area by the numbers and kinds of people involved. As Schnore points out, a human population is an aggregation of people that can be studied with respect to its size, distribution in space, and composition (the proportions of persons in various categories considered relevant to the analysis, such as age, sex, or ethnicity). Demographers study the interrelations of these three characteristics of a population, especially as they are affected by such processes as fertility, mortality, migration, and mobility, and can show how changes in one aspect necessarily or probably produce determinable changes in other aspects.[33]

Schnore's essay on population problems uses the idea of a population

---

[32] See Scott Greer, "Traffic, Transportation and Problems of the Metropolis," in Merton and Nisbet, eds., *op. cit.*, pp. 616–617; and Arthur L. Stinchcombe, "Institutions of Privacy in the Determination of Police Administrative Practice," *American Journal of Sociology*, 69 (September 1963), p. 158.

[33] See N. B. Ryder, "Notes on the Concept of a Population," *American Journal of Sociology*, 69 (March 1964), pp. 447–463.

INTRODUCTION   23

to search out the causes and consequences of such problems as economic growth, in both developed and underdeveloped countries, and it is in such analyses that we frequently find the concept explicitly used. But many of our authors choose theories connected with population models, as Neugarten does in an analysis of the aged population or Trow in considering trends in the numbers and kinds of people attending school.

What Can Social Science Contribute?

What does social science contribute to understanding and solving any social problem? It helps in several ways: (1) by sorting out the differing definitions of the problem; (2) by locating assumptions made by interested parties—assumptions belied by the facts; (3) by discovering strategic points of intervention in the social structures and processes that produce the problem; and (4) by suggesting alternative moral points of view from which the problem area can be assessed.

1. We have already seen that a social problem can be defined in many ways by different people and groups, depending on their customary way of interpreting social events and on how their interests are affected by the events considered. Public discussion of social problems is often confused because the participants in the discussion use differing definitions but fail to make those definitions explicit. Consequently, they talk past one another, and the mechanisms of discussion and compromise, thought by many to be among the chief ways of dealing with social problems, can never be tested. By uncovering the implicit definitions of the nature of the problem, the social scientist can provide a basis for reconciling definitions, so that discussion becomes possible; or alternatively, his analysis may reveal that definitions, and the interests on which they are based, are so divergent that no compromise is possible and discussion is futile.[34]

2. Clarifying assumptions and checking them against the facts constitute a second contribution. People interested (as citizens or professionals) in a social problem seldom do research before arriving at conclusions about the character of the problem and what ought to be done about it. Policemen do not do research on crime, and teachers do not make studies of educational problems. It is true that experts in police science or education make such studies, just as some psychiatrists and social workers do research on mental illness and poverty. But the practicing professional ordinarily does no research on the problems that he

[34] See, for example, Lewis Killian and Charles Grigg, *Racial Crisis in America: Leadership in Conflict* (Englewood Cliffs, N.J.: Prentice-Hall, 1964).

deals with, assuming that they can be fitted into the framework of researched fact and developed theory ordinarily used by his profession. To an even greater degree, public-spirited citizens rely on their personal experience, such knowledge as is provided by the public press, and "common sense" (what "everybody" knows) in assessing a social problem, rather than gathering relevant facts scientifically.

Typically, therefore, groups interested in a social problem make many assumptions (that could have been checked by research) about matters of relevant fact; and not surprisingly their assumptions, colored by prejudice and vested interest, are often wrong. Any diagnosis of a problem based on false assumptions is likely to be incorrect; any plan that rests on an incorrect diagnosis will probably fail. Careful social science research, by making false assumptions untenable, increases the odds that something useful can be done about the problem.

For example, the research of Walter B. Miller and his colleagues explodes the common stereotype that delinquent juvenile gangs ordinarily behave aggressively. Almost everyone supposes that any attempt to deal with delinquency effectively will have to cope with the tendency of gangs to engage in a variety of physically aggressive acts, including both isolated and spontaneous attacks on innocent persons and mass warfare between opposing gangs on the city streets.[35] Close and careful observations of a juvenile gang reveal that the supposition is untenable.[36] The members of the gang engaged in much aggressive behavior while they were observed, but most of it was verbal rather than physical; what physical aggression occurred was directed almost entirely at other members of the gang, rather than at outsiders, either innocent bystanders or other gangs. In fact, of the 1490 aggressive acts observed during one year in which the gang was observed, only 95 were physically aggressive acts, and physical aggression aimed at adults was almost nonexistent. Any plan of action designed to deal with physical aggression on the part of juvenile gangs is aimed at an overemphasized problem.

Similar examples can be cited. Many white people believe that Negroes, when they talk of integration and an end to discrimination, are primarily interested in *social* integration and particularly in intermarriage. If the belief is true, the problem is one kind of problem, to be handled with one set of means, for interested white groups. But re-

---

[35] See, for instance, Richard A. Cloward and Lloyd E. Ohlin, *Delinquency and Opportunity: A Theory of Delinquent Gangs* (Glencoe, Ill.: The Free Press, 1960).
[36] Walter B. Miller, Hildred Geertz, and Henry S. G. Cutter, "Aggression in a Boys' Street-Corner Group," *Psychiatry*, 24 (1961), pp. 283-298. See also Lewis Yablonsky, *The Violent Gang* (New York: The Macmillan Company, 1962).

search has shown that *social* integration is low on the list of Negro priorities; they are more interested in having the *political* rights of an American citizen—and equal *educational* and *economic* opportunities.[37] Similarly, research has exploded such commonly held assumptions as these: the use of marijuana leads to violent crimes;[38] when a minority group moves into a neighborhood, property values go down;[39] the incidence of mental illness has increased greatly over the last one hundred years.[40] In every case, social action can be planned more intelligently on the basis of facts rather than false assumptions.

3. A third contribution social science makes to the solution of social problems lies in the discovery of crucial points of intervention in the structures and processes that contribute to the problem. Before such a contribution can be made, the social scientist must arrive at his own definition of the problem, for intervention can be planned only when we know what the purpose of our intervention is and what particular set of consequences we wish to avert. But, if we know what we want, research and analysis can reveal the crucial points in the development of the problem, the points where intervention will be most effective and the points where it will be useless, dealing with superficial phenomena whose manipulation will have no effect.

If, for instance, we consider the chain of structural circumstances that produce the narcotics problem in this country, it is obvious that some links in the chain can more easily be manipulated than others. Let us define the problem as one where addicts engage in crime to support their habits, disrupting their own lives and the peace and security of the communities they live in. We hope that our intervention will result in a decrease in the crime of addicts and a consequent improvement of their lives and those of the community members. What steps will be most effective? What steps will be wasted, failing to accomplish the goal?

Suppose that our analysis of the problem suggests the following chain of relevant circumstances. People in socially disorganized areas find narcotics easily available and, since their lives seem to them difficult and pointless, are likely to try drugs frequently enough to activate

---

[37] Myrdal, *op. cit.*, pp. 60–67.
[38] Walter Bromberg and Terry C. Rodgers, "Marihuana and Aggressive Crime," *American Journal of Psychiatry*, 102 (May 1946), pp. 825–827.
[39] See Luigi Laurenti, *Property Values and Race* (Berkeley: University of California Press, 1960) and Erdman Palmore and John Howe, "Residential Integration and Property Values," *Social Problems*, 10, 1 (Summer 1962), pp. 51–55.
[40] Herbert Goldhamer and Andrew Marshall, *Psychosis and Civilization* (Glencoe, Ill.: The Free Press, 1953).

the physiological mechanisms of addiction. Once they become addicted, they tend to become involved in a way of life that makes them emotionally dependent on continued drug use. They then find that their ordinary sources of income are insufficient to pay for the drugs at current underworld prices; simultaneously, they find that there is no legitimate way for them to obtain the needed drugs. The high price of illicit drugs results from governmental prohibition against physicians prescribing drugs for addicts.

This analysis suggests several possible points of intervention. We might, for instance, attempt to alleviate social disorganization in the areas addicts live in. We might try to develop narcotics which are not physiologically addicting or attempt to substitute known harmless drugs for the addictive drugs now in use. We might attempt to cure the addict's emotional dependence on the drug through psychotherapy. And we might attempt to change government regulations so that addicts could obtain drugs legally, thus destroying the illegal market.[41]

Each of these measures is possible; but some are more difficult to achieve than others. Disorganized neighborhoods can conceivably be rehabilitated, but no one has ever mustered the massive resources that would be necessary for this. Pharmacologists have not yet discovered a nonaddictive drug with the same analgesic properties as the opiates; they may, but we cannot wait for them to solve our problem. Psychotherapy might help addicts overcome their emotional dependence, though there is no good evidence that it will; even if it can help, there are not enough trained psychotherapists available to be put to work at the task. The analysis suggests that the most strategic point of intervention is the government regulations, and this is the suggestion many social scientists have made.[42]

This extended example shows how a sociological analysis of a problem area can indicate the most useful points at which social action might be taken to deal with a social problem. The solution will not always be so simple as changing a government regulation. In some cases, analysis may indicate, in just the opposite fashion, that no such simple solution exists; to do anything useful, nothing less than a massive change in existing institutions will suffice. Where massive change is required, with the consequent heavy investment of resources which others would like to see used elsewhere and the inevitable conflict with

---

[41] This is a simplified sketch of a complex argument, useful only for purposes of the present discussion. See Isidor Chein, Donald L. Gerard, Robert S. Lee, and Eva Rosenfeld, with the collaboration of Daniel M. Wilner, *The Road to H: Narcotics, Delinquency and Social Policy* (New York: Basic Books, 1964), pp. 323–386.

[42] See *ibid.*, and the works cited in footnotes 9 and 12, *supra*.

other organizations and groups, laymen and professionals alike seek *panaceas:*

> schemes which will cause great changes in all the places that change is desired without in any way hurting anyone's interests or causing any basic change in the operating structure that now exists. . . . In any institution, one can make big changes only by making big changes. This is a truism about social organization, but one that is often overlooked.[43]

In other words, sociological analysis may show that the only useful point of intervention is the system or community itself, and that anything less will be useless.

4. Finally, the social scientist can help society deal with social problems by suggesting alternative moral points of view from which the problem can be assessed. Any definition of a social problem assumes some moral position from which the conditions or events regarded as problems are judged. The moral criterion may be one as mundane as efficiency, the standpoint from which engineers or urban planners often make judgments of problem areas. Or it may be a religious criterion, as in the temperance movement's opposition to alcoholic beverages or in Roman Catholic opposition to certain forms of birth control. Whatever the criterion involved, the social scientist's research may suggest to him the possibility of other moral criteria that might form the basis of an alternative judgment.

One example is found when social scientists, as a result of their research experiences, suggest that it will be useful to take the point of view of those who are defined as causing the problem instead of those who so define it.[44] Julius Roth, speaking of his experiences while studying tuberculosis hospitals, makes the point:

> "Why do patients leave the hospital against medical advice?" is a question often asked by tuberculosis hospital staff members and by social workers and social scientists interested in the TB hospital. But we might also ask (and should ask first): "Why do patients stay in the hospital?" The fact that the question is almost always asked in the first form shows a definite bias of the staff viewpoint in contrast to the patient viewpoint or, perhaps, a more objective viewpoint.
>
> The same is true of other aspects of the TB hospital. We hear of "cooperative" or "uncooperative" doctors or nurses. The patients have

---

[43] Howard S. Becker and Blanche Geer, "Medical Education," in Howard E. Freeman, Sol Levine, and Leo G. Reeder, eds., *Handbook of Medical Sociology* (Englewood Cliffs, N.J.: Prentice-Hall, 1963), p. 184.

[44] See Becker, *Outsiders, op cit.*, and Goffman, *op. cit.*

"problems" which the research psychologist may want to study or which the sympathetic doctor, nurse, or social worker may try to help him with. Yet many of these "problems" are a product of the social organization and the system of expectations of which the patients are a part, but the latter receive little or no attention. The patients are expected to do the "adjusting" to the hospital, the latter by implication being thought of as a given, unchanging quantity. Clinical psychologists want to do individual and group therapy with patients to help them deal with their handicap. The behavior of the patient is seen as something arising entirely from within himself (especially when he does something "wrong") and not as something arising from his relationship to the institution and its personnel.

This bias leads to a narrowing of both the understanding of the dynamics of the TB hospital and of practical decisions which are made in the hospital. Thus, when a patient leaves against advice, the reaction is, "What is wrong with him?" and no attempt is made to analyze the social situation of which the patient's characteristics are only one part. Because of the emphasis on the adjustment of the patient, little study is made of the significance of the behavior of the personnel except in cases of extreme or obvious abuse. The adjustment concept, furthermore, makes the assumption that there is a "best" way for a given group of people, e.g., TB patients, to act, or to be—an assumption that is certainly gratuitous and not at all helpful to the social science analyst.[45]

In our book, a striking example of this kind of contribution of social science analysis is found in Friedenberg's chapter on adolescence where, instead of asking what is wrong with adolescents, he asks what is wrong with the adults in our society that makes it difficult for them to accept youngsters as they are.

The Plan of the Book

Social problems can be classified in a great many ways, each of which might be useful and sensible from some point of view. We have chosen to organize the problems we consider on a scale of increasing size of the group involved. Some are problems of individuals, at least as they are popularly conceived, and we consider them in the context of the *life cycle* of the individual. Others are viewed as problems of individual *deviance*. Some problems are commonly found in the setting of the *community* or *nation*. Finally, there are problems, incapable of

---

[45] Julius A. Roth, "'Management Bias' in Social Science Study of Medical Treatment," *Human Organization*, 21, 1 (Spring 1962), p. 47. See also his *Timetables: Structuring the Passage of Time in Hospital and Other Careers* (Indianapolis: Bobbs-Merrill, 1963).

being contained in a national setting, which must be considered as *world* problems.

The life cycle. We begin by considering four aspects of the life cycle of Americans which are ordinarily viewed as social problems. Stages of the life cycle are defined by every society, whose culture describes certain events in a person's career as important, dangerous, and fateful.[46] It specifies appropriate kinds of behavior for people in each age grade and provides transitional mechanisms for moving from one age grade to the next. Although the problems that arise around stages of the life cycle seem to be personal, they are actually social in character, taking their form from the requirements society places on people at various stages in the life cycle. Life cycle problems typically arise from the inability of the society to deal with people moving into a new stage of the life cycle.

The four chapters concerned with social problems centering on stages in the life cycle begin with Friedenberg's discussion of the problem of adolescence; Trow then deals with problems of education and educational institutions; Wilensky, writing about problems of work, emphasizes the difficulties people have today as they search for satisfaction in their daily occupations; Neugarten, finally, rounds off our consideration of the human career with an analysis of the role of the aged in American society.

Deviance. Some social problems are publicly defined as problems of deviance. The important feature of the problem, as it is seen by both laymen and professionals, is that some individuals are thought to be habitual violators of important social rules. The concept of "deviance," as used in defining social problems, has much in common with the concept of a "social problem" itself. What is defined as deviant, as what is defined as a social problem, depends on who is making the definition. In this view,

> The central fact about deviance [is that] it is created by society. I do not mean this in the way it is ordinarily understood, in which the causes of deviance are located in the social situation of the deviant or in "social factors" which prompt his action. I mean, rather, that *social groups create deviance by making the rules whose infraction constitutes deviance*, and by applying those rules to particular people and labeling them as outsiders. From this point of view, deviance is not a quality of

---

[46] See Arnold van Gennep, *The Rites of Passage* (Chicago: University of Chicago Press, 1960); and Everett C. Hughes, "Cycles, Turning Points and Careers," in his *Men and Their Work* (Glencoe, Ill.: The Free Press, 1958), pp. 11–22.

the act the person commits, but rather a consequence of the application by others of rules and sanctions to an "offender." The deviant is one to whom that label has successfully been applied; deviant behavior is behavior that people so label.[47]

Two chapters consider problems of deviance. Wheeler's chapter on crime discusses the problem that arises with respect to people who are labeled as "intentional" deviants, those whose deviant actions are defined as having been done "on purpose." Duhl and Leopold consider the complementary problem of "unintentional" deviance, the kind of misbehavior that is defined as beyond the control of the person who commits it; mental illness is the chief example of such deviance in our society.

Community and national problems. Some of the problems that most involve the public are those that are conceived as problems of community or national organization. We might have included other problems in addition to those considered in the five chapters in this section, although it is difficult to imagine leaving out any of those included.

The problems in this section are those seen most naturally in the context of the local community or in the collection of communities and interstitial areas that make up the nation. They are problems that particularly involve questions of the use of governmental power and resources. For what purposes shall that power and those resources be used in solving problems of community organization? What means will be most effective in achieving those purposes? Mack (on race relations), Miller and Rein (on poverty), and Greer (on housing and urban renewal) study such questions.

Bloomberg's chapter on community organization takes up a more abstract problem. Why cannot our local communities organize themselves to deal more effectively with the many problems that confront them? He describes the variations in community organization, the way problems are made public issues in communities of various kinds, and the constraints that inhibit efforts to solve community problems.

The concluding chapter in this section, Gans's on mass culture, turns to a problem that is more clearly national in scope. Of all the authors, Gans perhaps goes furthest in relating his analysis to questions of social policy. By making explicit value judgments and attaching them to his

---

[47] Becker, *Outsiders, op. cit.,* pp. 8–9. See also Edwin M. Lemert, *Social Pathology: A Systematic Approach to the Theory of Sociopathic Behavior* (New York: McGraw-Hill, 1951), pp. 27–72; and the essays in Howard S. Becker, ed., *The Other Side: Perspectives on Deviance* (New York: The Free Press of Glencoe, 1964).

analysis as premises, he deduces a sociological standard of aesthetic judgment which provides the basis for imaginative policy suggestions.

World problems. The only context in which some problems can be adequately discussed is that of the entire world:

> During the last hundred years the external conditions of civilized life have been transformed by a series of inventions which have abolished the old limits to the creation of mechanical force, the carriage of men and goods, and communication by written and spoken words. One effect of this transformation is a general change of social scale. Men find themselves working and thinking and feeling in relation to an environment which, both in its world-wide extension and in its intimate connection with all sides of human existence, is without precedent in the history of the world.[48]

The final three chapters in our book deal with problems having worldwide scope. Schnore discusses population growth and its relation to the standard of living. Feldman treats a problem that is relatively new: the development of new nations from the former European colonies in Asia and Africa. Finally, we conclude with Horowitz's analysis of perhaps the most important problem of all: how to avoid thermonuclear war.

[48] Robert E. Park, *Race and Culture* (Glencoe, Ill.: The Free Press, 1950), p. 331.

Part One

Problems of the Life Cycle

1

Adolescence as a Social Problem

Edgar Friedenberg

THE French military leader Marshal Foch made a triumphal visit to the United States shortly after World War I; and, in the course of it, he attended the Ziegfeld Follies. This spectacle, astonishing to a civilized Frenchman, is said to have moved him to sum up his impressions of us as people by observing: "I had never seen such gay faces or such sad behinds!" In this respect, the ensuing half century has probably brought deterioration rather than improvement.

In America, moreover, the old seem usually to be in worse shape than the young: not merely, as might be expected, physically, but emotionally and morally as well. The increase in incidence and severity of emotional disorder with age that Leo Srole and his staff found characteristic of midtown Manhattan [1] appears not only to represent a wider sample but to be deeply embedded in the way our society works. Among us, by and large, the old have no dignity. The aged and abandoned in the subway or rooming house, or the hospital life of the elderly pictured by Jules Henry in *Culture Against Man*,[2] are pathetic and, indeed, tragic. But these, we may say, are scarcely representative. They are the victims of a way of life that most find benign, and cer-

---
[1] Leo Srole, Thomas S. Langner, Stanley T. Michael, Marvin K. Opler, and Thomas A. C. Rennie, *Mental Health in the Metropolis*, Vol. 1 (New York: McGraw-Hill, 1962), Chapter 9, pp. 157–171.
[2] New York: Random House, 1963, Chapter 10, "Human Obsolescence," pp. 392–474.

tainly the more successful, decked out in muumuus or Aloha shirts and leis, taking what they believe to be hula lessons on the decks of the *Lurline* or in the patio of the apolitical Town Hall of Sun City, a "paradise town" from which youngsters of school age are excluded,[3] are very different. They are more grotesque.

To be sure, the American aged are not usually as deracinated as rooming house or nursing home dwellers, or Senior Citizens of Paradise Town. But our lives run downhill and waste away into the sands often enough to suggest that growing up in America is not a process of maturation so much as of surrender; of atrophy and renunciation of the human qualities for spontaneous feeling, action, and commitment that, under more favorable social circumstances, would be the expected outcome of normal growth. The Senior Citizens of Paradise Town, pretending to themselves as long as they can that strangers, if friendly, are as good as friends and that heart attacks can be fun, are not, in their present form, a part of God's creation. They become what they are, as we all are doing, through such growth as is possible to them under the conditions of their life.

Much of what crucially happened or failed to happen to these people, as to all of us, occurred in adolescence; what we do then, or leave undone, becomes so deeply engraved into our identity that it is difficult to alter. When these people were adolescents, America was a different place indeed. But the pressures now on them are much the same as those on adolescents, with the critical difference that they can have no illusions—or nothing but illusions—about the future. Both the aged and the young in our culture are socially and economically marginal. Both the aged and the young are treated as helpless objects who require costly and profitable services to help them do what they are usually not allowed to do for themselves, or what they have lost the courage or initiative to try.

It is not, of course, primarily the elderly with whom adolescents must deal. In our society today, the old and young tend to avoid one another. The elderly, as in Paradise Town, often loathe the young and try to exclude them. Their rancor and suspicion can be understood, if not justified, as a form of envy for those whose lives are not yet forfeit. It is the middle-aged, with their own careers to make as schoolteacher, counselor, "attendance teacher"—as truant officers are now called in our continuous effort to make reality smile—or social worker who face youth directly in a quasi-professional capacity; while parents, of course, continue to face their own children as well as they can. The

[3] Calvin Trillin, "Wake Up and Live," *The New Yorker*, 40, 7 (April 4, 1964), pp. 120 ff.

middle-aged are less likely to respond to the young with acute hostility and irritation than with determination to be helpful. This makes them more dangerous.

Certainly, it cannot be said of middle-aged, middle-class America that it has no use for adolescents and wants no part of them. The *New York Times* for March 2, 1964, carried a full-page advertisement for Scholastic Magazines, Inc., which have, according to the advertisement, "served the schools, their teachers and students, for more than 43 years." Claiming twelve million readers, and that "Every issue of each magazine has an assigned place in the classroom programs on American Problems, Language Arts, Science and Homemaking," they undertake to "pinpoint young shoppers as a top priority, prime market; recognize them as an unprecedented factor influencing major family purchases, rather than as secondary targets of brand promotion *to begin* [italics theirs] at the time when the learning process is most acute." " 'The mind is capable of any kind of learning' " they note in a quotation from an unidentified article in the *Bulletin of the National Association of Secondary Schools* for April 1963, " 'and it is more supple than it will be in later years.' " American youth, the advertisement maintains in a quotation from a study published in 1962 by Social Research, Inc.—itself now a leader in the field of commercial programmed instruction—"generally feel relatively alienated from television. While they are not serious or strong critics, they have mixed attitudes about what it does or means to them." Like streptococci indiscriminately saturated with antibiotics, the next generation of Americans, according to Social Research, is developing an awkward degree of resistance.

This advertisement expresses a view of adolescents that strongly affects their place in American life. Only as a customer and, occasionally, as an athlete are adolescents favorably received. Otherwise they are treated as a problem and, potentially, a threatening one. No other social groups except convicted criminals and certified lunatics are subject to as much restriction, and there is strong political support for proposals that would increase these restrictions. If recommendations that the draft age be lowered to sixteen, the legal school-leaving age be raised in most states to eighteen, and paramilitary work camps be established as "schools" for the academically inept all become law, there will be no more male adolescents at large in the country.

And a great many American adults will—or so they now believe—sleep easier in their beds. Willing as they are to trade with him, they have no doubt that the "teen-ager" is an enemy, and they want him confined in schools or suitable recreational or military facilities. American adults are afraid of "teen-agers." They attribute to them a capacity for violence and lust; in this respect "teen-agers" serve the rest of us as the occasion both for wish fulfillment and for self-fulfilling prophecy. In their presence, generally sober policemen become trigger-happy and shoot to kill in sporadic outbursts of preventive war. The more miserable and underprivileged the adult is, the more likely he is to attribute outrages to the young. Numerous as sensational examples of this attitude are in press accounts of the activities attributed to adolescents, I can illustrate more precisely what I mean by the response of the elderly, ill-tempered doorman of my apartment house to a tragedy that occurred in the Times Square district of New York during the noon hour one day, when a middle-aged New Jersey underworld figure lost control of his car and drove through the plate glass window of a busy restaurant, killing several persons who were lunching there. Although news flashes were immediately broadcast, our doorman had not heard of it till another tenant mentioned it. Immediately, John's dull old eyes flashed with malicious delight. "Was it 'teen-agers'?" he asked happily.

Hostility does not come this easily to the middle class, which prefers to define any nuisance that it wishes to abate, or social situation that it finds threatening or embarrassing as a problem. Our youth problem is a notable accomplishment. We have made it ourselves, out of little, and now it is almost certainly the biggest youth problem in the world. Yet, we are not quite in agreement about what sort of problem it is.

Several Views of Adolescence

Many adults seem to use the terms "teen-ager" and "juvenile delinquent" as if they were synonyms;[4] to them, the youth problem is one of law enforcement or treatment for the emotionally disturbed and lies in the general province of "social work." At a more scholarly level this approach is obsolescent. There are still courses in *juvenile delinquency* in departments of sociology and especially in schools of social work and new textbooks dealing with the phenomenon continue to be written, but the concept has lost favor as an analytic tool. The obverse of the popular tendency to regard all adolescents as potential delinquents is a countervailing recognition in sociology that juvenile delinquents are merely one single category of adolescent, and not an especially useful one theoretically.

[4] It is very difficult to keep discussion of any topic related to adolescence from turning into a discussion of juvenile delinquency; I have even had participants, referring to a book I had written called *The Vanishing Adolescent*, identify it as *The Vanishing Delinquent*, without apparently noticing their parapraxis.

Of greater current influence, though also widely criticized, is the view best represented by James S. Coleman in *The Adolescent Society*.[5] Coleman, basing his conclusions on an extensive questionnaire study of nine high schools serving widely different clienteles near Chicago and one parochial secondary school in the city itself, maintains that teen-agers have succeeded in establishing in and around the school a separate society of their own which generates and maintains its own trivial values and interposes them, like a Southern governor invoking states' rights, between the youngsters and the serious moral and academic demands of the adult society. From this conclusion, he infers a mandate for the school to seek active dominance and control of the adolescent society for its own good and that of the culture as a whole. The most fundamental weakness in this position is, I should say, manifest in The *New York Times* advertisement already cited. Far from being independent of the larger society, adolescents are completely its subjects; and the triviality of teen-age life, though undebatable, is more a reflection of the determination of the adult society to exploit and corrupt it than of the stubborn determination of the teen-ager to resist.

Paul Goodman's *Growing Up Absurd*,[6] probably the most familiar and influential recent work on adolescents, does not attempt to establish a theoretical position. It is of great value as a provocative and highly insightful complaint against the indignity that modern life imposes on the young. Goodman does not suggest that this indignity is greater than that suffered by their elders—indeed, it is central to his point that it is not. He sees the entire process of growing up as a kind of *corruptio ad absurdum* that benumbs the young morally and intellectually, thus suiting them to the promise of the future. For Goodman, as for myself, the youth problem is an artifact, created by society in response to tensions and factors that affect us all, to which the young are simply more vulnerable.

Even after fifteen years, August B. Hollingshead's *Elmtown's Youth*[7] remains the most valuable presentation of, as the work's subtitle states, the impact of social class on adolescents. There has been much more change in the class structure itself—Elmtown, like so many other places, has become almost suburban in the past fifteen years—

[5] New York: The Free Press of Glencoe, 1961.
[6] New York: Random House, 1960. A detailed and penetrating essay-review of Coleman's, Goodman's, and my books, in which the three are critically compared, is Bennett M. Berger's "Adolescence and Beyond," *Social Problems*, 10, 4 (Spring 1963), pp. 394–408.
[7] New York: John Wiley and Sons, 1949.

than in the way young people are affected by it. The influence of social status on how a student is treated in school, on his self-image and, ultimately, on his life chances—for it was by life chances that Max Weber defined social class—remains essentially what it was and the source of much of the difficulty the young encounter and make for one another.

Two more eclectic works should finally be cited, both for their intrinsic worth and for their exceptional value as bibliographic sources. Perhaps the most useful work on adolescence to appear in a single volume is the set of essays included in the Winter 1962 issue of *Daedalus:* "Youth: Change and Challenge." [8] Including what is undoubtedly the most stimulating and original set of papers on various aspects of adolescence yet compiled, the essays by Bruno Bettelheim, Robert Jay Lifton, Reuel Denney, Kenneth Keniston and, of course, Erikson himself are especially notable; in addition, the essays are usefully annotated. In an altogether different vein, Rolf E. Meuss's *Theories of Adolescence* [9] is an excellent, comprehensive key to the connections between the literatures of adolescence and related areas of interest in the social sciences, especially psychology.

Despite the example of Meuss's work and the extensive psychological literature cited in it, it would, I believe, be fair to state that during the fifteen years since *Elmtown's Youth* was published social science has tended strongly to consider adolescence more in social and less in psychological terms. This shift is worth considering in itself. Clearly, it is not the result of any trend toward attaching less importance generally to human emotion and personality structure. On the contrary, such concurrent intellectual developments as the modification of pure Freudian theory to take greater account of the social circumstances in which growth occurs, as in the work of Erich Fromm, Harry Stack Sullivan, or Rollo May, make it clear that psychology itself is capable of response to social change without any loss in its essential character and emphasis. But the psychological categories in which adolescence used to be discussed almost exclusively were crudely normative. Psychology of adolescence usually meant, in fact, a psychology of adjustment to puberty and society generally. Adjustment meant normal adjustment, assumed to be desirable. Society, when it was explicitly considered at all, was not treated as a set of processes in which adolescents were involved in various ways, but as a given set of norms to which the adolescent was expected to adapt for his own good. This

[8] Subsequently published in hardcover by Basic Books, Erik H. Erikson, ed.
[9] New York: Random House, 1962.

naive and unfortunate view received a mortal blow at the hands of Holden Caulfield and has steadily languished since.

Adjustment, by now, has become a dirty word; the same school personnel who were pursuing maladjusted youth into thickets of therapy now talk with equal enthusiasm, and to much the same effect, about the adolescent identity crisis and the need for autonomy and self-definition. Conformity is discussed as a hazard, rather than a goal, and everybody who deals with youth claims to be avoiding it. The *New York Times* for March 14, 1964, in reporting that "A 16-year-old senior honor student at Wantagh High School was suspended from classes" for a week "because she refused to participate in a Civil Defense Drill," further reports of the Superintendent of Schools for her district that "Dr. Krum praised Miss Levenstein as a person, as well as her scholastic ability, but noted that 'She thinks we are trying to make her a conformist.' " She may well be right, even so. The replacement of psychological categories for dealing with adolescents by social ones has not really resulted in decreasing the pressure upon them to fit into the social group. In some ways it has increased it. Such little respect for human dignity and civil liberty as has taken root in our culture—and how little it is, among adolescents, is well established in H. H. Remmers' massive work [10]—applies entirely to the individual. No comparable respect for the folkways of divergent groups has become established in our culture. The objections to excessive and intrusive psychologizing that are expressed in current scorn for adjustment do not apply at all to socialization. It is just this which makes it possible for Coleman to recommend an aggressive effort to gain control of "the adolescent society" at a time when an equally determined effort to "improve the adjustment" of individual adolescents would meet with considerably greater resistance. We want individuality, but not if it blocks adaptation to current social demands. "Willy-nilly, all schools must work from the basis of Emile Durkheim's grim definition: 'Education consists of a methodical socialization of the young generation,'" Martin Mayer sadly asserts in *The Schools*.[11]

The Social Function of Socialization

But why should this socialization have become a matter of sufficient concern to generate within recent years a large and on the whole excel-

---
[10] *Anti-Democratic Attitudes in American Schools* (Evanston, Ill.: Northwestern University Press, 1963), Part I.
[11] New York: Harper and Brothers, 1961, p. 32.

lent body of scholarly literature? Why is it agreed that a "youth problem" of threatening dimensions exists? Why does a textbook on social problems include a section on adolescence at all? Why does puberty precipitate people into a recognized and recognizable group?

Individuals placed in a common position in society, dealt with by common institutions and exposed to common sanctions, develop common characteristics that lead others to see them as a group. As they gradually accept the definition of themselves society offers, either living within its terms or rebelling against them, they also come to see themselves as a group. Otherwise, no social group exists; it is quite true, as the Black Muslims maintain, that where there is no racial discrimination, there are no Negroes.

Nevertheless, grouping must make use of at least a putative, common characteristic; people classified in America as Negro do, by and large, have dark skins, or participate in the society in such a way as to define themselves as belonging among those who do. But people are not grouped unless their similarities present more powerful social elements with a problem, or provide them with an opportunity. People are grouped because it is worth someone's while to group them.

There are, to be sure, some characteristics so conspicuous and so relevant to every aspect of human behavior that no culture could overlook them. There is no society in which the living are not distinguished from the dead, or men from women. But people in the age range we call adolescent are not everywhere distinguished as a social group; and even where they have been, they are not always seen as a problem. All societies discriminate between children and adults, marking the division by the spectacular eruption of puberty. But it is rarer for a society to set aside a period of years after puberty, during which sexually mature individuals continue to be treated as a special kind of boy or girl, instead of accepting them as young, inexperienced adults with much to learn about the folkways but qualified to participate fully in society while they learn.

We often explain our practice by assuming that in a complex, technically developed society it takes time to teach boys and girls to be men and women, so that a transitional status is needed. But adolescence is transitional only in the sense that a gantlet is. The young must pass through it before they are allowed to reach adulthood; and they emerge at the end of it smarting with awareness of their dependence on and vulnerability to the social structure, and dulled by anxiety to their own strengths and potential. In our society adolescence is not an *intermediate* stage between childhood and adulthood but a status in most respects inferior to both; a position the postpubescent young are compelled to assume in order to expose them most completely to the effects of socialization and reduce their freedom to struggle against it effectively. Adolescents command less respect, arouse more hostility and mistrust, and are obliged to face difficult situations with less social support and greater risk to themselves than either children or adults of the same social class.

This is a paradox. In a highly technical society, age after puberty makes less difference in what a person is qualified to do than in a primitive society. Age and experience count for little in a rapidly changing world of mobile individuals that identifies people by the label attached to their job and rationalizes most jobs to require minimal skill or insight. There is less in our world than in an Indian village that a sixteen-year-old could not do as well as anyone else. Youths of sixteen can operate most machines, make love and care for children, and accept and discharge responsibility for more sensitive and complex tasks than most adults are ever called upon to perform—provided they are not incapacitated by a humiliating image of themselves as "teen-agers." What they lack in statesmanship they can often make up in compassion.

Adolescents are a problem to us primarily, I believe, because, unless forestalled, they tend to grow up to be more human than our society can accommodate—more passionate, more confident, more self-aware. Society has, at most, eight years to shape them up; after this it must, in the interests of its own continuity, somehow find a place for all those who do not become criminal or psychotic; and even these remain a burden. But the process creates severe problems; for many adolescents do indeed respond to the insult implicit in their socialization by developing traits of behavior and character that make them dangerous: apathy, a sense of worthlessness, and a sullen, hostile, and exploitive attitude toward the larger society. Even those who find a place for themselves in a dissident artistic or social-action group may be so crippled by resentment that their shared experience becomes relatively powerless to humanize them. Our respect for those of the young who devote themselves to a struggle for social purposes that we share but have largely abandoned, such as civil rights and integration, has led Jacob Fishman, currently director, Center for Youth and Community Studies, Howard University, Washington, D.C., to call their action groups "pro-social." This can be misleading. Such youngsters are pro-social in the important sense that they affirm the values the society officially esteems; they keep our soul alive despite our neglect of its obligations. But they are often more deeply and bitterly antagonistic to society than are ordinary delinquents; and that their feelings are justified does not make them less destructive. It is never simple to free slaves.

Peculiar difficulties arise because adolescence itself evolved as a social role, governed by a set of institutions that are obsolescent, though they still retain a measure of moral force. Traditionally, adolescence became established in cultures that took account of it as a period of self-definition and identity seeking, of passionate interaction with diverse individuals and experimentation with various social roles, under conditions where the adolescent was neither permitted as much freedom nor held as fully responsible as an adult would have been. Its function was to aid the youngster in

> finding out
> What you really are. What you really feel.
> What you really are among other people.[12]

In a society that values individual dignity and depends for social cohesion on individual commitment to those of its roles and goals that its members believe they have chosen to suit themselves, this is an indispensable and majestic function. From it, adolescence has sometimes derived the heroic quality so central to the character of Holden Caulfield or of Phineas in John Knowles' *A Separate Peace*. Yet these are fictional portraits, and both boys are portrayed by their authors as doomed through their very capacity for warmth and fidelity. Individual dignity and commitment have always been more prominent in the American cultural heritage than in our social practice; they present increasingly awkward obstacles to successful functioning in a mass society. Adolescent heroism still occurs, but the hero is now a literally quixotic figure.

From being a period provided by society for self-definition, adolescence is becoming instead a period, and a process, of thorough, though not consciously planned, grooming of youngsters to fit interchangeably, as adults, a succession of social roles that disparage their passions and their roots; and to accept, in the meantime, delays amounting to several years in attaining any meaningful social role at all. To most youngsters this is not especially painful. To many, the openness and instability of society promise opportunities more exciting than the permanent interpersonal attachments and deeply felt personal goals they have never experienced. Others, absorbed in friendships or early loves, or in a common devotion to sports, the arts, or just the routines of daily life in a community to which they have grown accustomed, do not notice the impersonality that surrounds and penetrates their enclave. The institutions that deal with them are skilled at making fun

[12] T. S. Eliot, *The Cocktail Party* (New York: Harcourt, Brace, 1950), pp. 30–31.

more attractive than joy. If the result is often a pervasive feeling of alienation and despair, it is even more often a cheerful and incoherent distraction whose very normality makes it seem reassuring.[13]

Socialization, however, is a lifelong process in every culture. The values and attitudes instilled in high school merely continue those whose foundations are laid in the elementary school; children's commercialized recreation is cute, while that provided for teen-agers features a teasing and inconclusive sexuality as bait for the adolescents' new physical maturity; but both are phony trade goods useful in luring the natives into the stockade, keeping them amused while they are held there, and getting a cut of their ten billion dollars a year in pocket money. All societies mold, deform, and seduce the personalities of their young into the kinds of human development they are accustomed to and can accept; and this process can only be really effective if begun in early childhood and continued fairly consistently. Why, then, does the advent of puberty create, in our society, a special class of individuals?

The Social Challenge of Puberty

What difference does puberty really make to the adolescent, or to the adults who deal with him? In any society the answer to this question combines economic and psychological elements of the greatest complexity. But in contemporary America the combination is peculiarly unworkable. No sexual arrangement other than that between man and wife is accepted as legitimate, nor are the children who may result. A family must be self-supporting to be self-respecting. In a society with a rapidly expanding economy and a growing demand for labor, this is perhaps an economically feasible way to organize a human community. In an increasingly automated society with no place to put new self-sufficient units, it is not. Adolescents are barred from employment by child labor laws for several years after puberty; when they are old enough for working papers, they are still restricted to marginal and poorly paying jobs. Even after they are old enough to require no special permission, union policy, the risk of being bumped for lack of seniority, and, in the case of young men, employers' reluctance to hire and train people subject to the draft make it difficult for late adolescents to find jobs or to keep them.

Our conception of the family, then, amounts to a syllogism. Only a man and wife may legitimately enjoy sexual relations; only economically self-supporting people may marry; only people of twenty-five or

---

[13] See Henry, *op. cit.* Chapter 7, "Rome High School and Its Students," for a detailed and perceptive discussion of this issue.

so have much hope of being economically self-supporting at a high and consistent enough level to be respected. Puberty, then, pushes the young into a decade of limbo; and adolescent behavior that adults call irresponsible simply reflects the failure of society to provide any responsible position for them. But the plight of the adolescent cannot be understood in purely negative terms, as a consequence of what is denied. Within this context of denial he is subject to powerful and sometimes destructive social forces.

It is important to understand precisely what *is* denied and what substitutes are offered in its place, how they work, and why they are generally unsatisfactory. Clearly, the crucial lack is not in sexual opportunity itself. Sexual moratoria, as Aristophanes suggested in *Lysistrata*, tend to be inherently unstable; and adolescents can usually evade them. Sex, in human beings, however, is not just a tissue need. We have institutionalized it as the basis for deep and permanent relations between individuals, whether lovers or parents and children. Puberty therefore carries with it a need for personal involvement and commitment, even though the emotional immaturity of the recently pubescent also requires that they be permitted and expected sometimes to go beyond their emotional depth and be forced to withdraw. But personal commitment and emotional involvement must be validated by society. The adolescent must be able to see their fruition in the lives of persons around him who are enough like him in age and status that he can accept them, not as models but as evidence that life as he is beginning to experience it can be trusted and lived. One factor that makes life harder for adolescents today than a generation or so ago is the decreased opportunity for friendly contact with young adults who already feel somewhat established, like older brothers and their wives, or for the casual friendships of older communities where people have been growing up for a long time, a complete range of ages exists, and age is fairly consistently related to status.

Just the contrary condition is common today. Young adults are not yet part of any established community. Career patterns take people out of their communities and replace them with strangers whose lives are unimaginable. There are age gaps in many suburbs, and even in urban neighborhoods, as families move onward and upward or into oblivion. The old residents are marginal—they are the people who have been left behind.

The adolescent therefore not only is bereft of legitimate means of establishing a sexual relationship, but has little opportunity to observe directly how sexual feelings become expressed in lasting love relationships, or how the young people who become sexually involved manage to set their relationship up on an adult basis. His own sexuality is likely to be channeled into either the anonymous promiscuity available in commercial roadhouses that cater to a teen-age clientele—the sort of thing Jules Henry illustrates in his account of "Tight-Pants Town"; [14] or, conversely, limited by the current high school convention of, as one student leader rather sardonically put it, "going steadily," reserving the phrase "going steady" for a relationship that might have more meaning if he were ever fortunate enough to encounter it. Many thoughtful teen-agers perceive "going steady" as a defensive maneuver they are forced into by the anonymity of mass education, although resenting it for being virtually as confining as marriage without, in fact, providing much legitimate social or sexual status. Youngsters who are nearly ready for a sensitive and responsible relationship to each other find "going steady" extremely treacherous, since it denies them the right to get to know each other before their peers assume that they have made a commitment. Especially in good, middle-class high schools, a boy who takes a girl out three times is likely to find that she is assumed to be his; if he breaks off the relationship, she is simply abandoned; and he is regarded and is likely to regard himself as heartless.

Adolescents, then, are likely to find it far easier to have sexual intercourse than sexual relationships—or, for that matter, relationships of any kind. *Relatedness* is just what is denied people in our social system; and though this is a general and vital deficiency of our culture, it bears especially hard on adolescents. The socialization of Americans, particularly if they are above working-class status, is now assumed to require that they accept much geographical and social mobility. This means, in effect, learning to be friendly to large numbers of shifting casual acquaintances; mastering an effective "presentation of self" [15] in Erving Goffman's phrase; avoiding emotional entanglements with people who will only have to be abandoned when the job is done and one moves on to the next. Yet, adolescents need strong, highly personal emotional relationships to become fully human.

I have already stated my conviction that adolescent status is defined as it is precisely to afford society an optimal opportunity to arrest the development of more human potential than it can accept in its adult members. It is hardly astonishing, then, that it should do so by restricting opportunity for an essential process of growth. But human beings need many different kinds of experience to grow on; and although all

---

[14] Henry, *op. cit.*, pp. 262–276.
[15] As in his book, *The Presentation of Self in Everyday Life* (Garden City, N.Y.: Anchor Books, Doubleday, 1959).

are essential, they are not equally pressing at every stage of life, as Erikson's familiar paradigm of maturation makes clear. Erikson's model [16] portrays maturation as proceeding through eight successive stages, each characterized by a specific developmental task. To the extent that any individual fails in one of these crucial aspects of development, he will be hampered in each successive stage. Insults to fundamental processes of growth, or serious deficiencies in affection or experience, cannot be made up altogether by subsequent compensation or enrichment; there will inevitably be some distortion throughout later stages of growth. Human needs are needs at a specific time for specific purposes of growth.

The aspects of development, which Erikson states as polar pairs representing success versus failure, range from the establishment of "basic trust versus mistrust" in the environment during infancy, through "identity versus role diffusion" in puberty and adolescence, "intimacy versus isolation" in young adulthood, to "ego integrity versus despair" in maturity. These stages are not norms but universals that would apply to any culture in which the specific stage of growth discussed is discernible. Puberty greatly intensifies—indeed, precipitates—the human need to fuse intimacy and prowess, to focus feeling expressively on a fully realized, valued object, and to love. Adolescence requires what Erikson has called "the strength of disciplined devotion," [17] both to other persons and to wider purposes, whether private or expressed through political or social action.

This need, of course, conflicts directly with the process of socialization for mobility to which I have referred. The conflict of the postpubescent young with society would therefore appear to be overdetermined. It is not simply a matter of subjecting the adolescent to a process of socialization that diminishes his humanness. Rather, the specific developmental process dominant in adolescence, if allowed to proceed successfully, would make him less fit for most available social roles. If our society had more use for disciplined devotion than for social interaction, it would doubtless bear harder on the immediately prepubescent youngster and more easily on the postpubescent, discouraging and disciplining the social jockeying of later childhood and subjecting children to a more rigorous educational content, to be used to penetrate more deeply into the meaning of subsequent experience. But, the values of our society being what they are, and related as they are to its underlying economic arrangements, it is the adolescent who is subject

[16] Erik H. Erikson, *Childhood and Society*, Chapter 7, "Eight Ages of Man" (New York: Norton, second edition, 1963), pp. 247–274.
[17] Erik H. Erikson, "Youth, Fidelity and Diversity," *Daedalus*, 91, 1 (1962), p. 23.

to the heaviest and most severe socializing pressure, and who is likely to feel himself least able to meet society's demands and most reluctant to accept the roles it makes available.

These demands are made sharper and more hostile by the unconscious dynamics that underlie adult attitudes toward the adolescent, and the conscious feelings through which they are expressed. It is not easy for us to pay the costs of our own socialization, or to admit them to ourselves. The process of socializing the young cannot but arouse in older persons a complex and generally distasteful mixture of emotions: jealousy of the vigor and emotional openness of the young; guilt over our own part in training these out of them; nostalgia for the lost power of our own youth; erotic attraction and erotic envy. Coupled with these are more prosaic sources of hostility: fear of competition and displacement and fear that the heedless energy and often truculent commitment of youth will disrupt useful and profitable administrative arrangements. The acerbity of competition between the generations, as Bettelheim demonstrates in a masterly analysis,[18] has been intensified by the discontinuity in modern life. Our interest in and solicitude for the young are likely to be greatest when we see them as our successors in a common personal or cultural enterprise of value to us both and we think of ourselves as passing our authority and our skill on to youth who share our values and retain the strength to defend and propagate them. If, instead, we see them as struggling to render us obsolete by their cleverness or superior technique, trying to get us out of the way so that they can re-create the world in their image and obliterate ours, or, probably worst of all, wearily accepting our weakness and limitation till it shall please God to remove us, it becomes more difficult to applaud and encourage their progress.

The difficulties of dealing responsibly with the young become insuperable when compounded by administrative responsibility. School officials, political leaders, and employers are subject to conflicting pressures and are obligated by the demands of their office to resolve conflicting interests. They have often been selected by social processes that penalize directness and moral courage and that give no advantage to wisdom. Yet they do know more about the actual conditions under which they must function than their critics, and more than they feel free to explain. Their jobs often require them to face young challengers whom they believe to be right and defend policies in which they feel themselves to be entrapped. High school or college faculty assigned as advisers to student newspapers, for example, know that the

[18] Bruno Bettelheim, "The Problem of Generations," *Daedalus*, 91, 1(1962), pp. 68–96.

school administration expects them to censor editorials and even news reports that might prove troublesome, while their own self-esteem depends on their retaining the respect and liking of the students who work on the paper and an image of themselves as defenders, in principle, of forthright journalism and a free press. Liberal but acquiescent personnel men for firms that practice clandestine discrimination must justify their decisions to militant young defenders of civil rights despite their own feelings of guilt. There is little such men can do except become evasive, pull rank, or disparage the intelligence or motivation of their charges, seeing them as misguided enthusiasts or as young conspirators. Which, unfortunately, young people sometimes are.

Between adolescents and their elders, then, there is more likely to be an uneasy truce covered by a generalized and fragile facade of goodwill than genuine affection, trust, and empathy. Both try to work out a modus vivendi; each tries to manipulate the other. Often the most positive element in the relationship is erotic; for only a thorough puritan can steadfastly deny the weight of this testimony to the value of the postpubescent young. Sense data may be repressed or distorted in perception; but they are there and must be dealt with. The young, ultimately, are by their physical presence their own best witness. Sexuality has been experienced in so many ways that it is difficult to say what its essential quality may be; but it is, among other things, reassuring.

Minority Status of Adolescents

The image of adolescent life reflected in the popular stereotype has less in common with the Botticelli *Aphrodite* than with the coarse festivities depicted by Pieter Brueghel; and a vocal minority of adults would go on from there to the fantasies of Hieronymus Bosch. Every newsstand has its supply of pornography purporting to depict what goes on among high school students; and although the picture presented is perhaps no more degrading than the reality, it is certainly much more erotic. The processes that menace the virtue of high school students are threatening, indeed; but they are social and intellectual for the most part. Yet the characteristic portrayal of adolescent behavior in the popular press, and the resulting public image, are revealing despite, or indeed because of, their distortion.

What is most interesting about this image is that it is so much like that of every minority group that has first entered this country, as immigrants usually do, in a low socioeconomic status. All these people, in their turn, are depicted as childish and irresponsible, warmhearted and lovable, but uncontrolled and unstable—their broad jollity shifts easily to whimsical and destructive brutality. They excel in crude expression, in dancing and jazz and sports; the spirit of Dionysos is barely contained in the body of Apollo.

This description is never, of course, wholly invalid for any people who are kept, despite their competence and vigor, in irresponsible and degrading isolation from the economic and social mainstream of the community to which they aspire. The exemption of Jewish and Chinese immigrants from this stereotype is probably because they usually did not aspire, at least at the outset, to anything like complete integration, but continued to sustain themselves on the fruits and folkways of their original culture. Being less frustrated by their exclusion, they behaved with less hostility and were then perceived as exotic, sinister, and potentially subversive, but not as childish, irresponsible, or potentially riotous and brutal.

The adolescent shares with the southern European, Latin American, and Slavic immigrant both the need to gain an economic place and the obligation ultimately to abandon whatever mode of life has become natural to him and consent to his own socialization. In the case of the adolescent, the threat to the larger society is probably even more severe than that presented by foreign immigrants, since his acceptance cannot in principle be long delayed. It must once have looked to proper Bostonians as if the Irish and Italians could be kept in their place indefinitely by sustained and coordinated exclusion. But nobody has this illusion about teen-agers, though the teen-agers, in desperation, do sometimes have it about themselves.

Hostility, while it lasts, is then based on even stronger anxiety and is likely to be even sharper, just as Southern white antagonism toward Negroes is currently exacerbated by its own obvious futility. This stereotypical hostility is functional; it does reduce economic competition. One of the most troublesome and threatening characteristics of adolescents is that they need jobs. The teen-agers much-discussed ten billion dollars a year breaks down to an average of about seventeen dollars a week for boys and a small fraction of that for girls, which does not go far among a group whose society provides them no economic function except that of an oversteered consumer. The jobs adolescents formerly found as elevator operators or delivery boys have been eliminated by automation and the mechanization of personal services. They now press directly on the shrinking unskilled and semiskilled adult job market; a stereotype that views them as alien justifies their rejection as inexperienced and irresponsible, whereas adults who accept the young and care for them as their own successors are obliged to help them gain the experience and develop a sense of responsibility.

Hostility to adolescents also, paradoxically, reduces adults' emotional conflict about them. Hostility helps any discriminator, be he a middle-aged critic of teen-age behavior or an American of earlier stock viewing recent immigrants, to stigmatize his own former characteristics as disgusting, thus both diminishing his tendency to relapse and giving him the furtive and nostalgic satisfaction of thinking about it. But, when special circumstances abate the economic threat, the erotic fantasy suddenly deflates. Our attitudes toward servicemen who are either adolescent or members of ethnic minorities strikingly illustrate this phenomenon. Soldiers and sailors are economically by definition *hors d'oeuvre* and *hors de combat*. Their status is officially subordinate; there is simply no question of regarding "our boys in the service" as men. Far from pressing competitively upon the job market, they are immured in a nonproductive status that supports the economy and creates employment for others. Their ethnicity, if any, then disappears, or is at least subsumed under the general inferiority of enlisted status. Soldiers and sailors are just Americans; even their own intergroup hostilities melt away as their military identity develops.

This attitude could be explained as the consequence simply of recognition, by the public and themselves, that their service to their country entitles them to full acceptance as Americans. But the same thing happens to adolescents who go into uniform, even if they are already as American as only an individual of completely Anglo-German origins can be. Adolescents who become soldiers are more likely than other adolescents to be the kind of youngsters who fit the stereotype of teen-age misconduct. Most adolescents who join the Army or Navy are working class or lower and have low educational aspirations. These boys are more likely than most to use poor and offensive language; their sexual behavior is freer; they are more likely to fight and less likely to argue. These are among the traits that get teen-agers branded as "troublemakers," but in servicemen they are not seen as offensive but as normal; they are elements of a positive *stereotype*.

Because what is disparaged in adolescents and ethnics is praised in the military men does not, I would suggest, indicate that the stereotype has changed its essential function. This remains what it was: to attest to their unsuitability to compete for adult status and full membership in the society and the economy. The difference is the same as that between a "good and bad nigger" in old Southern ideology: the "bad nigger" made himself dangerous and ridiculous by trying to become like a white man; the "good nigger" knew that he could not and obviously enjoyed just the characteristics that made it impossible. The first had therefore to be rebuffed and sharply reminded of his deficiencies, while the second was praised for his naturalness and humility, and even wistfully envied for his simple, happy, slave life.

The similarity between the status of the adolescent and the displaced "native" persists in the practice of subjecting both to legal restrictions not applicable to other members of society—even to discriminated ethnic groups. Teen-agers, Indians who live on reservations and thereby retain tribal status, and Australian aboriginals are forbidden to buy liquor when anyone else may. They are treated in various ways as wards of the state; there are impediments to their making contracts or conveying title to property; they may not apply for certain licenses that are available to ordinary adults, even when the license is awarded only after competence is demonstrated; many fifteen-year-olds have a virtuoso's mastery of automobiles, yet cannot become licensed drivers; teen-agers, like South African natives, are subject in many locations to a curfew. That these discriminatory practices are justified as necessary for the *protection* as well as the control of the young does not really tell us much; the Australian and South African governments make similar claims, and with evident sincerity. They also, however, display a simultaneous patronage and contempt for the objects of their solicitude, and a callous disregard for the same folkways they praise as attractively primitive, if these interfere with customary administrative practices.

As life becomes more philanthropic and bureaucratic, subordinate status becomes more onerous; General Custer, as Sitting Bull demonstrated with finality, was in the end easier to deal with than the Bureau of Indian Affairs has proved to be.[19] However benign the intent of authority may be, and however useful the services it provides, its institutional form makes it to some extent both a vested interest and a source of constraint. The legal definition of a class of juvenile offenders subject to special courts with special powers and procedures may, as was intended, make the treatment of young offenders more humane. But it also sharply reduces their access to due process and constitutional guarantees and blurs the distinction between justice and administrative intervention. Adolescents now sometimes find themselves legally in a twilight zone. They can be apprehended for behavior that falls short of the kind of overt act which is defined as a legal offense for adults: adolescents can be and often are confined for indefinite periods in a "juvenile hall" or "detention home" on accusations of incorrigibility or potential delinquency, even though no charge has been

---

[19] See Murray L. and Rosalie H. Wax et al., "Formal Education in an American Indian Community," SSSP Monograph Supplement to *Social Problems*, 11, 4 (Spring 1964).

proved against them. Indeed, no trial is held; they are committed at hearings with few formal safeguards and are subjected to judgments which, precisely because they are conceived and justified as more remedial than punitive, are left much more to the discretion of the official in charge—who may or may not be a judge—than any to which an adult defendant might have to submit. While an adult at least knows that, if convicted, he can only be fined, imprisoned, or executed, and that his punishment is limited by the statute governing his offense, a juvenile offender is subject to minor and whimsical indignities. He may be sent to a reformatory, but he may also be required to write a penitent and a patriotic paper or—as an Indiana judge has become famous for doing—coerced into accepting a public spanking in preference to incarceration.[20]

Nor are "problem" youngsters the only adolescents who find themselves under legal disability; to some degree all adolescents do.[21] We are so accustomed to viewing public education as a service to the young and a cost to the adult community that we do not recognize that it is also a severe and exceptionally protracted form of constraint. Public school attendance requirements constitute an odd form of guardianship. The school is not required to demonstrate that it benefits the young people who are obliged to attend it. Their status is essentially that of a conscript; they are protected by certain regulations governing the school and its personnel and procedures, and by certain standards which the school must maintain; but no breach of these can legally justify their withdrawal. This policy, like military conscription, is defended by saying that education is undertaken in the public interest. But the community also expects the adolescent himself to feel that he is receiving a service, that the school is serving his interests as well as the public interest.

These positions are not, of course, logically in conflict. It is necessary for an individual to function in the society he lives in, and what the society requires of him in order to make this possible may therefore be said to be in his interests. Whether compulsory school attend-

[20] Adolescents thus find themselves, like those classed as mentally ill, defenseless precisely because society has defined its constraint as a service and a kindness. This, I believe, is a central thesis of Thomas Szasz in *Law, Liberty, and Psychiatry* (New York: The Macmillan Company, 1963).

[21] To an increasing degree, all adolescents find themselves defined as "problems" for the purposes of the rapidly metastasizing bureaucracies set up to coordinate and orient them. See particularly Aaron V. Cicourel and John I. Kitsuse, *The Educational Decision-Makers* (Indianapolis: Bobbs-Merrill, 1963) for a chilling case study of the functioning of counseling in a large high school in a primarily upper-middle-class suburb of Chicago.

ance is good for an individual youngster or not, it is certainly an indispensable part of the socialization process by which he becomes an American adult. But it is nevertheless clear that laws compelling school attendance on the basis of age—and age alone—do certainly set the adolescent apart as subject to special constraint and create a unique category of legal sanctions to apply to him. It is also clear that, although the educational function of the school remains putative and hortatory, its custodial function is explicit and mandatory. Public education may be necessary to produce a citizenry competent to function in a democracy or a technically developed society. But we do not require that anyone attend school until he can demonstrate a particular degree of competence by examination, say, or performance in an internship. We demand that he attend until he reaches a specific age, and we attempt to induce him to remain longer if that is not long enough for him to obtain a certificate. The meaning of this certificate, and the basis for our concern with it, are the source of great conflict, for it has become impossible to go on simultaneously requiring that all adolescents try to earn it and pretending to define it as evidence of intellectual or academic achievement. The difficulty does not appear to lie primarily in any sort of native deficiency in ability—it is probably true that a very large majority of adolescents are capable of doing the work a good high school offers—but in the fact that no high school program specific enough to have rich meaning for certain of its students can mean much of anything to others whose experience of life has been altogether different.

The custodial function, then, predominates because it is residual. And again, its economic utility is disturbingly evident. Whatever else it is, or fails to be, the educational system in America is a superb way of keeping people out of production and out of economic competition. In the upper range of adolescence, this function is continued by college and graduate school for youth of higher economic aspirations, and by the army and simple, aimless indigence for those with less opportunity or a lower level of aspiration. When we refer to these processes, we usually speak of the rising educational requirements for employment in a technologically developed industrial society, rather than of contracting opportunity for people to earn a living at their accustomed, ordinary levels of skill. But this latter, after all, is what automation means.

By the devices I have discussed and others, we therefore finally deny adolescents any meaningful economic function. In an open, competitive society, this amounts to denying that they seriously exist. The result is to force them to choose among a number of discernibly different roles which share a strongly fantastic element—an "as if" quality which heightens the unreality of the experience and tends further to retard the development of the firm sense of personal identity that adolescents find so essential to their growth, and society finds so difficult to accept in its members.

The "Teen-ager"

The most normal—in the strict sense of the word—of these roles is that of the "teen-ager." A "teen-ager" is what adults expect adolescents to be; it is the role that the mass media, merchants, planners, and chaperones of school "activities" and commercialized entertainment, and especially parents, expect adolescents to fit. By becoming a teen-ager the adolescent reduces his conflict with the rest of society to a minimum. He also gains reassurance from the response of those around him that his growth is proceeding normally, and that he may expect to enjoy in adulthood the normal amenities of life in his culture.

There is much to be said for this. Being a teen-ager eliminates the superficial but nevertheless excruciating anxieties that come from feeling abnormal and involving oneself in continuous fights with authority. Authority today, moreover—especially if it is middle class—is likely to express itself benignly, and to respond to youthful recalcitrance with more disappointment and bewilderment than overt irritation or reprisal. The adolescent cannot fight it without becoming uncomfortably guilty and feeling that he is alienating people who are, on the whole, friendly and well-disposed toward him. This not only is a heavy price to pay but must also seem needlessly willful.

I encountered an especially disturbing example of this authority in a recent visit to a Juvenile Hall in a primarily middle-class, suburban county of California. The director of the institution had invited me to spend half a day in a seminar at his institution, which was a new, physically attractive building in the foothills of the coast range; it was late March, California's green and tender season. This director seemed to me a man almost ideally suited to his job: intelligent, tender-tough, realistic about kids, and devoted to them. He has managed to maintain a remarkably generous policy of furlough and a program of coeducational recreation among his charges, against constant and pressing community vigilance and anxiety. The staff are called "counselors" rather than guards, and they obviously *feel* like counselors rather than guards.

But this attitude must make the experience more confusing, as well as more humane for the youngsters. Nobody uses the word, but they are confined to cells. In the coast range hills their windows are sealed;

there is a tepid trickle of forced air and a prison stink. Since these are mostly middle-class kids of the kind teachers and counselors feel at home with, they are treated pleasantly and respond pleasantly in return; they follow visitors around curiously to the limit of their restricted orbit. They are under detention; they have not been convicted, or necessarily even charged with any offense. Most of the people they see are kind. Only they cannot open a window or go out even into the hall's fenced gardens unless taken there. The bulletin board in the main hall has on it a large facsimile of the Constitution. I asked the director what happened when a youngster read it. "Then," he replied with a grin, "we'd be in trouble!"

The advantages of teen-age status are not confined to making interpersonal relationships smoother and easier. Being a "teen-ager" makes life simpler in general for the adolescent. His requirements and interests are catered for; the clothes and the cars and the rest of the equipment he needs are widely available, though costly. He need not face the difficulties of trying to function alone in a mass society. By accepting the definition of himself as a teen-ager, the adolescent accommodates socially; the disadvantages, then, become those of social accommodation.

How serious these disadvantages are depends on how serious a distortion teen-agers are of what an adolescent might be, and how much is likely to be lost of what he might become. Being a teen-ager is certainly the most comfortable and efficient way of becoming a middle-class American adult; and if this is satisfactory, there seems no special reason to avoid it. If the limitations of middle-class social character are not acceptable, then to become a teen-ager makes an adolescent a kind of Uncle Tom, who gives up some of his dignity and modifies his private conception of himself to get along with, and ultimately into, the middle-class adult world. It is misleading, however, to discuss such an issue as though it could be faced as a conscious choice. To the teenager himself, a teen-ager is likely to seem the only thing there is for him to be.

Few features distinguish him sharply from the adult he is becoming. There is no genuine "adolescent society" or "peer culture" to be contrasted with that of the surrounding adult world. Adolescents have nothing like enough detachment to form one. People who have no homes or economic roots of their own, and who are constantly controlled and bombarded by a dominant social group into which they themselves know they must ultimately be absorbed, do not develop a culture or society. The most they do is devise, like prisoners, customs, insignia, and an etiquette with which to maintain a little freedom and privacy. Teen-age status does this much well. Because it accepts the basic social values of our culture, it merely annoys or amuses adults; it does not threaten them seriously. Yet, in its very extravagance, teenage behavior expresses elements of hostile self-parody, which are selectively emphasized and exploited by adult observers. The paperback books of jokes and cartoons about teen-agers that can be bought in any drugstore make a somewhat more archaic point than their topical emphasis suggests. Their characters, though decidedly faded, are still recognizable to those old enough to have known them. Here, reincarnate, are Amos and Andy, the Kingfish, and Madam Queen.

Is this caricature of adolescence false and malicious? To a degree, but the matter is not quite that simple. Like that of the Negro, the image of the teen-ager is produced by reflection, as if back and forth from the walls of a barbershop with distorting mirrors. There really is a customer who looks a little like this image and—which is much more serious—who recognizes himself only in such images, who has no other way of knowing what he does look like. There is also an entrepreneur, firmly convinced that he knows what the teen-ager should look like, after he has finished trimming him. The Negro has finally revolted, and a good deal of glass is being shattered; when it has been replaced it will reflect a different image of a different reality. But the teen-ager tends ruefully to accept the prevailing image of himself and cooperates with the efforts of school and society to make him match it.

The hostility in this caricature is less the result of adults' overt distaste for adolescents than of their need to portray some of the more unpleasant traits many adolescents do develop as innate rather than as evidence of successful socialization. The youngsters themselves sometimes resent the indignity of being regarded as teen-agers; but they also—like a successful Southern Negro undertaker of 40 years ago—exploit it and become accomplices in their own humiliation. A submissive subordinate does more than just reduce his anxiety and avoid conflict; he acquires certain positive immunities. A teen-age conclave can, if it wishes, make itself as impenetrable to parents or teachers as an enlisted men's canteen is to officers or a Negro dance hall in a Southern city is to whites. Conversely, low status makes people socially invisible without impairing their faculties; teen-agers know a good deal more about their parents and teachers than they could learn if adults took their presence seriously.

There are useful advantages in this system of defensive maneuvers that allow teen-agers to live with adults, observe how they operate, and still preserve a measure of privacy and self-direction. Such maneuvers do not, however, help adolescents to become aware of any alternative life style beyond that visible in adult models. Adults *can* and sometimes do provide adolescents with something more fundamental: with models of compassion, of autonomy, of authentic emotional response. But these, surely, are not the social skills we live by; and they are not what youth in America is encouraged to learn, or could learn, except from adults who respect them.

American education is no failure; it is one of the most efficient systems yet devised for turning out people suited to their culture. Teenagers are simply one of the stages in this process. The more conspicuous differences are between teen-agers' social and economic marginality. Teen-age groups, for example, tend to be even more completely attuned to consumption and sensitive to changing consumer patterns than adults. We interpret this as faddishness and triviality and complain of the conformity that makes them dress alike, amuse themselves in the same way, use the same catchwords, and dance to the same tune —different drummers get short shrift. But consumption is the only economic function in which teen-agers are engaged; they are either completely dependent on allowances or hold part-time, poorly paid, temporary jobs. Moreover, constituting as they do a large market whose individual members have little to spend, there is hardly any profit to be made by offering them a genuine choice among goods and services. To make any money from teen-agers, unit costs must be kept low, and the market saturated with cheap, uniform products. The teenage market is among the most thoroughly manipulated in our economy; for example, distributors of clothing and other fashionable gear customarily select high school or college students thought to be campus leaders and subsidize them in a small way to wear or otherwise promote the popularity of their product.

Adolescents who have adopted the teen-age style also show emotional marginality. Their behavior may range from sheer apathy, through cool cynicism, to orgiastic display, according to circumstances. But even their orgies are likely to be objectless; the popular singer of the moment is not loved for what he distinctly is; and the youngsters themselves know that they have made no commitment to him; their frenzy is wholly subjective. But adolescents, as "teen-agers," cannot regard themselves as authorized to make emotional investments. Occasionally, a sardonic youngster consciously parodies this alienated state; some collect campaign buttons for all the possible presidential candidates and wear them at once as jacket studs. The most creative of these to come to my attention, by a considerable margin, was a youth who, for several days during the emotional height of the Eichmann trial, wore around high school a large, homemade button proclaiming, "I like Eich!"

High school athletic contests provide especially rich opportunity for observing the pressures on the teen-ager and the emotional limitations of his role, in contrast to more authentic modes of adolescent emotional response. In small communities, at least, basketball and football games create for the high school a recurring crisis in public relations. No other function of the school arouses such strong and complex emotions in adults, ranging from real joy in the vigor and prowess of youth to the most vicious and destructive competitive feelings; and this is a situation that is notable in our culture for permitting comparative freedom of expression. Student response is an important element in this spectacle, and high schools do not risk leaving it to spontaneous self-expression; it is structured by pep rallies, cadres of cheerleaders, and other familiar devices. The result is that the young spectators whose individual responses might have been spontaneous but enthusiastic can no longer tell whether they are expressing their feelings or enacting their roles. They appear, however, to be more involved in projecting an "image" of enthusiastic support than in the progress of the game itself; they cheer goals and victory but not exceptional strategy or tactics except at the moment these pay off; and they watch one another to see how their enthusiasm is received.

But the team responds differently. Their athletic experience is genuine enough to prevent them from becoming "teen-age." If they are good, they share actual skills, esteem for competence, and a serious mutual undertaking. Their actions and their posture in defeat or victory are often mute evidence that they value what they are trying to do and value one another as contributors to doing it. Athletic skill seems especially helpful to adolescents in establishing their sense of who they are, their sense of self-esteem. This is not only because athletes win deference and sometimes even respect, or because successful athletes enjoy superior sexual opportunity, though they have both of these advantages. It is also because athletic prowess is self-validating. Athletic competence is possible only to one who is on intimate terms with his own body and who knows what it can do and how to use it; athletic achievement cannot be faked. For this reason an individual sport like track, in which the athlete judges his own performance against established standards rather than concentrating on the defeat of a particular adversary, probably contributes more to adolescent growth than does a team sport, and athletic activities that are carried on entirely outside the school or any formal administrative structure contribute most of all.

Such athletic enterprises, rare as they are, are implicitly pro-adolescent and anti-teen-age. A pointed illustration of this distinction is afforded by an exchange of letters in a recent issue of an interesting journal called *The Surfer*,[22] which caters to the specialized interests of the growing number of youngsters interested in the surfboard. Surfing is, as yet, an informal sport that is practiced individually or under the sponsorship of adolescent groups themselves; it is not a school sport or a highly competitive one—surfers compete only on form. In California, surfers and those who identify with them call ordinary teen-agers "hodads." A "hodad" wrote to the magazine:

> In your past issues of the SURFER you have printed letters saying, "Do away with Hodads and Gremmies," etc. To be frank with you, I am a hodad. I don't want to be, but I am. I want to do what everyone else is doing, but I can't seem to surf good. I think that this is the problem of most of the other hodads, and I think the surfers should give us a chance. If you publish this letter, I think the surfers will understand us hodads a little better.

The editor replied:

> To be frank with you, ——, the objection to hodads has come about because of the attitude that some bring with them—that surfing is one big, glorious rumble and an excuse for thefts and misdeeds. Fortunately, not all hodads are surfing for these reasons—and I think your letter makes that clear. One of the reasons some hodads don't surf well is that their boards are slippery—hair oil and other greases on a highly polished decorative-type surfboard make for a very difficult surfing. *To be a good surfer takes more than just a desire to belong to the group. It takes a lot of actual practice—surfing* [italics mine].

The editor's reply does much more than defend the dignity of his avocation. He also resists, courteously but firmly, the "hodad's" wistful invitation to be a good guy and more tolerant—there is a volume of unspoken social criticism in the editor's retention of "surf well" where the "hodad" says "surf good." But it seems evident to me that it is the "hodad" who is being more successfully socialized. It is he who will be patient and understanding when his wife feeds him on TV dinners and packaged, "gourmet-type" Noodles Romanoff. The editor may even expect his wife to learn to cook, thereby making her anxious and forcing her into therapy.

But despite their longing to be accepted into the surfers' enterprise,

[22] 3, 4 (May-June 1964), p. 4.

"hodads" do not genuinely respect them or understand what they get out of surfing. High school athletic teams, similarly, fail to command the respect of their teen-age spectators. Teen-agers in action as such cannot express such respect; they display a variety of advanced social skills rather than a coherent pattern of tastes and values. They do not see what the team is trying to do and may, as the following recent observations of half-time ceremonies at a "homecoming" football game illustrate, use the occasion for wholly incongruous purposes.

The home team represented a famous public school, which has justly become distinguished for exceptional academic quality; before this game it had lost four in a row. The library has a collection of which a small college should be proud, excellent in both range and political audacity. It is a national center for imaginative curriculum planning and manages to provide an atmosphere of trust, respect, and intellectual stimulation for students of a very wide range of ability. The model of scholarship it presents is both appealing and demanding and suggests as strongly as a school well can that intellectual interests are to be extended into daily life. Few if any of its students can be seriously hampered in using its resources by any anxiety or hostility caused by its treatment of them.

Efforts to arouse community enthusiasm, however, are artificial because the school serves a region of extreme geographical mobility. Many elderly people come there to retire and have no interest whatever in the school except as a possible basis for taxation. Economically, the area has exploded from near-destitution to a high rate of low-level employment in industries related to military and missile development. A high proportion of the inhabitants have moved into the area within the past few years, and many of the students are transfers from other high schools.

What the word "homecoming" means in such a context is unclear; it serves, however, as an occasion for remarkable ceremonial. At the half, the National Anthem was played. Afterward, the spectators remained standing and repeated the Pledge of Allegiance, while drum majorettes in gold lamé blouses and brief shorts held their batons rigidly in various positions of attention. There followed a small parade of five or six comic floats pulled by automobiles. The winning float depicted a large, papier-mâché bulldog—the symbol of the home team—dressed as a pugilist, revolving as it was towed along. The second prize winner seemed more imaginative and was certainly more elaborate. It bore three human figures, only two of which were visible at a time. A young athlete was ushered by another boy dressed in a white coat with a stethoscope and a big clipboard of charts into a large box labeled

TERRORIZING MACHINE. (The visiting team were called "Terriors.") A puff of smoke and a flash were emitted from the box, and a third boy who had been concealed in it staggered out, smudged and rag-clad, in an attitude of extravagant decrepitude.

The comedy finished, the solemn feature of the homecoming ceremony began. A throne was erected in the middle of the field. The band disbanded and reassembled as an orchestra seated behind the thirty-yard line. As it began playing, in slow tempo, a series of familiar popular favorites of yesteryear—the first was "My Funny Valentine"—a procession of some twenty-five or thirty teen-age couples began to cross the field, the girls in elaborate formals, the boys mostly in summer dinner jackets with a few dark business suits. Each of the girls had been nominated as a candidate for homecoming queen by the boys' organization whose president was now escorting her. The winner had been selected, though not publicly announced, at a pep rally that afternoon for which last-period classes had been canceled.

The girl chosen was a French exchange student who was spending a year at the school; the choice evoked marked and clearly genuine enthusiasm, apparently for the international gesture, since school had been in session less than two months and this girl, unlike most of the candidates who were regularly enrolled in it, could not have been well known personally. She ascended the throne, flanked by the girls who had been chosen for second and third place. The captain of the football team, covered with the stains of the playing field, then advanced on the throne and handed her a huge bouquet of roses.

From the sidelines, then, a boy in summer evening dress drove a new, black, Pontiac convertible that had been lent by the local dealer across the field to the throne. The Queen entered it, sat on the folded canvas of the top, like a political candidate, and graciously saluted the spectators as she was driven slowly around and around the asphalt running track. Meanwhile, however, it began to drizzle. The Queen, captive, held her position royally; but the girls and their escorts, who had been standing as an honor guard in their vulnerable finery, slunk off to shelter. They missed the second half of the game, which the Bulldogs won by an impressive margin.

Tribal customs often seem grotesque to extraneous observers who do not understand them. But this homecoming ceremonial seems more grotesque if one does understand it: what is troubling about it is its utter lack of integration. Individually, each of the values symbolized in the successive parts of the ceremony is valid in the sense that it is indeed powerfully held by the community; some of them may be bad values, but all are conspicuous in our way of life. Every culture expresses in its ceremonial some values that are destructive and growth inhibiting even on its own terms. Every culture includes discordant values and expresses their conflict in symbolic terms. Every culture is ambivalent about many of its most cherished attitudes.

But not every culture lumps secular, religious, patriotic, and exhibitionist motifs into one eclectic mess. Not every culture confuses its occasions for outdoor, body-contact sport and for display of ballroom attire. Not every culture translates its generosity to a foreign visitor into commercial display. Behind this disorder and heterogeneity one senses genuine apathy, the kind of neglect that has created a neon strip along the thoroughfares leading into every major American city: expensive, banal, repetitive, and enervating. The false-fronted villages Potemkin constructed to line the route of his sovereign's progress were empty frauds designed to delude Catherine the Great into thinking that her empire was flourishing. But Potemkin at least knew how a flourishing village ought to look. The image that he counterfeited was an image of organic growth.

The teen-agers in the high school where the Bulldogs play have at their disposal, more abundantly than most high school students, intellectual and cultural resources adequate to inform them who they are and where they come from, and to help them decide where they wish to go. They use them with marked enthusiasm. But when they wish to project a public image of themselves they include nothing of this in it; nor do they use it more subtly to give order and discipline to their way of arranging this display. One can hardly avoid concluding that their smiling confusion and taste for chaos have become cultural principles in themselves, serving to reassure them that life is made of interchangeable, replaceable parts and can be plugged in anywhere.

"Pro-social" Youth

Though only a small proportion of American youth behave as if strongly committed to any basic values, a high proportion of those Americans who show strong commitment are young. Some are adolescent, more are old enough to be considered young adults. They are included in this discussion because, characteristically, their friendships and associations are linked to their recent past rather than their future, which suggests that their identifications probably are also. They are campus-based; they think of themselves as, and usually are, "students."

These "pro-social" youth are a novel and, on the whole, a reassuring development. Until about 1960 American youth seemed devoid of political interests and incapable of social action, absorbed—at least since World War II—in the individual pursuit of not especially enlightened self-interest. Although young people in Turkey, Korea, Japan, Latin America, and the emerging nations of Africa and Asia appeared on the world scene from time to time as Youth on the March, American youth, like that of western Europe, more often settled for the role of Youth on the Make: an unedifying spectacle, especially to adults who had already "made it."

In this respect the vast majority of American youth have not changed greatly. Their careerism cannot, in any case, be thought of as primarily characterological. In the newer nations youth need not choose, for ideological commitment and passion may form the basis of a career, whereas in the older, relatively closed societies of Asia and Latin America the young cannot make the future appear more promising even by conformity. But in America, political passion and social commitment close paths of ascent that would otherwise be open; they do not open others. Young men here do not embark upon successful careers in politics, labor, education, or the ministry with spectacular ideological devotion.

Pro-social youth are therefore all the more remarkable. Their youthfulness is in part an artifact; other adults infer it from their political, social, or artistic and expressive interests, which are taken as evidence that they have not "settled down." But they are indeed pro-social, both in the sense that they assert themselves within the framework of existing institutions, which they seek to improve, and in the more profound sense that they maintain and defend democratic values officially endorsed but hopelessly compromised by society generally. The very factors that make them pro-social prevent their becoming, however, more than narrowly and empirically political. Like other American pressure groups, pro-social youth direct their energy toward a series of specific economic and legislative goals, avoiding direct challenge to fundamental polity. Liberal pro-social youth generally oppose elitist political philosophy and insist that a comparatively open society be opened still more widely to accommodate the ambitions of those hitherto denied access to social and economic opportunity. Most of their effort has recently been centered on the struggle for civil rights and equal treatment for Negro citizens, which began, at least in the present phase, as a youth movement in the form of sit-ins by college students and young "freedom riders," passing into the hands of older leaders after the younger people had demonstrated its feasibility by taking the initial risks, and had brought the movement to the point where it required more formal structure and continuous use of legal and economic technique. Simultaneously, self-styled conservative youth groups have appeared which, although not overtly anti-Negro, champion the existing American social order and resist any critical analysis of it. Lawrence F. Schiff, in one of the few studies of young American conservatives, has described these groups as composed of young people who are likely to feel themselves to be socially marginal and to be seeking "a symbolic identification with an historically, culturally, and socially well-defined and prestigeful American position," [23] a position from which they cannot afford to express dissent or criticism.

The situation of American pro-social youth appears therefore to be fraught with irony and potential political confusion. For in this country liberal attitudes on issues that are not specifically economic (such as socialized medicine) tend to be positively correlated with social status and income, and to be supported by the social institutions that are least responsive to popular sovereignty. Already, liberal pro-social youth has been forced to depend more and more heavily on judicial decision and a reluctant and vulnerable executive branch against the opposition of a recalcitrant legislature and entrenched local sovereignties, and to depend on policy decisions that large corporate structures have been more willing to make than able to implement locally against the bitter resentment of entrenched local opposition. This is an odd position for a liberal, empathetically disposed to attack the establishment, to find himself in. The young conservatives seem a bit out of place defending the century-old myths of classic liberalism, on which spokesmen for free enterprise still draw for ceremonial self-justification, with resources derived from insurgent and disaffected Texas oilmen and a deep, abiding, and probably well-justified faith that the common man, fearfully defending his hard-won increments of status and respectability, is on their side. Where liberal pro-social youth tend to be too resentful of privilege to recognize that the values they defend have deeply conservative roots and operate feebly if at all in the common life of America, the young conservatives tend to be too preoccupied with their status aspirations to recognize—and too canny to admit—that their values are exactly what make them "mass" and therefore give them strength in a mass society. Neither group is disposed toward the kind of radical critique of American political function that would be needed to make their position ideologically consistent.[24]

[23] In a working paper on "The Conservative Movement on American Campuses," prepared for the Conference on Youth and Social Action held at Howard University, October 3–6, 1963.

[24] During the period that this volume was in preparation, the emergence of new, more fundamentally critical youth groups, such as Students for a Democratic Society, has, however, brightened this picture.

Pro-social youth are themselves largely middle-class and collegiate; some are former teen-agers who developed an interest in the substance of politics through becoming familiar with its forms as "student leaders" in high school; others were never teen-agers and were alienated from most of their high school peers by their inappropriate social interests; a few attended secondary schools in which such interests were socially acceptable; and a very few attach themselves to pro-social groups while still in secondary school. Numerically they are insignificant in comparison to the teen-age population, or even to the portion of it that goes on to college. Their political role is also largely peripheral, though sometimes dramatic. But they are important as an example of what we might call the secondary defenses of society against the failure of adolescent socialization. For those who, despite the experience of secondary education, continue to sense that society is questionable and to find terms in which questions can be raised, the role of liberal pro-social youth serves to contain the questioner, preserve him from alienation, and perhaps even put him to limited use as a source of innovation. For those who dream the American dream too seriously and find that reality threatens to turn it into nightmare, the role of young conservative gives the nightmare form and style and prevents abrupt awakening. He, too, is preserved against alienation; before he can actually turn into a fascist, the Young American for Freedom is likely to find that he has made it to the suburbs and is as safe as he will ever be.

But what of those who turn antisocial—whose socialization does fail, who do not make it in school, and whose home is inadequate through poverty or emotional disorder to bring them into the mainstream of American life? Being a teen-ager is not the only way of growing up. There are other ways that less clearly reflect the values and usages of middle-class life and that do not so reliably promise the youngsters who follow them easy assimilation into middle-class status. Since these values are official to the society and dominate its institutions, they nevertheless have a strong influence on the lives and behavior of those who reject them—quite possibly a stronger influence than on those who accept them, since the dissident or rebel is trapped in the social order and has less room for maneuver than the teen-ager, but the impact has different results.

Aspects of Delinquency

The most familiar and widely publicized patterns of adolescent life, besides that of the teen-ager, are those classed as delinquent. Teen-agers, to be sure, also commit delinquent acts and form more or less protracted illicit relationships as a part of their experimentation in finding an identity for themselves; and there are certainly youths whom an observer could not classify either way with any confidence and who, indeed, may or may not turn permanently delinquent according to chance circumstances—such as getting caught and acquiring a record for a minor and comparatively isolated offense. Nevertheless, delinquent groups develop their own styles; they do not act much like teenagers.

Juvenile delinquency is, however, almost impossible to discuss with precision. There are too many slippery factors: there is variation from one location to another about what constitutes delinquency; there is variation in the rigor of law enforcement in different places and at different times, so that statements about trends in delinquency mean little. Adults who discuss delinquency, moreover, are usually concerned about aspects of adolescent behavior that seem to them disruptive or destructive, rather than with technical judgments about the legality of what youngsters do; and although this concern may sensitize them to deterioration in relations between the generations, it makes their responses valueless as objective indices of change; what seems delinquent to one adult may be defended by another as a sign of healthy spirit and juvenile vigor.

There are also subtler reasons why quantitative estimates of delinquency, even defined with more than usual caution, are likely to mislead. As has already been mentioned, certain categories of offenses can only be committed by juveniles, like truancy or buying liquor, and by their existence as legal categories make juveniles appear lawless in comparison to older groups. Other acts, like possession of marijuana, car theft, and certain sexual acts, though offenses if committed by adults, have a totally different meaning in the lives of adolescents who commit them than they have for adult offenders. In any case, adolescents, having generally less privacy and less status than adults, are far more vulnerable to detection and prosecution.

So to view juvenile delinquency with alarm is pointless; we cannot be certain just what is alarming. It is clear that there are many groups of young people who relate to one another in such a way that their socialization is much forestalled, and whose behavior is threatening to other persons, especially, perhaps, to other juveniles. It is equally clear that these groups are not alike but can be placed in quite different categories according to what they do and why they do it. What they have in common is that, from the adult point of view, the gang serves as a subculture and screens its members from the institutional pressures that more effectively draw teen-agers into an acceptable social orbit.

It is this alternative, and unacceptable, process of socialization that worries adults more than the actual delinquent acts. This is evident from the fact that a lone adolescent who commits an offense of the kind associated with juvenile delinquents is not usually regarded as one;[25] he is more likely to be treated as either a prankster or an emotionally disturbed individual—which in fact he is more likely to be. His action, though objectionable, does not arouse the apprehension that he may be growing up in a set of relationships that will alienate him permanently from legitimate society. Adults are even less apprehensive if the offenders are members of a group perceived as already firmly committed to middle-class culture: fraternity members and pledges during an initiation, for example, or college students on a panty raid.

This confusion of categories is probably the most important reason why the literature on juvenile delinquency tends consistently to complain that too little is known about delinquency among middle-class youth, despite the frequent recurrence of suburban outrage. But to become a delinquent gang requires more than a capacity for organized outrage; it requires the power to evoke in middle-class adult observers and law enforcement officials a response that middle-class youngsters do not trigger.

I am not at all implying that middle-class youngsters who commit antisocial acts are more likely than lower-status youngsters to be treated indulgently. They are quite as likely to be treated more harshly and resentfully, though unless abandoned by their parents they can usually afford a more able defense. The point is rather that their delinquent behavior alone simply is not enough in the presence of sufficiently powerful symbols of middle-class status, to put them in the same category as working-class or lower-class youth. The anxiety and hostility they arouse may be equally or more intense; but it is qualitatively different. They are not perceived as an alien growth with its own malignant values, rules, and source of authority, threatening to overwhelm legitimate society, disrupting public education, and turning public thoroughfares into a jungle. Their stake in the established order is assumed to be ultimately greater than their interest in creating disorder or a new lower order of their own.

Yet, though we know little for certain about the role juvenile delinquency plays in subsequent adult antisocial and criminal behavior, the

---

[25] For this perception, as well as many others I shall use freely in this section of the chapter, I am indebted to Richard A. Cloward and Lloyd E. Ohlin, *Delinquency and Opportunity* (Glencoe, Ill.: The Free Press, 1960).

relationship seems highly inconsistent. One type of delinquent gang that Cloward and Ohlin describe as a part of "the criminal subculture"[26] is certainly maintained and deliberately cultivated by organized crime as a bush league training ground. But the juveniles trained are unlike the popular image of a juvenile delinquent. Organized and syndicated crime has as little tolerance for deviant and impulse-ridden behavior as any other bureaucracy—less than most, since it can be more easily endangered by unreliable subordinates. Young members of criminal gangs are building careers in crime and are at least as wary as young men on the make in legitimate lines of endeavor; they commit no unnecessary violence, are shunned if they use narcotics, and learn to be as inconspicuous as possible. Detection, for them, is the ultimate failure; a boy with a criminal record is at a disadvantage in organized crime as well as in trying to go straight. Promising recruits are those who are known for their prowess to the neighborhood representative of the syndicate—but *not* to law enforcement officials. When statistics on delinquency are compiled, they are omitted.

Cloward and Ohlin's other major categories do get included in delinquency statistics—in fact, they largely compose them. But they are not serious candidates for important or policy-making positions in the adult underworld. Their "conflict gang" is the familiar lower-status, usually ethnically stigmatized corps of knights-errant sentimentalized in *West Side Story*. Such gangs as these tend usually to disintegrate as their members grow into adulthood and dire economic necessity. Furthermore, they seem to be an obsolescent model and are being replaced by smaller, looser, more sporadic groups of hostile boys whose guerilla tactics are better suited to evasion of policemen and social workers alike. In any case, what these gangs provide their members is a group in which they are not anonymous and insignificant, and in which the qualities that earn respect and status are the ones they have or can hope to acquire: strength, daring, "heart." Since they feel themselves despised and rejected by the larger society and are constantly tempted by its material goals, which are utterly beyond their reach, they are certainly often hostile, destructive, and mean; and the actions their hostility leads them into are often criminal, but they have no stake in crime as a career, and tend to disappear as adults into the world of the poor, which, though repugnant to persons trained to middle-class amenities, and a hard and perilous life, is not especially criminal.

Why, then, has juvenile delinquency been so highly visible and an object of such pervasive concern? There may, to be sure, have been an actual increase in juvenile crime, but social response to it has in any case been aggravated by a breakdown in social barriers that has not

[26] *Ibid.*, pp. 161–170.

been accompanied by a comparable increase in opportunity. A generation or two ago, few youths from the social classes most easily perceived as a source of delinquency would have had much access to middle-class people except on middle-class terms. High school especially would have seemed to those who remained in it a reliable if steep pathway to at least a modest footing in the establishment; those who dropped out either passed into unpromising but fairly steady working-class jobs or, if they became delinquent, were regarded and treated much as any criminal would be. Middle-class adults could more easily avoid confronting lower-status youngsters except when the youngsters were exposed by their roles as pupils or messengers or, in earlier days, chimney sweeps; and when they were better armed, like Dickens' more smug and offensive characters, with confidence in their own rectitude and viability. Even in *Oliver Twist*, there is no conception whatever of juvenile delinquency; the society pictured is not capable of that much self-doubt or compassion. Oliver is an object of solicitude because he is middle-class himself and a fallen victim of circumstances; but the other children are simply little criminals whose fate, though bewailed, is taken for granted. Only since World War I, and especially since the Great Depression of the 1930s, has the articulate middle class been forced to accept the fact that the society to which it is accustomed creates special difficulties for youth—though it usually interprets this ethnocentrically, as if youth were itself the source of the problem.

The elaboration of the idea of juvenile delinquency masks, I believe, a growing uneasiness that many of the conventional goals and values of American life are irrelevant and even grotesque when applied to the actual life circumstances of "culturally deprived" or "disadvantaged" youth. In an open society which does more and more of its unskilled and semiskilled work mechanically, these youngsters are conspicuous, and conspicuously unlike nice, accommodating kids. Only a small proportion may be delinquent, but "juvenile delinquency" serves less as a category to put them in than as a way of defining them as a problem to be solved by personal and social manipulation. This approach is less destructive than treating them as mere vagrants and criminals, but it still implies that middle-class social norms are morally right and are what the youngsters must be brought to accept.

The School-Dropout Conflict

As the middle-class position becomes clearly inadequate to deal with the hiatus between lower-status youth and middle-class society, interest shifts from the "juvenile delinquent" to the less pejorative category of "school dropout." The holding power of the schools, as judged by the proportion of all youth who do complete their course and graduate, is, in fact, still rising, as it has done since free public high schools were first established nearly a century ago. Yet the National Education Association, PTA groups, and the mass media down to and including the *Reader's Digest* continue to clamor for new ways of keeping adolescents in school till they finish.

Two factors account for the appearance of crisis. One is ephemeral, the large and rapid increase in the adolescent population resulting from the high birth rate following World War II. The other, however, is fundamental and has already been discussed, the rapidly increasing difficulty of finding any other social role for those who leave school, and any economic role for them at all. In school they are at least kept track of, sometimes given lunch and, occasionally, physical examinations whose results their parents can act on if they can afford medical care.

The resulting efforts to retain pupils are confused, and their results are ambiguous. Most dropouts have been more than willing to meet the school halfway. Most youngsters who leave school before graduation do not, astonishingly, drop out as soon as they legally can; they stay considerably longer, sometimes waiting till the army or some job possibility opens an alternative to school that they can picture, sometimes hoping to succeed in school until examinations in senior year come close enough to seem real. The schools, which are becoming alarmed at the prospective loss of their wide base of social support and at the certain loss of state aid figured on the basis of average daily attendance if large numbers of their clientele desert, have been making great effort to retain lower-class youngsters in school. These efforts, however, generally take the form of intensive counseling and propaganda about the economic advantages of remaining in school and getting a degree.

But the propaganda, though true in detail, is misleading in implication. Youth who do not complete high school have, certainly, dim economic prospects. But so would high school graduates if the dropout retention programs were effective. High school graduates who do not go on to college already overtax the number of jobs available; the economic advantages imputed to a high school education are dependent on the fact that many youngsters do drop out; and the advantage is not great enough to affect the individual's standard of living much unless he also goes on to and graduates from college. But this increment is also partly an artifact resulting from the comparatively smaller number of college graduates and from an inflated demand for educational credentials that relate less to what the candidate for a job is expected to do on it than to his ability to keep a clean record through sixteen years of rather intrusive and paternalistic education.[27]

What the schools generally do *not* do, in an effort to retain dropouts, or for any other reason, is discipline their own staffs to a more precise definition of their educational function and a broader conception of permissible behavior among their clientele. We usually find that the high school will finally settle for almost any kind of work as passing but relentlessly punishes normal aspects of working-class or lower-class conduct that are, strictly speaking, none of its educational business. To graduate from high school a student must know at least better than to use dirty words, or wear sexy clothes, or talk back to teachers, or carry himself too proudly and confidently. Beyond this, it is difficult to say.

Meanwhile, the schools, which have their own establishment to defend and which represent an enormous investment in the nearest thing to local autonomy that most communities possess, maintain a legal monopoly on the socialization of an increasingly heterogeneous body of students. To many of these students the schools' lower-middle-class folkways are unfamiliar and inappropriate—worse than useless when they leave the school building, and a humiliating imposition even while they are within it.[28] Society, which relies on the comprehensive public

---

[27] See Cicourel and Kitsuse, *op. cit.*, and the entire issue of *American Child*, 46, 3 (May 1964), "Should We Raise the School Leaving Age?," which is devoted to an examination and, in some cases, rebuttal of Secretary of Labor W. W. Wirtz's view that we solve the crisis in youth unemployment by doing so. Paul Goodman, James S. Coleman, and James E. Russell, Secretary of the Educational Policies Commission of the National Education Association, are among the commentators included.

[28] In the past few years there have been several exceptionally fine works on education that deal specifically with the plight of the lower-status student in the schools and that make concrete technical suggestions for improving his lot. None of these faces up, however, to the fact that lower-status youth are properly so-called. They do not seem to recognize that the middle-class school establishment treats working- and lower-class youth as it does precisely because it is, indeed, hostile to such people and can usually get by with treating them badly. It is true, however, that this immunity is being rapidly lost as out-of-school youth become a more serious threat and, particularly, as Negroes, who have been the most seriously deprived under present conditions, develop political force. Of these books, Patricia C. Sexton, *Education and Income; Inequalities of Opportunity in Our Public Schools* (New York: Viking Press, 1961) is an excellent and thorough study of the relationship between the income of students' families in Detroit and the educational facilities and services provided them in that city; Frank Riessman's misleadingly entitled *The Culturally Deprived Child* (New York: Harper and Row, 1962) is an excellent treatment of the conative and cognitive difficulties faced by poor children in the school, with specific suggestions for meeting them, though it is directed more at the elementary school pupil than at the difficulties of

school to serve as the melting pot in which awkward conflicts of background and tradition are resolved, has so far supported it. There have been many proposals recently for providing for adolescents who cannot accept school or succeed there: a domestic peace corps to assist in economically depressed areas, local programs for volunteer work, a paramilitary conservation corps. None of these is presented as an alternative to compulsory school attendance; they are rather viewed as emergency measures to meet the desperate needs of "school dropouts" for a pittance and some kind of ID card. The youngster is still perceived as a waste product of the school system. But, at least, the concept of "school dropout" suggests that the problem lies in the relationship between the youth and the social institution to which he had been assigned, and not in his personal aberration. For a society accustomed to concealing the deficiencies in its way of life by blaming its tragedies on their victims, this is a major step forward.

Valedictory

It would, I think, be presumptuous to speculate at this juncture on what the future has to offer American adolescents. If it were necessary to characterize our society in a single word, with all the oversimplification this implies, I should be forced to say its most notable characteristic is that it is *untrustworthy*. Our commitments to opportunity and individual success, when applied in a context of large, impersonal organizations which replace stable geographical communities and make binding judgments on the basis of fragmented data mechanically processed, make for a certain shiftiness of character and policy. If this judg-

---

the adolescent. *Education in Depressed Areas*, edited by A. Harry Passow (New York: Teachers College Bureau of Publications, 1963) is an authoritative collection of papers from a two-week Work Conference on this topic held at Teachers College the previous year. The collection is extensively annotated. A similar, useful, more recent, if possibly less distinguished, set of papers is included in *Guidance and the School Dropout*, edited by Daniel Schreiber (Washington, D.C.: National Education Association, 1964).

However, much the clearest and most useful source of information on the specific economic situation of the school dropout is a pamphlet by S. M. Miller, Carolyn Comings, and Betty Saleem, *The School Dropout Problem: Syracuse* (Syracuse: New York State Division for Youth and Syracuse University Youth Development Center, n.d.). This pamphlet is essentially a case study, distinguished by an unusually revealing and intelligent breakdown of the data presented by sex, work permit categories, residential patterns, and other relevant variables that more often stay concealed in the general figures. Especially valuable is the authors' demonstration that, despite a general assumption to the contrary, there is no simple correlation between school withdrawal and delinquency.

ment seems too harsh or cantankerous, we need only ask ourselves how much confidence we have, in fact, that the Atomic Energy Commission makes decisions in such a way that children really will be protected from fallout; that the CIA and the FBI willingly subordinate themselves to the needs of national policy and the orders of the executive branch of which they are a part; that automobile manufacturers are spontaneously concerned about the evidence that their product is unsafe. To expect all this would be naive, if not un-American.

This untrustworthiness affects prediction adversely in two ways. It makes the future contingent on details of policy formation and power seeking that are both concealed and transitory; we are forced to waste too much time and effort trying to figure out, from insufficient data, who is really doing what to whom. But it also makes the future blacker for adolescents, whatever turn it takes, because the social climate itself is inimical to personal clarity and commitment, which are the chief developmental tasks of adolescents. America, in short, is a hard country to grow up in and is getting harder. And most of the world is becoming more like us.

Personal isolation and a sense of abandonment are among the costs of constructing an open, technically advanced social system whose chief boast is the opportunity it gives its members to alter the circumstances of their lives. And they are costs that bear disproportionately on adolescents. They are not imposed by conscious decision, and they cannot be averted by an act of will; they are implicit in the developmental processes that have become established in our society. These are subject, of course, to alteration; but this alteration would also be costly. It would involve the sacrifice of some of our most widely held values—values, moreover, that America has come to symbolize in the rest of the world even as we betray them. Egalitarian democracy is not only an inspiring political concept. It is a powerful euphoric and hallucinogenic drug which often leaves its addicts disturbed and depressed. The plight of the adolescent is one of its side effects.

2

Two Problems in American Public Education

Martin Trow

Two Conceptions of Educational Opportunity

Social problems are social phenomena—patterns of behavior or belief or attitude—that some people who can make their voices heard think ought to be changed. Moreover, those who define a phenomenon as a "problem" usually see it as morally wrong, not merely as a technical difficulty in achieving some desired end. Thus a social problem changes not only with the prevalence or objective consequences of the social pattern so defined, but also with the size and importance of the groups concerned about it, and with the moral force of their condemnation of or concern with it. For example, the denial of civil rights to Negroes is a major social problem today in a way it was not 30 years ago, though the objective conditions of Southern Negroes were certainly worse then than today. On the other hand, "big city political machines" constitute less a social problem today than during the first decade of this century, though there is no evidence of less civic corruption now than then. Problems become problems when they are authoritatively defined as problems; the objective conditions themselves, their prevalence and consequences, are only one, though an important one, of the elements entering into such a definition.

In American education, the central problems today are the education of the culturally deprived and the academic preparation of those going on to higher education. The first centers on the elementary school, the second on the high school. Most of the issues that are discussed and debated—the preparation and credentialing of teachers, the organization and content of the curriculum, the location of schools and the composition of their student bodies, and so forth—derive from one or the other of these concerns. Though they address themselves to what appear to be diametrically different kinds of students—the most and the least academically able—nevertheless both problems are generated at least in part by the same forces in American society and American education. Both reflect the increased importance of formal education in our society. Both of them acquired their present urgency after World War II with the growth of mass higher education, broad changes in the occupational structure, and the revolution in the status of Negroes. Although the education of the urban slum child and the college preparatory student was certainly not worse after World War II than in the preceding decades, these other forces and developments outside education changed people's conceptions of the functions of schools, and thus also their notions of what constitutes an adequate or successful education, both for slum children and for those headed for college.

In both cases demands for reform arose outside the schools themselves. Pressure to strengthen the academic side of secondary education grew after World War II as the rapid expansion of college enrollments began to transform what had been for 50 years a system providing chiefly terminal secondary education into what was increasingly a system of college preparatory education. This development, in turn, created a growing body of parents concerned with their children's preparation for (and admission to) college. And these parents were (and are) the "attentive audience" for the growing numbers of academic men who mounted a sharp criticism of the quality of American secondary education.[1]

For the lower-class urban child, the demands came from Negro civil rights organizations and their growing numbers of white supporters. Perhaps most important, governmental agencies on the city and national level in the past decade have become increasingly concerned with the large numbers of poorly educated slum youth who are unemployed and in our economy unemployable, and who therefore constitute a danger to public order and a burden on local welfare agencies. These same governmental agencies are also sensitive to increasing political pressures to deal with this problem. In addition, the problem of school performance of Northern urban slum children assumed

[1] See M. A. Trow, "The Second Transformation of American Secondary Education," *International Journal of Comparative Sociology*, 2, 2 (September 1961), pp. 144–166.

greater urgency with the increasingly widespread demands of Negro groups for the abolition or reduction of *de facto* school segregation. Quite apart from the merits of any specific proposal to change the racial ratios of urban schools, such demands force people both inside and outside of schools to consider the comparative school performance of white middle-class children and Negro lower-class children. And when the performance of Negro slum children is compared with that of white children in the same city, rather than with one another or with Negro schools in the South, the very wide discrepancies are seen as wrong, as a violation of new and stronger conceptions of equality of opportunity, as a condition which we must do something about, as indeed, a social problem.

Attacks on the problem of the secondary education of college preparatory students have centered almost exclusively on the school curriculum, teacher training, and new modes of instruction, such as programmed learning designed to circumvent existing limitations of teachers and curricula. The education of the culturally deprived has called forth a more varied set of proposals reflecting the wider range of factors thought to be involved in their poor academic performance and high dropout rates. The difference in the character of the attack on the two problems lies in the assessment of their social and psychological sources. For the college preparatory student, it is assumed, the question is not of his motivation; he would not be planning to attend college if he were not motivated in some degree to meet the requirements of the educational system. Nor is the question raised of the adequacy of his experience or his present environment; these are assumed to be sufficiently beneficent or supportive to allow him to be knocking on the doors of a college. By contrast, the difficulties of the culturally deprived child are seen as having manifold sources—in early socialization, family attitudes, peer group influences, class and racial segregation, teacher attitudes, inadequate or inappropriate counseling—as well as in the curriculum itself. Moreover, college-bound youngsters typically come from families that are more or less successful in managing their own lives and those of their children; the only "welfare" agency they are usually served by is the school system, and it is to the school system alone that reformers look in seeking ways of strengthening the intellectual and academic preparation of college-bound youngsters. By contrast, the parents of culturally deprived youth are typically, and almost by definition, unsuccessful in their efforts to steer their own lives, or to gain even a modest share of the available material goods, or economic, familial, or emotional stability and security. They are, typically, the objects of attention by many agencies engaged in social welfare, and the discussions of the plight of their children naturally turn to the assistance that all these and additional projected agencies, as well as the school, can offer.

Although the sources of their difficulties in school lie in race, class, and family, and their effects on early experience, almost all the discussion of the education of the slum children is directed toward improving their academic performance, reducing the numbers who drop out before graduation from high school, and increasing the numbers who qualify for better jobs or higher education. This may appear a narrow criterion of success; certainly there are other important qualities of mind or spirit that those concerned with this problem want to enhance. "The fullest capacity to fulfill one's own talents and abilities" is one way to describe the broader aim that appears to give proper recognition to a wider range of qualities than is defined by performance in school. And yet it is the criterion of school performance against which the suggested reforms and innovations are always assessed. This is in part because school performance is more easily assessed than are the more subtle human qualities of spontaneity, emotional maturity, freedom and creativity in work and in relations with others. But it is also because in our society intellectual and emotional growth usually reflect themselves in satisfactory school performance, and even more because our society makes it extremely difficult for these other qualities to emerge *unless* the individual has done at least moderately well in school. There are certainly many happy and productive people in our society whose school careers were not marked by any high academic distinction. Yet, at the extremes, and it is the extremes we are discussing here, a career of repeated failure in school and early dropout from school is an extremely poor foundation for a happy and productive adult life.

We may think of potential talents as the biological and genetic endowments of people, their inherent and latent capacities for acquiring and using knowledge and skills in the service of themselves and others. Realized talent is the capacity actually to do these things. In contemporary America, potential talents are not often realized unless they are developed and certified through formal education, and increasingly, through higher education. However intellectually well endowed a child may be by nature, he is not likely to show evidence of his talents without the training and opportunities that schooling affords. Potential talent that is not cultivated and certified in schools is rarely evidenced; and this is increasingly true as formal education becomes to an ever greater extent the prerequisite for occupations and other adult roles in which many of these talents can be evidenced. When high potential intelligence is not developed and certified in the schools, it is usually aborted or frustrated. Thus the realization of talent is, at least in its early phases, in large part a matter of achievement in schools. And the social forces that work for or against the realization of talent are very much the same forces that work for or against achievement in school.

The discussions of the culturally deprived and the academically ambitious both center on what they learn in school; in the former the question is mainly of their capacities for learning as affected by forces both inside and outside the school; in the latter the question centers on how their assumed capacities are focused and developed by their teachers and the curriculum. But the two sets of problems differ in another important respect, that is, in the conceptions of equality of opportunity that provide the moral force in their definition. With the culturally deprived, there is increasingly applied a "radical" conception of equality of opportunity, whereas in the demands for the reform and extension of college preparatory work, we see applied an older "liberal" conception of equality of opportunity.[2]

The "weaker" conception—the traditional liberal view of equality of opportunity—would reduce or remove all external handicaps of birth or poverty which interfere with the translation of intelligence into academic achievement and thus into social, political, or economic leadership. In this view, intelligence is largely genetically given and substantially fixed; the demand is that intelligent children of humble birth be given access to preparatory schools and universities if they can show they are able. It is this conception of equality which was the driving force behind the Education Act of 1944 in Britain, which for the first time provided free secondary school places for all youth, as well as free places in the preparatory grammar schools for the academically able youth. It is also the conception that lies behind the stipends (or scholarships) awarded to nearly all students admitted to British universities, so that poor but able students will not be prevented from attending a university.

The radical conception of equality of opportunity sees intelligence as itself in large part achieved, and calls for equalizing the opportunities for gaining intelligence. This demand is also more radical in its implications, since it holds that intelligence has been determined to a large degree before the child ordinarily begins to attend school.[3] The policy

---

[2] See Anthony Crosland, *The Conservative Enemy* (London: Jonathan Cape, 1962), pp. 169–174. Crosland refers to these as "strong" and "weak" conceptions of equality of opportunity. Considering the enormous consequences of the "weak" conception and of its continuing strength and relevance to many educational problems, it seems preferable to use a term which stresses its roots in the liberal conception of society open to talent and self-help.

[3] This view is finding increasing support in psychological research. See Benjamin S. Bloom, *Stability and Change in Human Characteristics* (New York: John Wiley and Sons, 1964).

implications of this doctrine are active measures to help the family with the intellectual growth of children and additional measures to supplement the family's efforts through what might be called "compensatory socialization." This conception thus leads to a commitment by public authorities to help the child acquire intelligence despite the family's indifference or even active opposition.

A growing part of the political and educational leadership in the United States is increasingly committed to the radical conception of equality of opportunity. (This was a central though obscured issue in the presidential election of 1964.) This marks a profound shift in the dominant conceptions of equality in America and in the public policies necessary to achieve that equality. It certainly was not Jefferson's conception of educational opportunity when he proposed to "sift the rubbish heap" for the few ablest youth of humble origins whom the state should aid in gaining secondary and higher education. It was not even the conception of equality of educational opportunity that underlay the establishment of the common school in America, or that led to the natural extension of that policy in the creation of a free universal and comprehensive system of secondary education between the Civil War and World War II. The comprehensive public high school and the growth of the junior college and of mass higher education today can be seen as the fullest expression of the liberal conception of equality of educational opportunity. They are based on the recognition that the more advanced the *nonselective* education that is provided, the more attenuated are the handicaps of humble birth for educational achievement. Thus the free comprehensive secondary school, like the relatively unselective junior colleges and state colleges today, give more and more time for native talents to demonstrate themselves and to qualify for still further education. This liberal conception recognizes that the poor but able child does start with handicaps; his family is less able to pay for his schooling or for the kinds of social and cultural experience which would enable him to compete successfully in the school against children from wealthier homes. It is assumed that if public schooling is free, easily accessible, and prolonged, these handicaps of birth become attenuated the longer the child remains in school.

But the assumptions on which these institutions have been built are only valid if the deficiency in the home is financial and cultural,[4] and not motivational or emotional. When these conditions are met or approximated—when, that is, ambition and intelligence are randomly distributed in the population—the poor but able and ambi-

---

[4] "Cultural" in the sense of exposure to books, art, music, etc., rather than in the anthropologist's sense.

tious boy may need more time to translate his talents into achievement, using the school, the free public library, and so forth. But the society and the schools need do no more (and this is considerable) than to provide him with the time and the opportunities; his talents will reveal themselves even in the face of a culturally alien or impoverished home, indeed, even despite indifferent teaching and an obsolete curriculum.

Of course, the assumptions of the liberal concept of equality were never wholly or even substantially met in the United States; the poverty of the Irish, Italian, Polish, and Russian immigrants of the post-Civil War decades was a poverty not only of money but also of the resources for gaining intelligence. But those assumptions were close enough to being true, and the conditions of the immigrants close enough to the intellectual conditions and resources of native white Americans, so that the schools could be seen as providing opportunities for acquiring education and demonstrating intelligence, despite the handicaps of wealth, ethnic origin, or class.

There were in the writings of Dewey and his followers some hints of the stronger conception of equality of opportunity that is only now becoming dominant. They perceived that the urban slums did not provide children of the new immigrants with the intellectual and motivational resources that they remembered or imputed to the older small town and rural America. Many of their specific suggestions were aimed at generating in the school qualities of mind and interest that we could no longer assume were being created in the home or by the larger society. But these subtle and imaginative efforts to develop the intellectual and moral resources of slum children were not widely accepted by American public education. The elements of the Progressive doctrine which were accepted (often in debased and vulgarized form) were increased emphasis on the useful aspects of curriculum and de-emphasis of the traditional curriculum which, it was argued, was irrelevant to the great mass of students and beyond the attainments of most.[5] This selective adoption of Progressive teaching was also guided by a peculiar interpretation of the liberal conception of equality of educational opportunity, and led to an effort to reduce inequalities by bringing the content of public education within the reach of all. Broadly speaking, the stronger and earlier the emphasis on competitive academic achievement in the schools, the greater the weight of the home environment in academic achievement. Conversely, watering down the curriculum and reducing the element of academic achievement serve to reduce the initial competitive advantage of birth and home environment; and

---

[5] See Lawrence A. Cremin, *The Transformation of the School* (New York: Alfred A. Knopf, 1961), and Richard Hofstadter, *Anti-Intellectualism in American Life* (New York: Alfred A. Knopf, 1963), pp. 299–390.

there was a broad if uneven movement of American education in that direction between the two world wars. By not teaching too much in high school, final educational placement could be further delayed, and relatively unselective colleges and universities provided to give still another chance to children who start with an initial disadvantage to realize their potential talents. Our system of comprehensive high schools, "open-door" colleges, extension courses, and adult education means that these chances are not closed at age eleven, sixteen, eighteen, or even later for those who possess some motivation to "improve themselves."

Although a renewed emphasis on academic work over the past decade has increased the competitive tone, and to some extent selective "tracking," in the schools, the rapid expansion of American higher education has prevented this tendency from increasing the competitive advantage of birth or breeding. Rather, by extending formal schooling for more people still longer, its net effect is probably to reduce those advantages still further. At the same time, it makes the penalties for not having gained much schooling more severe.

The increasingly widespread acceptance of the radical concept of equality of opportunity is closely related to the growing recognition of the lower-class urban Negro as a major social problem after World War II. Their rapidly growing numbers, the Negro "revolution" and the demands that it makes for better education in the North as well as the South, coupled with the growing body of evidence of the wide gap in the educational performance of white and Negro children in Northern cities—a gap which increases the longer they remain in school—has been a severe shock to the liberal conception of equality of educational opportunity and to the belief in the unreformed public school as the chief vehicle for the assimilation and mobility of new groups entering the society at the bottom. The system of public education has earned considerable respect for having apparently coped so well with the mass immigrations of the late nineteenth and early twentieth centuries. In the Northern cities the lower-class Negro immigrants from the South were the system's first highly visible failure (apart from Soviet successes in rocketry for which it was unfairly blamed).

We are now coming to recognize that the persistent effects of slavery, discrimination, degradation, and exploitation result in handicaps to lower-class Negro children more profound than, and in some ways qualitatively different from, those of the children of European immigrant groups.[6] The growing recognition of these facts, together with the traditional American view of education as a central instrument for

[6] See Stanley M. Elkins, *Slavery* (Chicago: University of Chicago Press, 1959).

the achievement of social ends, leads directly to the acceptance of the radical conception of its role in the provision of equality of opportunity, a commitment which requires the school to see itself not merely as the arena where talent *realizes* and then *reveals* itself, but as the place where indeed for some children talent will have to be *created* and *nurtured* against strong counterforces in the child, his home, the community, and the larger society. This stronger conception is by no means universally accepted as the guiding principle of public education, either in the general population or by all teachers and educators. It is more widely held where the problems of the Negro slum child are felt most acutely—that is, in the large Northern cities—and by educators and social scientists most aware of the inadequacies of the traditional role of the school in meeting the special problems and disabilities of the Negro slum child. The uneven acceptance of the new role of the school by different professional and lay groups is the source of both social and political problems, and of conflicts within and around education itself.

A basic difference between the liberal and the radical concepts of equality of educational opportunity is the demands they make on the school for the success of the student. Under the liberal concept, responsibility for the student's success or failure is placed largely on his own shoulders; although the quality of the school and the teachers is thought to have some bearing on the matter, the primary cause of success or failure in school is seen to be the student's own moral and intellectual resources. Under the radical concept the student's success or, more commonly, failure is seen as the failure of the school or teacher, a failure to create in the child the moral and intellectual resources that lead to academic success. This view of the matter, of course, makes much more severe demands on the educational system and underlies the new stronger calls for educational reforms and the search for ways to intervene effectively in the socialization of the child. The pressure for new modes of intervention arises, then, out of the application of the strong concept of educational opportunity to schools attended by "groups whose characteristics are those of poor ability, scanty knowledge, and low levels of motivation, at levels of deficiency far below those 'normally' encountered in dealing with the 'standard' American school population." [7]

Rossi suggests that "For the practitioner (in education) the answer to how to intervene in order to reduce the spread of differences in the general population is given largely through an understanding of the

---

[7] Peter Rossi, "The Challenge of Group Differences" (Chicago: National Opinion Research Center, mimeographed, 1964), p. 10.

same mechanisms in which the social scientist has a more academic interest. Without understanding processes through which lower-class persons and Negroes maintain their characteristic differences from others it is not possible to make inroads into the problem." [8] Although this statement is broadly true, there are some important differences between the academic explanations of these differences and the practitioners' prescriptions for dealing with them. The social scientist's explanation of these differences necessarily puts heavy weight on historical and institutional forces—including the nature and consequences of American slavery for the slaves and their descendants, the long-range effects of discrimination and prejudice, changes in the economy and the occupational structure, and so forth—which the schools can do nothing about. Conversely, the practitioners and those social scientists directly concerned with their problems are likely to focus in much more detail on the aspects of education that they can manipulate.

Without minimizing the importance of the fuller understanding of Negro and lower-class disabilities being gained by historians and students of American society, it may be useful to look briefly at some characteristics of the slum schools and culturally deprived children that can be linked to the trouble these children have in school and that might be modified. I can point here to only a fragment of a broader discussion of the problem of poor and ill-educated youth, much of which centers on the question of what can be done outside the school. This includes some of the work on juvenile delinquency and youth unemployment; indeed, much of the federal poverty program is oriented to the problems of school dropouts through measures for their support and training outside the school system.

Within the slum school, increasing attention has been given to the teachers it recruits and retains, and to their conceptions and stereotypes of the students they teach. These attitudes shape the expectations teachers hold of their students and the climate of the classroom. We see in these discussions the subtle interplay between the child's own intellectual and emotional handicaps, the culture of the slum school, and academic achievement. These discussions are informed by the "radical" conception of equality and lead to new diagnoses and new prescriptions.

The Slum School and the Culture of Defeat

The quality of instruction in the slum schools is obviously affected by the quality and character of the teachers. By and large, slum schools cannot attract or hold the more able and experienced teachers. With

[8] *Ibid.*, pp. 10–11.

some notable exceptions whose numbers may now be growing, slum schools are staffed by new teachers who, because of lack of tenure and seniority, have to accept the least attractive posts, and by older teachers who have settled more or less comfortably into undemanding if not pleasant roles. As Becker notes, slum schools are for a variety of reasons less attractive to teachers than are middle-class schools; "it is typically the schools handling children of subordinate groups which are least desired, and teachers' careers tend to be structured in terms of movement away from such schools." [9] He continues:

> Such a pattern of movement means that the less desirable schools, those teachers want to avoid, get something less than an equal share of teaching talent. At the least, it typically means that they do not get the experienced teachers, for experience is almost always a ticket to a better job, whether through the workings of a seniority system or through the greater bargaining power it provides in bidding for jobs. In Chicago, many lower-class Negro schools are staffed almost entirely by teachers fresh from training school, the only ones who cannot choose their assignments; as soon as they build up enough seniority to move, they go, to be replaced by a new batch of beginners. More generally, it is probably true that, whatever the qualities a school system wishes to reward in its teachers, those qualities can be effectively rewarded only by assignment to the more desired schools, so that disadvantaged groups, who require the most skilled and experienced teachers, get the opposite and something less than an equal chance to an education.[10]

Another author notes that "thirty-four out of a hundred teachers appointed to the borough of Manhattan do not accept appointment to the schools to which they have been assigned. Some selected schools have much higher rates." [11]

The teachers' conception of the slum school as unattractive and depressing rather than challenging has been reinforced by school administrators who have used assignment to these schools as a form of pun-

---

[9] Howard S. Becker, "Schools and Systems of Stratification," in A. H. Halsey, J. Floud, and C. A. Anderson, eds., *Education, Economy, and Society* (New York: The Free Press of Glencoe, 1961), p. 99.

[10] *Ibid.*, p. 100.

[11] Vernon F. Haubrich, "Teachers for Big-City Schools," in A. Harry Passow, ed., *Education in Depressed Areas* (New York: Teachers College Bureau of Publications, 1963), pp. 246–247. This difficulty of recruitment and high turnover in lower class or slum schools is common in many countries. In some countries it takes the form of reluctance to leave the cities and teach in the poorer and isolated rural areas, and as an eagerness to return to the cities when the chance arises. See, for example, Ministry of Education, *Half Our Future* (London: HMSO, 1963), pp. 22–23 and 245–249.

ishment for teachers. "It is no secret that in many cities across the country, the depressed areas have been the 'Siberia' of the local school system, and those who for a variety of reasons were to be disciplined were sent to these undesirable schools." [12]

The high turnover of teachers drains the slum schools of much teacher talent, experience, and vitality. Among those who remain, along with a dedicated minority, are many teachers whose conception of their job works against the education of their pupils. A study of teachers in ten public schools located in depressed areas of a large Northern city found that "while there were some outstanding exceptions . . . the overwhelming majority of these teachers and their supervisors rejected these children and looked upon them as inherently inferior. For most, the teachers indicated that they considered these children to be incapable of profiting from a normal curriculum. The children were seen as intellectually inferior and therefore not capable of learning." [13]

There is widespread agreement that, as Carl Marburger puts it, "teacher expectations have surprising impact on pupil-achievement."

> The teacher who expects achievement, who has hope for the educability of his pupils, indeed conveys this through every nuance and subtlety of his behavior. The teacher who conveys hopelessness for the educability of his children usually does so without ever really verbalising such an attitude—at least, in front of his pupils . . . Certainly the expectations of the teacher for his pupils can determine, particularly in depressed-urban-area schools, the school survival or non-survival of the youth.[14]

If there is agreement on the importance of teacher expectations for pupil achievement, there is equally wide agreement that such expectations are commonly lacking. Many observers have identified the attitudes and stereotypes of teachers in slum schools as a major factor in the poor academic performance of children in those schools. As one observer notes,

> Not infrequently teachers, counselors, principals assigned to the depressed-area school have been people without any real concern for these children and with the common stereotype of them as children of low

[12] Mel Ravitz, "The Role of the School in the Urban Setting," Passow, ed., *op. cit.*, p. 19.
[13] Kenneth B. Clark, "Educational Stimulation of Racially Disadvantaged Children," in Passow, ed., *op. cit.*, p. 148.
[14] Carl L. Marburger, "Consideration for Educational Planning," in Passow, ed., *op. cit.*, p. 306.

ability. As a result of this low estimate of potential, the self-fulfilling prophecy went into effect. The children were not encouraged to learn very much; the teacher expended little energy on anything but maintaining order and bemoaning her lot; as a consequence, the children fulfilled the low expectation, which in turn reinforced the original assumption to prove the teacher was right.[15]

The view of slum children as mostly incapable of learning held by many of their teachers is a stereotype charged as often with pity as with hostility. But it is no less crippling in its effects on the teacher's behavior and ultimately on the child. As Frank Riessman observes,

> Another subtle form of discrimination is patronisation in all its guises . . . The specific forms of patronisation are manifold; the tendency to talk down to the deprived child—to speak his language, to imitate his slang and speech inflection; the assumption that these children are lacking in intellectual curiosity and conceptual ability; the lowering of academic standards, and the failure to set high goals for the deprived; the too-quick taking for granted that they are not interested in learning.[16]

Many forces shape the attitudes and stereotypes that teachers hold about slum children. Their own social origins, typically lower-middle or upper working class, do not equip them to view with understanding or tolerance the lower-class norms and culture of the slum. Moreover, even if a beginning teacher in a slum school does not have these attitudes, he often finds them the dominant attitudes among the experienced teachers whom he may look to for guidance. One commentator suggests that it is probably just as well that the beginning teacher is immediately assigned a full teaching load and therefore "rarely sees his colleagues except for a brief nod in the corridors or for a few minutes of casual conversation in the cafeteria."

> Even if there were time to confer seriously with his fellows it would probably be more debilitating than useful. In many lower-class schools, freer access to experienced teachers would simply shorten the time required for the beginner to water down his courses and to resign himself to drastically lowered aspirations of what youngsters can reasonably be expected to learn. The great majority of experienced slum school teachers seem to have grown wearily pessimistic and to have concluded that personal sanity requires coming to terms with the limitations of "reality." [17]

[15] Mel Ravitz, in Passow, ed., *op. cit.*, pp. 19–20.
[16] Frank Riessman, *The Culturally Deprived Child* (New York: Harper and Row, 1962), p. 22.
[17] Robert J. Shaeffer, "The Recruitment and Training of Schoolmen," paper read at the Conference on Quality and Equality in Education, Princeton, N.J., December 1964.

Shaeffer is describing what might be called "the culture of defeat," a set of attitudes shared by veteran teachers in slum schools, reinforced by bitter daily experience and serving to rationalize and justify classroom routines which they have evolved for dealing with (and surviving in) an unrewarding and difficult environment. Whether the new teacher encounters these attitudes immediately or in the course of time, they cannot but have great influence on how he or she views the task; they are, after all, the settled sentiments and approved practices of those whose survival in the slum school is itself the strongest testimony to success. And new teachers with higher goals than simple survival may find the older teacher not merely discouraging but actively hostile. Successful teaching in a slum school can be seen and felt as a distinct threat by an older group who have made their accommodations to its problems in other ways.

Reference to the culture of defeat in the slum schools should not obscure the real and discouraging difficulties encountered in teaching in them, nor should we ignore the devoted teachers who continue to struggle against those difficulties. But in many schools the teachers who have not surrendered to those difficulties are rare or isolated, and a beginning teacher with hopes as well as fears finds little support among his older colleagues for his plans and ideas. It would be difficult in any circumstances to sustain those hopes without support from one's peers; in the conditions of a slum school it is often close to impossible.

The improvement of teaching in the slum schools calls not only for changes in the curriculum, in teaching methods, and in materials, but also for an attack on the culture of defeat, and for the development of support for a teacher's own higher expectations of herself as well as of her pupils. Thus the director of a school improvement project in Detroit observes that "the involvement of an almost total staff, including administration, would seem then to be essential for innovation in curriculum, and for modification of behavior to insure truly effective teaching." [18] And he speaks of the necessity to reinforce continually the teachers' enthusiasm and hope for the educability of children in lower-class schools. One way to do that is to provide additional personnel and resources; another, proposed by Haubrich in describing the Hunter project, is for a teacher training institution to "adopt" one or more lower-class schools, and gradually increase the proportions of its trainees among the school personnel, with the school or department of education itself providing the continuing professional and psychological support for the students it places in its "adopted" schools.[19]

The attitudes of teachers toward lower-class pupils, and especially to-

---

[18] Carl L. Marburger, in Passow, ed., *op. cit.*, p. 307.
[19] Vernon F. Haubrich, in Passow, ed., *op. cit.*, pp. 248 ff.

ward Negro children, are reinforced by the widespread use of IQ tests as measures of "inherent" intelligence. As Ravitz observes,

> We now recognize that it is no longer sufficient to rely on traditional IQ tests as measures of innate intelligence, learning ability, or creativity. Much evidence suggests not only that the test itself is the product of middle-class attitudes and values, but that many children who take such tests are wholly unfamiliar with both the materials of paper and pencil and the language patterns used. We are beginning to suspect that if some youngsters who do poorly on IQ tests were to function in their familiar environment, we might well see their performances improve. Finally, we are slowly coming to appreciate that the real damage of the IQ test is its subtle influence on the mind of the teacher. Teachers, often unconsciously, expect the level of performance from the child that his IQ test indicated, a practice which, taking into account the weaknesses and inadequacies of these tests, really doesn't give some children half a chance to succeed. Paradoxically, the teacher herself may be the greatest impediment to the child's successful learning experience.[20]

The uncritical use of IQ tests reinforces the widespread stereotype of lower-class children as unable to learn much by presenting what is really a measure of "achieved" intelligence as a measure of latent or potential intelligence. The test results thus justify lower levels of expectation and lower standards of instruction by providing other convenient explanations for the student's low level of performance.

IQ tests have been criticized in two different ways—first, as "unfair" to the lower-class child since they test skills and knowledge he is not likely to have by virtue of his class or ethnically conditioned culture and experience.[21] The other criticism is more fundamental; the modes of thought, not merely the bits of knowledge and vocabulary, tested by IQ tests are themselves affected by the child's cultural background and by how he has been taught in school.[22] Vernon asserts that "the provision of higher education is not so much dependent on, as capable itself of raising the IQ." He cites "Husén in Sweden and Lorge in America who have, in effect, followed up children who were of the same IQ level at the presecondary stage and found that those who ob-

---

[20] Mel Ravitz, in Passow, ed., *op. cit.*, pp. 15–16.
[21] See K. Eells et al., *Intelligence and Cultural Differences* (Chicago: University of Chicago Press, 1951).
[22] See P. E. Vernon, *Intelligence and Attainment Tests* (London: University of London Press, 1960), and his "Pool of Ability," *The Sociological Review Monograph No. 7*, The University of Keele, October 1963, pp. 45–59.

tained a full secondary and university education scored adult IQ's averaging some twelve points higher than those who left school at the earliest opportunity and obtained no further education." [23]

Verbal skills are a prerequisite for academic success; they can be gained through education, as Vernon and others observe, but in turn they also heavily condition the success of formal instruction. Children who are "linguistically deprived" on arrival in school do not learn to read easily and begin very early a career of relative but progressive academic failure. Intelligence tests, such as the one designed by Davis and Eells, which try to reduce the influence of class (or more accurately, of the cultural and intellectual climate of the home) on test performance must minimize the effects of verbal skills. But these authors, although denying the relation of verbal skills to "pure" or "potential" intelligence, do not deny the relation of the class-influenced verbal skills that "ordinary" IQ tests measure to later academic performance. Therefore, if we sidestep what is probably a sterile quest for a way to measure "pure" or potential intelligence, we may find it more profitable to consider the ways in which early experience affects the resources of language that a child brings to school.

In a series of papers, Basil Bernstein, an English social psychologist, has explored the culture and socialization patterns of English working-class families that lead to a relative impoverishment of the language of their children in ways that have marked consequences for their formal education.[24] Bernstein's studies of English working-class children have relevance for American lower-class children as well, though the patterns and problems he points to take somewhat different and more extreme forms among some of our minority ethnic and racial groups. He shows that in English working-class families the language by which parents communicate with their children is much less differentiated, personal, and qualified than it is in middle-class families, but the role of nonverbal communication is greater ("shut up" versus "will you kindly be quieter"). The working-class child is the object of short commands and simple statements directed largely to specific objects and familiar events. There is less emphasis on the relation of immediate action to distant consequences, and thus less concern with the logical and rational connections between means and ends. Where in the working-class home things simply *are*, in the middle-class home "objects in the present are not taken as given, but become centers of in-

[23] *Ibid.*, p. 48.
[24] Basil Bernstein, "Some Sociological Determinants of Perception: An Inquiry into Sub-cultural Differences," *British Journal of Sociology*, 1, 2 (June 1958), pp. 159–174.

quiry and starting points for relationships."[25] The result is to intensify the child's curiosity and reward his explorations. By contrast, in the working-class home "sustained curiosity is not fostered or rewarded, as answers to questions rarely lead beyond the object or further than a simple statement about the object."[26] Correlatively, the absence in the language patterns of a relatively long time perspective organized in rational cause-effect terms makes more difficult the postponement of present pleasure for future gratification.

The poverty of language, the blunted curiosity, and the tendency to subordinate future to present gratification are familiar problems to all who have worked with or studied lower-class children. These characteristics of lower-class children are very heavy handicaps to them in school; as the Ausubels note, "Since schools place great emphasis on the learning of abstract relationships, and on the abstract use of language, lower-class children, on the average, experience much greater difficulty than middle-class children in mastering the curriculum."[27]

Many of the difficulties of lower-class children, including their language problems, can be traced to their attenuated relationships with their parents and other adults. Speaking of a group of first- and fifth-grade lower-class children, both white and Negro, Suzanne Keller is struck by how little attention is typically paid to them:

> There is clearly a lack of sustained interaction with adult members of their families.... Only about one-half, for example, regularly eat one meal with one or both parents, the rest either eat alone or with brothers and sisters only. This robs them of one of the important socializing and intellectually stimulating experiences of childhood.... Participation and interaction with significant others in an organized way helps shape the personality and sensitizes the participants to each other's needs and inclinations. Organized conversation helps shape the development of verbal facility and subtlety and determines a whole set of complex attitudes and feelings about the use of language. The family meal also serves as an acculturating agency, for, in their interaction, the members teach each other and develop a way of seeing themselves and the world in which they live.[28]

Keller sees the climate of indifference in the lower-class child's home as only one, though perhaps the central, element in a pattern of con-

---
[25] *Ibid.*, p. 165.
[26] *Ibid.*, p. 169.
[27] David P. Ausubel and Pearl Ausubel, "Ego Development Among Segregated Negro Children," in Passow, ed., *op. cit.*, p. 114.
[28] Suzanne Keller, "The Social World of the Urban Slum Child: Some Early Findings," *American Journal of Orthopsychiatry*, 33, 5 (October 1963), pp. 823–831.

stricted experience and monotonous repetition of activities, dominated by television and by play with other children. "This constriction of experience and the poverty of the spirit it engenders may account for the below-normal IQ scores of this group of poor children by the time of the fifth grade . . . confirming countless other studies that have shown a similar scholastic and verbal inferiority for children from underprivileged environments." [29] It is noteworthy that the average IQs of the group Keller studied were not merely low but also declined by some seven points between first and fifth grade.[30]

The social and psychological forces that handicap lower-class Negro children are generally found in extreme forms and with additional handicaps special to their condition. The Ausubels, who reviewed a large body of literature on the problem, point to a number of factors that inhibit the realization of potential talents of Negro youth.[31] Among these are (1) the high rates of family instability among Negroes, and the frequent absence of a father in the home; (2) the low self-esteem, flowing from the inferior caste status of Negroes, which, with confused feelings of hatred, both for themselves and others, is a major handicap to successful school performance; and (3) the greater and earlier freedom from parental supervision which Negro youth have in common with most lower-class whites and which makes for a precocious independence from the family, while greatly increasing the

---

[29] *Ibid.*, p. 829.

[30] The relative and often absolute deterioration of both achievement and measured intelligence of lower-class children during the years they are in school is gaining additional confirmation in many studies and situations. For example, a study done in England during the 1950s reports that, "At 11 years the average test scores made by children in the four social classes differ more widely than they did at eight. The two middle-class groups come closer together and move further away from the manual working-classes; this shows itself in intelligence tests as well as tests of school achievement" [J. W. B. Douglas, *The Home and the School* (London: MacGibbon and Kee, 1963), p. 46]. The combined and progressive effects of social origins and the social class composition of the school, both in primary and secondary schools, is shown in the Robbins Report, *Higher Education*, Appendix I (London: HMSO, Cmnd. 2154–I, 1963), pp. 46–50.

See also Patricia Sexton, *Education and Income* (New York: Viking Press, 1961), pp. 25–28; Allen H. Barton and David E. Wilder, "Research and Practice in the Teaching of Reading; A Progress Report," in Matthew B. Miles, ed., *Innovation in Education* (New York: Teachers College Bureau of Publications, 1964), p. 386, Table 10; and Martin Deutsch, "The Disadvantaged Child and the Learning Process," in Passow, ed., *op. cit.*, p. 165.

[31] See also Martin Deutsch and Bert Brown, "Social Influences in Negro-White Intelligence Differences," *Journal of Social Issues*, 20, 2 (1964), pp. 24–35; and the studies cited by Thomas F. Pettigrew, "Negro-American Personality; Why Isn't More Known," *Journal of Social Issues*, 20, 2 (1964), pp. 4–23.

socializing influence of the peer group whose values are usually opposed to those of the school.

Behind these patterns of Negro American life lies the destructive effect of what may well have been the most degrading form of slavery in history, followed by a century which did little to modify and much to perpetuate the political, economic, and social subordination of the descendants of the slaves. Where early efforts were made to counter the results of slavery and subordination, their effects are clearly visible. Horace Mann Bond, after documenting the almost total absence of Negroes among winners and runners-up in the National Merit Scholarship contests, links this to the paucity of Negroes among the educated professional groups which supply a hugely disproportionate number of the National Merit Scholars. He then raises the interesting question of the social origins of those Negro Americans who have demonstrated high academic talent by earning a doctoral degree.

> When the childhood residences of the parents and grandparents of my doctoral sample are located on a map, they cluster in certain localities; and these localities are likely to coincide with what had been the locations, immediately after the Civil War, of mission schools founded by Northern missionary societies, and principally staffed by the inimitable Yankee schoolmarms, gently bred women, either from New England itself, or from New England families transplanted to the Western Reserve.
>
> These women were available to teach former slaves because of the humanitarian zeal of the times; but also, because they represented, in their generation, a surplus of their class, when so many of the marriageable males had been killed in the War, or were adventuring far out on the Western frontier. For whatever reason, their availability and their devotion stand out unmistakeably on a spot-map of an emerging Negro intellectual elite, almost a century after they began their unsung labors among the Freedmen.
>
> Among the lessons to be drawn from their work is that teachers in the best intellectual tradition may have a tremendous effect upon the most deprived of populations. The emancipation of women has now long since made other occupations perhaps too strong a competitor for modern prototypes of these inimitable carriers of academic and moral culture.[32]

Bond's findings are not only a very powerful rebuttal of assumptions about the inherent intellectual limitations of Negro children, a corrosive and self-defeating stereotype that persists, as we have seen, even

---

[32] Horace Mann Bond, *The Search for Talent* (Cambridge, Mass.: Harvard University Press, 1959), p. 56.

among educators in our own time. But his observations and the historical experience of other ethnic groups which entered American society with at least some of the characteristics of Negro Americans suggest that the transformation of ethnic subcultures necessary for full participation in American society on equal terms may take several generations.

But in the changed moral and political climate of the United States, Negroes will not be satisfied with the prolonged gestation of talent in isolated communities that Bond describes. What is now demanded is more even than a very rapid extension of full social, political, and economic rights and opportunities for all Negroes, a demand flowing from the liberal conception of equality of opportunity for individuals. The more radical demand, flowing from the radical conception of equality of opportunity, is for interventions by the society to ensure that Negroes rapidly and as a *group* show distributions of achievement in all areas of life comparable to those of other groups in the population. The basis for this demand is that it is only equivalence of group distributions of performance that provides sure evidence of genuine equality of opportunity. These new and stronger claims (new in the sense that the older immigrant groups appealed to the liberal conception of equality and to individual achievement rather than group distributions) [33] are made at a time when the concentration of great numbers of poor Negroes in the urban slum ghettos provides a very difficult environment for the compensatory socialization and education that is required. In addition, rapid transformation of the occupational structure is destroying the kinds of unskilled work on which immigrant families established a stable pattern of life, enabling children to develop their abilities and aspirations for more education and better occupations than their parents. Furthermore, the rapid development of mass higher education is increasingly making college attendance a mark of respectability as well as a prerequisite for a decent standard of living, at the same time that it draws out of the public schools the kinds of teachers Bond describes. Today the rate of social and economic change is much faster than it was a hundred years ago; the question is whether the efforts we are now making to transform social and educational conditions that stunt and deform the abilities of so many Negro (and other culturally deprived) children can have equally rapid effects.

[33] Of course the older immigrant groups looked after the welfare of the group, through self-help societies, political pressure, and the like. But they did not claim group advancement as a right to be guaranteed by governmental agencies.

The "Problem" of American Secondary Education: Sources and Responses

As I have suggested, current thought on the educational problems of slum children reflects an increasing application of a radical conception of equality of opportunity with its strong stimulus to the study (and manipulation) of the social sources of intelligence. By contrast, the critical discussions over the past decade of the academic quality of our schools, especially high schools, reflect the continuing power of the older, liberal conception of equality of opportunity. American mass higher education is the natural extension of this liberal conception of equality of educational opportunity. And a secondary system geared to the preparation of students for higher education, that is, a system much more concerned than our high schools have been with the quality of college preparatory work, is a corollary of the extension of higher education to a majority of college-age youth.

It may be useful to raise the question of why the quality of academic work in the schools came to be seen as an especially acute problem in the mid-1950s, as a problem calling for major educational reforms and innovations. It may also be useful to look at one of the forms the response to this "new" problem has taken: the widespread and rapid growth of interest in new technical and organizational forms of instruction. Finally, we want to consider very briefly how this specific response to the problem has been conditioned; first, by the way the educational problem has been defined; second, by the nature of American public schools and their personnel; and third, by the values of the society in which it is put forward.[34]

The national discussion that has gone on in recent years about the quality of American public education is conventionally linked to the shock of the Soviet success in space exploration and rocketry, marked by its first successful satellite in 1956. Behind this, of course, lies the Cold War competition, a competition which generates worry about our pool of technically trained manpower and the relative merits of the Soviet and American school systems. But pressures for higher standards in American education would have developed even if the Soviets had not challenged us widely on scientific and military fronts.

---

[34] Much of the following is drawn from my essay on "American Education and the New Modes of Instruction" in Bruce J. Biddle and Peter H. Rossi, eds., *The Impact of New Communication Media on Education*, Chicago (Aldine Publishing Company, 1966).

The more basic sources of the new emphasis on the content of public education lie elsewhere.[35]

They lie first in the character and development of American secondary education. In the 50 years between 1880 and 1930, the numbers of students in public high schools in the United States roughly doubled every decade, rising from 110,000 to nearly 4.5 million. The new secondary education that emerged during those years was shaped both by the enormous increase in the numbers of students and by their social characteristics. Many of the new students were in school unwillingly, in obedience to the new or more stringent state compulsory education laws; many came from poor, culturally impoverished homes and had modest vocational goals; many were the sons and daughters of recent immigrants and seemed to observers greatly in need of "Americanization." These new students posed new problems for secondary education; these problems, and the answers which they engendered, transformed public secondary education, its philosophy, and its curriculum.

The creation of a system of mass secondary education could not simply be the extension of the old elite secondary system; it was different in function (terminal rather than preparatory) and in organization (publicly rather than privately controlled). Moreover, it needed its own curriculum and its own teacher-training programs and institutions because the sheer number of secondary teachers required by mass secondary education was far beyond the capacities of the traditional colleges to supply.[36] In the old academies the principals and masters were college products and often went on to teach in the colleges; there was no sharp break between the academies and the colleges, since they taught similar subjects to the same kind of students. This was no longer possible with the new terminal public high school; the students were different and the curriculum was not, by and large, preparation for college. New departments of education and state teachers colleges began to train the staffs of these new high schools.[37] These centers of profes-

---

[35] See Trow, "The Second Transformation of American Secondary Education," *op. cit.*

[36] The number of public high school teachers increased from about 20,000 in 1900 to over 200,000 in 1930. U.S. Office of Education, *Biennial Survey of Education, 1928–1930, Bulletin,* 20, 2 (1931), pp. 8–222.

[37] On the upgrading of normal schools to the status of four-year state teachers colleges and the establishment of departments of education in other colleges and universities in the decades before 1920, see Benjamin W. Frazier, "History of the Professional Education of Teachers in the United States," and E. S. Evenden et al., "Summary and Interpretations," U.S. Office of Education, *National Survey of Education Bulletin 1933,* 10, 5 and 6 (1935).

sional education were not identified with the older, elite traditions of higher education, but created their own traditions of education for life, for citizenship, for useful tasks, the traditions, that is, of the mass democratic terminal secondary system that came to full flower between 1910 and 1940.[38]

Since the end of World War II, American higher education has been undergoing a very rapid expansion which in many ways resembles the growth of mass secondary education in the first half of the century. As recently as 1940 our colleges and universities enrolled only about 1.3 million students, who comprised about 15 percent of the college-age population, the eighteen- to twenty-one-year-olds. (The same proportion of the high school age group—the fourteen- to seventeen-year-olds—were enrolled in high school in 1910.) By 1965 the number earning credits in our colleges and universities was over five million. This four-fold increase resulted largely from rising rates of enrollment, since the college-age population was almost exactly as large in 1940 as in 1960. The difference is that whereas the college enrollments in 1940 comprised about 15 percent of the age group, in 1964 that figure was over 40 percent and increasing at an average of more than one percent a year.[39]

The growth in numbers will be even faster in the decades to come because, in addition to rising enrollment rates, the rise in birthrates after World War II is even now greatly increasing the pool of college-age youngsters. College enrollments in 1970, projected from present trends, will be over seven million.[40]

The growth of college going is transforming what has, for 60 years or more, been predominantly a system of mass terminal education into one that is increasingly asked to prepare large numbers, and even majorities, of students for college work. By 1962 well over half of all high school graduates went directly to some form of higher education,

---

[38] "During the first half of the present century, while many liberal arts colleges turned their backs on the problems of teacher education, legal requirements for certification were established in nearly all states. . . . (W)hile the liberal arts colleges were preoccupied with other things, while they ignored the problems of teacher education, a like-minded group of school administrators and other professional educators came to agreement among themselves on the necessity for professional preparation for teachers and transmitted their convictions into law. It was during this period that the educators became imbued with a new philosophy of education, one far removed from the academic traditions of the liberal arts colleges." Paul Woodring, *New Directions in Teacher Education* (New York: The Fund for the Advancement of Education, 1957), p. 23. See also Merle L. Borrowman, *The Liberal and Technical in Teacher Education* (New York: Teachers College Bureau of Publications, 1956).

[39] American Council on Education, *Fact Book on Higher Education* (Washington, D.C., n.d.), p. 233.

[40] *Ibid.*

and in some parts of the country the proportion was much higher.[41] Thus transformation is being imposed on the secondary schools by forces external to it.

In the course of this transformation the high schools find themselves confronted not only with a different kind of student but also with a different kind of parent. During the formative years of the mass terminal secondary system in the United States, the teachers and educators who were building the system were dealing by and large with parents who themselves had gone no further than grade school. These people, many of them immigrants or of rural origin, whose children were going no further than high school, had neither the competence nor the motivation to be greatly concerned with the high school curriculum. And the debates about secondary education were carried on largely over the heads of these parents, among the professionals themselves (and between the educators and sections of the academic community). But increasingly, secondary school people are dealing with educated parents of preparatory students, parents who possess both the competence and the direct motivation to be concerned with the character of their children's secondary education. As recently as 1940 three American adults in five had never been to high school, and only one in four had completed high school.[42] By 1960 three in five had been to high school, and over 40 percent were high school graduates.[43] By 1970 over 50 percent will be high school graduates, and by 1980 it is estimated that figure will reach 60 percent.[44] Parents who themselves have been through high school, many of them through some years of college as well, feel themselves more competent to pass judgment on the secondary education of their children and are less likely to accept on faith the professional recommendations of school administrators, educators, and counselors. It is this rapidly growing group of educated parents whose children are going on to college that provides both the audience and the support for the academic critics of the secondary school and its curriculum. There is every reason to believe that parental interest will grow as competition among their children for the better colleges heightens.

The increased numbers of students going on to college, the resulting

[41] *Ibid.*, p. 253.
[42] See Donald J. Bogue, *The Population of the United States* (Glencoe, Ill.: The Free Press, 1959), Table 13-8, p. 343.
[43] Between 1940 and 1962 the average educational level of the whole American adult population rose from 8.7 to 11.9 years of schooling completed. See U.S. Bureau of the Census, *Current Population Reports*, Series P-20, Nos. 99 and 121 (1959), p. 5. See also Denis F. Johnston, "Educational Attainment of Workers March 1962," *Monthly Labor View*, Special Labor Force Report 30, May 1963.
[44] Bogue, *op. cit.*, Table 26-11, p. 779.

heightened interest among academic men in primary and especially secondary education, the increasing concern with scientific and technological manpower as an element in national power and economic growth, the large and growing numbers of educationally competent parents—all of these and other forces have since World War II created pressures for the improvement of the quality of education.

The responses to these pressures over the past decade have taken two distinct forms. One of these has been a variety of efforts to improve American education by working through the classroom teacher. Among these efforts has been the work, largely undertaken by college and university professors, to reshape the school curriculum, first in the sciences, and increasingly in foreign languages, English, and the social sciences, through the preparation of new syllabi, texts, and other teaching materials. All these efforts have been aimed at introducing new knowledge and conceptions into the classroom and bringing what is taught there closer to the academic disciplines as they are taught in colleges and universities. Along with these reforms in curriculum have gone efforts and proposals to strengthen the academic preparation of teachers, to ensure that they have been educated in what they teach and that they teach only what they know. Some states have revised credential requirements so that most new teachers must have a subject matter major. New and wider opportunities have been provided for older teachers to continue their education at National Science Foundation Summer Institutes. Working in the same direction, proposals have been made to reform teacher training to emphasize academic work and supervised teaching. Some schools and departments of education have tried to recruit better teachers by raising admissions requirements.[45] Not all these efforts can be attributed to the widespread concern about education that developed after World War II, but certainly the new climate of criticism has reinforced and accelerated these efforts. What they all have in common is that they are addressed to the education and training of the teachers.

The other major response to the pressures for strengthening the academic side of American education has been the enormous interest in

[45] On the reforms of the curriculum, see the essays in *The School Review*, 70, 1 (Spring 1962). Proposals and current projects looking toward the improvement of teacher education can be found in James D. Koerner, *The Miseducation of American Teachers* (Boston: Houghton Mifflin, 1963); James B. Conant, *The Education of American Teachers* (New York: McGraw-Hill, 1963); and Paul Woodring, *New Directions in Teacher Education, op. cit.* On programs of inservice education, keyed to curriculum reforms, see "Secondary School Curricular Areas," *The Bulletin of the National Association of Secondary School Principals*, 47, 286 (November 1963).

and development of new technical and organizational forms of instruction, notably classroom television, teaching machines, and team teaching. They represent attempts to strengthen education not primarily through the teachers but, to a considerable extent, independently of them. These efforts are a product of the disparity between what it is widely felt needed to be done and the possibilities of doing it quickly by improving the performance of 1.5 million classroom teachers.

Efforts to raise the quality of education by strengthening the school curriculum and teacher training—that is, by raising the quality of the teacher's performance in the classroom—are agonizingly slow to take effect. They are slow partly because the enormous institutional complex, represented by the schools, departments of education, credential requirements, and the like, has great inertia and powers of resistance to innovation. The men and women who staff the teacher-training programs and lead the state departments of education and the state and national educational associations are, by and large, the people (or students of the people) who with great dedication and devotion created the system of mass terminal secondary education, and who hold with almost religious fervor the values associated with terminal education, the values of education for life and for useful work that characterized American secondary education for 50 years or more. Many of them are less than enthusiastic about the new emphasis on academic performance and the changes it is bringing to the curriculum and to instructional methods. Commenting on a National Education Association report on new approaches to instruction, Fred Hechinger observes that:

> The startling fact—as one looks over the list of innovations covered by the report—is that few, if any, of the experiments were begun by public school educators or, having been started, welcomed by the rank and file Team teaching, TV and the use of non-professional teacher aides appear to have sprung from Ford Foundation research; the mathematics reform movement was initiated by the Carnegie Corporation, the physics, chemistry and biology curriculum reform was born at the universities, and not predominantly at their schools of education.[46]

But over and above the inertia and resistances of teachers and educators, efforts to upgrade the curriculum and the education of teachers are slow to take effect because the academic qualifications and abilities

---

[46] See *New York Times* (Western Edition), October 16, 1963. One study done in Ohio in the early 1950s found that "teachers were more likely to resist significant curriculum change than either administrators, students, or parents." Cited in Ronald Urick and Jack R. Frymier, "Personalities, Teachers, and Curriculum Change," *Educational Leadership*, 21, 2 (November 1963), p. 108.

of teachers are relatively low compared with other professional and college-educated groups.

Many high school teachers of academic subjects are inadequately prepared in the subjects they teach. A study conducted by the National Council of Teachers of English of over 7000 high school English teachers, whose average experience was nine years, reports that "only 50.5 percent had majored in English. One-third majored in a field with no relationship to English. Two-thirds rated themselves as poorly prepared to teach composition and oral skills, 90 percent said they were poorly prepared to teach reading, and almost 50 percent said they were poorly prepared to teach literature." [47] A national study of junior and senior high school science and mathematics teachers sponsored by the National Science Foundation in 1960 and 1961 concludes that "a teacher who has less than eighteen semester hours of college work in a science does not have a substantial education in it, and we have seen that two-thirds of the physics classes, a third of the chemistry classes, and more than a fifth of the biology classes and upper level mathematics classes (and over half of the junior high mathematics classes) are taught by such teachers." [48] The proportion of teachers with inadequate preparation in these subjects is even higher than the proportion of classes taught by them.[49] A study by the U.S. Office of Education in three states in the late 1950s showed that 39 percent of the teachers in the study who were teaching one or more courses in high school mathematics had not studied the calculus or a more advanced course in mathematics, and 7 percent had studied no college mathematics at all.[50] At about the same time, 35 percent of California students in mathematics classes were being taught by teachers who had neither a major nor a minor in mathematics.[51]

With respect to abilities, the pattern of negative selection to teaching below the college level has been abundantly documented. The extensive studies done with national samples by the Educational Testing Service and others show that students who major in education score lowest on comprehensive tests of verbal and mathematical competence

[47] See *New York Times* (Western Edition), December 30, 1963.
[48] See *Secondary School Science and Mathematics Teachers: Characteristics and Teaching Loads* (National Science Foundation, Washington, D.C., 1963), p. 11.
[49] *Ibid.*, p. 8.
[50] See K. E. Brown and E. S. Obourne, *Qualifications and Teaching Loads of Mathematics and Science Teachers in Maryland, New Jersey, and Virginia*, Office of Education, Circular 575 (1959), Tables 20 and 22, p. 46.
[51] See J. A. Kershaw and Roland M. McKean, *Teacher Shortages and Salary Schedules* (New York: McGraw-Hill, 1962), Table 13, p. 91.

as compared with majors in almost every other field.[52] In a review of some sixteen studies of the ability of teacher education students, extending from 1928 to 1958, and in many different populations, North found without a single reversal that teacher education students were in general less able academically than other college students.[53] The negative selection to teaching is even more marked for men than for women, and this has special significance for college preparatory work in the high schools, where men comprise about half of all teachers.[54] Moreover, among those who go into education, there is a further negative selection of those remaining in classroom teaching. A follow-up study done in 1955 by Thorndike and Hagen of 10,000 Air Force cadets who had taken comprehensive aptitude tests during World War II shows that of all those who went into public school teaching after the war, "those who were academically more capable and talented tended to drop out of teaching and that those who remained as classroom teachers in the elementary and secondary schools were the less capable members of the original group."[55] Both the men who remained in education as administrators and those who had left education completely showed more ability on the Air Force tests of reading comprehension, arithmetic reasoning, and mathematics than did those who stayed in the classrooms.

The lower incomes of teachers, as compared with the incomes of school administrators, of men who leave education, and of most other occupations requiring a comparable amount of education, account for

[52] See Henry Chauncy, "The Use of the Selective Service College Qualification Test on the Deferment of College Students," *Science*, 116, 3001 (July 4, 1952), p. 75; Dael Wolfle and Toby Oxtoby, "Distribution of Ability of Students Specializing in Different Fields," *Science*, 116, 3013 (September 26, 1952), pp. 311–314; and Dael Wolfle, *America's Resources of Specialized Talent* (New York: Harper and Brothers, 1954), pp. 189–208.

[53] Robert D. North, "The Teacher Education Student: How Does He Compare Academically with Other College Students?" in NEA, National Commission on Teacher Education and Profession Standards, *The Education of Teachers: New Perspectives* (Washington, D.C.: 1958).

[54] North, reporting on the results of the 1956 College Qualification Test, which was administered to more than 24,000 freshmen in 37 colleges and universities across the country, notes that: "Norms for college freshmen in programs leading to the degree in education are given for a group of 274 men and 583 women. Comparison of these norms reveals that in the education group about 80 per cent of the men and about 60 per cent of the women had scores below average on the general norms. In contrast, only about 40 per cent of the freshmen in programs leading to the B.A. degree ranked in the lower half of the general norms" (*ibid.*, p. 283).

[55] R. L. Thorndike and Elizabeth Hagen, "Men Teachers and Ex-Teachers: Some Attitudes and Traits," *Teachers College Record*, 62, 4 (January 1961), p. 311.

much of this unfortunate pattern of recruitment and retention of male teachers. Moreover, the relatively low status of teaching below the college level, which is both a cause and a consequence of the low salaries, also helps to explain why teaching attracts and holds too few of the most able men. And although teachers' salaries are rising, it is unlikely that the gross differentials in pay and prestige between high school teachers and other occupations requiring a college education are likely to be significantly narrowed in the near future.[56] On the contrary, there is reason to fear they may be widened. The continued extension of opportunities for higher education to able students, through public and private scholarships, the expansion of public higher education, and the like are offering to able young high school students a wider range of educational and occupational alternatives, many of which carry greater prestige and higher income than does teaching.

In the past a career in teaching was often the only intellectual occupation (aside from the ministry) open to serious young boys from farms and small towns; and the local normal schools or state teachers colleges were often the only educational avenues of mobility open to such boys. Able young men and women with academic interests are more likely to be drawn to schoolteaching when their opportunities are limited by poor or immigrant or rural backgrounds, by scarce employment, or by the difficulties or expense of getting a higher education in other than a teacher training institution. The able students whose horizons and aspirations were formerly bound by a local normal school now have wider opportunities and higher aspirations. This, together with the continued growth of the "intellectual occupations," is almost certain to make the competition for able men keener in the years to come.[57] Our society's demands for scientists, engineers, and

[56] Over the six years between 1955–1956 and 1961–1962, the average salaries of all public school teachers, principals, and supervisors rose by 37 percent. But during the same period the salaries of college teachers in all ranks rose by about as much, and in most categories of institutions by more. From data in *Fact Book on Higher Education, op. cit.,* pp. 105, 106, 239.

[57] Between 1940 and 1950, "professional, technical and kindred workers," which is the census category for the occupations that require at least some part of a college education, rose from 7.5 percent of the labor force to almost 12 percent. In the decade 1950–1960 that category grew by 48 percent while the whole labor force was growing by only a little over 10 percent. It is estimated that the category is increasing during the 1960s by an additional 40 percent, from about 7.2 million to about 10.4 million. Stella P. Manor, "Geographic Changes in U.S. Employment from 1950 to 1960," *Monthly Labor Review,* 86, 1 (January 1963), Table 4; U.S. Bureau of the Census, *Historical Statistics of the United States: Colonial Times to 1957* (Washington, D.C., 1960), p. 74, Table D72–122; *Fact Book on Higher Education, op. cit.,* p. 146.

technically trained people of all kinds appear insatiable, and the rewards for such work are usually considerably more generous than they are for schoolteaching. Of even greater importance, the very rapid expansion of higher education currently underway, and the enormous demands for college teachers that it creates, constitutes perhaps the strongest set of competitive opportunities for young men and women who want to teach. Junior colleges, in particular, draw a substantial proportion of their faculties directly from the high schools, and they get the more academically oriented teachers at that. The continued expansion of the colleges and junior colleges cannot help but impoverish the teaching staffs of high schools.

Substantial increases in pay for public school teachers may ameliorate, but are not likely to reverse, the pattern of recruitment of academically less able men to high school teaching. Thus, no matter how teacher education and secondary school curricula are reformed to strengthen the college preparatory function of the high schools, a substantial part of the actual teaching itself will be carried on by relatively poorly paid, low-status, and academically less able people. This may not have mattered so much when secondary education was largely terminal—at least it can be argued that qualities other than academic ability, for example, a deep interest in young people and skills in working with them, are more important for teachers of students whose interests are not academic or intellectual.[58] But this claim can hardly be made for teachers of college-bound youngsters whose success in college will rest very heavily on the knowledge and intellectual habits they acquire in secondary school.

Consider the lot of the high school teacher today, as described by Francis Keppel, then Commissioner of Education:

> In many cases, his salary and social status are still only slightly above those of an office worker. The public tends to consider him neither a scholar nor a man of affairs, but a compromise between the two who could probably succeed at neither. His working day, while theoretically short, is packed with teaching assignments, corridor patrol, or lunchroom supervision. His chances for advancement, either in rank or salary, are limited and usually require him to leave the classroom, where he is badly needed, to enter administration, which also has a shortage of qualified men.
>
> He has little academic stature compared even to the lowliest college instructor. His contacts with the main stream of American intellectual life are limited, if not non-existent. If he is conscientious, he may spend

---

[58] Although many critics argue that it is precisely the weaker students who need the most serious attention to academic subjects in secondary school. See the publications of the Council for Basic Education.

many after-hours correcting papers or preparing for future classes. More often, he will find that he has to pump gasoline at a filling station. During the summer, he frequently has to work at a non-teaching job rather than take additional studies that he can afford only by starving his family. The university courses he does take are likely to be chosen for their accessibility and economy (or for their effect on the salary schedule) rather than for their contribution to his knowledge in his teaching field. When he looks at the years ahead, he often sees a future of mediocrity and stagnation rather than one of achievement and challenge. The contrast to many other walks of life is all too evident. . . . Under these circumstances it is little wonder that the high schools have not attracted their proper share of able young men and women with a commitment to teaching. It is not surprising, either, that many new teachers come to their jobs with inadequate preparation either in academic knowledge or professional skill. Nor should we marvel that a discouragingly large proportion of the 67,000 who begin high school teaching each year soon leave it for greener fields.[59]

It is significant that this description is part of an article in which Keppel recommended programs which offer the master of arts in teaching to a relatively small number of very able students in elite colleges and universities, such as Harvard, Oberlin, and Reed. The graduates of the program, Keppel reports, seem to be "on the way to well-paid and responsible positions that make education an attractive career for the able and dedicated candidate."[60] It is clear that Keppel saw these programs as a way of recruiting considerably larger numbers of students from the strong selective undergraduate colleges which in the past had not "provided their fair share of potential teachers."[61] Much the same concern with improving the quality of education by recruiting relatively small numbers of highly able teachers who could occupy posts of special responsibility and reward lay behind Keppel's early interest in team teaching. He believed team teaching could offer genuinely able recruits (such as the products of the master of arts in teaching programs) a "career"—a hierarchical series of steps in teaching—comparable to that offered by other professions. As Keppel

---

[59] Francis Keppel, "Masters of Arts in Teaching," in Paul Woodring and John Scanlon, eds., *American Education Today* (New York: McGraw-Hill, 1963), pp. 146–147. Mr. Keppel's predecessor as U.S. Commissioner of Education shares these concerns: "It is a national tragedy that the generality of our teachers are not fully qualified to assume the burden of responsibility that we must place upon them in the future. Many are lacking the native talent demanded by the art of teaching. Others in large numbers are inadequately prepared by general education or education in their teaching specialties. Sterling M. McMurrin, "A Crisis of Conscience," in Woodring and Scanlon, eds., *op. cit.*, p. 22.
[60] Keppel, *op. cit.*, p. 253.
[61] *Ibid.*, p. 248.

put it, "if the schools were organized in teaching teams, I could go to Amherst and say, 'You will start as an intern, and you can work up to Master Teacher—at a salary, I'd hope, of ten to twelve thousand dollars a year.' We have a million and a quarter teachers. I'm prepared to believe that the American people will pay ten to twelve thousand a year to two hundred thousand—but not to a million and a quarter." [62]

In a sense, all the new modes of instruction I have been discussing—programmed learning, classroom television, and team teaching—are efforts to use to best advantage the elite of talented and well-educated teachers that Keppel wants to recruit or identify. These innovations all involve the creation of a hierarchy of skill and reward among teachers, coupled with a division of labor and function aimed at increasing the educational impact of the minority of the ablest teachers—the most talented, energetic, committed, and academically well-grounded.

Stiles and Chandler make the connection between the new modes of instruction and the development of a hierarchy among teachers explicit:

> Urban schools in the future will offer multiple opportunities for professional service, specialization, and advancement. Although it is to be expected that guild organizations will exert persistent pressures to prevent the professionalization of teaching services in city systems, it is highly probable that differentiations will be developed in the quality and utilization of teaching competence that will permit outstanding teachers to be rewarded for professional competence and contributions. Examples of such recognition of quality teaching are already available in television teachers, instructional team leaders, and specialist teachers in some school systems. In the future, it is likely that the uniform scale salaries that educational guilds defend so vigorously will apply only to the lowest echelon of teaching. Others who prove their professional competence will be able to advance within the function of teaching to higher assignments that carry greater professional responsibility and greater financial rewards.[63]

Stiles and Chandler do not distinguish among the several new approaches to instruction by the elite groups they create within teaching; they refer rather casually to rewarding outstanding teachers who can "prove their professional competence." But teaching machines and

---

[62] Quoted in Martin Mayer, *The Schools* (New York: Harper and Brothers, 1961), p. 388.
[63] Lindley J. Stiles and B. J. Chandler, "Urban Schools for the Future," in B. J. Chandler, Lindley J. Stiles, and John I. Kitsuse, *Education in Urban Society* (New York: Dodd, Mead, 1962), p. 260. See also Judson T. Shaplin, "Team Teaching," in Woodring and Scanlon, eds., *op. cit.*, pp. 214–215.

classroom television differ from team teaching in this respect, which may partly account for the relatively easy acceptance of television and teaching machines by the schools, as compared with the spotty and slow progress of team teaching.[64] Teaching machines and television have built into them fairly clear technical skill criteria for differentiating among teachers. Moreover, the elite teachers, the programmers and television teachers, are rarely the classroom teacher's colleagues and do their work outside the teacher's own school. The "differentiation" between elite and ordinary teachers arising out of programming and television develops in the *occupation*, but typically not within any given *school*. By contrast, team teaching brings these distinctions into the school, where the selection of the master teacher or team leader runs into all the difficulties involved in assessing the processes of classroom teaching. Teachers and their guild organizations are traditionally highly suspicious of efforts to differentiate among them on the basis of their abilities as teachers. We can see this attitude in the enormous resistance teachers put up to schemes for merit pay and the tendency to link pay differentials to criteria other than the invidious distinctions between better and poorer teachers—most commonly to seniority and credit hours in schools of education.[65]

All three of the new modes of instruction distinguish between elite and ordinary teachers, but compared with the visible technical skills of the machine programmer or television teacher, the distinction within a team of teachers is likely to be felt as illegitimate, invidious, and arbitrary, for the basis of the distinction is not a technical skill but merely somebody's judgment of how able one teacher is in relation to his peers. And it is not surprising that in some schools where team teaching has been introduced, the hierarchical principal has been successfully resisted; the teams, after a period of floundering, have "organized themselves as groups of subject-matter specialists or in patterns as close as possible to those prevailing in the self-contained classroom." [66]

[64] The acceptance of television and teaching machines is also due in part to the vulnerability of school administrators to external demands for greater efficiency and higher productivity in education. See Raymond E. Callahan, *Education and the Cult of Efficiency* (Chicago: University of Chicago Press, 1962).

[65] An NEA study done in 1960 showed that between 1938–1939 and 1958–1959, the proportion of large school districts studied having a merit pay plan in operation had fallen from 20.4 percent to 6.2 percent. Of the districts that had tried such a plan but had dropped it, a third reported that they had done so because of the difficulties of evaluating teachers, another third because the plans had created dissension among teachers, "Why Few School Systems Use Merit Ratings," *NEA Research Bulletin*, 39, 2 (May 1961), pp. 61–62.

[66] Mayer, *op. cit.*, p. 390.

The Impact of New Modes of Instruction on the Classroom and Profession

The impact of the new forms of instruction will be conditioned by the characteristics of the craft on which they impinge.[67] Among these characteristics are three of special importance: the indeterminacy of the teacher's product, the relatively low visibility of the teaching process, and the limited control teachers have over their working conditions.

The new forms of instruction modify, in their different ways, each of these characteristics of the teacher's job. They affect what teachers do, how they are related to one another, what rewards they can gain from their work, and ultimately, the kinds of people who will be recruited and retained in the classroom. Indeed, it is likely that an important source of the support for these new forms of instruction lies in their potential for reshaping the nature of instruction more directly and more drastically than is possible through the traditional efforts to improve the quality of the teachers themselves or their training.

We generally recognized that it is extremely difficult to assess the effectiveness of the classroom teacher. Teaching aims to transmit bodies of knowledge, develop habits of logical inquiry and critical reflection, contribute to the child's psychological well-being, cultivate social responsibility and "good citizenship," encourage enduring interests—the list can be extended almost indefinitely. Many of these desired results are difficult if not impossible to measure; moreover, the teacher's impact is difficult to distinguish from all the other influences on the moral and intellectual development of the child. And finally, a teacher's most important effects on students may not be visible, and thus assignable, in the short run, but may bear fruit long after the student has left his classroom.

Coupled with the indeterminacy of his effectiveness is the relatively low visibility of his efforts. The teacher in his classroom is insulated both from the general public and from his fellow teachers and administrators. As Lortie notes, "The witnesses of a teacher's mastery of the processes of teaching are primarily legal minors whose testimony and judgment are somewhat suspect."[68] The process of teaching is invisible in another sense, in that it is obscured by all the other

---

[67] For a number of these ideas I am indebted to a penetrating essay by Dan C. Lortie, "Craftsman, Professional, Bureaucrat," Interpretation Project, AACTE Studies Committee (mimeographed, n.d.).
[68] *Ibid.*, pp. 9–10.

forces affecting learning. Even when we observe a teacher at work, the responsiveness or apathy of his students can rarely, with any confidence, be attributed to the teacher.

Nevertheless, teachers, like other craftsmen, seek and find rewards in their work. The societal rewards, in pay and prestige, are typically felt to be deficient. Moreover, as teachers recognize, these rewards cannot be closely linked to their effectiveness as teachers, in large part because of the indeterminacy of the product and the difficulties of assigning credit for success. Lortie's research leads him to suggest that, in their search for rewards in their work, teachers substitute "proximate, somewhat accessible goals for the ultimate goals stressed in the rhetoric of educational philosophy."

> The individual teacher works out his own definition of his desired product and monitors his performance in terms of that production definition. Since this process is undertaken individually (and largely without official sanction), it leads to a diversity of product definitions among teachers. One teacher will get his rewards of craft pride from seeing that his classes obtain a high average score on college board examinations where another will influence youngsters to choose teaching as a career.[69]

Although for some the rewards of raising the intellectual capacities, or academic performance, or career aspirations of their students will be central, for many their chief rewards lie in their ability to relate to students as persons. For these "their pleasure at indications that their students like and enjoy them, and the affective response they obtain" [70] is the chief pleasure they find in teaching, when their own dispositions, training, and the characteristics of their students all work to reduce the rewards from the intellectual and academic content of the teaching itself.

The indeterminacy of the product and the invisibility of the process of teaching both increase the importance of the personal characteristics of teachers for the goals they set for themselves and the rewards they seek in the classroom. Insofar as these definitions of success are private, they are highly variable, affected very greatly by a teacher's temperament, intellectual ability and training, and history of intellectual success or failure. Many teachers have not themselves been liberally educated, nor have they enjoyed or done well in their academic careers. Such people are not likely to find their chief rewards in the intellectual

[69] *Ibid.*, p. 4.
[70] *Ibid.*, p. 20.

growth of their students or to see their students' academic achievements as a major goal and an important criterion of their own success as teachers.[71] Nor, until recently, have such criteria been strongly urged and supported by school administrators and boards.

One function of educational philosophies is to shape and justify the product definitions of teachers. But the absence of any consensus among educational philosophers about the aims and priorities of education has diminished their influence on what the teachers themselves take to be important. Vulgarized versions of progressivism certainly helped to demolish the authority of the classical tradition but gave little support to the notion that the distinctive function of the schools is intellectual training.[72] Rather, these versions of "progressivism," most notably the life adjustment movement, tended to justify the private product definitions of teachers, especially those that minimized the importance of academic achievement.[73]

Underlying the widespread criticism of American education over the past decade is a mistrust of the private product definitions of teachers and of the educational philosophies, formal and implicit, which legitimate them. The new modes of instruction, reflecting this mistrust, insert themselves directly into the classroom and take the definition of the product out of the hands of the teachers (and to some extent out of the hands of professional educators), centralizing it and making it more visible.

Programmed learning, for example, focuses the student's attention on a body of material to be learned. A student attending to a program of instruction is not at that moment engaged in "interpersonal relations with the teacher," or in a group discussion whose character and direction are far more vulnerable to the teacher's notions of success and to his private search for gratification in his work. Insofar as the programs themselves are written by subject matter experts, their product definitions are introduced more directly and forcefully into the classroom than has heretofore been possible. (To an important extent, programmed instruction not only substitutes one set of definitions of success for whatever set the teacher may have held, but by directing the teacher's as well as the student's attention to the program, may in fact modify the teacher's conceptions of desired outcomes, and thus his sources of intrinsic gratification in his work.)

[71] See Edgar Z. Friedenberg, "The Gifted Student and His Enemies," *Commentary*, 33, 5 (May 1962), pp. 410–419.
[72] See Cremin, *op. cit.*
[73] See Hofstadter, *op. cit.*, pp. 299–390.

Similarly with televised courses; television makes the teaching process widely visible,[74] and the televised teachers themselves more likely to be subject matter specialists, with aims closer to those of their counterparts in the colleges. It is true, as Lortie notes, that television could conceivably become an instrument of the individual teacher who uses it very much as teachers use films today, to supplement the teacher's own instruction and demonstration. But this, in his view, is unlikely:

> The high costs involved in equipment and technical personnel, however, make it more probable that television facilities and transmission will be centralized at the school system level or in larger units of cooperating systems. Under such circumstances, television will become a central office function and it is also likely that with time, it will lead to a specialized role of television instructor. Such television becomes an instrument for projecting the teaching of one teacher into many classrooms.[75]

The televised teacher is far from representative of teachers as a group, and is much closer in temperament, talent, and training to the models projected by the critics of contemporary education. He is more likely to have the grasp of the subject demanded by the curriculum reform groups, a sense of the structure of the discipline called for by Bruner, and the creativity and imagination in presentation admired by Mayer. Unworried by discipline problems, with time and resources for scholarly preparation unknown to the classroom teacher, and debarred from the rewards flowing from personal relationships with the students, the televised teacher, more nearly than the great majority of classroom teachers, can meet the demands for intellectual challenge and academic achievement that accompany the growth of mass higher education and the concomitant transformation of secondary education.[76] And similarly, the master teacher or team leader, at least in

---

[74] One observer has expressed concern precisely about the increased visibility of teaching by television, which he sees as inhibiting the presentation of controversial or original material. For this and other criticisms of televised teaching, see Richard Franko Goldman, "The Little-Read Schoolhouse," *Columbia University Forum*, 4, 1 (Winter 1961).

[75] Lortie, *op. cit.*, p. 23.

[76] However, some observers have doubts about the extent to which watching a master teacher on television will help the classroom teacher's own teaching effectiveness: "the television teacher often pitches his presentation above the level of the classroom teacher's competence, showing the latter at a disadvantage and exposing him or her to student questions that he cannot answer. This kind of embarrassment doesn't necessarily motivate improvement; rather it increases tensions and the fear of threat to the classroom teacher's authority. Resistance rather than learning may derive from this experience; the dynamics of the individual sit-

theory, will be a subject matter specialist, abreast of advanced work in his discipline.[77]

These new approaches to instruction are, each in its own way, a response to the pressures for upgrading the quality of American education in the face of the very considerable difficulties of raising the quality of performance of the great mass of American teachers. In addressing themselves to the technology and organization of production, rather than to the level of skill or effort of the individual workers, they represent a measure of rationalization of production which involves, at least to some degree, the transformation of a labor-intensive craft into a capital-intensive industry.[78] And in this respect these innovations represent the application to education of a characteristically American tendency to circumvent shortages of labor or skill by the more efficient utilization of what labor or skill is available.[79]

The "technological revolution" in education involves forces working both to raise and to lower the status of teachers. Where teaching remains a craft, where the skills, training, and abilities of classroom teachers are strengthened and cultivated more intensively, and where teachers are in control of the new technology of instruction, teaching will assume more of the characteristics of a profession and the teacher's activities will be governed more by professional norms, rules, and his own discretion than by orders from above. By contrast, where the new media come to play a major role in instruction, where they supplant rather than come under the authority of the classroom teacher, the

---

uation are not taken into account in the more optimistic predictions"[John Fritz, as reported by Lester Asheim, "A Survey of Informed Opinion on Television's Future Place in Education," *Educational Television: The Next Ten Years* (Stanford, Calif.: The Institute for Communication Research, 1962), p. 27]. But we have very little knowledge of the effects of television on the classroom teachers, or how they deal with the problems which the master teachers on television create for them.

[77] See Shaplin, *op. cit.*, pp. 211–217.

[78] An English economist, commenting on the use of teaching machines and television in American schools, observes: "In these and other experiments a complex procedure of replacing labour by machines to subdivide the teachers' tasks is proceeding just as it did in Adam Smith's pin factory. The unpleasantness of individual experiments to those of us more accustomed to the easier, more slipshod labour-intensive methods of ordinary education should not blind us to the historical trend which is inevitable in a society where capital is more abundant (relatively) than skills" [John Vaizey, *The Economics of Education* (London: Faber and Faber, 1962), p. 80].

[79] On the relation of scarcities of labor and skill to technological innovations in nineteenth-century America, see H. J. Habakkuk, *American and British Technology in the Nineteenth Century* (Cambridge: Cambridge University Press, 1962).

teacher will have less and less the characteristics of a professional. In the short run this seems likely to be the more common tendency in elementary and high schools.

The more centralized and extensive the planning of instruction through the new media, the more important will be the planning and administrative staffs in city, county, and state departments of education. These staff people already rank higher in status and salary than classroom teachers. The gap will be widened, and these central staffs will come to include more people directly involved in teaching (as television or master teachers) or in developing instructional materials (programmers). But in addition to the widening of status differentials, the rationalization of instruction will centralize power as well. The classroom teacher now has relatively narrow discretion in the shaping of the curriculum and the choice of materials. The new media, if governed from above, will further narrow the scope of his discretion. By reducing the calls on him for other than routine skills and custodial functions, the new media will lower the status of the non-elite teacher.

In any event, the consequences of these innovations will certainly be greater than their intended effects on the quality of instruction. They are likely to affect the structure of the teaching profession, replacing a unitary status by a hierarchy of profession and status; they may affect the rewards of teaching by reducing the scope for private "product definitions" and by standardizing criteria of success; and ultimately they will affect the patterns of teacher recruitment by establishing within education different tracks for different groups and strata.

Summary and Conclusion

In this essay I have discussed, more illustratively than exhaustively, two broad "problems" faced by American education. One of these is the education of culturally deprived children; the other is the academic preparation of the growing numbers of students headed for colleges and universities. These problems have both similarities and differences.

In both cases the emergence of the problem was not associated with a worsening of the education of the groups in question; the education of culturally deprived and college-bound children was no worse (and almost certainly better) in 1955 than in 1925 or 1935.

In both cases the emergence of the problem was associated with changes in what was expected of the schools by large or influential groups outside the schools. The slum school, over the past decade, has come to be seen as the institution through which society can attempt to reduce in the children of slum dwellers the damage, emotional and intellectual, resulting from poverty and deprivations of many kinds in their homes. At the same time the high schools have come to be seen as preparatory schools for college, rather than as the termination of formal education.

The changes in the demands made on the schools reflected changes in the larger society which also created the attentive audiences for the critics who defined the problems and pressed the demands. The new demands on the slum school were part of a major change in the position of Negro Americans and were made by civil rights organizations, parents organizations, and social scientists professionally interested in the social psychology of learning. These demands found support among public officials who were responsive both to the political pressures involved and to the social dangers posed by large numbers of school dropouts for whom the economy was providing fewer and fewer jobs, who were creating major problems for police and welfare agencies, and whose potentialities for violence and crime constituted a major danger to urban life.

The new demands in academic education were voiced by the growing body of parents of college-bound children, by academic men increasingly aware of the inadequate preparation of many college students, by scientists concerned with the gulf between their subjects as taught in the colleges and as taught in the schools, and by public officials concerned with the quality of education and its bearing on national strength and our resources of skilled manpower in the context of a global competition with the Soviet Union.

The two conceptions of equality of opportunity which provided the moral force behind the new demands on the schools are different. For the culturally deprived, a radical conception demanded that the schools devise ways of strengthening the child's cognitive, intellectual, and motivational resources for dealing with formal schooling. For the college-bound student, the older liberal conception of equality of educational opportunity demanded that schools respond to the growth of higher education by improving the quality and content of their academic curriculum.

Action to meet the two defined problems, initiated to a considerable extent outside the educational profession, has been conditioned by the nature of the schools and their teaching and administrative staffs. The "culture of defeat" noted by so many observers as an obstacle to the education of the slum child has been especially difficult to modify. Other efforts are made to circumvent existing school routines and attitudes by extending and improving preschool education for slum children and by training ancillary and specialized personnel able to develop forms of education that supplement the ordinary curriculum and are designed to improve the child's chances of coping with the regular schoolwork.

In the problem of the high school and its academic program, the response has taken two forms: efforts to improve the skills and knowledge of the teachers themselves, and other efforts to improve teaching through measures relatively independent of the teachers' own abilities or limitations. Of these latter efforts, the technological innovations in instruction have met with less resistance in the schools than have such innovations as team teaching which modify the status and authority relations among teachers and administrators.

The progressive and meliorist values of American society, coupled with its rapid rate of social change, tend sooner or later to convert almost all aspects of national life into "problems," at least as defined by some. A "problem" implies reform, or change, and places established institutions and customary procedures in question. In education, demands for reform are made on the institutions of education and on their professional personnel. The clash between the forces for educational change and the relatively conservative educational institutions results in a very large number of educational innovations, such as the ones which attempt to circumvent the school and the teacher by reaching the child either before he enters school, outside of school, after he drops out of school, or directly through technical or organizational devices, during regular school hours. These efforts, and parallel efforts to reform the educational practices of the schools and teachers themselves, can be understood as attacks on the two problems under discussion. Their "solutions" will surely be marked by new educational problems, defined by new groups and audiences, reflecting other changes in the society and calling for further changes in the forms and functions of American education. Just as the educational philosophies, institutions, and practices which were the responses to yesterday's problems are themselves part of our current difficulties, so our present solutions will be seen as sources of the educational problems of the future.

3

Work as a Social Problem

Harold L. Wilensky

>Captain, Captain give me my time
>Tired of workin' in damned ol' mine
>Captain, Captain can't you see
>This pick and shovel is killin' me
>
>>—American folk song
>>Auburn, Alabama, 1915
>
>Work
>Thank God for the Might of It!
>The Glory, the Strength,
>The Delight of It!
>
>>—Sign beneath clock in sixth-grade schoolroom,
>>New Rochelle, New York, 1930
>
>I may Look Busy, but I'm Only Confused.
>
>Your Call Has Climaxed
> an Already Dull Day.
>
>Time Is Valuable—
> Why Waste It Working?
>
>>—"Noninspirational mottoes" in
>>business offices, 1950s

---

* Based on H. L. Wilensky, *Work, Leisure, and Freedom: The Gains and Costs of Abundance*, Parts I and II, forthcoming. Used by permission of the Free Press of Glencoe, a division of The Macmillan Company. Part of a program of research—the "Labor-Leisure Project"—made possible by grants from the National Institute of Mental Health (M-2209), 1958–1963, and the generous support of the Center for Advanced Study in the Behavioral Sciences and departments of sociol-

WORK is a social problem for four reasons. (1) Every society defines it as a central obligation for most of the population, but in modern society some men cannot obtain enough of it. The existing skills and talents of the population never perfectly fit the demands of the technology and the economy. The degree of incongruity between the cultural and genetic characteristics of the human material and the work roles to be performed is greatest in rich countries where occupations are numerous, specialized, and subject to rapid change. At any given time many adults are incapable of working or cannot find work; they must be trained or retrained, or the work must be changed to fit their capabilities, or they must be otherwise taken care of. (2) Many men are discontented with the work they do. (3) Employers and officials often feel that their subordinates are not doing enough work or good enough work. Hardworking portions of the population sometimes complain that others are "featherbedding" or "goldbricking." (4) Lack of work or alienation from it can place a heavy hand on the quality of life. Attitudes and practices developed in one sphere can spill over into another —killing time at work can lead to killing time in leisure, and apathy in the workplace can become apathy in politics.

Think of the Detroit auto worker: gripped bodily to the main line for eight hours, doing repetitive, low-skilled, machine-paced work that is wholly ungratifying, he comes rushing out of the plant gate, helling down the superhighway at 80 miles an hour in a secondhand Cadillac Eldorado, stops off for a beer (when commuter traffic piles up) and starts a barroom brawl, goes home and beats his wife—and in his spare time throws a rock at a Negro moving into the neighborhood. It is possible that his routine of leisure is an explosive compensation for the deadening rhythms of factory life and for the frustrating journey to work. Or consider another hypothetical auto worker: he goes quietly home, collapses on the couch, eats and drinks alone, belongs to nothing, reads nothing, knows nothing, votes for no one, hangs around the house, watches the "late, late" show, lets the television programs shade into one another, too tired to lift himself off the couch for the act of selection, too bored to switch the dials. It is possible that the mental stultification produced by his labor permeates his leisure. If such observations are accurate, work and its discontents have implications for every other

ogy at the University of Michigan and the University of California at Berkeley. The project conducted long interviews with 1354 men in various occupational groups and strata, focusing on their styles of life. The samples include lawyers, professors, engineers, a cross section of the middle mass (lower-middle and upper-working classes) of the Detroit area, and two samples of underdogs, 81 Negro and 105 white.

social problem discussed in this book—from teen-age delinquency to racial conflict, from mental health to poverty.

To understand the meaning and place of work is to understand some of the major questions about the social impact of affluence. Exploring such a social problem is a good way to grasp the shape of modern society. Is America becoming a leisure-oriented or consumer-oriented society characterized by the decline of the "Protestant Ethic," a general withdrawal from work, and an intensified search for substitute leisure commitments? Or are Americans typically responding to the "new leisure" by going into home production, working overtime, seeking spare-time jobs, and generally engaging in feverish economic activity? And what of the psychology of work: are Americans becoming more and more contented with their jobs as incomes and security rise, occupations become professionalized, and skills are upgraded? Or is joy in work declining, as jobs become more technical, disciplined, and specialized?

The questions are too simple and the data to answer them are limited. In this chapter I shall trace the major meanings of work through history; assess evidence of satisfaction and dissatisfaction in modern work; introduce a sociological conception of work alienation, indifference, and attachment; and, finally, speculate about the impact of automation on work as a social problem. I shall argue that in the perspective of many centuries, economic growth everywhere appears to foster ideologies increasingly favorable to work. If there is a recent withdrawal from work, it is not occurring mainly through rapid decline in the average work week or any urgent push for shorter hours; it is instead subjective, subtle, and it varies according to the work situation. I shall further argue that given modern doctrines of work, men who do not have it or are alienated from it are squeezed out of the mainstream of community life and thereby constitute a potential threat to political democracy. The picture that emerges will be more complicated conceptually than commonsense approaches to the sources and effects of job satisfaction, but it will reflect more accurately the ambiguities of the human condition.

From Curse to Craft

Men have attached meanings to their work as wondrously varied as the meanings they have attached to sex and play.[1] To the ancient

[1] The best history of philosophies of work remains Adriano Tilgher, *Work: What It Has Meant to Men Through the Ages* (London: George G. Harrap and Company, 1931), on which I draw for classical conceptions. See also the interpretations

Greeks, whose economy was slave based, work was a curse. According to Homer, the gods hated mankind and out of spite condemned men to labor. Although Greek thinkers conceded that agriculture might be tolerable for a citizen, because it could bring livelihood and independence, they deplored the mechanical arts as brutalizing the mind. In general, the Greeks, like the Romans to follow, saw work as a painful, humiliating necessity.

Similarly, the early Hebrews conceived of work as dismal drudgery, but they added the notion that man was obliged to suffer it as punishment for original sin, and in this sense work was accepted as an expiation, a way to regain lost spiritual dignity. In fact, Rabbinical literature held that no labor, however lowly, is as offensive as idleness.

What of the early Christians? Again, scorn is heaped upon prudent work and the cultivation of wealth. Jesus tells us, "Behold the fowls of the air, for they sow not, neither do they reap nor gather into barns; yet your Heavenly Father feedeth them. Are ye not much better than they?" If labor was to be avoided as diversion from the service of God, wealth, too, was temptation, a peril to the soul: "No man can serve two masters. . . . Ye cannot serve God and Mammon." And, "It is easier for a camel to go through the eye of a needle than for a rich man to enter the kingdom of God." Jesus, although he did not in the aristocratic Greek manner condemn work as a tragic necessity, set no value at all upon the world's goods and their pursuit. Primitive Christianity admitted only that work might be a means to charity, and possibly to the health of body and soul (for Christians shared the Hebrew view that idleness could do more mischief than labor). Even St. Augustine, who approved of handicraft, tilling the soil, and commerce on a small scale (if it conformed to the "just price" and involved no interest), held that work was obligatory only for monks and condemned anything that went beyond simple subsistence. In a word, as Tilgher puts it, "That work is best which least fills men with thoughts of profit and loss, which least distracts man from God."[2] The "work" most honored by early Catholicism was pure, passive contemplation—the gaze fixed on the world to come. Related to this was increasing tolerance for intellectual activity (reading and copying manuscripts), especially that done in a religious order. Toward work in the great world, neutrality or indulgent charity was the Catholic stance.

From the eleventh to the fourteenth century, Catholicism drew

---
of work, labor, and leisure by Hannah Arendt, *The Human Condition* (Chicago: University of Chicago Press, 1958).

[2] Tilgher, *op. cit.*, p. 34.

closer to society and community, granting a larger place to labor and its fruits. The view of St. Thomas Aquinas is not far from that of the Catholic Church today: work is a natural right and duty, the sole legitimate base of society, the foundation of property and profit, of guilds and corporations (according to divine plan), but it is always a means to a higher spiritual end. Carvings in the great European cathedrals depict the humble daily toil of the peasant, serious and suffering; high above stand the images consecrated to learning and contemplation.

In general, a radical split between religious piety, expressed in meditation and prayer, and worldly activity, expressed in labor, was maintained until the Renaissance and the Reformation, when work began to be defined explicitly as a duty for all—the *only* way or a major way of serving God. Idleness and the contemplative life alike were now seen as unnatural. This gradual shift toward a more activist view of man came at a time when developments in science, technology, and exploration were laying the groundwork for the vast economic expansion of the sixteenth and early seventeenth centuries. Doctrines of work, rooted in the pattern of entrepreneurial opportunities and motivation that emerged with economic growth, found sanction in the theology, especially, but not exclusively, of ascetic Protestantism and the Free Church sects (e.g., Quakers, Huguenots, Methodists, Unitarians, Congregationalists, Baptists, Scottish Presbyterians). This is the period in which the Protestant Ethic, together with other strands of Christian doctrine, meshed with the "Spirit of Capitalism" to form, ultimately, a secular religion of work.

Scholars have debated whether the modern zest for work has its origins in religion in general, or Protestantism in particular, or neither. Those who support Max Weber's position have argued that beginning with Luther's pronouncement of the equal spiritual value of all varieties of labor and his emphasis on the best performance of one's vocation or profession as the highest duty, followed by Calvin's stern doctrine of predestination (which, oddly, developed into the idea that hard work—rational, methodical, disciplined—placed one among the elect), Protestant theology gave religious sanction to worldly achievement. Weber's analysis of "ascetic Protestantism" suggests that the concept of the "calling" reflected a basic attitude toward worldly activity—a positive approval of active, rational mastery over things and ideas; a view of hard work as a virtue and profit making as obeisance to God. The Protestant Ethic, in Weber's view, was an injunction to ceaseless effort to make the earth the mirror of divine majesty. And if the effort required a change of occupation or class, or brought one riches, that was all right, too; it was everyone's duty to seek work that would bring to him and to society the greatest return.³

That such ideas were part of the climate of opinion for the philosophical discussion of work from about the sixteenth century on seems clear. That they were a major causal factor in the rise of capitalism, that they are specifically religious or unique to Protestantism, seems dubious.⁴ It is closer to the mark to say that Protestantism, insofar as it dealt with economic problems, never gave up the insistence on subordinating economic activity to the requirements of Christian morality. Indulgence or acquiescence toward worldly success and luxury is as far as modern Christian doctrine goes—like medieval Christianity, neither encouraging nor obstructing the spirit of capitalism. It is true that the ideas Weber labels "ascetic Protestantism" have some affinity with other systems of thought in which economic growth and the belief in a better future for nations or individuals are central. In the perspective of several centuries, however, the Protestant Ethic merged with a

---

³ Max Weber, *The Protestant Ethic and the Spirit of Capitalism* (New York: Charles Scribner's Sons, 1930); Max Weber, *The Theory of Social and Economic Organization* (New York: Oxford University Press, 1947); Talcott Parsons, "H. M. Robertson on Max Weber and His School," *Journal of Political Economy*, 43 (1935), pp. 688–696.

⁴ Among Weber's critics, see R. H. Tawney, *Religion and the Rise of Capitalism* (New York: Harcourt, Brace and Company, 1926), R. M. Robertson, *Aspects of the Rise of Economic Individualism: A Criticism of Max Weber and His School* (Cambridge: Cambridge University Press, 1933), and Kurt Samuelsson, *Religion and Economic Action* (New York: Basic Books, 1961). In a lively, somewhat injudicious attack on Weber, concentrating wholly on his early work, Samuelsson argues that the idea of "the calling" preceded the Reformation, which introduced no sudden ideological break with the past; that the Benedictine, Franciscan, and Jesuit orders come close to Calvinism in their asceticism and exceed it in their exhortations to joy in work; that the great Puritan teachings, mistrusting riches and the temptations of this world, were anything but capitalistically inclined; that thrift and diligence were virtues preached as zealously in Catholic France as in Puritan Scotland or New England, and in any case are more relevant as an ideological base for small traders and artisans than for large commercial and industrial entrepreneurs, the symbols of modern "capitalism"; that hardworking, successful men have everywhere, whatever their creed, elevated their industry and prosperity into religious virtue; finally, that the desire for riches and power, as well as the qualities of initiative and rationalism, are everywhere correlated with economic growth, in nations of every religion, in men both secular and devout. Weber's critics are especially persuasive on (1) the lack of a clearly Protestant or Puritan religious core for the ideology that is alleged to have interacted with increased mobility opportunity to produce capitalist and industrial forms of organizations; (2) the failure of certain empirical predictions (for example, the lack of a relationship between Protestantism and successful entrepreneurship—in some places even in the "take off" period of industrialization, in most places afterward).

mélange of doctrines that preceded it (e.g., mercantilist abomination of "idle and unprofitable persons," including nonworking children) and that followed it (for example, the rationalism of the Enlightenment, the "survival of the fittest" notions of social Darwinists such as Spencer and Sumner, the laissez-faire liberalism of American captains of industry such as Carnegie, Rockefeller, and Ford). The breach between religious piety and worldly activity *was* reduced, but this represents, first, the increasing autonomy of economic life as it was emancipated from feudal and church control and, later, the increasing control of economic life by the nation-state, together with the adaptation of religious doctrine to the hard realities of economics and politics.

On the issue of the importance of work, nineteenth-century socialism was at one with ascetic Protestantism and free-wheeling capitalism. In the society of socialist dreamers, work is central, natural, and an end in itself. Socialist *ideologues* generally went a step further: freed from institutional constraints, exploitation, avarice, and fraud, work could become a joy; workers, freely associated, managing in common the means of production, would throw themselves into it, endlessly transforming the material environment; the world would become a happy beehive. In the early writings of Marx and Engels, during their humanistic stage, work in the utopia of the classless society would acquire the free, fluid character of leisure: "society regulates the general production and thus makes it possible for me to do one thing today and another tomorrow, to hunt in the morning, fish in the afternoon, rear cattle in the evening, criticize after dinner, just as I have a mind, without ever becoming hunter, fisherman, shepherd or critic." [5]

The dominant modern philosophies of work have in common a positive approval of labor—whether it be a means to active mastery over matter (in an up-to-date phrasing, "the road to economic growth") or an ultimate value in itself. All modern states have developed ideologies giving work a positive central place. For modern fascists work is a social duty, carried out through the guided collaboration of various occupations and classes so that the nation may achieve its highest development. The Soviets call themselves the republic of workers, peasants, and soldiers, glorifying manual labor as the highest human dignity. Modern Protestant countries in the free West still draw on the liberal economics of yesterday to defend the free market, private property, and (in America) minimum government as the formula for releasing the productive energies of the people. Catholic idealizations of labor continue to emphasize its roots in the natural order and its utility

---

[5] Karl Marx and Friedrich Engels, *The German Ideology* (New York: International Publishers, 1939), p. 22.

in the attainment of higher spiritual ends. French humanists define labor as man's confirmation of himself against nature (whatever it does to make life easier and longer or useful and beautiful).

In compressing some 2500 years of changing philosophies of work into a few paragraphs, we will do well to remember that the modern enthusiasts for work had their precursors. In 1516, the original utopian, Sir Thomas More, anticipating Marx, pictured a world where no man was idle and all men took their turns at all kinds of work. Such utopias abounded in the early 1800s—intellectual responses to the rise of industrialism. In the writings of those intense system builders whom Frank Manuel calls the "Prophets of Paris," [6] work in general and physical labor specifically were given new value. The rich fantasies of Charles Fourier culminated in a utopia designed to overcome the boredom of industrial civilization and produce harmony. This would be accomplished by giving expression to the twelve basic passions, which, in various combinations, became 810, each finding accommodation in ingenious social arrangements conducive to love, labor, and play. Work would vary partly by stage of life. The way to get dirty work done, for instance, was to let those who might enjoy it do it. " 'The natural penchant of children for filth,' he wrote, 'becomes the charm and bond of the series [of freely chosen work assignments]. God gave children these strange tastes to provide for the execution of various repulsive tasks. If manure has to be spread over a field, youths will find it a repugnant job but groups of children will devote themselves to it with greater zeal than to clean work.' " [7] Similarly, in an early analysis of the problem of personality and occupation, Fourier found a place for "naturally ferocious" men, any "bloodthirsty characters" who might be about: they would be hunters and butchers.

"All men shall work" was the rule in the industrial scientific utopia of Saint-Simon, too, and again there was a concern with matching the job to the man. His system was a class society based on occupation. Occupation in turn was to be based on the natural capacities of men—acting, thinking, and feeling (which, he argued, tend to be mutually exclusive)—rather than the accidents of birth and chance. In Saint-Simon's new world, men would engage in motor activity either as administrators or as workers, pure rational activity as research scientists, or emotive activity as moralizers and inspirers (in the ministry and the arts). In a flash of prophetic insight, Saint-Simon suggested that since the engineer combined the characteristics of both adminis-

[6] Frank Manuel, *The Prophets of Paris* (Cambridge, Mass.: Harvard University Press, 1962).
[7] *Ibid.*, p. 233.

trator and scientist, he would have a strategic role in implementing the grand design. Each basic class, however, would be represented in "the high administration of society." The goal: maximum production through maximum use of individual capacities—each man allotted his natural functions.[8]

Since the Greeks expressed their scorn for toil, the doctrines have shifted drastically. Anchored in religious orthodoxy, work became a duty or an expiation for sin; freed from religion, it became important for its own sake, the nucleus of the Renaissance image of man as creator, and by the nineteenth century almost a secular religion.

The Modern Propensity to Work

These modern philosophies of work both reflect and reinforce a highly developed propensity for the activity itself; despite talk of the leisure-oriented society, and in the face of affluence for the majority, modern populations remain busy—with some groups becoming busier.

As I have shown elsewhere,[9] the average man's gain in leisure has been exaggerated by selective comparison of gross daily or weekly averages in working hours with those of the "take-off" period of rapid economic growth in England, France, and America—a time of blood-curdling schedules and conditions. Estimates of annual and lifetime leisure and comparisons with earlier times suggest a different picture. The skilled urban worker has now achieved the position of his thirteenth-century counterpart, whose long workday, seasonally varied, was offset by many holidays, rest periods, and long vacations; annual hours of work now, as then, remain in the range 1900–2500.

People in the upper strata have lost out. Even though their work lives are shorter and their vacations longer than those of lower strata, they work many hours, week after week—sometimes reaching a truly startling lifetime total. Top leaders in political and economic life, in the military establishment, education, aesthetics, and entertainment, show a marked preference for income over leisure. At less exalted levels, millions of ambitious men adopt a similar way of life. Considering both moonlighting and all hours worked on the main job, the data of the Labor-Leisure Project suggest that there is a slowly growing minority of the male urban labor force in the United States who usually work 55 hours a week or more; at least a third of the lawyers, professors,

---

[8] *Ibid.*, especially pp. 121–126.
[9] H. L. Wilensky, "The Uneven Distribution of Leisure: The Impact of Economic Growth on 'Free Time,'" *Social Problems*, 9, 1 (Summer 1961), pp. 32–56.

small proprietors, and middle managers in our samples work that long.[10]

Any discussion of trends in the propensity to work must consider those who have most apparent choice in the matter—women. Increased rates of nonagricultural female labor force participation are a concomitant of economic growth; for women in all the rich countries, both opportunity and motivation to work run high. This, of course, excludes the "work" of home and family. It seems plain that emancipation, while it has released women for the labor market, has not to an equal extent released them from housewifery. Studies of the weekly round of women report a range of averages of 50 to 80 hours a week in housework, child care, and paid labor. If a woman takes a job today, she has to figure on adding her work week to a 40- or 50-hour "home-making" minimum.

Labor-saving devices, more light and heat, better safety and health, speedier transportation—these have perhaps cut back on the minimum hours necessary to maintain the home. And despite talk of "outdoor housekeeping" in suburbia, the new burden of more elaborate home maintenance, the running and repairing of machinery, and an increase in financial management, physical drudgery has surely been reduced—both for housewives and for their teen-age daughters. The potential gain in free time, however, is offset by work (especially at the two peaks of labor force participation, ages 20 to 24 and after 40), a general increase in the demand for competence in child rearing, and an infectious rise in consumer expectations that keeps women busy on the shopping front.

On balance, the female "workweek" may be as long as it was a century ago, and pace-setting elites, the main carriers of cultural traditions and values, have probably increased their time at work.

It is not so much the general level of economic activity that has changed in the modern era as its distribution and the meaning vested in it. In order to grasp this we must first look at the new poor, whose employment opportunities are limited, and then at the ways in which the more secure majority approach their jobs.

Men Without Jobs: Clues to the Primordial Meaning and Function of Work

If a man's ties to work are so tenuous and his changes of job and employer so frequent and unpredictable that he never feels he has a job he can call his own, it does not make sense to speak of his work and its

[10] *Ibid.* See also footnote to Table 1.

discontents. The central fact of his work experience is job chaos—the lack of any stable work milieu, organizational context, or career to which he can respond in a cheerful or alienated way. Such is the condition of a large minority of the American labor force, and perhaps of marginal workers in every advanced country. There is a kind of forced withdrawal from work among (1) the involuntarily retired, (2) the intermittently unemployed, (3) the chronically unemployed—three segments of the population that are increasing in numbers.

Since 1890 there has been an accelerating decrease in the labor force participation rates of men in Great Britain, Canada, Germany, New Zealand, and the United States. Men aged 65 and older have reduced their participation rates far more than any other age category, mainly because of declining opportunity.[11]

Reduced opportunity is a function chiefly of:

1. Educational and occupational obsolescence. Employers are reluctant to retain or hire older men when stronger, better-trained, and often less costly personnel are available. Much of the displacement of older men has been due to the increased availability of middle-aged women for clerical, personal service, and professional jobs and of young high school and college graduates in all fields. From this situation flow compulsory retirement policies and age discrimination in hiring. As Long says, these practices were common decades ago, but there is clear evidence that they are more likely to prevail in larger firms—and an increasing fraction of the labor force works in such firms. Furthermore, if concern over unemployment increases and is intensified by the rising rate of new entrants, union sentiment for imposing or lowering compulsory retirement ages will grow.

2. The decline of "old men's" jobs in proportion to the number of old men. Older workers are concentrated in occupations that are dying out or declining—farmers, tailors, and locomotive engineers.[12] The

[11] Two excellent reviews of the evidence are C. D. Long, *The Labor Force Under Changing Income and Employment* (Princeton, N.J.: Princeton University Press, 1958), and M. Gordon, "Work and Patterns of Retirement," in R. W. Kleemeier, ed., *Aging and Leisure* (New York: Oxford University Press, 1961). All facts and inferences on this point are from these sources unless otherwise specified. Long states that "No statistical evidence could be found . . . that the decline has been the immediate result of increases in real income, extension of pensions and social security, physical deterioration (compared with elderly men in earlier periods), or of changes in self-employment, the pace of industry, or the level of employment" (*op. cit.*, pp. 13, 23), although older men have dropped out in periods of *very* high unemployment.

[12] D. J. Bogue, *The Population of the United States* (Glencoe, Ill.: The Free Press, 1959), pp. 498 ff.

number of guards, doorkeepers, and watchmen is not increasing as fast as the number of elderly men who want such jobs.

Do older workers retire not only because they lack opportunity but because they prefer leisure? A desire for leisure could express itself if both financial security and health among the aged were at high levels, but this test has not come. The evidence, while not conclusive, points (as in the past) to ill health as the main reason for "voluntary" retirement, and income as the main reason for staying on full time.[13] At least in the short run, as opportunities decline, the number of men who want to go on working and cannot is likely to increase.

The partially unemployed and the chronically unemployed in all age categories perhaps account for more life-span "leisure" hours than any group except women. Job insecurity under the most prosperous conditions is common. In 1957, when the national rate of unemployment averaged only 4 percent, at least 15 percent of persons who worked at some time that year experienced one or more episodes of unemployment.[14] Part-time work patterns are also frequent. Although much part-time work is involuntary, some of it is no tragedy—witness the partially retired professional, the housewife or student with a spare-time job, the moonlighter with two jobs. Long-term unemployment is another matter, and it is becoming more acute. An increasing number of people are condemned to idleness by the changing economic structure. Unemployment is concentrated among low-status service workers and unskilled and semiskilled manual workers in construction, manufacturing, and trade. Growth in these labor force categories has been slower than that in all other categories except farming; an accelerated decline in most of these jobs is in the offing. The unemployed are also disproportionately young, elderly, nonwhite, or foreign born, and the reproduction rate of some of these minorities, at least in the recent past, has been on the high side. Moreover, a very large fraction of the numerous children of the less skilled do not acquire the training and ability, information, and motivation to break out of the poverty circle. An old paradox becomes more prominent: those whose productivity is highest will work longer hours partly to support the forced leisure of men rendered obsolete by the activities of long-hours men.

[13] Gordon, *op. cit.*, pp. 31 ff., and F. A. Pinner, P. Jacobs, and P. Selznick, *Old Age and Political Behavior* (Berkeley: University of California Press, 1959), pp. 65–67. There is also an increase in part-time, unstable patterns of work among the aged (Gordon, *op. cit.*, p. 46). By 1956, one-fourth of male workers 65 and over and more than 40 percent of female workers of the same age were part-time employees, and their reasons were *non*economic (Bogue, *op. cit.*, p. 450).

[14] Bogue, *op. cit.*, pp. 642, 644.

These extremes of deprivation—the unemployed and the retired—dramatize the meaning and function of work for all men. Given modern doctrines of work, what happens to people who are cut out of the labor market?

In 1960 we interviewed 105 able-bodied white men, 25 to 45 years old, living with their wives and children, men who had been in Detroit at least five years, had been unemployed for at least one year, and were on relief. The Detroit Department of Public Welfare, squeezed by a rising welfare load and limited funds, is by any standard "tough" (but not punitive). Like many agencies in hard-pressed areas of chronic unemployment, it adheres strictly to the rule book. Some signs of the right moral fiber are required (for example, all recipients must have been completely self-sustaining for twelve months in the city; even a free medical exam in a clinic disqualifies). Relief investigators check need thoroughly, and most applicants never receive as much as an emergency food order. For those who pass the screening, total relief is held close to subsistence. Nonroutine allotments, such as children's clothing, are carefully controlled; pressure is sometimes applied to make the recipient move to cheaper quarters such as public housing. Cars, of course, must be sold before any relief is received. Most important, for our purpose, the Department of Public Welfare conducts a work-relief program. All recipients who are physically and mentally capable, according to doctor certification, earn the cost of subsistence received by working on special municipal projects; they are assigned as cleanup men in parts, janitor's helpers in city buildings, and the like. The pay: $1.98½ per hour, the lowest rate for a regular city laborer. The hours: not to exceed 72 in two weeks. Only men with many children are given the opportunity to earn that much relief.

We discovered that the Republican mood, expressed in such labels as "welfare chiselers" and assertions that reliefers drive about in second-hand Cadillacs, contains an ironical truth. Some of these men indeed "never had it so good." Their biographies are so peppered with layoffs, long stretches of unemployment, and fruitless efforts to obtain work and avoid charity that the chance to earn even bare subsistence and bus chits by tending furnace and erasing blackboards at a local school for a few months struck a few of them as the most stable and productive "employment" ever offered them. It was not uncommon for those working at high schools to use the shop after "work" to make ashtrays and similar knickknacks that they used for home decoration, gave away, or (violating another welfare rule) sold.

One man, the father of thirteen children aged 2 to 20, had been in and out of the army three times and had tried trucking and painting and decorating on his own in the 1930s and 1940s. Since World War II he has been intermittently employed in various construction jobs. On and off welfare since the mid-1950s (his work relief mainly consists of cleaning alleys), he does not regard himself as unemployed. He hopes to get "a little bit better, easier job, more money" such as the temporary construction job he had lined up for next week.

We could not, of course, find one case of comfort on relief. No one in these samples is maintaining a standard of living possible for men with steady jobs; all have had to cut back on expenses. Insofar as anyone becomes "adjusted" to this life, it is the adjustment that says, "Irregular work is better than none at all." Experience has taught these people that the choice is not work or welfare; it is occasional work, on or off welfare, or no work.

These men, like the underdogs of other studies, are extremely isolated. Half can name no close friends; half never visit neighbors; organizational memberships are rare, organizational activity negligible—all in contrast to social life among our samples of employed men.

Our data, together with studies using a great variety of samples and techniques, are consistent with this picture: in rich countries of the modern era, work, whether it is becoming more or less central as a source of personal identity and social solidarity, still remains a necessary condition for drawing the individual into the mainstream of social life; wherever work ties are severed, there is a decline in community participation and a related sense of isolation. For instance, excluding churches, there appears to be a general curve of participation in formal associations which closely parallels a job satisfaction curve—a sharp drop for people in their early twenties, especially among hard-pressed married couples, a climb to a peak in the middle years, a slight drop-off, and then a final sag when people reach their sixties—and these cycles seem to be interdependent, although good longitudinal data are as usual lacking.[15] More important, those persons and groups with the most tenuous ties to the economic order—from men squeezed out of the labor market (older workers, retirees, and the unemployed) to "unemployables" who seldom get in (skid row bums, adolescents of the slum) —are also the most isolated in community and society.[16]

[15] H. L. Wilensky, "Life Cycle, Work Situation, and Participation in Formal Associations," in Kleemeier, ed., *op. cit.*, pp. 213–242.

[16] On the effect of unemployment, see E. W. Bakke, *The Unemployed Man* (New York: E. P. Dutton and Company, 1935); E. W. Bakke, *Citizens Without Work* (New Haven, Conn.: Yale University Press, 1940); E. W. Bakke, *The Unemployed Worker* (New Haven, Conn.: Yale University Press, 1940); B. Zawadski and Paul Lazarsfeld, "The Psychological Consequences of Unemployment," *Journal of Social Psychology*, 6 (1935), pp. 224–251; P. Eisenberg and Paul Lazarsfeld, "The Psycho-

Variations in Job Satisfaction among Men with Jobs

How about the meaning and function of work among the great majority comprising the dominant America—the men whose information, opportunity, motivation, skill, and education enable them to find a solid place in a modern economy?

Money and the Cheerful Worker

At first glance, the surveys of job satisfaction seem to yield a picture of general contentment. For instance, the Roper poll in 1947 asked 3000 American factory workers, "On the whole would you say that your job is really interesting and enjoyable, or would you say that it is all right but not very interesting, or would you say that it is dull and boring?" More than two-thirds said "interesting"; another 23 percent, "all right"; only 7 percent were willing to label their jobs as "dull." In literally several hundred studies in which such general questions were asked (for example, "Taking into consideration all the things about your work, how satisfied or dissatisfied are you with it?"), the clearly "dissatisfied" response seldom exceeded 20 percent.[17]

Investigators are virtually unanimous on a second point: the lower

---

logical Effect of Unemployment," *Psychological Bulletin*, 35 (1938), pp. 358–390; M. Komarovsky, *The Unemployed Man and His Family* (New York: The Dryden Press, 1940). Cf. W. Kornhauser, *The Politics of Mass Society* (Glencoe, Ill.: The Free Press, 1959). On the position of youth, see S. N. Eisenstadt, *From Generation to Generation: Age Groups and the Social Structure* (Glencoe, Ill.: The Free Press, 1956). On the decline of participation with aging, see citations in H. L. Wilensky, "Life Cycle, Work Situation, and Participation in Formal Associations," *op. cit.* On the isolating impact of another form of economic deprivation or discontinuity, chaotic "careers," see H. L. Wilensky, "Orderly Careers and Social Participation: The Impact of Work History on Social Integration in the Middle Mass," *American Sociological Review*, 26 (August 1961), pp. 521–539. For evidence that economic deprivation is cumulative in effect, see H. Pope, "Economic Deprivation and Social Integration Among a Group of 'Middle Class' Factory Workers," unpublished Ph.D. thesis, University of Michigan, 1962, which shows that in our sample of "middle-class" factory workers who survived successive cutbacks in a parts-supplying firm, the more job dislocation experienced in the past, the less contact with formal associations and relatives in the present.

[17] These studies are reviewed in detail by F. Herzberg et al., *Job Attitudes: Review of Research and Opinion* (Pittsburgh: Psychological Service of Pittsburgh, 1957). Cf. R. Blauner, "Work Satisfaction and Industrial Trends in Modern Society," in W. Galenson and S. M. Lipset, eds., *Labor and Trade Unionism* (New York: John Wiley and Sons, 1960), pp. 339–360. Only brief illustrations from the evidence will be used here.

we go on the social scale, the less joy in work we find and the more often we encounter the starkly simple response, "What do I get out of work? The money!" For instance, Lyman, studying 250 employed men in several Illinois towns, found that blue-collar workers tend to rank economic rewards high; white-collar workers favor the work itself and such factors as autonomy on the job or a chance for self-expression.[18] This contrast held for both satisfied and dissatisfied workers.

Some of these studies show that earnings rank below several other factors when men tell what they like most about their work.[19] Initially, such findings appear to support the folklore of enlightened management, namely, the belief that income is not the most important incentive for work. When the focus is on reasons for dissatisfaction, however, wages lead the list.[20] As many writers have indicated, if workers receive the going rate in industry or community, they are likely to take money for granted and to rate other factors higher; when they receive less than their just deserts, they tend to rank money at the top.[21] It is the same with "security," a top-ranking source of satisfaction in these attitude studies. Surveys in several countries suggest that the working class more often than the middle class will choose certainty of income over more money with less stability.[22] Security is of more concern to workers than to professional and administrative people; in relative terms, the latter already have it.

Majorities in these samples at every social-economic level are generally satisfied; the proportion showing at least moderate satisfaction

[18] Elizabeth Lyman, "Occupational Differences in the Value Attached to Work," *American Journal of Sociology*, 61 (September 1955), pp. 138–144.
[19] Herzberg et al., *op. cit.*, p. 44.
[20] *Ibid.*, p. 48.
[21] Robert Dubin, *The World of Work* (Englewood Cliffs, N.J.: Prentice-Hall, 1958), pp. 240–241. See also the sensitive portrait of economic man in action, a study of machinists as canny calculators, preoccupied by economic rewards, by Donald Roy, "Quota Restriction and Goldbricking in a Machine Shop," *American Journal of Sociology*, 57 (March 1952), pp. 427–442. For a review of European studies see Georges Friedmann, *Industrial Society: The Emergence of the Human Problems of Automation* (Glencoe, Ill.: The Free Press, 1955). Cf. Arendt, *op. cit.* Karl Mannheim's remark that "the proletariat works mainly in order to earn a living, while the middle classes, once their primary wants have been supplied and their need for security satisfied, work mainly for the sake of increased power and prestige . . . the intelligentsia is . . . only happy when [they have] work which is in keeping with [their] special interests and qualifications" seems well supported. Karl Mannheim, *Man and Society in an Age of Reconstruction* (London: Routledge and Kegan Paul, 1940), p. 315.
[22] Alex Inkeles, "Industrial Man: The Relation of Status to Experience, Perception, and Value," *American Journal of Sociology*, 66 (July 1960), pp. 10–11.

increases with increased occupational status; and whatever the general feeling about work, the lower the status, the more prominent the economic meanings of work.

Such findings, of course, merely scratch the surface. First, the questions are unsophisticated. Assuming a cultural bias toward expressing contentment ("Be a booster, not a knocker"), the respondent may hide dissatisfaction or simply be unable to report it. There may also be class and group differences in norms of expression—the working class, the military, and college students griping about work, upper-strata feeling constrained to play up its creative side. Second, the data bear little relation to the preoccupations of social scientists, social philosophers, and *ideologues* through the ages: service to God or community, mastery over nature, fulfillment of self. Only the crudest commonsense notions of satisfaction guide such studies. Third, jobs for perhaps a majority are ephemeral and variable; job satisfactions are more so. The most significant meanings of work are anchored in *a social context* (the nature of the work role, workplace, and community, and the place of work in the daily round), *the identity of the person* (does the work affirm the self or deny it?), and *the life cycle* (his time perspective and stage in the family cycle and his career, if any). The study of job satisfactions apart from these social and psychological roots is superficial.

Indirect Questions, a Longer Time Perspective, and Less Cheer

Several students of modern work have tried to overcome such deficiencies. Indirect approaches have uncovered more discontent. For instance, recognizing that job satisfaction is linked to satisfaction with position attained (in relation to aspirations past and present), we can ask, "What type of work would you try to get into if you could start all over again?" "Why would you prefer this to the work you are doing now?" We can follow up with more specific questions about self-employment aspirations, past and present, actual attempts to go into a different line, and so forth.

Results of our investigation of these matters among ten occupational groups and strata are summarized in Table 1, with comparable evidence from other studies. The general level of "job satisfaction" turns out to be fairly low by such measures: only one in four men of the upper working class in the Detroit area would try to get into anything like their present work; well over half of the lower-middle class (clerks, salesmen, technicians, office supervisors, small proprietors, etc.) would try something else. The range of "satisfied" is from about nine in ten of the professors and mathematicians to 16 percent of the

Table 1 There Are Large Variations among Occupational Groups in the Proportion Who Would Try to Get into a Similar Type of Work If They Could Start Over Again

Professional and Lower White-Collar Occupations	Percent	Working-Class Occupations	Percent
Urban university professors *	93	Skilled printers	52
Mathematicians	91	Paper workers	52
Physicists	89	Skilled auto workers	41
Biologists	89	Skilled steelworkers	41
Chemists	86	Textile workers	31
Firm lawyers *	85	Blue-collar workers, age 30–55 *	24
School superintendents †	85		
Lawyers	83	Blue-collar workers, age 21–29 *	23
Journalists (Washington correspondents)	82	Unskilled steelworkers	21
Church university professors *	77	Unskilled auto workers	16
Solo lawyers *	75		
Diversico engineers *	70		
Unico engineers *	70		
White-collar workers, age 21–29 *	46		
White-collar workers, age 30–55 *	43		

* All probability samples or universes of six professional groups and a cross section of the "middle mass" (lower-middle class and upper-working class) in the Detroit area, stratified for comparability with respect to age, income, occupational stratum, and other characteristics. The size of each sample is given in Table 3. The lawyers, engineers, and professors had college degrees and were 30 to 55 years old when interviewed in the first half of 1960. The "don't knows," or missing data, affecting few cases, were assigned to the mean of the group. For details see H. L. Wilensky, "The Uneven Distribution of Leisure," *Social Problems,* 9, 1 (Summer 1961), pp. 32–56. No asterisk indicates data on manual workers from a Roper survey of 3000 factory workers in 16 industries or from studies of professionals that provide inadequate information on sample size and characteristics. These studies are listed in Blauner (*op. cit.,* p. 343), and contain no information on missing data.

† From a 48 percent sample of all school superintendents in Massachusetts, 1952–1953. Of these, 43 percent gave a "definite yes," 42 percent a "probably yes." Neal Gross et al., *Explorations in Role Analysis, Studies of the School Superintendency Role* (New York: John Wiley and Sons, 1958), p. 354.

unskilled auto workers.[23] A poll of Germans, using a similar question, produced similar results—about 40 percent of a cross section would "choose their present occupation" if they were fifteen years old and could start again. In this sense, three in four professionals, one in three lower white-collar workers, and one in ten unskilled manual workers were "satisfied." [24]

Other attempts to probe the deeper meanings of work remind us again of the primordial function of work at the same time that they suggest widespread indifference and discontent. Weiss and Kahn find that at every occupational level a large proportion—half to three-quarters—of those men who report that work does "nothing" for their sense of importance and usefulness say that they would nevertheless continue to work in the absence of economic need.[25] Morse and Weiss report similar findings on a national sample of 401 employed men.[26] A fantasy question about inheriting enough money to live comfortably without working yields 80 percent who would go on working anyway. Asked why, a third said "to keep occupied," another third gave "negative" reasons (would feel lost, bored, go crazy, get in

[23] Among the questions we used to tap feelings about work was: "We've been talking about the way you spend your time. Now, what would you do if you had more time than you actually have? If you had two more hours in the day—a 26-hour day—what would you most like to do with the extra time?" Two in three professors, one in four lawyers, one in five engineers, and only one in twenty of the middle mass mentioned work or work-related activity. A factor analysis suggests that these responses, together with the "do it over again" response, measure general job satisfaction as part of the respondent's view of his total lifetime. This concept and measure of job satisfaction is independent of concepts and measures of work alienation and attachment described later in this chapter; it is also independent of direct questions which yield the high levels of contentment described earlier.

[24] Inkeles, *op. cit.*, p. 6, compares these German answers with answers to direct questions about job satisfaction in other countries and concludes that the general level of job satisfaction varies among countries at roughly the same level of development. As our results suggest, however, the contrast between the large majorities "satisfied" in the United States and the 40 percent who would "choose their present occupation" in Germany is mainly a matter of different phrasing. Inkeles' point that there is a cross-cultural uniformity in the relative job satisfaction of broad occupational strata is nonetheless well supported. The major deviation is that skilled craftsmen fare slightly better and small entrepreneurs slightly worse on both prestige and satisfaction wherever official ideology celebrates manual labor and denigrates free enterprise, e.g., in Poland. A. Sarapata and W. Wesolowski, "The Evaluation of Occupations by Warsaw Inhabitants," *American Journal of Sociology*, 66 (May 1961), pp. 581–591.

[25] R. S. Weiss and R. L. Kahn, "On the Evaluation of Work among American Men," unpublished manuscript, 1959.

[26] N. E. Morse and R. S. Weiss, "The Function and Meaning of Work and the Job," *American Sociological Review*, 20 (April 1955), pp. 191–198.

trouble, etc.). Only 9 percent explained their answer in terms that could be coded, "I enjoy the kind of work." What the vast majority seem to be trying to say is that they want to remain among the living.[27]

Supplementing these more sophisticated surveys are close observational studies of men at work; they confirm that less-skilled factory work, especially on old-fashioned assembly lines, is wholly ungratifying, devoid of every value the doctrines of work have emphasized, whatever its function as a means of livelihood.[28] The incidence of this type of work situation is now small and may be declining. The new technology will free many men on the assembly line for something better; others, obsolete, will join the new poor.

Job Satisfaction and Life Satisfaction

Few studies focus directly on the place of the job in the total round of life. Few analyze job satisfaction in relation to satisfactions derived from other life areas. Two studies that provide data on manual workers are suggestive; both indicate levels of satisfaction similar to those in Table 1. Analyzing the "central life interests" of 491 relatively low-skilled workers in small Midwestern cities, Dubin[29] found that only one in four could be classified as mainly job-oriented—about the same proportion who, in samples of comparable categories, would choose the same work if they could start over again.[30]

---

[27] Data on the impact of unemployment, from Lazarsfeld's study of Marienthal, Austria, in the 1920s to Bakke's study of Greenwich, England, confirm the idea that severing the work tie constricts all contact with mankind, both for economic and for noneconomic reasons (see footnote 16). Freud, of course, saw work as the chief means of linking the individual to reality. The wide recognition of the integrative function of work has led to a myth about the older worker's dying faster upon retirement than his age-mates who go on working. A four-year panel study of 1260 older men, however, found that health (both self-reported and doctor-diagnosed) among those who retired was more likely to improve; physical decline (at least as self-judged) was more frequent among men of the same age who went on working. W. E. Thompson and G. F. Streib, "Situational Determinants: Health and Economic Deprivation in Retirement," *Journal of Social Issues*, 14, 2 (1958), pp. 20–21. Men die socially, not physically, when they are squeezed out of the labor market.

[28] C. R. Walker and R. H. Guest, *The Man on the Assembly Line* (Cambridge, Mass.: Harvard University Press, 1952); F. H. Blum, *Toward a Democratic Work Process* (New York: Harper and Brothers, 1953); Eli Chinoy, *Automobile Workers and the American Dream* (Garden City, N.Y.: Doubleday, 1955).

[29] R. Dubin, "Industrial Workers' Worlds: A Study of the 'Central Life Interests' of Industrial Workers," *Social Problems*, 3, 3 (January 1956), pp. 131–142.

[30] The measure may be weak. Dubin, *ibid.*, p. 134, defines "central life interest" as "the expressed preference for a given locale or situation in carrying out an activity."

The second study, a careful assessment by Arthur Kornhauser of the mental health of factory workers in thirteen large and medium-sized automotive manufacturing plants, shows variations by skill level strikingly similar to those in Table 1.[31] About half of the most skilled (men like the printers and paper workers) scored "good" mental health compared to only about a third of the "ordinary semiskilled" and one in eight or ten of the "repetitive, machine-paced, semiskilled" workers. The measure of mental health, validated by six experienced psychotherapists, as well as by reports from the workers' wives, is based on questionnaire responses indicating absence of anxiety and emotional tension; trust in and acceptance of versus hostility toward people; sociability and friendship versus withdrawal; self-esteem versus negative self-feelings; personal morale versus *anomie* or social alienation; overall satisfaction with life. Mental health was best among those high in education and occupation, poorest among those low in both. The popular view that educated men in low-level jobs have the poorest adjustment receives no support. Most important, the relationship between skill level and mental health remains strong at each of three educational levels and among men of greatly varied personality and prejob background.[32] If we assume that job satisfaction and life satisfaction are inseparable, this study suggests that the portrait of the cheerful worker derived from more direct approaches to job satisfaction is grossly overdrawn.

In 40 questions workers were given such alternatives as these: "I would most hate (1) missing a day's work; (2) missing a meeting of an organization I belong to; (3) missing almost anything I usually do." "I would rather take my vacation with (1) my family; (2) some friends from work; (3) by [sic] myself." "I prefer to join a club or a lodge (1) where there are people from my neighborhood who are members; (2) where there are people from work who are members; (3) where the members come from all over." Workers who chose the workplace or fellow workers for an activity in at least half the questions covering each of four "sectors of experience" (technical, formal, informal, general) were classified as job-oriented. Dubin's assumption that each question represents an activity that is as likely to occur "in connection with some aspect of the job or workplace" as "at some definite point in the community outside of work" (p. 134) seems dubious. Furthermore, it is possible that a friendship in the neighborhood or a social club was originally formed in the workplace, and many "community" answers should have been coded "job-oriented." However, the Labor-Leisure Project, which relates feelings about work to actual patterns of social life, supports Dubin's polemic: though work accounts for slightly more hours than the mass media and mass entertainment, and though the workplace activates friendships for large numbers, the core of life for most men in the middle mass is not the job. (See footnotes 9, 15, and 16.)

[31] Arthur Kornhauser, "Toward an Assessment of the Mental Health of Factory Workers," *Human Organization*, 21, 1 (Spring 1962), pp. 43-46.
[32] *Ibid.*, pp. 45-46.

The Problem of Work Alienation

A final limitation of existing studies of job satisfaction is that they seldom tap useful traditions of social thought; our data on the meaning of work tend to be irrelevant to the classic debates about labor and leisure. This is not merely a matter of the inevitable distance between the philosopher and the ordinary citizen, the social scientist, and the workers interviewed. The great difficulty is measuring abstract ideas in field studies and the consequent bias of students of work against trying.

The big ideas in this area are found in discussions of work alienation, principally deriving from Karl Marx and such neo-Freudians as Erich Fromm, but also developed independently by sociologists and social psychologists. The departure point for Karl Marx's treatment of alienation was Hegel's treatment of the problem of freedom, a condition in which man was self-willed, possessed of his own "essence." The main attribute of human nature that threatens freedom, according to Hegel, is alienation—the radical dissociation of self into both actor and thing, into a *subject*, an "I" that strives to control its own fate, and an *object*, a "me" that is manipulated by others.[33] Marx, giving alienation social content, located it in modern labor, where man loses control of process and product and, under the property system of capitalism, becomes a commodity, an object used by others. "Labor," said Marx, ". . . is external to the worker, i.e., it does not belong to his essential being; . . . in his work, therefore, he does not affirm himself but denies himself. . . . His labor is . . . merely a *means* to satisfy needs external to it"; it ". . . is not his spontaneous activity. It belongs to another; it is the loss of self." [34] Alienation, as Bell points out,[35] was initially conceived by Marx as a process whereby an individual lost his capacity to express himself in work.[36]

It is this idea of loss of identity that has formed the basis for a humanistic interpretation of Marx best exemplified in the work of Fromm and Arendt.[37] Writing of the "marketing orientation" Fromm says,

---

[33] Daniel Bell, *The End of Ideology* (Glencoe, Ill.: The Free Press, 1960), p. 338.
[34] Karl Marx, "Estranged Labour," *Economic and Philosophic Manuscripts of 1844*, in C. W. Mills, ed., *Images of Man* (New York: George Braziller, 1960), p. 500.
[35] Bell, *op. cit.*
[36] Weber, too, although he was often doing battle with the ghost of Marx, saw modern work as a threat to individuality; the bureaucratic accent on formal rule and rational calculation, while it might be fair and efficient, would strip work of what personal involvement and enchantment it had.
[37] Erich Fromm, *Man for Himself* (New York: Rinehart, 1947); Erich Fromm, *The Sane Society* (New York: Rinehart, 1955); Arendt, *op. cit.*

The principle of evaluation is the same on both the personality and the commodity market: on the one, personalities are offered for sale; on the other, commodities. Value in both cases is their exchange value. . . . We find that only in exceptional cases is success predominantly the result of skill and of certain other human qualities like honesty, decency, and integrity. . . . Success depends largely on how well a person sells himself on the market, how well he gets his personality across, how nice a "package" he is; whether he is "cheerful," "sound," "aggressive," "reliable," "ambitious." . . . Since modern man experiences himself both as the seller and as the commodity to be sold on the market, his self-esteem depends on conditions beyond his control. If he is "succesful," he is valuable; if he is not, he is worthless.[38]

Nisbet suggests that the vocabulary of alienation—mass man, unattached, marginal, obsessive, isolated, frustrated, anxious, insecure; communities fragmented, normless, lacking in stable organization or firm moral values—has become a dominant form of discourse in the social sciences and literature. "The disenchanted, lonely figure . . . incessantly striving to answer the question, 'Who am I, What am I,' has become, especially in Europe, almost the central literary type of the age." [39] The quest for community lost or community to be gained is the other side of the alienation coin. The alienated man of contemporary literature and political philosophy seeks to overcome his estrangement by searching for ethical significance in the smallest of things, compulsively striving for certainty, immersing himself in fanatical faiths of nation, class, race, or church—not to conquer but to be conquered, not to win freedom but to escape from it. Such ideas about alienation and community integration have guided much recent social research on deviance (crime, suicide, mental disorder) and social disorganization (political extremism, susceptibility to demagogues).[40]

---

[38] Fromm, *Man for Himself, op. cit.*, pp. 69–70, 72. Cf. C. W. Mills, *White Collar* (New York: Oxford University Press, 1951), pp. 182, 188.

[39] R. A. Nisbet, *The Quest for Community* (New York: Oxford University Press, 1953), p. 12.

[40] Some major referents of the concept of alienation, as specified by M. Seeman, "On the Meaning of Alienation," *American Sociological Review*, 24 (December 1959), pp. 783–791, are (1) *powerlessness*—the expectation that one's own behavior cannot determine the outcomes one seeks in the social order (in politics, work, or world affairs, for instance); (2) *meaninglessness*—the expectation that satisfactory predictions of the outcomes of one's behavior are impossible because one does not know what to believe; (3) *normlessness*—the expectation that socially disapproved behavior is required to achieve one's goals; (4) *isolation*—the low rating of goals or beliefs highly valued in society (a sense of estrangement from the culture); and (5) *self-estrangement*—which Seeman defines as "the degree of dependence of the given behavior upon anticipated future rewards," i.e., the failure to engage oneself in activities which seem worthwhile in themselves (to work only for the

The critics of modern society who have developed the vocabulary of alienation differ in their definitions of the phenomenon and their explanations of its roots, but most of them invoke some aspect of the social and technical organization of work—its discipline, mechanization, specialization, hierarchy, or social relations—and see it as a threat to personal identity. The term "alienation," burdened with ideological freight, has evaded clear definition and integration into sociological perspectives. My aim in this section is to reformulate these classic views by bringing alienation within the framework of role-self analysis as it has developed since Cooley and Mead [41] in the writing of Sullivan, Gerth and Mills, and Goffman,[42] and then to show how a social survey so guided can locate the sources of alienation in modern work.

A Sociological Concept and Measure of Work Alienation

The problem is to link specific attributes of social structure in the workplace to the private experience—the troubles, the joys—of the person. Let us define social alienation as the feeling that routine enactment of role obligations and rights is incongruent with prized self-image, for example, the kind of fellow I am at my best is not the kind of fellow I am obliged to be as assembler in work crew, father in family, member in church, union, or voluntary association.

To measure social alienation we must first measure prized self-image, the central attributes of self-concept to which strong positive feelings are attached. Then we must relate attributes of some specific role (recurrent behavior which expresses the rights and duties of a social position) to these central attributes of self. We may speak of the man whose work role poorly fits his prized self-image as work-alienated.

To tap prized self-image in relation to work role in a survey interview is difficult but not impossible. The labor-leisure study tried the following measure. In the context of the respondent's description of recent contacts with relatives, friends, neighbors, and right after dis-

---

money, to cook only to eat, to play "customers' golf," etc.). This last idea, alienation of self from role, is most relevant for the present discussion; in a more precise sociological form it was the basis for a measure of work alienation in our interviews in 1958–1959, reported later.

[41] C. H. Cooley, *Human Nature and the Social Order* (New York: Charles Scribner's Sons, 1902); G. H. Mead, *Mind, Self and Society from the Standpoint of a Social Behaviorist* (Chicago: University of Chicago Press, 1934).

[42] H. S. Sullivan, *Conceptions of Modern Psychiatry* (New York: Norton, 1940); H. Gerth and C. W. Mills, *Character and Social Structure* (New York: Harcourt, Brace and Company, 1953); E. Goffman, *The Presentation of Self in Everyday Life*, Monograph 2 (Edinburgh: Social Science Research Centre, University of Edinburgh, 1956).

cussion of his three best friends—that is, after evoking an image of those most likely to affirm his better self—we asked, "Almost everyone has a pretty good idea of the way he is seen by the people he likes and feels comfortable with. How about you—for example, are you known as a good mixer, a person who likes to get together with other people?" (Yes, No, Don't Know.) If yes: "Would it make much difference to you if you weren't known as a good mixer?" This general format was used for five attributes of self-image which we thought could be most clearly validated or violated by the work role: sociable, intelligent, conscientious (competent, efficient), independent-autonomous, and ambitious.[43] Later in the interview, in the context of questions about work (and in an effort to avoid "halo" effect) we covered six features of the work situation that could be related to these attributes of self-image. For instance: "About how often during an average day do you talk to the people you work with about the things *not* required by your job—you know, just shooting the breeze? Would it be every few minutes, once or twice an hour, four or five times a day, or less often than that?" If at least four to five times a day: "Would it make much difference to you if you didn't have a good chance to talk that way?" If less often: "Does it bother you a lot that you don't have much of a chance to talk and joke around?" The following match was made in constructing an index of work alienation-indifference-attachment.

Attribute of Prized Self-Image (both perceived and valued)	*Attribute of Work Situation* (both perceived and valued)
Sociable	Can talk sociably on the job (shoot the breeze) at least four or five times a day
Intelligent	Plenty of chance to use own judgment
Conscientious (competent, efficient) —person who believes that if a thing is worth doing, it is worth doing right	Chance to do work well—do a good, careful job Chance to do the things you're best at—use the kinds of skills that you have
Independent—a man who won't hesitate to go it alone when he thinks he should	(For those with a boss) Boss not always breathing down your neck —not watched too closely
Ambitious—person who tries hard to get ahead	Good chance for promotion where you work

[43] These were selected from a longer list of eleven we used in 147 long interviews with a group of "middle-class" factory workers in 1958–1959. For sample characteristics see H. L. Wilensky, "Work, Careers, and Social Integration," *International Social Science Journal*, 12, 4 (1960), pp. 543–560.

If a man's friends think of him as a "good mixer" and it would make a difference to him if they did not, and if, further, his job affords a good chance for sociability and it would make a difference to him if it did not, the fit is good and he receives a point for "attached." On the other hand, if sociability is part of his prized self-image, the job blocks it, and that bothers him, he receives a point for "alienated." Any other combination scores "indifferent." (A man who is indifferent may complain about one or another condition of work, but such gripes are unrelated to major attributes of his better self.) Or take intelligence: the alienated man is saying, in effect, (1) "I am reasonably intelligent and it's important to me that I be seen that way"; (2) "Going through these motions on the job is a dumb show and any strong moron could do it"; (3) "What is a guy like me doing here?"

The Incidence and Sources of Work Alienation, Indifference, and Attachment

Feelings about work are anchored not only in job-relevant aspects of personal identity but in the social and technical organization of work. In what work situations should we expect to find a high incidence of work alienation or attachment? What are the structural roots of such feelings? Variations in job satisfaction by broad occupational strata are a clue, but we must characterize the work environment more precisely than such classifications permit. (Even one of the more homogeneous categories in the United States Census occupational classification, "professional, technical, and kindred," covers authors and draftsmen, striptease artists and mechanical engineers.)

By our stringent measures, relating work role to prized self-image, the incidence of alienation is low: only 177 of our 1156 employed men score "alienated" on even one of the six possible attributes of the work situation; only 51 are alienated on two or more attributes, eleven on three or more.[44] The data also support the guiding hypothesis: work role, occupational group, and organizational context (and associated variations in job freedom and status and the stability and predictability of job patterns) are more powerful sources of alienation and attachment than is social class.

[44] It should be remembered that the scoring system yields three indices. A man may be attached to one aspect of the work role, alienated from another, indifferent to a third. The column headings in Tables 2 and 3 indicate only the portion who were "alienated" on one or more dimensions (no one scored "alienated" on five or six dimensions), "attached" on four to six, two or three, or (a low score) one or none. Indifference is reported only for those scored neither "alienated" nor "attached" on *all* dimensions.

High economic, occupational, and educational status together form a leading predictor of strong attachment and the absence of alienation. Table 2 shows that 13 percent of the highest of four strata are at all alienated to some extent, compared to 26 percent of the bottom stratum; 26 percent of the top are strongly attached to their work, compared to 6 percent of the bottom. Note, however, that this good measure of social class makes little difference among the top three strata; only the 35 less-skilled blue-collar workers with the very lowest income and education stand out. And if, in contrast to previous studies, we hold class constant and pinpoint variations in work milieu, career, and organizational context, we see that both extremes—the strongly alienated (Unico engineers) and the strongly attached (firm lawyers) —appear in higher strata (Table 3).

The best independent predictors of work alienation are (1) a work situation and organizational setting that provide little discretion in pace and schedule, and a tall hierarchy above (low freedom, high pressure), (2) a career which has been blocked and chaotic, and (3) a stage in the life cycle that puts the squeeze on (the measure combines "large numbers of children living at home" with "low amount of savings and investments"). Strong work attachment has similar but not identical roots; it is most frequent among men of medium to high status, 30 to 39 years old, whose careers have been orderly and whose present jobs provide much opportunity for both sociable talk and getting ahead of the work load. (The causes of alienation need not be the causes of low attachment. For instance, blocked mobility, life-cycle squeeze, and a large number of superior levels of authority foster alienation, but their absence does not assure strong attachment. Furthermore, restricted sociability on the job is apparently not a source of alienation, but plentiful sociability is a source of attachment.)

Most important, the difference between occupational groups within the same occupational stratum is greater than the difference between groups two strata apart. For instance, Table 3 shows that 30 percent of Unico engineers but only 6 percent of urban university professors are at all alienated; the figures are 19 percent for Diversico engineers and 18 percent for upper blue-collar workers matched for age. The heavy incidence of both strong alienation and weak attachment is among engineers and blue-collar workers.

The special disaffection at Unico confirms the general picture in that this company was sampled for the type of organizational context it provided for engineering work: an enterprise dependent on one product, increasingly subject to competition, with a record of erratic sales

Table 2 *Percent of Men in Various Social Strata, Work Milieux, Organizational Contexts, and Careers Who Are Work-Alienated, Attached, and Indifferent* *

Rank as Predictor of Strong Alienation†	Rank as Predictor of Weak Attachment	Variable and Measure	N	Work Alienation			Work Attachment			Work Indifference	
				Some (1-4)	None (0)	H (4-6)	M (2,3)	L (0,1)	Indifferent on All Items	Not Indifferent on All Items
		SOCIAL AND ECONOMIC STATUS									
1	2	Low SES	35	26%	74%	6%	29%	66%	46%	54%
		Low-Medium	473	16	84	19	38	44	28	72
		High-Medium	331	16	84	27	42	31	18	82
		High SES	317	13	87	26	47	28	13	87
		LOW FREEDOM, MUCH DISCIPLINE									
2	8	*Number of Levels of Authority above the Respondent*									
		None	286	7	93	22	47	31	19	81
		One or two	163	15	85	25	40	35	21	79
		Three	707	19	81	22	39	39	23	77
3	6	*Control of Work Pace*									
		Cannot get ahead of work load	229	25	75	18	39	42	21	79
		Can get ahead of work load	927	12	87	24	41	35	22	78
9	17	*Control over Work Schedule*									
		Fixed schedule	657	19	81	20	40	40	24	76
		Has some control	499	11	89	26	42	32	18	82
20	3	*Frequency of Sociable Talk on the Job*									
		Every few minutes or once or twice an hour	243	16	84	25	37	38	23	77
		Four or five times a day	550	12	87	25	44	30	17	83
		Less often	363	18	82	16	40	44	28	72

144

Table 2 (Continued)

Rank as Predictor of Strong Alienation[†]	Rank as Predictor of Weak Attachment	Variable and Measure	N	Work Alienation			Work Attachment			Work Indifference	
				Some (1–4)	None (0)	H (4–6)	M (2,3)	L (0,1)	Indifferent on All Items	Not Indifferent on All Items
		ORDERLINESS OF JOB PATTERN									
		Blocked Mobility									
7	23	R has not experienced blocked mobility	1039	14	86	22	42	36	21	79
		R has experienced blocked mobility	117	24	76	23	36	41	22	78
		Chaotic Work History									
6	5	Least orderly	227	20	80	14	33	52	32	68
		Partial orderly	244	17	83	24	37	40	25	75
		Most orderly	685	13	87	25	46	30	17	83
		CONSUMPTION PRESSURE AND STAGE IN THE FAMILY LIFE CYCLE									
		Life-Cycle Squeeze									
15	19	Low	111	10	90	19	40	41	23	77
		Low-medium	622	14	86	25	41	34	21	79
		High-medium	374	19	81	19	43	38	21	79
		High	49	20	80	24	35	41	27	73

* Combined samples of labor-leisure study (see footnote to Table 1).
† Rank based on a "multiple classification analysis" of 23 variables thought to be sources of or effects of work orientation. Only the relative importance of the leading sources is mentioned here. The computer program and its assumptions are described in J. N. Morgan et al., *Income and Welfare in the United States* (New York: McGraw-Hill, 1962), pp. 508 ff.

Table 3 *Work Orientation Is Shaped by Occupational Group and Organizational Context More Than by Occupational Stratum* *

Occupational Group	N	Work Alienation			Work Attachment			Work Indifference	
		Some (1-4)	None (0)	H (4-6)	M (2,3)	L (0,1)	Indifferent on All Items	Not Indifferent on All Items
Upper-Middle-Class Professionals Age 30-55									
Solo lawyers	100	10%	90%	20%	51%	29%	16%	84%
Firm lawyers	107	8	92	34	49	18	8	92
Church university professors	31	10	90	32	45	23	16	84
Urban university professors	68	6	94	22	46	32	9	91
Diversico engineers	93	19	81	28	45	27	14	86
Unico engineers	91	30	70	22	45	33	15	85
Middle Mass									
Lower white-collar, age 21-29	69	13	87	20	45	35	22	78
Lower white-collar, age 30-55	252	13	87	25	35	40	25	75
Upper blue-collar, age 21-29	53	23	77	15	46	39	22	78
Upper blue-collar, age 30-55	293	18	82	16	35	49	36	64

* See footnote to Table 1 for samples.

and a reputation for being local, a dead end for engineers who might want to move to central headquarters. Its employees are heard to complain that both the factory and its product are outmoded (although this is far from a marginal firm).[45]

Implications

Obviously, work alienation may be more widespread than this strict measure indicates. Many aspects of male identity (such as masculinity) were not tapped, although it is possible that work situations can confirm or deny them. Direct questions, as we have seen, discourage admission of discontent. The questions used may have provoked anxiety; for instance, many interviewers felt that the "self" battery went less smoothly than the rest of the interview, although no unusual number of respondents took the escape route of "don't know." Insofar as the wide separation of "self" and "work" questions failed to overcome halo effect, there may be an additional bias against expression of discontent on matters of importance; a man may feel he is admitting that he is spineless or a failure if he pictures himself as staying in a job that violates his most positive self.

Despite its limits, this index of alienation has the great merit of relevance to the classic discussions of work alienation in the social sciences. It is a useful device for linking social structure to the social self. I am inclined to take the amount of alienation uncovered as the minimum that exists, to attach weight to the differences among groups variously situated as to work and career, and to say that the results reflect a generally effective system of placement—such that most people either adjust their identity to the demands of the role (they acquire the proper "occupational personality") or shift out of those roles that tend to punish them.

On the assumption that the "attachment" category is exaggerated by the directness of the measure, the principal finding, consistent with the evidence just reviewed, is that the vast majority of the middle mass and almost a majority of the engineers—swiftly growing categories of the labor force—are generally indifferent to work in the precise sense that their jobs neither confirm their prized self-image nor deny it for most

---

[45] Tables not here reported control for social and economic status (SES) and relate work alienation to an index of freedom comprised of control over schedule, number of levels of authority above the respondent, control over speed of work and frequency of sociable talk. The main findings: (1) men in the highest social-economic stratum have by far the most freedom on the job, but (2) at every level, restricted freedom fosters work alienation.

of the attributes analyzed. In the middle mass, more than one in five of the young white-collar men and one in three of the older blue-collar men score indifferent on *all* attributes (see Table 2). Populations excluded from these samples—the lower half of the working class, the very young, men over 55, and women of any age—have less opportunity to become attached to work; their indifference would surely be more widespread. On balance, the vast majority of Americans are "playing it cool," neither strongly wedded to the job nor feeling it to be an intense threat to their identity.

Our review of data on the roots of discontent points to important gaps in the evidence and to probable trends in the meaning and function of work. Three promising areas for research I will mention are (1) national variations in job discontent by level and rate of economic growth; (2) those occupational and industrial variations that have most relevance for the emerging economy (such as the feelings of those in defense industries that symbolize the lavish manufacture of unused products, and jobs in the tertiary sectors that often involve client or customer contact); and (3) the impact of automation on job satisfaction. I will then speculate about work as a social problem in the short-run future of the 1970s.

Economic Growth and Job Discontent

The level and distribution of job discontent in a society will, of course, be affected by its level and rate of economic development. Is the misery that drives peasant populations out of run-down rural areas in developing countries replaced by the misery of rising consumer expectations pressing against meager job rewards? Or does a low-freedom, high-discipline job providing no chance to move up seem pleasant to the new industrial worker in Mexico or India, when he compares it with opportunities in the village from which he escaped? Even if contentment is dominant at the beginning, later, when the underdeveloped country develops and the majority are on the move in an environment of expanding opportunity, the same semiskilled operative, now more literate, more eager for a freer life, may become alienated.

What about the effect of continued growth in the rich countries? The evidence is mixed: we have seen that overeducated assembly-line workers are less alienated than their fellow worker; but the alienation we find among engineers may be symbolic of a growing population of college graduates in high-paying jobs whose demands for "more, more, more"—more freedom, more authority, more status—exceed anything Samuel Gompers dreamed of, as well as anything the emerging economy can provide. In all this, we need data going beyond those in Table 1—comparative studies of work discontent by stage of life cycle and career, by work milieu, occupational group and organizational context, in various countries and communities.

Variations in job discontent by occupational group and industry suggest this hypothesis: the highest levels of alienation occur where work routines provide the most pressure and the least freedom—for example, on the assembly line. In the service occupations, especially at the more professionalized levels, workers display more work attachment. But my previous discussion of the limits of typical survey questions about job satisfaction suggests caution. The salesman who sells vacuum cleaners must first convince himself; the general emphasis of service establishments on public relations and positive thinking may permeate not only work but the survey interview. Even casual observation indicates that most customer- or client-contact jobs—in sales, business repair services, public administration, entertainment, recreation, and the professions—require considerable repression of hostility and control of aggression. As the functionary tries to keep his distance from the object of commercial appreciation, the chance for dissociation of self from role is clear. The frozen smile of the receptionist may impartially mask both alienation and indifference; the affectation of involvement among conferees noted for their teamwork may hide boredom. If such work roles become central to the identity of the person —commanding in both leisure and work—generalized self-hatred can develop. For instance, jobs in business, politics, and the mass media sometimes require a hard-boiled, manipulative outlook—a view that the world divides itself into two kinds of people, those who can be led by the nose and those who can be bought. Such job-fostered cynicism, the contempt for audience or customers, can spill over into job-determined leisure, and in time become contempt for self. Typical surveys do not tap this psychological underworld; of happiness and despair we need more subtle measures.

If job cynicism is common in the commercial markets of the free West, think of the situation in the political markets of modern totalitarian nations. Where education is party-controlled and state schools are the main road to success, the necessity of ideological conformity may produce the same dissociation of self from work. We will never know how many professionals and technicians, civil servants and party leaders in the Soviet Union become alienated in the course of their training and career. To endure dull Marxist propaganda and to play it back on exams requires not merely endurance but subterfuge, and among sophisticated men may foster contempt for official socialist morality. There are enough of these ideological endurance contests in American education and job training to give us all a sympathy for people who experience them fully organized.

Affluence, Useless Work, and Job Discontent

An undercurrent of cynicism and boredom may be matched by feelings of uselessness peculiar to the affluent society. The theme that much modern work is frivolous and destructive is an old one. Since the 1830s, English writers such as Pugin, Ruskin, and Morris have lashed out at industrialism not only for production processes that alienated men from their work but also for industrial products that were useless by their standards of right and valuable function.[46] The indictment is more persuasive today than a century ago. As societies get richer, they become more careless about the uses of abundance; only the affluent society can afford to waste its human resources on such a grand scale. In modern economies there are three main expressions of manpower waste: (1) featherbedding; (2) hoarding of labor (most prominent in market economies with heavy military budgets but apparent elsewhere too) and "planners' tension," or the demand for overfulfillment of production plans (most prominent in command economies); and (3) the proliferation of antisocial specialties, notably in entertainment and promotion, some of them quasi-legal or illegal. Each involves activities that some men experience as demeaning.

Least important and most discussed is the waste of featherbedding —work that is done, paid for, but goes unused, as with the printer who resets advertisement copy already printed outside the shop and promptly melts it down ("dead horse") or with unnecessary workers who simply stand by while machines designed to replace them do the work (for example, the "featherbird pilot," a fourth man squeezed into a three-man cockpit during a dispute between flight engineers and airline pilots over who should occupy the third seat). Featherbedding is most discussed for obvious reasons: unions are usually involved, and antilabor spokesmen find the slogan convenient in campaigns for restrictive labor laws. It is least important because a management determined to eliminate it usually does, and its cost where management tolerates it is usually not high. First, recall some cases involving heavy labor costs: the occupational death of the firemen on diesel-electric locomotives took only a decade after the diesel was widely adopted in the early 1950s. The airlines dispute was settled only four years after

---

[46] Raymond Williams, *Culture and Society, 1780–1950* (Garden City, N.Y.: Anchor Books, Doubleday, 1960), pp. 145 ff.

the "featherbird" was put aboard, and now three men man the cockpit.[47] Standby musicians as a strategy for coping with recorded music in broadcasting, where the practice was most burdensome, lasted only six years. Considering that these cases were matters of life and death for the workers and unions involved, the life cycle of featherbedding seems short indeed. Of course, occupational death can be achieved more speedily if Draconian measures are used—kulaks can be liquidated, machine tractor stations abandoned, urban co-ops wiped out, with no full-page advertisements in *Pravda*, no parades in Red Square, no arbitration hearings, no strikes. So long as freedom of association and its attendant conflicts persist, however, featherbedding will continue to be a short-range response of workers threatened by technological unemployment.

Second, consider the cases in which such practices persist. When we look carefully at work rules labeled "featherbedding," they often turn out to make sense (an oversize paint brush may look efficient, but it tires the arm and slows up the job); or if the rules represent employer inefficiency or union restrictions designed to increase employment, either their cost is slight or they soon give way to new methods. For instance, the most systematic study of labor relations and productivity in the building trades concludes: "While there are one or two trades, such as bricklaying and tile setting, where techniques have remained substantially unchanged over the past thirty or forty years, and one or two more where new techniques have not been of great importance, the overall increases in productivity from the use of power equipment, new materials, and prefabrication have been of major importance in excavation, cement work, carpentry, the mechanical trades, and most of the finishing trades," bringing a long-run upward trend in productivity.[48] One reason is union concern over competing labor and materials. For instance, the painters' union, worried about do-it-

---

[47] That feelings ran high in this dispute is suggested by the engineers' reported threats to release photographs of pilots at work with stewardesses on their laps. Paul Jacobs notes that the fight over the third man resulted in "at least six strikes, an unsuccessful attempt by the pilots' union to prevent Federal Aviation Agency inspectors from riding in the cockpit, the appointment of 40 neutrals to presidential commissions and emergency boards that have been unable to resolve the problem, five commercial airlines flying with four men crammed into a cockpit designed for three, fist fights between crew members, and hundreds of grievances filed against each other. . . ." *Dead Horse and the Featherbird* (Santa Barbara, Calif.: Center for the Study of Democratic Institutions, 1962), p. 41. In the end engineers were given a choice of pilot training or severance pay.

[48] William Haber and Harold M. Levinson, *Labor Relations and Productivity in the Building Trades* (Ann Arbor: Bureau of Industrial Relations, University of Michigan, 1956), pp. 202–203.

yourself homeowners as well as the rapid rise in the use of materials requiring no painting, has recommended greater acceptance of the spray gun. This study estimates that in building construction, the standout case of archaic methods, the complete elimination of *all* union work rules would mean a reduction of on-site labor costs of only about 5 percent.[49] If more substantial gains are possible, management typically goes after them aggressively—as in West Coast longshoring where a mechanization and modernization agreement gave employers a completely free hand in return for job security for regular dock workers.

Finally, it should be noted that featherbedding is far from popular; most men despise such nonwork. With rapid technological change, it is likely to become a smaller fraction of all work.

More important than "dead horse" and the "featherbird," and a more accurate guide to future sources of discontent, is the "malallocation" of high-level manpower—a euphemism for managerial and professional featherbedding. In the United States the defense and space programs are the main seat of high-level featherbedding, and scientists and engineers are the typical groups, but the phenomenon spreads beyond these industries and occupations, beyond our private-enterprise economy. Some waste motion, some squandering of talent is inevitable in all military research and development. As Arthur M. Ross notes, military technology changes so fast that it may be entirely rational never to produce an item after spending billions to develop it. "Moreover, this is a situation where the customer does not know in advance exactly what he wants; the supplier does not know in advance what he can really deliver; the serviceability of the product will not be entirely clear until it has been developed and tested."[50] But such ambiguities cannot explain the extraordinary concentration of manpower in these programs. The federal government pays for two-thirds of all research and development in the United States; most of it goes to defense and space. It was widely predicted that our space program alone, if pursued on the scale projected in the early 1960s, would absorb all the new graduates in mechanical, electrical, and aeronautical engineering, physics, and mathematics that our universities could possibly produce during the decade.

---

[49] *Ibid.*, p. 250.
[50] Arthur M. Ross, "How Do We Use Our Engineers and Scientists?" in *Toward Better Utilization of Scientific and Engineering Talent: A Program for Action*, Report of the Committee on Utilization of Scientific and Engineering Manpower (Washington, D.C.: Printing and Publishing Office, National Academy of Sciences, 1964), p. 87.

This reflects not merely a chronic shortage of intellectual manpower, common to all rich countries, not only our astonishing indifference to development of the civilian sector, public and private alike, but also a system of program planning, contractor selection, and contract negotiation and administration that assures an allocation of talent to the featherbed. Ross [51] summarizes the argument: (1) it is unlikely that the increment of military advantage justifies the large number of costly weapons systems that we develop but never produce; (2) contract awards emphasize technical and design superiority, so each contractor lacks pressure to minimize costs; (3) we maintain duplicate capabilities in specialized fields—a wasteful competition for contracts among large numbers of companies, each with its own staff of scarce scientists and engineers; (4) in this scramble, perhaps 5 to 10 percent of all research and development personnel in defense industries are assigned to preparing and selling proposals; and (5) manpower is "loaded" or "hoarded" so that each company is in a position to accept new contracts, which naturally leads to (6) the assignment of scientists and engineers to subprofessional and administrative duties.[52] The net result is persistent complaints by professionals that they cannot use their skills and judgment—a theme uncovered in our interviews with engineers (see Table 3) and repeated in similar surveys of job satisfaction.

America may have developed the fine art of managerial and professional featherbedding further than other countries of the free world. If so, the explanation lies in our bloated defense budget and in the heavy concentration of intellectual manpower in large firms in a few manufacturing industries serving space and military needs. In contrast, virtually all research and development personnel in western Europe and Japan work in the civilian area, where manpower waste is less prodigious. This is doubtless no small factor in the success of Germany and Japan in world markets. To the vanquished go the consumer markets; to the victor, the military featherbed.

In some ways the command economies of modern totalitarian nations are close to the United States in their waste of intellectual manpower, but the structural causes are different. Where the enterprise aim is not profit (or better, the avoidance of loss) but the fulfillment of a plan (or better, the hitting of high-priority physical output targets), "planners' tension" will pervade the work routines of middle and

---

[51] *Ibid.*, pp. 87–88.
[52] Manpower waste is characteristic of military operations. A measure of our tolerance for it is the storm of criticism evoked by Secretary of Defense McNamara in the early 1960s when he made efforts to change the system here described.

top echelons. By "planners' tension," following Wiles,[53] I mean the pressure of the planners' impossible demands—an excess of administratively ordered output over capacity output—typical of Soviet-type economies. Soviet manpower waste takes the form of an immense apparatus for communicating and enforcing orders, a complicated system of unofficial expediters and fixers who try to circumvent the orders so that goals may be met (creating a demand for more planners to keep track of what is going on), and considerable antiplan crime, including black marketing and black production. In a brilliant dissection of the command economy Wiles describes pro-plan fixers in action: "As the output targets are always the most important part of the plan, and the director's bonus depends mainly on his fulfillment of them, he is always violating the rest of the plan for their sake. Black markets, or rather black bilateral transactions, occur in raw materials and labor, and firms secretly barter services among each other (you repair my furnace, I'll lend you some aluminium until next quarter)." Since all expenditures are tightly controlled, "these activities mean squaring the accountant and probably also the auditors, and in reply the authorities constantly reshuffle directors and accountants before they get to know each other." Directors also violate wage regulations to obtain scarce help, and they hire permanent agents, *tolkachi*, who are supposed to know whom to talk to, which forms to use, etc., to reduce the plan targets and expedite or increase supplies. The party official attached to the local plant to keep the director in line knows that all this scrambling about is aimed at fulfilling the plan, so he joins in it: "the Vanguard of the Proletariat . . . goes grubbing . . . for belting and sulphuric acid on the director's behalf." [54] Some planned violations are not so "constructive" but are direct attacks on the plan which capitalize on the irrational pattern of allocation. A light engineering factory secretly works overtime producing sewing needles and sells them at a great profit, until the director and the accountant are put in jail. Entrepreneurial citizens with time on their hands queue up for scarce goods (it helps to be tipped off on the arrival of a consignment); they buy at state prices and resell at a profit. Naturally the combination of exhortation to plan fulfillment, evasion to fulfill, and antiplan sabotage is widely understood by the population: "by theft, embezzlement and 'speculation,' by refusing to buy this and refusing to work there, even perhaps by complaining and queuing, the citizen fights back." [55] Thus

---

[53] P. F. D. Wiles, *The Political Economy of Communism* (Oxford: Basil Blackwell, 1962).
[54] *Ibid.*, pp. 134–135.
[55] *Ibid.*, p. 132.

planners' tension wastes manpower, takes the joy out of work, and encourages corruption.

Useless work and its hypothetical correlate, job cynicism, are not confined to centralized collectivist economies or to defense programs; the civilian sectors of decentralized market economies produce much of it, too. In the one case, the root difficulty is the impossible demands of the planner; in the other, the zealous search for markets. The superfluous work of Soviet planning engineers who spend their time arguing with the engineers assigned to keep the machinery running is matched by the useless work of excess advertisers and promoters in America who spend their time creating a demand for products no one needs, using methods that might well make any grown man ashamed of himself. As Paul Goodman suggests, the people on television who demonstrate the product and sing the jingles "are clowns and mannequins, in grimace, speech and action. . . . the writers and designers are human beings thinking like idiots; and the broadcasters and underwriters know and abet what goes on—

> *Juicily Glubbily*
> Blubber *is doubbily*
> *Delicious and nutricious*
> *Eat it, kitty, it's good.*" [56]

Today our outlays for advertising are almost equal to our current expenditures on public schools (elementary and secondary)—about eleven billion dollars annually.[57] Additional billions go to public relations and the like. The more abundance, the more activity to increase the desire for it. Little is known, however, about the feelings of those who man this enormous and growing machinery of promotion.[58] We do

---

[56] Paul Goodman, *Growing Up Absurd* (New York: Random House, 1960), pp. 25–26.
[57] Fritz Machlup, *The Production and Distribution of Knowledge in the United States* (Princeton, N.J.: Princeton University Press, 1962), p. 104.
[58] Systematic studies of job discontent provide contradictory clues. A detailed occupational breakdown of our middle-class sample shows that the least work-attached (by the measure in Table 3) are young salesmen (21 to 29 years old) but older salesmen (30 to 55) display the opposite tendency. For instance, only 7 percent of the young men in sales are strongly attached to their work compared to 44 percent of the older group. The most likely explanations are that the older men have better sales assignments, suffer less life-cycle strain, and have been more effectively inducted into the boosters' culture. Second, there are some hints that the glamorous side of the mass entertainment and communications industries, their "show business" character, evokes a positive response from their employees. Observing and interviewing film workers in Hollywood and Chicago gives Joan W. Moore the impression that film carpenters, electricians, and other craftsmen

not have job satisfaction surveys that compare the general population with the network of talent scouts, booking agents, and studio buildup men who sustain the celebrity cult or with the ad men and press agents who sustain the promotional uproar.

Modern society—whatever the political-economic system—casts up a large number of specialists who do not fit the "square" world and for whom the opportunity to express their deviance in quasi-legal institutionalized ways is great. America and the Soviet Union alike provide hundreds of jobs where expense account chiseling, kickbacks, payoffs, tax or price evasion, touches of larceny or fraud are all in a day's work.[59] Many of these jobs are as highly pressured, as tightly disciplined as the most oppressive assembly-line operation.[60] Perhaps decentralized market economies of rich countries are unique only in the large number of jobs they devote to the manufacture and promotion of products which are dangerous (quack cures), frivolous (fur-lined toilet seats), or deliberately designed for speedy obsolescence (toys, cars). Untapped by our surveys are the feelings of an estimated 80,000 door-to-door salesmen busy pushing fake health aids, of the editors of associated magazines, of the staffs of racketeers in religion, economics, and politics, of the managers and workers in industries making products publicized as water polluting, like pesticides, or danger-

---

feel superior to comparable craftsmen in more mundane industries. Even writers in the industry who lose identification with the film or teleplay produced from their scripts retain a strong identification with the industry itself: both elite and rank-and-file enjoy the glamor of the industry and its output (personal communication). Another clue is the flow of writing and editorial talent into jobs which combine glamor and money. A study of younger alumni of the Columbia University School of Journalism notes that two-thirds go to newspapers and wire services but that six years after graduation only half have remained with these jobs; the others moved into broadcasting, public relations, or magazine publishing, where they express greater job satisfaction than those who remained on newspaper staffs. Leo Bogart, "Newspapers in the Age of Television," *Daedalus* 92, 1 (1963), pp. 116–127.

[59] Orrin E. Klapp, *Heroes, Villains, and Fools: The Changing American Character* (Englewood Cliffs, N.J.: Prentice-Hall, 1962).

[60] Consider, for instance, the blackjack dealer in Las Vegas, the most closely supervised worker in the American economy—the pitboss and his assistants a few feet away at all times, peepholes above manned at unpredictable intervals, the work routine prescribed, the workpace frantic. It will be interesting to see whether the automatic "21" dealer, a machine, an improved version of which is now being tested in Nevada, will displace these skilled workers. Erving Goffman suggests (in a personal communication) that while managers of gambling establishments would like to use machines to eliminate dealer stealing and reduce labor costs, the effects on the psychological pleasures of the game are unknown, and the machines themselves are not immune to cheaters or to those who exploit malfunctions.

ous, like tobacco. In short, do men take special pride, derive special dignity from working on products their fellows view as unequivocally good and useful; and do they feel any shame, experience any restiveness, when they work on products viewed as useless or harmful? Or are the rewards of task, workplace, and career central, the uses of the output a minor incidental in the psychology of work?

Automation and Job Discontent

Because we do not know how widely and quickly automation will spread, we cannot be sure that this picture of the organization and meaning of work, which I think accurate for the last decade, will apply for the next decade. The technological developments covered by "automation" are numerous, the costs and gains variable; the precise manpower demands are a matter of guesstimates.

Three major developments are (1) integration, or the linking together of conventionally separate manufacturing operations into lines of continuous operation through which the product moves untouched by human hands; (2) the use of feedback control devices or servomechanisms that compare the way work is actually being done with the way it is supposed to be done, coupled with a device that automatically makes any necessary adjustment in the work process (think of the living room thermostat); and (3) computer technology that records, stores, and processes information (EDP or electronic data processing). Together these three developments ultimately mean the spread of virtually automatic factories—EDP for bookkeeping and accounting chores in the office and laboratory, matched by industrial control computers directly connected to the instruments and controls of a plant process. In factory, office, and store alike, and at every level —blue-collar and white, supervisory and managerial, semiprofessional and professional—the new technology can transform work and its rewards. I will not try to describe the technology [61] but will merely suggest some likely changes in the abilities required of the labor force that have most import for our problem. These are:

1. *An increased demand for responsible work performance among men of the working class.* An accent more on mental clarity and alert-

[61] For a stimulating description and evaluation of automation see M. Philipson, editor, *Automation: Implications for the Future* (New York: Vintage Books, 1962), especially the essays by D. N. Michael, N. W. J. Diebold, N. Wiener, and E. M. Kassalow. For a sober assessment of the impact on top management and staff, see Herbert A. Simon, *The New Science of Management Decision* (New York: Harper and Brothers, 1960).

ness than on physical strength or manual dexterity. It is often said that automation means a general "upgrading of skills." But if when we say "skill" we evoke the image of a skilled carpenter who does beautiful cabinet work with great pride of craft, we may be misled. Although the label exaggerates, the new worker may be something of a quasi-engineer, who can sense connections among processes, remain vigilant, in some cases spot trouble when it is developing, in all cases give close and regular attention to signals that tell him how well machines are doing man's work—a worker who, when the technical and organizational system is changed by engineers, planners, and programmers in the head office, can quickly learn new signals and new trouble spots in new automatic machines. The watchwords in these tightly integrated systems of production are "discipline," "reliability," and "adaptability"—what managers mean when they say "good work habits."

2. *Both upgrading and downgrading of skills in clerical, sales, supervisory, and accounting jobs.* The net effect may be a slight shift downward. The insurance adjuster finds himself attending only to troublesome, challenging cases; office mechanization takes care of the routine semiclerical tasks that once burdened him. On the other hand, the office manager once in charge of 30 subordinates in a payroll department, now confronting an electronic brain programmed and run by others, has only two girls working under him. The lesson of case studies of the changeover to EDP is that we have grossly exaggerated both the indispensability and complexity of many office jobs. The white-collar pyramid is flattening out, with a heavy concentration of workers at the low end of the salary scale—for example, in keypunching jobs which are themselves being automated.

3. *Both upgrading and downgrading of managerial and administrative jobs.* If we combine the rapid handling of information by computers, the application of mathematics and statistics to administrative problems (mathematical programming, simulation, and operations research), and the recruitment and training of better-educated managers who are smart enough to use the staff to put these methods to work, then we have a formula for revolution in the middle bureaucracy, and perhaps ultimately in top management, too. It means greater centralization of authority, clearer accountability of subordinates, a sharper distinction between top management and staff and the rest of the organization, and eventually a transformation of the planning and innovating functions.

Automation thus far seems to increase pressure and rigidity in scheduling, require more disciplined work, and reduce freedom on the job.

Drudgery and danger are reduced, but so is sociable talk. The slack is going out of the system. For instance, compare the characteristics of jobs on old assembly lines (on the main moving conveyor belt) with those on newly automated lines.[62]

	Old Lines	Automated Lines
Freedom	Low sociable interaction	Lower sociable interaction
	Almost complete predetermination of tools and techniques	Complete predetermination
	Machine pacing, but can work ahead sometimes, take breaks	Machine pacing timed more rigidly
	Surface mental attention	Closer attention, sometimes intermittent, sometimes constant
Status	Low skill, little responsibility	More responsibility
	Low income, status	More income for men who get the new jobs?
	Low community visibility	Low community visibility

If jobs with low freedom and high pressure foster alienation and jobs affording plentiful sociability and control over the work strengthen attachment (see p. 142), automation on balance may increase discontent and indifference.

A note of caution must be sounded. Extrinsic rewards—money, job security—may be greater for the workers who successfully make the shift. Further, the evidence on freedom and pressure is not all on one side. Some of the jobs allow variation in sequence of tasks. A factor offsetting reduced freedom in most automated factories is the increase in sophisticated maintenance jobs. Some of these jobs require that men patrol the plant alone on a fixed round but many permit freer sociability. And although operators are often more isolated from their peers, they are more integrated with engineers and technicians—if not by fraternity, at least by information flow.

[62] Charles R. Walker and Robert H. Guest, *The Man on the Assembly Line* (Cambridge, Mass.: Harvard University Press, 1952); Charles R. Walker, *Toward the Automatic Factory: A Case Study of Men and Machines* (New Haven, Conn.: Yale University Press, 1957); William A. Faunce, "Automation in the Automobile Industry: Some Consequences for In-plant Social Structure," *American Sociological Review*, 23 (August 1958), pp. 401–407; and William A. Faunce, "The Automobile Industry; A Case Study in Automation," in H. B. Jacobson and J. S. Roucek, eds., *Automation and Society* (New York: Philosophical Library, 1959), pp. 44–53.

If we consider all the variations in automation, we lack the necessary evidence to make a judgment about the long-run effects on intrinsic job satisfaction. Men now bothered by the combination of high pressure and low freedom are in the midst of a transformation; we do not know how their successors will feel. Ultimately all these trends may produce a new man who is well adjusted to the new milieu—a meticulous, disciplined man who abhors unpredictability. The dilemma of the future would then be that the new jobs foster intolerance for ambiguity, and yet the new economy necessitates quicker adjustment to unpredictable change.

Jobs in the service sector are subject to a similar process of rationalization, depersonalization, and centralization. Although some of these changes are not linked to automation but result from mechanization of a primitive sort or from changes in the structure of the workplace, they move in the same direction. For instance, retail clerks are becoming heavily concentrated in large food and drug chains. Fewer of them are women; fewer of the men expect quick promotion. For many salesmen the personal sales relationship has eroded: the swing is from sales talk to check-out counter and charge plate, from customer contact to materials handling. The "proletarianization" of white-collar workers is doubtless a factor in the spectacular rise of the Retail Clerks International Association, now one of the eight largest unions in the United States. Thus one of the favorite generalizations of social science—that modernization puts an ever-larger proportion of the labor force in "tertiary" jobs requiring customer or client contact—is no longer valid. Farm, factory, office, and store—primary, secondary, and tertiary alike—increasingly conform to the same mold of technology and organization.

Automation, Unemployment, and Job Discontent: A Postscript on Prospects and Solutions

No student of automation has suggested that the new technology spells less discipline on the job, less accent on hierarchy in the workplace, although some think that it means more impersonal, and hence smoother, human relations. The major sources of alienation and indifference will thus become more prominent in the future organization of work.

Is this a matter of public concern? Should it be?

Solutions to Job Discontent

Job discontent is not high on the list of American social problems. Surely in importance the population explosion as it affects the quality of daily life and nuclear weapons as they affect the prospects of civilized survival rank higher. Work is instead like the second major user of time, television. The dominant feeling about it is ambivalence; strong alienation is rare; more pleasant alternatives serving the same functions at the same cost are not readily available; without a vision of a better way of doing things, there is a tendency to accept the world as it is constituted.

Insofar as intellectuals or workers have become concerned about work (not the lack of it) as a problem, they have advocated three major types of solution: (1) develop patterns of creative, challenging leisure to compensate for an inevitable spread of stultifying labor; (2) offer vastly better compensation for those condemned to alienating work situations; (3) redesign the technology and workplace to invest work with more meaning and hence enhance the quality of leisure.[63] The first solution is unrealistic; labor that requires little investment of self tends to go together with leisure that is full of malaise. As I have shown elsewhere,[64] the leisure style of short-hours men at every level (engineers, blue-collar workers) is like that of men who have no work at all: its main theme is the compulsive absorption of gargantuan amounts of shoddy television as a time-filler. Generally, men whose time at work is limited have time on their hands; they cope with restless malaise by an unsatisfying retreat to violent, escapist programs. One qualification is in order: a great majority of men with a high-quality college education display high leisure competence (if we can take their uses of the mass media as a clue). But these fortunate men tend overwhelmingly to work long hours at gratifying work—and their leisure competence is accordingly high. To solve the problem of leisure we must solve the problem of work; what is necessary is a heavy investment in institutions that prepare people for both.

The second solution is the trade union strategy of more money for less working time—pay and play within the framework of existing technology. Testifying to the popularity of this solution are the scores of ways of compensating for unpleasant work provided by the typical union contract—from rest periods to vacation pay, from premium rates for dangerous work or night work to renegotiation when job content is changed (it is usually assumed that any change is for the worse and ought to be paid for). Managerial variations on the theme

---

[63] David Riesman, in the course of his seminal writings of the past decade, has advocated all three strategies and has become discouraged by each in turn. See the stimulating analysis by Georges Friedmann, *Où va le Travail Humain?* (Paris: Gallimard, 1950).

[64] H. L. Wilensky, "Mass Society and Mass Culture: Interdependence or Independence?" *American Sociological Review*, 29 (April 1964), pp. 173–197.

include plant tours to give the overspecialized worker an overview of the plant or product, participation programs to give workers a sense of belonging (for example, suggestion plans, profit sharing), supervisory training in human relations to secure a less strained acquiescence to authority. Such solutions are attempts to increase the rewards of admittedly frustrating work without changing the work itself.

The third strategy includes attempts to (1) enlarge the job, for example, by combining the work of skilled setup men and inspectors with that of routine machine operators; and (2) to rotate jobs, for example, by shifting teams of operators from one set of jobs to another daily, increasing the individual's pay as he masters each new block of operations. Despite some evidence that job enlargement or rotation can both reduce job discontent and increase efficiency—through improved quality and quantity of output, a more flexible work force [65] and, less surely, reduced labor turnover—these programs are rarely adopted in American industry, and then mainly in small plants headed by latter-day Owenites. To fit machine systems to the man is an idea foreign to most employers. Those who consider it are repelled by the training costs and managerial effort required and are doubtful about the gains to be won; complete mechanization that eliminates the vagaries of human labor is far more attractive, and, together with consolation prizes for the surviving workers, remains the main strategy of the change-prone modern manager.[66]

Automation, Alienation, and Community Disruption

Automation may for a time reduce the magnitude of management's tasks in human relations, as several observers argue, but if it increases pressure and reduces freedom on the job, and spreads fear of displacement and job chaos, the savings from reduced payrolls and reduced human error may be offset by growing alienation and indifference among the dwindling portions of the labor force. The possibilities can be glimpsed in the responses of discontented workers at every level of mechanization. Left to their own devices, workers often find the "compensation" solution wanting; they say that they could reorganize the technology and task more efficiently on their own, or they actually do so. One survey of production workers in heavy industry reports

---

[65] Louis E. Davis and Richard Werling, "Job Design Factors," *Occupational Psychology*, 34 (April 1960), pp. 109–137.

[66] Insofar as automation requires enlarged, multiple-skilled jobs, it may make management more receptive to programs of job design which tap more of the data from studies of the impact of specific types of job enlargement. See Louis E. Davis, "The Effects of Automation on Job Design," *Industrial Relations*, 2 (October 1962), pp. 53–71.

that two in three of the respondents felt that their work could be done better if they had more chance to make suggestions about such matters as the design, layout, or setup of their own work.[67] In a study of industrial work groups, Sayles [68] found that many workers, in defiance of plant rules, tried to gain variety by exchanging jobs. The traditional ingenuity of machinists who invent and hide cutting tools that do the work more efficiently than the tools provided, and thereby permit more worker control of the pace, is matched by the exquisite genius of men who sabotage machine-paced operations. The auto worker on an old-fashioned assembly line throws a few bolts inside the door panel, and auto dealers are mystified by a rash of customer complaints about loud rattles in their new cars. Lately the phenomenon has appeared among tabulating-machine operatives and other office workers threatened by EDP. The trick is to restrict the flow of information to be fed to the computers, fail to meet deadlines, let errors go through, and announce that "the job just can't be done that way." [69] Finally, in one large automated oil refinery, the most careful and instantaneous records of gasoline output did not stop a disaffected manager from diverting thousands of gallons of gasoline to his private enterprise. We have not yet probed the depths of human ingenuity in the sabotage of these highly integrated systems, nor have we gauged the motivation for it.

Perhaps all this is transitional. Even if the will to sabotage increases, the opportunity is more and more restricted; tasks will become not merely more fixed and explicit but more unavoidable, more closely monitored. If so, the discontent, like the workers, will be displaced. The stably employed who cannot express their alienation and indifference in tightly run workplaces will do so elsewhere, in the family and neighborhood. And those with no place in the new economy—untrained adolescents and older men made obsolete or prematurely retired—may one day disrupt community life in ways that no computer, no automated system can cope with. If the protest of the job-disaffected and job-denied remains scattered, a succession of individual adjustments to individual tragedies, the problem will not rock the nation. But obviously there is some rate of insecurity and some rate of unemployment that can produce collective protest instead of self-

[67] Survey Research Center, *Attitude and Opinions of Hourly Employees* (Ann Arbor: University of Michigan, 1950).
[68] Leonard R. Sayles, *Behavior of Industrial Work Groups: Prediction and Control* (New York: John Wiley and Sons, 1958).
[69] Ida R. Hoos, "The Sociological Impact of Automation in the Office," *Management Technology*, 1 (December 1960), pp. 10–19.

blame. Negro ghettos of the early 1960s, with a majority of their young men out of school and out of work, provide a preview of the possibilities of community conflict. We cannot count on Ghandian doctrines of nonviolence to prevail among the growing populations, white and nonwhite, who now look at the tight, closed world of work from the fringe, from the outside.

Summary

Whatever the attitude of the common man, philosophies of work have through the ages become more favorable to labor and its fruits. Popular sociology has labeled this tendency the rise of the Protestant Ethic. The generalization relating ideas and economic action that can withstand a cross-cultural test, however, may be this: wherever economic growth is sustained, societal values which acquire a sacred cast and are favorable to economic growth will appear, furthering and reflecting that growth. Thus the well-known puritanical drive of the Soviet managerial elite, the entrepreneurial spirit of skilled immigrants in developing countries (Nisei in America, Huguenots in Amsterdam, Jews everywhere) reflect not a Protestant Ethic but a doctrine of work, tied to Communist ideology and an expansionist totalitarian state in the one case, to ethnic-religious tradition and marginal status in the other.

The nineteenth-century secular religion of work may be attenuated in the affluent society, but work itself remains central in two senses. First, considering all hours worked—moonlighting and the main job, overtime and straight time, as well as the increased labor force participation of women—modern economies command an impressive amount of disciplined work, and there is no sign that the trained population is suffering a markedly decreased willingness to log those hours. Second, the primordial meaning and function of work is dramatized by the narrow range of social contact of men squeezed out of the labor market; the aged, the school dropouts, the unemployed, and the underemployed are isolated from the mainstream of community life. Employment remains symbolic of a place among the living.

Once we eliminate the growing minority who have no steady work to which they can respond (something studies of job satisfaction usually fail to do), we find large variations in levels and kinds of gratification and discontent, depending on the measure, the time, and the place. Direct questions yield a misleading picture of cheerful majorities, although they also suggest the prominence of economic meanings of work among lower strata. More indirect approaches and some consideration of the balance between rewards and aspirations and their chronology over the work life uncover more discontent. They also suggest that job satisfaction is part of life satisfaction, and, less surely, that job discontent spreads to create other discontents.

The classic problem of work alienation has received little systematic study. Feelings about work are anchored both in personal identity and in the technical and social organization of work. A fruitful way to join debate about what work is doing to or for modern man is to compare men variously situated and ask how well their prized self-images fit their work roles. Relating measures of alienation, attachment, and indifference that tap prized self-image to specific attributes of work role and workplace and to the careers and occupational groups that cut across them, we find that a work milieu that provides little freedom, a career that has been blocked and chaotic, and a stage of life where consumption pressures outrun income foster work alienation. Control over the workpace, opportunity for sociable talk on the job, and an orderly career foster work attachment. The most alienated groups in our study are blue-collar workers (all have above-average family incomes) and engineers (many of them have high salaries). The most attached are lawyers in firms and professors in a denominational university. The general impression from these and other data is that the typical American man is lightly committed to his work. He may be reliable and disciplined on the job, he may talk it up or gripe about it, but he neither throws himself into it nor feels that it violates his better self.

The central tendency is to view work with detachment, but there are variations on the theme. If we go beyond the limits of our measures and data, we uncover signs that job cynicism and feelings of uselessness are growing in the defense industries of all countries, among planners and their competitors in command economies, among hucksters in market economies—more generally, among men busy at useless work with useless products.

The diverse innovations going under the label "automation" are spreading; they may ultimately affect every industry, every occupation, and every social level. But their impact is most dramatic in factory and office where no one is immune, neither workers, staff experts, middle managers, nor supervisors.

The net effect on the organization of work may be to increase discipline and reduce freedom on the job, centralize decision making, and accent hierarchy in the workplace, reliability and flexibility in the employee. The effect on the meaning of work will be to encourage the spread of indifference, and perhaps alienation. Although the displacement effects have not been adequately gauged, they will hit hardest the swiftest-growing populations, the young and the old. In the 1960s we are combining an urgent demand for work-oriented, literate employees with millions of school dropouts entering the labor market for the first time—an explosive mix.

The future will include large, centralized bureaucracies of government, business, and education run by an elite of sophisticated science- and system-oriented managers with unparalleled command of information. Serving them will be a vast apparatus of communications specialists and an underlying population controlled increasingly from the center. The stably employed masses whose attitudes and capacity to learn fit the needs of the economy will be subject to clearer and more consistent direction, but they will be increasingly incapable of understanding the nature and purposes of their work, of the esoteric bases of decision—incapable, for instance, of judging one computer program against another or the "why" of policies that flow from the top. This is not to say that they will move to man the barricades; there are many compensating rewards—possessions, leisure, multiple ladders for mobility—that function to dampen protest and keep the employed population quiescent.

For those squeezed out of the labor force entirely, the problem is not job discontent and indifference but a generalized alienation from the core of American life. In general, the new technology is likely to create a greater chasm between expert and official and between official and the rank and file worker-consumer-voter. The heroes of such a society will probably be logical and authoritarian types, managers who cannot stand the variability and unpredictability of human behavior and who will try to program it out of existence—in short, men who are intolerant of the ambiguities of a pluralist society and a democratic polity.

4

The Aged in American Society

Bernice L. Neugarten

WHEN this century was new, four of every hundred persons living in the United States had reached or passed the age of 65. Sixty years later the proportion of old people in the American population had more than doubled; in 1965 it exceeded 9 percent. Although the percentage is not likely to rise much more, there are expected to be about 24 million older people in the country by 1980 and over 28 million by 2000. This astonishing population explosion has vastly increased social awareness of the problems of aging and the aged.

How does society meet the needs of older people? How does their increasing presence affect other groups in the society? What new relationships are being generated between young and old? More and more Americans are asking these questions in their professional as well as in their private lives. Biological and social scientists have evolved a new science, *gerontology*;[1] the medical profession has developed a new

* Prepared with the assistance of Jacqueline M. Falk.

[1] In the mid-1950s the term "social gerontology" was introduced into the social sciences, and with the publication of the *Handbook of Social Gerontology*, Clark Tibbitts, ed. (Chicago: University of Chicago Press, 1960), came to denote those areas of inquiry which deal with societal aspects of aging. A companion volume, Ernest W. Burgess, ed., *Aging in Western Societies* (Chicago: University of Chicago Press, 1960), summarized underlying economic and social trends as well as the policies and programs developed by several European nations in dealing with problems of the aged. The distinction has therefore been drawn between social gerontology, on the one hand, and those aspects of aging, both social and psychological, in which the individual, rather than the society at large, is the focus of attention. The research literature dealing with the aging individual has been summarized in another volume of this series, James E. Birren, ed., *Handbook of Aging and the Individual* (Chicago: University of Chicago Press, 1959).

specialty, *geriatrics*. Social workers are perfecting new types of services for older clients. Educators are now attempting to serve the older as well as the younger adult in adult education and have also instituted special training programs for those who as teachers, administrators, and counselors will deal with the aged. Recreational workers are trying a variety of leisure-time programs for old people. In the business world corporations pay close attention to retirement policies and often concern themselves with preparing middle-aged workers for the adjustments they must make after retiring. Further, the federal government has introduced an increasing amount of legislation intended to meet the economic and social needs of old people, and commissions, committees, and government agencies proliferate at the local, state, and national levels to cope with these problems.

The Aged as a Social Problem

Some people define a social problem as a state of affairs in society which the public thinks is wrong and needs to be corrected. On this basis the number of aged persons is not in itself a social problem. Few would seriously maintain that it is wrong to have many older people in any given population or that remedial steps should be taken to pare their numbers. On the contrary, nations prize longevity and count it an accomplishment, not a failure, that increasing numbers of men and women live to old age.[2] The social problem is rather the lag in adapting social institutions to the needs of older people without disrupting the machinery of the whole society. The problem lies in the dislocations occurring in the society because it is not prepared for the "sudden" appearance of large numbers of aged. From this point of view, the gravest aspects of the problem are posed for those persons who formulate social policy at local, state, and national levels. To take but one example, we can now fill several five-foot shelves with the published hearings by Congressional committees on various problems of the aged; and a prominently placed federal official commented recently that he could not manage even to read all the titles of legislation currently under consideration.

Populations (as opposed to individuals) age as the benefits of industrialization, rising standards of living, and modern medical research

---

[2] A historical view of changes in longevity is to be found in Louis I. Dublin, A. J. Lotka, and M. Spiegelman, *Length of Life* (New York: Ronald Press, 1949). Information on growth of population, age distributions of national populations over the world, and other demographic data are published by the Population Reference Bureau, Washington, D.C.

lead to longer life expectancy and as the proportion of old people increases in relation to the number of children. This societal aging, common to all industrialized nations, appeared in Europe earlier than in the United States. Table 1 reflects the trend through a ratio of the number of persons 60 years old and over to the number of children under 15 (known as an index of aging). As the table shows, at midpoint in the nineteenth century the population of the United States resembled that

Table 1 Index of Aging and Census Dates for Selected Countries

	Index of Aging
Underdeveloped:	
Thailand, 1947	9.9
Brazil, 1950	10.2
Semi-industrialized:	
Japan, 1950	21.8
Industrialized:	
Mid-nineteenth century:	
United States, 1850	10.0
Great Britain, 1851	20.7
Sweden, 1850	23.8
Mid-twentieth century:	
United States, 1950	45.3
Sweden, 1950	64.0
Great Britain, 1951	69.8

SOURCE: Adapted from Henry D. Sheldon, "The Changing Demographic Profile," Chapter 2 in Clark Tibbitts, ed., *Handbook of Social Gerontology* (Chicago: University of Chicago Press, 1960), p. 28.

of contemporary underdeveloped countries, and today the "aging process" is more advanced in some European populations than in the United States.

This social problem is a sword with two edges. First, a certain proportion of older people suffer from poverty, illness, and social isolation. These people, whom we shall call the needy aged, create acute problems in the field of social welfare. Second, broad problems stem from the need of all individuals in the society to adjust to the new rhythms of life that result from increased longevity. All members of society must adapt to new social phenomena such as multigenerational families, retirement communities, and leisure as a way of life. Thus this second set of social problems relates to the innumerable questions of social policy that arise as the whole social fabric accommodates itself to the new phenomenon of large numbers of aged. Most of this chapter will deal with the latter set of problems. Although the line of demarcation between the two sets is not clear, the distinction should be kept in mind, for many of the current American stereotypes of the aged are based on the needy rather than on the typical aged.

Inevitably, we must engage in broad generalizations and postulates using averages and overall trends. It should always be kept in mind, however, that old people are extremely diverse. Each person has a unique life history which with the passage of time makes him *increasingly* distinct from others in many of his habits, customs, and values. The millions of individuals who constitute the aged in American society include wealthy as well as poor, healthy as well as sick, contented as well as discontented, privileged as well as deprived. As a recent government publication noted,

> The faces [of the aged] are those of:
> . . . Three ex-Presidents.
> . . . Nearly 10 percent of the entire United States population.
> . . . Nearly 1½ million people living on farms.
> . . . More than one out of four United States Senators.
> . . . Almost 2 million people working full time.
> . . . Two of the nine United States Supreme Court Justices.
> . . . More than 10,000 people over 100 years old.
> . . . Over 12½ million people getting social security benefits.
> . . . Over 2.3 million war veterans.
> . . . More than 3 million people who migrated from Europe to the United States.[3]

Only in a general sense can "the aged" or, perhaps more precisely, "people who have grown old" be said to have certain common characteristics which differentiate them from the young and the middle-aged, and which accord them a unique place in American society.

The Position of the Aged in American Society

The social position of any group can be viewed from a number of perspectives, including economic, social-psychological, and political. The aged may first be seen from two time perspectives: *calendar time* (the characteristics of the aged in successive historical periods) and *life time* (the characteristics of the aged as compared with other age

[3] President's Council on Aging, *The Older American* (Washington, D.C.: U.S. Government Printing Office, 1963), p. 1.

groups). These two views overlap; the relations between old and young are determined by the social attitudes learned by both groups, and social attitudes are in turn determined by life experiences that vary with historical circumstances.

The Historical Setting

The persons who now constitute the aged population in the United States are different from those who will follow because the world in which children grow up is constantly changing. People aged 65 or over in 1965 were born for the most part between 1880 and 1900 and grew up during a period of great economic expansion and general optimism in America. Although the frontier had disappeared, its spirit was still prevalent. A lengthy education was the exception rather than the rule; for the average person, formal schooling ended with the eighth grade. Many unskilled jobs existed for youth and for the large numbers of foreigners who came to make a better life in the New World. A young man could get ahead, or so the rags-to-riches novels of Horatio Alger told him, with persistence, thrift, good manners and morals, and, of course, a bit of luck. A man expected to work hard—and to work all his life. If an able-bodied man failed to make a living for his family, it was considered a disgrace and an indication of personality defect. Pension plans and social security did not exist, but if one put aside a bit of money regularly, one presumably would be protected against any illness that might come with old age.[4]

The people who are old in the 1960s and 1970s were already adult in the period of rapid technological and industrial change which marked the first half of the twentieth century. In those decades the proportion of agricultural workers dropped from 30 percent to less than 10 percent of all workers, and work skills became subject to rapid obsolescence. Between 1900 and 1935 many Americans lost the conviction that the world was constantly improving. World War I did not make the world safe for democracy, and the Great Depression of the 1930s brought the realization that the individual's economic success or failure did not depend solely on his strength of character. Many of today's aged lost their occupational moorings during the Depression; and, of these, some did not recoup during the period of prosperity ushered in by World War II, nor did they build up sizable equities under the

[4] For an interesting journalistic description of the changes in values and attitude systems that have occurred over the past 75 years in American society, see Frederick L. Allen, *The Big Change: America Transforms Itself, 1900–1950* (New York: Harper and Brothers, 1952). See also Henry S. Commager, *The American Mind* (New Haven, Conn.: Yale University Press, 1950), and David Riesman et al., *The Lonely Crowd* (New Haven, Conn.: Yale University Press, 1950).

federal social security program that developed in the 1940s and 1950s.

In succeeding decades, more and more older people will have been native-born Americans, will have grown up in urban areas, will have had the advantages of regular medical care during their lifetimes, will have had high school and college educations, will be unacquainted with widespread economic catastrophe, and will be likely to take for granted pension programs, social security, and government assistance programs of all types.

These paragraphs are perhaps sufficient to indicate not only that the future aged in America will be different from the present aged, but also that different age groups at the same point in calendar time have different experiential bases for their behavior. Although older people, just as younger, go on learning throughout their lives and continually change their minds and their ways of life, different generations may be expected to have somewhat different attitudes and values, so that, as the sociologist Karl Mannheim put it, the presence in society of different generations produces a "non-contemporaneity of the contemporaneous."[5] In other words, persons of different ages who live together at a given moment in history have been molded by different historical events and different cultural climates and therefore have different attitudes and sentiments.

The Age-Status System

These differences among age groups come to be reflected in the age-status system of the society, the system of implicit and explicit rules and expectations that governs the relations among persons of different ages. In all societies there are rights, duties, obligations, and privileges which are differentially assigned to children, adolescents, young adults, the middle-aged, and the old.[6] Certain behaviors are regarded as appro-

[5] Karl Mannheim, "The Problem of Generations," in *Essays on the Sociology of Knowledge* (New York: Oxford University Press, 1952), pp. 276–322.

[6] In addition to the paper by Mannheim, major sociological analyses of age-status systems and age-sex roles include: Ralph Linton, "Age and Sex Categories," *American Sociological Review*, 7 (October 1942), pp. 589–603; Ruth Benedict, "Continuities and Discontinuities in Cultural Conditioning," *Psychiatry*, 1 (1938), pp. 161–167; Kingsley Davis, "The Sociology of Parent-Youth Conflict," *American Sociological Review*, 5 (August 1940), pp. 512–535; and Talcott Parsons, "Age and Sex in the Social Structure of the United States," *American Sociological Review*, 7 (October 1942), pp. 604–616.

Anthropological classics include Arnold van Gennep (1908), *The Rites of Passage* (Chicago: University of Chicago Press, 1960); and Robert H. Lowie (1920), *Primitive Society* (New York: Harper and Brothers, 1961). More recently, A. H. J. Prins, *East African Age-Class Systems* (Groningen, Djakarta: Wolters, 1953) has analyzed the concepts and terms in use among anthropologists.

priate or inappropriate for each age group; and the relations among age groups are based on dimensions of prestige, power, and deference. Older children have prestige in the eyes of younger; adolescents, in at least some ways, recognize the power of adults; and both children and adults, in at least some ways, show deference to the old. Within the total society each age group may be said to occupy a given status. The age-status system undergoes certain alterations in line with other social, economic, and political changes in the society.

In America today, the aged generally occupy a position of lower status than the middle-aged. In many ways older persons are accorded less prestige and less deference than they presumably were accorded in earlier historical periods. For the most part, they possess less economic and political power than the middle-aged. The position of the old in America has often been compared unfavorably with that of the old in other societies. In Imperial Chinese society, for example, individuals as they aged are said to have drawn to themselves greater and greater amounts of respect and deference. There is reason to doubt, however, that in earlier times, either in Western or non-Western societies, the aged were uniformly valued as a group. Their status has probably always had both positive and negative elements, as shown in a recent study of three traditional villages in India where the position of the aged was analyzed with regard to prestige, authority, power, and security.[7] A wide gap was found to exist between the ideal norms and actual practices: the old lose status with the death of a spouse; many older people feel neglected; only a small minority of old people of upper socioeconomic status play leadership roles in the village; control of family affairs and participation in community affairs are generally relinquished after middle age. This picture is not unlike descriptions of the status of the aged in contemporary America.

Such studies raise doubts about the generalization that the aged lose status as a direct consequence of urbanization and industrialization.

More recent works on age status include S. N. Eisenstadt, *From Generation to Generation* (Glencoe, Ill.: The Free Press, 1956); and papers by Bennett M. Berger, "How Long Is a Generation?" *British Journal of Sociology*, 11, 1 (March 1960), pp. 10–23; Bruno Bettelheim, "The Problems of Generations," *Daedalus*, 91, 1 (1962), pp. 68–96; and Bernice L. Neugarten, Joan W. Moore, and John C. Lowe, "Age Norms, Age Constraints, and Adult Socialization," *American Journal of Sociology*, 70 (May 1965), pp. 710–717.

[7] William H. Harlan, "Social Status of the Aged in Three Indian Villages," *Vita Humana*, 7, 3/4 (1964). See also Leo W. Simmons, *The Role of the Aged in Primitive Society* (New Haven, Conn.: Yale University Press, 1945); and Robert A. LeVine, "Intergenerational Tensions and Extended Family Structure in Africa," in Ethel Shanas and Gordon F. Streib, eds., *Social Structure and the Family* (Englewood Cliffs, N.J.: Prentice-Hall, 1965).

Nevertheless, it is true that our society has come to be characterized as one where the primary value has been placed upon youth and where the aged are often disparaged. Some sociologists have written at length about the "roleless role" of the aged. They mean that as older persons retire or are retired from the labor market, they become removed from active participation in other areas of society and are thus relatively isolated and ignored. This view has become a stereotype of the aged and like all stereotypes is only partially true.

Whether the aged in America are less respected today than they were, say, 50 or 100 years ago remains a matter of opinion. There is little empirical evidence by which to judge the matter. The relations among age groups were probably more formal in the nineteenth century than in the twentieth, but the extent to which formalities accurately reflect underlying power or prestige is a moot point.

There is fairly good evidence, on the other hand, that in successive decades the aged have become more clearly delineated as a group. In this respect there is a certain parallel between adolescents and the aged. As technological progress has caused a dramatic growth in economic productivity, both age groups moved from producer to nonproducer roles in the economy. During the Great Depression adolescents were removed from the labor market to create more jobs for adults. More recently, in a period of economic affluence, rising population, and automation, the labor of the aged has become increasingly superfluous. The situation has been created in which the old are now beginning to form a distinct group in somewhat the same way as adolescents first did in the 1930s.

The increased delineation of both adolescents and the old as special age groups has led to the question of whether these groups may be said to constitute subcultures, in the sense that members of each group are interacting more with one another than with persons of other ages and are thereby creating their own institutions, codes, manners, and customs.[8] A related question is the extent to which the old, like adoles-

---

[8] The delineation of a youth culture has been discussed by Ernest A. Smith, *American Youth Culture: Group Life in Teenage Society* (New York: The Free Press of Glencoe, 1962); by various contributors to "Teen Age Culture," an issue of the *Annals of the American Academy of Political and Social Science*, 338 (November 1961); and in Erik H. Erikson, ed., *Youth: Change and Challenge* (based on the Winter 1962 issue of *Daedalus*) (New York: Basic Books, 1963). A book which speculates about the future of American youth in the rapidly changing social and economic setting is *The Next Generation*, by Donald N. Michael (New York: Vintage Books, 1965).

Discussion of a subculture of the aged can be found in Arnold Rose, "The Subculture of the Aging: a Topic for Sociological Research," *The Gerontologist*, 2,

THE AGED IN AMERICAN SOCIETY

cents, are becoming age-segregated as well as age-separated. We shall return to these questions after we have examined the status of the aged within several different social institutions.

The Economic Status of the Aged

The period through which our present aged population has lived has been one of rapid social and technological changes. These changes have had far-reaching effects upon all age groups, but the effects on the old have been especially dramatic. We have already commented upon the increased numbers of older persons, but the numbers need to be examined further in relation to the economic status of the aged.

Longevity and the Economics of Health

Since 1900 advances in medical knowledge and rising standards of living have brought about a sharp increase in life expectancy. The year 1961 marked the first time that life expectancy at birth for the population at large exceeded 70 years. (The increase has been greater for

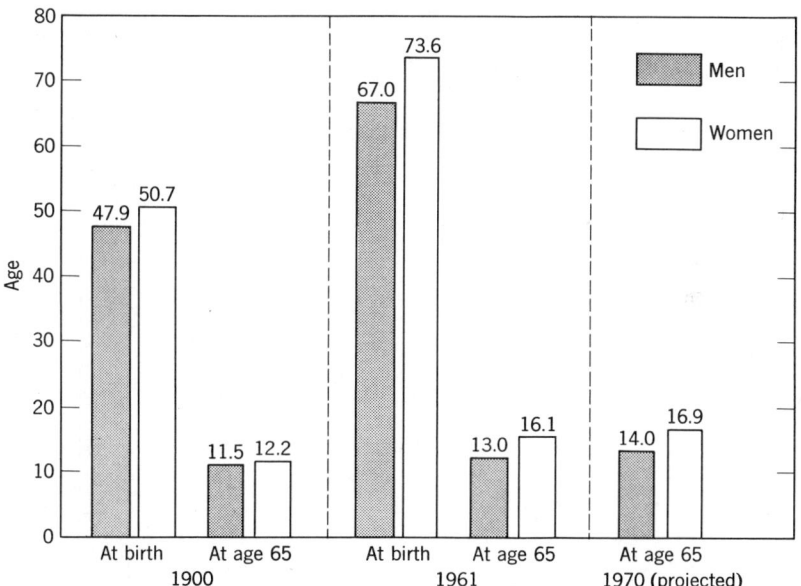

Figure 1 Expectancy of life in the United States. From *Health, Education and Welfare Trends, 1963*, p. 13.

---

3 (September 1962), pp. 123–127; and in two papers in Tibbitts, ed., *op. cit.*: Eugene A. Friedmann, "The Impact of Aging on the Social Structure," pp. 120–144; and Richard H. Williams, "Changing Status, Roles, and Relationships," pp. 261–297.

the nonwhite than for the white population, but there is still a gap of almost seven years, with the expectancy for nonwhites approaching 65 and that for whites, 72.) This change has been brought about primarily by greatly increasing life expectancy in infancy and childhood through bringing under control such contagious and epidemic diseases as diphtheria, influenza, whooping cough, scarlet fever, and poliomyelitis. Medical science has not yet conquered the diseases that are now the major causes of death, often designated as the diseases of old age: heart disease, high blood pressure, and cancer. Consequently, the human lifespan itself has not increased markedly. Persons who reached 65 in the 1960s could expect to live not much longer than their counterparts in 1900, as Figure 1 shows. Nevertheless, the effect of new medical knowledge and public health practices on the population has been considerable. Not only are more people living to old age, but the older population is itself growing older. As seen in Figure 2, the number of men and women in the advanced age group 75 and over is growing at a faster rate than the group aged 65 to 74. In addition, more women than men live to a very old age. (Of all persons aged 65 and over, there are 121 women for every 100 men; but in the group aged 85 and over, this ratio is 156 to 100.) As we shall see later, it is elderly women especially who constitute an economically deprived group.

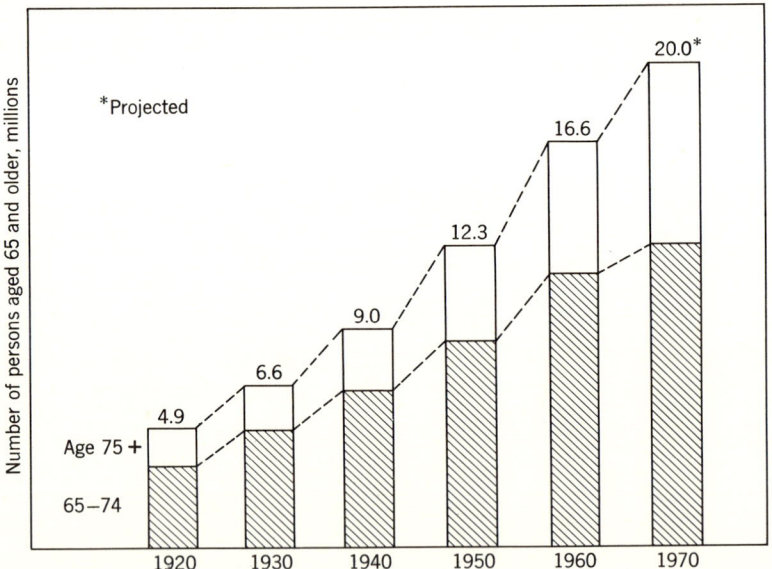

Figure 2   Proportion of the very old in the elderly population. From "The Older Population," *Health, Education and Welfare Indicators* (November 1962), p. v.

When people live to old age, they are likely to be unusually healthy individuals, and yet they are afflicted with chronic and degenerative diseases. This state of affairs is at odds with the popular conception of the health of the elderly. The image of old age today is as likely to be that of the vigorous, white-haired man on the golf course as it is that of the toothless grandsire in his rocking chair. Since we are focusing on the older population as a whole, we must first consider the health status of the aged in general before looking at the problems of those who are ill.

Over three-fourths of persons over 65 have some chronic health condition, almost twice the proportion found in the population as a whole (Table 2). Chronic health problems, however, do not suddenly appear when people pass the age of 65. Three-fifths of middle-aged persons (45 to 64) also have one or more chronic health conditions, which indicates that the elderly are likely to have lived with their health problems for a long time. Rather than the number of persons

Table 2 Percent of Population Limited in Activity and Mobility by Chronic Health Conditions: * *By Age*

	Percent Distribution		
	All Ages	Aged 45–64	Aged 65 and Over
Total population	100.0	100.0	100.0
Persons with no chronic conditions	58.1	38.7	21.3
Persons with one or more chronic conditions	41.9	61.3	78.7
Persons whose condition limits activity	10.9	18.3	45.1
Hindered in going to school, working, or keeping house	5.8	10.4	22.8
Prevented from going to school, working, or keeping house	2.3	2.9	15.5
Other limitation	2.8	5.0	6.8
Persons whose condition limits mobility	2.7	3.7	17.8
Trouble in getting around alone	1.6	2.5	9.9
Unable to get around alone	0.6	0.6	4.1
Confined to house	0.5	0.6	3.8

* The National Health Survey definition of a chronic condition is a very broad one. Many of these conditions are health complaints such as stiffness in the joints, chronic catarrh, and so on.
SOURCE: Adapted from *Health, Education and Welfare Indicators* (October 1962), p. xxi.

with chronic conditions, however, a better measure of health is one that is based on limitations of function. How many people cannot perform the tasks normal for their age? How many cannot move about freely because of illness or disability?

On these points Table 2 shows that of every 100 persons over 65, 45 have conditions that limit their activity in some way, for example, a weakened heart, arthritis or rheumatism, or a visual impairment. Only sixteen of these persons, however, are prevented from working or from keeping house. Eighteen cannot get around as they should, but only four are confined to their homes. Figures such as these can be interpreted as good or bad, depending on the reader's values and on whether one focuses on the present instead of the past, or the achievements instead of the potentialities of the society.

For old people who require more than routine medical care, the costs are likely to be major. For example, one of every six old persons is hospitalized during a given year; the average hospitalization is twice as long as for a younger person, and the average hospital bill is twice as large.[9] Until 1966, the old person was, furthermore, much less likely to have part of the costs defrayed by insurance. It was this situation which underlay the political controversy of the mid-1960s over providing hospital insurance for the elderly through social security, a controversy in which the issues were often obscured by the difficulties in drawing a line between the needy aged and *all* the aged. With the passage in 1965 of the federal legislation known as Medicare, the problems of the aged in meeting the economic costs of illness are likely to be greatly mitigated, even though it is as yet too soon to assess the full effects of the new legislation.

There are, of course, medical needs and costs other than hospitalization. There are physicians' and surgeons' fees, medicines, costs of nursing homes and convalescent homes. Because the economic aspect of health and disease constitutes a central problem for most older persons, we have introduced it first in discussing the economic status of the aged. Its significance can be assessed, however, only by viewing it in the context of other data that bear on the economic position of older people. The perspective must be broadened even further if we are to understand how the economic status of the aged relates to the changing economic and technological base of the society.

The Changing Economic Structure

Some people are alarmed at the growing numbers of the elderly and worry lest society be unable to support all the economic nonproducers,

[9] "The Older Population," *Health, Education and Welfare Indicators* (November 1962), pp. v–xii.

that is, persons who are under 18 or over 65. In 1963 those who fell outside the productive age group constituted about 46 percent of the population. This is a high proportion, but it is considerably smaller than it was in 1900 when children constituted a larger proportion of the population than now. Until 1985, because of the high birthrates of the 1940s and 1950s, people in the productive ages will continue to outnumber those in the preparatory and retirement age periods. It is also anticipated that a higher proportion of those in the productive age range will actually be in the work force, for more women will probably hold jobs both before their children are born and after their children are in school. This projection is based on the assumptions that the economy will continue to expand as the population grows, and that the forces of automation will not destroy old job classifications at a speed much greater than that at which they create new ones.

Men and women have also been working longer because they have been living longer. In 1900 a man could expect to work 32 years, and a woman about 6 years. Half a century later, the average work-life had risen to 42 years for men and to 18 for women. At the same time, productivity per man-hour has soared, so that the great proliferation of goods and services has occurred simultaneously with a cut in working hours. A striking juxtaposition is that a century ago a man worked a 70-hour week and had an average life expectancy of 40 years, whereas now these numbers have been reversed and a man works a 40-hour week and has an average life expectancy of 70 years.

The most recent changes in the economy have been brought about by cybernation, a term which means not only automation but also computer control and analysis, and the changes in design and production brought about by computer technology.[10] By the new methods, for example, a machine can form units of production, can adjust itself to compensate for wear, and can even replace its own worn parts, all with only cursory inspection by a human worker. A computer tells a manufacturer which styles sold best during the preceding week and sends instructions for production to the factory, just as another computer controls the path of a missile to the moon.

At present we can only guess about the effects this new industrial revolution will have on society and on the aged. It seems likely, however, that the American economy will be able easily to produce enough goods and services to support the growing number of older people as well as the growing number of children. The economic difficulties are likely to continue to lie in distribution and not in produc-

[10] The pamphlet by Donald N. Michael, *Cybernation: The Silent Conquest* (Santa Barbara, Calif.: Center for the Study of Democratic Institutions, 1962) provides a particularly interesting discussion of this topic.

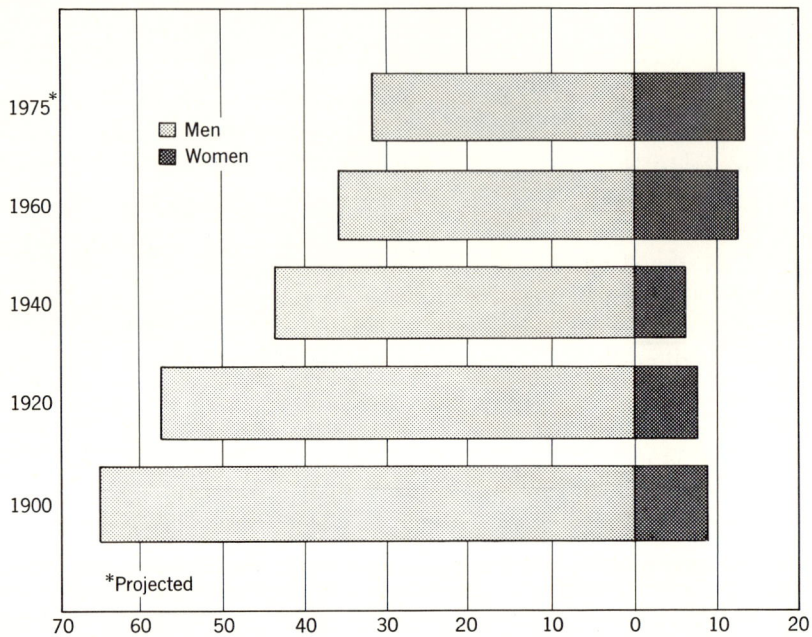

Figure 3 Percentage of men and women aged 65 and over in the labor force, 1900 to 1975. From the President's Council on Aging, *The Older American* (Washington, D.C.: U.S. Government Printing Office, 1963), p. 21.

tion. Predictions beyond this are obviously shaky, since there is every indication that the rate of social change is becoming even more accelerated than in the past few decades.

Yet it is clear that the period of economic change through which the present older generation has already lived has had a significant effect upon its employment status. Because the labor of all persons able to work is no longer required or even desired in the economy, the old as well as the young are encouraged to stay out of the labor market—the young, by staying in school; the old, by retiring.

Work Force Participation and Retirement

The sixty-fifth birthday has come to be regarded as the beginning of the retirement years (and thus as the beginning of old age), mainly because the first social security laws made benefits payable at age 65 and because private pension plans followed the same pattern. The trend since 1900 has been for men over 65 to leave the labor force (Figure 3). In part, this decline in proportion of aged male workers reflects the decline of agriculture and of small family businesses, in which it is relatively easy for an older man to keep working on a part-time basis. In the large companies that dominate the economic world today, it is becoming more common for all salaried workers to be retired at 65 or before, and for only younger workers to be hired. In several recent labor contracts that affect large numbers of workers, men are eligible for retirement at age 55. Consequently, some older men who want to continue working are being arbitrarily retired, and others are retiring voluntarily as social security and private retirement plans enable them to do so.

Figure 3 shows also that, contrary to the trend for older men, there are more older women in the labor force today than there were in 1900. Many of these women have gone to work to supplement their husband's retirement income; others have kept on working past retirement age. They work primarily in traditional women's service occupations which have as yet been little affected by automation. They are, for example, clerks, salesladies, and office workers—often working part time rather than full time.

Retirement itself is a recent economic and social fact. Industrial pension plans began to appear in the nineteenth century, but they covered relatively few workers, and most such plans foundered in the Great Depression. By the mid-1940s, some ten years after the passage of the Social Security Act, less than 4 percent of the aged were benefiting from social security, but almost 25 percent were drawing Old Age Assistance. Old age at that time was commonly regarded as calamitous. The older person, supposedly forced to retire and without financial reserves, was unable to find another job because of age or health.

In the succeeding 20 years, the economic position of the elderly improved steadily. As more persons retired with longer periods of steady work behind them, social security checks automatically became larger. In addition, benefits were extended and increased. Private pension plans also became more common and were established on a sound financial basis. By the early 1960s, over two-thirds of all older people were receiving social security benefits, whereas the proportion depending on Old Age Assistance had dropped by one-half.

In coming years more workers will retire before, rather than after, they reach 65. As of 1966, amendments to the Social Security Act (which will eventually cover almost all workers) make it possible for retirees to draw benefits starting at 62 and for widows to draw pensions at age 60. Most of the large private pension plans also provide for early retirement, and studies show that more workers are electing to retire early, at the same time that more companies are adopting compulsory retirement rules. The retired population as a result will become younger.

Retirement as a Social Problem

A commonly held belief has been that men want to work as long as they possibly can and that retirement is therefore harmful. Self-respect, so this argument runs, is bound up with earning a living. Without the economic function to perform, a man loses much of the meaning in life, feels worthless, perhaps depressed; in turn these feelings may lead to a decline in physical health.

There seems to be little empirical evidence to back up this belief. Research has shown that at higher levels of the occupational ladder the extra-economic meanings of work are increasingly important, and that a man's identity is closely tied up with his work career; but at lower occupational levels work tends to be less engrossing. As a result, attitudes toward retirement vary with occupational level. At present, highly skilled white-collar workers, executives, and professionals are the most likely of all to have the desire as well as the opportunity to keep on working beyond 65.

Indications are that the retired are in poorer health than workers of the same age, but research findings also show that illness more frequently develops before, not after, retirement, and that poor health is a major cause, not a result, of withdrawal from the labor force. There is also some evidence that health improves after retirement.[11]

The majority of persons retiring in the 1960s, reared in a social atmosphere in which the values and judgments of the Protestant Ethic prevailed, measure self-worth to a great extent by size of income and consider hard work a sign of moral virtue. Future generations will be more accustomed to leisure and are likely therefore to have less difficulty in adjusting to retirement. But it is still debatable whether retirement constitutes a major psychological trauma for most workers even at present.[12]

---

[11] Gordon F. Streib and Wayne E. Thompson, "Adjustment to Retirement," *Journal of Social Issues*, 14, 2 (1958), whole issue.

There are many recent studies of retirement. Two major researches which set the pattern for current empirical work, and whose findings are still relevant, are Eugene A. Friedmann and Robert J. Havighurst, *The Meanings of Work and Retirement* (Chicago: University of Chicago Press, 1954) and Guy Hamilton Crook and Martin Heinstein, *The Older Worker in Industry* (Berkeley: Institute of Industrial Relations, University of California, 1958).

For a good survey of the issues, see Margaret S. Gordon, "Work and Patterns of Retirement," in Robert W. Kleemeier, ed., *Aging and Leisure* (New York: Oxford University Press, 1961), pp. 15–53. See also Juanita M. Kreps, ed., *Employment, Income, and Retirement Problems of the Aged* (Durham, N.C.: Duke University Press, 1963).

[12] See Kleemeier, *op. cit.*, for a noteworthy collection of papers that deal with leisure and the meaningful use of time. See also Max Kaplan, "The Uses of

Retirement, as it is now occurring in the lives of most Americans, requires major changes in the pattern of life, with consequent reorganization of the use of time, and with different social relationships which usually involve not only the loss of working colleagues but also concomitant changes in family and community roles. Whereas for some

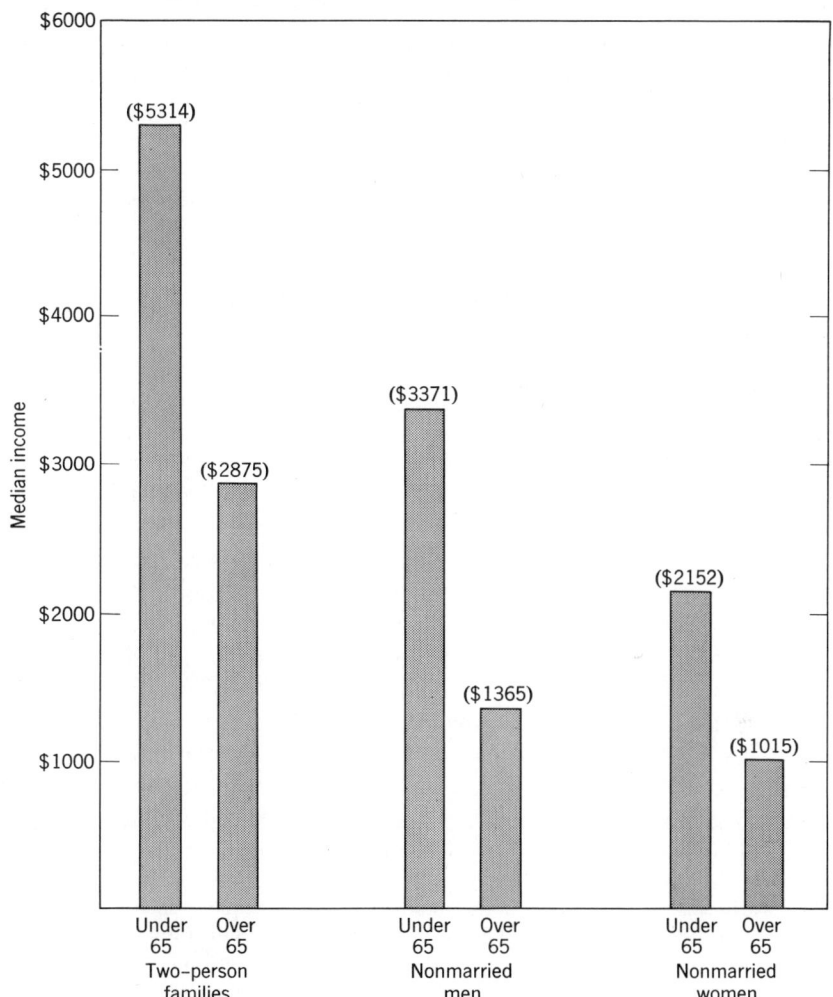

Figure 4 Comparison of median incomes of persons over 65 with those of persons under 65. Data for persons under 65 from 1960 Census, for persons over 65 from 1963 Survey of the Aged. From Lenore A. Epstein, "Income of the Aged in 1962," *Social Security Bulletin*, 27, 3 (March 1964), p. 8.

Leisure," in Tibbitts, ed., *op. cit.*, pp. 407–443; and James C. Charlesworth, ed., *Leisure in America: Blessing or Curse?* (Monograph 4) (Philadelphia: American Academy of Political and Social Science, April 1964).

persons retirement is a highly unwelcome event, for others it is welcome. Adjustment to retirement depends on different factors for different individuals, but for the average worker it depends largely on the amount of income he maintains after he stops working and the extent to which the drop in income is felt to create hardship or deprivation.

As a group, older people, of course, have much less income than younger people, for the majority over 65 do not work, and many of those who do work are employed only part time. Comparative incomes are shown in Figure 4, with the data for persons aged 65 and over based on a special government survey carried out in 1963.[13] Because comparable data for younger persons are available only for 1960, the comparisons are not altogether accurate. Median income for persons under 65 had undoubtedly risen in the intervening few years, so that the differences between age groups are probably greater than those indicated.

It is, of course, not the actual amount that is important, but the adequacy of the income to the person who receives it. Is the income of the elderly adequate to meet the current cost of living? Can it provide not merely subsistence, but the style of life older people themselves consider necessary for a dignified, respectable old age? Can it take care of emergencies?

These questions are difficult to answer. Poverty is relative; different people have different ideas of what it takes to live decently. There is great variation in income which is obscured by these median figures. For example, 5 percent of all elderly couples receive 10,000 dollars or more a year, while 5 percent receive less than 1000 dollars.

In order to obtain some objective measure of the adequacy of income, the United States Bureau of Labor Statistics worked out a budget that would enable an elderly couple or a single person living in a city to maintain an independent household at a "modest but adequate" standard of living, assuming good health. This amount for a couple is

---

[13] For various reasons, the economic status of older people was not accurately reflected in 1960 census data. The Social Security Administration therefore in 1963 undertook a special survey to investigate the income and other economic assets, the living arrangements, and the medical-care needs of older people. Analyses of these data have appeared in installments in the *Social Security Bulletin*. Various analyses of the economic status of the aged which appeared in the early 1960s and which were based upon the 1960 census data, including Michael Harrington, *The Other America* (New York: The Macmillan Company, 1962), and Harold L. Ohrbach and Clark Tibbitts, eds., *Aging and the Economy* (Ann Arbor: University of Michigan Press, 1963), have for the most part drawn too bleak a picture of the economic status of the aged and stand in need of qualification.

2500 dollars; for a single old person it is 1800 dollars. If we arbitrarily take these figures as the criteria, we find that 72 percent of elderly couples have enough income, but only 32 percent of single men and only 17 percent of single women have adequate income.[14] The financial position of nonmarried women over 65, most of whom are widows, is thus especially poor.

Amount of annual income is only part of the picture. For one thing, older persons are favored by the income tax; the most recent laws grant them additional personal exemptions as well as extra medical expense deductions, so that a great many older people pay no federal income tax. For another thing, one of the greatest worries of old age, that of paying the costs of prolonged or catastrophic illness, has now been assuaged by the 1965 changes in the Social Security Act that provide medical care for persons over 65. Older people, when compared with younger adults, have more savings, more frequently own their own homes, and less frequently have installment debts. On the other hand, those aged persons who have the lowest incomes are also those who have the fewest assets.

Because of these and other complicating factors, the economic status of the aged is not easily assessed. It is even debatable whether a comparison between the old and the young is justifiable, since material needs are so different at successive stages in the life cycle. Although it is exactly about economic status that the greatest controversy exists between those who are and those who are not convinced that most of the aged are needy, it is probably a fair conclusion that the financial position of most aged persons is not comfortable. Whereas the majority of married couples can manage on their incomes, the great majority of the single, especially the widows, do not have sufficient income to live independently.

Predictions for succeeding decades are even more difficult. Certainly the small incomes of elderly women will improve as more women earn social security benefits in their own right. Both men and women in future decades will retire after having earned higher wages for longer periods of time than is true for those retiring today, and after having built up greater social security and pension benefits. These factors are operating to raise retirement income, but other factors are operating to depress it. For instance, more workers are retiring before age 65 and taking reduced benefits; the cost of living is rising; in the next two decades, probably fewer than a third of the aged will enjoy private pension benefits; and finally, the elderly population is growing fastest

[14] Lenore A. Epstein, "Income of the Aged in 1962: First Findings of the 1963 Survey of the Aged," *Social Security Bulletin*, 27, 3 (March 1964), p. 3.

in those age brackets where the lowest incomes are found. More and more elderly widows will be added to the aged population; and although their incomes may be expected to improve, there is little likelihood that they will improve enough in the foreseeable future to meet a "modest but adequate" budget for independent living.

From a long-range perspective, unless there is some major reversal of social values, the aged in American society may be expected to gain a more equitable share of the goods and services of the economy. They are likely in the long run to benefit somewhat more than younger groups if the war on poverty is successful and if the society as a whole becomes more affluent.

The Aged in the Family Setting

Within the institution of the family, the status of the aged has been affected, first of all, by changes in timing of the events of the family cycle. These changes have been dramatic over the past decades. Age at marriage has dropped. Children have been born earlier in the marriage. With increased longevity, the duration of marriage has increased. As shown in Table 3, with analyses based primarily on census data, parenthood is occurring earlier and the period of child rearing is becoming shorter. Children are not only being born increasingly soon after

Table 3 Median Age of Husband and Wife at Successive Events in the Family Cycle

Stage	1890	1940	1950	1959
Median age of wife at				
First marriage	22.0	21.5	20.1	20.2
Birth of last child*	31.9	27.1	26.1	25.8
Marriage of last child	55.3	50.0	47.6	47.1
Death of husband	53.3	60.9	61.4	63.6
Median age of husband at				
First marriage	26.1	24.3	22.8	22.3
Birth of last child	36.0	29.9	28.8	27.9
Marriage of last child	59.4	52.8	50.3	49.2
Death of wife	57.4	63.6	64.1	65.7

* It is suggested that these ages are probably too young by a year or two for all dates, according to Bureau of the Census data, collected in August 1959, based upon cohorts of women.
SOURCE: Paul C. Glick, David M. Heer, and John C. Beresford, "Family Formation and Family Composition: Trends and Prospects," paper read at annual meeting of the American Association for the Advancement of Science, Chicago, December 1959, p. 12.

marriage, they are also apparently being spaced more closely together (though not shown in the table) and are growing up and leaving home at an earlier age. As a consequence, grandparenthood is also occurring at an earlier chronological age than in preceding generations.[15]

Historically, the family cycle may be said to have quickened, for marriage, parenthood, and grandparenthood all occur earlier now than in 1900. Yet widowhood tends to occur *later* than before. The trend, therefore, is toward a more rapid rhythm of events through most of the family cycle, followed by an extended interval (now some fifteen to seventeen years) in which husband and wife are the remaining members of the household, a period which has come to be called the period of the *gerontic* family.

The significance of the gerontic family can perhaps be assessed by noting that the post-child-rearing period for older couples is now approximately two-thirds as long as the child-rearing period itself. It is then followed by a long period of widowhood, especially for women who, because of their disproportionate number, do not remarrry at the same rate as men. (Approximately 25 percent of men but 55 percent of women are widowed in the age group 65 and over.)

Although relatively few studies have thus far been made of marital relationships in the gerontic family, of adjustment to widowhood, or of remarriage patterns, intergenerational relations now constitute a growing area of research for sociologists who are interested in the family. Theoretical positions have changed in the past few years as large sets of empirical data which relate specifically to the presence or absence

---

[15] Despite the fact that the family constitutes a major area for sociological research and that sociologists have given much attention to marital and parental roles, there has been surprisingly little research on the role of grandparent. Exceptions include Ruth Albrecht, "The Parental Responsibilities of Grandparents," *Marriage and Family Living*, 16 (1954), pp. 201–204; and Bernice L. Neugarten and Karol K. Weinstein, "The Changing American Grandparent," *Journal of Marriage and the Family*, 26 (1964), pp. 199–204. The latter report suggests that grandparenthood is becoming a middle-age more than an old-age phenomenon, and that styles of being a grandparent vary consistently with age of grandparent. A cross-cultural study by Dorrian Apple Sweetser, "The Social Structure of Grandparenthood," in Robert F. Winch, Robert McGinnis, and Herbert B. Barringer, eds., *Selected Studies in Marriage and the Family* (New York: Holt, Rinehart and Winston, 1962), pp. 388–396, shows that among the 51 societies studied, those in which grandparents were removed from family authority are those in which grandparents have an equalitarian relationship with grandchildren, but in those societies in which economic power rests with the old, relationships between grandparents and grandchildren are formal and authoritarian. Peter Townsend, *The Family Life of Old People* (London: Routledge and Kegan Paul, 1957), reports that among working-class Londoners, although many grandmothers maintain responsibility for the care of a grandchild, the relationship between child and grandparent is one, by and large, of "privileged disrespect."

of the extended family network in modern America have become available.

Intergenerational Relations

It is often said that at the beginning of this century, when the society was more rural than urban and when transportation and communication were more limited, a large proportion of children grew up and settled near the parental home; and that as a result the typical American family of the early 1900s was a large and extended social unit. Children, parents, and grandparents (and often aunts, uncles, and other family members) presumably lived close to each other on nearby farms, or small towns, or within the same city neighborhoods.

Some persons tend to look back with nostalgia to earlier historical periods. It is often said, furthermore, that there was greater family solidarity 50 or 100 years ago, that adult children willingly assumed economic support of aged parents, and that they generally showed more respect and devotion than they do today. This view has not been merely a stereotype held by the uninformed; sociologists in the 1940s and 1950s stressed that the nuclear family (husband, wife, and children) living independent from kin had become the typical family structure; that it was the one required in a developing industrial society in which both geographical and occupational mobility are prevalent; and that a true historical change had therefore occurred in family structure. In this view, aged parents, living in separate households from their children, had become socially and psychologically isolated from their children, from their more distant kin, and—because of the anonymity of modern urban life—from the community as well.

No doubt with increased urbanization the nuclear family unit has become the dominant household pattern; but, given the empirical evidence that is accumulating, there is good reason to question whether the nuclear unit ever replaced the extended family network. For one thing, it is not so clear that the large household of the extended kinship family was ever the prevailing one. In a study of New York City households in 1703, for example, only 4 percent could be considered three-generational, and the investigator concluded that "we do not know whether a majority of the aged were ever cared for in this manner in our country's history." [16] Nor is the three-generation household itself the only issue at question. It is not clear, either, that there has been historical change in regard to the geographical proximity between aged parents and children. American life has always been char-

---

[16] Eugene A. Friedmann, *op. cit.*, pp. 130–131.

acterized by high rates of geographic mobility, not just with the onset of industrialization and urbanization, but from early in our history with the opportunity for sons to leave the parental household to establish their own homes on the frontier.

There are studies, furthermore, which indicate that currently an exchange of aid among family units flows both within and between familial generations, with the greatest portion passing between parents and children. Contrary to what many believe, the flow is downward from parents to children rather than upward from children to parents.[17] This assistance takes many forms. Parents finance college educations after their children have married, assist young couples in establishing homes, give business advice, gifts and loans, and take care of grandchildren. Families stand ready also to house relatives temporarily and to locate jobs for kin who are planning to move into their area.

Along with this aid should be included the social supports supplied by the kin. The difficulty in establishing close friendships in urban areas often gives special importance to social activities with relatives; indeed, informal visiting between relatives appears to be more important to city dwellers than visiting with neighbors, fellow workers, or friends, especially at lower-class levels. It has become clear that in modern America the extended kinship system still occupies a position of considerable importance. Therefore it seems more realistic to consider the nuclear family as the basic unit of the kin system rather than as an isolated social unit.

The family network also extends between generations, involving a variety of services to old persons, with younger members giving physical care, escorting, shopping, and performing household tasks. Such patterns are characteristic of the middle as well as the lower class. Recent studies have shown not only that extended family relations are possible in urban society, whether or not family units live in close proximity, but also that in many ways the family structure is one that may properly be called a *modified* extended kin family, in which various units give aid to other units and thereby facilitate, rather than block, geographical and occupational mobility of both old and young.[18] Given this view, the gerontic family unit is not isolated but forms part of the extended family network.

[17] One study showing this is Marvin B. Sussman, "The Help Pattern in the Middle Class Family," *American Sociological Review*, 18 (February 1953), pp. 22–28.

[18] This interpretation of the structure of the modern family, as well as the empirical studies on which the interpretation is based, is discussed at greater length in Marvin B. Sussman, "Relationships of Adult Children with Their

Living Arrangements

It is customary for old people today to maintain their own households as long as they are able. Over half of those 65 and over were living independently at the beginning of the 1960s, as shown in Table 4. This arrangement is the preferred one in the opinions of both younger and older generations, and does not necessarily isolate the older person.

Table 4   Living Arrangements of Persons 65 and Over, 1961

	Total 65 and Over	Men	Women
	Percentages		
Married, spouse present	50.9	31.2	19.7
Living with a relative other than spouse	23.1	6.0	17.1
Living alone or lodging	22.3	6.1	16.2
In institutions	3.7	1.5	2.2
Total	100.0	44.8	55.2

SOURCE: Adapted from *Health, Education and Welfare Indicators* (November 1962), p. xv.

The data in Table 5 indicate that older parents generally live near at least one child, and modern highways and the telephone make communication easy. In one recent survey, 83 percent of the older people interviewed said they preferred their own households, and about the same proportion said they saw their children at least once a week.[19]

Although many older people are concerned lest they become financially dependent on their children, most adult children are willing to assume responsibility for aged parents, to help with medical bills, and to find new housing when it is needed; some move their own homes in order to be near aged parents.[20] Married daughters more often than

---

Parents in the United States," in Ethel Shanas and Gordon F. Streib, eds., *Social Structure and the Family* (Englewood Cliffs, N.J.: Prentice-Hall, 1965). Among the empirical studies, two by Eugene Litwak are of particular interest: "Occupational Mobility and Extended Family Cohesion," and "Geographic Mobility and Extended Family Cohesion," *American Sociological Review*, 25 (February 1960), pp. 9–21, and (June 1960), pp. 385–394.

[19] See Ethel Shanas, "Older People and Their Families," in *The Health of Older People* (Cambridge: Harvard University Press, 1962), pp. 107–141; also Sussman, *op. cit.*

[20] Shanas, *op. cit.*; also Sussman, *op. cit.*

married sons will share their homes with widowed or ill parents. In general, intergenerational ties are strengthened more often than weakened by widowhood, illness, or the onset of extreme old age.

Living arrangements of the elderly are, of course, directly related to health and age. Old persons in poor health are less likely to be living alone than persons with good or fair health; and by the time people reach age 85, fewer than 20 percent live alone (about 20 percent are still living with their spouses, and over 43 percent are living with a relative other than spouse).

Table 5 Location of Nearest Child of Persons 65 and Over *

	Men	Women
	Percentages	
Child in same household	23	32
Ten minutes or less distant	33	33
Ten to 60 minutes distant	25	21
More than 60 minutes distant	19	14
Total	100	100

* Based on a nationwide sample of 2442 noninstitutionalized older people, 82.4 percent of whom reported living children. Data subject to sampling variation.
SOURCE: Adapted from Ethel Shanas, "Family and Household Characteristics of Older People in the United States," in *Age with a Future,* Proceedings of the Sixth International Congress of Gerontology, Copenhagen, 1963 (Philadelphia: F. A. Davis Company, 1964), pp. 449–454.

In one respect there has been a major, long-range shift in the relations between generations. The economic support of the aged has become the function, not of the family but of government and economic institutions, through the growth of social security pension plans. There is little evidence, however, that social and emotional ties between parents and children have lessened.[21] We do not mean that there are not isolated older people; however, they are in the minority, not the majority. Among this minority are many who were probably isolated before they reached old age because of their lack of family ties or because of

[21] See Alvin L. Schorr, *Filial Responsibility in the Modern American Family* (Washington, D.C.: Social Security Administration, U.S. Department of Health, Education and Welfare, 1960).

psychological reasons. Old age does not automatically bring loneliness and social deprivation.

Thus far, we have not mentioned persons living in institutions. Although the proportion of the institutionalized rises with age, even in advanced old age (among those 75 and over) the number does not exceed a few percent of the total. It is because of the absolute increase in numbers of the very aged that there has been a recent proliferation of homes for the aged, nursing homes, and convalescent homes.[22] Actually, the growth of other forms of congregate living, such as special housing projects and retirement villages both for low- and high-income groups of aged, may more properly be regarded as a new historical phenomenon. We shall return to this point presently.

Prospects

In viewing the status of the aged in American society, we have chosen certain perspectives and social institutions and omitted others. We should return, however, to consideration of the aged in the overall age-status system. In pointing out certain parallels between adolescents and the aged as two age-separated groups, the question was raised whether the aged constitute a subculture.

The matter is debatable. The increase in the proportion of those who are retired has made the aged a socially visible group which has become a focus for both social service and political action in recent decades. As yet, however, evidence of a developing subculture of the aged is equivocal at best. There are, to be sure, some tendencies toward residential segregation. There are disproportionately large numbers of the aged in rural counties, chiefly in the Middle West, in the older neighborhoods of large cities, and in older suburbs. There are a growing number, although still a small proportion, who migrate to retirement communities in California, other Southwestern states, Florida, and Mexico. In such retirement communities a subculture of the aged may be developing, oriented to the use of leisure, as suggested by some observers who point out that socioeconomic, sex, and ethnic differences have less influence upon the social relationships of the inhabitants

[22] For a discussion of social policies about care of the aged (in particular, the issue of institutionalized care) within the British setting, see Peter Townsend, *The Last Refuge* (London: Routledge and Kegan Paul, 1962) and Barbara E. Shenfield, *Social Policies for Old Age* (London: Routledge and Kegan Paul, 1957). Many of the issues apply equally to the United States. See also, for various American points of view, Jerome Kaplan and Gordon J. Aldridge, eds., *Social Welfare of the Aging* (New York: Columbia University Press, 1962).

in retirement communities than is characteristic for other American communities.[23]

The next generation of retired people will be different from the present one in income, education, and ethnic backgrounds. Whether these older persons will become increasingly segregated, by choice or not, cannot be determined. Higher incomes, better health, and more years of retirement may well stimulate the further development of a subculture of leisure for the aged—a development which may, by making old age a more attractive period of life, raise the prestige of this age group.

Related to the question of residential separation is the question of political separation. There has been a great deal written, pro and con, on whether there is a politics of age developing in the United States. Most political sociologists tend to agree that, for groups under 65, other factors (geographical, ethnic, religious, educational) override age in influencing political and voting behavior; but there is a rising controversy over the extent considerations of age are beginning to dominate the political views of groups over 65. Some suggest that, with increased numbers of retired persons living on fixed incomes, and with the host of other economic and social changes that lead to increasing visibility of the aged as a group, a social movement is being created in which consciousness of age is the dominant feature. This movement is predicted ultimately to have political overtones.

The opposite point of view is put forth with equal conviction. Some political analysts point to the short-lived character of political movements among the aged in the Depression years (the EPIC, Ham-and-Eggs, and Townsend movements). They regard the growth of the McLain movement in California in the late 1950s as stemming from a set of special circumstances and point out that no political movements of the aged seem to be developing in areas where the aged form a large proportion of the stable population. Old people seem thus far to be inclined to "vote their age" only on such issues as medical care; and even on that issue evidence was ambiguous that by the mid-1960s the aged were indeed voting as a bloc.[24]

---

[23] Calvin Trillin, "Wake Up and Live," *The New Yorker*, 40, 7 (April 4, 1964), pp. 120–177, describes the tempo of life in one of the 250 retirement communities that now exist in the United States. See also Ernest W. Burgess, ed., *Retirement Villages* (Ann Arbor: University of Michigan Press, 1961) for descriptions of various forms of congregate living seen from the perspectives of sociologists, economists, architects, and others.

[24] Data on political participation by age, and various interpretations of the data, are to be found in Angus Campbell, "Social and Psychological Determinants of

It remains to be established whether a politics of old age will emerge on the American scene, and if so, whether it will be more than a temporary phenomenon; or if the aged will in the long run continue, as now, to be integrated into existing political parties.

It is a somewhat different question, however, to ask whether America is moving toward a gerontocracy, a society in which economic and political power rests in the hands of individuals who are old. The trend has indeed been for political leaders, like economic leaders, to become older from decade to decade, up to 1960.[25] In general—and despite some striking exceptions—the more recently elected the official, and the more his responsibility, the older he is. On the state level, representatives are younger than senators, and both are younger than governors, which reflects not only the underlying increase in longevity but also seniority. United States Senators have not aged much but they have been a relatively senior group since 1900 (the average age of Senators in 1899 was 56.8; in 1962 it was 58). The average age of Representatives, however, had risen from 48 to 53 in the same period of time. Cabinet members have also tended to become older in successive decades; the median age of all cabinet members was 55 in the period from 1900 to 1924; it rose to 60 in the next 25 years.

The aging trend is most notable in the judiciary, especially at the state supreme court level. To take but one example, a century ago (in the period from 1838 to 1868) justices of the Iowa Supreme Court were 37 years old, on the average, when they took the oath of office. During the period from 1933 to 1961, however, the average was 58. For federal Supreme Court justices, the average beginning age reached a high of 59 during the period from 1920 to 1932, then declined to 54 from 1933 to 1961.[26] This reversal probably reflects an

---

Voting Behavior," in Wilma Donahue and Clark Tibbitts, eds., *Politics of Age* (Ann Arbor: Division of Gerontology, University of Michigan, 1962), pp. 87–100; Angus Campbell et al., *The American Voter* (New York: John Wiley and Sons, 1960); Robert E. Lane, *Political Life* (Glencoe, Ill.: The Free Press, 1959); and Seymour M. Lipset, *Political Man: The Social Bases of Politics* (Garden City, N.Y.: Doubleday, 1960).

[25] The average age of business executives has risen steadily since 1870, when average age of the business elite was 45 (it is now approximately 54). In the shorter interval between 1928 and 1952, the increase was from four to six years. See Francis W. Gregory and Irene D. Neu, "The American Industrial Elite in the 1870's," in William Miller, ed., *Men in Business* (Cambridge, Mass.: Harvard University Press, 1952), pp. 193–211; and W. Lloyd Warner and James C. Abegglen, *Occupational Mobility in American Business and Industry, 1928–1952* (Minneapolis: University of Minnesota Press, 1955).

[26] These data on age of state representatives, governors, congressmen, cabinet members, and judges have been culled from a variety of sources, including John C.

important political issue that arose in the 1930s when President Roosevelt's proposals for enlarging the Supreme Court as a means of overcoming its political conservatism (the so-called "court-packing" proposals) became an attack upon "nine tired old men."

Although the age of political leaders or the judiciary seldom becomes controversial, old age became a source of anxiety at least twice in the recent past: with the death of President Roosevelt and the illnesses of President Eisenhower. It may be that public attention focused more upon the health of presidential candidates and incumbents than upon their age per se. Yet some observers see significance in one of the oldest American presidents, Eisenhower, being followed in office by one of the youngest, Kennedy; and they perceive a reversal of the long-term trend toward gerontocracy in American government in such occurrences as the average age of cabinet members dropping ten years, from 58 for the Eisenhower Cabinet to 48 for the Kennedy Cabinet. It remains to be seen whether these events indicate that a significant change is taking place in the age-status system of American society, a change that represents a reaction against the investment of political and governmental power in the hands of the aged.

We should, however, in closing this discussion of the aged, turn from the leaders of society (who, because of their personal qualities, are likely to be atypical in a great many respects) and consider once again the ordinary American citizen who is passing from middle to old age. There is no doubt that, with continuing rapid technological and social change, the age-status sytem will also continue to change, and that social complexity is likely to increase rather than decrease in the next several decades. Life styles are likely, as a consequence, to become more varied among the aged just as they become more varied among the young. As society recognizes a greater number of life styles for older people, present stereotypes about the aged are likely to break down and a climate of increasing permissiveness may come to characterize life for the elderly. The older person of the future is likely to have a healthier, more vigorous, and longer life ahead of him than his counterpart of half a century or a century ago. Moreover, he will have

---

Wahlke, Heinz Eulau, William Buchanan, and Leroy C. Ferguson, *The Legislative System* (New York: John Wiley and Sons, 1962); John K. Gurwell, "Governors of the States," *State Government*, 14 (July 1941), p. 157; Harvey C. Lehman, "The Age of Eminent Leaders: Then and Now," *American Journal of Sociology*, 52 (January 1947), p. 342; "Aging in General," *The Gerontologist*, 2, 2 (June 1962), pp. 104–105; and John R. Schmidhauser, "Age and Judicial Behavior: American Higher Appellate Judges," in Wilma Donahue and Clark Tibbitts, eds., *Politics of Age* (Ann Arbor: Division of Gerontology, University of Michigan, 1962), pp. 101–116.

open to him more ways in which to spend his time. It is not impossible that "old age" may in the future come to mean life beyond age 75 rather than 65, and "the aged" may come to mean merely a great many different types of people who have grown old.

Part Two

Problems of Deviance

5

Delinquency and Crime

Stanton Wheeler

UNLIKE some problems in this book, there has never been serious disagreement about whether crime is a social problem. Crime's social and economic costs are too great; nor is crime a recent problem. And unlike problems created by urban growth, international tensions, and possible nuclear war, crime has long been with human societies, and efforts have long been made to control it. As a result, everyone is an amateur criminologist, with views about the causes of crime and potential remedies for it.

Despite centuries of concern, there are few settled solutions and few indisputable facts. This chapter reviews some of the leading problems and issues in the objective study of crime. We will see how social scientists have developed their perspectives on crime causation and control, and what current issues stir the minds of those whose occupation is the study and control of crime. Sometimes these issues are questions of fact, and sometimes questions of value. But in both cases there are exciting problems that often go far beyond an immediate criminal act. The limits of a chapter are such that there can be no thorough examination of each issue and problem; however, nothing prevents a student from exploring them further on his own.

Crime and criminal law. Crimes are distinguished from all other forms of problematic or deviant behavior by their legal character. Crimes are defined by the legislative and judicial branches of a governing political area, such as a state or the federal government. The label "criminal" provides the justification for invoking the full powers of such reactive agencies as the police, the courts, and prisons. Defining an action as criminal allows the *legitimate* use of force by the state against its citizens and may lead to deprivation of liberty and, in some jurisdictions, of life *with* due process of law.

Yet not *all* patterns of conduct of which we disapprove are defined as crimes. What, then, distinguishes those disapproved lines of conduct that find their way into our legal codes from those that do not? Legal scholars and philosophers have tried to find a rationale that provides clear guidance in deciding which disapproved acts should be labeled criminal and which should not. A major question concerns the appropriate balance between a purely *moral* component of the criminal law and a *secular* concern for social harms and damage to the community.

Some persons find the dominant aim and purpose underlying the criminal law in the moral traditions or "mores" of the community. As one authority puts it, crime is "conduct which, if duly shown to have taken place, will incur the formal and solemn pronouncement of the moral condemnation of the community."[1] The community labels as criminal those lines of conduct it sees as immoral, and its official actions amount to a pronouncement of moral condemnation, whatever penalties are attached signifying the degree of condemnation that offense deserves.

An alternative line of reasoning lays stress not on the moral dimension of conduct, but rather on its social danger for the community. Crimes are acts dangerous to the community, quite apart from their moral character. In this view there should be a clear distinction between crime and sin. A crime is an action dangerous to the community. Sin is the business of the home and church; the inculcation of proper moral values is not the prime purpose of the law.[2]

These two lines of reasoning apply equally well to much of our traditional criminal law, since that law typically refers to conduct considered both dangerous to the community and morally wrong. All societies have apparently found it necessary to establish some limits on the willful destruction of life and limb, the destruction or theft of property, and the free use of deceit, trickery, and lying in human affairs.[3] When our courts continue to enforce the rules that form part of our cultural heritage, or when legislative bodies pass criminal statutes referring to and perhaps clarifying traditional elements of the common law of crimes, we can see a reasonably close connection between the law on the books and the organized sentiments of a community. Although many may violate these rules, there are few in

[1] Henry M. Hart, "The Aims of the Criminal Law," *Law and Contemporary Problems*, 23, 3 (Summer 1958), pp. 401, 405.
[2] Wolfenden Report in Parliament, *Criminal Law Review* (England), 1959, p. 38.
[3] H. L. A. Hart, *The Concept of Law* (London: Oxford University Press, 1961).

most modern societies who do not agree that they *are* legitimate rules.

As social life becomes more complex, as societies move from a simpler and more homogeneous community life, as subcultures develop within segments of society, it becomes more difficult to sustain a close bond between the legal and the moral orders. As these social changes occur, two new conditions change the traditional relation between the criminal law and its moral and social underpinnings. First, new products, inventions, and modes of thought arise and exert influence in areas where there is no settled community opinion. The presence of the new elements and the absence of a fixed opinion help break down the traditional relationships, since the new conditions become defined by special segments of the population and may fail to reflect settled legal or social opinion. Three brief examples will be noted in the areas of white-collar crime, sex offenses, and narcotics addiction.

New forms of commerce, trade, and industry have brought about the need for controls to prevent their misuse. This need, in turn, has brought about the passage of laws administered primarily by federal regulatory agencies, such as the Pure Food and Drug Administration, the Federal Trade Commission, and the Anti-Trust Division of the Justice Department. But the technical economic and legal issues involved in decisions concerning such matters as unfair advertising practices and corporate attempts to set prices in violation of federal legislation involve highly complex problems about which the public cannot possibly be well informed. In such cases, then, the final forms of the statutes and their administration depend primarily on informal bargaining and power relations among the various interested parties. These factors are one reason why illegal gains resulting from the crimes of corporations are treated differently, with fewer penal sanctions, than are the more obvious but much less profitable endeavors of thieves and burglars.[4]

Special legislation that defines some sex offenders as psychopaths, to be treated in a manner unlike other traditional criminal violators, emerged only after there were new ideas in psychiatry and psychological diagnosis.[5] The concept of a sexual psychopath, who engages in sexual offenses in a pathological and conscience-free manner, arose during the early part of the twentieth century and was used as a basis for special legislation. Most often this legislation was written by those in the psychological specialties and was passed uncritically by state legislatures, responding to states of fear in the community. Among other problems was the vagueness in the definitions in these laws so that, unlike most

[4] Edwin H. Sutherland, *White Collar Crime* (New York: Dryden Press, 1949).
[5] Edwin H. Sutherland, "The Diffusion of Sexual Psychopath Laws," *American Journal of Sociology*, 56 (September 1950), pp. 142–148.

criminal legislation, the laws were difficult to apply. The diagnostic techniques themselves were also defective because they lacked a capacity to distinguish the truly dangerous from the relatively harmless sexual offender. Again, however, social changes leading to new ideas about diagnosis and treatment, in company with a state of fear in the community, led to new forms of criminal legislation in areas where the general public could not be expected to have a traditional, settled response.[6]

Still another pattern emerges in the case of legislation imposing punitive taxes on marijuana and bringing it under the control of the federal Treasury Department. Unlike the opium derivatives such as heroin and morphine, marijuana is not a physiologically addictive drug. It is not certain from current evidence whether smoking marijuana is more dangerous to health than smoking popular brands of cigarettes or drinking alcoholic beverages. Indeed, before the 1930s, only a few states had laws restricting the sale or use of marijuana, and there was no great evidence of community abhorrence of the drug. Passage of uniform state legislation outlawing marijuana use, and of the marijuana tax act was not, therefore, a simple reaction of legislators to the organized sentiments of the community. In this instance those very sentiments were themselves shaped and reinforced by the Federal Bureau of Narcotics. Whatever the case regarding the objective social danger of marijuana, the passage of legislation controlling its use was dependent on the activities of the Bureau, which generated enough support for the legal controls.[7]

Thus it is evident that in those areas where recent legislation has been enacted, we do not find a settled relation between either moral or social danger and the legal structure, except as that relationship is interpreted and specified by various segments of the community who typically have some interest in the outcome and are in a powerful enough position to make their influence felt. In these areas, as distinguished from our more traditional criminal law, the close tie among moral order, social danger, and legal order does not prevail.

Second, the same processes of social change that produce the unsettled relationships just described have the further consequence of secularization leading to a clearer separation of the traditional moral order from secular activities. This potential separation, and problems of defining the boundary between the moral and legal, arise insistently in more secularized societies, and have their influence on the criminal law

[6] *Ibid.*
[7] Howard S. Becker, *Outsiders: Studies in the Social Control of Deviants* (New York: The Free Press of Glencoe, 1963), pp. 135–146.

as on other parts of the social order, including civil rights legislation.

Perhaps the clearest current indication of the significance of this distinction is the legislation concerning sexual relations between consenting adults. Historically in America our criminal codes have made a criminal offense of almost every form of sexual relationship other than marriage. Some statutes, however, prohibit *all* sex relationships deemed unnatural. Fornication, adultery, lewd and lascivious cohabitation, to say nothing of homosexual relations between consenting adult partners —all are violations of the criminal codes in most of our states.

Efforts to develop a model penal code in this country and efforts of a special committee in England are directed to removing these "offenses" from our criminal law.[8] Advocates of the new legislation say that these acts are of moral but not of legal interest, because, provided the relationships are between consenting partners of mature age, they create no social danger. These persons desire to restrict the criminal sanctions to those instances that are clearly harmful to the social order. To quote from the American Law Institute's Model Penal Code: "The Code does not attempt to use the power of the state to enforce purely moral or religious standards. We deem it inappropriate for the government to attempt to control behavior that has no substantial significance except as to the morality of the action."[9] So far, few of our states have enacted legislation based on these principles; the important point in the present context is that there is increased support for such legislation among members of the bar both in England and the United States. Passage, however, depends on the success of the plea that the activities involved are of purely moral concern.

When the Wolfenden report was presented to the English House of Commons, there was general acceptance by members of Commons that conduct not injurious to society falls outside the legitimate concerns of the criminal law. But members of the House of Commons were uncertain that homosexuality between consenting adults was not injurious to society. There was fear that others might be easily corrupted if the act were not criminal, and that removing the legal sanctions might imply condonation of homosexuality.[10] So despite the lack of apparent social danger in acts between consenting adults, there remains the possibility of long-term harmful consequences. Arguments to this effect can always be made and are hard to refute empirically, especially if the pre-

---

[8] For a fuller description of laws regarding sexual offenses and efforts to change them, see Stanton Wheeler, "Sex Offenses: A Sociological Critique," *Law and Contemporary Problems*, 25, 2 (Spring 1960).
[9] *Model Penal Code* 207.1, comment at 207 (Tent. Draft No. 4, 1955).
[10] *Model Penal Code* 277–278 (Tent. Draft No. 4, 1955).

sumed effects take place over a long time span. Thus, in the absence of any evidence of social danger, moral considerations are likely to affect the perception of what is or is not dangerous. The attempt to draw a firm line between the two criteria may clarify the arguments, but is unlikely to resolve them.

Unfortunately, because there are few comparative studies of the process by which the criminal law is formed and modified, it is impossible to go further than a few illustrations of the instances of change or controversy, such as those just given. Hopefully, in the next few years there will be careful studies of how legislatures behave, given pressures to modify their criminal and penal codes, and the structure of the major groups proposing various forms of legislation will be examined. Such studies should provide us with better evidence for generalizations about the social foundations of criminal law and the forces that shape its change.[11] In the remainder of this chapter, we consider existing criminal law and turn our attention to those who violate it.

The data of criminology. Why do some men commit acts the law defines as criminal while others do not? This is perhaps the question most frequently asked in criminology. It is an intellectually stimulating question concerning human lives and the events that influence them. And it is a question of practical importance, for if we could answer it, we might be able to control crime. Yet it is a difficult question to attempt to answer adequately; after decades of data gathering and theorizing, it is not evident that our capacity to answer the question has improved significantly. We know much more than we did, but the knowledge is fragmentary. It has only rarely been possible to isolate crucial causal patterns, or to gather evidence in such a way that we can reject some ideas and accept others.

The chief reason why it is difficult to determine why some persons commit crimes is that it is difficult, if not impossible, to get a clear, reliable measure of who has and who has not committed a crime. We cannot know of all acts in violation of the criminal law, since many of them are never reported, either by those who commit them or by their victims. Given this lack of knowledge, most studies have relied on some official record of crime, such as police or court statistics. The moment we shift from the theoretical entity called the true crime rate to substitutes such as the rate of arrest or conviction, we introduce a new dimension in the analysis. Then we are assessing the activities of

[11] These problems are part of the broader issues involved in the study of sociology and law. For our recent review and bibliography see "Law and Society," supplement to *Social Problems*, 13, 1 (Summer 1965). See also Jerome Hall, *Theft, Law and Society* (Boston: Little, Brown, 1935).

the official agents of crime control—not simply the activities of criminals. There is a vast range of evidence documenting the *differential* detection of crimes and enforcement of the law, varying with the character of individual policemen, their departments, and the community where they work.

The labeling of a criminal, then, is the product of an *interaction* between citizens and officials, influenced by the character of both the potential law violator and the community. Among a group of 100 boys, for example, it is likely that some of those who have violated the law will not be detected in their violation while others will. If study shows that the percentage of Negro boys who violated the law was higher than the percentage of white boys, it may indicate one of two things: Negro boys, at least in this group, committed more violations; or Negro boys were detected more often. It is even possible that the white boys committed more offenses but were less often detected, so that the "true" rate is the reverse of the "official" rate.

This example illustrates the dilemma posed by official statistics of crime and criminals. They may not be directly related to the actual rate of crime; that rate, in turn, may never be known. Any study of variations in the "true crime rate" that uses official criminal records must recognize this problem. In the face of it, investigators have followed one of three paths.

1. Some have conducted studies of crime independent of official crime data. Perhaps the leading example of this sort of investigation is the work of Nye and Short.[12] These investigators developed a scale of reported delinquency based on questions asked a large sample of youths attending public schools. They then developed an index of reported delinquency based on the youths' answers to such questions as whether they had ever "taken little things (less than two dollars in value)," "defied parents to their face," "destroyed property," and so on. Then they compared the backgrounds of youths who score "high" on such an admitted delinquency scale with those who score low. The results, some of which we note later, indicate a number of the correlates of delinquency. One problem with this method is that it tends to discriminate among persons at a relatively low level of delinquency, but because few report serious offenses it appears less useful for studying the more serious, patterned, repetitive delinquent activities.

A related procedure is to question those who work closely with youths. In one study, gang workers used a checklist and noted all the

[12] F. Ivan Nye and James F. Short, Jr., "Scaling Delinquent Behavior," *American Sociological Review*, 22 (June 1957), pp. 326–331.

offenses that had been committed by each boy they knew well enough to rate.[13] Such questioning, dependent as it is on the skills and knowledge of the workers, is not altogether reliable, but it is free of the major bias produced when the informant is a member of a law enforcement agency.

2. A more frequent approach is to use the official records as an assumed approximation to the true crime rate, taking care to select the specific measures in a way that comes closest to removing the possible biases introduced by the law enforcement procedures themselves. Those who have worked closely with the official statistics have concluded that some are much more reliable than others and better serve the purposes of crime index construction. A chief procedural rule is that the further removed from the actual crime incident, the less reliable the statistics.[14] Thus indices based on police data are better than those based on court actions because the latter include the additional biases involved in the selection of cases for court action.

The index usually regarded as best is compiled by the Department of Justice and published annually by the FBI, along with related material, under the title "Uniform Crime Reports." [15] These reports are compiled from records sent to the FBI from 90 percent of urban and over 75 percent of rural areas. The reports list the type of offense and other pertinent data including date of offense, loss of property, and so on. When someone has actually been arrested for the offense there are additional data about the arrested person—primarily age, race, and sex. Arrest data are available currently for some two-thirds of the population areas of the United States. These two indices, "Crimes Known to the Police" and "Crimes Cleared by Arrest," provide the most frequently used source of official data about crime in the United States, the former for studying the volume and type of crime, the latter for studying characteristics of the offenders.

In addition to the attempt to avoid bias by using data closest to the commission of the act, most investigators use data for only those crimes likely to be most fully reported. The FBI index of major crimes is restricted to the following seven categories: murder and nonnegligent homicide, forcible rape, robbery, aggravated assault, burglary, larceny over 50 dollars, and auto theft. Many other types of

[13] James F. Short, Jr. and Fred L. Strodtbeck, *Group Process and Gang Delinquency* (Chicago: University of Chicago Press, 1965), pp. 77–101.
[14] This and other principles regarding the use of official statistics are thoroughly reviewed in Thorsten Sellin and Marvin E. Wolfgang, *The Measurement of Delinquency* (New York: John Wiley and Sons, 1964).
[15] Federal Bureau of Investigation, United States Department of Justice, "Uniform Crime Reports," *Crime in the United States*, 1963.

offense, such as shoplifting or certain types of sex offenses, are simply not fully enough reported to be even moderately reliable indicators of the number of such crimes.

Internal checks can often be used to supplement the official data. For example, data on the cause of death in mortality statistics can be used in comparing one jurisdiction with another, to supplement the data yielded by the police statistics. This provides data on crime victims comparable to that sought by the police.

Finally, for the study of variations in crime rates in different jurisdictions or of the background characteristics of those who do as opposed to those who do not commit crime, the important element is comparability. If the amount, type, or direction of bias is consistent and moderate across different groups, we can draw valid conclusions. The difficulty, of course, is that it is just those variables believed likely to produce genuine differences in the probability of criminal acts that are also most likely to be *differentially* reported and responded to by police. For example, if the delinquency rate is lower in the suburbs than in central cities, lower among middle-class than among lower-class youths, and lower among children from intact rather than broken homes, is it because these factors truly prevent crimes, or is it because police are less likely to take official actions against suburban, middle-class youths? Unfortunately, there is simply no way to avoid this problem short of accumulating as much evidence as possible, from a variety of sources, to demonstrate that (in the case under study) the actions of the police or other agencies are not contributing a major portion of the variation in outcome.

3. An alternative way of using official data is to assume that in fact they tell us more about those who participate in reporting and compiling the data than they do about the lawbreaker. Under this alternative, we turn the problem around and ask: What is there in the nature of the individual police officer, the police department, court jurisdiction, or the community each serves that leads one person or jurisdiction to arrest or prosecute more offenders than another? We look, in our efforts to explain variations in the official crime data, to the persons and systems who participate in the detection and official labeling process. For example, it is commonly felt among persons in police work that young officers are more likely to make arrests than are older officers. If this is true, youths living in an area patrolled by younger officers are more likely to be picked up than are their peers in other areas. Differential arrest rates would then reflect a characteristic of the police system rather than a characteristic of the offenders. Understanding and explaining variations in the arrest rate would lead us to inquire

into the processes by which officers are assigned to districts, rather than to the processes by which youths commit crimes.

This third alternative has only recently been explored. The differential handling of offenders by police or judicial officials was formerly viewed simply as a problem of bias and discrimination—hence injustice —or as a problem of inadequate criminal statistics. Differential response was not viewed as an event worthy of explanation in its own right. Partly as a result of increased funds for the study of the administration of criminal justice, partly as a result of methodological analyses, such studies are beginning to appear with greater frequency.[16]

These studies, of course, must face the same problem as those carried out under the second approach, except that now the problem is reversed: they must control for differences in the actual rate of offenses when they study the system of reactions, since they aim to express the reaction as a function of the reactors and not the offenders. An adequate methodology for the future will include study of the *interaction* between types of offenders and their social and personal backgrounds on the one hand, and types of reactors and their personal and social backgrounds on the other. This methodology will provide a rich matrix of possibilities as various types of offenders come in contact with various police or judicial structures and hence are treated in varying ways. Since, however, there are few such studies to date, and many studies that are designed to explain crime as a function of the criminal and his background, the following review of the structure of crime in America and the analysis of its causes will draw heavily from the latter. The few studies that inform us about differentials in the reactive procedures will be discussed within the broader context of the total system of reaction to crime.

Crime in American Social Structure

Given the limitations of official criminal statistics, it is perhaps unwise to attempt to set forth the seemingly most important facts about crime in the United States. It is conceivable that with adequate and valid measures many of these "facts" would change drastically. Nevertheless, there seems to be enough evidence, gathered from a variety of sources, by diverse methods, to support at least the following brief description of crime in the United States.

[16] Suggestions for a reformulation of the problems of criminal statistics along these lines are contained in Stanton Wheeler, "Criminal Statistics: A Reformulation," paper given at the proceedings of the American Statistical Association, 1965.

1. Crime rates are high, and may be getting higher. To say that a rate of crime is high is to suggest a criterion that distinguishes a high rate from a low one. Here we mean simply that crime rates in the United States are apparently among the highest in industrialized societies. Because of the lack of strict comparability of crime statistics from one political system to another, this judgment rests largely on informal observation of persons familiar with crime problems in a range of countries. Particularly with regard to violent crimes, there is relatively little doubt among such persons that the problem of crime in the United States is greater than in most other countries.

The number of persons officially charged with being delinquent or criminal in any one year is, however, small. In most analyses it ranges from one to 4 or 5 percent of the population. If we ask, however, how many persons will either have been arrested or have appeared in court during their lifetime for a delinquent or criminal charge, the rate is of course substantially higher.

Evidence for the rise in the crime rate in recent years comes largely from the official statistics compiled by the FBI. Taking only those offenses they believe most reliably reported, as discussed earlier, the crime rate for 1963 is up some 30 percent over the rate for 1958.[17] The actual number of crimes increased about 40 percent, whereas the population of the United States increased only 8 percent over that time period, leaving an overall increase in the crime rate of approximately 30 percent. Most of this increase was due to an increase in property crime; the rate of increase for murder, forcible rape, robbery, and aggravated assault was only 12 percent.

2. The vast majority of offenses are property crimes. This judgment is especially subject to the limitations of official statistics, because offenses against the person, notably those involving mutual consent, such as many types of sex offenses, are unlikely to be reported to the police. In any event, the work of the police, the courts, and the prisons is primarily with property offenders, rather than offenders against the person. Of the total of 2,259,081 offenses treated as most serious in the "Uniform Crime Reports," 77 percent involved the property crimes of burglary, larceny of 50 dollars or over, or auto theft, and of the remaining 23 percent, about one-third involved crimes of violence against the person, apparently committed for *reasons* of gaining property, that is, robberies.[18]

---

[17] Here and in following sections, official FBI data are taken from "Uniform Crime Reports," 1963.
[18] *Ibid.*

3. Despite a preponderance of property crimes among the more serious offenses, the amount of personal violence is high—probably higher than in most Western nations, a view which necessarily rests on subjective comparison as well as evidence. Specifically, our homicide rates are much higher than those of European countries, as are our rates of assault.

4. A characteristic feature of American criminality is the presence of organized crime—the development of large-scale organizations for criminal activities. Traditionally, what has been organized is the control and distribution of illicit goods and services—alcohol during prohibition, narcotics, prostitution, and gambling. In addition, there are the organized efforts to control various legitimate business activities, such as labor unions, vending machine operations, and the like. Although the total number of major crimes charged to "organized crime" is probably small, its cost and its pattern within our central urban areas provide a distinctive element of American society.[19]

5. The United States has much youth-gang crime. Here again, it is the patterning, rather than the total numbers, of such crime that is important. Gang violence in our major urban centers has been a prevalent part of the American urban scene. It is found especially in our largest cities such as New York and Chicago, but it is far from unknown in other areas as well. In recent years similar patterns appear to be developing in western Europe, as represented, for example, by the Mods and Rockers in England, the *raggeri* in Sweden, and similar youth groups elsewhere.

These features—the high proportion of property crime, and the amount of violence, organized crime, and youthful gang activity—are salient characteristics of crime in the United States. A parallel series of characteristics emerges when we examine those charged with commission of crimes.

1. Crime rates are many times higher for males than females. The 1963 FBI data suggest an overall arrest ratio of eight males for each female. The ratio of male to female crime is greater for property offenses than for personal offenses, and the ratio tends to decline under conditions when crime rates are at their highest. That is, the ratio of male to female crime tends to decline in our urban centers among young people, and among other segments of the population that tend to have higher crime rates.

2. Official crime rates tend to be highest among those in the lowest

[19] Gus W. Tyler, *Organized Crime in America* (Ann Arbor: University of Michigan Press, 1962).

socioeconomic groups. Whenever studies have been conducted that relate crime to one's location in the socioeconomic order, those at the bottom tend to have the highest rates. The extent to which this is true varies under different conditions, but the general point has been made in many studies. It is the case, however, that the impact of socioeconomic status shows its effect most strongly the further one goes into the criminal adjudication process. Nye and Short, using the self-reported delinquency method described earlier, found no evidence of higher delinquency rates among their lower-class adolescents.[20] Their finding has recently been confirmed for a large urban area by Akers.[21] At the most serious level tapped by this self-reporting measure, however, Akers' lowest socioeconomic group did report higher rates of offense. Thus the apparent relation of socioeconomic status to crime probably indicates both some true difference in the amount of serious crime committed by lower- and middle-class persons, and an impact of police and judicial procedures that is likely to lead to higher rates of arrest, court action, and conviction among those socially and financially less capable of fighting for their release.

Not all the seemingly discriminatory action is chargeable to negative bias or the lack of funds, however. Many court officials feel that, especially among delinquents, removal from poor environments into institutions may be more beneficial than leaving them in unfavorable environmental settings. Such action is taken in the name of humanity and therapy, but its consequence is the application of what society regards as a more severe reaction. Again, an important feature of the relationship between crime and socioeconomic status is that "white-collar crime," for reasons indicated earlier, is not likely to be included in these statistics.

3. Crime rates tend to be highest during middle and late adolescence, declining rapidly with the onset of adulthood. Here again, it is difficult to obtain adequate measurement, because adolescents are frequently handled by special administrative procedures. They are less likely to be fingerprinted, and less likely to have official records with the FBI. But such evidence as is available suggests strongly that crime is primarily a young man's activity.[22]

4. Crime rates tend to be highest in the central areas of our major

[20] F. Ivan Nye, James F. Short, Jr., and V. J. Olsen, "Socio-Economic Status and Delinquent Behavior," in F. Ivan Nye, *Family Relationships and Delinquent Behavior* (New York: John Wiley and Sons, 1958).
[21] Ronald L. Akers, "Socio-Economic Status: A Retest," *The Journal of Research in Crime and Delinquency*, 1, 1 (January 1964), pp. 38–46.
[22] See the data described in Walter B. Miller, "The Impact of a 'Total-Community' Delinquency Control Project," *Social Problems*, 10, 2 (Fall 1962), p. 168.

cities, with the rates being much lower in small towns and rural areas. This differential is especially true for property crimes, much less so for offenses against the person, where the differential between rural and urban rates is far less extreme.[23]

5. Crime rates tend to be higher than average among certain minority groups, and lower than average among others. Most forms of crime tend to have relatively high rates among Negroes, Puerto Ricans, and Mexican-Americans living in our large urban areas; the rates tend to be lower than average for populations of Japanese and Chinese ancestry. A large portion of the differential rates for the minority group members appears to be related to the frequent concomitants of minority group status, especially those already enumerated, living in the central sectors of cities and low socioeconomic status. Additional features that may partly account for the differentials between the Oriental and Negro rates relate to typical family structures, which are usually solid and strong among Orientals and more frequently weak or broken in the Negro population. In those few attempts that have been made to compare rates among different racial groups, holding constant such features as socioeconomic status, there still appears to be some differential in the rates by race, although it is difficult to find comparable units because of the association between race and poor socioeconomic conditions.[24]

This brief list of characteristic features in American crime invites the question: Why? What is there about the character of American society that gives it these specific properties? A convincing and thorough answer to this question is impossible at this time, since so little is objectively known about how we compare with other countries, and since in any case it is so difficult to attribute *causal* significance to one or another of the ways in which we differ. It can be shown, for example, that the homicide rate in Norway is much lower than in the United States. But in attempting to tell why Americans kill each other at a higher rate than Norwegians do, we might list a combination of *any* of the vast number of other ways Norway differs from the United

---

[23] For a review of area differences, see Terence Morris, "A Critique of Area Studies," reprinted in Marvin E. Wolfgang, Leonard Savitz, and Norman Johnston, eds., *The Sociology of Crime and Delinquency* (New York: John Wiley and Sons, 1962), pp. 191–198.

[24] Guy B. Johnson, "The Negro and Crime," *Annals of the American Academy of Political and Social Science*, 271 (September 1941), pp. 93–104; Earl R. Moses, "Differentials in Crime Rates between Negroes and Whites Based on Comparisons of Four Socio-Economically Equated Areas," *American Sociological Review*, 12 (August 1947), pp. 411–420.

States: growth rate, size, nature of the political system, rate of industrialization, racial composition, rate of urbanization, average level of income, range in level of income, differences in patterns of child rearing. Or among characteristics that are conceptually closer to crime, there is the difference in police systems, in public attitudes toward law and its enforcement, differences in the severity of punishment for offenders, in the rate of their detection, and so on.

Occasionally there are techniques for statistically controlling some of these forms of variation, thus removing their influence, so that we can see whether the effect still remains. In this instance, for example, we might be able to compare homicide rates among rural and urban people in both Norway and the United States, to see whether the overall difference is caused by the varying rates of urbanization. Typically, however, such comparisons are difficult because the necessary data are lacking. It is thus nearly impossible at present to explain the characteristic features of American crime in an intellectually compelling and satisfying way. But we are not prevented from using the knowledge that can be gathered in an attempt to piece together a plausible account of the characteristic differences. It should serve to forewarn us, however, of the possibility of error and of the great need for more systematic comparative studies that make possible a clearer assessment of the conditions related to crime in different societies, and an explanation of changes in volume of crime over time and place.

In presenting and assessing these accounts, we should remember that some are addressed to the *general character* of crime in America—its various types and amounts. Others are addressed more to an explanation of the *distribution* of crime among various segments of the population. (These differences correspond roughly to the different sets of facts just noted.) The theories also differ in generality; some point to features common to modern industrial societies and are useful in explaining why crime patterns may be different in such societies from the patterns found in the preindustrial or developing nations; others point more directly to factors that distinguish the United States from other industrial nations.

Finally, the arguments reviewed here are designed to explain differences in the rate or quality of crime, not to describe in detail the process by which a given person becomes criminal. Even for social categories in which rates are highest, some individuals do not commit offenses. It requires a more detailed review of their personal background experience to explain why, within the same broad category, some persons do and others do not become criminal. We turn to some of these problems in a later section.

The disruption of social relationships. Some efforts to account for variations in crime rates focus on disrupted social bonds and the consequent weakening of motives for conformity to conventional standards.[25] The central notion is that personal stability and willingness to abide by conventional norms depend on the stability of social patterns and relationships. Individuals bound up closely with persons from groups that they know and admire would be unlikely to violate the norms of such groups. And for most groups, most of the time, the norms include conformity to the law. Proponents of this view hold that any condition that leads to a weakening of social bonds, or to the development of conflict and dissension in place of cultural uniformity and homogeneity, may so weaken motives for conformity that individuals are willing to commit criminal acts.

Such conditions are typically found in modern industrial societies. First, rates of social change are rapid, so that new generations face new conditions. This means a possible breakup in the continuity of training and socialization, and therefore a potential weakening of ties across age-graded positions in the life cycle.

Second, not only is there rapid change in general social conditions, but there is also likely to be rapid change in the position of given individuals in the social order. High rates of social mobility, either upward or downward, produce disrupted social relationships and a weakening of solidarity.[26]

Third, increasing social differentiation and heterogeneity may lead to the disruption of social relationships among groups occupying differing statuses and engaged in different functions, even though there may be stable bonds *within* such groups. When the bonds are broken between them, the possibility of variant group values and interests emerges, along with conflict among the various segments. Such relationships may allow the development of deviant subcultures giving expression to values opposed to those of the conventional society. Clear examples in our own society include those sorts of urban subcultures devoted to organized crime, gang delinquency, and the like. Adolescence appears crucial here, since so much of the adolescent's time is spent with his peers rather than with those directly engaged in tradi-

[25] This is the general position of those who stress social disorganization as a cause of crime. For a relevant review, see Albert K. Cohen, *Delinquent Boys: The Culture of the Gang* (Glencoe, Ill.: The Free Press, 1955), Chapter 1. See also Ralph H. Turner, "Value Conflict in Social Disorganization," *Sociology and Social Research* (May–June 1954), pp. 301–308.

[26] The original argument is found in Emile Durkheim, *Suicide: A Study in Sociology*, trans. by John A. Spaulding and George Simpson (Glencoe, Ill.: The Free Press, 1951).

tional adult roles. Under these conditions it is not surprising to find an upward surge of deviant movements, either political, delinquent, or bohemian, among adolescents and young adults.[27]

It is important to note three things about this reasoning. First, it is not necessary to argue that only those persons who personally face these conditions are likely to feel the weakening of the social and normative order. Rather, when these conditions are found in society, many will be exposed to their indirect consequences. For example, even though a youth may grow up with a stable family life and retain most of his childhood friends, he is still likely to be exposed to rapid changes in communication and transportation systems, the occupational and educational structure, and other major institutional settings.

Second, as Cohen and others have clearly noted, this line of reasoning does not explain why motives for the commission of crimes are present in the first place.[28] Only if there is a relatively steady (although perhaps random) push or motivation toward the commission of criminal acts will these conditions of disrupted social relationships result in crimes.

Third, these conditions are general, whereas crime is specific. The same conditions are alleged to be related to the production of mental disorder, suicide, the formation of deviant political groups, revolutions, and almost all other forms of behavior defined as socially deviant. It would not be surprising to find that many of these forms of deviation have elements in common and therefore are responsive to common conditions. The question remains: Why do these conditions sometimes lead to the commission of crimes, sometimes to radically different forms of deviance? Part of the answer may be suggested below.

The nature of role and status definitions. Other ideas focus on the major status and role structures of society. The definitions of appropriate behavior for males versus females, adolescents versus adults, lower-class youths versus middle-class youths, may predispose, if not require, characteristic forms of criminal behavior. One of the leading reasons for the predominance of male over female crime is that males are expected to provide material goods and services. They are also expected to play more aggressive and instrumental roles, whereas females are expected to be more passive and expressive. The combination of these role definitions provides a basis for expecting high rates of male crime compared to female crime, especially since the bulk of all crimes

[27] See David Matza, "Position and Behavior Patterns in Youth," in Robert E. L. Faris, ed., *Handbook of Modern Sociology* (Chicago: Rand McNally, 1964), pp. 191–217.
[28] Cohen, *op. cit.*

is property offense. We might also expect that where *different* definitions of male and female roles emerge, there should be changes in the rates of crime between the sexes. Thus it has been argued that as women's roles become more masculine, as in some labor forces, the female crime rates also rise.[29]

When we look more closely at the manner in which crimes are committed, this difference between male and female role definitions appears clearly. In an interesting analysis of male and female crime, Grosser showed that delinquent girls' pattern of participation in delinquent activities was radically different from that of delinquent boys.[30] Not only are the girls much less likely to become involved in delinquent activity at all, but when they do become involved, it is typically with sexual promiscuity, or with helping males engaging in offenses. It is uncommon for girls to be involved in the more serious patterns of delinquency except through their participation in heterosexual affairs.

Another set of role and status definitions that may influence rates of crime are those associated with different positions in the social stratification system. Since today many of those Americans who compose the lower levels in the stratification system are members of ethnic and cultural minorities, these patterns of role definitions are in some respects tied in with ethnic status. Some investigators, such as the anthropologist Walter Miller, feel that there is a core set of values and problems in lower-class culture that distinguishes it from other levels in the system and increases the probability that anyone raised in that culture will engage in violations of the law.[31] On the basis of long-term experience in the study of lower-class street corner groups, Miller has arrived at a set of what he calls "focal concerns" of lower-class culture that differentiate it clearly from other positions in the social order. These include:

1. "Trouble"—various forms of unwelcome or complicating involvement with society's agents, such as police, welfare investigators, and others.

2. "Toughness"—skill in physical combat plus a surrounding set of values that emphasizes the ability to "take it," lack of sentimentality and a contempt for anything smacking of femininity.

3. "Smartness"—being able to outwit, dupe, and in general outsmart others.

[29] Edwin Sutherland and Donald R. Cressey, *Principles of Criminology* (Philadelphia: Lippincott, fifth edition, 1955), pp. 111–114.
[30] George Grosser, "Juvenile Delinquency and Contemporary American Sex Roles," unpublished Ph.D. dissertation, Harvard University, 1952.
[31] Walter B. Miller, "Lower Class Culture as a Generating Milieu of Gang Delinquency," *Journal of Social Issues*, 14, 3 (1958), pp. 5–19.

4. "Excitement"—a value placed upon thrills, taking chances, and flirting with danger.

5. "Fate"—a value that assumes most of the important events in life are beyond one's control and governed by chance, destiny, or circumstance.

6. "Autonomy"—on the level of expressed values, though not necessarily in actual behavior, an emphasis on the importance of not submitting to others' demands, a resentment of external controls or restrictions—especially coercive authority.

Miller's point is that an orientation toward this set of concerns will necessarily involve some in unlawful activity such as fighting and disturbing the peace, and that it creates situations in which unlawful activity is likely to emerge. The craving for excitement leads to auto theft, or the stress on toughness leads to the return of verbal insult with physical attack. It is not that lower-class cultural values *demand* violation of the law, but rather that they help create circumstances where violation is more likely.

Culturally defined expressions of appropriate behavior also relate to crime through what some have called the "subculture of violence."[32] It appears that Negro communities and Southern white communities are more likely to condone the use of aggression as a response to problems. Rates of homicide are generally higher in the South than in the North, even when racial differences in homicide rates are removed. Many homicides result from initially innocuous arguments among intoxicated persons. No clearcut set of social controls keeps a verbal dispute from becoming physical, a physical dispute from becoming a fight with deadly weapons, and so on. Indeed, according to a study of some 500 homicides in Philadelphia over a five-year period, 26 percent were "victim precipitated"—the person who was killed *began* the dispute that led to his death.[33]

Role and status definitions, like our previous category of disrupted social relationships, do not operate uniformly on all members of a given status category. Some persons more deeply internalize the norms of their settings, and others are in positions where these normative pulls or pushes are felt less strongly. These processes do give a basis, however, for expecting higher rates of delinquent and criminal behavior among some segments of the population than among others.

The struggle for success and the response to failure. One of the most influential sets of ideas about crime causation has been developed by a

---

[32] Thomas Pettigrew and Rosemary Spier, "The Ecology of Negro Homicide," *American Journal of Sociology*, 67 (May 1962), pp. 724–730.

[33] Wolfgang, Savitz, and Johnston, eds., *op. cit.*, p. 329.

long list of scholars, stemming primarily from the French sociologist, Emile Durkheim, with a major restatement by Merton and additional contributions by Cohen, Cloward and Ohlin, and others.[34] These ideas about crime are typically embedded in a broader series of issues about the genesis of other forms of deviant behavior; we shall restrict our account to the portion bearing most closely on crime and delinquency, and for the most part to Merton's statement of the problem.[35]

The central notion involves a distinction between cultural goals and the institutionalized and legitimate means by which they may be achieved. The goal is what is worth striving for—the item or condition of value toward which we direct our activity. The legitimate means are the various procedures by which we can seek to achieve the goal without violating social or legal norms.

Merton's argument derives from this distinction in two ways. First, societies differ in the relative emphasis they give to the goals themselves, or to the institutionalized means for achieving them. Some, which we might think of as "rule-oriented," heavily stress proper and correct procedures—the norms telling how one is allowed to compete for the goals. Others place the emphasis on the goals rather than the legitimacy of the means for their achievement. Second, people *within* a society differ in their proximity to the legitimate means for achieving the goals. Some are in positions that provide easy access to the goals through legal means for achieving them; others are in positions where access to such means is difficult. The central concept here is one of *differential* opportunity or access.

By combining these ideas, we can arrive at predictions about the relative rates of crime within and between societies. In comparing different societies, for example, the prediction must be that societies placing emphasis on personal goal attainment, without similar emphasis on the legitimate means for achieving the goals, will tend to have generally high rates of crime and other forms of "innovating" behavior designed to achieve the goals by whatever means. Merton has argued that the United States is such a society—that we have extolled the value of success without a balance of attention being given to the legitimate means for achieving it. If opportunities were easily accessible to all, there would be no problem, since it would be possible to achieve the goals by legitimate means. But no society has so eliminated the struggle, and it is questionable whether the goal would be worth striving for if everyone could easily attain it. It is, of course, difficult to test these

[34] Durkheim, *op. cit.*
[35] Robert K. Merton, "Social Structure and Anomie," *American Sociological Review*, 3 (October 1938), pp. 677–682.

notions because we have no measure of the extent to which a society emphasizes, in its cultural values, goals versus means. No thorough attempt has been made to rate societies on these dimensions. Nevertheless, this idea is one of the important bases for expecting differential rates of crime among societies.

This line of reasoning is applied more frequently to individuals within the same society. Here the argument is straightforward: crime rates will differ according to the extent of "disjuncture" between the goals persons internalize and their socially structured opportunities for achieving them. In American society, where the goal of material success seems dominant, and where the legitimate means to such success typically call for high levels of education and professional training, we would expect high crime rates among those least able to obtain good vocational or professional training.

It is important to note that our prediction does not imply that, anywhere and everywhere, persons of lower socioeconomic standing will have higher rates of crime. This will only be true, so the argument goes, when a cultural goal is set for them and is therefore in most instances internalized by them as an important aim in life, at the same time that their position makes it difficult to compete for this goal. If the society stresses some other goal, say spirituality, and if lower-status persons are in no worse position to compete for this goal than others in society, we would not expect a differential rate of deviant behavior on these grounds. Or, to take a more familiar case, if the goals held out to members of society differ depending on their location in the system, as in some caste systems, we would not necessarily expect the same result. For it is where they stand *in relation to the goals which they seek* that we use to predict their rate of deviant behavior, not where they stand in any absolute sense.

As a plausible account, this reasoning goes far in helping us interpret some of the findings already discussed. Certainly it is true that persons in the lower part of the social order are disadvantaged in their capacity to compete for monetary success. And since that success, on the basis of other values in American society, is expected to be won primarily by males rather than females, we could expect a greater drive toward crime among males. If ethnic and racial minorities have been exposed to the same value or goals, we would expect their crime rates to be higher. Indeed, we might expect relatively well-organized paths of criminal behavior to emerge as routes to financial success for those less likely to attain it through legitimate patterns. Such paths are suggested by the disproportionate ties of political corruption and organized crime to lower-status ethnic groups in our society.

This theme has been criticized, modified, and extended since its original publication in the 1930s. Some have questioned whether the cultural goal of success is indeed held out to all or even a large percentage of persons across the social strata; they have pointed to the evidence that persons in lower social strata do not expect their children to proceed far up the educational ladder, are less likely to expect to hold professional jobs, and so forth.[36] The question is what number of persons hold such achievement goals *compared to the number of available positions;* the balance between the two is difficult to judge.

A closely related issue is the extent to which upward mobility is closed to those near the bottom. Current programs that provide support for poor but talented students, that provide retraining for school dropouts, that provide special nursery school training as a preparation for entering elementary school, are all designed to achieve greater equality of opportunity. To the extent that such programs are successful, *and* to the extent that this theory is correct, crime rates should fall as more persons are given access to opportunities for developing their skills and talents. In any event, the question here is primarily one of magnitude since there is little question that some persons, because of their ethnic, cultural, or personal family backgrounds, are in poorer positions to struggle for success than others. And it is largely in such groups that relatively high official crime rates are found.

Another important modification of the theory has been offered by Cloward.[37] Cloward raised the question: What are the opportunities for success in the criminal world? If we can ask how opportunities for achieving success by legitimate means are distributed throughout the social structure, does it not make sense to ask the same question about illegitimate means? Crime is not a simple reflex action emitted without any prior training or preparation. Most crimes are not of that form, and many persons are not in positions where they can learn to use the necessary means effectively. How many students who read this chapter can hotwire a car, find a fence for stolen property, have the audacity to be a successful con man, have the manual dexterity and training to be a successful pickpocket or safecracker, have the social ties to gain entry to organized gambling syndicates? The question is not silly and the point is clear. Many students would find it difficult to acquire such

---

[36] Herbert Hyman, "The Value Systems of Different Classes: A Social Psychological Contribution to the Analysis of Stratification," in Reinhard Bendix and Seymour Martin Lipset, eds., *Class, Status and Power* (Glencoe, Ill.: The Free Press, 1953).

[37] Richard A. Cloward, "Illegitimate Means, Anomie, and Deviant Behavior," *American Sociological Review*, 24 (April 1959), pp. 164–176.

skills, even if they were motivated to learn. To draw any clear predictions about the probable rates of crime in differing social statuses, we need to know what access the various statuses provide their occupants for both legitimate and illegitimate opportunities.

These (and other) qualifying ideas suggest that the theory of illegitimate or deviant means has been rich in its capacity to create new thoughts, leading to refinements and modifications in the theory. Unfortunately, evidence providing efficient tests of these ideas is more difficult to come by. Hopefully, evidence will emerge from current efforts to provide equal opportunities and the associated effort to evaluate such programs.

A historical tradition of lawlessness. A final set of ideas about crime in America uses an historical mode to explain the seemingly high rate of crime and violence. It does seem that a combination of historical factors has given rise to conditions with less effective restraints on crime than those in other countries. Our Puritan heritage meant that many human vices were strongly condemned. Emphasis on legal control has meant that laws have been passed to prevent them. Thus gambling, bookmaking, the use of alcohol, premarital and extramarital sexual relations, and other forms of behavior are criminal in many, if not all, jurisdictions of the United States. One pressure toward higher crime rates has come from the simple fact of passing numerous laws in an attempt at legal control of personal conduct.

At the same time, the settling of a vast country required strength, aggressiveness, and manliness. The most successful man was likely to be the most aggressive and powerful, rather than he who lived closest to the letter of the law. Moreover, many of those who settled the country did so partly to escape past histories of failure or deviance. Some of the early settlers of our country arrived here after being banished from England for criminal offenses. In short, the condition seemingly necessary for successful expansion and settlement of the country, coupled with the personal backgrounds of many of the early settlers, was hardly supportive of a passive, mild, and peaceful way of life.[38]

Our methods for responding to criminal behavior were equally aggressive and violent. In the absence of settled legal and protective institutions, local groups often took the law into their own hands, and lynch law emerged as a form of violence supported by many elements in the social order, including lawbreakers and law enforcers. Such activities are by no means limited only to our historical past, as is obvious from recent events in connection with the civil rights movement.

[38] Mabel A. Elliott, "Crime and the Frontier Mores," *American Sociological Review*, 9 (April 1944), pp. 185–192.

With the settling of the West many of the central problems of crime reappeared in our growing cities. Here the combined forces of ethnic immigration and corruption in politics led to high rates of organized crime in urban machine politics. And again, lest we imagine that such problems died in the 1920s and 1930s with the Capone era, evidence suggests that there were large numbers of gangland killings in such cities as Boston in the 1960s. The pattern of violence has been traced clearly for one county in southern Illinois—admittedly not a typical instance. From the late nineteenth century to the early part of the twentieth, Williamson County had a pattern of violence that included a massacre of strikebreakers in connection with union strife and several murders precipitated by family feuds, the Ku Klux Klan, and gangster rivalry.[39]

It is thus possible to argue that America is a society with violent traditions. The forms of violence have varied with the changing conditions of social life, especially the settling of previously unsettled land and the growth of major cities. Currently, a great deal of attention is given to violent youth crime. It is receiving the attention previously devoted to the gunmen of the West and the corruption in the syndicates of our urban areas. This recent attention is in no sense the first time public concern has been expressed about youth crime. For example, here is an account of youth gangs in late nineteenth-century New York City:

> The gang fights of those days were fearsome. On the Fourth of July in 1857, the Dead Rabbits from the Five Points district [now being torn down for an urban renewal project] clashed with the Bowery Boys in Bayard Street. Sticks, stones and knives were freely used. Men, women and children were wounded. A small body of policemen, sent to quell the disturbance, was repulsed after several of these were wounded. Finally, the Seventh Regiment was summoned from Boston, and the city militia called out. By the time the riot was put down, late in the evening, six had been killed and over a hundred wounded.[40]

The amount of violence may also vary by region of the country. There is good evidence, as noted earlier, that the violent tradition is more widespread in our Southern regions than in other areas. Not only are the actual rates of violent behavior such as homicide higher in such areas, but values supporting the use of weapons and guns appear to be stronger. A recent public opinion poll showed that 53 percent of

[39] Paul M. Angle, *Bloody Williamson* (New York: Alfred A. Knopf, 1952).
[40] Wayne Phillips, "The Relative Rumble," *Columbia University Forum*, 5, 4 (Fall 1962), p. 40.

Southerners believed it should be legal to have loaded weapons in homes, compared with smaller percentages in other regions.[41] There is even one study suggesting that those who migrate from the South to the North or West show the effect of their Southern heritage in that they have higher rates of homicide in the Northern communities than do those who have always lived in the North.[42] These observations have the character of variations on a theme and should not obscure the fact that violent traditions are part of our total cultural heritage.

This set of ideas differs from the previous ones primarily in that it is less general as an explanation of high crime rates. It pertains to historical conditions unique to the United States and is thus of little help in explaining variations in rates of crime in other countries. But it is clear that many of its elements have much in common with the three sets of ideas presented above. Sharpening, modifying, extending, and clarifying the relevance of these plausible accounts is one of the major tasks confronting social scientists interested in crime.

The Social Psychology of Delinquency and Crime

Even if there were much better evidence than we have indicated, we still might feel quite unhappy with our interpretations. For one thing, crime is a general concept. Included under it are actions we sense to be different—petty theft and violent rape, illegal gambling and armed robbery. General explanations of overall rates may conceal these differences. Even where offenses are legally identical, the circumstances in which they occur suggest important differences in their causes. One assault with a deadly weapon results from a quarrel between husband and wife, another as part of a gang's attack on a rival group. We would not feel satisfied with an explanation of crime that did not pay attention to these significant differences.

Furthermore, it is only at the extremes of the distribution of crime rates that we might feel satisfied we have put our problem to rest. Even in the highest delinquency rate areas of our urban centers, only about one-fifth of the male youths are likely to be arrested in any one year. If we shift our measure and ask how many of such youths, by the time they reach the age of 18, will have been arrested or have appeared in court at least once, the rate may go up as high as 65 or 75 percent.[43]

[41] Thomas F. Pettigrew, *A Profile of the American Negro* (Princeton, N.J.: Van Nostrand, 1964), p. 148.
[42] Pettigrew and Spier, *op. cit.*
[43] Miller, "The Impact of a 'Total-Community' Delinquency Control Project," *op. cit.*

But in either case, we are left with many who do not fit the pattern—those who did not become delinquent when the majority did, and those who did when the majority did not. A closer look at these youths and their social circumstances is necessary to account for such differences.

Finally, our analysis of delinquent or criminal conduct is likely to be diffuse and atomistic unless we strive to identify processes of development over time. Although a given delinquent or criminal act may occur in a matter of minutes or seconds, the circumstances that lead up to the act may develop over a long time period. Some persons are criminals only briefly; others remain criminals. It is only when we look for criminal careers and processes of development that we can begin to understand these matters.

Social scientists from many fields have studied these problems. In our account of different types of delinquency and crime it is necessary to look not only at the results of studies but also at who conducted them, for the nature of the studies and some of the leading ideas are partially determined by the doctrines and ideologies of professions that study the problem. Since preventive efforts are also linked to different types of offenders and different professional groups, we shall discuss preventive efforts along with types of offenders. And because juvenile delinquency and adult criminal patterns differ in important ways, we shall discuss each separately.

Varieties and Types of Delinquency

Persons who carry the label "delinquent" exhibit a bewildering variety of styles of conduct and forms of deviant behavior. Our discussion will be somewhat arbitrarily limited to four different patterns of delinquency. Each of the patterns has been emphasized by one or another theorist, and each may fit some delinquents though not all. Our account will include a description of the relevant behavior pattern and its social context, the causes that are alleged to bring it about, and the forms of prevention or treatment most often suggested as appropriate for the pattern in question.

Patterns of individual delinquency. Since shortly after the turn of the century, there have been a number of works designed to locate the causal processes of delinquency within the individual delinquent. Most of these contributions have come from clinicians working in psychiatric clinics. Their argument is that delinquency is a solution to psychological problems stemming primarily from faulty or pathological family interaction patterns.

The research of Healy and Bronner during the 1930s provides an excellent example of this approach.[44] These investigators compared delinquent youths with their nondelinquent siblings, to see what differences there were between them. The most important finding was that over 90 percent of the delinquents compared to 13 percent of their nondelinquent siblings had unhappy home lives and felt discontented with their life circumstances. The nature of the unhappiness differed: some felt rejected by parents; others felt inadequate or inferior; others were jealous of siblings; still others were affected by a more deepseated mental conflict. Delinquency was seen as a solution to these problems. It brought attention to those who suffered from parental neglect, provided support from peers for those who felt inadequate, brought on punishment and therefore reduced guilt feelings.

The general theme is clear: unfortunate, unhappy family circumstances, leading to personal psychological problems of adjustment for the youth, which in turn are in some way solved by the commission of delinquent acts. This study, although published in 1936, is still the prototype of studies following what may be called a psychogenic model —studies that search for the causes of delinquency in the psychological makeup of the delinquent, typically resulting from specific styles of family interaction.

Later studies have more clearly identified detailed aspects of family relations that seem important but have not altered the fundamental point of view. In a recent investigation Bandura and Walters gathered detailed interview data from adolescents with records of highly aggressive actions, and compared them with a control sample of nondelinquents.[45] Because they wanted to focus specifically on family pathology rather than cultural processes, they restricted their sample to intact families of white boys with no clear sign of economic hardship or related problems. Their investigation suggested that the delinquent youths differed from the nondelinquent controls relatively little in their relationship with their mothers, but that they had much less identification with their fathers. Unlike some earlier studies within the psychogenic tradition, in this study father-son rather than mother-son relations seemed most crucial. The delinquent boys failed to internalize a set of moral values, apparently in part because of the absence of good role models in their fathers. In addition, discipline was meted out in a harsher manner. Although the more aggressive, delinquent boys had

[44] William Healy and Augusta F. Bronner, *New Light on Delinquency and Its Treatment* (New Haven, Conn.: Yale University Press, 1936).
[45] Albert Bandura and Richard H. Walters, *Adolescent Aggression* (New York: Ronald Press, 1959).

poor relations with their peers, the boys with healthy family relations had stronger peer relations.

In both these studies we can note the psychogenic model in operation. Because of interest in family relations, other types of influences are controlled and cannot appear as causal elements; one way is by comparing siblings, the other by selecting cases in such a way that community disorganization variables cannot come into play. Attention focuses on the boy, his family, and their problems. Less information is available on the nature of the delinquent or aggressive behavior and the situations in which it occurred.

The treatment model in cases of this sort has been derived from the standard situation of counseling and guidance. Since the problem centers on the boy and his own feelings, the treatment model is clinical, emphasizing the rebuilding, through psychotherapeutic processes, of more normal and healthier response systems. Efforts may be made to help the youth see his problems more clearly, and especially to help the youth's family understand how their own methods of dealing with him may be contributing to his problems of adjustment. The counselor may have considerable professional training or be simply an older, more mature person.

One of the few attempts to test the effectiveness of such a counseling system occurred in what is known as the Cambridge-Somerville Youth Study.[46] In that study youths who seemed headed for trouble were divided into matched pairs, one member of the pair being assigned to a counselor and the other serving as a control. It was assumed that the efforts of the counselors would prevent delinquency in at least some of the cases, leading therefore to a lower rate of crime for the treated cases. The results in this study, however, did not show any systematic effect of the counseling. Other studies designed to test programs similar to the Cambridge-Somerville Youth Study have not yet produced methods that reduce significantly the rate of crime in treated cases.[47]

Group-supported delinquency. At about the same time that Healy and Bronner and others were studying the psychogenic sources of delinquency, another set of investigators studied other sources. Social scientists at the University of Chicago during the 1920s and 1930s were

[46] Edwin Powers and Helen Witmer, *An Experiment in the Prevention of Delinquency: The Cambridge-Sommerville Youth Study* (New York: Columbia University Press, 1951).
[47] Henry J. Meyer, Edgar F. Borgatta, and Wyatt C. Jones, *Girls at Vocational High: An Experiment in Social Work Intervention* (New York: Russell Sage Foundation, 1965).

impressed as much by the force of culture and social disorganization in a rapidly expanding city filled with immigrants and other minorities as the psychiatrists were with the trauma of family background. In a series of investigations of crime rates in the urban area, it was found that rates of delinquency were stable from one period to another, that the largest percentage of youths committed their delinquencies in companionship with others, and that a series of sociocultural characteristics were typically associated with the areas where high rates were found. The studies of Thrasher and of Shaw and McKay report both evidence and argument in line with this tradition.[48] These characteristics included rapid turnover of population, a sizable portion of the land used for industrial buildings, high rates of minority group membership, and high rates of social disruption as reflected in broken homes, suicide, alcoholism, and the like.

In the face of these characteristics, it was natural for students of delinquency to see important causes residing, not in the youth's family alone but in the cultural context of his home and neighborhood. Living in such areas, a boy's "natural history" was to participate in delinquent careers. No specific psychological block seemed necessary; patterns of delinquent and criminal action were all around. Joining in these patterns would be natural for all except those restrained by close family life, strong ties to conventional community institutions such as the school, or other such influences. In fact, contact with youthful groups that sometimes got into trouble was meaningful and important, partially because of the surrounding disorganization of family and community life.

The key concept for understanding why youths became delinquent was association and companionship with other youths already delinquent. This was later put very clearly by Sutherland, who developed the theory of *differential association*.[49] This theory argues that youths become delinquent to the extent that they participate in settings where delinquent ideas or techniques are viewed favorably, and that the earlier, the more frequently, the more intensely, and the longer the duration of their associations in such settings, the greater the probability of their becoming delinquent. Unlike the psychogenic theories, this set of ideas focuses on *what is learned* and who it is learned from, rather than on the problems that might produce a *motivation* to com-

---

[48] Edwin W. Thrasher, *The Gang* (Chicago: University of Chicago Press, 1936); Clifford R. Shaw and Henry McKay, *Juvenile Delinquency in Urban Areas* (Chicago: University of Chicago Press, 1942); Clifford R. Shaw, *Natural History of a Juvenile Career* (Chicago: University of Chicago Press, 1930).
[49] Sutherland and Cressey, *op. cit.*, pp. 74–81.

mit delinquencies. Support for this theory has been found both in studies using the method of self report,[50] and those using official crime data,[51] although it is difficult to obtain adequate measures for the different types of association.

One of the critical reasons for emphasizing patterns of association is that our ties, especially those that are most frequent and intimate, provide the mirror that reflects our self-image, and our conception of self is highly important in guiding behavior. In one sense, the importance of delinquent contacts is that they enable the person to commit acts he might otherwise feel uneasy about, without losing self-respect and pride. His friends may value him even if others do not. One study, closely linked to the differential association tradition, found that boys who held a favorable self-conception seldom became delinquent, even though living in areas with high rates of delinquency.[52] The suggestion is that for these boys the cost of losing the parents' favorable image was too great to risk through delinquency.

Models of prevention or treatment that emphasize group contacts and interaction are difficult to apply, although some of their elements are clear. When a delinquent youth's mother desires to change her residence in order to "get Johnny away from the bad influences around here," she is applying the differential association principle, as are parole boards when they try to restrict associations among ex-prisoners. More generally, applications involve encouraging the person to accept as legitimate sources of values and norms those persons who are conventionally oriented, that is, who do not themselves provide support for delinquent belief systems. In organized gang settings, the person may be a social worker assigned to work with the gang; part of his job may be to encourage other types of associations with nondelinquent contacts. It is assumed that direct work on the interpersonal networks will pay off in prevention or control of delinquency; there is less emphasis on the delinquent's internal problems, his strains and his emotional disorders, except as these can be seen to affect directly the sources of his ideas about delinquency.[53]

---

[50] James F. Short, Jr., "Differential Association as a Hypothesis: Problems of Empirical Testing," *Social Problems*, 8, 1 (Summer 1960), pp. 14–25.

[51] Albert J. Reiss, Jr. and A. Lewis Rhodes, "An Empirical Test of Differential Association Theory," *The Journal of Research in Crime and Delinquency*, 1, 1 (January 1964), pp. 5–18.

[52] Walter Reckless, Simon Dinitz, and Barbara Kay, "The Self Component in Potential Delinquency and Potential Non-Delinquency," *American Sociological Review*, 22 (October 1957), pp. 566–569.

[53] Donald R. Cressey, "Changing Criminals: The Application of the Theory of Differential Association," *American Journal of Sociology*, 61 (September 1955), pp. 116–119.

At least until the early 1950s, these two perspectives were the dominant forms of theory attempting to link given individuals with delinquency. In at least one important early investigation, support for both patterns was found. Hewitt and Jenkins studied youths sent to a child guidance center in Michigan and analyzed the interrelations between their behavior patterns and their backgrounds.[54] They found two distinct syndromes of behavior that are relevant to our distinctions. One, which they called the *unsocialized aggressive* pattern, identified youths with some combination of the following traits: assaultive tendencies, initiatory fighting, open defiance of authority, malicious mischief, or inadequate guilt feelings. These characteristics are close to those that appear in the Bandura and Walters study, and another study of aggressive children which space does not permit us to review in detail, *Children Who Hate*.[55] The backgrounds of these youths often included signs of extreme rejection and lack of love, with high rates of illegitimate births and frequent foster home placements.

A different pattern was found for another group of boys. This one included association with undesirable companions, cooperative stealing, habitual truancy, running away from home, and staying out late at night. The authors called this a pattern of *socialized* delinquency, since it seemed to involve so much that is normal, peer-oriented delinquency. As we might expect by now, these boys showed less individual pathology, but they more frequently were raised in areas of high delinquency and lacked parental supervision. The parents were lax but not basically hostile and mean. In summary, youths raised in situations of great interpersonal conflict and parental rejection more closely fit the individual delinquent model, whereas those raised under lax supervision in areas with delinquent traditions more frequently fit the socialized delinquency model.

Just as those studying individual delinquents were biased in their orientation by failure to see the delinquent in his surrounding social context, so those emphasizing the context typically had little detailed information on relationships within the family or on the youth's personality makeup. The description of two types found in the Hewitt and Jenkins study gives added weight to the assumption that both orientations may be correct, though for different segments of the delinquent population. And of course in many cases the two sets of problems are found together and may work in a common process to

[54] Lester E. Hewitt and Richard L. Jenkins, *Fundamental Patterns of Maladjustment: The Dynamics of Their Origin* (Springfield, Ill.: State of Illinois Printers, 1947).
[55] Fritz Redl and David Wineman, *Children Who Hate—The Disorganization and Breakdown of Behavior Controls* (Glencoe, Ill.: The Free Press, 1951).

generate both internal motives and external pressures to engage in delinquent acts.

The organized delinquent gang. It is not surprising to find that adolescents often develop formally organized groups within which they carry out their activities. Nor is it surprising to find that these groups sometimes engage in delinquent activity. As noted earlier, the phenomenon of delinquent gangs is by no means new, in the United States or elsewhere. In the decade of the 1950s, however, attention was drawn to gang activities more insistently than in the past. Partly this was because of the increase in the amount of violence and crime engaged in by such groups; in part it seemed to reflect the somewhat changed structure and function of such groups. In any event, there are enough differences between the formally organized gangs studied and reported on during the 1950s, and the somewhat looser aggregates usually referred to in the earlier studies to justify a separate analysis.

The central concept that emerged during the 1950s to encompass the phenomenon of the gangs is that of the *delinquent subculture*. The concept culture refers to the set of values and norms that guide the behavior of group members; the prefix "sub" indicates that these cultures often emerge in the midst of a more general all-encompassing system. Delinquent subculture refers, then, to a system of values, beliefs, and practices encouraging the commission of delinquencies, awarding status on the basis of such acts, and specifying typical relationships to persons who fall outside the groupings governed by group norms. It suggests a broad, systematic form of gang activity.

The first person to call renewed attention to delinquent subcultures and to explore theoretically their possible sources and character was Cohen, in *Delinquent Boys*.[56] Cohen argued that the subculture of delinquency was based on a set of norms and standards defined in direct opposition to those of the conventional society. Its most prominent characteristics are that it is nonutilitarian, malicious, and negativistic— it denies many of the values usually associated with middle-class respectability.

In theorizing about the conditions under which groups supporting such a normative system will come into existence, Cohen departed from the earlier traditions of Sutherland by asking a different question. Sutherland asked, in effect: Why does this or that boy take on the pattern of delinquency? Cohen asked: Why is the pattern of delinquency there to be taken on in the first place? He was not satisfied to stop with an explanation of participation in a delinquent system; he wanted to

[56] Cohen, *op. cit.*

explain the system's presence. He found an important clue in the seemingly malicious and negative character of gang activity. It had this character, he suggested, precisely because it is an attack upon the conventional value system. Motives for the attack arise in much the same manner as that described in Merton's theory of deviant means. That is, they arise among youths in the lower order of the status systems who are confronted with "middle-class measuring rods," to use Cohen's phrase, in school, at work, and elsewhere. Their cultural and family backgrounds leave them unprepared for such things as the delay of gratifications, obtaining an education, the importance of study, and the like. Faced with such problems, they typically wind up at the bottom of the heap in the status systems of the schools. They do not like being at the bottom of the heap and are therefore in the market for a solution to status problems. Through subtle interactive processes, they locate other youths having the same problems, and together they establish a system that rewards them for the characteristics they do possess rather than denying them status for attributes they cannot easily attain. Aggressiveness, fighting, attacking the school, all become part of the valued activities of the subculture.

Cohen's work stands between the earlier contributions and later ones, since the groupings he had in mind did not necessarily resemble well-disciplined units organized around a specific form of delinquent activity. That such processes do take place and are an important part of the delinquent culture in our largest urban areas is the burden of the argument in another important work, that by Richard Cloward and Lloyd Ohlin.[57] These authors detailed three *different* delinquent subcultures, one organized around fighting and attacks against rival gangs, another around predatory theft, and a third around narcotics and other forms of escapist activity. Cloward and Ohlin argue that although all three may be found in our largest urban areas and have their basic roots in a kind of reaction formation similar to that described by Cohen and by Merton, each has its own distinctive conditions under which it flourishes. The theft subculture is found most often where there are strong ties between the adolescent and adult world in the urban slum, so that youths who get involved in organized crime and the rackets may move upward to higher positions. The conflict subculture, on the other hand, is likely to arise when there are few ties to the adult world—the conflict gives expression to the frustrations brought on by lack of legitimate opportunity when there are no chances for illegitimate gain through organized theft and crime. They further

[57] Richard Cloward and Lloyd E. Ohlin, *Delinquency and Opportunity: A Theory of Delinquent Gangs* (Glencoe, Ill.: The Free Press, 1960).

argue that the narcotics subculture is likely to be found among those who are "double failures"—those who, in Cloward's scheme of legitimate activities, are failures in both spheres.

There are other important distinctions that cannot be reviewed here, but the essence of the argument is clear. There is much concern in the works stressing subcultures for the influence of social values and for life outside the family. In fact, the family receives relatively little attention, especially in Cloward and Ohlin's work. But, like the more psychogenic interpretations, delinquency or delinquent subcultures are seen as solutions to problems. In the psychogenic tradition these problems are mental stress, anxiety, and feelings of deprivation and rejection; in the sociogenic tradition they are solutions to problems of status and position in society. In one tradition they take an individual form, and in the other they take a collective form. But the ties to both of the previous traditions should be clear.

There are two critical questions to be raised about the subculture theory. First, how extensive are delinquent subcultures with the vigor and complexity described by Cloward and Ohlin? Groups of the nature they describe seem to be found predominantly in our very largest urban areas. It seems that only in such areas, New York and perhaps Chicago, with the extremely high-density population of the urban slums, do we find the proliferation of different organizational forms, the systematic organization for the protection of "turf," and the like. It seems possible that their theory of the origins of such subcultures is correct, but there may be severe limits in the range of applicability of these ideas. Some investigators have concluded that the formally organized delinquent subcultures are much less frequently sound than journalistic accounts would have us believe.[58]

Second, it is still an open question whether groups embodying the distinctive values pointed to by Cloward and Ohlin, with the clear separation of conflict-oriented, theft-oriented, and retreatist subcultures, can be found with any frequency even in the largest urban slums. In one of the most important studies of delinquent gangs, search was made for groups embodying these distinctive value patterns, but they were rare. The investigators in this study, under the direction of James Short, have noted that most of their groups were versatile, engaged now in one form of delinquency, now in another, and so on in a flexible pattern. These matters are just now gaining the systematic research they deserve.[59]

[58] L. Yablonsky, *The Violent Gang* (New York: The Macmillan Company, 1962); H. W. Pfautz, "Near-Group Theory and Collective Behavior," *Social Problems*, 9, 2 (Fall 1961), pp. 167–174.
[59] Short, Jr. and Strodtbeck, *op. cit.*

The models of prevention suggested by the analysis of delinquent subcultures are different from those suggested by either of the two approaches described earlier. Since the principal problem appears to be the absence of the opportunity for educational and occupational training that enables one to compete more effectively, the principal direction of preventive programs is to attempt to increase opportunities available to the disadvantaged youth. Programs to accomplish this end have been supported by the President's Committee on Juvenile Delinquency and Youth Crime, an arm of the Department of Health, Education, and Welfare. The program of that group has been guided by the theory of legitimate and illegitimate opportunity structures, and is aimed, in several cities, to develop programs that increase legitimate opportunities for advancement. The program known as Mobilization for Youth in New York City has developed job placement and training programs, programs of intensive remedial education for persons who are retarded in their schoolwork, and other activities to increase the skills and abilities of the youths in the Lower East Side of Manhattan. Part of their effort has been directed at increasing a sense of competence on the part of the adults as well as the youths in such areas, in the belief that the best solutions to problems of urban slums will be found when people facing the problems can organize more effectively for their solution, so that apathy and a sense of powerlessness are reduced.[60]

It is still too early to judge the success of efforts of the type carried on by Mobilization for Youth. They are broad-gauged programs, designed to have impact on a whole community; the linkage to immediate reduction in acts of delinquency is not direct. The basic assumption is that the reorganization of urban slum communities is required before any systematic dent will be made in a host of problems, including delinquency and crime. It is a bold experiment that will have to await further analysis and testing before firm conclusions about its efficacy can be drawn.

The situational delinquent. The conceptions, theories, and preventive programs outlined all have one quality in common. In all of them, delinquency is viewed as having deep roots. In the psychogenic tradition these roots lie primarily within the individual, but in the sociogenic traditions they lie in the structure of the society, with emphasis either on the ecological areas where delinquency prevails, or on the systematic way in which our social structure places some individuals in

[60] Mobilization for Youth. *A Proposal for the Prevention and Control of Delinquency by Expanding Opportunities* (New York: Mobilization for Youth, Inc., 1961).

a poorer position to compete for success. But no matter where the emphasis is laid, it is clear that delinquency must be regarded seriously, requiring as it does a fundamental reorganization of the psyche, the social structure, or the culture.

The conception of the situational delinquent provides a different perspective. Here, the assumption is that delinquency is not as deeply rooted as suggested by the theories just discussed, that both the motives for delinquency and the means for controlling it are often relatively simple and near the surface. We do not mean that the forces outlined in these theories are not at work; in many cases they may be heavily at work, and in others they may be at work enough to break the ties to the conventional social order so that it no longer restrains those who are tempted to commit delinquent acts. But if a young man can commit such acts without having a deep commitment to delinquency, if he can engage in them periodically without making an emotional investment in their expression, then perhaps deep underlying forces may not need to be present in order for delinquency to occur.[61]

One of the critical reasons for believing that these forces are not as insistent and deeply rooted as our theories sometimes lead us to imagine is the precipitous decline in delinquency as the disadvantaged youth moves into adulthood. We would not expect deeply rooted patterns to be so easily erased while growing up; thus the question arises whether they were so deep originally. We would expect them to be acted on primarily by those whose impulse control is less developed, those whose family restraints are less firmly and consistently reinforced, those who have less supervision or surveillance from adults, and of course by those who are doing relatively poorly anyway and so have relatively little to lose even if caught. This is a form of opportunity theory concerned with the simpler and more immediate opportunities for action, rather than the opportunities that provide a young man with the chance to change his status and position in life.

To the extent that such reasoning is correct, we may be able to prevent delinquency, not by acting directly upon the person who may be delinquent but rather by acting on his social and physical environment. The rate of burglary ought to fall with an increase in burglary protection, the rate of auto theft to fall with an increase in the proportion of automobiles on the street that are locked, the rate of rape to fall with the decline in the number of unlighted doorways and passageways, and so forth. None of these things would happen if the motives for crime were deeply rooted, for surely persons would travel far and wide to find circumstances where these conditions did not prevail, or would be

[61] David Matza, *Delinquency and Drift* (New York: John Wiley and Sons, 1964).

moved to commit their acts even in the presence of such conditions. Such an approach to delinquency prevention would be much less costly than any program operating on individual predelinquents. Such programs have never been tested systematically, but that does not distinguish them from the theories reviewed earlier. If anything, it is an argument for their trial, for at least they have not been proved failures.

There have been modest, unsystematic, and unevaluated attempts at such efforts, and what reports are available on them suggest that they might work. For example, in the Scandinavian countries all drivers know that they may be stopped without cause at any time, that a test may be run on the alcohol content of their blood, and that they are subject to a jail sentence if the percentage of alcohol in the bloodstream is above a very low level. Note that in this system the authorities do not wait for an accident to occur. A person may be driving perfectly safely when stopped, arrested, and jailed. An apparent result is that few persons drive while drinking, and there are few deaths on the highway because of drunken driving. Such benefits are won, unfortunately, only at the cost of some loss of civil liberties.

In Denmark during the war, there was a period when there were literally no police on the streets.[62] If such things as the mere presence of the policemen have no impact, there should have been no change in the crime rate. The evidence is that the crime rate rose for property crimes, though it did not rise for crimes such as rape and armed robbery, where the offender is visible to his victim. There have been no similar tests, either experimental or otherwise, of the effects of streetlighting campaigns, burglar protection for automobiles and homes, and the like.

The concept of situational delinquency is undeveloped and as yet of unknown relevance to the problem of delinquency causation and control. In part this is because the rest of our theories direct us to gathering data about personal characteristics of the delinquent and his family, or the social pathologies of the areas in which he resides. It is much more difficult to obtain adequate data on the circumstances in which offenses occur, their ecological properties, what was occurring five minutes before the act took place, and so forth. Yet it is these facts, rather than the others, that would be relevant for those instances in which a situational model applied. And of course it would be a supplement to, rather than a replacement for, the other notions. To the extent that delinquency represents a fundamental attack on the values of the society, or a deeply rooted mode of expression of personal prob-

---

[62] Johs Andenaes, "General Prevention, Illusion or Reality?," *Journal of Criminal Law, Criminology and Police Science*, 43, 2 (July–August 1952), pp. 176–198.

lems, the situational forces and circumstances are unlikely to be effective in modifying the response. But if much delinquency is episodic, unplanned, an expression of fun and thrills rather than resentment, then programs based on the logic just developed would seem to be worth trying.

The four patterns we have stressed—individual delinquency, group-supported delinquency, the organized delinquent gang, and situational delinquency—are simply one way of looking at research and theory regarding delinquents. Some delinquent patterns may involve components of all four processes, and in other cases each process may describe one kind of delinquent pattern but not the others. Each pattern may also be seen as a way in which the pressures from the broader social structure become implicated in the particular careers of particular boys.

It may be evident from our review that the most systematic work on delinquency has been theoretical work, with carefully organized and well-thought-out accounts of the process of delinquency, each of which is highly plausible. A critical remaining task is to gather systematic and objective data regarding delinquent patterns that can be used to assess the truth value of the various conceptions and theories.

Patterns of Adult Criminal Activity

One of the important properties of the delinquent condition is that it does not last long. It is a condition of adolescence. The extent to which delinquent patterns persist into adulthood is difficult to determine. In at least one study, only one-third of a cohort of youths with official court records as delinquents was also found to have an adult arrest for something other than a traffic offense.[63] In another study the figure was about 60 percent, but this was for youths who also had been referred to a psychiatric clinic for severe emotional disturbance.[64] One of the great needs of current criminology is for detailed study of the transition from adolescence to young adulthood, so that we can better understand why some abandon their delinquent careers and others continue.

A reasonable guess is that the strongest single set of forces making for a decline in delinquency is the assumption of adult roles. As the

---

[63] Robert E. Stanfield, "The Family and the Gang in the Aetiology of Delinquency," unpublished Ph.D. dissertation, Harvard University, 1963.
[64] Lee N. Robins, Harry Gyman, and Patricia O'Neal, "The Interaction of Social Class and Deviant Behavior," *American Sociological Review*, 27 (August 1962), pp. 480–492.

young man nears the end of his teens, as friends marry and the corner group begins to wither, there is less hold on those who would remain. The insistent demands to get a job and bring in a paycheck, or the need to support a child, may transform the delinquent attitude into a relatively steady, if grudging, participation in standard working-class family and occupational roles. There is nothing like responsibility to make persons responsible, and it is not surprising that prison inmates consist disproportionately of single, unemployed males. Thus the role demands of adulthood may be the single strongest force making for the decline in rates of delinquency and crime as adult status is assumed.

Although youth crime attracts more public attention and more concern for prevention and corrective efforts, adult criminal careers present some of the most intriguing problems of analysis and explanation. In part this is because the patterns of adult crime are more various and differentiated than are those of youthful offenders. Indeed the variability in types of criminal careers is so great that they defy summary in any brief form. Specific types of adult crime have been the subject of book-length monographs, and books have been devoted to problems of developing adequate criminal typologies.[65] In the brief space available here, it seems best simply to describe some of the dimensions of variation and suggest some of the problems and prospects in the analysis of criminal careers.

Amateurs and professionals. One of the very important ways adult crime patterns may be differentiated is the degree to which their participants have a professional orientation toward their work. To say that someone has a professional orientation suggests several things—first, that special skills and techniques are involved which the professional can apply in a manner unlike that of the amateur. The skills may be manual, like those of a surgeon or a safecracker; or they may be verbal, like those of a psychiatrist or a confidence man. In any event, there is a technology involved in crime as in other pursuits, and the professional is distinguished from the amateur by his ability to employ that technology effectively.[66]

The professional is also distinguished from the amateur by the degree to which he has pride in his skills and achieves status through them, albeit in the eyes of a restricted group. Like the distinction between the professional and the amateur in athletics, the professional

---

[65] Don C. Gibbons, *Changing the Lawbreaker: Principles of Treatment for Delinquents and Criminals* (Englewood Cliffs, N.J.: Prentice-Hall, 1965).

[66] A good if somewhat outdated account of professional theft may be found in Edwin H. Sutherland, *The Professional Thief* (Chicago: University of Chicago Press, 1937).

in crime is likely to work at his trade full time, while the amateur pursues it intermittently, when his legitimate employment breaks down or under other special circumstances.

Finally, professional crime typically involves careful organization that distinguishes it from the more frequently hit-or-miss qualities of amateur offenses. Successful professional crimes typically involve more than one offender and careful planning, both in the commission of the offense and in the sale of stolen goods or property if the "take" is not in cash. The distinction between amateur and professional depends also upon quality and not simply quantity. A person may steal frequently and yet not think of himself as a professional thief. A good example comes from a recent study of shoplifters by Mary Owen Cameron.[67] She notes that the great bulk of shoplifters are women who use shoplifting as a means of supplementing the family budget. They do not think of themselves as criminals, and once caught by store officials are unlikely to continue. Only a small number are professionals whose major source of income is shoplifting and who develop the skill as a high art.

Professional offenders, because crime is literally their way of life, are likely to have well-developed value systems which justify their activity by exploiting the defects in the value system of the conventional world. The professional burglar, for example, may argue that he is no more "criminal" than politicians and corporation executives. The only difference he sees is that they make their profits by exerting special influence and by clever legal schemes that find loopholes in the law, whereas he, because of his lack of formal education, must use less subtle and more direct methods. The professional confidence man can argue effectively that he never took from anyone who did not have larceny in his heart, since confidence games typically involve the willingness of the victim to get something for nothing. The importance of such value systems for the professional offender is that they provide him with clear defenses against the introjection of guilt and with a rationale that enables him to explain this conduct to himself. Together with pride in his workmanship, these features may enable him to engage in systematic criminal activity without suffering the self-doubts and troubled conscience that often characterize other types of offenders.

Manual dexterity or verbal dexterity. Most of the offenses aimed at monetary gain involve the use of either manual or verbal skills. The

[67] Mary Owen Cameron, *The Booster and the Snitch* (New York: The Free Press of Glencoe, 1964), pp. xii–202.

successful safecracker (now apparently a dying breed, what with new safety devices such as time locks and an abundance of cash available outside of safes) is perhaps the prototype of the criminal with well-developed manual skills. A variety of techniques for safecracking have been developed to a point of genuine craftsmanship; it takes many hours of "trade training" to master the techniques. Offenses such as burglary, safecracking, and robbery are known as "heavy theft," since they typically involve the use of some force or the threat of force to complete the offense.

Such offenses are clearly distinguished from those that involve a preponderance of verbal skills, trickery, fraud, and deceit. Although the evidence is by no means clear, these differences in style appear to be related to stable differences in the social backgrounds of offenders. Heavy thieves are more likely to come from urban slums and often have records of crime and violence in their youth. Grifters, on the other hand, appear more frequently to emerge from middle-class backgrounds, apparently from families where verbal skills were practiced. They are likely to have more formal education, and according to some reports, higher intelligence. One highly suggestive but as yet unverified theme is that confidence men frequently emerge from families of marital strife and conflict, where the youthful offender learns to use deceit to turn parental feuds to his own advantage. He becomes highly skilled in verbal manipulation.[68]

Periodicity and chronicity in criminal careers. The professional career offender, committed to crime as a way of life, is apparently a small minority among the total population of offenders. Another minority may be found at the other end of the continuum. Here are the offenders whose crimes appear to be the result of extreme pressure in highly emotionally charged circumstances, or the result of accident, fate, and the like. Offenders of this type are unlikely to remain permanently in trouble with the law because the circumstances that produce their offense are situational and unlikely to recur. Examples include assaults and homicides arising from marital triangles and other amatory circumstances, and negligent homicide as a result of drunken driving. Closely related to this pattern are crimes of persons whose misdeeds are concentrated in a short period of time and are in a sense multiple expressions of the same immediate problem. An example is the pattern of embezzlement under the pressure to repay gambling debts.[69]

[68] Richard L. Jenkins, "The Budding Grifter," in *Breaking Patterns of Defeat* (Philadelphia: Lippincott, 1954).
[69] Donald R. Cressey, *Other People's Money* (Glencoe, Ill.: The Free Press, 1953).

By far the most frequent pattern, however—at least within the categories we think of conventionally as criminal—is an episodic movement into and out of criminal activities as employment circumstances and other conditions vary. This is even true among the felons who are imprisoned in our state and federal penitentiaries. A recent investigation of such offenders by the sociologist Daniel Glaser refers to the "zigzag path" of the criminal's career and notes that "at least 90 percent of the felons who are imprisoned would be viewed more realistically if we thought of them as men who keep alternating from criminal to noncriminal means of pursuing economic or other objectives, rather than as persistently criminal." He suggests that for adult offenders employment conditions appear to be one of the critical contingencies that effect the decision to move into and out of crime.[70]

The problem these features present for criminological theory is that we may find it difficult to explain criminal careers by reference to the personal characteristics of the offenders, except where the career is adopted as a way of life. For the "one-time loser" and the occasional offender, such background conditions are not of much use, for they may explain equally well both the noncriminal and the criminal career phase. The critical problem for further research is to study in detail the conditions under which persons turn from one to the other mode of activity.

Victim involvement. Because our standard ways of processing criminals tend to dissociate them from their victims, there is little systematic knowledge about the relationship between the victim and the offender. European criminologists have shown more concern for this problem and indeed have suggested the development of a science entitled victimology. Such knowledge as is available does indeed suggest that victims may play far more than a passive role in crime. We have already noted that in over a quarter of homicides occurring in Philadelphia over a five-year period, the eventual victims played an important role in the initiation of the offenses. Victim participation is essential in the success of confidence games and swindles, since it is only by agreeing to participate in fraudulent endeavor that the victim loses his money. In cases involving sexual offenses, there is often some evidence that offenses such as rape may occur after a period of drinking, petting, and mutual sexual arousal. Thus the concept of "victim proneness" may be applied to crimes as well as to accident research, for victims are no more randomly distributed than are those who victimize

[70] Daniel Glaser, *The Effectiveness of a Prison and Parole System* (Indianapolis: Bobbs-Merrill, 1964), p. 466.

them. Indeed, in some assaults and homicides, denoting one person as the victim and the other as the criminal may be highly arbitrary, except in a strictly legal sense.

Another way in which victims become important is that properties of the victims may determine reactions to the offender. As Garfinkel showed years ago, and as others have noted more recently, sentences in homicide cases differ depending on the race of the offender and the victim.[71] Another study suggests that theft from large corporations is not viewed as negatively as is theft from small businesses.[72] And if we can notice differentials of this type, it seems fairly safe to assume that offenders may do so also, and may use their estimates to guide them in deciding whom, what, and where to offend.

Explaining Adult Criminal Careers

The range and variability in adult crime patterns is so broad that it defies any simple explanation. It seems no accident that theories purporting to account for juvenile delinquency are more clearly set forth and perhaps are more amenable to the test of evidence than are those for adults. Two reasons for this seem paramount. First, delinquents are still in some form of contact with their parental families, and the relevance of family problems is obvious to most of those searching for the causes of delinquency. Even in the most extreme sociological formulations of the causes of delinquency, the family is still viewed as playing a role, if only because of the lax supervision that enables youngsters to learn the street culture. With adults, however, ties with the parental family have often been broken, and it is more difficult to note any clear causal linkage, either speculatively or in fact.

Second, the great bulk of all delinquency, both male and female, involves group participation. This provides a common focus of interest for most theorists and enables them to identify points of agreement and disagreement. The theorists may differ in their analyses of the detailed structure of youth groups, in their attribution of causes for the structure of the groups, or in their analyses of the content of group culture, but they do not disagree on the fundamental importance of group involvement, social pressures, contagion, and social influence in the making of adolescent delinquents.

One approach to bringing order out of the chaos of adult criminal

[71] Harold Garfinkel, "Research Note on Inter- and Intra-Racial Homicides," *Social Forces*, 27 (May 1949), pp. 369–381.
[72] Erwin O. Smigel, "Public Attitudes Toward 'Chiseling' with Reference to Unemployment Compensation," *American Sociological Review*, 18 (February 1953), pp. 59–67.

patterns is to develop criminal typologies—classifications of offenders into relatively homogeneous groups such that persons in any one category appear to have much in common both in the nature of their criminal activity and its causes. This approach has been systematically employed in the work of the sociologists Don C. Gibbons and Donald Garrity, and is also found in less systematic form in the work of many others.[73] Space precludes the laying out, even in brief form, of such a typology. Rather, we shall identify some of the leading processes that appear to be relevant to many types of offenders. Each might be thought of as part of an answer to the question why adult criminals continue to commit crimes.

Continuity. One theme is that whatever factors produce budding youthful offenders will continue to operate on the adult offender. Since many adult offenders have records of juvenile offenses, the notion of continuity seems reasonable for some cases. The problem is that many who were juvenile offenders have not moved on to adult crimes; we must explain why. Conceivably, it is only those who are most intensively and frequently involved in crime as youths who continue to be criminal in adulthood. It is also conceivable that they are the ones unable to move into legitimate adult roles through marriage and the labor market. In any event, it is clear that continuity does not operate in any simple and direct way even for those who continue in crime. Among youthful incarcerated offenders now being intensively studied, extremely few indicate any desire to continue with their delinquent and criminal careers, although a somewhat larger number feel that fate is against them and that they will indeed become involved with the law once again, even if not from any deep motivation on their own part.[74]

Differential opportunity. Especially for males, a particular location in the occupational structure makes certain criminal activities possible and others difficult. Within the unskilled labor categories, from which a large segment of the adult criminal population is drawn, there appears to be immense variety and great differentials in the probability of coming into contact with criminal patterns, whether a person is motivated to find them or not. Thus bellhops and taxi drivers are in a good position to learn about and participate in various petty rackets or frauds, including pimping, illicit distribution of liquor and narcotics,

[73] Don C. Gibbons and Donald L. Garrity, "Some Suggestions for the Development of Etiological and Treatment Theory in Criminology," *Social Forces*, 38 (October 1959), pp. 51–58. See also Gibbons, *Changing the Lawbreaker, op. cit.*
[74] Martha Baum and Stanton Wheeler, "Becoming an Inmate," in Stanton Wheeler, ed., *Controlling Delinquents* (to be published by John Wiley and Sons, 1966).

and the like. Stevedores and men holding similar jobs, on the other hand, have opportunities to rob and pilfer from warehouses, stock rooms, and parked automobiles. Currently, Negroes apparently have lower rates of embezzlement than whites, because they are less often in situations where embezzlement is a possible alternative. Rates of narcotics addiction are reported to be high among members of the medical profession who have easy access to narcotics.

In short, whatever the motives for engaging in criminal activity may be, some positions in the social order make certain forms of activity more probable than others. Therefore much of the variability in patterns of crime appears to result from differential location in the social and ecological order, which systematically enhances opportunities for some types of crime while lowering opportunities for others. Although there is probably no one who lives in a totally crime-free environment, there are likely to be vast differences in the extent to which criminal opportunities are available, regardless of their form. Thus these considerations may go far in explaining why, among members of a particular social status position, some commit crimes while others do not.

Contingency and the role of rationalization. Like the situationally oriented delinquents examined earlier, many adult offenders appear not to be driven by any deeply rooted urge to commit crimes. Whatever their position in life, they have typically entered that position with no expectation that crime will be a part of their future careers. Circumstances change, however, and contingencies emerge that make crime appear to be a viable solution to a problem. We have already illustrated this by mention of the embezzler, who may begin to take funds from his employers with every intention of repaying them after getting himself out of debt.[75] A related instance occurs among drinkers who write checks to cover the cost of their alcohol and other expenses. Such offenders often begin with the simple expedient of postdating checks, with every intention of providing funds for payment. But as the drinking pattern increases and as fewer days are put in at work, income falls and costs rise. At this point the drinker, like the embezzler deeply involved in covering up, is forced to realize that he cannot easily extricate himself from the circumstances.

In both of these instances and in other related ones, a necessary element in enabling the offender to continue with the commission of offenses appears to be a set of rationalizations or justifications that enable him to engage in the crimes without destroying his conception of himself as a basically conventional person. The means for doing so are

[75] Cressey, *Other People's Money, op. cit.*

frequently available in cultural themes that receive support from conventional members of society. The embezzler may conceive of himself as a borrower rather than a thief, since he fully intends to pay the money back. The fact that it is technically illegal is a little like driving with an out-of-date driver's license. That, too, is illegal, but if you get the new license before you are stopped, who cares? The offenders in white-collar and corporation crimes have many similar rationalizations. Doesn't everyone pad his expense account? Cut corners on income tax? Aren't these simply ways of fighting the federal government, red tape, and bureaucracy?

Although it is difficult to pin down the precise time order in which such rationalizations appear, it makes a great deal of difference in our theories of criminality whether we assume that they appear before an act or only after it. Perhaps the most frequent psychiatric interpretation is that such claims bear no fundamental relation to the act itself, and appear only afterward, as a means of reducing one's guilt for committing the act. The sociological interpretation usually has it that the rationales precede the act, and indeed are integral to it in the sense that the person could not bring himself to commit the act unless he had convinced himself that it was justifiable in some way. For these rationalizations are, in the words of Sykes and Matza, "techniques of neutralization," that is, means by which the moral force of society can be neutralized and therefore removed from consideration, thus allowing more expedient and immediate forces to operate.[76] But these techniques can operate only if they receive a fairly wide degree of tacit support from various sectors of the social order. For most of our offenders are not hallucinating, not capable of such systematic delusions as to be persuaded by reasons that no one else would accept. Persons otherwise conventionally oriented will commit a breach of the law in circumstances where many of those around them provide some justifications for it. These modes of rationalization are an important part of what is learned through the process of differential association.

The place of psychopathology. Until now we have said little about the role of mental or emotional disorders, except when we discussed the model of the individual delinquent in an earlier section. It should be clear from the discussion that there are many forces other than severe psychopathology that lead to the commission of criminal acts. But that is no reason to assume that personality disorders and related

---

[76] Gresham M. Sykes and David Matza, "Techniques of Neutralization: A Theory of Delinquency," *American Sociological Review*, 22 (December 1957), pp. 664–670.

disturbances bear no relation to crime, for the evidence, although shaky, suggests too strongly and insistently that they do. The clinical reports of Freud, Alexander and Staub, Healy, and Aichhorn suggest that there are indeed neurotic criminals who commit their acts in a search for punishment, compulsive offenders who appear driven to their acts by deep psychic needs, and psychotic offenders who may be legally sane, but only because of legal rather than psychiatric formulations of sanity and insanity.

Although instances of these phenomena may occur with great frequency in a clinic population, they are infrequently found in more representative samples of offenders. Estimates differ widely because of vagueness in the application of such labels as neurotic, compulsive, and the like, but it seems clear by now that few of the persons convicted of crimes fit such a pattern.

There does appear to be one type of offender with an identifiable form of psychopathology, although again there are frequent disagreements about meanings and interpretations. These are those offenders who carry the label psychopath or sociopath, referring primarily to the absence of internalized norms to guide conduct.[77] These are offenders who in our common vocabulary "have no conscience." They are distinguished by their inability to feel empathy for their victims, or their inability to feel sorrow or guilt for harm done to relatives; more generally, they have failed to internalize the normative demands of the society. Any prison contains some inmates who fit this sort of description fairly well, and so for that matter does almost any college or university. For not all such persons engage in criminal acts. Indeed, most will probably find it expedient not to if they can avoid it. But the lack of inner normative controls means that one of the restraints on the commission of offenses is absent, should the motive or need to commit an offense ever arise. It is just for this reason that we are more likely to find the guiltless, conscience-free individual in prison than in many other settings. But it is the relative infrequency of this type even in a criminal population that makes the processes of neutralization and rationalization so important.

Stigma, labeling, and deterrence as determinants of criminal careers. So far we have treated the causal processes as though they operated relatively independent of the stage in which we find the offender. Such a treatment would be justifiable only if the events of arrest, adjudication, and incarceration had no impact upon the offender's future career.

[77] For a review of relevant work, see William and Joan McCord, *Psychopathy and Delinquency* (New York: Grune and Stratton, 1956).

Most students agree that these events are important but disagree about the direction of their effect.

It is the burden of argument, in one line of reasoning, that these events have only negative consequences. The argument is straightforward: any time a person is caught, arrested, and brought into court for an offense, he is being publicly identified as a criminal. Such a public identification has the character of a "degradation ceremony." [78] In any event, the offender is branded. He must fill out routine papers that require him to answer questions about arrests and court appearances. When he travels, there is always the chance someone will know of his record. This is likely to lead him to think of himself as a delinquent or criminal, and others will also think of him in this way. In addition to this moral reconstruction, people may also make it difficult for him in more direct and immediate ways, for example, by refusing to employ him. The sum of all these forces is a negative effect of labeling, of public identification of the offender, and its consequence is likely to be a further identification of the offender with those who fall outside the moral boundaries of society. A suggestive phrase for this whole process is "secondary deviation." [79]

This is a compelling, significant argument, for it suggests that we are at an impasse in our attempts to control crime with current techniques. If we pay no attention to the offender, he may continue to offend for whatever reasons he began with. If we do pay attention to him, however, he may suffer the consequences of labeling and continue to offend for that new reason. Those who offend once and suffer the indignities and stigma of the labeling process, yet offend no more, emerge as heroic figures, able to withstand more than the society had any right to expect.

The counterargument is that the process of arrest, trial, and adjudication will have a deterrent effect on persons so processed. They will not like being treated like criminals and will therefore refrain from committing criminal acts. The rationale of deterrence is currently in low repute, partly because a humanitarian value system has led to reduction of extreme forms of punishment and torture, many of which were justified on grounds of deterrence. Note that the argument concerns the *effect* of rejection, not its existence. Indeed, it is the sting of this rejection that led many to believe in a philosophy of deterrence.

---

[78] Harold Garfinkel, "Conditions of Successful Degradation Ceremonies," *American Journal of Sociology*, 61 (March 1956), pp. 420–424.

[79] Edwin M. Lemert, "Social Structure, Social Control and Deviation," in Marshall B. Clinard, ed., *Anomie and Deviant Behavior* (New York: The Free Press of Glencoe, 1964), pp. 57–98.

Who would commit an offense in the face of rejection? Who, having done so once, would risk further rejection by *repeating* the offending behavior? The alternative question is who, having faced the rejection, will not instead reject his rejectors? So the issue is not over whether some rejection may take place in connection with the handling of deviants, although even here there is little knowledge of the extent and types of rejection and how it may differ for differing types of deviance. The issue is over the offender's *response* to the rejection, *relative to his response if there is no detection of his deviance in the first place, and hence no official action taken about it.*

It is difficult to test these alternatives empirically. Many persons have used the relatively high rates of relapse among mental patients, and recidivism among inmates, to support the labeling argument and as evidence of the futility of deterrence. But relapse equally supports an argument that the initiating causes simply have not been removed. Whatever produced the initial response recurred again to reproduce deviant behavior. The only effective way to test these alternatives is through experimental research in which we vary the critical variables of detection, degree of labeling, and amount of consequent rejection, and of course such research itself involves practical and moral problems. The obvious pragmatic importance of the potential effects of stigma and labeling means that this problem is currently a critical one for criminology.

The Reaction System

Our focus now shifts from the delinquent and criminal to those officially charged with responsibility for delinquency and crime control. A full understanding of crime requires, as we noted earlier, study of the reactions to crime as well as study of the reactions of criminals. It is necessary simply because the processing of offenders by the official reaction system in many ways determines the nature of the crime problem as it is publicly defined. It is also crucial from a more immediate and practical point of view, since there is a great search for systems of control and adjudication of criminals that will reduce the rate of crime.

The reaction system is an abstraction that stands for a large and complex network of individuals, groups, and institutions. A brief review of the central problems and issues in the study of reaction systems cannot do justice to the complexities involved. As for the causes of crime, detailed book-length monographs have been devoted to each of the separate elements in crime control. Thus students seeking a detailed treatment must look elsewhere. Our major aim in the remainder of this chapter will be to identify critical issues and problems in the organization of reaction to crime and delinquency. The three major institutional networks involved in the reaction system include the police, the courts, and correctional agencies.

The Police

Police are the most conspicuous agency officially charged with the detection of delinquent and criminal behavior. It is important in gaining an appropriate perspective on police systems, however, to recognize that they are only one part of the social control network. Indeed, in the small and homogeneous communities of preindustrial times, police played only a very small role, if any, in the control of misbehavior. The "first line of defense" rested in the internal controls of the individual, the second line of defense in the social pressures of community opinion, gossip, and similar informal mechanisms. It is primarily in instances where such mechanisms break down that public agencies such as the police are felt to be necessary as means of social control.

It still appears to be the case that, in communities or neighborhoods characterized by strong social bonds among the families, much social control is organized on informal lines. In an interesting comparative study of low- and high-delinquency areas found within the low-income districts of a large urban center, Maccoby and others note that the area with a low delinquency rate was characterized by high amounts of interaction among the neighbors.[80] Most of them knew each other by name, were willing to borrow from and share with each other, and in other ways demonstrated signs of cohesive community life. In areas with a high delinquency rate these signs of social cohesion were much less evident. These differences in the degree of social cohesion apparently led to important differences between the two areas in their residents' mode of responding to trouble of various sorts. In the low-delinquency-rate area, parents and others would intervene when they saw someone else's property being damaged, but in the high-delinquency-rate area the adults were much less ready to make any efforts at control. The plausible suggestion from these results is that official delinquency rates were lower in one area because the unofficial and informal social control system of the neighborhood operated efficiently. Youths in the community learned what the standards were, and learned to keep their behavior within those standards most of the time. In the area with a high delinquency rate, in contrast, predatory

---

[80] Eleanor Maccoby et al., "Community Integration and the Social Control of Juvenile Delinquency," *Journal of Social Issues,* 14, 3 (1958), pp. 38–51.

and destructive acts could continue unabated, growing in seriousness until youths were caught up in the formal police machinery. The suggestion is that the differences in the rates of crime in the two areas, then, were due primarily to the differences in the way in which these communities were structured for social control.

These differences were observed between two contiguous areas in the same city. Similar processes apparently operate to account for some of the large differences often found between different communities in the rates of police contact and court referrals. Nathan Goldman studied police handling of juveniles in each of four different communities in Allegheny County, Pennsylvania.[81] He found wide variations in the rates of arrests and also of court referrals in the different communities. In some communities police apparently act quickly, arresting many children for relatively minor offenses, but seldom refer the children to the juvenile court. In others there may be little police action on minor offenses, but a high proportion of arrests lead to court referrals. An especially important difference across the communities is in the handling of the less serious offenses, which apparently reflects the closeness of the relation between the police and the court on the one hand, and the police and community attitudes on the other, both integral parts of the social control system.

It is precisely in the areas of our largest cities characterized by anonymity and the relative absence of strong social bonds that problems of police control loom greatest. Spectacular instances of cries for help unheeded by the public demonstrate the extent to which the public in some areas has abdicated its role as an agent of social control to formal agencies such as the police.[82] These incidents also demonstrate how difficult it is for police agencies to assume the total burden of response to crimes.

The police and the public. Police stand in a delicate relationship to their local communities, for in a sense they are both servants and masters. They are employees of the community, supported by its taxes. At the same time they are expected to control other members of the community. This is a role with much strain. An important source of variation among police systems is found in the diverse ways in which this strain is handled. At one pole, police may encourage warm and friendly relations with the townspeople, so that they are recognized as "good

---

[81] Nathan Goldman, *The Differential Selection of Juvenile Offenders for Court Appearance*, National Research and Information Center, National Council on Crime and Delinquency, 1963.
[82] Several incidents of this type were publicized in New York City during 1963–1965.

Joes" and are responded to on the basis of personal ties to members of the community rather than because of their uniform. At the other extreme, police may attempt to avoid the problems posed by close personal contact with those they may some day have to control; they may adopt a more abstract and distant role as authoritative agents of the city or other governmental unit in question. The British sociologist, Michael Banton, has compared police systems in Scotland and the United States and suggests that the systems found in Great Britain more closely approximate the abstract role, with officials serving as direct agents of the Crown and thus being protected by social distance from the pressures created by undue familiarity. Police in many American cities, according to Banton's observations, tend toward the more personal approach.[83]

These different postures of police systems in relation to the public are likely to create diverse consequences. As agents of the community, the police are expected to take action on the basis of generalized standards and are not supposed to be swayed by personal ties and friendships. Yet a system that plays down these ties and friendships may make it more difficult for police to provide support when it is demanded by members of the community. These latter demands are likely to be important. In a recent study researchers analyzed 800 incoming telephone calls at the police complaint desk of a metropolitan police department.[84] In classifying the calls, they found that more than half appeared to involve requests for help and some form of support for personal or interpersonal problems. The police are often involved in guiding complainants to people who can solve their problems, or in attempting to solve them directly either by providing information, offering sympathy, or helping to resolve interpersonal disputes. Thus much police work includes tasks other than those suggested by the view of the police as pursuers of criminals. The personal relations encouraged by the supportive roles are often similar to those that merge into systems of corruption.

Problems of police-public relations have become increasingly important because the ordering and controlling functions of the police are no longer restricted to areas beyond the pale for middle-class citizens. Perhaps the single most important technological advance that has led to change in the relations between the police and the public is the automobile. A large part of police work involves traffic control, and many

---

[83] Michael Banton, *The Policeman in the Community* (New York: Basic Books, 1964).

[84] Elaine Cumming, Ian M. Cumming, and Laura Edell, "Policeman as Philosopher, Guide and Friend," *Social Problems*, 12, 3 (Winter 1965), pp. 276–287.

persons otherwise not in contact with the police are brought into such contact through parking and speeding violations and the like. Coupled with this change is the more immediate and dramatic role of the police in handling problems of public demonstrations and civil disobedience. These features mean that the work of the police, as well as that of other agencies of control, is increasingly accessible to observation and criticism. These broad-scale social changes are very likely to leave their impact on the relations of the police and the public.

The internal organization of police systems. In any police system other than those servicing small communities, one is likely to find a highly differentiated system of roles required by the diversified functions of the police in modern society. The traffic division, patrol division, detectives, special services, narcotics control, women's divisions, and children's services are only some of the labels suggesting the range and variety of functions the police must serve. Any one of these departments may have further subdivisions within it, as when detectives work as specialists on bunco or check details, homicide, burglary, and so forth.

This functional division of tasks is likely to be accompanied by both spatial and temporal divisions. The larger cities typically have the police function divided into separate precincts, often with their own buildings, offices, and facilities. Within each of these divisions the general social control functions of the police require the posts to be manned 24 hours a day; thus we find three shifts within the various departments.

The allocation of these diverse tasks and coordination of the differentiated parts require a high degree of skill and efficiency in organization. Police systems are massive and complex bureaucratic structures not unlike giant industries on the one hand, or other governmental agencies, such as schools, on the other. Supervision and coordination are complicated, however, because unlike the factory or educational system, the operatives in the police department are typically in the field and are not available for direct supervision. Furthermore, since they are dealing with problematic and unplanned events, it is often less feasible to schedule activities in routine ways. These and related problems of internal organization in police departments can only be touched upon in the present context. Works on police administration provide detailed accounts of the administrative theory and principles underlying some of these problems of organization.[85]

There are, however, different modes of organization that apparently

[85] O. W. Wilson, *Police Administration* (New York: McGraw-Hill, 1963).

make for a radically different character of police operations in different cities. One of the principal ways in which police systems differ has been described by the political scientist James Q. Wilson, and is related to the dimensions of social immediacy and distance referred to in our earlier discussion of police relations with the public.[86]

In examining police systems in differing communities, Wilson found that an important variation appeared to be the *professional* police department at one pole and what he refers to as a *fraternal* department at the other. In a professional department general impersonal rules prevail and govern the actions of the police, independent of the specific characteristics of the individuals with whom the police are dealing. The fraternal department on the other hand relies to a much greater extent on particularistic judgments. Related to this principal distinction are a series of other differences. Professional departments are likely to recruit members on the basis of demonstrated performance and achievement, but nonprofessional departments are likely to draw only from local citizens and may base their choice in part on such considerations as political connections, race, or religion. Professional departments are also more likely to provide formal training for their men, to insist on enforcement of the law without preferential treatment, and, in decisions about promotions and status within the police system, to depend on achievement rather than on seniority or personal contacts.

Differences such as these make for radical differences in the way in which police justice is administered. Wilson found that these differences appear to be related directly to the rate of arrest, as well as to less formal features of police operations. In an analysis of delinquency control in two cities, one fitting the professional model and the other the fraternal model, he found that the professionally oriented system led to a larger number of arrests and formal charges of delinquency than did the fraternal system. This was true despite the fact that the professionally oriented police had a more sophisticated and less directly punitive orientation toward delinquents. Apparently the professional system brought a closer concern for legal violations and an unwillingness to change this system into an informal and more permissive structure. The result is that youths living in these two different types of city are exposed to quite different risks of treatment as delinquents. If there are negative consequences of the labeling process, one effect of the more professional system may be to produce a larger number of stigmatized delinquents.

[86] James Q. Wilson, "The Police and the Delinquent in Two Cities," in Wheeler, ed., *Controlling Delinquents, op. cit.*

But the important thing to stress is that these matters are just now opening up for investigation. Some police systems are beginning their own programs of research into police activity in an effort to better understand their operations. Some are beginning to cooperate with social scientists and others. This trend appears to be part of a broader change, discussed later, toward closer scientific examination of the administration of criminal justice.

Interaction between police and offenders. In the classical conceptions of the administration of criminal justice, the police and other officials react to the nature of the offense and not to the offender. Similar legal violations are to be treated similarly without a show of discretion on the basis of qualities extrinsic to the act. In important ways, this principle has been modified so that police are expected to pay attention to characteristics other than those surrounding the actual commission of a delinquent or criminal act. Thus in most police systems only some detected law violations lead to arrest. The police perform a quasi-judicial role by sorting out offenses into those that are sent on to the courts, those that are handled informally by the police system, and those that are forgotten. Statistical analyses indicate, for example, that among all persons caught by the police, those of lower socioeconomic status are more likely to be referred to court.

A recent study in which the investigators actually observed the police in interaction with youth provides some suggestions that may help explain the statistical evidence. The observers noted that in a large number of encounters with youth, those youths who most frequently took on what we might call a delinquent stance or demeanor were officially handled as delinquents. Among youths originally stopped by investigators for the same offense, those who appeared contrite, who spoke politely to the police, who agreed to follow the policeman's suggestions or strictures, who bore few of the outward symbols of the delinquent culture, were more likely to be treated with leniency. Those who were defiant, who wore their hair and clothes in manners associated with a delinquent tradition, were more likely to be treated severely. Although this does not come as a surprise, it does indicate the importance of characteristics not intrinsically involved with the act that may become a basis for official action on the part of the reactors. In these instances police were implicitly estimating that youths of one type were likely to get into further difficulty and those of the other type were not.[87]

[87] Irving Piliavin and Scott Briar, "Police Encounters with Juveniles," *American Journal of Sociology*, 70 (September 1964), pp. 206–215.

Civil liberties and police efficiency. Judged solely in terms of their capacity to catch criminals and thereby to solve crimes, most police systems are not too efficient. As we saw in the introductory section to this chapter, the bulk of all crimes reported to the police are never cleared by arrest, and many of those that are cleared by arrest do not lead to prosecution. But just as there are legitimate and illegitimate ways of earning a conventional livelihood, so there are legitimate and illegitimate ways of catching criminals. One reason why the rates of arrests and prosecution are not higher is that the police are constrained from using highly efficient but illegal means of solving crimes. Indeed, some of the most important recent constitutional decisions arrived at by the United States Supreme Court have concerned issues of legitimate and illegitimate police operations—illegal arrests, the use of wire taps, unreasonable search and seizure. As with many of the guarantees and protections involved in court investigations, our legal system has typically recognized the vast difference in power between an individual and the state by placing the bulk of the procedural safeguards on the side of the individual. One of the costs of providing such safeguards is a less than maximally efficient police department.

There are, of course, additional problems of police efficiency that cannot be explained by legal constraints against the use of various mechanisms of detection. Many police forces have been shown to have members, both corrupt and not, who fail to arrest offenders clearly violating the law. But it is interesting to note how often the failure to "invoke the criminal process" occurs around nonvictim crimes: abortion, alcohol and narcotics offenses, gambling, voluntary homosexuality, and prostitution.[88] As one professor of law has put it, "Almost every case in which the law calls upon the enforcement agencies to stamp out conduct that involves a willing seller and a willing buyer . . . is a situation that contains the seeds of police corruption and demoralization." [89]

On the one hand, instances of nonvictim crimes provide rationalizations for the police officer who knowingly allows the conduct to continue. Who is really hurt, the policeman may ask, by the placing of a bet with a bookie, the purchase of alcohol after hours, and related

---

[88] Edwin Schur, *Crimes Without Victims* (Englewood Cliffs, N.J.: Prentice-Hall, 1965); for a very recent account of police practices in making arrests and investigations, see Jerome Skolnick, *Justice Without Trial* (New York: John Wiley and Sons, 1966).

[89] Joseph Goldstein, "Police Discretion Not to Invoke the Criminal Process: Low-Visibility Decision in the Administration of Justice," *Yale Law Journal*, 69 (March 1960).

types of offense? On the other hand, when there are strong pressures on the police to control criminal activity that typically does not involve a victim in the usual sense, such as narcotics offenses, one is likely to find the wholesale use of informants who are protected in their habit by their willingness to reveal the habits of others. And if direct evidence of criminal activity is hard to come by, as in prostitution cases, police may attempt some control through harassment of suspected offenders. Thus some of the problems of police organization seem to result from the nature of the laws the police are required to enforce, and so we return full circle to questions of what acts ought to be made criminal.

It is a truism that members of any occupation or profession are likely to look at the world from a perspective influenced greatly by the typical problems they face in their work. The police are no different from other occupational categories in this regard, and it is not surprising to find that the police are frequently upset at the difficulties placed in front of them by constitutional safeguards designed to protect civil liberties. Further, in their roles as citizens, parents, and more generally members of the community they serve, it would be surprising to find them immune to the beliefs and prejudices toward minorities, including the minority of criminals, that are held by civilians in their own communities. Yet our value system requires that in their role as police they must strive to remain free of the biases, must simultaneously work hard to protect the community from crime while working within a framework that also protects civilians from the dangers inherent in police power. It seems almost unnecessary to note that this is indeed a stringent set of demands.

Administration of Criminal Justice

Few areas of our domestic social life capture more public attention and interest than the administration of criminal justice. Typically, when persons are faced with the application of actual sanctions, a great amount of attention is focused on the problem, and a number of penetrating questions may arise: whether it is right to punish people in certain ways, whether certain acts ought to be punished, whether the quality of justice is fair, how much evidence there must be in order to convict, and a host of other questions. Indeed, the theme of the courtroom drama is familiar to most Americans, although few are actual participants at criminal hearings and trials.

Since the administration of criminal justice tells us much about the quality of life in a society, and raises basic and often heated issues, it is important for us to attempt to arrive at an objective view of the processes involved, the underlying philosophies, and the actual consequences of the actions taken in the name of criminal justice. In order to do so we must begin historically, for there have been fundamental changes within the short space of the last 100 years in American society's mode of adaptation to problems of criminal justice.

Changing conceptions of criminal justice. Historically, the prime purpose and function of criminal law and its administration were to distinguish the innocent from the guilty and to impose penal sanctions on the latter. The purpose for imposing the penal sanction was both to punish the wicked and to deter those who might but for the fear of punishment engage in the forbidden activities. This statement is an oversimplification, of course, and there are many refinements of conception underlying the application of criminal sanctions and justifying alternative rules for insuring safeguards to the innocent. But the nub of the problem is clear.

Much remains of this central argument, but much has been added to it over the years. Although the changes are intertwined and difficult to disentangle, there are at least three important types of changes in our conception of and attitude toward the administration of criminal justice. First, there has been a growing spirit of *humanitarianism.* When criminals could be viewed as part of the lower elements, different in kind from conventional members of society, and especially from those who man its administrative tribunals, it was possible to treat the criminal as a thing rather than as a person, and consequently to justify harsh actions against him. As one illustration, it was only 180 years ago that there were over 200 capital offenses in English law. The last few decades have witnessed a great reduction in both the number of capital crimes and the number of persons actually receiving capital punishment.

Second, scientific study has been added to moral judgment as a basis for decision making in the field of criminal justice. This change is perhaps best symbolized by noting the frequency with which we now ask "Why did he do it?" and "Will he do it again?" No longer is it enough to know that what the person did was morally wrong. We assume that what he did had its causes, that they were determinable, and that knowledge of them will lead us to greater understanding and greater wisdom in our actions.

Third, and clearly interrelated with the other two, is the growth in what one author calls "the rehabilitative ideal." [90] Above all, we have

[90] Francis A. Allen, "The Juvenile Court and the Limits of Juvenile Justice," *The Borderline of Criminal Justice* (Chicago: University of Chicago Press, 1964), pp. 43–61.

come to think of the purpose of our actions regarding the offender as including therapy or rehabilitation. Sometimes this reaction is seen as the opposite of punishment: "Our purpose is not to punish the offender but to reform him." Although it is not necessary to see these two as opposed (and indeed one of the early Italian penal reformers, Garofalo, saw the possible therapeutic functions of punishment), it is a relatively new idea to consider as one primary goal of the system of criminal justice the therapeutic effect of that system on the person who is processed through it—on his well-being, his personality, and more generally his future life.

Changing institutional structures. The shift in philosophy has produced changes in the actual social structures through which criminal justice is administered, changes which are designed to enable the new philosophy to work. Although the impetus for some of the changes may have been quite concrete and particular to the immediate circumstances, they do reflect in greater or lesser degree a broader overall change in philosophy. Four specific changes can be noted here.

1. *Alternatives to imprisonment.* Throughout the late nineteenth and twentieth centuries we have seen an increase in the use of alternatives to imprisonment as a means of handling offenders convicted by our courts. The most prominent of these are the increased use of probation and parole. Probation and parole programs are typically justified in terms of the rehabilitative ideal, and to the extent that they reduce the number of persons who go to prison or the length of time they stay there, they also reflect the humanitarian tradition.

2. *Growth in administrative discretion.* There have been changes in the sentencing structure designed to increase the discretion of the court and simultaneously to increase the extent to which the court can consider factors other than the seriousness of the crime in the determination of the sentence. Under the classical free-will doctrine, persons were for the most part able to calculate precisely the penalty for any crime they might commit, so that they could assess whether the possible gain from committing the crime was worth the cost of the penalty if they were caught. Individual differences in the personality, social and criminal background, or other features of the offenders were of little relevance; the offense was the critical incident. Penal codes written according to these values typically had what are known as "definite sentences," which means simply a specified length of time to be served in prison for the particular offense in question. Little freedom was given to the sentencing authorities to alter the sentence depending on specific facts about either the crime or the offender.

The indeterminate sentence provides opportunities for the judge to consider subtle facts that may have influenced the individual. In particular, it enables the judge to consider features of personality that may influence the extent to which the offender is assumed to be capable of reformation. Unlike the earlier system, two offenders who have committed precisely the same offense may be sentenced to differing terms in prison, or one may be given probation while the other goes to prison, such actions being justified on grounds of the differing probabilities of reformation of the two offenders and other related considerations. In some jurisdictions the increased discretion is in the hands of the judge; in other jurisdictions the sentence is set by an administrative board after the individual has arrived in prison and more is known about him. In both cases the general effect is increased discretion and power for the sentencing authority.

Along with this change in sentencing structure there has developed a change in the sources of information available to the judge or other sentencing authority at the time action is taken. Increasingly, they have available social histories and backgrounds on the offenders, based upon a "presentence investigation" typically conducted by a probation department. And in some instances they may have access to psychological or psychiatric records. This change, then, signifies the broadening of the informational base assumed relevant to the actions to be taken, along with the broadening of the alternatives available to the sentencing authorities, whether judge or administrative board. The result is an increase in administrative power, and a relative reduction in the extent to which actual sentences are determined by the original legislative action establishing crimes and penalties.

3. *Changing rules for establishing criminal responsibility.* The historic distinction between the criminal and the sick has been challenged by the influence of modern psychiatric concepts and the more general influence of positivism as a body of thought in the Western world. The result is a blurring of the distinction both in the rules of law and in the social arrangements that give expression to those rules.

A historic principle for application of criminal sanctions (one beclouded by issues too technical and complex to be discussed here) is that the person must have criminal intent. This does not mean that he must know that the act is a crime, but rather that he must have a conscious intention to commit the act. A chief condition for finding the person criminally irresponsible and therefore incapable of criminal intent is that, at the time the person committed the act, he was "labouring under such a defect of reason, from disease of the mind, as not to know the nature and quality of the act he was doing; or, if he did know it, that he did not know he was doing what was wrong." [91] This is the McNaghten rule, the classical doctrine relating mental illness to the criminal law. The wording codified the principle generally in effect at the time the case in which it was enunciated was decided. That case, the *Queen v. McNaghten,* is exceedingly important, for the rule of application of an insanity plea established at that time has remained in effect in almost all our jurisdictions until the present day. To it was added, at a later time, a doctrine of irresistible impulse, to enable a finding of insanity in cases where the person had cognitive knowledge of his act but was driven by the strongest of emotional compulsions to commit the act anyway.

Psychiatrists and others approaching legal issues from a medical-scientific perspective have found it difficult to work under the McNaghten rule because it poses a seemingly extreme, unrealistic, and outmoded test of mental functioning. The result has been considerable agitation over many decades concerning a possible reformulation. In 1954, in Washington, D.C., the Court of Appeals established a different basis for deciding issues of criminal responsibility.[92] This new ruling, the Durham rule, was more in harmony with modern psychiatric concepts, and the presiding judge in the court in which it was established, David Bazelon, has received awards from the American Psychiatric Association for his wisdom in supporting such a rule. Other jurisdictions, however, have found the rule vague and wanting in several respects, and by and large have failed to follow the Durham decision. The precedent set by the decision, however, testifies to the increased concern for the rules of criminal responsibility and for the possibility of extending the realm in which persons are found to be acting without full responsibility for their actions. The tendency is toward a broadening of the use of mental illness as a defense against criminal liability.

The same trend is exhibited in legislation concerning sex offenders; as noted earlier, some statutes require certification by medical authorities before those sentenced under the special sex offender laws can be released from penal institutions.[93] The general haziness of any clear boundary between the criminal and the sick is further evidenced by

---

[91] The McNaghten rule is presented and discussed in Richard C. Donnelly, Joseph Goldstein, and Richard D. Schwartz, *Criminal Law* (New York: The Free Press of Glencoe, 1962), pp. 734–777.
[92] *Ibid.*
[93] Wheeler, "Sex Offenses: A Sociological Critique," *op. cit.*

legislation in several states allowing relatively free transfer of offenders from prisons to mental hospitals at the discretion of administrative and medical officials.

The full institutionalization of many of these changes is clearly evident in other Western nations. In Norway, for example, of all persons serving time in institutions, only a minority have been sentenced under the classical criminal sanctions. A certain number are placed in institutions for "preventive detention"—where they are classified as not fully responsible for their actions but are being detained for the prevention of further crime.[94] Another large segment are alcoholics who are sent to a workhouse institution, presumably for their care and treatment. There are also special rules for processing youthful offenders. The result is that the new forms and structures have come to dominate, at least numerically, the penal system.[95] Some consequences of these new structures will be considered later.

4. *Emergence of the juvenile court.* A major change in criminal administration was brought about by the introduction of the juvenile court as a separate administrative agency for processing young offenders. The juvenile court began roughly at the turn of the century in the United States, and has been extended so that all our states have separate procedures for processing juveniles, although only the larger jurisdictions have special juvenile courts with full-time juvenile court judges.

The impetus for the establishment of the juvenile court was clearly a combination of the changed philosophies just outlined. The major premise underlying it is that the juvenile, like the mentally ill person, is not fully responsible for his actions and should not be held accountable for them in the same manner as adult offenders. Instead, the court should serve the best interests of the youth in question; its aim should be reform rather than punishment. In actual practice, the incorporation of the rehabilitative ideal and action in behalf of the child has meant that the formal austerity of the criminal courtroom is not found in most juvenile hearings. Conferences may be held in the judge's chambers, the judge may shed his robe for civilian dress, and the juvenile is less likely to be represented by defense counsel. Questions and problems are likely to concern the nature of the boy's character, his family upbringing, parental disharmony and the like, with a withdrawal of systematic attention to the specific conduct leading to the youth's appearance in court. Indeed, little formal effort may be exerted

[94] For a study of one such instance, see Thomas Mathieson, *The Defense of the Weak* (Ph.D. dissertation, University of Oslo, Norway, 1965).
[95] I am indebted to Nils Christie, Institute of Criminal Law and Criminology, University of Oslo, for information on institutions for alcoholics in Norway.

to establish the fact that the youth has actually committed a specific offense.[96]

The social consequences of the changed ideology and institutions. It is one thing to establish a changed philosophy and its incorporation into actual social arrangements. It is quite another to come to a balanced assessment of the consequences of the change, both for the community at large and for those individuals directly exposed to its operations. One might anticipate that some of the changes are in line with the intentions of those who created the new institutions, but that others have been unanticipated and often seemingly at odds with the underlying philosophy.

There is no question that the trend has been accompanied by a reduction in the more extreme forms of direct brutality and physical punishment. The rate of executions in the United States has declined, and the prisons in which we hold persons who might previously have been put to death show signs of a more humanitarian regime. Less often than in the past do we build them in dark and forbidding styles, nor do we emphasize quite as heavily the clearly incapacitating features of the prison such as high walls, fences, and guards. In the more progressive states the large portion of inmates are likely to serve out much of their sentence in honor camps or farms where they live in dormitories, rather than in old bastilles, living in cell blocks. These and many other changes do indeed give expression to the modern rehabilitative ideal.

These same changes, however, have had other consequences that are not so clearly in line with the original objectives. The emphasis upon scientific study of the criminal and on the character of the offender rather than his offense has led to a withering of concern for some of the fundamental elements of civil and political liberty in connection with criminal actions. Use of the indeterminate sentence, for example, has apparently led to sentences at least as long as those prevailing under the older, seemingly more punitive doctrines.[97] It is clear that once concern is transferred from the nature of the offense to the probability that an offender will repeat it, there may be a basis for keeping a person in prison for a long time even though he may have been convicted of a minor crime.

These problems appear in direct form in juvenile court proceedings. If we can effectively argue that we are acting on behalf of the child

---
[96] A number of works treat the history of the juvenile court in some detail. For one such treatment, see Paul W. Tappan, *Juvenile Delinquency* (New York: McGraw-Hill, 1959).
[97] Francis A. Allen, *op. cit.*

rather than on behalf of the community and that we are providing therapy rather than punishment, it is but a short step to arguing that we should feel free to keep the individual in an institution for a long time if his needs seem to warrant it, since what we are doing is beneficial to him and is not determined by a punitive ideology.

Thus we can question the meaning of a humanitarian or therapeutic approach if we find an increasing deprivation of the individual's liberty. Here it is extremely important, both for decision makers and those exposed to their decisions, to distinguish between the intentions that motivate actions, the actions themselves, and their social consequences. If one person is "treated" by a year's confinement behind walls and bars, while another is "punished" by six months behind similar walls and bars, we might well ask which is the more benign, humanitarian, therapeutic setting. And it is important to look closely at what goes on behind the walls and bars and not simply at the vocabulary used to discuss it. A program of rehabilitation may mean spending one hour, out of the approximately 120 waking hours a week, talking to a guidance counselor. Or vocational rehabilitation may mean being one of 40 inmates assigned to a shop designed for ten, working with equipment that is no longer used in private industry.

The point of all this is merely to accentuate the fact that intentions are not enough, and that the consequences of alternative programs and courses of action cannot necessarily be known in advance. An important feature of the modern administration of criminal justice, and of our efforts to find an appropriate balance between the varied and conflicting values guiding that administration, will be detailed and carefully designed research which can trace the objective consequences of the actions we have taken.

The quality of justice. If many of the historical changes in our ideologies about the administration of criminal justice can be caught up in the phrase "the rehabilitative ideal," the problems now on the horizon may be caught up in the phrase "the quality of justice." In part because of the problems already mentioned and the seeming withdrawal of concern for justice in the name of therapeutic programs, and in part for more immediate reasons, there is a renewed and growing concern for the concepts of justice and fairness in relation to the administration of criminal law. Although this concern is likely to appear in relation to many different aspects of criminal justice, it currently receives its greatest impetus from concern for equality of justice for the poor.

It is evident on many counts that, despite values supporting the concept of even-handed justice for all, many aspects of the actual administration benefit primarily those with greater financial resources and greater education. Persons of greater education are likely to have greater knowledge and awareness of what their rights are, and hence to recognize instances in which these rights are violated by others. They can also call on resources from educated friends, as well as on financial resources, in order to assure that their legal interests are protected. It often appears that these conditions do not obtain for the poor.[98]

A prime example of the effect of income on the quality of justice administered may be drawn from recent studies of the bail system in the United States. In our legal system the typical means used to ensure that an accused person will not flee to avoid prosecution and will appear for his trial is the bail system—the posting of money so that the accused will have a financial interest in appearing in court. A person accused in a criminal proceeding will either be jailed until his trial or released on bail. If he is financially incapable of posting bail, he is detained in jail. To quote from a recent report on bail in the United States, "Each year, the freedom of hundreds of thousands of persons charged with crime hinges upon their ability to raise the money necessary for bail. Those who are freed on bail are released not because they are innocent but because they can buy their liberty. The balance are detained not because they are guilty but because they are poor." [99] Clearly, this system discriminates against persons on the basis of their income.

Recently, the Vera Foundation conducted studies designed to test the effectiveness of alternatives to the bail system. In the "Manhattan Bail Project" persons arrested for felonies are interviewed by law school students before their arraignment in court. If the offenders appear to be residentially stable, have a reasonably stable employment history, have family contacts within New York City, and have no extensive prior criminal record, they stand a good chance of being released without posting bail. The defendants are released on their own recognizance—they promise to appear without any further security. In the Vera Foundation study, of the persons released under these circumstances, fewer than one percent failed to show up in court. It appears that at least two-thirds of all felony offenders might be released under similar proceedings. Further, nearly 60 percent of those recommended for release were later either acquitted or had their cases

[98] *The Extension of Legal Services to the Poor* (Washington, D.C.: U.S. Department of Health, Education and Welfare, December 1964).
[99] Daniel J. Freed and Patricia M. Wald, *Bail in the United States: 1964,* National Conference on Bail and Criminal Justice, 1964, p. vii.

dismissed. It thus appears that such procedures may be effective alternatives to the bail system, thus helping to provide equality of justice administration.[99]

The Bail Study offers one good example of the way in which carefully designed policy research can produce evidence that makes a rational evaluation of policy possible. Other issues involving the quality of criminal justice administration that either have been or might be given similar objective study include the role of the public defender's office;[100] the process of bargaining between prosecution and defense attorney that sets the actual crime for which the person will be charged, and thus often determines the character of his penalty;[101] and the study of factors leading to differential dispositions by different judges operating within different jurisdictions.[102] In all these areas, it seems fair to say, we are really just beginning to understand the nature and consequences of judicial and administrative actions.

The problem of general prevention. In the movement toward a more humanitarian, scientific, and therapeutic orientation to criminal justice, some deeply rooted issues which provide part of the underpinning for most of our system of criminal justice administration have been neglected. Chief among these is the problem of ascertaining the effects of criminal justice administration, including the punishments meted out for crimes, on the general population. European scholars have referred to this as the problem of *general prevention*, to distinguish it from questions of "individual prevention"—the effects of criminal justice administration on the persons who themselves are being charged with crimes.[103]

Historically, invoking the criminal process was assumed to have its effect not only on the particular criminal in question but also on law-abiding citizens who might be potential criminals. The latter effect has been viewed as operating in two quite different ways. The first and most commonly cited way is by simple deterrence: applying penalties to criminals will deter others who might themselves have engaged in the crime but for the fear of receiving the penalty. The simple assumption is that we learn from witnessing the experiences of others as well

---

[100] David Sudnow, "Normal Crimes: Sociological Features of the Penal Code in a Public Defender Office," *Social Problems*, 12, 3 (Winter 1965), pp. 255–276.
[101] Donald Newman, "Pleading Guilty for Considerations: A Study of Bargain Justice," in Norman Johnston, Leonard Savitz, and Marvin E. Wolfgang, eds., *Sociology of Punishment* and *Correction* (New York: John Wiley and Sons, 1962), pp. 24–32.
[102] Edward Green, *Judicial Attitudes in Sentencing* (New York: St. Martin's Press, 1961).
[103] Andenaes, *op. cit.*

as from experiencing events directly ourselves. For those who have not deeply internalized the standards of right conduct proposed by the criminal law, or when the law itself has no strongly binding moral quality, deterrence is thought to be an important social control. We may stop at a stop signal because we believe it morally right to follow all laws, or we may stop because of fear of an accident, or we may stop because if we go through it, a policeman might give us a ticket. To the extent that we stop for the latter reason, we are witnessing the deterrent effect of the penalties assigned to violation of the law.

A second way in which general prevention is assumed to operate is through a more positive interpretation of the effects of criminal laws and punishments. Citizens, it has been argued, need to be reminded of the law and its binding powers, and in particular require periodic reinforcement of their moral commitments. An important social function of punishment is that it calls attention to the moral code by locating instances of its violation, and to the sanctity of the code by calling attention to the punishments that attach to its violation. The punishment of violators shores up the moral conscience of the community and provides an opportunity for highlighting and dramatizing the importance of its moral code.[104]

Despite the rise in the number and quality of objective studies of crime and its consequences, we know little about the efficacy of either of these lines of reasoning. It has been much easier to test the effects of programs on the individuals directly exposed to them it has been to test their indirect effect on others. Some work has been devoted to studies of the death penalty as a deterrent to murder, and such evidence as emerges from these studies suggests that there is little relation between the nature of the penalty and the rate of homicide.[105] But the emotional involvements often found in murder cases and surrounding the issue of capital punishment make it a poor basis for forming general conclusions. It seems quite likely that general prevention, in either or both of the senses mentioned, will operate differently for different types of offenses and to differing degrees in different people. Of course, the probability of being caught in a crime is a critical issue as well as the nature of the punishment. In any event, here is another area where the criminal law rests upon presumptions about human motives and the structure of social control that are at best poorly understood at this time.

It seems unlikely that the various problems we have discussed,

[104] Emile Durkheim, *On the Division of Labor in Society*, trans. by George Simpson (New York: The Macmillan Company, 1933).
[105] Karl Schuessler, "The Deterrent Influence of the Death Penalty," *Annals of the American Academy of Political and Social Science*, 284 (November 1952).

including the philosophy underlying the operation of our courts, the nature and consequences of the actual administration of criminal justice, the quality of justice, and the role of deterrence, will ever be resolved once and for all. Most of these questions get to some of the core problems of the society, and the solutions are likely to be intimately entwined with the nature of the society itself and therefore subject to change as the society changes. What does seem characteristic at this period in American history is that many questions previously resolved by premature closure are now being opened for legitimate scientific investigation. Hopefully, our knowledge will be a basis for bringing criminal justice administration more in line with the values and philosophies that undergird it.

Correctional Systems

After offenders have been convicted of crimes, something must be done with them. An important part of the reaction system in the United States is the prison. It was not always so, for prisons have been an important form of reaction to crime only for roughly two centuries. In earlier periods various forms of physical punishment and torture were used, along with capital punishment and banishment to foreign places, and there was no concept of using imprisonment as a long-term device for punishment or therapy. That notion developed primarily as the humanitarian device to replace the rack, flogging, and other means of corporal punishment. And although at one time it was the only primary substitute for these other devices, new ones such as probation and parole have been added as part of the general humanitarian and rehabilitative trend. Probation and parole deserve detailed comment, but space prohibits such a discussion here.

Approximately one-quarter of a million Americans are currently serving felony sentences in one or another of our state or federal prisons. Our brief treatment will be restricted to four critical areas of concern about prisons: (1) the nature of the prison as a social system, (2) the character of inmate culture and social structure, (3) the relation between the prison and the external community, and (4) the effects of imprisonment on those imprisoned and on the broader society.

The nature of the prison as a social system. Although prisons have often been thought of as unique institutions, they have very clear similarities to other types of organizations, and hence have similar problems and structures. First, they are part of the class identified by sociologist Erving Goffman as "total institutions"—walled establishments wherein all or almost all the needs of residents of the establishment are met on a 24-hour a day basis.[106] Other examples include mental hospitals, monasteries, military camps, and the like. Perhaps the chief characteristic of such establishments is the division between those who are paid to run the establishment and those who are there for other reasons. This distinction is suggested by the concepts of rulers and ruled, keepers and kept, staff and inmates, staff and patients, officers and men. Such establishments typically develop a complex social structure with a number of formal status distinctions among differing staff positions, and a rich informal system among the inmates.

To the extent that the prison attempts to accomplish something with its inmates, to change them in some way while they are there, it also resembles other institutions in our society such as the school or the university and the treatment-oriented mental hospital. All these institutions are socialization settings, where efforts are made to train, educate, or in other ways modify the responses of members of the inmate, patient, or student category. Again it is typical to find the division between the teachers and the taught, and so it is not surprising to find a good deal of similarity between socialization settings and total institutions, often with the same concrete organization having both functions. When we emphasize the total institution quality of such settings, attention is often focused on the general nature of the relationship between the two groups. When we focus on the socializing features of the settings, the critical question is whether what the recruits to the setting are learning is what the staff in the setting are teaching.[107]

Let us compare the college student with the prison inmate. College teachers often want their students to learn new ways of thinking; the students are sometimes more concerned solely with the grade, since grades rather than abstract concepts and ideas may determine the student's later life chances. Similarly, prison staff are often hopeful that their inmates will learn new values or new means of self-control as a result of participation in prison programs; the inmate's own participation, however, may be geared much more toward simply getting out of prison as soon as possible. A chief fact about imprisonment is that it is a deprivation of liberty; it is not surprising that inmates are more motivated to regain their liberty than they are to change their personality or values.

A characteristic feature of the prison as a social system is that it is

---

[106] Erving Goffman, *Asylums* (Garden City, N.Y.: Anchor Books, Doubleday, 1961).

[107] Stanton Wheeler, "The Structure of Formally Organized Socialization Settings," in Orville G. Brim, Jr. and Stanton Wheeler, *Socialization after Childhood* (New York, John Wiley and Sons, 1966).

designed to fill a multiplicity of goals, and there is likely to be a conflict among them. We have already commented elsewhere on the Bastille-like character of prisons. Despite a great change in conception since the nineteenth century, there is still a strong emphasis on security measures. One of the prime functions of the prison is of course to protect society from persons who have violated its rules in serious ways, and some correctional administrations are likely to be highly attentive to the problem of escape. It is difficult to make a prison absolutely escape-proof and at the same time convey the feeling that it is a benign therapeutic setting. Neither staff nor inmates are likely to miss the apparent contradiction between group therapy settings on the one hand and manned gun towers on the other; between the stress on a sense of individual responsibility and dignity and the mass features of imprisonment such as identical cells and uniforms.

In these and in other ways the conflict between protection of society and rehabilitation of offenders stands out clearly. The social system that comprises the prison gives expression to this conflict, with some officials hired largely to contain inmates and others to treat them. What inmates are allowed to have in their cells, how often they may visit with relatives, whether all inmates who violate a given rule receive the same penalty for its violation, whether inmates wear standard uniforms or are allowed to adopt some forms of civilian dress—decisions about these and other details of inmate life often depend on our broad premises about the role of free will, punishment, rehabilitation, and the like. Prisons are by no means the only social system that serves a multiplicity of functions and goals, but they are certainly one where great conflicts appear.[108] Perhaps this is one reason why careful studies designed to test the effectiveness of social casework and counseling programs in institutional settings so often fail to demonstrate real effectiveness.

The recent trend of imprisonment has surely been toward a greater emphasis on the training, treatment, and therapeutic functions of the prisons. Those correctional systems that are thought of as embodying the best in correctional philosophy exhibit concern for these features. Our federal prison system has long emphasized vocational training programs, and some of the state systems, such as that in California, have recently given great attention to group counseling as a possible therapeutic device. But so long as imprisonment involves the deprivation of freedom and free movement, to that extent, apparently, it can never be completely therapeutic.

[108] Richard E. Cloward et al., *Theoretical Studies in the Social Organization of the Prison*, Social Science Research Council Monograph 15, 1959.

Inmate culture and social structure. Of all the possible prison problems that might have captured the attention of social scientists, the one that has most often done so is the nature of inmate society in prison. Without attempting to review all the relevant studies, we can at least single out some of the important questions that have been raised.

1. To what extent do inmates form a society of their own characterized by its own values and social order? Some investigators have found that the character of inmate society is largely atomistic, that its members fail to participate meaningfully in social relations with one another, and that therefore it has only a relatively loose form of social order. This is one of the findings of a classic monograph on inmate life, Donald Clemmer's *The Prison Community*.[109] Others have suggested that inmate life is more cohesive and ordered than suggested in Clemmer's account, and that the depriving character of the prison fosters the development of an inmate culture which can ward off the deprivations of imprisonment and provide self-esteem to members of the inmate community, in much the same way as the delinquent gang is said to provide such esteem to lower-class boys in slum neighborhoods. This theme characterizes another distinctive work on prisons, Gresham Sykes' *The Society of Captives*.[110]

Other investigators have questioned both of these views of the operation of the inmate system and have moved toward a more pluralistic conception of the inmate system in which a variety of possibilities short of either extreme are seen to emerge under differing conditions. One treatment, for example, suggests that some inmates are oriented largely to the criminal culture outside the walls, and that for these prisoners inmate life is not a dominating force. Other inmates are assumed to get their rewards primarily from life within the institution and therefore adapt differently.[111] What appears to happen is that any or all of these patterns may be found, depending on a variety of other conditions, including the social composition of the inmate population, the nature of the staff and program of the prison, the broader cultural setting in which the prison is located, and so forth.

2. To the extent that inmates do form a coherent social order, is the *content* of that order supportive of or hostile to that of the official establishment of the prison? Until recent years the principal answer to

[109] Donald R. Clemmer, *The Prison Community* (New York: Rinehart, reissue of 1940 edition, 1958).
[110] Gresham Sykes, *The Society of Captives* (Princeton, N.J.: Princeton University Press, 1958).
[111] John Irwin and Donald R. Cressey, "Thieves, Convicts and the Inmate Culture," *Social Problems*, 10, 1 (Summer 1962), p. 142.

this question has been that the content appears to stress values in opposition to the staff: "Don't inform on fellow inmates, help the staff no more than necessary, and be loyal to your fellow inmates." In one of the first sociometric studies of the prison, Schrag found that inmates chosen by others as leaders were typically inmates who had committed more crimes before entering prison, who had longer sentences to serve, and who in other ways appeared to be more criminally oriented.[112]

Recently, researchers have found that this structure is by no means inevitable. In a sociometric study of inmates in minimum security camps, Grusky found that inmates chosen as leaders by others were typically those who had more positive attitudes toward the staff and their programs.[113] Street, in a report on a larger study of seven juvenile correctional institutions, found that the extent to which the inmate system was supportive of the staff depended on the character of the institution itself: inmate leaders were more likely to support the staff in institutions that were benign and treatment-oriented.[114] Thus the substance of the values supported by the inmate system, like the degree of coherence of the system itself, appears to depend on a variety of conditions and is not a simple and uniform function of prison experience.

3. What changes take place in inmates as they are exposed to imprisonment over time? This is a critical question that has not been met with any simple answer. Clemmer's pioneering work some years ago introduced the concept of "prisonization" to refer to the process by which the inmates take on the values of the criminal world the more thoroughly they become exposed to inmate life. In an attempt to study the notion, Wheeler found that Clemmer's propositions appeared to be true but did not give the full picture. In addition to taking on the values of the prison, inmates appear to shed those values as they prepare to leave the institution, so that the net effect of imprisonment on their attitudes is much smaller than suggested by the prisonization concept.[115] Yet neither of these patterns is exhibited in any simple way in a later study of Scandinavian prison inmates.[116] Another investigation

[112] Clarence C. Schrag, "Leadership among Prison Inmates," *American Sociological Review*, 19 (February 1954), pp. 37–42.
[113] Oscar Grusky, "Organizational Goals and the Behavior of Informal Leaders," *American Journal of Sociology*, 65 (July 1959), pp. 59–67.
[114] David Street, "Inmate Social Organization: A Comparative Study of Juvenile Correctional Institutions," unpublished Ph.D. dissertation, University of Michigan, 1962.
[115] Stanton Wheeler, "Socialization in Correctional Communities," *American Sociological Review*, 26 (October 1961).
[116] This statement is based on research in process. A review of the project will appear in a forthcoming issue of *Scandinavian Studies in Criminology*.

under way seeks to trace in detail inmates' subjective feelings about the impact of imprisonment on them, and hopefully will provide a clearer picture of the way imprisonment is actually experienced by those who go through it.[117]

The prison and external society. Prisons give the appearance of being completely cut off from the broader society because of their walls, bars, and fences, and often by their location in rural counties and isolated areas. But at several different levels they are of course intimately linked with the broader social world. Indeed, a careful study of all the connections between the prison and the broader environment would be illuminating.

For the individual inmate an important part of his adjustment depends on the nature of his relations with primary group members outside the prisons. But perhaps even more significant for an understanding of the prison itself are the ties between the prison system as a whole and the political structure of the state or other jurisdiction in which it is located.[118] The budget provided for imprisonment depends typically on action by state legislatures, and the way in which that budget is cut is likely to depend heavily on a central prison administration, and not solely on the staff at a given institution. For these reasons it is essential to understand the interplay among these various units. State legislators, with a range of heavy demands for limited state funds, are unlikely to allocate more than a minimum amount of funds to prisons unless prison riots or other special circumstances draw public attention to prison conditions. Prisons are of course in competition with other state endeavors such as highway and educational programs, yet the pressure groups supporting prisons are unlikely to have the same strength and position in the state as those backing, say, state universities. The differential allocation of resources of course reflects, in part, different ideas of what is important. In any event, one reason for the frequent gulf between precept and practice in the field of corrections is that the costs of putting our precepts fully into practice are often greater than most states are willing to support.

The effects of imprisonment. Of the three prime objectives often cited as justifications for the existence of the prison as a reaction device—protection of society, deterrence, and reform of the inmate—there is good evidence that the prison is effective on the first of these criteria but little or no evidence about its effectiveness on the other two. The rate of escape from prison is typically less than 2 percent of

[117] Baum and Wheeler, *op. cit.*
[118] See Lloyd E. Ohlin, "Conflicting Interests in Correctional Objectives," in Cloward et al., *op. cit.*

the inmate population, and therefore there is little question but what the society is protected from crimes the inmates might commit were they not locked up. It is unclear, of course, how many crimes of such a type there might be, since there are no accurate estimates of the offenses that might have been committed had inmates not been imprisoned. Undoubtedly, some might have committed no further offenses, but others may well have continued a pattern of frequent offenses. And our statistics on offenses do not enable us to estimate with any degree of precision how many of the total number of offenses are committed by persons who have served time in institutions.

There are a number of reasons why being in prison should make men more criminal, others why imprisonment should have the opposite effect, and little real evidence either way. It is difficult to make any systematic assessment of the effects of imprisonment without conducting controlled experiments, and such experiments might well be judged inhumane in terms of our American value system of equality of justice for all. An offender or his family might well resist a system in which important decisions regarding the offender depended on the role of a die or on a selection from a statistical table of random numbers.

Short of true experimentation on imprisonment itself, we can experiment with different types of prison programs. It is sometimes difficult to draw reasoned conclusions from such experiments, because there are many different reasons for program failure. The ideas may have been good but their implementation poor. Perhaps the staff were not carefully selected, or perhaps there was not an intensive enough exposure to the treatment. Such experiments as have been conducted so far suggest that no program has yet been found that consistently results in lower rates of parole failure after release from institutions.[119]

Short of experimentation, we can try to compare parole outcomes for persons who have been exposed to different prison programs, holding constant their most relevant background characteristics. Here again one finds a relatively pessimistic conclusion. The best research done on this problem so far has been conducted by the California correctional system. They have worked up what is called a base-expectancy table expressing the probable rate of parole violation for a group of offenders depending on their backgrounds before entering prison. They then compare men who have been in different prisons, after first taking account of the type of men who went into the prison. Major differences in rates of outcome between different programs should suggest that one program is more effective than another. There

---

[119] For a general review of studies of the impact of corrections, as well as a specific evaluation of the federal correctional system, see Glaser, *op. cit.*

are sizable differences in the type of institutions, ranging from minimum-custody establishments like the California Institution for Men at Chino, to the maximum-custody prison at Folsom. But after one removes whatever effects stem from the backgrounds the men bring to prison, there is little difference among the institutions. No one program seems demonstrably more effective than another.[120]

At the present time, then, there is little evidence that being sent to prison makes a man either more criminal or less criminal. It seems likely that the prison will have a rehabilitative effect on some inmates and an incapacitating one on others, depending on the conditions under which they enter the prison, their backgrounds, the nature of the prison program, and what life holds for them after release. This latter variable would seem to be very important, for it may well be the image of the prison in the mind of the society that determines what happens to persons who have been there, more so than anything going on during the individual's stay.

Preliminary interviews with incarcerated young offenders suggest that they see the impact of the prison largely in these terms. Some feel that the stay in prison may help them, for the mere deprivation of liberty will "teach me a lesson." Here at least is a verbalization of the direct deterrent effect of the prison on the individual. Those who feel the prison will harm them are likely to refer, not to the negative features of imprisonment during the time they are serving their sentences but rather to the fact that getting a job after release may be difficult. More generally, then, it may be the status of the prison in society, rather than what happens to the individual while he is going through imprisonment, that is important in determining his reactions after he leaves it. But on most of these matters, we are just beginning to gain meaningful empirical evidence.[121]

Conclusion

Every society has rules prescribing minimum standards of conduct that appear essential, in terms of the values of that society, for the maintenance of orderly social life. No society has remained free of persons who either occasionally or systematically violate such rules. The violations call for some form of reaction.

The most important intellectual and practical questions raised by the

---

[120] Robert F. Beverly, *An Analysis of Parole Performance by Institution of Release*, Research Report 40, California Youth Authority, March 1965.
[121] Brendan Maher and Ellen Jacobowitz, "The Delinquent's Perception of the Law and the Community," and Martha Baum and Stanton Wheeler, "Becoming an Inmate," in Wheeler, ed., *Controlling Delinquents, op. cit.*

field of criminology are suggested by these simple facts. Of all the behavior patterns in this society, which ones are to be labeled criminal? How does this labeling come about, and how does it change over time? Of all the individuals and groups in a society, which ones are most likely to engage in conduct that has been labeled criminal? By what process do they become engaged in it, and how do they differ from those who do not become so engaged? Finally, among the variety of possible reactions to criminals, what accounts for the dominance of certain reactions, for the differential application of the reactions to different types of offenders, and for the structure of the whole reaction system itself? Satisfactory answers to these questions would put us in a good position to answer the most important practical questions: What can be done to prevent crime, to reduce the number of criminals, or to return those who are criminals to a law-abiding way of life? What would be the economic and social costs of doing those things?

This last question is deceptive, for it might appear that the costs of crime control are purely economic, and that lack of knowledge is the only thing that stands in the way of more adequate crime control. But crime is an integral feature of modern society. It is a normal phenomenon, as Durkheim noted nearly three-quarters of a century ago. Annually we make estimates of budgetary and personnel needs which are predicated on our assurance that a certain volume of crime will occur: estimates for police, for judges, for prison cells and staff. Crime seems as clearly a product of the society in which it occurs as is any other part of that society—family life, the educational system, the economic order, the functioning of the legal and medical systems. We may anticipate that changes in the society sufficient to produce a great reduction in the rate of crime are likely to have other consequences that might not be regarded as happy. We have already seen that the presence of some criminals may serve useful functions for others in society, and that some police inefficiency may be a consequence of other values we strive to maximize. These are enough to suggest that we are unlikely to find panaceas for crime.

These problems need not concern us yet, for we are still far from achieving true explanatory power. But the practical problems are important and the search for explanations intriguing. Indeed, one of the very interesting though less important consequences of crime is the emergence of occupations designed not only to control it but to understand it. The accomplishments and problems of such groups have been the subject of this chapter.

6

Mental Illness

Leonard J. Duhl, M.D.,
and Robert L. Leopold, M.D.

THE vital sociological importance of mental health and illness is twofold. (1) Mental illness is so prevalent in our society that it constitutes a social problem simply because of its potential for disrupting the social system. (2) Mental illness has substantially more social determinants and components than many, if not most, widespread diseases, both in its causation and in its management.

This chapter is more directly concerned with the second point, the relationship between mental health (or illness) and the social environment. To discuss that relationship in all its myriad ramifications would be a monumental task; we introduce only some major considerations.

The Issue

A few statistics will convey the magnitude of mental illness. It is estimated that each year in this country from 125,000 to 150,000 patients are admitted to public mental hospitals. An additional 200,000 are admitted to general hospitals for the treatment of mental illness; 14.5 percent of all beds in general hospitals are used as "mental beds." These figures do not include outpatients at mental health clinics, who in 1962 numbered approximately 741,000. It is estimated that during 1963 a total of 1.853 billion dollars in governmental funds *alone* (federal, state, and local) was expended on the care of the mentally ill. In addition, although no reliable figure is currently available, we can assume that the private psychiatric bill was enormous.

* This chapter was prepared with the assistance of Dorothy S. Kuhn.

Such figures indicate that mental illness is widespread enough and expensive enough to constitute a major social issue. It is staggering just to think of the living quarters that have had to be provided for so many hospitalized patients, of finding sufficient personnel to treat and care for so many sick people, of the interruptions and dislocations of the social system that occur when illness cuts such a wide swath across society. Endless speculation is possible about the breakdowns in family life such a widespread incapacitating disease must cause and about the whole new series of social problems set in motion by these breakdowns. Yet, we still speak here as if mental illness were similar to any other widespread disease; we have not begun to consider the social aspects that make it sociologically more significant than other diseases. Furthermore, as appalling as the statistics seem, they do not tell the whole story. Who are the mentally ill? There is no way to ascertain the number of persons under treatment by private psychiatrists (or other mental health specialists), but even if there were, and even if we could add this number to the number of hospital and clinic patients, would we have counted all the people who are mentally ill? If not, where are the others?

Almost everyone knows people who are regarded (openly or by implication) as "mentally ill" by their families, their friends, or their working associates. Yet, they are not patients receiving professional help. Many of these people may not be ill by psychiatric standards; but many others are ill indeed and uncounted in the statistics. Thus official figures on hospitalization, treatment, and so forth are inadequate measures of the extent of mental illness.

As we talk of the number of people who are mentally ill, we become aware that we are speaking of a disease not easily defined. What *is* mental illness? Since illness has full meaning only in relation to health, we also want to know what mental health is. It is necessary to produce some reasonable working definitions that will serve as a basis for discussion.

For most people the terms "health" and "illness" have medical overtones and refer to bodily conditions. Only recently, in relatively small and sophisticated circles, has it become customary to refer to a psychologically disturbed person as "sick" or "ill" without a qualifying word to indicate that his condition is not physiological. In general, "health" and "illness" suggest problems which belong within the province of medicine, albeit with many exceptions (for example, in some cults and religious denominations); these problems, if they are not readily manageable by the individual or the family, are taken to persons associated with the medical profession.

But the moment we speak of "mental" health, we add a number of connotations. There is usually, of course, a medical overtone nowadays, but for most people there appear to be several other possible connotations: religious, philosophical, social, and psychological. The ambiguity is increased by the presence of feelings and moral values that are usually absent for *most* bodily illnesses.

Why should these terms be so encumbered? We must investigate this matter, for how people think and feel about mental illness is an extremely significant social factor in determining how and by whom the victim will be managed, and to a large extent the course his illness will take.

Historical Perspective

A society's attitudes are, of course, conditioned by inheritance from the past. Thus it would seem reasonable to look to the past to find some of the answers to our original questions. To clarify our thinking, let us assume that society has always regarded certain conditions of man's psychological being (by which we mean that part of his being that can only be described in terms of his thoughts, his feelings, and the behavior which manifests his thoughts and feelings) as "normal," that is, as conforming to accepted standards, and that such behavior represents mental health; that society has always regarded other conditions of this being as "abnormal," that is, as deviating from its accepted standards, and that such behavior represents mental illness. But it must be emphasized that these are *not* definitions but rather descriptions of behavior devised for the purpose of our brief historical investigation.

Today a recognized branch of medicine, psychiatry, deals with mental illness. This has not always been so. Mental illness, indeed, has not always been a concern of *any* branch of medicine. Throughout our history, all illness has had strong elements of mystery. The mystery stemmed from man's ultimate lack of control over his own being. But even primitive cultures learned to explain bodily ailments in concrete terms because of obvious physical manifestations. Mental illness, however, most frequently expresses itself in deviant behavior. Since primitive cultures could not usually see a physical reason for this behavior, they explained it in magical terms: the victim must be possessed by the supernatural powers which control men's destinies.

If the victim was possessed by supernatural powers, he was too sacred to be tampered with by anyone except those appointed or sanctioned by society to negotiate with these powers, namely the **priests**. Even after there were primitive doctors to care for the needs of the sick body, mental illness remained a thing apart, and the mentally ill remained the responsibility of the priests. Doctors were accorded no place in the propitiation of those spirits that could damage society. In other words, it appears that very early in human history an unwritten law prevented the intervention of doctors in matters of the mind.

Until the beginning of the twentieth century this attitude impeded scientific investigation and treatment of mental illness. Even when the actual management of the mentally ill was turned over to doctors, the rationale for such management was devised by nonmedical disciplines. The mystical speculations of the priest were replaced (or supplemented) by philosophical formulations, both secular and religious.

Philosophies cannot provide a scientific rationale for the treatment of mental disease. They depend for their conceptualization on intuition and speculation rather than on carefully observed and recorded clinical data. By their very nature they imply the use of a value system, a set of moral criteria in their conceptualization of the disease which must preclude objective scientific investigation and treatment, and which must imply further that man has a free choice with respect to the disease, that his will cannot be impaired by sickness. The ultimate expression of this belief in the immunity of the will to disease was seen during the era of witchcraft when hundreds of thousands of mentally ill were slaughtered on the grounds that they were possessed by the devil, and that they had chosen to be so possessed. Since they had made a bad choice, they had to be punished; the community had to be freed of the evildoers, and their souls had to be redeemed by the purification of fire.

Society's restrictions against true medical intervention deprived doctors of the traditional right accorded them with most other diseases, the right to base treatment on objective scientific investigation of all the factors involved. Furthermore, insistence that the human mind is the rightful domain of philosophy and religion served to reinforce and perpetuate the notion that mental illness—since philosophy and religion judge it in terms of moral values—must be evidence that the victim is "bad" rather than sick.

Thus, for most of our history, mental illness and the mentally ill have been regarded with awe, fear, and hatred. The mentally ill, long after they ceased to be tortured and burned at the stake, continued to be abused and derided. Those who were deemed too dangerous to roam at large, or to be hidden away in the home, were confined in chains and fetters in institutions which were, with rare exceptions, places of horror and degradation.

A wave of social reform brought considerable relief to the institutionalized mentally ill in the late eighteenth century. We have had many such institutional reforms since then and, regrettably, many regressions which have persisted well into the twentieth century. Nevertheless, these reforms have made society more acutely aware of the problems of mental illness.

We can best examine twentieth-century attitudes toward mental health and illness in the context of modern medical psychology. The work of Freud (as well as that of his immediate predecessors and of his followers) in exploring the unconscious by means of psychoanalysis is, of course, at the base of this psychology. The influence of modern medical psychology on society's current attitudes toward mental health cannot be overstated. Its basis in scientific investigation, its insistence that psychological manifestations are simply natural phenomena (neither good nor bad), its recognition that mental illness may exist even in the absence of demonstrable psychical impairment—all these have made possible a view of mental illness less superstitious, less weighted with mystery and moral judgment. Modern medical psychology's attention to the mildly disturbed patient as well as the dramatically sick person has helped to make mental illness appear less fearful in the sense that it can now be seen as something that may happen even to ordinary people like oneself. Acknowledgment that mental illness can impair the will, even when it does not impair the ability to think, has engendered at least a tentative belief that some kinds of behavior may be sick rather than "bad."

Of special sociological significance are the environmental and developmental aspects of the Freudian view, which sees man as a biological whole, all parts of which are in constant and reciprocal interchange with each other and with every part of the environment. At various stages of personality development, these interchanges are more dramatic and more influential than at others. These aspects have suggested the possibility of altering the environment and intervening in the development so as to forestall or ameliorate pathological development. Belief in this possibility has led to a more hopeful attitude, a shift in emphasis from mental illness to mental health, from treatment to prevention.

We must also note other developments in the twentieth century which have helped to foster these changes. For example, various physical methods of dealing with mental illness, notably the use of drugs, have seemed to make mental illness more understandable as a medical condition. The increase in the number of psychiatrists and the fact that these medical specialists have emerged to a great extent from behind hospital walls, to practice in more familiar and more accessible areas, also seem to have made mental illness appear less mysterious and less threatening.

The shift in emphasis from treatment to prevention reflects the tremendous interest in public health that has characterized this century. Public health focuses its attention primarily on the control of developmental and environmental factors in order to promote health and prevent illness. Many current mental health activities may be viewed largely as extensions of the public health movement; at the same time, the public health movement itself reflects many aspects of twentieth-century medical psychology.

Society's attitudes toward mental health and illness have been greatly affected by the great wave of social reform which has covered the world in this century. These reforms, or attempts at reform, are an expression of mounting dissatisfaction with such ancient social evils as poverty, unemployment, poor education, high medical costs, and discrimination against minorities. Not only are these socioeconomic ills conducive to mental illness, but they also militate against its effective management.

We cannot separate the problems of mental illness from the problems of social illness. Some people continue to talk as if they could. It is difficult to escape the conclusion that they prefer this attitude to an uncomfortable awareness of the changes in the social system that would be necessary if these problems were seen in their correct relationship to each other.

The developments we have recorded in twentieth-century thinking about mental health and illness seem to be directed toward enlightenment and progress. But such attitudes are far from universal; the millennium has not arrived. Today, most popular concepts about mental health fall into one of two broad categories. One usage refers to a variety of community activities and responsibilities and implies action or a need for action. This meaning is evident in the phrase "the mental health movement" and suggests that for many people mental illness is much like certain widespread killing or crippling physical diseases; that is, subject it to a specific, frontal attack, and we will eventually eliminate it or at least mitigate its devastating effects. That this view represents an extreme oversimplification need not be elaborated here. We mention it simply to indicate that "mental health" suggests programs concerned with the prevention and treatment of mental illness, research in mental illness, raising funds for mental health activities, and the like, thus underscoring the complexity of the term.

The second popular usage of "mental health" refers to personal states of being and is usually used to mean "good" mental health. But what is a "good" state of being? Opinions are many and varied and frequently contradictory. Does "good" mental health mean contentment, serenity, satisfaction with one's society and one's role in society? If it does, what becomes of the view that it is "good" to seek improvement in one's own lot and in society? Does the urge to reform, to help, to change evil then become evidence of mental illness? Is the man who functions efficiently by the rules of a given social structure mentally healthy? If so, what becomes of this view if the social structure happens to be a highly organized criminal subculture? Does not the view then contradict a religious view of mental health, concerned with moral rectitude? Is a person mentally healthy if he has pursued a successful career? If he is, what happens to this view if his success has been achieved at the sacrifice of values often considered the criteria of positive mental health? A book by Marie Jahoda investigates other current concepts of positive mental health.[1]

The Psychiatric View

Regardless of such complex questions, it is the responsibility of the authors, both psychiatrists, to present for the purpose of this discussion a psychiatric view of mental health. Basically, the psychiatrist sees mental health as the ability of the individual to cope with his environment. Each human being must use his internal resources in a social context. In American society the environmental stresses are complex and require the individual to develop complex techniques for dealing with them. These techniques will depend in part on internal psychological adaptive mechanisms and in part on education in the most total sense —that is, in the sense of a learned ability to deal with social interactions and the challenges of the social environment. Mental health, then, presupposes the development of such techniques.

Mental health must also be considered from the standpoint of the relationship between environmental stresses and coping resources. Given a low order of stress, a person with few coping resources can exist quite comfortably. Given highly developed resources, an individual can deal with much greater environmental complexities and still maintain the integrity of his personality. In some instances a person's internal adaptive mechanisms can be redeveloped so that he compensates, in the face of environmental stress, for a lack of learned ability in his total armament of coping resources. But it must be remembered also that the social environment, apart from the stresses it imposes on the individual, can play a part in determining mental health. When the individual is faced with damage to his personality because his coping resources are inadequate to meet a stressful situation, the damage can

[1] Marie Jahoda, *Current Concepts of Positive Mental Health,* Joint Commission on Mental Health and Illness, Monograph Series, no. 1 (New York: Basic Books, 1958).

be arrested if the social environment provides sufficient compensatory supports.

Thus mental health involves interaction among the individual's strengths, the stresses imposed by the social environment, and the supports provided by the environment. We may use the head of a family as an illustration. Suppose there is stable family life that gives him little cause for mental conflict. Suddenly a child becomes seriously ill. The head of the family has to call on his internal resources to cope with his own concern over the sick child, with the disorganization of the household generated by the illness, and with the conflicts and anxieties aroused in the mother and in other family members. The stresses of the environment make unusual demands on his coping apparatus. He has to deal both with feelings and with practical necessities. Mature adults have learned during the course of their lives how to deal with conflicts of feeling in themselves and others by using devices called the mechanisms of defense. These mechanisms are healthy if they are not overused. In this instance overuse would consist of denying the severity of the illness and taking no realistic and necessary action; healthy use would consist of denying the severity sufficiently to keep the father and the family under practical emotional control. It should be noted that to cope adequately does not mean there may be no expression of emotion. (It is appropriate and healthy, for example, to feel deep grief after the loss of a loved one; it is not healthy to grieve for years.) The mentally healthy father allows himself to feel and to express his feelings appropriately, at the same time that he deals realistically with his own and his family's stressful situation. In stating that he is mentally healthy, we also assume that he has some idea of what realistic action must be taken, and that if he does not, he will consult someone who can help him determine what should be done.

Mental health, viewed in this way, connotes a flexible capacity to adapt to changing circumstances, often full of stress, without fleeing from them, becoming physically or emotionally ill, or taking precipitate action. Furthermore, this view of mental health includes an ability to create a stable family structure such that other members of the family develop a similar flexibility and adaptability (within the limits of their age and experience) in handling stressful situations. Thus the family itself becomes strong enough to provide the external supports and strengths that will complement the internal coping apparatus of each member when an emergency threatens any individual or the family as a whole. We may take this concept a step further by saying that to be mentally healthy a community structure ought to provide means whereby the family in stressful circumstances can receive external supports and strengths from the community to complement its own coping devices whenever this extra help is needed.

The ability of any individual at any time to make decisions for his own life, as well as for the lives of others, is a major indicator of his mental health and of that of the community. Traditionally, psychiatry has tended to measure the mental health of an individual with reference to internal psychological structure alone, neglecting the relationship of that structure to the social environment. Only recently has the significance of environmental factors for mental health and illness begun to emerge in psychiatric thinking. The psychiatric view of mental health presented here emphasizes how the complexities of the internal psychological apparatus derive not only from the constant interchange within the individual system, but also between the system and its surroundings.[2] This theme runs through our entire chapter; we see mental health not as an isolated phenomenon of an individual or a society, but as a state of being which reflects the complicated relationships between the individual and his social environment.

We have noted previously that mental illness in some contexts is seen as a disease susceptible to the direct frontal attack applied to various major physical diseases. This view is an oversimplification, as should be apparent from the preceding discussion of the complex interchanges between individual and social environment that enter into the psychiatric view of mental health.

In other contexts, the meaning of mental illness depends on who is using the term. In many quarters there is a disposition to label as mental illness anything that is not liked or is too threatening. On the community level this view is expressed by unwillingness to deal directly with the genuine issues involved in the most serious social problems of the day; it is easier to call them problems of mental health or mental illness. For the moment we wish merely to emphasize that certain kinds of behavior often called "mental illness" may be, from the psychiatrist's point of view, normal responses to damaging situations. Hence it becomes a moot question whether he regards these as evidence of mental illness or of mental health. Even when he minutely examines the context of the behavior he finds no easy answer.

The disposition to label "mentally ill" anything that is not liked is found in many interpersonal relationships: between husband and wife, doctor and patient, lawyer and client. It must also be noted that in

[2] Erik H. Erikson, *Identity and the Life Cycle* (Psychological Issues, vol. 1, no. 1, Monograph 1, 1959).

interpersonal relationships the reverse situation often holds true: actual mental illness may be called by other names until it has progressed to a critical stage.

This point is illustrated in the reports of the Clausen studies [3] concerning the impact of mental illness on the wives of hospitalized mental patients. A schizophrenic patient, for the three years of his marriage before his hospitalization, had behaved in many strange ways. Yet his wife perceived his behavior as a psychiatric problem only when it became so bizarre that she felt thoroughly threatened. Before that, she had always adapted herself to his behavior, rationalizing it in one way or another and building up other strong defenses against it. Even after she began to recognize the seriousness of the situation, she tried to accommodate to his behavior. The husband was finally hospitalized following a public disturbance and police intervention.

The studies pointed out that the delay in recognizing mental illness on the part of a wife is conditioned by many factors working together in a complicated way. For instance, the kind of conception a wife has of psychological processes and the nature of emotional disturbance, and the degree of tolerance she herself has for emotional disturbance, determine how she will label her husband's behavior. Furthermore, the social environment provides many supports for maintaining a wife's picture of a husband's normality. Intoxication on payday or occasional abuse of a wife is not unusual in a certain milieu. Such behavior would not be perceived as mental illness until it had become markedly excessive. In a social environment where these manifestations are rarely seen, they would be called mental illness much earlier.

It should be apparent by now that the meaning of mental illness is open to much contradictory discussion. Nevertheless, as with mental health, it becomes obligatory for the psychiatrist to state his view of mental illness.

Mental illness is not seen by the psychiatrist as the simple antithesis of mental health. Rather, the psychiatrist uses this generic term to indicate any point between normal functioning, as represented by our view of mental health, and the complete personality disintegration of the most regressive forms of schizophrenia. Mental illnesses may be categorized in many ways. For example, we may speak of them as neuroses or psychoses; as mild, moderate, or severe; as incapacitating or non-incapacitating; as involving physical impairment or not. There are many other distinctions, but to the psychiatrist *all* kinds of mental

---

[3] John A. Clausen and Marian Radke Yarrow, eds., "The Impact of Mental Illness on the Family," *Journal of Social Issues*, 11, 4 (1955), p. 4.

illness represent points between the two extremes. To him, mental illness connotes the breakdown of a series of systems which an individual and a community mutually establish to promote reasonably smooth functioning. In this view mental illness occurs when an overwhelming stress is imposed on any part of the system. It has been said that "every man has his breaking point." This implies that no man is so psychologically healthy that overwhelming stress cannot cause him to be mentally ill, however briefly. This is a somewhat broader view of mental illness than a more traditional one that sees a person as mentally ill only when his loss of ability to cope with his social situation is so complete that he must be cared for by others.

In mental illness the mechanisms of defense are overused or used inappropriately. For example, all of us make use of denial (we have seen its appropriate use in serious family stress) and occasionally overuse it. As mental illness becomes more serious, denial is used so extensively that it isolates the patient from reality and makes it impossible for him to deal with practical problems because he denies their very existence. Similarly, all of us are at times somewhat circumspect or suspicious, but under threat of personality disorganization people may actually project their own feelings outward and attribute them to others. It is important to understand that personality disorganization occurs in stages, that people pass from one inadequate means of coping to another even less adequate. Thus, in current psychiatric thinking, rigid diagnostic differentiation on the basis of symptoms alone, formerly seen as extremely important, has begun to lose much of its meaning. Indeed, the young psychiatrist quickly learns that the better he knows any patient, the more difficult it is to give a categorical diagnosis of his condition.

Mental Retardation

Mental retardation is often confused with mental illness. In fact, in some childhood disorders it is extremely difficult to differentiate severe retardation from an early schizophrenic reaction. Differentiation between mental retardation and mental illness is made, in general, along these lines: the mentally ill person usually has difficulty in psychological areas primarily concerned with emotions and with ability to cope with social situations and interpersonal relationships; for the mentally retarded the major problem is a lack of the intellectual and cognitive skills needed for dealing with the environment. Differentiation is complicated because both conditions may have their origins in biological and physical damage to the brain system, in psychological or social conditions which inhibit growth and development, or in crises which are beyond the coping capacity of the individual. In addition, retardation and mental illness can occur concurrently in the same individual.

The difficulty of discussing current concepts of mental health and illness, and the confusions and complexities surrounding the subjects, suggest a related area of public confusion and, indeed, of considerable ignorance—the roles and functions of the psychiatrist. This public confusion and ignorance in itself constitutes a significant social problem. For one thing, it makes many persons reluctant to seek psychiatric aid; and for another, it makes many—even professional people—reluctant to believe that the psychiatrist concerns himself with mental health as well as mental illness, that he can prevent mental illness.

Conclusions

Let us sum up with the following points.

1. The psychiatrist, when called on to treat what is termed by society "mental illness," acknowledges that in all such disturbances there is some degree of failure in the ability of the individual's internal psychological apparatus to cope with his environment, but he also recognizes some failure in the social environment (either immediate, or in the community beyond the individual's home) to provide certain elements which might have prevented or ameliorated the breakdown. He also recognizes that various elements in the social environment will influence the effectiveness of his treatment.

2. The environmental determinants and components of mental illness frequently reflect pressing current social problems. This fact is not acknowledged by many persons, primarily because they prefer to relegate these problems to the mental health–mental illness field exclusively, rather than face the necessity for drastic social change.

3. The psychiatrist, like other medical practitioners, concerns himself with the prevention of the illness he is called on to treat. But the psychiatrist, perhaps more specifically than any other medical practitioner, must look to the social environment.

These statements provide a basis for the following discussion. Themes that derive from them and will be pursued throughout the balance of this chapter include the roles and functions of the psychiatrist in therapeutic and preventive work; some social considerations pertinent to mental hospitals; the relationship between mental illness and some significant, current social issues; aspects of the current attack against mental illness; and other closely related topics.

The Psychiatrist—What He Is and What He Does

A discussion of the psychiatrist and certain aspects of his work may help to illuminate the areas of confusion and ignorance we have alluded to previously. At the same time it will serve as a focus for considering the connection between the psychiatrist's field of competence and social planning for mental health.

A psychiatrist is a specialist in a branch of medicine, psychiatry, which deals with the prevention, diagnosis, and treatment of mental and emotional disorders; he holds the degree of doctor of medicine. In addition to the usual year of internship training in general medicine, he has had advanced training as a psychiatric resident in a hospital (part of his residency is usually spent in a mental hospital) during which he has had intensive experience in the diagnosis and treatment of mental and emotional disturbance.[4]

The Psychiatrist in Therapeutic Work

In discussing how the psychiatrist handles his patients, we will not give an exhaustive account of psychiatric medicine but rather point out the most prominent aspects of the psychiatrist's therapeutic work. We focus on the classical procedures that involve the one-to-one relationship between the psychiatrist and the patient. Whether this relationship occurs in a private practitioner's office, a clinic, a hospital, or another setting, it has the following features: the psychiatrist's main contact is with the patient; his primary responsibility is to the patient in a mutual effort to help him cope with the problems he presents; and the psychiatrist's role is the classical role of the physician in which the

[4] The public often confuses the terms "psychiatrist," "psychoanalyst," and "psychologist." A *psychoanalyst* is anyone trained in the specific method developed by Sigmund Freud for treating mental illness. At first, most psychiatrists rejected psychoanalysis, and as a result a number of early psychoanalysts were "lay analysts" (not medical doctors). But psychiatry today, especially in America, has largely accepted psychoanalytic theory and method. American psychiatrists under 50 years of age have had specialized training in psychoanalysis as part of their advanced work in psychiatry. Most psychiatrists are not psychoanalysts, however, and some noted psychoanalysts are not psychiatrists but lay analysts (e.g., Erik Erikson, Erich Fromm, Bruno Bettelheim). The *psychologist* studies mental states and processes in animals and humans; psychologists who specialize in the study and treatment of mental illness are called *clinical psychologists*. Some clinical psychologists are lay analysts, but others use different types of psychotherapy.

See Wesley Allinsmith and George W. Goethals, *The Roles of Schools in Mental Health*, Joint Commission on Mental Illness and Health, Monograph Series, no. 7 (New York: Basic Books, 1962).

confidentiality between doctor and patient is unbroken, thus giving the psychiatrist access to the innermost secrets and psychological processes of the patient.

A variety of procedures, known generically as the psychotherapies, are built upon this basic relationship. They involve different intensities of contact between doctor and patient. In some instances the patient is seen regularly but infrequently; in others (more intensive and more expensive) the patient is seen as often as five or six times a week The choice of procedure has several determinants: the kinds of problems posed by the patient and the degree of his difficulty in meeting them; the goals of treatment as expressed by the patient; the social class and the education of the patient; and his ability (in part determined by his social class and his education) to participate in the available psychological procedures.

Whatever the procedure, its principal ingredient is talk. The patient is encouraged to talk to the psychiatrist as if he, the psychiatrist, were various key persons in the patient's life experience; the patient is encouraged to direct toward the psychiatrist feelings about these people which he has never been able to express satisfactorily, and which may be the cause of many disabling conflicts. Thus he establishes with the psychiatrist what may be called sample relationships. In these he has an opportunity to ventilate his feelings and eventually to release some of his troublesome conflicts. (In psychoanalytic techniques of psychotherapy the feelings about the therapist tend to become quite intense, and older and deeper conflicts are uncovered.) Following ventilation, the psychiatrist attempts some clarification. He never makes value judgments about anything a patient tells him; but he does offer such psychological explanations as the patient requires and can understand. After ventilation and clarification, patient and therapist together try to work out patterns of action based on the patient's newly acquired understanding of his feelings rather than on old and hampering conflicts.

Although the primary mechanism of the therapeutic relationship is personal interaction, the psychiatrist may use other tools, in accordance with individual patient need, to supplement psychological procedures. These include a wide range of drugs (such as barbiturates, energizers, and tranquilizers), electroshock treatment, and other general medical procedures.

Since the patient's problems are only partially the result of internal mechanisms, the therapeutic relationship may explore the complex relationships among the individual, his family, and the larger social environment. As these relationships become understood, the psychiatrist, either directly or through other professionals (a social worker, for example), will work with the family and with the community and its social institutions to make changes in the environment that may help the individual to deal with his current problems. The psychiatrist may enlist the aid of many people, both professional and nonprofessional, inside and outside the clinical setting. These include the psychologist, the psychiatric nurse, the psychiatric aide, the occupational therapist, the physical therapist (occasionally), family physicians, teachers, ministers, counselors of various kinds, and others who serve in "helping" or "caretaking" roles. All these people can help the psychiatrist in various ways.

In some instances the patient's illness, in combination with the total social situation in the family and community, may be such that he cannot remain in the situation without endangering himself, the family, or other community members, either psychologically or possibly physically. He must then be removed from the situation. Thus hospitalization, whether voluntary or not, may become a necessity.

The hospital facilities available for the mentally ill cover a wide range, from the psychiatric section of the general hospital (which is used more often for temporary management of acute cases than for long-term treatment) to the vast state hospitals and certain similar federal institutions. Between these there are many private, and some public, hospitals of various sizes. In general, it may be said that the smaller and more expensive the hospital, the more likely it is that the treatment of the patient will include a regular program of individual psychotherapy on a frequent basis; the larger the hospital, and the less expensive, the more likely it is that the patient will receive little or no private therapy. Although shock therapy, drug therapy, other medical procedures, and group therapy may be used in hospitals of all sizes, there is likely to be more emphasis on these in the larger institutions than in the smaller, and especially in those maintained largely by public funds.

Some Social Considerations about Mental Hospitals

We must pause here to consider at least a few of the staggering social implications involved in the hospitalization of the mental patient. To understand them even on the most elementary level, we must ask ourselves what mental hospitals were originally designed for. Historically, since the mentally ill were believed to be connected with demonic evil influences, or with criminality, the hospitals' primary purpose was to protect society from actual or apparent danger. Thus, in this very real sense, the mental hospitals were agents of the community rather than of the sick person. Indeed, mental hospitals did not replace jails, generally speaking, until the end of the eighteenth century and the beginning of the nineteenth century.

Unfortunately, treatment of *illness* has been, and still is, a secondary purpose in the majority of hospitals. The mental hospital today has many features it inherited from the jail, features that are far from being therapeutic but that are accepted by many people who continue to view the primary purpose of the hospitals as custodial. We can now begin to see that mental hospitals, with rare exceptions, have been designed and operated largely to meet three needs that derive from their original primary purpose: (1) maximum security; (2) the convenience of a staff which remains always united, not only to maintain maximum security but to insure a minimum of disturbance within the hospital; and (3) training of personnel who will continue the tradition of custodial care.

It is small wonder, then, that many mental hospitals have the characteristics of "total" social institutions so graphically described by Goffman.[5] Central to Goffman's characterization is the movement of whole blocks of people through time and space in rigidly designed bureaucratic processes; the circumstances under which the inmates work, eat, sleep, and play involve a degree of surveillance, control, and enforced close association with others that is in sharp contrast to ordinary life situations. The total institution is planned so that relatively few supervisory personnel can see to it that all inmates do exactly what is required of them; individual infractions will stand out in bold relief against the regimented performance of large groups of inmates. Privacy does not exist and all personal needs are subjugated to the overall purpose of the institution. These features obviously serve the custodial goal of prisons; we must bear constantly in mind that this goal is hardly distinguishable historically from the primary purpose of mental hospitals.

Until World War II, despite the introduction of various kinds of treatments in many hospitals, with apparent benefit to some patients, the psychotic patient remained relatively isolated from the medical caretaking systems of society. Then the shortage of military manpower made it necessary to take a new look at mental hospitals. When skilled military personnel became psychiatrically ill, the services could not afford to let them receive only custodial care. Every possible means had to be used to restore them to normal functioning and send them back to service. The general community also pressured for the return of patients to keep urgent wartime jobs filled. It became mandatory to use hospitalization for rapid treatment and rehabilitation.

[5] Erving Goffman, *Asylums* (Chicago: Aldine Publishing Company, 1962).

New Trends

Thus, under circumstances of wartime urgency, psychiatrists became more aware than before of the curious fact that even with only custodial care, patients in some mental hospitals seemed to recover spontaneously. Similarly, in some other hospitals, patients did not seem to improve regardless of treatment. The accelerated interest in these phenomena was also a corollary of the psychiatrists' increasing attention to the social environment as a factor in preventive and therapeutic work. The mental hospital was conceptualized as a social system, and an attempt was made to find out what elements of the system were significant in patient progress or regression. For example, psychiatrists began to wonder whether certain behavior manifestations might not be a reaction to the totalistic features of the hospital environment itself rather than continuing symptoms of the illness which led to hospitalization.

With the help of other disciplines (notably psychology and anthropology), they began to study the workings of the hospital social system and to look for ways to use them therapeutically. Among a number of outstanding studies in this area, those of Stanton and Schwartz [6] and Caudill [7] are representative. The data contributed by these studies have had great value in the introduction of new approaches to the hospitalization of mental patients.

Two major trends can now be identified in the study of the social environment. The first views the patient as part of the small, tightly woven social system of the psychiatric ward. The ward is, in turn, part of a larger social system—the hospital. And the hospital itself, since it cannot exist without supplies of persons, materials, and information from the outside world, is part of the social system of the community. Since all parts of any social system are of necessity in a state of continuous reciprocal interchange with each other, the patient must be affected by anything that goes on within the system and subsystems—most of all by the ward system, to a slightly lesser extent by the hospital system, and to a more limited, but still significant extent, by the social system outside. So viewed, the patient's behavior must be considered as conditioned not only by his psychological history but also by the way he is treated, what is said to him, how it is said, and countless other circumstances of his daily life. It is possible, furthermore, to see

---

[6] Alfred H. Stanton and Morris S. Schwartz, *The Mental Hospital* (New York: Basic Books, 1954).
[7] William A. Caudill, *The Psychiatric Hospital as a Small Society* (Cambridge, Mass.: Harvard University Press, 1958).

that the workings of the social system can be altered in ways that will help strengthen the patient's internal resources, rather than present him with stresses that are beyond his already inadequate capacities for coping.

This view emphasizes privacy, with its implicit requirement that respect for the dignity and integrity of the individual will be maintained, despite the often repellent manifestations of severe mental illness. The patient is no longer seen as an automaton, but as a person whose interactions with staff (and other patients) can be used to build up rather than to tear down his trust in humanity. Toward this end, all staff (not only those officially designated as psychotherapists), and especially those who are in the most prolonged daily contact with the patient, must be trained to value and use a therapeutic as well as a custodial role.

The second trend lies in the recognition that the patient usually must return to his community, with all its stresses. Thus there is a need to prepare him for return via gradual contacts with the larger social systems beyond the ward. As his ability to deal with stresses grows, he is allowed to move more freely within the hospital. Mental hospitals are being moved from their historic rural isolation into the general community, so that the patient may feel less isolated from the outside social system and be given opportunities, under controlled circumstances as his health improves, to test his ability to move about in it. Several alternatives to the "total" mental hospital are also being developed: the day hospital where the patient is treated by day but is allowed to return to his family at night; the night hospital where he is treated at night but works in the community by day; the "halfway house" where the patient, no longer needing hospital care but not yet ready for adjustment to his family, can live while finding his way back into the community social system.

These developments are certainly far from widespread, but they are gaining ground. The use of drugs that help the patient to maintain control during periods of acute illness has been of enormous value in expanding these developments.

Efforts are also being made to keep the family in closer touch with the hospital; this is one reason for moving the hospital bed into the community. The family must be helped to understand and accept its responsibilities toward the patient returning to the community. It is quite possible that the rate of return to mental hospitals may be as much related to family attitudes about the returned patient as to anything that occurs in the hospital itself. The patient must learn to live with the social system of the family, but the family must learn to mitigate the stresses on the returned patient. Helping the family to learn this is part of the social systems approach to mental hospitalization.

There are still far too many prison-type hospitals. Fortunately, in responsible quarters, they are now perceived as outmoded. The federal grants currently being made for state mental health programs envisage caretaking facilities which we can hope will transform mental "institutions" into true hospitals.

The Psychiatrist in Preventive Work

A most fruitful area for preventive psychiatry is the social institution whose members function, from the psychological standpoint, in a reasonably healthy way. Such institutions have been designed for other purposes, but mental health programs have been built into their operation; these include the military service, some industrial organizations, some schools and colleges, various social service agencies, and the Peace Corps.

Both authors of this chapter have served the Peace Corps since its inception and feel qualified, therefore, to discuss its mental health program. This discussion will reveal some functions of the preventive psychiatrist and also suggest one possible model for a practical community approach to mental health. The program has been described fully elsewhere;[8] only its most pertinent aspects will be reviewed here.

There is no separate division of the Peace Corps labeled "mental health program." The program cuts across many areas of Peace Corps structure and operation. The psychiatrist is a consultant to the entire Peace Corps program as well as to the medical division.

The mental health program may be reviewed in relation to three major areas of Peace Corps function.

1. *Selection.* Survivors of a preliminary screening are invited to enter training. Training closely approximates the conditions of actual service. The Trainee (after selection for overseas service, he is called a Volunteer) is observed and evaluated in these circumstances; his performance determines his final selection or rejection. At each training site consultant psychiatrists, along with other professional personnel, observe his performance and the final decision is based on the joint recommendation of psychiatric and nonpsychiatric personnel.

[8] Robert L. Leopold and Leonard J. Duhl, "The Peace Corps: A Historical Note on a New Challenge to Psychiatry," *Journal of Nervous and Mental Diseases*, 137, 1 (July 1963), pp. 7–13; "New Frontiers in Psychiatry: The Peace Corps," *Psychiatric Studies and Projects*, 2, 1 (January 1964), pp. 1–9; and "A Mental Health Program for the Peace Corps," *Human Organization*, 23, 2 (Summer 1964), pp. 131–136.

2. *Training*. The kind of psychological stresses that may be expected in service are deliberately included in training. The Trainee learns to handle himself effectively in such stress circumstances. The psychiatrist at the training site works with educators and administrators to make certain that these training stresses are used as fully as possible. He also leads group sessions in mental health education. These classes use the daily training experiences to explore and express the kinds of feelings that may be expected to develop in actual service and are another way of preparing the Trainee to handle the expected psychological stresses of service.

The training site psychiatrist also helps Trainees develop sensitivity to the psychological needs of their co-workers and to learn how to give psychological "first aid" to those in difficulty. In addition, he is largely responsible for the mental health orientation of those charged with the well-being of the Volunteer overseas, that is, the Peace Corps physicians and other professional staff.

3. *Overseas support*. Overseas, the Volunteer may turn for emotional support to a fellow Volunteer, to staff members, or to a Peace Corps physician. The help he receives may be emotional first aid, counseling, or more intensive psychiatric treatment. Consultation for Peace Corps representatives and physicians is provided by psychiatrists serving in Washington. At intervals these psychiatrists visit Peace Corps sites overseas to discuss problems and to collect and report various data to Washington. Such data are used to improve the operation of the Peace Corps, especially the mental health of its workers.

Obviously, the mental health program had to be designed to serve the special goals of the Peace Corps. But we may view it from a more general perspective. Elimination of psychologically unsuited candidates tends to prevent individual breakdown by keeping people away from precipitating circumstances; at the same time, the program points out their weaknesses and the kinds of stress they must avoid; and it suggests the possibilities of seeking psychiatric help. In addition, the psychological conditioning of training adds to the individual's internal resources for dealing with many kinds of problems after Peace Corps service is over. The psychological support he receives overseas can also affect his mental health in later life.

A Fundamental Concept of Prevention

The last statement of the preceding paragraph is based on a concept fundamental to preventive mental health work in the Peace Corps and elsewhere, the concept known as *crisis theory*. Each human being throughout his life will encounter periods of unusual stress. When these stresses are acute, unexpected, not susceptible to ready solution, or beyond the individual's coping ability, the situation may be called a "crisis."

Crises may be termed "pathological" if they are essentially the result of internal psychological processes. The external situation may appear to cause them; actually, it simply triggers them. Such crises rarely occur in Peace Corps experience because the rigors of the selection process tend to eliminate applicants who are predisposed to them.

Another type of crisis, called "idiopathic," includes those that normally arise from the death of a loved person, from severe illness or injury, or from various types of disaster. Such crises occur in the lives of Peace Corps workers just as they do in the lives of others. But special types of idiopathic crisis may be expected in Peace Corps service. The sudden change from one culture to another, the difficulty of communicating with other people across a cultural barrier, the changes in self-image caused by an unfamiliar setting, re-entry into one's own culture, having to make a career decision on termination of service—all may cause crises. No matter how carefully the Peace Corps worker has been conditioned psychologically in training, there will be many situations for which he lacks adequate coping resources.

The essence of emotional crisis is a short upset in psychological equilibrium. In order to restore the equilibrium, the individual in crisis must discover and use new methods of coping and problem solving. During crisis periods there is an opportunity for healthy personality changes as well as risk of unhealthy change. If, during crisis, the individual chooses a course of action that is based on reality, produces the least possible damage to himself and others, and makes the best use of available resources, we may say not only that he is mentally healthy (as we did of the hypothetical father of a critically ill child) but that his mental health will actually improve as an outcome of the crisis, because he has added to his internal resources for coping effectively with the stresses of life. If, on the other hand, the individual's actions are based on fantasy, on magic, or on excessive use of denial or other mechanisms of defense, or if he uses other pathological means of avoiding the problems attendant on the crisis, we may say not only that he is mentally ill but that his mental health will actually deteriorate as a result of the crisis, for he has increased his potential for dealing ineffectively with his problems, for passing from one inadequate means of coping to others that may be even less adequate.

During crisis the path chosen depends on the interplay among several forces: the personality patterns of the individual, the state of his personality assets, the effect of his past experience, and his interactions with other people.

We are most concerned here with the interactions of the individual with others. These interactions will largely determine how much outside support he will receive in solving the crisis problems. The balance of all the forces involved in the individual's reaction to the crisis may be tipped toward his mental health or toward his mental ill health by the immediate help of these significant others. Here, perhaps, we are simply restating our view, as psychiatrists, that both mental health and mental illness are expressions of extremely complicated relationships between the individual and his social environment.

The rise of tension that occurs during crisis is an important factor in the outcome of the crisis. As tension during crisis increases, the motivation to seek help increases, and at the same time the manifested signs of distress seem to stimulate others to come to the individual's aid. The individual in crisis is more susceptible to influence than at other times in his life—a factor of prime importance in preventive mental health work. It gives great emotional leverage to the helping person in the situation and offers an enormous potential for affecting the future mental health of the person in crisis.

To whom do most people turn for help in time of crisis? For a variety of cultural and economic reasons, few turn to a psychiatrist. Most people usually turn to family members, friends, ministers, family doctors, and attorneys. In Peace Corps work, as we have intimated, other Volunteers, staff members, and the physician are included. The Peace Corps believes that amateurs in the field of psychological help can become quite skilled with minimal training. It tries to develop such skills in all these people—skills known as techniques of preventive intervention.

Preventive intervention is restricted; it provides the minimal assistance needed to steer the individual toward healthy problem solving. It is used only when an individual is observed to be using inappropriate responses, and it attempts to influence him to adopt more effective responses. It does not attempt to find out *why* he is using inappropriate responses, but only to tip the balance of forces in a healthy direction, to insure only that he behaves appropriately in the particular situation.

Preventive intervention, obviously, should not actually solve the problems behind the crisis. The intervener, if his intervention is to be truly preventive, should simply lend the kind of support which the person in crisis needs in order to work out solutions himself. For example, the intervener may discuss a number of possible solutions with the individual, help him to see all the considerations involved, to weigh them, and finally to choose the most desirable; or the intervener may simply listen attentively while the individual in crisis talks through his problems and airs some feelings which may be hampering his efforts to find a solution. In some instances preventive intervention may consist of helping to *share* a work load which seems insurmountable at the moment, thus giving the individual in crisis a breather, so to speak, which enables him to work out his own solution; or it may be advisable to let a depressed person work out the guilt feelings which are the very essence of depression by allowing him to carry an *increased* work load. Sometimes, simply to offer help in crisis is enough evidence of caring that the individual finds strength to work out his own difficulties.

Preventive intervention not only forestalls pathological developments in the current situation. It adds effective problem-solving and coping techniques to the individual's repertory which will be available to him in future stress situations.

Crisis theory and preventive intervention have many implications for community mental health work. Preventive intervention maximizes the use of available psychiatric manpower, by disseminating professional knowledge "downward" through a wide variety of caretaking agents. Of course, specialized psychiatric skill will always be needed in certain kinds of mental illness; in fact, preventive intervention may mean simply recognition of the need for more professional aid and helping the person to get it. Thus training in preventive techniques must include orientation to the basic guideposts of serious disturbance. But it is also true that help given in time of crisis may avert the need for eventual psychiatric help; and even if it does not avert the need, it may reduce the amount and the intensity of psychiatric assistance that will be needed.[9]

The Peace Corps, conscious of the importance of prevention during transitional periods, seeks to meet the psychological needs of persons whose development itself is at a critical point. These are mainly young people who may need a "moratorium" in which to deal with the problems connected with finding their own identities; but many are older people who face the problems of retirement, and there are other special groups. Government planning is currently directed toward other institutions, in addition to the Peace Corps, for meeting various transitional needs. The possibilities such institutions present for promoting positive mental health are as significant as any socioeconomic values involved.

Perhaps most important of all, the Peace Corps philosophy, with its

[9] Gerald Caplan, *Principles of Preventive Psychiatry* (New York: Basic Books, 1964).

emphasis on the worth and dignity of the individual, on giving help to others as well as learning to help oneself, seeks essentially to create a social environment in which the individual can achieve his highest potential. Such an environment is, or should be, central to the ultimate goals of any mental health program.

The psychiatrist's Peace Corps work underscores a new conception of his roles and functions. This conception involves his potential contribution as a behavioral scientist. The psychiatrist may be regarded not only as a physician who treats and strives to prevent mental illness, but also as an observer of human behavior and the effect of the social environment on behavior. Certainly, he may be regarded as an informed observer. His participation in programs which involve psychologically healthy people puts him in an even better position to fulfill his potential as a behavioral scientist, for he is then able to add to his clinical insights his observations of relatively normal behavior and interactions in a nonclinical social system. The implications here are manifold. They suggest that eventually the psychiatrist may work extensively with other behavioral scientists who seek means of adjusting the social environment in the interests of mankind. On this basis, we can visualize the psychiatrist as making his ultimate contribution to mental health work by helping to promote social conditions that are least conducive to mental illness, and that, when it must inevitably occur, make it most amenable to treatment.

Mental Illness in Relation to Some Current Social Problems

There is no simple, one-to-one relationship between clinical mental illness and any given significant social factor or set of factors. But epidemiological studies of mental illness, such as those of Hollingshead and Redlich [10] and others,[11] have demonstrated that certain social phenomena greatly increased the risk of mental illness in segments of a population consistently exposed to them.[12]

It will help our understanding of this increase in risk if we recall that

---

[10] August B. Hollingshead and Frederick C. Redlich, *Social Class and Mental Illness* (New York: John Wiley and Sons, 1958). A good review of Hollingshead and Redlich may be found in S. M. Miller and E. Mischlev, "Social Class, Mental Illness and American Psychiatry: An Expository Review," *Milbank Memorial Fund Quarterly*, 37 (April 1959), pp. 174–199.

[11] F. Riessman, J. Cohen, and A. Pearl, eds., *Mental Health of the Poor* (New York: The Free Press of Glencoe, 1964).

[12] Jerome K. Myers and Bertram H. Roberts, *Family and Class Dynamics in Mental Illness* (New York: John Wiley and Sons, 1959); Ernest M. Gruenberg, "A Review of Mental Health in the Metropolis: The Midtown Manhattan Study," *Milbank Memorial Fund Quarterly*, 41 (January 1963), pp. 77–94.

the psychiatrist views mental illness and mental health in terms of individual coping resources, the stresses presented by the environment, and the supports provided by the environment to supplement individual strengths. Extending this view somewhat, we should now consider how an individual's coping resources are developed. This is a complicated subject which is not entirely understood, but there can be no doubt that the development of individual coping capacities depends to a significant extent on supplies, so to speak, furnished to him by the environment.

Perhaps a more graphic way to label the sum total of an individual's internal resources for dealing with his environmental stresses is to use the term "skills of living." Obviously, these skills include the ability, in an adult, to earn a living. But much more is involved. In the current context, one of the most significant skills is knowing where to turn for help when one's own resources are inadequate. The lack of this skill is a major factor in converting relatively minor psychological disturbances among the poor, the uninformed, and the misdirected into serious mental illness.

If we narrow our thinking about the skills of living down to one community agency which presumably should help to provide them, we may think of education in the sense of formal schooling. But there is far more implied in acquiring such an education than can be learned in our schools as they currently and generally exist. It must be kept constantly in mind that today's American world is a verbal world whose social exchanges and processes are largely conditioned by abstractions of thought which can be expressed only in extremely complex language and language symbols. A child reared in a relatively nonverbal-, nonlanguage-oriented home will not develop the language skills essential to successful coping with that kind of world.[13] In fact, he will be unprepared even to use the opportunities provided by the schools for developing coping strengths. Indeed, he will be excluded from participation in many other early experiences which could help him work toward intellectual and emotional maturity. Because of his poor background in the skills of living, he will have limited opportunities for employment and for continuing growth in adult life. He will place very low in the power structure which must inevitably develop in any community; he will have very little access to or communication with the powerful. Thus his opportunities will also be limited for participation in efforts to correct the very conditions that have contributed to his limitations.

It takes little imagination and relatively little grasp of social prob-

---

[13] See especially Martin Deutsch, "The Disadvantaged Child and Learning Process," in Riessman, Cohen, and Pearl, eds., *op. cit.*, p. 172.

lems, then, to comprehend the variety of social conditions in which only limited help comes from the environment in developing these skills of living. Poverty; lack of opportunity because of racial segregation; the failure of education to compensate for the cultural deprivation of the home; the mass living, the mass education, and the mass working conditions which are so depersonalized that the individual is deprived even of the learning opportunities provided by continuing contact with preceptors and "pacesetters"—all these and others not only are conducive to individual failure to acquire the skills of living but tend to *perpetuate* such failure. Moreover, the conditions that nurture such failure appear to be the very conditions that present the individual with some of the most devastating stresses the social environment can manifest. It must be apparent that the population which is at greatest risk of clinical mental illness is the group that on the one hand is exposed to the most serious environmental stresses and on the other has had the most limited opportunities to develop the skills of living.

The upper-class or middle-class family, in contrast to the lower-class family, is able to give its children opportunities to enlarge their coping resources, enhancing their ability to deal with the adult world. They can qualify for a larger variety of jobs; they learn to identify and seek out sources of power, of help, of advantages in the community; they "know their way around."

The Caretakers

The greater incidence of mental illness in the lower class tells only one side of the story, however. Studies such as those of Hollingshead and Redlich also demonstrate that people who are in psychological difficulty seek help in relatively predictable ways. The private psychiatrist is usually sought out by middle- and upper-class patients. Psychotherapy is not only expensive; to be effective it requires considerable psychological understanding and education—a grasp of language and of language symbols without which it is extremely difficult for the patient to comprehend the meaning of his inner conflicts and their connection with his current problems. All too often the lower-class patient considers concrete action more potent than words. Indeed, to go to a psychiatrist at all, particularly voluntarily, implies some sophistication—at least enough education to be aware of what a psychiatrist is and does, and the ability to overcome the ancient fears and superstitions concerning mental illness that have already been discussed.

But lower-class people turn to various other caretakers. These may be official or semiofficial: welfare and health departments, voluntary social service organizations, the courts, health departments, the church, and, more rarely, the school. Frequently available service is not of the highest quality or geared to meet the particular needs of the patient. The professional attitudes too often prove to be a barrier for the poor and keep them from achieving psychotherapeutic help. (In addition, they often seek out unofficial, but implicitly recognized, neighborhood caretakers, such as bartenders, storekeepers, and barbers. It is one of the sadder elements of modern urbanization that the availability of such caretakers is being decreased by forced moves from old familiar neighborhood settings to more remote shopping centers.) When the resources of the individual and the caretakers are inadequate, and the individual becomes clinically ill, he more often than not ends up in a state hospital for the mentally ill.

In this connection the Clausen studies previously referred to throw a peculiarly poignant light on the ways in which mental patients get to mental hospitals, and show that this path is beset with dangerous and traumatic delays for both patient and wife. Clausen observes that the hospitalization of the 33 patients studied was seldom accomplished efficiently, that the patient who was severely ill of a physical ailment would generally come under medical care or be hospitalized with much greater dispatch. In physical illness there are relatively clearcut patterns for diagnosis and treatment. These are not readily apparent in mental illness, nor is the patient likely to be very cooperative about his own treatment, as a physically ill person usually is. Thus the delay in getting treatment, often caused by a wife's failure to identify the nature of the husband's difficulty, was usually increased by a lack of clarity about which way to turn for help, or what to do if the patient refused to cooperate. Indeed, several wives were told by friends, or personnel in hospitals and clinics where they sought help, that there was nothing they *could* do unless the husbands got into trouble with the police.

Clausen emphasizes the difficulty for most of these wives in knowing who in the community were the "gatekeepers" to psychiatric care. Some doctors, clergymen, and policemen were able to recognize the nature of the husband's difficulty and to help deal with it effectively. Others were less well informed about mental illness, less able to recognize it and assist the family. Even this small study indicates that our society is lacking in firm supports, often in the very quarters where one would expect to find them, for those whose internal resources are insufficient to cope with stresses.

More hospitalized mental patients are from the lower class than from the upper and middle classes. Among patients in psychiatric treatment outside the hospital, the reverse is true. One reason seems to be that the lower-class patient does not enter the psychiatric treatment system when his difficulties are minimal but only when he is in severe distress —close to, or actually in, a state of personality disorganization. Social and economic class determines, at least in part, not only the pathway to mental illness, but also the pathway the individual takes when he becomes ill. We can now begin to visualize an attack on mental illness, on a social basis, which starts with the needs of an entire community. We can begin to think of these needs in two ways: first, by expanding the opportunities whereby individuals can develop their own resources for dealing with the complex stresses of modern living; and second, by providing resources which will support the individual when his own resources are inadequate to meet these stresses. It becomes increasingly clear that programs for dealing with mental illness and programs for social reform have much in common.

Utopia or Non-utopia?

Mental illness is so significantly related to the social environment that efforts to combat it widely can be discussed only in terms of the major social issues of the day. But thinking of this kind should not blind us to the fact that mental illness has elements which are not entirely derived from the social structure. The assumption that in a perfect social environment there would be no more mental illness is a utopian ideal, impractical and unrealistic.

One frequently encounters another kind of thinking which represents almost an opposite view. From this position, mental illness is seen as an inescapable fact of life, regardless of its social determinants and components. The psychiatrist must, in this view, treat the illness with the best tools at his disposal and within the environment as it is, not as he might wish it to be. Thus the serious social obstacles he may encounter in treatment must be handled on an individual basis; on this basis, what cannot be changed readily must stand, and the patient must be helped to live with an unfavorable environment by whatever means are available. This line of thinking fails to take account of the possibility of social reform in the interest of prevention or amelioration. Thus, ultimately, it must lead to a defeatist and negative attitude.

To the authors, the realistic and positive approach lies between these extremes: it renders all possible immediate aid to the individual victim at the same time that it seeks to adjust the social environment in the interests of prevention. It recognizes that mental illness probably can never be eliminated entirely, but that every possible medical and social means must be used to lessen it.

Utopias are notoriously impossible to achieve, primarily because of the difficulty in defining what utopia is. Furthermore, medical history shows that a disease-free environment is virtually impossible. The very means taken to control a disease may promote the persistence of predisposition to the disease, or guarantee the appearance of other diseases. René Dubos has explored this subject in fascinating detail in his *Mirage of Health*.[14]

One may equate social utopias with medical utopias. We have evidence to demonstrate that some social reform, although it may be expected to ameliorate certain kinds of mental illness, often has quite unexpected and unfavorable results. Slum clearance is a case in point. In most major cities of the United States, city planning efforts have recently been directed at urban renewal problems in the central core of the cities. Central-city areas have become primarily residential areas for the bulk of the poor from minority groups and for a few well-to-do childless persons who like the convenience of city living. In city after city, areas classified as slums have been cleared through major governmental action, in order to increase the tax base of the community and bring "life" to the central-city area (thought to be decaying).

The decisions to clear these areas and relocate the populations have been largely based on economic, political, and design expedience. The criteria used to classify them as slums have been expressed in terms of physical deterioration and, implicitly, social deterioration and pathology. In actual fact, many slum communities *can* be shown to have high rates of social pathology and severe mental illness; the extensive use of social agencies, the mounting cost of police and fire protection, and many other factors bear ample witness to the presence of countless social evils historically associated with the slums. Nevertheless, it is clear from studies made of slum clearance projects, such as the one in the West End of Boston, that not all slums which have the *physical* appearance of deterioration are of necessity *social* slums.[15] In some slums the social structure is such that the population can be considered extremely healthy in its ability to cope with most of its problems. Thus it is obviously necessary to differentiate slum communities when we say we must "clean them up." Some have high levels of pathology, and some, like the West End of Boston, have minimal levels.

The urban renewal program for the West End required the clearance of a large area in order to build high-rise luxury apartments

[14] René Dubos, *Mirage of Health* (New York: Harper and Brothers, 1959).
[15] Marc Fried, "Grieving for a Lost Home," pp. 151–171, and Edward J. Ryan, "Personal Identity in an Urban Slum," pp. 135–150, in Leonard J. Duhl, ed., *The Urban Condition* (New York: Basic Books, 1963); Herbert Gans, *Urban Villagers* (New York: The Free Press of Glencoe, 1962).

which would attract middle- and upper-class people back to the center of the city and increase the tax base and the beauty of the city. From the standpoint of economics, political expedience, and physical planning, the city might be expected to benefit in every way. Moreover, the relocation of the slum population would be to their advantage. But the population was forced to disperse and relocate with minimal assistance. Their social structure, their total social fabric, was torn up and destroyed. When this happens, the individual must either increase his internal strengths in order to cope with the problems of transition and life in the new community or, if he is unable to develop this strength, he must turn to others for help. A large segment of the West End population, after its dispersal, became increasingly dependent on a wide variety of social agencies for such support.

If we measure costs to the community in social terms, it may, in fact, be extremely expensive to tear up communities with a strong sense of community ties—more expensive than planning comprehensively for human needs, social as well as physical. This kind of planning means taking into account a slum's positive as well as its deteriorating elements; it means retaining its devices for supporting social and mental health. Such planning may be complicated and costly since it is difficult to keep a community's social structure intact while its physical structure is being drastically changed. But it can be done, and it is only expensive if immediate financial cost is a greater consideration than ultimate social cost.

Comprehensive planning requires the planners to understand the social structure of each community. For example, the values of a slum community like the West End may be quite different from those of a Negro slum in New York's Harlem. And both these slums may have values entirely different from those of the middle-class urban settings from which most planners and politicians emerge, or whose values they represent. The West End studies explore the psychosocial processes involved in urban renewal and pose some critical questions. They offer no hard and fast rules, no complete solutions. But they do emphasize that social planning involves the tremendous risk of disturbing a social structure which may be less pathogenic than the effects of its disruption.

Although a social utopia may be unattainable, the social reformer is obliged to continue his search for ways of eliminating social evils. A medical utopia may also be impossible, but the doctor must go on looking for ways to treat and prevent disease.

Social Reform and Psychiatry

Obviously the psychiatrist must concern himself with the purely medical developments of the day. But the peculiarly social elements of mental illness imply that he must also concern himself, as a doctor, with social change. Not only must he keep himself informed of current social developments; he must also use his citizen's rights and opportunities to participate in social reform. Furthermore, we believe firmly that he is obligated to develop his potential as a behavioral scientist.

The problem of urban renewal illustrates how the psychiatrist, as a behavioral scientist, can make a significant contribution to social reform. Obviously, the psychiatrist must be aware of the impact of such major social decisions as urban renewal on the population from which at least some of his patients may come. True, he can never be the major person concerned with changing urban renewal policy at any governmental level. But his awareness of the complex nature of the total social situation involved in this policy should be added to that of his colleagues in other disciplines and made available to the people who shape the policy. Their joint knowledge and experience can be used by the policy makers to evaluate more carefully than they do now the psychosocial costs of urban renewal; at the same time, they can use this information to find ways and means of helping those in the population who lack adequate internal resources for coping with the stresses of relocation. It must be emphasized that this help only rarely necessitates the services of a psychiatrist; rather, it implies the help of a number of existing social agencies which can be adapted to this purpose, or possibly the creation of new agencies.

It must be emphasized further that the psychiatrist can contribute only his own special knowledge and insight. Furthermore, he should not be held responsible for the success or failure of any program beyond the area of his own contribution. Contrary to many popular misconceptions, he is not a magician; his profession simply requires him to observe human behavior with greater care than that required of some other mortals. This close observation qualifies him to contribute to social planning conducted in the interest of mental health.

Where Are We Now, and Where Are We Going?

How has our sense of social responsibility translated itself into legislation for mental health? The passage of the National Mental Health Act in 1946 was a milestone which led to the creation in 1947 of the

National Institute of Mental Health in Bethesda, Maryland. NIMH is devoted to the pursuit of knowledge: the causes, diagnosis, and treatment of mental illness; the care and rehabilitation of the mentally ill; and the prevention of mental illness and the promotion of mental health. It makes grants for these purposes for research, for professional training, and for the development of community mental health programs. Its research grants are made not only in psychiatry and psychology but in the social sciences, thus acknowledging that mental health and illness are closely related to major social issues. NIMH also maintains various statistical and other information services for those concerned with mental health.

Another national legislative advance was the passage by Congress in 1955 of the Mental Health Study Act. This act called for a nationwide analysis of the human and economic problems of mental illness and the methods for solving them, and the formulation of recommendations for better use of our resources for reducing mental illness and promoting mental health. A nongovernmental study group, the Joint Commission on Mental Illness and Health, which had been originated earlier in 1955 by the American Psychiatric Association and the American Medical Association, was assigned the task. Representatives of many related disciplines, including nonmedical personnel, were included in the group, emphasizing the growing awareness of our century that the problems of mental health and illness are exceedingly complex and involve far more than narrow medical concerns.

The work of this task force led to the publication of various reports, including a comprehensive volume, in 1961, entitled *Action for Mental Health*.[16] The book reports on a wide range of problems—research, personnel, care and treatment facilities, rehabilitation, dissemination of information to the public, and many others. It recommends governmental action at national, state, and local community levels, as well as private voluntary action; it discusses the cost of its proposals and suggests ways of meeting those costs, as well as a strategy of implementation. Certainly, its summary of recommendations is important reading for every student and every American citizen who feels any sense of social responsibility for mental illness.[17]

---

[16] Joint Commission on Mental Illness and Health, *Action for Mental Health* (New York: Basic Books, 1961).

[17] Other publications growing out of the work of the Joint Commission are of great interest and significance. See Jahoda, *op. cit.*; Rashi Fein, *Economics of Mental Illness*, Joint Commission on Mental Illness and Health, Monograph Series, no. 2 (New York: Basic Books, 1958); George W. Albee, *Mental Health Manpower Trends*, Joint Commission on Mental Illness and Health, Monograph Series, no. 3 (New York: Basic Books, 1959); Gerald Gurin, Joseph Veroff, and Sheila Feld,

The Congress and President Kennedy reacted sympathetically to the report and initiated a further study of the problems posed. Many of the major reports which followed proposed solutions which were unrealistic, both legislatively and practically. Nevertheless, these reports, together with the Joint Commission's report, forced on the American people and the Congress, particularly, the need to take an entirely new look at the whole problem of mental illness, and focused attention on the many critical issues involved: how to meet the mental health needs of *all* segments of our population rather than those of a privileged minority; whether to improve and duplicate existing facilities or to eliminate them gradually and substitute radically different kinds; how to augment the existing psychiatric manpower reservoir; and how to extend psychiatric help to groups and organizations operating with little or none; how to coordinate and unify existing and contemplated programs and efforts; and countless others.

Subsequently, President Kennedy proposed a series of comprehensive community mental health centers throughout the United States, and the Congress approved planning grants to the states for this purpose. It is expected that the states will develop these centers as part of a unified, state-organized program of services for the mentally ill, covering case finding, diagnosis, care, treatment, and rehabilitation. It is hoped that these programs will make readily accessible (both geographically and financially) not only all direct mental health services but also other social service facilities which supplement psychiatric treatment and insure comprehensive care; and that they will go beyond care to develop programs of mental health education and consultation for all relevant community agencies. Special consideration is envisioned for the needs of communities where professional manpower is minimal in the face of maximal need—thus emphasizing the needs of the poverty-stricken. Integration of some mental health programs with various programs designed for general social welfare is also foreseen.

It is rather difficult not to feel optimistic in the face of all the mental health activities, private and public, going on today in research, build-

---

Americans View Their Mental Health. A Nationwide Interview Survey, Joint Commission on Mental Illness and Health, Monograph Series, no. 4 (New York: Basic Books, 1960); Reginald Robinson, David F. DeMarche, and Mildred K. Wagle, *Community Resources in Mental Health,* Joint Commission on Mental Illness and Health, Monograph Series, no. 5 (New York: Basic Books, 1960); Richard J. Plunkett and John E. Gordon, *Epidemiology and Mental Illness,* Joint Commission on Mental Illness and Health, Monograph Series, no. 6 (New York: Basic Books, 1960); Allinsmith and Goethals, *op. cit.;* and Richard V. McCann, *The Churches and Mental Health,* Joint Commission on Mental Illness and Health, Monograph Series, no. 8 (New York: Basic Books, 1962).

ing of facilities, training of personnel, education of the public, preventive programs, and so on. In spite of many gaps and failures, many anomalies and contradictions, many costly duplications, much is being accomplished.

What remains to be done, however, staggers the imagination. Among the almost self-evident problems involved, money and manpower are paramount. The problem of money, obviously, is not peculiar to the mental health and illness issue but is rather a part of the vast political, social, and economic issues inherent in public responsibility for the welfare of the individual. The authors feel that they are not qualified to discuss these issues.

As for manpower, we can only underline the need for training ancillary personnel for mental health work, as so succinctly set forth in *Action for Mental Health*.[18] The Peace Corps model described earlier is representative of a number of systematic efforts made in recent years to use more extensively than is known in traditional psychiatry the help of persons *outside* the usual clinical milieus. These efforts must be expanded far beyond their present limits. Our society has a vast reservoir of persons untrained in mental health principles and practices who are already giving help to the mentally disturbed primarily because of the lack of better-trained personnel. They are already strongly motivated to help. With proper training clergymen, public welfare workers, teachers, and a host of other persons engaged in caretaking activities can become skilled mental health counselors. We must train them to serve the needs of the population most vulnerable to mental illness; they must be taught not only mental health principles and practices but how to communicate effectively with people whose language skills are severely limited.

Other persons who are fully and professionally trained in the mental health professions—psychologists, social workers, some family physicians, and psychiatrists with a particular interest in community service—can be made available for systematic consultation with mental health counselors to provide on-the-job training, professional supervision, and moral support and reassurance.

It has been suggested also that we may need an entirely new category of mental health worker, that is, "case managers," people who can be trained to direct the uninformed to the best sources of psychiatric help. The caretakers to whom the uninformed first turn for help can be taught to cooperate with these case managers and to report to them the first signs of mental disturbance which requires specialized professional help. The case manager would then see to it that the pa-

[18] *Op. cit.*

tient entered the treatment system in such a way that he would receive the full benefit of professional service. Although the case manager is needed mainly by the poor, he could play a vital role even for the middle-class family, bringing it information which it may otherwise lack.

The existing reservoir of potential ancillary personnel can probably never meet the need. Ways must be found to interest young people in mental health careers, as well as in other professions which involve mental health training. Most of these occupations pay notoriously less than many others. Here is another social problem within a problem.

The term "organizational sclerosis" designates another kind of obstacle. It is well known that institutions tend to perpetuate themselves in order to fill needs other than those for which they were designed. President Kennedy's program proposed some radical departures from traditional approaches to mental illness; it could well involve not only major changes in existing institutions but elimination of some. The mental health facility fills the needs of many people other than the patient: staff, those who support and encourage the institution, those who maintain programs for training its professional personnel, and others involved in countless social mechanisms centering around its operations. Changes that may benefit the patient may also play havoc with these needs: it may be easier to deal with the patient in a changed situation than to work with persons who have a tremendous psychological and economic investment in the institution. All too often the decision to preserve existing institutions is made for the sake of people other than the patients.

Organizational sclerosis also presents itself as an emphasis on efficient operation at the expense of long-term goals. Thus a comfortable alternative keeps institutions from facing the challenge of change and its effect on long-term goals. Such sclerosis characterizes many mental health activities and is difficult to deal with since it is often covered by an aura of business and "doing good."

Social Problems or Mental Health Problems?

Perhaps the greatest danger of all is the current tendency in the United States to gather under the umbrella of the "mental health movement" vast social problems which can be dealt with realistically only if they are called by their real names. When abnormal behavior which is a manifestation of widespread social stress is treated as a separate problem, rather than as a symptom of that social stress, it is implied that the goal of treatment is individual "adjustment" to the status quo. If we continue to treat all mental illness in terms of this individual "adjustment," we shall continue to spend on mental illness ever-increasing sums which perhaps should be used to alter the status quo.

We do not know the answers to all the questions about mental illness; we do not fully know why some individuals react to social stress with illness while others do not. But we do know that the social environment plays a vital role. Hiding the problems of that environment will not solve them.

Much current research is concerned with the relationship of these evils to mental illness. This is a proper beginning, embodying both a medical and a social perspective. But it is one thing to discover what is wrong in the environment and another to correct it. Certainly we have had, and continue to have, major social reforms in this century. Many of them may be seen as mental health measures. But they do not *necessarily* represent action taken as a result of mental health research. It is precisely this lack of recognition of the relationship between action for mental health and social action that makes it possible for the "mental health movement" to obscure social issues and retard social progress. There is no intention here to impugn the motives of those who fight the war against mental illness on any front; we need all fronts—medical, educational, social. But we must somehow base the war on honest awareness of all the issues involved, and somehow make it a war carried on by all responsible segments of the community, lest it become a series of minor skirmishes rather than a total war.

The major issue, then, appears to be this: How are we to take what is discovered in research and translate it into social action? The process of conversion necessarily involves extremely complex problems. They go beyond any single field of knowledge, any single science, any single branch of human activity. We have no answers to these complexities, but we do insist on the need to face them in every dimension. We believe that the only hope of resolving them lies in organized, rational planning, planning in which not only government but various relevant nongovernmental groups and agencies play prominent roles, planning which leads to political decision. Ultimately, political decision, made through our democratic processes, must effect the necessary conversion.

Societies, like individuals, encounter crises in their development. Societies as well as individuals can make their crises opportunities for growth and maturation. In our current social crises we can fall back on old and ineffective patterns of behavior, or we can find entirely new ones which are compatible with our democratic structure, our ideals, and our traditions—patterns which lead to progress rather than to regression. In attacking mental illness, medicine and social reform must search together for these patterns in every field of human endeavor.

There can be no perfect answer to the problems of mental health and illness. But to search for the answer in terms of *all* their determinants and components would seem to best represent the most humanistic aspects of social and medical history.

Part Three

Problems of Community and Nation

7

Race Relations

▼▼▼▼▼▼▼▼▼▼▼▼▼▼▼▼▼▼▼▼▼▼▼▼▼▼▼▼▼▼▼▼▼▼

Raymond W. Mack

EVERYWHERE, men manage to believe that their group is superior to others. Human beings in any group tend to think that their culture, their way of doing things, their way of thinking is not only the best way but perhaps the only right way. It is difficult to consider that the fellows in the other political party could have the better platform. It is hard to conceive that the God being worshipped in a different language by strangers halfway around the world might be the true one, and that the God one's parents believe in could be a fiction. Most tribes have a word for themselves and a less flattering one for outsiders: Jews speak of gentiles, Greeks of barbarians, Americans of foreigners.

This human tendency to judge other groups by the standards of one's own is called *ethnocentrism*. It is by no means limited to tribes, nation-states, and total societies. All sorts of groups have a higher opinion of themselves than of others, whether nations, street-corner gangs, religious denominations, universities, treaty alliances, or families. Caplow, in a study of 33 different types of organizations, found that raters overestimated the prestige of their own organization (as evaluated by others) eight times as often as they underrated it.[1] Research at two Strategic Air Command Air Force bases revealed that more than half the squadrons were ranked first in prestige by their own members, and that all squadrons ranked themselves higher than people in other squadrons ranked them.[2] A study of 122 university departments

---

[1] Theodore Caplow, *Principles of Organization* (New York: Harcourt, Brace and World, 1964), pp. 213–214.
[2] Raymond W. Mack, "The Prestige System of an Air Base: Squadron Rankings and Morale," *American Sociological Review*, 19 (June 1954), pp. 281–287.

showed that 51 percent of the departments were rated by their own department chairmen as among the first five in the country; only 5 percent even considered themselves below average.³

One consequence of this aggrandizement is that members of one group tend to underrate and even to reject the achievements of members of another group. A disproportionately large number of Jews are found in the high-prestige professions of medicine and law; but many European and American Christians cite this, not as evidence of valued traits such as ambition, intellectual ability, or success, but as proof that Jews are characteristically pushy, clannish, and aggressive.

People may even reject another group when the other group is helping them. Since World War II, acute labor shortages in the industrialized nations of northern Europe have been alleviated by mass migrations of laborers from Spain, Portugal, and Italy into France, Sweden, Switzerland, and, especially, Germany. There are 900,000 foreign workers in the German labor force. A common view among Germans is that the foreigners, especially Italians, are lazy, unproductive workers. Yet the fact is that Italian workers in Germany average only 13.7 days of absenteeism for sick leave per year, while native-born German workers take an average of 20.6 days.⁴

Refusal to credit the achievements of people outside one's own group is only one consequence of ethnocentrism. Another consequence of great significance for social policy is resistance to social change. Human beings resist innovations that pressure them to alter their socially shared values and beliefs.

For most persons social facts are considerably more emotion-laden than physical facts. When physicists announce that they have learned something new about atomic behavior, most people are not much excited about the discovery. They are not personally acquainted with any atoms; their parents did not teach them that good, moral atoms behaved in a certain way; and they feel no obligation to revise their day-to-day thinking or behavior because of the physicists' discovery. But when sociologists announce that they have learned something new about how human groups behave, people are likely to be agitated. They feel that their own observations are as valid as the studies of social scientists. Because their parents have taught them that good, moral human beings behave in a known way, new scientific knowledge about human beings may oblige them to revise their habits of thought and behavior. It takes a conscious effort to abandon customary ways of thinking. Most people will resist acceptance of new knowledge, even

³ Theodore Caplow and Reece J. McGee, *The Academic Marketplace* (New York: Basic Books, 1962), Table 5-5.
⁴ See *Newsweek*, "Slow Melting" (August 3, 1964), p. 37.

though rationally arrived at, in favor of superstitions or prejudices that they have been taught to accept. If we have long believed that rural people are happier than city people, or that whites are more intelligent than Negroes, or that contact between groups of persons who resent and distrust each other will dispel their hostility, it is easier to reject the social scientist who informs us that these beliefs are prejudices and superstitions than it is to abandon our beliefs because the scientific evidence runs counter to them.

This failure to accept new ways of thinking and behaving is especially strong when the stability of the social order is reinforced by overlapping social factors. If race and class mean almost the same thing—if being Negro means almost automatically that you are lower class—it is difficult to change the stratification structure because that would interfere with racial beliefs and racial etiquette, and it is hard to convince people that they should alter their attitudes about race, because those attitudes are reinforced by life chances and the evidence of social class differences.

The traditional caste system of India, for example, is a social structure where race and class mean almost the same thing. The word "caste" derives from the Portuguese *casta*, meaning lineage; kinship is a basic factor in the maintenance of Hindu class gradations. The Hindu word for caste is *varna*, meaning color; in India, skin color and the order of arrival of immigrants over the centuries have affected the definitions of caste boundaries. The power of tradition and the magnitude of the resistance to changes in group boundaries are attested in a recent research report.

> New Delhi, June 27 (AP)—Begumpur, a village 12 miles from the capital, has handed the Indian government a shock. A census study of Begumpur's 840 residents shows they either ignore or never have heard of one of the government's best publicized campaigns.
>
> This is the 17-year campaign to wipe out untouchability, an ancient form of social discrimination that relegates an estimated 60 million persons throughout India to lowest-class lives of scorn, menial jobs and in some villages near-animal existence.
>
> Beginning with Mohandas K. Gandhi, Indian government officials, educators, politicians, and writers have thundered against untouchability. The constitution outlaws untouchability and the courts assess heavy fines occasionally against people convicted of practicing it.
>
> But, the study shows, 38 per cent of Begumpur's residents never have heard that untouchability is illegal.
>
> In Begumpur untouchables must sit on the ground while speaking to Brahmins or other high castes. They cannot draw water from the community's well. . . .

In large cities untouchables have been able to blend somewhat with higher-caste Indians. But untouchable colonies still exist in the capital and untouchables live apart in Calcutta, Madras and Bombay.

In remote areas, discrimination is rampant.

There are government reports of forced labor—akin to slavery—in six states. Investigators in Rajasthan State found children working to pay off debts of their long-dead parents—and getting deeper in debt to money-lenders. . . .[5]

Every society has a category of people who are dominant. In some societies there are people who look or act differently from the members of the dominant class. Such people, identified as different, are excluded from full participation in the society. People discriminated against (in other words, accorded differential treatment) because they are believed to be inherently different from the dominant members of the society are called by sociologists a *minority*. The word does not necessarily mean that they are a numerical minority. The Bantu-speaking natives of South Africa are a minority because, although there are fewer Europeans, being European is normative for the society. The Europeans are in power; they control the society, and the Bantu are excluded from full participation in the culture.

A number of people may be defined as a minority by the dominant population on grounds of race (they are physically different) or of ethnicity (they are culturally different because they share learned behaviors, such as language, religion, dress, or diet, which set them off from the rest of society). Despite efforts of social scientists to set up logical, analytical concepts, the whole issue is confounded by two facts. (1) Defining a race as a minority isolates them from the mainstream of the culture to an extent that they tend to *become* ethnic—that is, they tend to develop patterns of behavior peculiar to the race. (2) Defining an ethnic category as a minority leads the dominant group to attempt to justify discrimination by imputing some immutable characteristics to that minority. It is not unusual, therefore, for dominant people to refer to ethnic minorities as races. In short, the treatment that they receive tends to make minority races "ethnic," and people are inclined to call ethnic minorities "races."

American Racial and Ethnic Minorities

The history of the United States is a history of minorities. A racial or ethnic population becomes defined as different and emerges as a

[5] *Atlanta Journal and Constitution*, "India Works to Solve Problems of Untouchables" (June 28, 1964), p. 17.

minority in one of four ways: through annexation, colonialism, voluntary migration, and involuntary migration. The entire population of the United States is derived from one or another of these four minorities.

The bulk of people who have occupied minority status in the United States became minorities through voluntary migration. These immigrants, in turn, made the American Indians a minority through the colonial pattern of political and economic subordination of native populations. Our relations with the native populations of Cuba, Alaska, Puerto Rico, Hawaii, and the Philippines have been, in greater or lesser degree, toward the creation of colonial minorities. Our most notable case of creating a minority through annexation occurred after the Mexican War (1846–1848) when the Mexicans in Texas, California, and the Southwest were taken into the United States. Negro slaves entered the United States, of course, via involuntary migration. We can say, then, not only that all four of the patterns of minority emergence have contributed to the growth of the United States, but that every contemporary American is either a member of a minority or the descendant of someone who was.

Although minorities comprise a significant proportion of America's social structure, the ethnic fabric of our society is undergoing extensive changes. Who our minorities are, where they fit into the social structure, the rate at which they are encouraged to assimilate, and their impact upon such major institutions as education and government—all these are in a state of flux.

A striking change in the American role of minorities is the declining significance of European ethnic minorities. There are two reasons: the number of Europeans entering the United States has decreased markedly, and those already here and their descendants are becoming assimilated.

Most people who became members of a minority in the United States did so as a result of voluntary migration. The primary source of voluntary migrants has been Europe—northern Europe before 1890 and southern and eastern Europe since that time. Over 37 million immigrants have entered the United States in the past century. Fewer than one million of these came from Asia and Africa. In short, from the past century most of the country's minority population has been comprised of foreign-born immigrants of European extraction. This is no longer true; the children born in the coming decades will be the first in the history of the United States to be reared amidst a population that is over 95 percent native-born.

At the turn of the twentieth century, immigration was nearly as great a factor as the birthrate in increasing the nation's population. Even in the period from 1840 to 1880, immigration from Europe accounted for over one-fourth of our total population increase per decade. From 1880 to 1890, immigrants comprised over 40 percent of the total population increase; between 1900 and 1910, 55 percent of the population growth came from immigration. Since the adoption of the Immigration Act of 1924, the number of people entering minority status in our society through voluntary immigration from Europe has been negligible. In 1850, we were admitting over fifteen immigrants per thousand of population; during the past 25 years, we have averaged well under one immigrant per thousand of population. Clearly this alone would account for a marked decline in the significance of foreign-born Americans in the total picture of minorities in the United States.

There is, however, another reason why we can ignore the foreign-born and their descendants in projecting future trends in dominant-minority relations. European immigrants, in general, have been encouraged to assimilate. Americans have been critical of national minorities who have segregated themselves and retained their "foreign" institutions. The immigrant considered most desirable has been the one who teaches his children the culture patterns of his adopted country and becomes "Americanized."

The assimilation rate into the dominant population is influenced by how recently the immigrant arrived, how different his native culture is from his adopted one, how concentrated he and his fellows are in one part of his adopted city or country, and whether or not he is physically different from the dominant population. All four of these assimilation-deterring factors add up to one thing: how visible is he? The more recently he has arrived, the less time he has had to learn a new language, mode of dress, and other culture patterns, the less he acts like dominant people and the more identifiable he is. The similarity of the culture in which he was reared to the one where he had immigrated is a factor in his rate of assimilation for the same reason: the more different he is, the more identifiable he is. A large number of different people in one area is considerably more noticeable than a few would be. Because they are different and noticeable, there seem to be even more of them and they are more likely to inspire fear, to be singled out as a threat to our way of life, to have stereotypes built up about them, and to become objects of prejudice and discrimination. Concentration in the population makes them visible; visibility slows their rate of assimilation.

European immigrants have not been as visibly different as our other minorities, so they have been able to assimilate faster than other minorities. The next generation of their descendants—native-born, playing in American city streets, attending American public schools, exposed to movies and television which explicitly and implicitly teach the ways and the desirability of American culture—this rising generation of descendants of immigrants will be assimilated at an even faster rate than their parents and grandparents. They will be less concentrated in the population; they will carry little of the burden of cultural differences; they will be natives, not new arrivals; they will, in most ways, not be visibly different from the dominant people, and they will therefore assimilate.

Does this combination of rapidly increasing assimilation with drastically curtailed immigration mean the end of ethnic minorities as a significant feature of the American metropolitan social structure? It does not. The waning of European immigration and the assimilation of the immigrant generation serves only to focus our attention more pointedly on three new urban minorities.

The second major change involving the place of "ethnics" in the social structure is the emergence of three new minorities in our metropolitan areas. The first are the Puerto Ricans. Legally, Puerto Ricans are not immigrants; they can pass freely from the island to the mainland without a passport, just as one can cross a state line. Sociologically, of course, they fall into the category of voluntary migrants, becoming a minority as they move out of the culture where they were reared and appear—concentrated, newly arrived, culturally different, and visible—in a new land.

Puerto Ricans are not widely distributed on the mainland. They are concentrated in a few large cities, most notably New York. By 1956 there were over 550,000 Puerto Ricans in New York City, or, to use a journalistic cliché, there were more Puerto Ricans in New York than in San Juan, the largest city in Puerto Rico. Of the new minorities, the Puerto Ricans are the most like their European predecessors as immigrants in that they are marked off from the dominant population by language and religion. They have one difficulty, however, with which few of our previous minorities have had to cope: racial ambiguity. Some Puerto Ricans have physical characteristics considered in the United States to be white; others are classed as Negroes.

The second new minority is not only English-speaking but white and native-born. Its members are nonetheless an ethnic minority, unprepared by their upbringing (by the values and patterns of behavior they have learned) to be assimilated readily into metropolitan life. These are the Southern white mountaineers, commonly known as hillbillies, recent migrants to the Northern industrial city.

Like the Puerto Rican, the Southern white mountaineer has all of the characteristics of an ethnic minority except the technicality of foreign birth. He comes to the city from an area where the culture is different, where different behaviors are rewarded and punished. He has recently arrived. He has come from a poor environment, seeking economic opportunity, and hence will be found concentrated in an old, run-down section of the city. Both his speech and his behavior make him visible, and many people in the dominant population consider him inferior and undesirable.

The third new minority deserves most of our attention, since it is by far the largest. Everything we have said about the Southern white mountaineer as a minority applies to him, with one exception: he is more visible, and his visibility is not so easily shed, because he is Negro. It may be contended that the Negro is not a new minority, which is true; but he is a newly urbanized minority, and hence is of concern to us. To see that the Negro as an urban dweller is a new minority, one need only note how ill-equipped our metropolitan areas are to deal with him. He compounds the problems of being racially visible with those of the rural person attempting to become part of an urban milieu.

Throughout the three centuries of Negro residence in the United States, most Negroes have resided in the country. As recently as 1900, 90 percent of the Negroes in the United States lived in the South, and over 80 percent of all Negroes in the United States in 1900 lived in rural areas. By 1950, 63 percent of the Negroes were urban dwellers; outside the South, over 90 percent lived in cities, which is to say that Northern Negroes are more urban than whites.

The changing distribution of minorities in America's metropolitan social structure can, then, be summarized. For 150 years, European immigrants comprised most of our minority population; their most important learning task on the road to assimilation was the exchange of their native culture patterns for the ways of the Americans. Now, and for the foreseeable future, most of our minority population is composed of United States citizens: Negroes, Puerto Ricans, and Southern whites. Their assimilation depends on adjusting to urban life and on exchanging rural values and behaviors for city ones. The overwhelming majority of them face the additional block to assimilation of a visibly different skin color.

If the members of a society are to exclude some of their fellows from full participation in the culture and define them as a minority, the people who comprise the minority must have some visible characteristic, brand, badge, or stigma by which they can be identified. The

Negroes of the Ituri Forest can treat the pygmies as a minority because they can tell by a man's stature that he is a pygmy. New England Yankees can treat local French-Canadians as a minority because the latter's speech and family names set them off from the dominant people. A minority's identifiability may result from speaking a different language, having a different skin color, possessing different eye color, or attending a church different from that attended by the people in the dominant category. In other words, either they can be different physically, they can be labeled as different, or they can behave differently, but one or the other is necessary if they are to be identifiable, and they must be identifiable if they are to be discriminated against as a minority. This is why the Nazis forced the German Jews to wear armbands so that they could be more easily detected.

If only a man's behavior makes him identifiable, he can become socialized into a new culture and be assimilated. But physical differences are more permanent; if his skin color identifies him, no amount of socialization into the dominant culture will remove him from minority status. Racial minorities are therefore less able to lose their identity and escape minority status than are ethnic minorities.

Racial minorities, unlike ethnic ones, have been discouraged from total assimilation. Many states have laws against intermarriage between whites and Negroes or Mongoloids. All the culture patterns that keep racial minorities separate from the dominant category—segregated housing, schools, churches, and so on—deter total assimilation which would mean biological amalgamation and intermarriage.

Identifiability is the key to the rate and degree of assimilation of a minority. The basic difference between European ethnic minorities and Asian and African racial minorities is a function of the degree their identifiability is changeable. The Polish immigrant who learns English and changes his name will rear children who not only will not be *identifiable* as Polish; they will not *be* Polish. Their visibility as a minority depends entirely on culture patterns. If American culture patterns are substituted for Polish ones, such visibility vanishes. But no matter how completely a Negro is "American" in his thoughts, language, religion, name, and behavior patterns, he is identifiable as a member of a minority because his visibility depends on his physical features, not his learned behavior.

The Southern white mountaineers who currently seem such a problem to the city fathers of Chicago and Detroit are therefore the most easily dismissed from our discussion of the new urban minorities. They are visible only because they are rural people from one region who have come to dwell in the cities of another region. As soon as they have learned the behaviors that are Northern and urban, and substituted these for the culture patterns that are Southern and rural, they will be assimilated.

Those Puerto Ricans whose racial ancestry allows them to be considered white will be the next to assimilate. They have a little more to learn, a few more changes to make, than do the Southern whites. Where the Southern white need only change his accent, the Puerto Rican must learn a new language. If he does not look Negro, only the need to learn new ways of behavior blocks him from total assimilation.

The Negroid Puerto Rican, however, like the Southern Negro migrant to the city, remains a visible member of a minority no matter how complete his cultural assimilation. It seems safe to predict that those defined as racial minorities will be the last to assimilate, and that they will not do so in our lifetime or, for that matter, in our children's.

Race as a Social Problem

Americans need hardly be told that relations between the races constitute a social problem in the United States. In some ways the position of the Negro in American society is caste-like. A person may work his way up in the class structure, but he cannot work his way up from Negro to white. Efficient social barriers keep most Negroes from moving into white neighborhoods in Northern cities, and the barriers to full participation in the community are even more rigid in the Deep South. In recent voter registration in Louisiana, Negro applicants were disqualified for such offenses as an error of one day in computing the applicant's age by number of years, months, and days; misspelling the word "birth"; answering either "brown" or "Negro" in a blank reading "My color is ——"; leaving out a middle name; or underlining "have not" as well as crossing out "have" in a series of character statements including: "I have not (have) given birth to an illegitimate child within five years." [6]

It is not difficult to see that race relations are a problem in a society that guarantees equal rights under the law, and encourages the ideal of equality of opportunity, yet allows widespread racial discrimination in voting, housing, employment, religion, and even education. People see race relations as a social problem, but they are less likely to see that discrimination is a different problem depending on who you are and where you stand in the society. Race relations are a problem for a Negro Congressman from Harlem and for a white Congressman from

[6] *The New Republic*, 150 (April 4, 1964).

Mississippi, but the problem is different for each; racial discrimination seems a problem to a Methodist minister in a Northern suburb, to a Methodist minister in a Southern metropolis, and to a Black Muslim, but the three men see different problems.

That one's perspective on race as a social problem varies with his situation is aptly illustrated by the findings of a survey made for the Institute of International Education.

The problems and attitudes of young Africans studying in America have been probed by a comprehensive study throughout the country.

And a major conclusion, regarded as surprising by the survey makers, is that African students don't get on as well as expected with Negroes.

At the same time, however, according to the survey, the Africans resent the fact that they receive better treatment from white Americans than Negroes do in situations of racial discrimination.

The survey made for the Institute of International Education reported that 20 percent of the Africans at Southern schools had no American Negro friends.

"This is particularly significant," the study observed, "since all but one of these schools were Negro institutions."

In Northern schools, it was reported, 45 percent of those questioned said they had no Negro friends. The study identified 1537 Africans at 366 colleges, obtained written replies from 1010 and included 208 personal interviews.

Of the almost two-thirds of the Africans who felt friction with Negroes, 19 percent said American Negroes were unfriendly and 13 percent said Negroes felt superior to them.

In a recent study a series of ten stereotypes about Negroes was set before white people, who were asked which statements they agreed with and which they rejected. Table 1 reveals how the response patterns of the nationwide sample of whites differ from the sample of Southern whites, and how both differ from samples of those who had had social contact with Negroes. For example, over half of white Southerners believe that Negroes are inferior to whites; fewer than one-third of the nationwide sample believe this, and only 15 percent of those with previous social contact with Negroes hold such a view.

People not only disagree on when or where or why race is a social problem; they disagree on the nature of the problem itself. For the white man who is afraid that his daughter will marry a Negro, race is a sexual and familial problem. For the Negro who is excluded from membership in a union controlling access to jobs, race is an economic problem. For the London landlord who raises rents in the face of the Pakistani demand for housing that is in short supply, or for the Chicago realtor who charges higher rents to Negroes than to whites while helping restrict the supply of housing available, race discrimination is not a "problem" at all: it is a chance to make more money.

Often, of course, race relations pose dilemmas. Does the Golden Rule mean that a Christian employer should hire Jewish clerks—even if it costs him the patronage of some of his anti-Semitic customers? How is an Irish-American mother supposed to feel when her daughter brings home an Italian-American fiancé—unhappy he's not Irish or glad he's not Protestant? Is a Negro clergyman obligated to urge his flock to turn the other cheek? Or should he risk the financial support he receives from the white community by criticizing its acceptance of racial discrimination?

Table 1 White Stereotypes about Negroes

Agree with Statement:	Nationwide, percent	South, percent	Previous Social Contact Group, percent
Negroes laugh a lot	68	81	79
Negroes tend to have less ambition	66	81	56
Negroes smell different	60	78	50
Negroes have looser morals	55	80	39
Negroes keep untidy homes	46	57	31
Negroes want to live off the handout	41	61	26
Negroes have less native intelligence	39	60	23
Negroes breed crime	35	46	21
Negroes are inferior to whites	31	51	15
Negroes care less for the family	31	49	22

SOURCE: William Brink and Louis Harris, *The Negro Revolution in America* (New York: Simon and Schuster, 1964), pp. 140–141.

This would be confusing enough, but as it happens, people are not even agreed on what they mean by race. Brazilians, South Africans, Americans, and Jamaicans are all vitally interested in the question of who is a Negro, but for each group the term "Negro" has a different meaning.

Nasser frequently speaks of the Arab race. Much of his success in unifying the Arabic-speaking peoples has come from his stress of the need for racial unity. Meanwhile, across Egypt's border lives another group of people hated as much for their racial difference from Arabs as for their religious difference—the Jews. If the race hatred between

Arabs and Jews had not cost so much in bloodshed and bitterness, it would be amusing, for our most valid biological classification system not only places Arabs and Israelis in the same racial category (Caucasoid) but consigns most Arabs and most Israelis to the same subclassification (Semitic) of that category.

Race means many things to many people. Hitler wrote with passion of the need to keep the Aryan race pure, but scientists tell us that Aryan is a language group, not a physical type. Hitler included the Japanese with the Germans as Aryans; yet he rejected the Americans from his honorific category despite the fact that Germans constitute the second largest component in the American stock. It would be well to stop and ask what we are talking about. Just what are races?

Are Races Real? The Biology of Race

Scientists mean by "race" a number of humans who share a set of innate physical characteristics. People often assume that members of a race share a set of physical characteristics which are unchangeable and set them apart permanently from other races. This is not true. Human races are subject to the same processes of genetic change as all other living organisms.

An ideal system of classification is one in which all the cases can be categorized (the system is exhaustive) and in which there is no overlap in the categories (the categories are mutually exclusive).[7] But we have no such system for humans. Because all human beings are members of one species and because the various stocks in that species have been mixing with one another for hundreds and thousands of years, biologists have no set of "racial" categories which are both exhaustive and mutually exclusive.

A biologist's classification system for races is concerned only with factors that are of scientific interest to the biologist. Religious beliefs do not come through the genes. Nor can political ideologies, or customs, or beliefs be inherited. So the biologist must reject such factors in classifying races. A biologist is concerned with genetic relationships, with what is hereditary, and deals only with the physical properties that may be transmitted through the genes. Among such properties are the color of eyes, skin, and hair; the form of nose, head, hair, and stature.

[7] The discussion in this section draws on Raymond W. Mack, *Race, Class, and Power* (New York: American Book Company, 1963). For more detail and illustrative data on the weakness of racial classifications, see *Race, Class, and Power*, pp. 33–94.

Human individuals differ from one another in various traits: stature, curl of hair, size of hand, length of toes, and so on. Clusters of similar features can be found distributed among a group of people who have lived together in some region for a long time in relative isolation from other groups. People who live in cool climates have, on the average, lighter skin than those who live in the tropics. Many people in the Far East have coarse black hair. Europeans generally have softer, less tightly curled hair on their bodies than most Asians or Africans. Many of the millions of people in Asia (and some in eastern Europe) have a skin fold over the inner corner of the eye which gives the eye the appearance of being slanted.

But all these are minor differences, less notable than, for example, the range of variation among black bears. It would be easy for a biologist to categorize men if their heads came in two distinct shapes, round and square. It would be easy if three distinct nose forms could be found, or distinctly different skin colors of a small number and variety. But nature does not oblige. Head shapes vary along a continuum from round to narrow and cannot be grouped into sharply different categories. Nose form, eye shape, hair type, hair color, and eye color also differ infinitesimally along a gradual scale, and skin coloring is almost infinitely divisible into variation along a color continuum.

Another complication is that sets of physical factors are not necessarily associated with each other. A man with a round head may have black skin or white skin. A man with a ruddy complexion may have a flat nose or a sharp one. A man may have dark brown skin, a medium long head, dark eyes, straight hair, and a sharp nose. The combinations and permutations seem virtually infinite.

Hence the use of biological concepts to classify men into races must be extremely arbitrary. At what point along the continuum of skin color do we make a cutoff, deciding that skin lighter than this will be called Mongoloid and skin darker than this Negroid?

Human beings are a single species; hence the basic body structure of men is the same all over the world. All human beings have the same kind of lungs, the same kind and number of bones, the same complex nervous systems, the same delicate sensory organs for tasting, smelling, touching, hearing, and seeing. All men have the same bloodstream and, although there are slight differences among individuals in blood chemistry, they are not related to skin color: a doctor handed a vial of type O blood has no way of ascertaining whether the donor was white or Negro, and no laboratory test of the blood can determine the donor's hair type, eye color, or other external physical traits.

Nevertheless, physical anthropologists and biologists have somewhat arbitrarily divided mankind into three major categories: (1) the whites or Caucasoids, who were inhabitants of Europe, North Africa, and Southwest Asia, but in recent centuries have spread pretty well over the globe; (2) Negroids, black or brown people, often having curly hair, who originally were mostly Africans but now constitute a high proportion of the population of the Western hemisphere; and (3) Mongoloids, yellow to brown people with straight, black hair, originally heavily concentrated in Asia and islands of the Pacific.

Table 2 Physical Characteristics of the Three Main Races of Mankind

Trait	Caucasaoid	Mongoloid	Negroid
Skin color	Pale reddish white to olive brown; some dark brown.	Pale yellow to yellow-brown; some reddish brown.	Brown to brown-black; some yellow-brown.
Stature	Medium to tall.	Medium tall to medium short.	Tall to very short.
Head form	Long to broad and short; medium high to very high.	Predominantly broad; height medium.	Predominantly long; height low to medium.
Face	Narrow to medium broad; no projecting jaw.	Medium broad to very broad; cheekbones high and flat.	Medium broad to narrow; frequent projecting jaws.
Hair	Head hair: color light blond to dark brown; texture fine to medium, form straight to wavy. Body hair: moderate to profuse.	Head hair: color brown to brown-black; texture coarse; form straight. Body hair: sparse.	Head hair: color brown-black; texture, coarse; form light curl to woolly or frizzly. Body hair: slight.
Eye	Color: light blue to dark brown; occasional side eye fold.	Color: brown to dark brown; fold of flesh in inner corner very common.	Color: brown to brown-black; vertical eye fold common.
Nose	Bridge usually high; from narrow to medium broad.	Bridge usually low to medium; form medium broad.	Bridge usually low; form medium broad to very broad.
Body build	Slim to broad; slender to rugged.	Tends to be broad; occasional slimness.	Tends to be broad and muscular, but occasional slimness.

SOURCE: Adapted from Wilton M. Krogman, "The Concept of Race," in Ralph Linton, ed., *The Science of Man in the World Crisis* (New York: Columbia University Press, 1945), p. 50.

The magnitude of the difficulties can be seen by noting the vagueness of the categories in Table 2. Loose as this three-way classification is, it does not cover all the races of man. African Bushmen-Hottentots, for example, have Mongoloid eyes. Australian aborigines have Negroid skin and Caucasoid hair. Some Polynesians have white skin and some dark brown skin; most have wavy hair, but there are many with straight or kinky hair. Some have broad and short faces, others long and narrow features. Since there is no such thing as a pure race among human beings, we obviously cannot set up a classification scheme for pure races and expect the data to correspond to the theory.

The uselessness of categories as loose as Negroid, Mongoloid, and Caucasoid as a basis for generalizations is obvious. Since the categories are based on gross averages, differences within categories are often greater than differences between them. There is more difference between the lightest and the darkest "Negroid" or between the lightest and the darkest "Caucasoid" than between the lightest "Negroid" and the darkest "Caucasoid." The differences even within a geographic region are often as marked as the variations among the great groups that are called "races." The Mojaves of the American Southwest average nearly six feet in height; their neighbors the Hopi average five feet four inches. Both the longest and roundest human heads are found among American Indian tribes. The tallest and shortest people in the world, the Watusi and the Pygmy, live within a few miles of one another; both have black skin and kinky hair—but some blond Norwegians also have kinky hair.

These three categories are neither exhaustive nor mutually exclusive. Slight differences have grown up among groups living in relative isolation in various parts of the earth over a considerable period of time, but the basic physical structure of all human beings is the same. How useful, then, is the exercise of classifying human beings into races and subraces? Differences between races are averages, because the boundaries between the races exist only by definition. We can say that Negroes *on the average* are darker than whites or Mongoloids, but being darker is only part of what we mean by being Negro. We have used the physical differences to define the racial boundaries. The next question is: What else is true about people who are darker and have curlier hair than other people?

What about language? Are there systematic differences, by race, in such a basic cultural element as the means by which people communicate? There are not. Any group of human beings can learn to speak any known human language. Consider, for example, the contemporary

English-speaking population of the United States: here we find Negroids, Mongoloids, and Caucasoids from all over the world who have learned in only a few generations to share a common culture and a common language. Although many Americans retain a few items from the culture of their grandfathers, whether Chinese-Americans or Hungarian-Americans, all read the labels on the same frozen foods at the supermarket and cheer in the same language at a baseball game.

Can you know a man's race from his religion or predict his religion from his race? No; as with language or any other learned behavior, any normal human beings can learn the belief system of a religion. People sometimes speak of "the Jewish race," but there is no more a Jewish "race" than a Christian one. Judaism arose among Semitic Caucasoids in the Near East, people of the same race and subrace as the Arabs, who spread their belief in Mohammed. But there are Chinese Jews, African Jews, European Jews, and American Jews. The American who wonders whether Jews are a race need only look at the blond, blue-eyed American Jews who came from North Germany and the swarthy, dark-haired American Jews who came from Turkey or Spain to be reminded that there are Mongoloid converts to Judaism living halfway around the world from him, and that all these believers can hardly be considered a biological race. Islam, too, has made converts all over the world; and there are Japanese Christians, Nigerian Christians, and English Christians.

Nationality and race are also matters not necessarily related to each other. Again, the United States affords an example of a single nation made up of all the major racial stocks. Similarly, the Soviet Union combines in a single nation people ranging from the Mongoloid Eskimos of eastern Siberia to the swarthy residents of Turkestan to the blond Nordic Caucasoids in northwestern Russia.

We can classify people by the color of their skins, the length of their noses, the language they have learned, the country in which they live, or the place of worship they choose, but we should remember that these are five separate and distinct methods of grouping human beings, and that the categories have no necessary relationship to one another.

Race, Social Structure, and Culture

Racial differences may seem a good explanation for the behavior of members of a given group at a moment in time. With some historical perspective a better explanation seems to be provided by the group's position in the social structure.[8] American Negroes, for example, score lower on IQ tests and other measures of ability and achievement than American whites. What we need to know is whether this is a racial trait or a difference attributable to the Negroes' position in American society.

In Army aptitude tests during World War II, Northern soldiers did better than those from the Southern states. We would expect this, because we know that education influences the results of such tests, and schools are, on the average, superior in the North. Northern Negroes excelled Southern Negroes; this would be expected because of the differing quantity and quality of their formal education. But these data pose a challenging question. When we know that (1) rural schools have lower standards and poorer facilities on the average than urban ones and that (2) the quality of formal education in the Southern states is poorer than in the North, *and* that (3) at the time of World War II most American Negroes had been born and reared in the rural South, how should we interpret the finding that Negroes averaged lower test scores than whites? Was this a consequence of race (heredity) or of social structure (environment)?

It is a more complicated problem than it seems at first, for Negroes and whites in the United States simply do not share a comparable environment, even if we ignore region and urban-rural differences. A typical Negro child attending the same school with whites in a Northern city is not in the same environment they are in: his parents had less formal education than most of the white parents, and education of inferior quality; he does not have the same things at home as the white children have; he lives in a poorer, more crowded neighborhood than the white children; his teachers treat him with less patience and sympathy than they give their white pupils; his fellow students exclude him from their evening homework sessions, especially if their parents insist. The Negro child lives in an environment of discrimination.

It is extremely difficult to compare racial abilities in a situation of experimental control. What we can do is contrast the performance of representatives of the two races in differing environments. Such a contrast casts doubt on any generalizations about race differences. Negro draftees from New York, Ohio, and Illinois averaged much better on Army literacy and aptitude tests than white soldiers from Georgia,

[8] See, for example, the data in S. Kirson Weinberg and Henry Arond, "The Occupational Culture of the Boxer," *American Journal of Sociology*, 57 (March 1952), pp. 460–469; or Raymond W. Mack, "Ecological Patterns in an Industrial Shop," *Social Forces*, 32 (May 1954), pp. 351–356.

Arkansas, and Mississippi.[9] We do not conclude from this that Northern Negroes are a smarter "race" than Southern whites. It simply means that where there are better opportunities, Negroes, like whites, profit from them.

From what we have been able to learn from the best tests we have, controlling for regional differences, urban-rural differences, and other cultural influences on opportunity and motivation, we cannot conclude that social science research offers us any evidence that there are inborn differences in ability between races. We know that representatives of all races are found throughout the range of intelligence: there are Negroid, Mongoloid, and Caucasoid geniuses, and there are Negroid, Mongoloid, and Caucasoid imbeciles.

But white men do seem to be in charge of things. If Caucasoids are not a breed superior to Mongoloids and Negroids, how can we explain the European dominance of Asia and Africa for several centuries? A glance at the patterns of colonial expansion during the seventeenth, eighteenth, and nineteenth centuries seems persuasive evidence of the superiority of the white race. The answer to this riddle is that one can easily believe in natural racial superiority—he needs only ignorance of history.

Whatever the causes of the rise and fall of civilizations, race, over the span of human history, seems a poor explanation. The ancient Egyptians were a mixture of Negro and Semitic stocks. Kingdoms of Negroid Africans and Mongoloid Asians were at the forefront of civilization when Caucasoid Europeans were hunting in forests and living in caves. Even after Europeans had risen to the heights represented in ancient Greece and the Roman Empire, centuries followed during which Caucasoid Europeans were unable to defend themselves against the Mongoloid might of Attila and the Khans.

Various races and subraces have proved capable of expansion and consolidation of power when given fresh ideas in a favorable setting. As the sum of what men know has increased, each society has built on the knowledge of its predecessors and neighbors.

To the extent that various tribes are in touch with one another, knowledge is diffused. There is a pyramidal building of learning and skill. The discoveries, social inventions, technology, and organization of one society furnish a foundation for the building of the next. As time goes by, the arts and inventions pioneered by one people become the common property of their neighbors and of faraway tribes with

[9] Robert D. North, "The Intelligence of American Negroes," *Research Reports*, 3 (1955), pp. 2–8.

whom they trade, and people of the next civilization are able to devote their imagination and energies to further advances in organization and application.

The power that results from new knowledge has been the force in creating the great civilizations. Therefore, when a people is isolated from the most advanced societies of its time, it is cut off from opportunities for rapid cultural growth. When African civilizations flourished, English and German tribes were unaware of them and remained relatively primitive. During the period when the Industrial Revolution was changing the social fabric of northwestern Europe and the United States, most Africans and Asians were completely isolated from these developments. The Mayan Indians had a decimal system, but no wheel; the Romans had a wheel, but no concept of zero. Hence the Mayas made greater advances than the Romans in astronomy and mathematics; the Romans exceeded the Mayas in transportation and conquest.

People of every race have at one time or another achieved high place, held sway over their neighbors, and advanced in knowledge beyond what was generally known among other races at the time.

The most important thing to realize about racial classifications is that they do not correlate with either social structures or culture patterns. High cheekbones show some relationship to reddish-brown skin; brown-black hair is associated with brown-black skin. But none of these is associated with intelligence, or a caste structure, or musical ability, or inventiveness, or a belief in one God, or the practice of polygamy, or anything else except each other. The inherited physical characteristics on the basis of which races are classified are not even correlated with other inherited physical characteristics, much less with social behavior.

Biologists and physical anthropologists classify mankind into major physical stocks and further divide us into subraces on the basis of physical characteristics. But these physical characteristics do not biologically cause anything else. The combination of a wide nose, kinky hair, and dark skin does not make one innately a prize fighter; straight hair and a skin fold at the inner eye do not make a man a Buddhist; the prevalence of blond hair and blue eyes in a population does not cause it to industrialize.

All human beings belong to a single species. The races of man which today inhabit the earth probably developed through a combination of mutations (some of which permitted survival more easily in one environment than in another), long periods of relative isolation which facilitated inbreeding, and a selection resulting from various cultural standards of what were and were not desirable physical traits. The major groups of races formed through mutation, isolation, adaptation, and selection have not remained unchanged, because the peoples have not remained absolutely isolated. Since the earliest period of human history, individuals, armies, traders, and whole tribes have migrated and intermarried with other physical types, thus breaking up the distinctive hereditary patterns.

Consequently, there are no pure races within the human species. It is impossible to devise a system of classification for behavioral science on the basis of inherited physical traits.

Are Races Real? The Sociology of Race

Race in the biologist's sense of the word has no biologically caused consequences, but what men *believe* about race has social consequences. In other words, most of men's discussions about race are discussions of their beliefs, not of biological fact. As Horowitz says: "Attitudes toward Negroes are now chiefly determined not by contacts with Negroes, but by contact with the prevalent attitude toward Negroes." [10] Most of men's actions about race are based on what they have been taught to believe about it, not on what scientists know. Race is usually not a biological concept. It is a social concept.

To see how social definitions work, let us examine the natural history of race as a social problem in the United States. Then we can see how the need to define slaves as property led white Americans to treat Negroes so differently from other Americans that the social category, Negroes, was actually transformed into a social group. Negroes were so systematically excluded from full participation in American society that they became a social class, virtually a caste, in the American stratification structure.

The first American Negroes came as explorers with the Spanish, French, and Portuguese, in the party of Vasco Nuñez de Balboa when he discovered the Pacific Ocean, with Hernando Cortes when he explored Mexico, and with Hernando de Alarcón and Francisco de Coronado in New Mexico, and accompanying the French in the settlement of the Mississippi Valley.

In 1619 a Dutch vessel brought to Jamestown, Virginia, 20 Negroes, who were sold by their captain for needed provisions. These Negroes were sold into service for a set length of time, like "indentured" white persons. During the first 100 years in the colonies the complete owner-

[10] Eugene L. Horowitz, "Development of Attitude Toward Negroes," *Archives of Psychology*, 194 (1936), pp. 34–35.

ship of Negroes by white masters, or slavery, did not become important. When white indentured servants stopped coming from Europe, in 1688, many Negro slaves were brought into the colonies. By 1715 there were 58,850 slaves in the colonies, and 60 years later the number had grown to 501,000. In 1807, at the request of President Thomas Jefferson, Congress voted that no more slaves should be brought into the country, but many were brought in against the law. The Negro population reached 2,300,000 in 1830 and was 4,400,000 by 1860.

There was a great difference between being an indentured servant, whose time of service was limited, and being a slave. As a slave, the Negro (1) could be sold or given away by his legal owners; (2) could be seized for debt; (3) could be separated from his family; (4) could own no property; (5) had no right to vote; (6) could not hold office; (7) could not testify in a court of law, except in suits for his own freedom; (8) could not legally marry; (9) could not trade or make contracts; (10) could not move about without permission; (11) could be given bodily punishment and even killed by his master in some cases; and (12) was not permitted to learn to read and write.

Not all Negroes remained slaves. A slave could be given his freedom as a reward for some outstanding service or acts and a master at his death sometimes gave his slaves their liberty. Some slaves bought their freedom with money saved from their own labor; others bought freedom for their families. By 1790 there were 59,311 free Negroes, nearly 8 percent of the total Negro population of the states.

Although these Negroes were called "free," they still suffered many handicaps. In the South they could not vote, give testimony in court cases involving white persons, purchase white servants, or intermarry with white persons. A free Negro might buy land; he might buy his wife and children if they were slaves; and he might have one gun to protect his home. Free Negroes owned property in the North and South. In the North as well as the South, however, the free Negro was restricted: the separate schools maintained for his children were often poorly equipped; he was not permitted to work in many of the trades; and in churches, places of amusement, and public conveyances Negroes usually were kept separated from white people.

Toward the end of the eighteenth century slavery became less important. Then, suddenly, the whole picture was changed by Eli Whitney's invention of the cotton gin in 1793. This simple device for separating cotton fiber from seed mechanically and quickly made slavery much more valuable to the South, for Negroes were needed as never before to cultivate the fields. The center of slavery shifted from the tobacco fields of Virginia and other states to the cotton fields of the

RACE RELATIONS 339

Old South—South Carolina, Georgia, Alabama, and Mississippi. Slaves were so necessary that they were bred within the country. Negroes in the United States increased by 200,000 in the ten years between 1790 and 1800, by 300,000 in the next ten years, and by more than 500,000 between 1820 and 1830.

Each Southern plantation was a little community. Although the mass of the slaves were field hands, a few were needed for other tasks as well. Some slave women learned to spin, weave, sew, cook, nurse, and even practice medicine (after a fashion). Slaves became carpenters, blacksmiths, painters, bricklayers, cobblers, engineers, typesetters, and mechanics.

Slavery continued in the South but was not successful in other sections of the country, mainly because the South was almost entirely agricultural and the other sections were not. Slaves made their owners the largest profits on the plantations where tobacco, cotton, rice, and sugar were grown.

Although slaves had no vote, during the slave era free Negroes voted in many of the colonies. Gradually, however, free Negroes were restricted more and more, and some colonies, such as Virginia in 1723, took away their right to vote.

On January 1, 1863, President Abraham Lincoln's Emancipation Proclamation became effective, setting free all slaves held in the Southern states, which were at the time at war with the Union. Freedom was extended to all slaves by the thirteenth amendment to the Constitution, which became effective on December 18, 1865. By these measures, more than 4,000,000 Negro slaves were set free.

The fourteenth and fifteenth amendments to the Constitution (1868 and 1870) gave Negroes the right to vote. The Federal Civil Rights Act of 1875 forbade keeping Negroes out of public conveniences and places of entertainment because of their color, but the United States Supreme Court ruled this act unconstitutional because it took over the rights of the states. Civil rights of Negroes were therefore left to the states, a decision which resulted in widespread discrimination in the former slave states. Whites and Negroes were usually separated by law in schools, railway trains, streetcars, restaurants, hospitals, jails, and graveyards, and by law or custom in hotels, theaters, elevators, lecture halls, libraries, and churches. Intermarriage was forbidden in a number of states.

After emancipation the Negro exercised political rights in the South between 1865 and 1895. The fourteenth amendment to the United States Constitution sought to penalize any state which restricted the right to vote, and the fifteenth amendment made it illegal to use race and color in the qualification of voters. The result of these amendments, and of the very large Negro population in the South, was to throw the government of the Southern states largely into the hands of the freedmen during 1866–1876. For a time Negroes controlled all Southern state governments, except Georgia. Eight Southern states were represented by Negroes in Congress between 1870 and 1891; for seven years Mississippi was represented in the United States Senate by Negroes.

The white people of the South were violently opposed to Reconstruction government. In 1865 a secret organization, called the Ku Klux Klan, was formed to oppose Reconstruction measures and to frighten the Negro, and thus to keep him from voting. The Negro governments were overthrown after the Reconstruction period. From that time to the present the Southern Negro has been prevented from voting by various means. About 1890 a movement arose in the South to deprive the Negro of his vote by legal enactments or state constitutional amendments. This was done by insisting on certain qualifications, the lack of which barred the citizen from voting. Voters were disqualified if they were illiterate, or did not possess 300 dollars' worth of taxable property, or had not paid the poll (head) tax, or did not have a regular occupation, or had not served in the army, or were not persons of "good character," or if they or their ancestors could not vote before January 1, 1867 ("grandfather" clause), or did not understand properly a clause of the Constitution and could not explain it when it was read to them. Some provisions of these laws were unconstitutional, and the "grandfather" clause was declared null and void by the Supreme Court of the United States.

The chief method used in preventing the Negro from voting in the Southern states has been a difficult educational test as a qualification for voting, which includes the ability to "interpret" any part of the state constitution. The other constitutional means of preventing Negroes from voting are property qualifications and taking away the right to vote for having committed such crimes as obtaining money under false pretenses, petty larcency, and wife beating.

At emancipation the Negro was given freedom of his person only. He had no land, tools, or farm animals, and most Negroes had little skill and experience in independent farming. The best land already belonged to white plantation owners. There developed the system of tenancy and sharecropping, with the owner supplying tools, machinery, and seed, and the tenant or sharecropper buying on credit and selling the crop. The tenant or sharecropper could not leave the plantation until he had paid his debt to the landlord, which was often difficult to do.

Negroes have continued to be a mainstay of Southern agriculture, but many Negro farmers are moving to the North and the West and to Southern cities. Before World War I, 90 percent of the Negroes in the United States lived in the South, and most of them were farmers. World War I gave many Negroes their first acquaintance with factories: the need for workers was great, foreign immigration was cut off, and Northern industries advertised for workers. At least 500,000 Negroes went to the North between 1915 and 1918. After World War I, Negro workers were needed less in the skilled trades and in industry. During the Depression they lost their jobs to white workers in the skilled trades and even in some of the service jobs.

World War II again brought a demand for labor and a great migration of Negroes out of the South. Figure 1 shows the redistribution of the Negro population which occurred in the United States between 1900 and 1960. By now a majority of American Negroes live in the North, and almost all Northern Negroes live in cities. New York City has over a million Negroes; Chicago has nearly a million, and Philadelphia and Detroit each contain about half a million Negroes.

The Negro was a slave into the latter half of the nineteenth century. As such, he was forced to remain at the base of the social structure. Nonetheless, he was freed from slavery, and one might expect that at this point the Negro would follow the same pattern of assimilation as the waves of immigrants. But the Negro was to be an exception for two major reasons. First, the condition of slavery had an effect on the way the dominant majority regarded Negroes. Many whites found it difficult to endure the idea that they had been subjecting their fellowman to the degradation of slavery. They began to save their consciences by asserting that the Negro was subhuman. As is often the case, many began to believe their own assertions and to transmit this belief to succeeding generations.

Thus freedom from slavery could not be regarded as a single act that wiped away all concomitants of slavery. The nation could not forget that the Negro had been a slave.

Race as Subculture

Minority status is as changeable as the characteristic that makes the minority identifiable. If the only thing that confers minority status is a person's surname, he can change the name and no longer be identifiable as a member of the minority. If, however, his skin color is the basis for discrimination, he is permanently consigned to minority status.

Social definitions of minorities vary from society to society, but the process of social definition is the same everywhere. It consists of establishing group boundaries and identifying individuals as members or

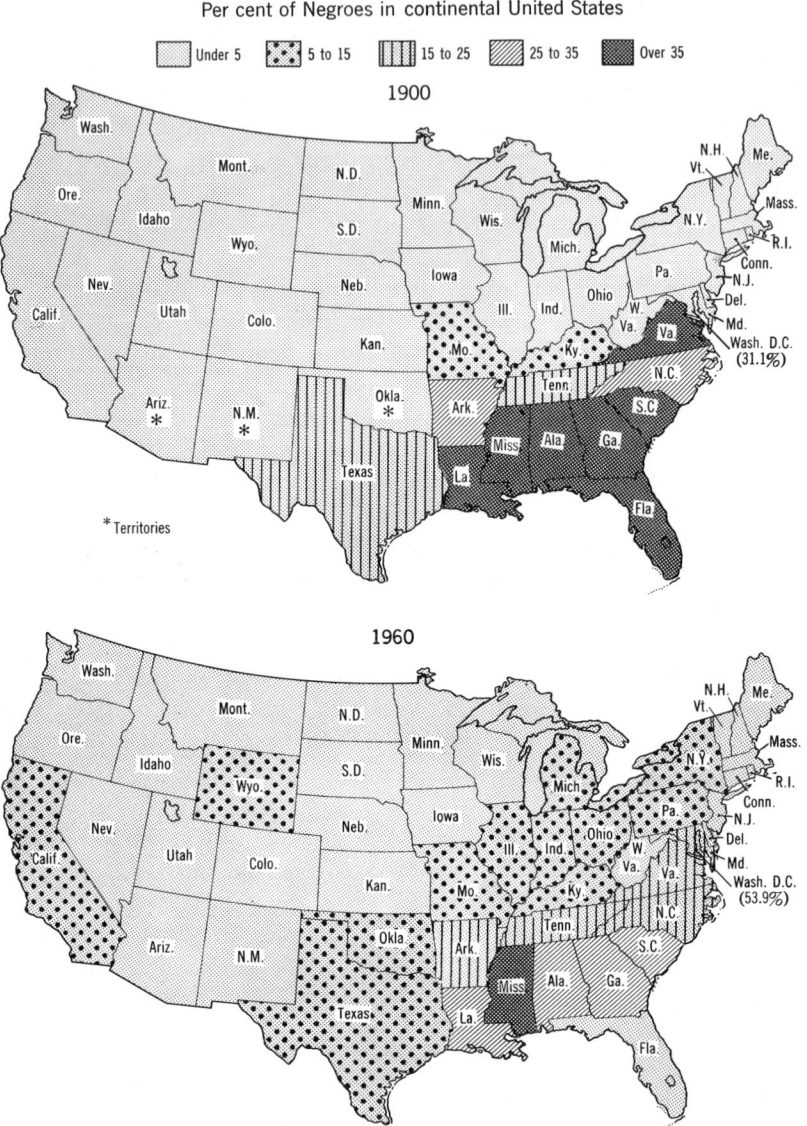

Figure 1 The Negro in the United States. From *New York Times*, June 2, 1963, p. 8E.

nonmembers. Hitler contended that Jews were so different from other Germans that they would subvert the society and weaken the culture, and since they were so different, that they should be required to carry identification cards so that people could tell which Germans were Jew-

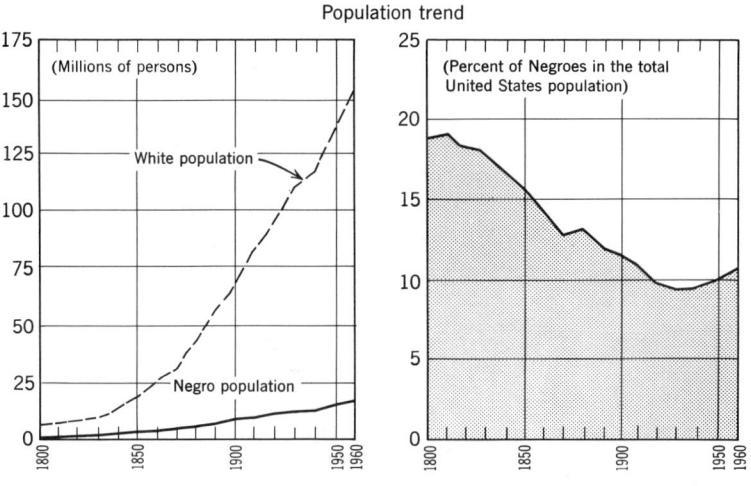
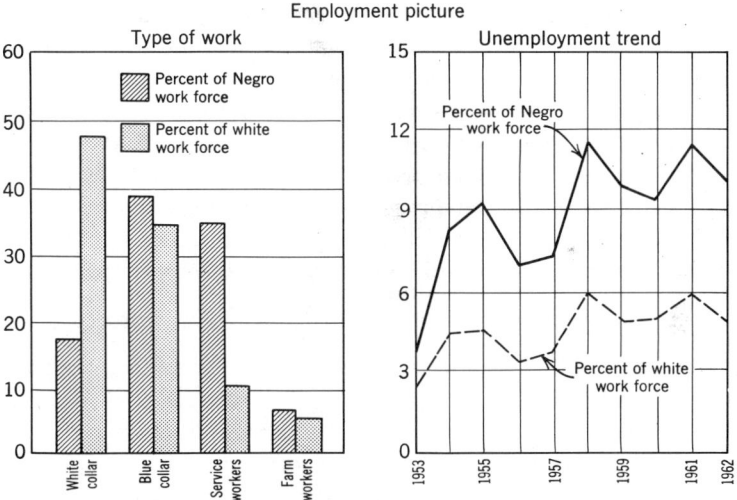

ish. Today, the question of what Jewishness is plagues Israel. Brother Daniel, a Carmelite friar who was born Oswald Rufeisen 40 years ago in Poland, has sued for Israeli citizenship. He is a convert to Catholicism, and calls himself a Christian by religion and a Jew by nationality. Israel has denied him citizenship on the ground that a man who abandons the Jewish faith quits the community too. Brother Daniel's attorneys reply by quoting the rabbinical law that no man born a Jew can ever cease being a Jew.

A minority status (such as Jewishness) is no less important because it is socially rather than biologically defined. Social definitions constitute a social reality, and they have social consequences. Such beliefs are translated into behaviors which often have far-reaching effects on the distribution of political and economic power. White Americans have believed for years that Negroes are less capable of learning than whites, that they are innately less intelligent. Given this belief, a "rational" course of action for the dominant whites is to provide inferior schools and teachers for Negroes—which means Negroes average lower than whites on intelligence tests. By the very fact of believing that Negroes cannot perform as well as whites, whites have made this so.

When power is exercised on the basis of this kind of definition of a situation, it generates opposition: it raises questions whether authority is being abused or influence is being overestimated. Here lies one argument for suspending or violating the rules, and converting competition into conflict. The disappointment of losers sometimes leads them to question the fairness of the competition; here is another argument for overthrowing the rules. Note that the obverse of these situations can serve equally to provide conflict potential: having authority may lead one to abuse it; enjoying influence may induce one to overestimate it; being a winner may encourage one to impose unfair rules.

Differentiation, stratification, and constraint lead to the creation of subcultures. In other words, subcultures arise from the exercise of power. Subcultures stem from isolation and shared fates, and power isolates and imposes shared fates. Hence power also contributes to the potential for conflict both a field for ethnocentrism and a basis, through style of life, for visible differences between groups.

Class Reinforcement of the Social Definition of Race

From the sociologist's point of view, most traits that people cite as typical of a minority are actually typical of people at or near the bottom of the economic ladder. This is why people must frequently defend their stereotypes by consigning some specific case to the category of "an exception to the rule." When someone who is convinced that Negroes do not take care of their property is driven through a middle-class Negro residential area, he has to concede that these Negroes are exceptions to the rule. A simpler way to interpret these data is to observe that lower-class people do not take as good care of their property as middle-class people.

Sociological research indicates that social distance declines with increased socioeconomic status. The higher a person's occupational prestige, or the higher his income, or the more formal education he has, the less likely he is to be an ardent segregationist, or to condone violence as a weapon in dominant-minority relations. Social distance is least when both Negro and white have high socioeconomic status; social distance is greatest when both Negro and white have low socioeconomic status.[11]

Given the constantly increasing educational attainment of our population, both Negro and white, our steadily rising level of living, and the fact that the cities are drawing as in-migrants the better-educated members of the Negro minority, it seems reasonable to predict a decrease in the social distance between the races. Most claims used to justify the treatment of the Negro as a minority are descriptions of lower-class behavior: poverty, disease, ignorance, irresponsibility, poor property upkeep, and so on. Most American Negroes at present occupy a relatively low socioeconomic status. As Figure 2 shows, this relatively low socioeconomic status has consequences ranging from a short life expectancy to reduced likelihood of completing higher education. As more and more Negroes achieve the education, income, and behavioral prerequisites of middle-class respectability, they will not automatically escape from their minority position, but the beliefs which justify keeping them at a distance will be greatly weakened.

What creates and maintains group boundaries? Sanctions do: social rewards and social punishments. People want to affiliate with the groups that offer them rewards: business associations that will increase their profits, unions that will increase their wages, parties that will promote their platforms, the denomination that seems to have the inside track to salvation, clubs in which they will find friends, friendship groups in which they may find love, colleges that will educate them, fraternities that will help them get jobs, families that will improve their power, neighborhoods that will convey prestige.

People not only seek rewarding associations but avoid the punishing ones. They decline the invitation to the dull tea, the ineffectual commerce association, the low-prestige country club. A man may date, but not marry, the girl from the wrong side of the tracks; he may study, but will reject, the erroneous theology. In the same way, he will try to protect the prestige of his reward system by keeping the "wrong" people out. Indeed, excluding them is itself a reward. My wife claims to have been vice-president, at the age of five, of a three-person organization which had its stated purpose: "To keep Bob Kingsley out." Neighborhoods band together to exclude those who might lower property values; sororities blackball candidates with foreign names; colleges discriminate against applicants with low College Entrance Board scores; churches excommunicate heretics; debutantes who

[11] Frank R. Westie, "Negro-White Status Differentials and Social Distance," *American Sociological Review*, 17 (October 1952), pp. 557–558.

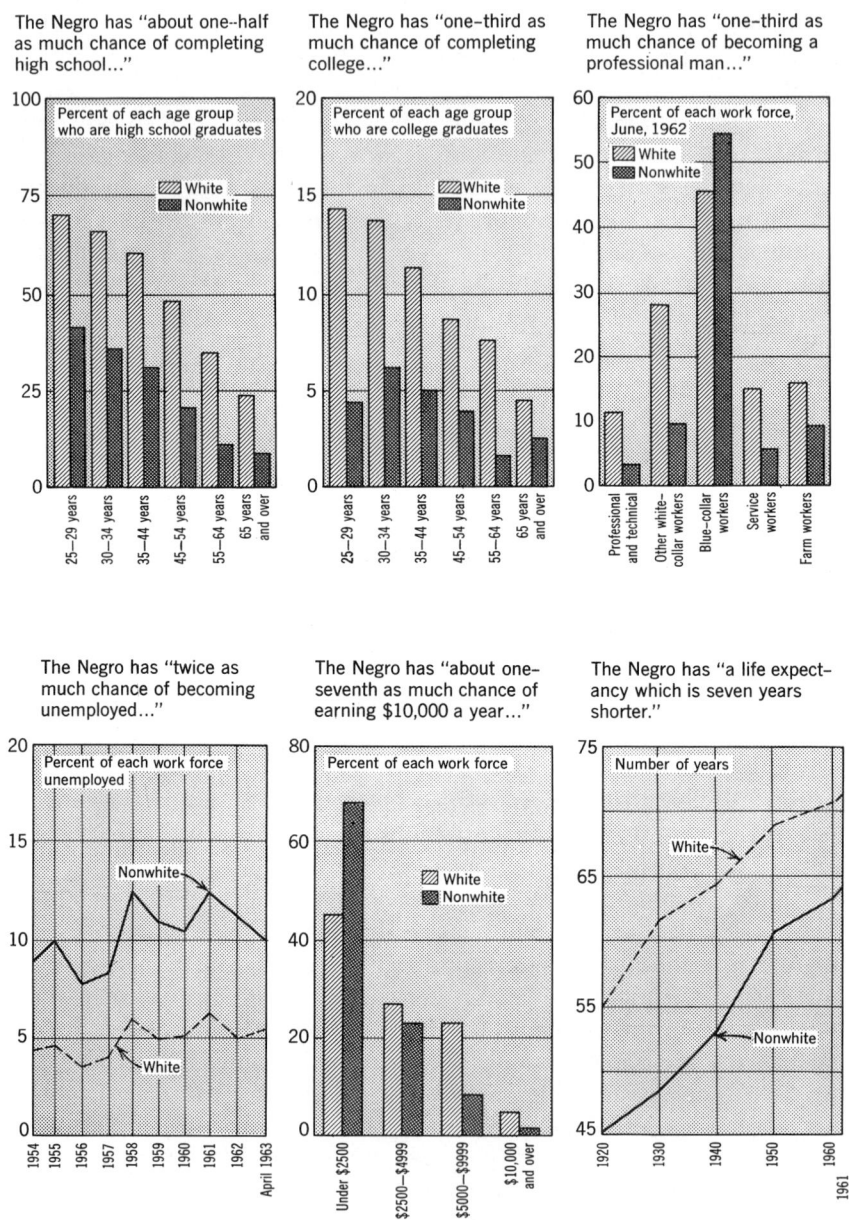

Figure 2 The status of the Negro in the United States today. From *New York Times,* June 16, 1963, p. 3E.

RACE RELATIONS

marry inappropriate spouses are dropped from the social register.

Rejection in turn creates walls of defense. Discrimination creates a reaction to itself. Institutionalized exclusion spawns a culture of antidiscrimination. For example, the formation of Jewish clubs that exclude Christians is a function of the same process whereby minorities retaliate against rejection by inventing epithets for the dominant population. If a man must bear hearing himself referred to as a "spade" or "coon" or "nigger," he can at least enjoy the luxury of jeering about "ghosts" and "ofays."

Thus are group boundaries born and guarded. Men seek rewards, avoid punishments, and band together for both purposes.

Race becomes socially meaningful in creating and maintaining group boundaries when the society associates racial status with another status or characteristic which conveys sanctions. Race becomes socially meaningful when biologically inherited characteristics are correlated or tend to match up with social characteristics considered especially desirable, such as education, or particularly undesirable, such as low income. When a condition that is rewarding or punishing, such as social class with its concomitant life chances, is highly correlated with race, then race is a convenient shorthand for specifying the boundaries of groups enjoying or suffering that condition.

Desegregation: Social Change in American Race Relations

Where an efficient segregation system minimizes one's exposure to members of a minority who do not conform to the stereotype, a culture of discrimination can flourish. Since most of the Negroes with whom many white Americans deal conform to their stereotype of Negroes—that is, that Negroes are poor, ignorant, and subservient—it is easy for white Americans to think of the term "Negro" as a synonym for poor, ignorant, and subservient. If people are isolated from the mainstream of society, as many whites are in the Southern states, this culture of discrimination can become a norm in itself, further isolating its members from "outsiders" who do not share their belief in Negro inferiority, or do not share it with the same intensity and conviction. When discrimination is basic to the culture, when it is part of a people's "way of life," it is easy for them to think of it as a natural, even an inborn, trait. Thus people may justify racial discrimination as a consequence of the "natural human aversion" to differentness, rather than the learned behavior that it is.

Since the Supreme Court desegregation decision of 1954, many people have become familiar with the social science data on Army Alpha tests of intelligence by race and region. Whites from Arkansas, Kentucky, and Mississippi scored significantly lower on these tests than Negroes from New York, Ohio, and Illinois. These research results do not mean that Southerners are innately inferior to Northerners, any more than similar contrasts should be interpreted to mean that urban-

Table 3   State Spending for Education, 1963

Average Annual Expenditure for Education per Pupil	State	Average Annual Expenditure for Education per Pupil	State
Less than $300		Less than $300	
$255	Alabama	$297	North Carolina
279	Arkansas	237	South Carolina
298	Georgia	262	Tennessee
275	Kentucky	297	West Virginia
230	Mississippi		
$300 to $399		$300 to $399	
$347	Florida	$395	North Dakota
382	Hawaii	342	Oklahoma
314	Idaho	390	South Dakota
379	Louisiana	379	Texas
338	Maine	354	Utah
355	Nebraska	362	Vermont
399	New Hampshire	335	Virginia
$400 to $499		$400 to $499	
$445	Arizona	$405	Missouri
437	Colorado	459	Montana
422	Kansas	441	Nevada
405	Indiana	421	New Mexico
414	Iowa	422	Ohio
469	Maryland	464	Pennsylvania
465	Massachusetts	467	Rhode Island
447	Michigan	488	Washington
481	Minnesota	467	Wisconsin
$500 or more		$500 or more	
$620	Alaska	$556	New Jersey
516	California	645	New York
522	Connecticut	502	Oregon
502	Delaware	510	Wyoming
526	Illinois		

ites are smarter than farmers or that Negroes are inferior to whites. They simply emphasize the consequences of unequal educational opportunities. As Table 3 shows, nine states spend less than 300 dollars per pupil annually on education, and everyone of the nine is a Southern state.

The products of regional educational inequalities are immediately apparent in statistics. Only eleven states in the continental United States have a rate of adult illiteracy of over 15 percent. Every one of them is in the South, one reason that literacy tests for voting can be skillfully used as instruments of racial discrimination there.

The social cost to the nation of this kind of inequality is documented in research on desegregation by Tumin suggesting that "the hard core" of Southern resistance to desegregation lies among the poor and uneducated.[12] The outstanding characteristic of those most willing to resort to violence to defy the law of the land is a below-average amount of schooling. The violence-prone, hard-core people are as stable in residence patterns as their neighbors; they belong to churches in about the same proportion and attend about as frequently. But their earning power is significantly lower than that of their neighbors, partly because a much smaller proportion of them have completed nine or more years of school. The wider society impinges much less directly on them. They are less influenced by newspapers and magazines. They are less prepared than their fellow citizens to adjust to rapid social change.

At present, the swift change in the social fabric wrought by desegregation seems concentrated in the South. This makes it more difficult, since the South is characterized by the very factors that make resistance to change part of its way of life. The South remains predominantly agrarian, with a high birthrate and a low level of formal education. It is the most rural section of urban America, the least-schooled region in a highly educated society, the least-industrialized portion of a technologically oriented nation.

Desegregation is a problem belonging not only to the South, although there it is focused and there it at present causes the most disruption of living patterns. Fifty years ago, 90 percent of all American Negroes lived in the states of the Confederacy. One measure of the swiftness of the change in the Negro's status is that half our Negro population now lives in the cities of the North and West. New York City is now 14 percent Negro; Chicago, 24 percent; Philadelphia, 26 percent; Detroit, 29 percent; and Newark, 35 percent Negro. These tremendous migrations create problems at both ends of the line. Mississippi lost one-fourth of its total Negro population in the 1940s. Al-

[12] Melvin M. Tumin, "Readiness and Resistance to Desegregation: A Social Portrait of the Hard Core," *Social Forces*, 36 (March 1958), pp. 256–263.

though some Mississippians might laughingly claim that migration promises the ultimate solution to their problem at the North's expense, this is not so. It is the Negroes Mississippi can least afford to keep who stay at home. Those most likely to migrate are the young people with a better-than-average education. And every year these people are packing into already overcrowded Negro ghettos in Northern cities, their residential segregation ensuring segregation in schools and other facilities.

In the long run, therefore, the problem of desegregation will hit the whole country. The South, at present, is particularly vulnerable to rapid change, for the Southern states depended for segregation on laws that have been declared unconstitutional. The North does not yet feel the same pressures, because its segregation is accomplished informally through residential patterns and is more difficult to strike at through the courts. But race relations are not a Southern problem; they are what Gunnar Myrdal called them—an American Dilemma.[13]

The upheaval of desegregation imposes strains on our social system far beyond the immediate results of human inertia and resistance to change. Within a generation we have projected into urban life the majority of one-tenth of our population, many of whom were brought up to live in feudal fiefdom. Although enormous strides are being made in education and other endeavors, enormous prices are also being paid for the swiftness of emancipation. As Hauser points out, "Tossing an empty bottle on an asphalt pavement in the city has quite different consequences from tossing it into a cotton field. Using physical force, including a knife or gun, in the resolution of personal conflict receives much more attention and has a much greater impact on the community in the city than it had in the rural south. The patterns of family and sexual behavior that the Negro inherited as a product of his history and his share in the American way of life have created the many complications connected with the administration of Aid to Dependent Children, in the urban setting."[14]

Over 20 percent of the Negro children in the United States are born out of wedlock, whereas the illegitimacy rate for whites is 2.1 percent. The consequences of the cultural heritage and social customs of a caste society produce other grim statistics. Negroes constitute only 10.5 percent of the population of the United States, but they commit over one-half of the murders, nearly one-half of the rapes, over one-third of the

[13] Gunnar Myrdal, *An American Dilemma* (New York: Harper and Brothers, 1944).
[14] Philip M. Hauser, *Population Perspectiveness* (New Brunswick, N.J.: Rutgers University Press, 1960), p. 150.

aggravated assaults and robberies, two-thirds of the burglaries and larcenies, and three-fourths of the auto thefts. In New York City in 1955, Negroes accounted for 12 percent of the population but they constituted 38 percent of the public housing and relief rolls. At the same time in Chicago, Negroes comprised 17 percent of the total population, but 70 percent of the public housing population, 75 percent of those on relief, and 65 percent of those in jail.

Other immigrant groups have in the past reacted to urbanization with comparable personal and social disorganization. But it is a foolish disservice to the minority and to the society to state that, or act as if, no problem exists. There *is* a Negro problem. But it is a problem born not of biology but of rapid social change.

Whose American Dilemma?

Until recently the Negro has been *in* America, but not a part *of* it—an alien in a hostile land. Ralph Ellison writes with telling accuracy of the American Negro as *The Invisible Man*. Only within the past 25 years has American society begun to concede that its Negro citizens are actually there. The *New York Times Index* for 1940 lists under "Negroes" only "See also Lynching." In 1960 the *New York Times Index* contains under "Negroes" more than two hundred subentries. Things have been happening.

As recently as 1950, only eighteen states prohibited segregation in transportation and recreation facilities. Now the Interstate Commerce Commission has outlawed all racial barriers on trains and buses and in terminals that are involved with interstate commerce.

In 1950 there were more states in which segregation in the public schools was mandatory than there were states in which school segregation was prohibited. The Supreme Court outlawed public school segregation in 1954. Seven years later there were only three states that had not begun to comply with the order. (One of them was the site of the original lawsuit that resulted in the Court's decision.) Today, in every state at least token compliance has begun.

Twenty years ago the white primary kept the majority of the Negroes in the United States out of the elections that counted in the South. The Supreme Court struck at white primaries in 1954, and in 1957 Congress passed the first civil rights act in 80 years, empowering the Justice Department to bring suits to win the ballot for Negroes. The apportionment decision of March 1962 by the Supreme Court reduced the rural dominance of a number of Southern state legislatures.

The Presidential Committee on Equal Employment Opportunity is pressuring government contractors to employ Negroes in skilled jobs.

In 1870, 80 percent of all American Negroes could neither read nor write. That illiteracy rate has been reduced to 7 percent. The proportion of college graduates among young Negro adults has tripled in the past 20 years.

These objective changes in the status of the American Negro are themselves important catalysts for change. Interracial tensions in the United States stem in part from the uneven rates of change in different segments of the social structure. Although American Negroes have been urbanizing and achieving legal rights, it remains true that the

Table 4 Percent Distribution of Income of Families by Color for United States, 1945–1961

Total Money Income Level	1945		1961		Percent Change in Ratio over 1945	
	White	Nonwhite	White	Nonwhite	White	Nonwhite
Under $4000	75.5	90.1	27.7	60.2	−63.3	−33.1
$4000–$5999	16.8	6.1	22.4	19.7	+33.3	+233.0
$6000 and over	7.7	3.8	49.9	20.1	+548.0	+429.0
Total	100.0	100.0	100.0	100.0		

SOURCE: U.S. Department of Commerce, *Current Population Reports*, Consumers Income, Series P-60, No. 2, March 2, 1948, and No. 38, August 28, 1962.

deprivations of their past in this country have kept them from gaining some fruits of change in American society—and that in some respects they are *losing* ground in relation to whites.

As Table 4 shows, throughout the United States whites have been getting out of the bottom income bracket faster than Negroes have, and a higher proportion of whites than of Negroes has been moving into the top income category. Furthermore, as can be seen in Table 5, the products of centuries of racial discrimination appear in the relationship between education and income. White Americans who have completed elementary school average higher lifetime earnings than Negro Americans who are college graduates.

In the entire United States the gap separating Negro and white citizens is *widening* in critical areas of social life.

We have experienced 25 years of rapid and extreme change in the social and economic structure of the United States, an era encompassing some notable changes in race relations. In assessing this revolution, we ought not to make the error that we fell into so easily in our attempts to understand the industrial revolution: the mistake of assuming that a process is completed when it has only begun. We no longer teach from the naively written textbooks that reported the industrial revolution "occurred" about 1800. We realize in 1965 that the industrial revolution is still in full swing, and that it will be our privilege and burden to live during it. If we guard against mistaking early growth for maturity, we may realize that the social revolution in civil rights is not ended but just beginning.

Table 5 Male Lifetime Earnings by Race and Education (in thousands)

Highest Grade Completed	White	Negro	Negro as Percent of White
Elementary School			
Less than 8 years	$157	$ 95	61
8 years	191	123	64
High School			
1 to 3 years	221	132	60
4 years	253	151	60
College			
1 to 3 years	301	162	54
4 years	395	185	47
5 years or more	466	246	53
Average	241	122	51

SOURCE: Employment and Earnings, Bureau of Labor Statistics, February 1964.

All we know of the sociology of revolution indicates that, contrary to the popular fiction that people rise up against their masters when they are too downtrodden to bear further oppression, a group is most amenable to revolution when its status has been improving. Galley slaves do not revolt; they have neither the opportunity nor the strength. The French *bourgeoisie* overthrew the social structure, not because they were a crushed and miserable minority but because they had gained so many concessions and were doing so well that it seemed to them their world might be an even better place if they took it over and ran it. The Thirteen Colonies which united to throw off the yoke of English oppression in the 1770s were probably the best and most generously governed colonies in the world at the time. For centuries the Russian serf lived under conditions of political and economic subjugation almost impossible for us to imagine and was too busy just staying alive to question the justice of his lot, much less begin any effective protest against it.

Three conditions are necessary for intergroup conflict: the groups must be (1) in contact with each other, (2) in competition with each other, and (3) visible to each other. All three of these conditions will obtain in Negro-white relations in the United States in the coming years. The conditions that define city life—crowding and rapid movement, for example—will throw the groups into closer and more frequent contact than was customary when the Negro was a rural dweller. Every improvement within the status of the Negro throws him into more direct competition with the white. Visibility, contact, competition—all are intensified in the urban environment. Add to these the uncertain definition of the situation, the ambiguity of role expectations that is a concomitant of urban life and of rapid social change, and you have an almost ideal situation for engendering conflict.

Conflict, the struggle for dominance, promotes the formation of groups. American Negroes used to be a social category after the fashion of "males" or "people in the labor force aged 19 through 44." Thirty years ago interested citizens who were not sociologists asked, "What do American Negroes want?" Thirty years ago the question was relatively meaningless, because American Negroes were a social category, not a group. Negroes, however, were taught the rules of competition within the American social structure and, within the past generation, had our society abided by the rules, many of them would have won. But they found that American society refused to play by its own rules. We refused to pay rewards to winners in the mobility sweepstakes if they were Negro. Moreover, we meted out punishments to nonlosers simply for being Negro and, worst of all, punished rather than rewarded insistent competitors. Contrary to what one might believe from reading many current editorials, the whites, not the Negroes, initiated conflict. The whites violated the rules of the competition for status and its rewards in the United States. As a result, American Negroes joined the conflict, violating economic and political rules with boycotts and sit-ins—and in the process were transformed from a social category into a group. Nowadays, the pollsters can get meaningful answers to questions about what American Negroes want, because a social category has been transmuted into a social group—by conflict.

In one shameful sense, as Willhelm and Powell point out,[15] the de-

---
[15] Sidney M. Willhelm and Elwin H. Powell, "Who Needs the Negro?" *Trans-Action*, 1, 6 (September–October 1964), pp. 3–6.

mands of the civil rights protest movement *are* revolutionary. The American Negro has been so disadvantaged economically and socially that a real attempt to bridge the gap would require a reallocation of resources that would indeed be revolutionary.

Negroes in America are better off on the average than villagers in India and Bushmen in the Kalahari Desert. The question is whether Americans find such relative measures comforting, or whether they have in mind some more absolute measures of justice and of equality of opportunity.

A Negro boy in America today has about half the chance to graduate from high school that a white boy has; one-third the chance to finish college or become a professional man; one-seventh the chance of earning 10,000 dollars a year; and twice the chance of becoming unemployed. A Negro American's life expectancy is seven years shorter than a white American's. In 1960 the median money wage was 3058 dollars for Negroes and 5425 dollars for whites. Only 39 percent of white families earned less than 5000 dollars; 71 percent of Negro families had incomes below 5000 dollars. And the relative gap between Negro and white family income has been increasing since the mid-1950s.

With perhaps intentional irony, President Johnson described the race relations situation in the United States admirably in his report on the 115 companies participating in President Kennedy's Plans for Progress hiring program.[16] "Within those companies whose reports have been received, the ratio of white salaried employees to nonwhite dropped from 61 to 1 at the beginning of the reporting period to 60 to 1 at the end. We still have a long way to go."

It is precisely because the American Negro has achieved so much in the past 20 years that he is so dissatisfied. The civil rights protest movement has been sparked by people who have achieved the education and income to entitle them to be middle class, but who are denied access to middle-class perquisites.

> It got under way and took on mass as a struggle for the equal right to consume goods and services—food, transportation, education, housing and entertainment. This is a goal of people with at least some money to spend and with the aspiration to spend as others do. The Negro Americans who led those first sit-ins were indeed so American that they seem more humiliated by not being able to spend the dollar than they would be at not having a dollar to spend. "My money is as good as the other fellow's," is probably the ultimate expression of American democracy. Here we meet the great paradox in American social structure. While our race line is,

[16] *New York Times*, December 6, 1963.

next to South Africa's, the world's tightest, we have times-over the largest Negro middle class in the world, and the largest group of Negroes approaching middle-class western tastes and with the money to satisfy them in some measure. This may be due to the fact that we are that country in which industry first depended upon its own workers to be its best customers, and in which movement has gone farthest in that direction. Handicapped though Negro Americans are in employment and income, they are well-enough off to resent the barriers which prevent them from keeping up with the white Joneses. This reflects a great change in the Negro social structure itself; goal and social structure are doubtless functions of each other.[17]

Some whites resolve the American dilemma for themselves by coming to the rationalized position that the stratification system is a consequence of a just, free, and open competitive system. Negroes, according to this position, get what they deserve and deserve what they get: the bottom rung. But the free and open character of the social system is an illusion developed out of lack of personal exposure to the decision to discriminate.

One sector of American society now experiencing extremely rapid change is the realm of majority-minority relations. We are a nation conceived by religious and political minorities, and we are presently constituted of racial, ethnic, and national minorities and their descendants. Over the years the American melting pot has assimilated millions of national and cultural minority people who came to our shores as immigrants. But we have not successfully assimilated our racial minorities. Negroes, Orientals, and American Indians are not accepted by many Americans as citizens with equal rights. This situation places a severe strain on the American ethic of equality of opportunity. Racial discrimination pinches our pride in democracy, embarrasses our dedication to the brotherhood of man, and maims a motivational system based on fair play for every citizen striving for success.

Bibliography

Allport, Gordon W., *The Nature of Prejudice* (Reading, Mass.: Addison-Wesley, 1954). A fine work on the psychology of prejudice.

Banton, Michael, *White and Coloured: The Behaviour of British People Towards Coloured Immigrants* (New Brunswick, N.J.: Rutgers University Press, 1960). Fascinating data on the difference between attitude and behavior, between prejudice and discrimination.

Brink, William and Louis Harris, *The Negro Revolution in America* (New York:

---

[17] Everett C. Hughes, "Race Relations and the Sociological Imagination," *American Sociological Review*, 28 (December 1963), pp. 879–890; quotation from p. 885.

Simon and Schuster, 1964). An analysis of a nationwide survey on what American Negroes want, how they feel about whites, and what whites think of Negroes and of the protest movement.

Broom, Leonard and Norval D. Glenn, *Transformation of the Negro American* (New York: Harper and Row, 1965). An assessment of the position and prospects of the American Negro, based upon a tracing of the change in Negroes' values and in their socioeconomic status.

Clark, Kenneth B., *Dark Ghetto: Dilemmas of Social Power* (New York: Harper and Row, 1965). A sensitive description of the economics, politics, and psychology of ghettos in general and Harlem in particular, with an especially valuable chapter on "Ghetto Schools: Separate and Unequal."

Drake, St. Clair and Horace R. Clayton, *Black Metropolis* (New York: Harcourt, Brace and Company, 1945). A sociological profile of the segregated Negro community in Chicago, with an especially good treatment of class differences among Negroes.

Elkins, Stanley M., *Slavery: A Problem in American Institutional and Intellectual Life* (New York: Grosset and Dunlap, 1963). The best study of the history of American slavery.

Frazier, E. Franklin, *Black Bourgeoisie* (Glencoe, Ill.: The Free Press, 1957). A penetrating study of the social adaptation of middle-class Negroes as they try to cope with the problems of being middle-class by some criteria but are excluded from the middle of the social structure on racial grounds.

Frazier, E. Franklin, *The Negro in the United States* (New York: The Macmillan Company, revised edition, 1957). A detailed discussion of the history and present institutional structure of the American Negro community.

Glazer, Nathan and Davis McEntire, *Studies in Housing and Minority Groups;* Eunice and George Grier, *Privately Developed Interracial Housing;* Luigi Laurenti, *Property Values and Race;* Davis McEntire, *Residence and Race;* and Chester Rapkin and William G. Grigsby, *The Demand for Housing in Racially Mixed Areas* (Berkeley and Los Angeles: University of California Press, 1960). Five volumes on invasion, succession, and the current status of the American Negro in the housing market.

Goldwin, Robert A., ed., *100 Years of Emancipation* (Chicago: Rand McNally, 1963). Articles viewing race relations as a contemporary social problem in the context of its source in slavery.

Gordon, Milton M., *Assimilation in American Life* (New York: Oxford University Press, 1964). Argues the thesis that the concept of structural pluralism is a useful tool for understanding the role of religion, race, and ethnicity in the United States.

Hughes, Everett C. and Helen M. Hughes, *Where Peoples Meet: Racial and Ethnic Frontiers* (Glencoe, Ill.: The Free Press, 1952). A set of brilliant essays on social definition, status inconsistency, and acculturation.

Humphrey, Hubert H., *School Desegregation: Documents and Commentaries* (New York: Thomas Y. Crowell, 1964). Traces the legal history of desegregation and illustrates the complexities of enforcement in various regions and institutions.

Kuper, Leo, *An African Bourgeoisie* (New Haven, Conn.: Yale University Press, 1965). An analysis of the incongruity between the high occupational status and the low racial and political status of South African colored professionals and businessmen.

Mack, Raymond W., ed., *Race, Class, and Power* (New York: American Book Company, 1963). Contains articles on minority-dominant relations and social stratification as elements of tension in the American value system.

Myrdal, Gunnar et al., *An American Dilemma: The Negro Problem and Modern Democracy* (New York: Harper and Brothers, new edition, 1962). A complete description and incisive analysis of the cultural paradox provided by the descendants of slaves in an equalitarian society.

Rose, Peter I., *They and We* (New York: Random House, 1964). A sprightly introduction to patterns of racial and ethnic relations in the United States.

Taeuber, Karl E. and Alma F. Taeuber, *Negroes in Cities* (Chicago: Aldine Publishing Company, 1965). A description of historical and contemporary patterns of Negro residential segregation and of change in urban neighborhoods.

Tumin, Melvin M., *Desegregation: Resistance and Readiness* (Princeton, N.J.: Princeton University Press, 1958). A provocative research report on the social correlates of attitudes toward desegregation.

UNESCO, Department of Mass Communication, *What Is Race? Evidence from Scientists* (Paris: UNESCO, 1952). A simple, readable discussion of genetics and the development of human differences.

Vander Zanden, James W., *Race Relations in Transition* (New York: Random House, 1964). A discussion of the impact of desegregation and social change on traditional Southern patterns of segregation.

Williams, Robin M. Jr., *The Reduction of Intergroup Tensions* (New York: Social Science Research Council, 1947). Perhaps the single most important work in summarizing research in race relations and extending theory by posing important questions.

Young, Whitney M. Jr., *To Be Equal* (New York: McGraw-Hill, 1964). A description by the Executive Director of the National Urban League of the present status of the American Negro, and a set of proposals for altering this condition.

8

Community Organization

Warner Bloomberg, Jr.

> . . . I view great cities as pestilential to the morals, the health and the liberties of man. True, they nourish some of the elegant arts, but the useful ones can thrive elsewhere, and less perfection in the others, with more health, virtue and freedom, would be my choice.
>
> —Thomas Jefferson, 1800

> The complicated problems which the great city develops are now seen not to be beyond the control of aroused public sentiment; and practical men of affairs are turning their attention to working out the means whereby the city may be made an efficient instrument for providing all its people with the best possible conditions of living.
>
> —D. H. Burnham and E. H. Bennett, *Plan of Chicago,* 1909

For those who have shared the agrarian conviction that cities are by nature sinful, there would be little merit in asking how best to organize the urban community. One might just as well discuss the proper governance of Hell. For those reformers whose work after the turn of the century established the modern tradition of city planning, organizing the community meant developing its physical plant and fiscal resources to solve problems of traffic, zoning, deterioration, recreational space, industrial growth, and the like. Today, a new approach to urban reform seeks to induce in city dwellers the democratic virtues that Jefferson assigned automatically to a romanticized agrarian society and denied forever to the urban masses. Without denying the importance of the city as a physical instrument for meeting material needs, emphasis is shifted to how people are organized to recognize the problems that confront them in their common social and physical environment, to decide on courses of action to meet those problems, and to bring the needed resources into the service of their plans and proposals. Until communities are adequately organized to carry out these functions and tasks, they will be unable to meet the other problems whose solutions require effective community action.

The term "community" itself may not be used as much in the everyday rhetoric of American public life as "peace with justice" or "brotherhood," but it surely runs a close second. Especially in this period of our history, when most of our pressing domestic problems are, one way or another, "city problems," more and more people are worrying aloud and often loudly about the state and fate of "our communities." This poses a special problem for those who attempt to study community problems scientifically: they must give familiar terms narrow and technical definitions that may make them mean both more and less than everyday usages.

When terms are not defined, the social scientist and his reader may inadvertently misunderstand each other. For example, the psychologist who points out gains from a modicum of "permissiveness" in child rearing may be interpreted by some readers as advocating that "kids be let run wild"; those in positions of executive authority may read into the proposals for "greater participation" made by an expert in management science the suggestion that they "abdicate" their leadership roles and relinquish their power over subordinates. So it is important that we understand each other thoroughly when we use terms such as "community" and "organization" in this chapter.

The Concept of Community: Ideology and Reality

The social scientist usually includes everyone who resides within the town or city as part of *the* community, but a great many of its residents would consider some local inhabitants as "outside" of what they mean by *our* community—such unwanted people as dope addicts, prostitutes, gangsters, and so on. Ideological boundaries for "our community" may be even more confining, making "outsiders" of racial, religious, or nationality minority groups against whom there are strong prejudices, even though these people have long had their homes in the locality.

The social scientist strips away such ideological components from his definitions. He seeks to describe what a community *is* as an ongoing social system, not what some people, himself included, may think it *ought* to be. It is fair to suggest improvements in community life, but one should not build proposed improvements into definitions of community or organization. It would therefore be best to set aside certain of the most common ideological components in the everyday use of these concepts before attacking the semantic difficulties created by social scientists themselves.

"Community" in the Rhetoric of Traditional Organizers in America

Long before anyone was specifically trained and paid to "get things done" in our towns and cities, to elicit the involvement of citizens in the solution of the problems faced by the community, and even to designate the conditions that ought to be considered problems, there were individuals who played these roles, not full time but occasionally. Indeed, they still do so, for the professional community organizer has taken over only a small part of the total task. Included among these nonprofessional, occasional organizers of the community are prestigeful business and civic leaders, top local governmental officials, newspaper editors, leaders of major interest groups in the locality, and the official or unofficial heads of such "solidary" groups as religious or nationality minorities characterized by a high degree of cohesion, self-identity, and the like. These traditional community organizers normally infuse the concept of community with one or more ideological components that should be examined at least briefly.

The myths of community. Not so long ago the industrial community of Stacktown, a middle-sized city in the Midwest, had a celebration to mark its fiftieth year.[1] Men grew beards, women wore dresses of allegedly turn-of-the-century vintage, the local newspaper featured biographies of founding fathers and famous local characters, and the entire production was topped off with a pageant that portrayed the history of the area from the days of the Indians to the present. The objective observer must note that a somewhat distorted version of the community's history was presented. Left out were the brutalities of early industrial management, race riots, violence during union-organizing days, vicious conflicts among different immigrant groups, fascinating periods of political corruption, and so on. The objective observer

[1] For additional information on Stackton, see Warner Bloomberg, Jr., "The Power Structure of an Industrial Community," unpublished doctoral dissertation, University of Chicago, 1961. Aspects of the community's political life are also described in Phillips Cutright and Peter H. Rossi, "Grass Roots Politicians and the Vote," *American Sociological Review*, 23 (April 1958), pp. 171–179.

might also point out that this public mythology about the city's past, like much of the celebration, was created under the direction of a private corporation which had its office in a distant metropolis and specialized in producing public extravaganzas to celebrate municipal anniversaries.

Such a distorted history is not surprising, for most American cities, as Greer has pointed out, ". . . were built on land which had no history and no hallowed memories," and their names recall no cathedrals of bishops, royal strongholds, or ancient Roman camps.[2] Lacking a "history" in the European tradition, Americans have tended to manufacture images of their past that the events themselves cannot provide. Nostalgic editorials about "the good old days" are part of the American journalistic stock in trade, though the same newspapers may also applaud the wholesale destruction of fine old structures in order to make way for the "progress" embodied in great new office buildings or sprawling housing projects. And some of the most ardent-sounding boosters of civic loyalty are individuals whose tenure in the community depends entirely on the promotion and transfer policies of the top management of the national corporations for which they work and for whom they carry on policies of "good community relations."

And so the word "community" is often used almost as an incantation to conjure up feelings of loyalty to locality among the most geographically mobile people in the world, and to bring forth a kind of ectoplasm of intergenerational continuity where actual history has been both brief and fitful. It may even represent a kind of wistful yearning for what we never were and can never be. Scientific usage must eliminate such connotations, just as community organizers must work with the episodic realities and low-level loyalty that characterize most American cities today, although they too may avail themselves rhetorically of the "gospel of community."

The nonpartisan justification of partisanship. A second use of the word that embodies an ideological distortion of reality is illustrated by many projects promoted "for the good of the community." They range from fund-raising campaigns by charitable groups to proposed changes in city charters or county tax rates. Close examination reveals that in almost all cases *some* people in the community benefit, but not all; and sometimes benefits accrue to some at the expense of others. Expressways are advocated to relieve "the community's" traffic jams, and

---

[2] Scott Greer, *Governing the Metropolis* (New York: John Wiley and Sons, 1962), p. 17.

urban redevelopment projects are proposed to clear out "the community's" slums. Both types of projects have the consequence of dislocating low-income residents from areas that are razed. Often they must move into housing just as inadequate and costly as the tenements they were inhabiting and must also endure the disruption of whatever social life they have built up around nearby kith and kin.[3] Most ardent advocates of expressways and slum clearance are from middle- and upper-class segments of the community and usually overcome easily such opposition as may be voiced by low-income, dependent inhabitants of the slums and the petty entrepreneurs who operate shops there.

Some activities are indeed genuine community-wide projects, and almost all members of the community will be aided by them and none harmed. For example, free distribution of antipolio vaccine would seem to qualify as generally helpful to a locality's inhabitants. But more often than not the assertion that some public or private agency's program includes a "community project" merely attaches the claim of universal benefit to an activity that actually will promote only the interests of some groups within the community and may even be viewed as harmful by others. Such usage pretends that the community has no special-interest groups, no factions, no conflicts, no major disagreements over means and ends. It may be useful as political rhetoric, but it makes for poor social science.

Communities within the community. Gans has used the term "urban villagers" to designate ethnic enclaves whose members lead a life different enough from that of the larger society that they may usefully be considered a community or "subcommunity"; they identify with each other and with a specific area of residences and attendant shops, stores, and taverns.[4] Such groups may persist for a long time in metro-

---

[3] Other negative consequences include marginally better housing at a cost in rent far out of proper proportion for the family's budget and loss of property-owning status. Guidance from relocation offices at best reduces these problems somewhat. Fully adequate studies of these problems have not, to my knowledge, been published; but see Herbert J. Gans, "The Human Implications of Current Redevelopment and Relocation Planning," *Journal of the American Institute of Planners*, 25 (February 1959), pp. 15–25; Nathaniel Lichfield, "Relocation: the Impact on Housing Welfare," *Journal of the American Institute of Planners*, 27 (August 1961), pp. 199–203; Harry W. Reynolds, Jr., "The Human Element in Urban Renewal," *Public Welfare*, 19 (April 1961), pp. 71–73, 82; and "What Do We Know about Our Experiences with Relocation?" *Journal of Intergroup Relations*, 2 (Autumn 1961), pp. 342–354.

[4] Herbert Gans, *Urban Villagers* (New York: The Free Press of Glencoe, 1962).

politan areas, even though they lose many of each new generation into the mainstream of the local society.[5] Enough elements of their daily round of life are distinctive that these groups may usefully be designated as having their own "subculture."

But these are clearly not the characteristics of the "business community," the "Christian community," or the "legal community." Such groupings include all those who have a common vocation or affiliation, even though many of them do not have any close ties to one another built up around this particular commonality. Such alleged communities also lack spatial boundaries and usually involve people more as individuals than as families with their friends. They do not rest upon extensive interdependence and continuing interaction as much as upon adherence to belief and doctrine or common practical interests to be secured and safeguarded. When their representatives call them "communities," they do so to impute to the members levels of common identification, group commitment, and personal involvement that simply do not obtain for many, often most, of those members. Indeed, the assertion that a city's businessmen, union members, Christians (regardless of sect), or political party adherents do constitute a "community" may be as much an effort to create an expectation that members will be committed and involved and identified with one another as to present a desirable "image" of the grouping to the larger society. Once again the social scientist must take care to distinguish between image and actuality, between wish or expectation and performance.

"Community" in the Vocabulary of the Social Sciences

The traditional community organizers in American towns and cities have thus dealt most often with the problems of suppressing conflict and discontent, promoting a "booster" spirit by means of myths and symbolic manipulation, advancing partisan programs and projects as if they were activities of universal benefit, and seeking to strengthen specific interest groups and institutional sectors by categorizing them as communities or subcommunities within the larger society. Most social

[5] Glazer and Moynihan note that ethnic identities tend to outlast residential enclaves, though the rate at which the latter disappear and the extent to which they may to some degree be reconstituted varies from group to group. See Nathan Glazer and Daniel P. Moynihan, *Beyond the Melting Pot* (Cambridge, Mass.: M.I.T. Press and Harvard University Press, 1964); also, Francis A. J. Ianni, "Residential and Occupational Mobility as Indices of the Acculturation of an Ethnic Group," *Social Forces*, 36 (October 1957), 65–72; and Stanley Lieberson, "Suburbs and Ethnic Residential Patterns," *American Journal of Sociology*, 62 (May 1962), pp. 673–681.

scientists have avoided importing such ideological components into their conceptions of community, but this does not mean they have achieved a consensus on just what the term denotes. One specialist in the area of the community once delineated some 94 different definitions of the term available in the social science literature on the subject![6] Fortunately it is not necessary to resolve this apparently endless professional dispute to arrive at a working definition appropriate to a concern for designating certain conditions as "community problems" involving "organization." It will be useful, however, to note the variation among the available social science definitions.

Definitions of community: What's in a name? Murdock has asserted that the local community is a universal human social group "founded on residential propinquity, and whatever additional bonds of kinship, economic cooperation, or political organization may in individual instances intensify its unity . . . a peace group, characterized by internal order, social solidarity, and a common culture . . . within which individuals normally experience most of their more meaningful social satisfactions."[7] Given this definition, cities in the United States today in many ways should be thought of not as communities, but as "states" or units created by states: structurally complex, formally organized, corporate collectivities. Consider the ephemeral, purely contractual relationship between the individual in Chicago who telephones an order into Sears, Roebuck and the clerk who records it and starts it through the assembly-line process that terminates with a mailman known to neither the clerk nor the customer delivering the package. Although these people are interdependent parts of a local segment of a vast economic system, there is nothing in their relationships to one another that Murdock would recognize as "communal."

By way of contrast, many "ecologists" consider any localized aggregate, even a vast, sprawling metropolis, a "community" precisely because its members are interdependent and share a definable local area. The forms of their social organization are considered the product of varying demographic, technological, and environmental pressures.[8] One need not get tangled up in considerations of social interaction pat-

[6] George A. Hillery, Jr., "Definitions of Community: Areas of Agreement," *Rural Sociology*, 20 (June 1955), pp. 111–123; and "A Critique of Selected Community Concepts," *Social Forces*, 37 (March 1959), pp. 240–242.
[7] George P. Murdock, "Feasibility and Implementation of Comparative Community Research," *American Sociological Review*, 15 (December 1950), pp. 713–714.
[8] Otis Dudley Duncan and Leo F. Schnore," Cultural, Behavioral, and Ecological Perspectives in the Study of Social Organization," *American Journal of Sociology*, 65 (September 1959), pp. 132–146.

terns, interpersonal relations, values, symbols, or expressive behavior to describe and understand the community so defined.

Just as the electrical engineer may draw upon generalizations produced by advocates of both wave and quantum theory, leaving it to the theorists to resolve the apparent incompatibility between the two, so those of us interested in the understanding and solution of social problems will find it useful to draw on both of these conceptions of community. Certainly economic interdependence is inevitable among any sizable population who, inhabiting a local area, manage with some success to continue generation after generation those routine activities we call our "round of life"—who work and play, worship and politick, make friends and fight with kinfolk, meet, mate, marry and rear children, age, die, and are buried. It is equally inevitable that any aggregate of people who carry on these activities together will have some common language, shared beliefs and feelings, and common standards of conduct which make their interactions with one another predictable. The likelihood that the community will persist or in time vanish, grow or decline, be a place of satisfaction and contentment or of strife and despair may depend a great deal on how interdependent its members are, each with all the others or one group with another, or upon how many values they share and how deeply they feel commitments to one another and involvement in the various affairs of the community.

This chapter will focus on problems of community organization found typically in middle-sized and large metropolitan areas—not because such places are more or less "communities," but because an increasing proportion of our total population lives in them. It will inquire into the ways citizens of such local settlements attempt to meet problems arising out of their interdependence or lack of interdependence, and out of their common beliefs and commitments or lack of consensus with respect to such values. It will be concerned, not with how the boundaries of a community ought to be conceptualized for theory, but with the consequences that the absence of sensible community boundaries may have for efforts by citizens to change conditions. It will raise questions about the effectiveness of these efforts and about how democratic they are. It will ask how present patterns of community organization affect the social structure of the locality, on the one hand—the patterns of interdependence and dependency, of hierarchy and social cleavage—and how they affect the culture and subcultures of the inhabitants, on the other hand—their beliefs, feelings, identities, and commitments.

A smorgasbord of theory. Craftsmen develop their understanding of the problems they face by intuition and trial and error, and often do not share their most successful techniques with one another. The so-called "pure scientists," on the other hand, concerned only with establishing explanatory models of the world of experience, use scientific procedure as rigorously as possible and have a tradition of publicizing their findings as widely as possible, at least within the profession. The engineer stands between the two, seeking to apply the theory of the scientist to the practical problems of the world of action, whether it be to cure diseases, to build missiles, to reduce unemployment, or to expand community services. This whole volume clearly deals with such "applied science." To what bodies of theory, then, should we turn for tested propositions, or if these are not available, for useful concepts and relevant information and insight based on research?

Books by sociologists who take "the community" as their subject usually attempt to sum up in a single volume the present wit and wisdom developed within the discipline and by other social scientists with respect to all major aspects of community social structures and cultural patterns.[9] These efforts are necessarily eclectic, for there can be no "theory of communities" any more than there can be a "theory of mammals" or a "theory of rocks and stones." Some of them use an underlying "theme" or "orientation" for bringing an interpretive focus to their concern for all the institutions and the patterns of action and interaction that occur within the local settlement.[10] Such theory as may be discernible in these compendia either is too broad for application to the problems confronted in this chapter or is not directly relevant.

It is necessary, then, to look for information, ideas, and theory that deal directly with the emergence of issues in community settings, the processes of group organization, the recruitment of people into action groups, and the like. Some social science knowledge is organized according to these concerns, but for the rest we must browse among the available offerings, selecting whatever we can find from published research that suits the specific intellectual appetite represented by the topic of this chapter.

[9] Two recent examples of this approach are Alvin Boskoff, *The Sociology of Urban Regions* (New York: Appleton-Century-Crofts, 1962) and Nels Anderson, *The Urban Community: A World Perspective* (New York: Henry Holt, 1959); the latter has more of a cross-cultural approach than most such texts.

[10] For example, Irwin T. Sanders develops a systemic functionalist orientation in *The Community* (New York: Ronald Press, 1958). Jessie Bernard's revised edition of *American Community Behavior* (New York: Holt, Rinehart and Winston, 1962) continues the emphasis on conflict and competition of the 1949 edition. The changes in American communities accompanying the urbanization and increasing national integration of the larger society provide a basic theme for Roland L. Warren's *The Community in America* (Chicago: Rand McNally, 1963).

The "higher ideology" of professional organizers. In addition, there are two bodies of literature that combine these social science concerns with "normative theory" or doctrine about organizing citizens to solve community problems. They are, in many ways, rudimentary theories of social engineering interwoven with the ideologies of professional experts. In the profession of social work, "community organization" has been recognized as a field of specialization for a quarter of a century.[11] The field of "community development" is newer as a profession with a body of doctrine; it owes its existence in the United States to the convergence of concern about modernization in the towns and villages of the developing nations with the teaching and action programs of adult education and extension services of some urban universities, the work of some agricultural agents in rural areas, and efforts by a variety of urban organizations.[12] These may be thought of as "higher ideologies" because they involve more systematically developed conceptions of the community than provided by the traditional community organizers and because they embody strong commitments to the goals of social and political democracy and very little sheer self-interest or preservation of the *status quo*.

The development of social work doctrines for community organization has roots in the 1920s when community chests and councils of social agencies were already becoming widespread. Steiner proposed that this should be an area of professional concern, emphasizing the continuous process of accommodation and adjustment among more or less antagonistic groups and elements in the community.[13] Almost fifteen years later the Lane Report proposed this as a special field in social work, recognizing that social workers were only one group among many—churches, chambers of commerce, political parties, and the like—trying to "organize" the community.[14] In social work this organizing was to apply specifically to building cooperation and collaboration in the discovery and definition of welfare needs, in the de-

---

[11] Ernest B. Harper and Arthur Dunham, eds., *Community Organization in Action* (New York: Association Press, 1959), p. 51.

[12] See, for example, the various agencies in the text and footnotes of Otto C. Hoiberg's article, "Contributions of the Social Scientist to Community Development," in Marvin B. Sussman, ed., *Community Structure and Analysis* (New York: Thomas Y. Crowell, 1959), pp. 130–143.

[13] Jesse F. Steiner, *Community Organization* (New York: The Century Company, 1925).

[14] Robert P. Lane, "The Field of Community Organization," *Proceedings of the National Conference of Social Work, 1939* (New York: Columbia University Press, 1939), pp. 495–511.

velopment of preventive and corrective programs for social pathology, and in the constant mobilization and readjustment of community resources to meet the changing content of these needs and programs. Although it recognizes the importance of general public support, the emphasis in this approach is on relating functional agencies and "interested groups of nonclients"—the latter often turning out to be those "nonprofessionals" whom Kurtz has recognized as "always having the last word." [15]

This is the heart of the matter. Hunter's seminal volume, *Community Power Structure*, whatever its flaws, provides an authentic display of the beliefs of many agency executives and community organizers that they are too much under the thumbs of nonprofessionals. These people of personal wealth, community prestige, and corporate power are the most important sources of funds for private agencies and constitute majorities on most boards of directors.[16] In his improved but neglected second book on this subject, Hunter places somewhat less emphasis on "the power structure" *per se* in accounting for inadequate community efforts to solve welfare problems, and underscores the divisive inclinations of individuals and groups to use community programs to advance their own particular interests. He discusses the absence of any community-wide rationale for developing welfare services, the resistance even to perceiving problems whose solution might well require fundamental changes in values or social alignments, and the largely negative response of the citizenry in general to apparent opportunities to participate in forming goals and programs, as when open meetings are held.[17]

Given this reality, much of what has been said and written about "proper procedures" and "democratic process" for social work community organizers strikes Hunter as a set of vague and empty pieties. What can be used effectively are such tactics as collecting a broad cross-sampling of people around a table to discuss the problem at hand

[15] Russell H. Kurtz, "The Range of Community Organization," *Proceedings of the National Conference of Social Work, 1940* (New York: Columbia University Press, 1940), pp. 400–412.
[16] Floyd G. Hunter, *Community Power Structure: A Study of Decision Makers* (Chapel Hill: University of North Carolina Press, 1953). For a summary of extensive and severe criticisms of Hunter's theory and method, see Nelson W. Polsby, *Community Power and Political Theory* (New Haven, Conn.: Yale University Press, 1963), especially pp. 45–56.
[17] Floyd Hunter, Ruth Conner Schaffer, and Cecil G. Sheps, *Community Organization: Action and Inaction* (Chapel Hill: University of North Carolina Press, 1956), especially the two concluding chapters.

and selling established business and civic leadership on any proposed solutions; this is the "bellwether principle." [18] Having discovered that the system is seriously flawed, the community organizer must learn how best to work within it.[19] Ross asserts that the community organizer must therefore be dedicated to the development of a cooperative, collaborative, democratic community process within the subcommunity of the neighborhood and the "functional community" of welfare institutions and agencies, but he probably must accept and work within the established political framework of the geographical community.[20]

There are some striking contrasts between this ideology of community organization and the doctrines of community development, so heavily influenced by efforts to bring both modernization and democracy into the lives of town and village people in the new nations of Africa and Asia. But if we compensate for language differences that derive from one group talking about large communities in the most industrialized nation and the other about small communities in the least industrialized societies, it would appear that community development philosophy assumes exactly the procedures and reform efforts that most professional community organizers in American social work have turned away from.

Community development asserts that projects should be initiated in response to the expressed needs of people, in effect giving power to "the clients"; that attitudinal change among the people is as essential as material progress; that new leadership must be cultivated, especially among previously powerless groups such as women and youth; that governmental aid, technical assistance, and a wide range of resources must be put at the disposal of essentially self-help projects; that institutions of local governance themselves may have to be reformed; and that the national government must play an important role in furthering community development.[21]

Those who view the problem of community organization from the perspective of community development in the villages of the nonindustrial societies with their minimal resources emphasize self-help programs to meet pressing, obvious, and largely material and physiologi-

[18] *Ibid.*, pp. 242–258.
[19] For one of the best efforts to resolve this dilemma, though it fails to do so, see Kenneth L. M. Pray, "Social Work and Social Action," *Proceedings of the National Conference of Social Work, 1945* (New York: Columbia University Press, 1945), pp. 348–359.
[20] Murray G. Ross, *Case Histories in Community Organization* (New York: Harper and Brothers, 1958), p. 29.
[21] *Social Progress Through Community Development* (New York: United Nations, 1955), pp. 5–13.

cal needs among people who have been physically and culturally isolated from the mainstream of state and national events.[22] Those whose orientation is to the American community, even one that is economically depressed and stagnant, focus especially on creating patterns of citizen participation and the accompanying acquisition of motivation and skill. Improvement in physical facilities or in provisions for welfare is less a goal in itself than a means of establishing an activist citizenry for whom involvement in community affairs becomes part of their way of life.[23]

Both schools agree (1) that the unit of organization for each development program must be small enough to enable citizens to relate to one another and experts to relate to participants in fairly direct and individualized ways (which of course means that in the large city the subcommunity or a potential subcommunity would have to be the locus of effort); (2) that lethargy and lack of interest result from, rather than cause, the exclusion of the majority of citizens from participation and leadership; and (3) that local resources, organizational skills, and individual commitment will expand together, making possible community projects that are increasingly large, sophisticated, and cosmopolitan rather than local in scope.

Summing up. Traditional organizers in American communities have usually portrayed their local social systems in ways distorted by ideology, presenting myths about the settlement's past, promoting the belief that what's good for one interest group is good for the whole community, portraying interest groups as genuine subcommunities, and reinforcing beliefs and judgments which effectively read some local inhabitants out of the community. The social scientist strips away such ideology in establishing his working definition of a community. Social workers and workers in the newer field of community development accept the realism of social science research but combine it with ideologies about the "good community" and doctrines about how to attain it. Both judge the existing organization of the community to be inadequate. Community organization doctrine emphasizes working mainly within the existing system of institutions and established organizations and power relationships. Community development doctrine in effect challenges that system by calling for direct involvement of the

[22] For example, Carl C. Taylor, "Community Development Programs and Methods," *Community Development Review*, December 1956 (Washington, D.C.: International Cooperation Administration), pp. 34–42.
[23] A good example of this perspective is William W. Biddle's "The Developmental Concept," in Sussman, ed., *op. cit.*, pp. 116–128.

organizer with the rank-and-file citizenry in order to produce new patterns of involvement and power.

Community Organization and the Social Organization of the Community

To be dissatisfied with the way a community is organized is not the same as to assert that the community is "disorganized." For the social scientist the "social organization" of a community is evidenced by the extent to which life in the locality follows predictable routines and changes in ways that theory and research make it possible to anticipate, whether or not these patterns are considered desirable.[24] Clearly, the problem of community organization is concerned with only a small part of all the behavior that taken together would constitute the social organization of the community.[25] Trying to understand this aspect of community life by itself is somewhat like describing and analyzing the functioning of the respiratory system as if it were unaffected by other organ systems, and then taking the lungs and inquiring into their character and activity as if they were not continuously affected by other parts of the respiratory system. We must, then, focus on the problem of community organization without forgetting the links between that aspect of urban behavior and the rest of the social organization of the locality.

The Formal Social Organization of the Community

All community organizers, both traditional and professional, must operate within the context of the existing social organization of the locality or else attempt to change it. Much of that established pattern results from deliberate efforts by some people to manage the behavior of others through formally organized institutions.[26] We sometimes for-

[24] Although deliberately pitched at an elementary level, one of the nicest explications of this concept is found in Scott Greer, *Social Organization* (New York: Random House, 1955), Chapters 3 and 4.
[25] For an effective historical sketch of the development of urban social organization in which a concern for citizenship and community leadership is especially evident, see Oscar Handlin, "The Social System," *Daedalus*, 90, 1 (1961), pp. 11–30.
[26] The major "institutional sectors" of the local community have been categorized as business, labor, education, religion, political parties, government, society (in the sense of organized "high society"), independent professions (such as law and medicine), mass communications, recreation, welfare, and culture (in the sense of the organized arts and crafts and related facilities such as museums). A rigorous theoretic critique would display the inadequacy of such a list, but it serves here the purpose of definition by illustration. Moreover, some modest success has been had in predicting community decisions on the basis of evidence as to the "activa-

get the extent to which our daily life is formally organized (if we are typical city dwellers), for the rules of the various organizations have become part of our personal habits.

Except for the self-employed, the place and time of work, to say nothing of the work routines themselves, are established largely by the rules and plans of formal organizations. Most of those who worship in a church also follow a program of action established through a formal, corporate organization. The traffic signs and lights that to some degree control those who drive to work or to church, like the buses on which they may ride, are scheduled by formal organizations. Municipal recreational facilities, such as movies and bowling alleys, are also managed through formal structures. Newspapers, radio, and television all have their contents established by the work of individuals in formal collectivities. And so it goes. Even much of what goes on in informal groups—in the family, in friendship cliques—takes place within a set of conditions partially if not largely established by the formally organized institutions of urban society.

It is important to remember that most of this organizing of the citizen's normal activities is a means to other ends. Governmental officials seek to maintain social order and public facilities, as well as their tenure in office. Industrial executives, labor leaders, and businessmen are all involved in organizing the production and distribution of goods and services to gain for themselves and those they represent a fair share of the price of those goods and services. Councils of social agencies attempt to maintain some overall planning and setting of professional standards among diverse private welfare organizations, while community chests and united funds concentrate on raising and allocating funds to support the programs of the various agencies. Those who own or manage newspapers, radio stations, and television outlets try to gain and hold a regular audience as a means of stimulating the advertising without which most of them could not continue to operate. Churchmen espouse a theological position, maintain an organization to support it, provide certain rituals and types of aid for its members, and for this receive their contributions. One observer has called the resulting pattern of action about community problems an "ecology of games"—the largely unplanned outcome of the pursuit of special institutional and

---

tion" of these various sectors. See Delbert C. Miller, "The Prediction of Issue Outcome in Community Decision Making," *Proceedings of the Pacific Sociological Society—Research Studies of the State College of Washington,* 25 (June 1957), 137–147; and Robert C. Hansen, "Predicting a Community Decision: A Test of the Miller-form Theory," *American Sociological Review,* 24 (October 1959), pp. 662–671.

individual goals with no major agency or organization attempting to see and evaluate the effects of each on the whole.[27]

There are times when a strong effort is made through a formal institutional structure to elicit at least some interest and activity from a great many citizens, as when charitable organizations launch campaigns for funds or political parties for votes. But this is clearly an example of using the energy and resources of the citizenry to implement policies arrived at by the officials and the small core of activists at the center of these main institutions in the community. In education, for example, citizens who do not hold positions of authority in the school system rarely have a hand in shaping the role of the public schools in the community, but in many districts all parents are urged to participate in the PTA or other organized groups of officially sanctioned spectators and boosters.[28]

To make our point explicit, there are *no* major formal organizations in the community which have as a central function the cultivation of citizenship. No institutional sector is devoted primarily to motivating participation in community affairs, developing the needed skills among the citizenry, and facilitating and organizing their involvement and participation in the recognition, definition, and resolution of community problems and issues. It is assumed that growing up in the United States almost automatically includes acquiring the motives and competences of citizenship, and that members of the community in the normal course of events will become genuinely concerned from time to time about one or another community problem and will react vigorously. With the exceptions of elections and referenda, our ideology of local democracy would therefore seem to depend for its implementation more upon an informal and always emergent organization of community members than upon the formally organized institutional sectors.

The Informal Social Organization of the Community

Much of the daily round of life does remain emergent rather than administered or managed. There are large areas of voluntarism in the American social fabric, and these become patterned or organized through the myriad choices of individuals and small informal groups in interaction with one another. When one stands back, so to speak, and views families, friendship cliques, gossip chains, and the like from a dis-

---

[27] Norton Long, "The Local Community as an Ecology of Games," *American Journal of Sociology*, 64 (November 1958), pp. 166–177.
[28] Warner Bloomberg, Jr., and Morris H. Sunshine, *Suburban Power Structures and Public Education* (Syracuse, N.Y.: Syracuse University Press, 1963), pp. 70–74.

tance, a mosaic of relationships may be discerned that can be represented abstractly as a part of the social organization of the community. These informal relationships, whether casual or intimate, develop inside formal organizations as well as in those segments of life less subject to the rules and regulations of bureaucratic structures. They help to determine not only the productivity but also the very quality of life within factories, schools, government bureaus, and so on.[29]

A person's standing in the community, sense of belonging to the whole community or some subcommunity, and concern for community affairs are all affected by the character of this informal social organization. Each of these in turn affects the extent and character of the citizen's involvement in, neutrality toward, or withdrawal from community problems.

Social science writings and the application of social science concepts and techniques to widely published attitude and opinion surveys have accustomed most Americans to thinking of our society as a broadly stratified pyramid with upper, middle, and lower classes, a substantial majority of people being in an extended middle range that includes the more skilled, "respectable working class," as distinguished from "the poor." [30] Our place in this socioeconomic pyramid is likely to have important consequences, not only for opportunities for education, occupation, income, and other "life chances," but also for behavior in such private matters as watching television or sex relations.[31] But there is some degree of circularity in this since our place in the social class hierarchy is affected not only by such central components as the occupa-

---

[29] The "human relations in industry" literature abounds with examples of the effects of small groups within large organizations on attitudes and interaction. Such effects are reviewed in a variety of settings in the excellent paperback by W. J. H. Sprott, *Human Groups* (Baltimore: Penguin Books, 1958); see especially Chapters 3, 6, 8, and 9. Another excellent source of examples (though this is certainly not its main purpose!) is George C. Homans, *Social Behavior: Its Elementary Forms* (New York: Harcourt, Brace and World, 1961), Chapters 5 through 17.

[30] Russell Lynes, Vance Packard, Samuel Lubell, George Gallup, Elmo Roper and other pollsters and popularizers of sociological research have contributed much to making this imagery acceptable, though the three-class structure is sometimes further oversimplified by collapsing it into the blue-collar–white-collar dichotomy. Historians of American thoughtways, however, may give special mention to prestigeful *Fortune* magazine's report on its survey of attitudes in its issue of February 1940 as an important step in making his kind of imagery publicly acceptable.

[31] For a brief overview of correlates of class status, see Kurt B. Mayer, *Class and Society* (New York: Random House, 1955), Chapters 4 and 5. Also see the articles in Part IV, "Differential Class Behavior," of Reinhard Bendix and S. M. Lipset, eds., *Class, Status and Power* (Glencoe, Ill.: The Free Press, 1953).

tional prestige of the head of the household and the income enjoyed by the family, but also, though to a much smaller degree, by evidence of our canons of taste, by membership in voluntary associations, by residential location, by the social standing of our friends, and even by the education and occupation of our children and the prestige of the kinship ties they acquire through marriage.[32]

This stratification system in the United States is characterized by flexibility and the absence of clearcut boundaries between higher and lower categories of people, except perhaps at the top and bottom of "the class ladder." [33] This stratification in turn contributes to a lack of polarization in American political life, to the absence of issues on which almost everyone takes sides in accordance with his class position.[34] Although more blue-collar voters are likely to cast their ballots for Democrats than white-collar voters, both the rank-and-file of the Democratic party and its formal leaders and active core in most localities include many white-collar types, including a substantial number of professionals and even some financial or industrial executives. On the other hand, the Republican party counts among its faithful in various localities labor leaders, Catholics, Jews, and Negroes, though the majority in each of these categories is likely to vote for Democrats.

What is underscored here is that a person's social standing, though affected by the matrix of local formal organizations, is not mandated by them. With the enactment and enforcement of civil rights legislation the last vestiges of *formally* established restrictions on social mobility and political rights are disappearing. The correlations which may obtain between social and economic standing in the community and the role played in community affairs or the position taken on community issues must therefore emerge through largely *informal* relationships. That they reflect deeply entrenched values and habits of association is not to be denied, for these are exactly the building blocks of the informal social organization of the community.

The decline of clearcut boundaries between classes, the emergence of a rather flexible and often ambiguous pyramid of strata which merge one into another, has been accompanied by a withering of class-conscious ideologies in politics. Even many young intellectuals today

---

[32] Talcott Parsons, "A Revised Analytical Approach to the Theory of Social Stratification," in Bendix and Lipset, eds., *op. cit.*, pp. 118–121.

[33] Parsons, *op. cit.*, pp. 121–125; also see David M. Potter, *People of Plenty* (Chicago: University of Chicago Press, 1954), Chapter 4, "Abundance, Mobility, and Status."

[34] Ralf Dahrendorf, *Class and Class Conflict in Industrial Society* (Stanford, Calif.; Stanford University Press, 1959), pp. 272–278.

reject doctrinal "isms," replacing them with a frequently expediential pragmatism, holding that political positions, if taken at all, should reflect individuated personal judgments rather than social standing.[35] It is a view that fits well with the myths of community and the suppression of conflict which, as indicated earlier in this chapter, have so often been the stock in trade of the traditional community organizers. Only those in the lower reaches of the socioeconomic pyramid tend to see the world as composed of distinctive classes ("we" and "they") rather than as a system of interlocking strata through which one, or at least one's children, may rise.[36]

Social and spatial mobility are often correlated. The residential segregation of people with similar ethnic, racial, and class backgrounds in Northern cities is largely an informally sustained ecological pattern. People not only move into what they believe to be better houses in better neighborhoods, but they also move to get away from those whose proximity they view as a threat, if not to personal security, then to property values or social prestige.[37] In most urban communities we can see a change in the social scenery by traveling a mile or two; we can also see the change by staying in the same place for a decade or two. Intercity migration has also increased a great deal, and movement from one suburb to another is now a major form of migration.[38] There are still people with a strong localistic orientation just as there are clearcut cosmopolitans, but more and more people display declining loyalty to what is presently their "hometown."

Thus the informal dimensions of the social organization of American

[35] The current doctrine of the "hip" and the "cool" is a nearly perfect apolitical, or even antipolitical, ideology, simplifying ideas and providing paradoxically a locus of commitment for those who passionately eschew all other passionate commitments. Today's campus radicals are pro-civil rights and anti-military involvement abroad, but few of them are "class-conscious" in the traditional sense of the term.

[36] Dahrendorf, *op. cit.*, pp. 283–289.

[37] See Joshua A. Fishman, "Some Social and Psychological Determinants of Intergroup Relations in Changing Neighborhoods," *Social Forces*, 40 (October 1961), pp. 42–51; Arnold Rose, "Inconsistencies in Attitudes Towards Negro Housing," *Social Problems*, 8, 4 (Spring 1961), pp. 286–292; Eleanor P. Wolf, "The Invasion-Succession Sequence as a Self-Fulfilling Prophecy," *Journal of Social Issues*, 13, 4 (1957), pp. 7–20.

[38] This follows as a conclusion from the fact that out-migration from the suburban rings has not helped to diminish the increasing status differentiation between central city and suburbia resulting from the migration of higher-status central-city residents to suburbs in their own or other metropolitan areas. See Karl E. Taeuber and Alma F. Taeuber, "White Migration and Socio-Economic Differences Between Cities and Suburbs," *American Sociological Review*, 29 (October 1964), pp. 718–729.

urban communities do little to motivate or facilitate involvement in community affairs on the part of a majority of citizens. On the one hand, the correlates of social standing militate against social action by a majority of American urban dwellers (a point which will be explored more fully). On the other hand, the lack of clearcut cleavages in the stratification system and its flexibility reduce any tendency on the part of categories of people, such as blue-collar workers, to become solidary groups sharing a common point of view about community issues rationalized according to an ideological interpretation of a seemingly fixed place in the social, political, and economic hierarchy. People move around often, and our informally generated value system includes little strong identification with the local community or preoccupation with its problems and issues.

Voluntary associations: another smorgasbord. Somewhere between the formally organized, large-scale institutions of the community and its largely informal social structure and value system lie the voluntary associations. Such an association is "a relatively lasting collectivity, somewhat formally organized, whose members belong by their own choice." [39] A friendship clique is too informal to fit into this category. A factory is too formal in its organization; besides, it is more difficult to choose just where to work, to say nothing of whether or not to work (especially for adult males and unmarried females), than to choose which fraternal association to join, or whether or not to join at all. A church membership is somewhat less compulsory in our society than a job, but in many groups and strata social pressures make membership in a religious organization difficult to avoid. The Ladies' Sodality or the Men's Temple Club would correspond more to the definition of a voluntary association than the church itself. Union membership also often lacks the highly voluntaristic quality denoted by the term, voluntary association, and again the organization is quite formal. But the Masons with its mass membership and highly formalized organization would generally be included in the category because, for those who are acceptable as members, whether or not a man joins and how long he remains a member, are highly voluntary decisions. These complexities indicate why social scientists are far from agreed exactly what organizations should be included and why.

Voluntary associations in the United States are many and varied. "A great part of our recreational, educational, philanthropic, political pro-

---

[39] George A. Lundberg, Clarence C. Schrag, and Otto N. Larsen, *Sociology* (New York: Harper and Row, third edition, 1963), p. 303. This text has one of the best sections on voluntary associations in the introductory literature.

tective, and social activities are now carried on not by the family or by the single individual but by participation in a great variety of organized groups. . . ."[40] Not only do such clubs and associations differ in size, purpose, and degree of formality in organization, but they also vary in the extent to which they establish prerequisites for membership (such as age, sex, race, religion, occupation, and so on) and the degree to which they emphasize instrumental activities (those undertaken to achieve or maintain some valued condition outside the organization itself) as against expressive activities (those undertaken for their own sake, such as recreational events of skill development among members).[41] Such groups also may vary greatly in the extent to which members feel personally involved and in the degree to which they participate in the organizations' activities or share in formulating policies and programs.[42]

Voluntary associations appear to be formed to provide the means for experiences and accomplishments which the members cannot obtain through either the small, informal groups which make up the mosaic of the informal social organization of the community or the extensively bureaucratized and often somewhat coercive major institutional sectors that provide the community's formal social organization.[43] If American citizens were continuously creating such voluntary organizations to deal with our continuously emerging community problems, associations characterized by a participative, committed, and democratically organized membership, we might well conclude that much has already been done to solve the problem of organizing urban places into effective, rather than merely formalistic, democratic communities. Some believe that just this condition has in fact been largely attained.

> There are at least 200,000 organizations, associations, clubs, societies, lodges, and fraternities in the U.S., along with innumerable social groups and *ad hoc* committees formed for specific causes. Except for the few intellectuals who don't believe in "joining," and the very, very poor who can't afford to, practically all adult Americans belong to some club or

[40] Herbert Goldhamer, "Voluntary Associations in the United States," in Paul K. Hatt and Albert J. Reiss, Jr., eds., *Cities and Society* (Glencoe, Ill.: The Free Press, 1957), p. 592. This essay was originally published in *Third Year Course in the Study of Contemporary Society*, Vol. 1 (Chicago: University of Chicago Bookstore, September 1942).
[41] C. Wayne Gordon and Nicholas Babchuk, "A Typology of Voluntary Associations," *American Sociological Review*, 24 (February 1959), pp. 22–29.
[42] William M. Evan, "Dimensions of Participation in Voluntary Associations," *Social Forces*, 36 (December 1957), pp. 148–153.
[43] Handlin, *op. cit.*, pp. 15–16.

other, and most of them take part in some joint effort to do good. This prodigious army of volunteer citizens, who take time from their jobs and pleasure to work more or less unselfishly for the betterment of the community, is unique in the world. It is, in a way, the mainspring as well as the safeguard of democracy. For, whatever the silly rituals and earnest absurdities of some of their organizations, and the self-interest of others, the volunteers are always ready to work and fight for what they think is right. Some of the organizations are primarily pressure groups—certain business, farm, labor, and veterans' organizations, for example—but they manage to do a lot of research and educational work too. Often, at the local level, they take on a share of the civic and charitable burden. In addition, there are countless organizations dedicated to the betterment of the community—the so-called "service" clubs, such as Rotary, Kiwanis, Lions, and local luncheon clubs of various kinds. The motives of the members, who meet, eat, and sing every week, may be selfish, in the sense that this mixing with other businessmen in the town is good for one's individual business; but at the same time these organizations do help to uphold standards of business ethics and carry out specific programs for the less privileged—to promote, as the Kiwanians put it, "righteousness, justice, patriotism, and good will." The fraternal orders—Moose, Elks, Eagles, Odd Fellows, etc.—are mutual-benefit societies and social clubs, but they also enter into local fund-raising campaigns and charitable projects. The 1,350,000 members of the 17,000 clubs grouped together in the General Federation of Women's Clubs are into everything, of course, with their music and art and literature committees, study, education, and legislative groups, better-community campaigns and general uplift and do-goodness. . . . Men may join an organization for business or political reasons, or because they find security in belonging to a group, or because they believe in accepting responsibility. They have learned that their own welfare rests in the welfare of all, and they contribute not only money to ameliorate misfortune, but brains and time to solve problems that reach far beyond old-fashioned charities.[44]

If this statement is true, it would appear that voluntary associations already have built into the existing social organization of the community adequate means and motivations for the continuing organization of the citizenry to discern and dispose of community problems with vigor and effectiveness. In that case the problem of community organization posed by professional community organizers in social work and community development would appear to be illusory. It is therefore important to examine carefully the extent to which citizens do use the established voluntary associations to meet community problems and the effectiveness of these efforts.

[44] The Editors of *Fortune, U.S.A.: The Permanent Revolution* (Englewood Cliffs, N.J.: Prentice-Hall, 1951), pp. 131–133.

A Reprise and a Preview

Let us review the argument: much of the social organization of American cities is accomplished through the major formally organized institutional sectors, but other important dimensions of behavior are patterned through informal relationships. Neither of these sources of social organization in the urban community appears to facilitate the direct and extensive participation of the citizens themselves in the definition and solution of community problems. Some citizens may be concerned over this, and traditional community organizers—formal and informal leaders of the major institutional sectors and solidary groups—sometimes expound the pieties of citizenship and wish aloud for greater civic virtue. Yet the evidence of word and deed suggests that this alleged condition is viewed as a highly significant social problem mainly by those who comprise the emerging profession of community organization and development in social work, in adult education, in university extension services, and in some governmental and private agencies. The development of voluntary associations to motivate and effectuate citizen concern about community problems appears to offer one solution to the problem. Some observers believe such associations already exist to an extent that the problem delineated by the professional community organizer would appear to be a gross exaggeration of the facts (though no doubt useful in promoting the growth of the profession).

We shall now examine in more detail how far American urban dwellers are organized to face up to the problems confronting their communities. How they participate in both the formal institutions of the community and its voluntary associations will be assessed, with an emphasis on who is involved as well as how many. Some determinants of both extent of participation and effectiveness will be suggested. The detrimental consequences of traditional patterns of community organization will be underscored. This discussion will lay the empirical and theoretic foundation for proposed new approaches to community organization with which this chapter will conclude.

Community Organization: Who Gets Organized about What?

Problems are creatures of our discontents, of our negative evaluation of some existing condition. But the link between "having a problem" and "doing something about it" may be far from simple and direct. To solve a problem of low grades, a student needs the intelligence requisite for performance that teachers will approve of, the skills required to apply that intelligence to the tasks set by the teachers, the time and energy and the materials and environmental conditions necessary to facilitate that application, and, of course, enough emotional and ideological "push" to motivate the acquisition and use of those skills, personal qualities, materials, and conditions in ways conducive to academic productivity. To put the matter in social science jargon, if a situation is to be perceived as a problem by a group of people and they are to engage in some efforts to solve that problem, then they must be organized in symbolic and expressive terms, on the one hand, and in instrumental terms, on the other—they must have both the motivation and the means for action. Applied to the urban community, this means that community conditions will be recognized as problems by the citizens and action involving the citizenry taken to solve them only if the means exist for most members of the community to become informed about such conditions, to evaluate them, and to act collectively on the basis of those evaluations, and if among these urban dwellers there is attentiveness to such matters, concern about them, and a belief that effective citizen action is possible.

How well, in these terms, are American communities organized? Do citizens perceive the problems facing the urban settlement, do they care about them, do they act upon them? What are the consequences of the existing patterns of community organization and development for the conditions of life in American cities? The research needed for complete and definitive answers to these questions has yet to be accomplished. However, a great deal of information is available on the basis of which tentative answers can be framed, albeit on a high level of generality.

The City of the Social Critics: Trouble and Sorrow

If we consult the glowing annual reports on the accomplishments of their administrations put out by most mayors of large cities, and then read the evaluations of the state of our cities prepared by social scientists and respected social critics, it seems that completely different places have been described. For most professional researchers and commentators conclude that the city has largely failed as a community and a polity.

Hardly a major recognized problem has been dealt with effectively without federal intervention. Slums have reached such proportions that only the bulldozer can dispose of what honest and vigorous inspection and law enforcement might once have prevented along with earlier and more extensive provision of subsidized shelter for the economically deprived. Predictable and predicted traffic jams destroy whatever possibility might obtain for making pleasant or efficient use of the private vehicle in the inner city and many other areas.

The poor and the "colored" minorities have been confined to ghettos by the policies of both governmental agencies and private real estate interests; little has been done to ameliorate their deprivation or to protect them from brutal treatment by some policemen and exploitation by some merchants. Now many cities risk a riotous social explosion—as if there had never been race riots in the past from which something might be learned. Indeed, what seems a kind of collective inability to learn and innovate appears almost endemic among the traditional community organizers as they confront such problems.

The welfare services and aid provided by largely local public and private agencies have had little effect on the status of the disadvantaged except in minimal material terms; some have become habituated to dependency and others have simply become more tractable. Problems of unemployment, which obviously cannot be dealt with by gross national inputs alone, have been almost completely neglected by urban leaders, although all efforts at retraining, relocation of workers, and the creation of new "muscle-motor" jobs for the nonintellectual, visceral types must be carried on in and through local agencies.

The list could be extended over many pages. Only a few of the most essential and easily organized services are provided for with some adequacy in most cities—garbage collection, water, electricity, and the extinguishing of fires. Much also has been done to protect the profits of major real estate investors and to keep the managers of major resident industries happy (it seems some of them are always about to "leave town"). And at least modest gains have been made for those more affluent segments of the society who desire centrally located luxury apartments or expressway access to outlying suburbs and great shopping centers to service them. Otherwise, it is difficult to find solid ground for defending the present modes of community organization as the best means for solving the problems of urban settlement.

The City's Citizens: Nobody Sees the Trouble That's Known

Yet a majority of American citizens appear either to be living in an urban paradise or else to lack even the rudimentary information and insight for stating a brief list of pressing problems and needed improvements. Only about a fifth of them name three or more conditions about which they are dissatisfied or want changes.[45] Among those who

[45] John C. Bollens and Henry J. Schmandt, *Metropolitan Challenge* (Dayton, Ohio: Metropolitan Community Studies, Inc., 1959), p. 291. Because they provide so much

believe that all may not be right with their cities there is a lack of consensus as to what ails them, a fragmentation of concern; the most clear-cut publics are the contented and the uninformed.[46] From a quarter to two-fifths of these urban dwellers admit little or no interest in local government, while only 10 to 20 percent profess great interest in it.[47]

The community, then, is poorly organized simply in perceiving the existence of problems and having some active concern about them. Still less is done to motivate action about its problems or even a demand that someone else do something. Only about a third to half of those who are actively discontented with some condition bother to complain to someone in a relevant institutional setting—no more than a sixth of the city's citizens. Many who "feel like complaining" do not, and even more claim to be dissatisfied but just do not *feel* like making a complaint! [48] The complaints made usually deal with sanitary services and utilities in or around the place of residence, not with more basic community problems.[49]

The Word and the Deed

Of course, people may underestimate or overestimate their concern for community affairs, and there are many other ways to become involved with local problems besides complaining to some city office or official. The easiest and simplest form of action is to vote in local elections and referenda, but close to a third of the city's adults do not; local elections often attract far fewer than two-thirds of the potential voters, and large turnouts in school bond, tax, and budget elections usually produce a negativistic, protest vote.[50] No more than 30 to 40 percent of our urban "citizens" engage in voting plus one other relevant activity, such as trying to convince someone else or attending a meeting; indeed, only about half take sides in their own minds, barely

---

relevant empirical detail about larger urban places, extensive reference is made to this volume and to the study of St. Louis by John C. Bollens, ed., *Exploring the Metropolitan Community* (Berkeley and Los Angeles: University of California Press, 1961). Their findings fit well with those of other studies, such as Robert A. Dahl, *Who Governs?* (New Haven, Conn., and London: Yale University Press, 1961) and Robert Presthus, *Men at the Top* (New York: Oxford University Press, 1964).

[46] Bollens, *op. cit.*, pp. 186, 206–207; Bloomberg and Sunshine, *op. cit.*, p. 154.
[47] Bollens and Schmandt, *op. cit.*, pp. 234–235.
[48] *Ibid.*, pp. 242–243; Bollens, *op. cit.*, pp. 189–208.
[49] Bollens, *op. cit.*, p. 189.
[50] *Ibid.*, p. 183; Bollens and Schmandt, *op. cit.*, pp. 231–232; Richard F. Carter and William G. Savard, *Influence of Voter Turnout on School Bond and Tax Elections* (Washington, D.C.: U.S. Government Printing Office, 1961).

more than a quarter trying to persuade others to their point of view.[51]

What about the much publicized and praised voluntary associations? Do they provide the means whereby citizen concern for community problems is organized and expressed? Nationwide surveys conducted in 1953 and 1955 indicated that in 47 percent of American families no one belonged to a voluntary association and that 64 percent of the adults either belonged to no organization or to a union only. In another 31 percent of the families no one belonged to more than one association; among adults taken individually, another 20 percent belonged to only one organization other than a union. Only 9 percent of the families and only 7 percent of the individual adults hold membership in three or more voluntary associations.[52] After reviewing the research literature, J. C. Scott concluded that at any one time about two-fifths of the adult population had no membership in voluntary associations other than a church and that no more than a third of the citizens, if that, were active in the achievement of organizational objectives or personal fulfillment in the associational context. Although leaders in most of these associations must be especially sensitive to members' beliefs and wishes, since those who have chosen to belong may also choose to quit, it is nevertheless true that direction of such groups is typically concentrated among those few of the minority of active members who serve on committees and hold office.[53]

Researchers in one metropolitan area concluded: "It falls upon the one-fifth of the residents who attend meetings at least once weekly (one-half of whom attend two or more meetings a week) to make their organizational rounds and thus maintain the complex network of voluntary organizations in the community. Therefore, while organizational activities take up relatively little time of most residents, the commitments of a small minority are substantial—without them the organi-

---

[51] Bollens and Schmandt, *op. cit.*, pp. 231–232; also see V. O. Key, Jr., *Public Opinion and American Democracy* (New York: Alfred A. Knopf, 1961), p. 193. As subsequent references indicate, the wealth of empirical evidence collated in this excellent volume frequently reinforces the findings of Bollens, Schmandt, and others cited.

[52] Charles R. Wright and Herbert H. Hyman, "Voluntary Association Memberships of American Adults: Evidence from National Sample Surveys," *American Sociological Review*, 23 (June 1958), pp. 286–287.

[53] J. C. Scott, Jr., "Membership and Participation in Voluntary Associations," *American Sociological Review*, 22 (June 1957), pp. 315–326, especially pp. 325–326. For other references see Scott's footnotes. More recent studies indicate variety in detailed patterns from one place to another but do not alter the basic generalizations.

zational fabric would collapse."[54] The "Busy, Busy Citizen" envisaged by the editors of *Fortune* turns out to be one of an overorganized minority, while the majority remain, from the perspective of community organization, highly underorganized. Moreover, most voluntary associations seldom become involved in community affairs; they serve other individual and institutional goals, most often religion, economic security, or simply sociability and recreation.

There is, then, a low level of citizen involvement even in such relatively low-effort activities as obtaining information about the problems of the city, caring enough to take sides or to complain, joining a relevant voluntary association, and voting. Perhaps, then, we should not be surprised to learn how few citizens play more direct roles in actually shaping community decisions. For a condition in a community to be recognized as a problem requires "initiators" to identify it as such and place it on the city's "civic agenda"; then efforts to meet the problem must be developed and promoted by the "formulators," "programmers," "legitimizers," and "negotiators-facilitators" who establish alternatives, marshal and allocate resources, justify action, and work out whatever communication and horse trading must go on among various groups involved.[55] Eventually the commitment to action is completed and implemented through one or more of the formal institutional sectors.

Extensive research in Syracuse, New York, to determine who had played any direct part in 39 such community decisions over a five-year period led to the conclusion that *less than one per cent* of the adult population actually have a discernible role in community decision making apart from elections and referenda.[56] The decisions studied included those made by government, by welfare and service organizations, by major voluntary associations, and by business and industrial corporations. On the basis of a similar study of 83 public and private community decisions in four upstate New York suburbs, it was concluded that *no more than 3 percent* of the adults were for all practical purposes managing and administering the affairs of these smaller, simpler communities.[57] Even if the skeptic intuitively affirms these re-

---

[54] Bollens and Schmandt, *op. cit.*, p. 227.
[55] This typology of functional roles in community decision making has been suggested to me by my colleague, David T. Livingston, based on Ernest A. Barth and Stuart D. Johnson, "Community Power and a Typology of Social Issues," *Social Forces*, 38 (October 1959), pp. 29–32.
[56] Linton C. Freeman et al., *Local Community Leadership* (Syracuse, N.Y.: University College of Syracuse University, 1960), pp. 26–27.
[57] Bloomberg and Sunshine, *op. cit.*, pp. 70–71. The calculations determining the percentage of adult population represented by the numbers of decision makers re-

search findings to be too conservative and arbitrarily doubles or trebles the number found to be involved in defining community problems and organizing human and material resources to meet them, at least 90 percent of the adults of the community remain outside of the process. At most, they are either the docile implementers of policies and plans established by those who manage (and mismanage) the affairs of the community or the sometimes vaguely refractory objects of these community decisions—the coolies and the kulaks of community affairs.[58] As Dahl has said of New Haven, "The first fact, and it overshadows almost everything else, is that *most citizens use their political resources scarcely at all.*" [59]

Participation and Performance

Are these two conditions—low participation and poor performance in solving problems—related? No simple answer to this question can be validated directly. What we can do is examine more carefully those who participate and then see whether the most and least active are also the most and least successful in having their needs met through community institutions.

For example, compared with those who vote, take sides, try to persuade others, and the like, those who do not even vote tend to be from the younger, less educated, less residentially stable, lower-income segments of the society—the "problem people." [60] These correlations, however, are far from strong enough to prove the point by themselves.

---

ported here will be provided in a forthcoming report on suburban and metropolitan leadership.

[58] Students in a class can test these generalizations impressionistically by finding out what roles, if any, their own parents and those of their friends have played in establishing community conditions as problems and determining what action should be taken. Since college students generally come from the more advantaged families, their parents should be much more active in community decision making than the general population. Care should be taken not to count trivia, such as building a new lodge at a Scout camp, as a community decision.

[59] Dahl, *op. cit.*, p. 276; the italics are his. Dahl's major concern in this section of his book (pp. 276–281) is with party politics and elections in New Haven. Also see the data on individual participation provided by Presthus, *op. cit.*, pp. 258–264. Case studies also lead to the conclusion that direct participation in community decision making, as distinguished from spectatorship and mere voting, normally involves only small and usually specialized cadres of local citizens. For example, see Robert J. Mowitz and Deil S. Wright, *Profile of a Metropolis* (Detroit: Wayne State University Press, 1962); Roscoe C. Martin et al., *Decisions in Syracuse* (Bloomington: Indiana University Press, 1961); Wallace S. Sayre and Herbert Kaufman, *Governing New York City* (New York: Russell Sage Foundation, 1960).

[60] Bollens, *op. cit.*, pp. 227, 249–251, 434–435, 445; also see Bollens and Schmandt, *op. cit.*, pp. 235–237.

What about voluntary associations? Manual workers participate less than nonmanual, women less than men, Catholics less than Protestants; membership is correlated with education and with socioeconomic status in general.[61] Although the total number of lower-middle- and lower-class individuals participating in associations is undoubtedly greater than the total number from the much smaller upper-middle- and upper classes, the latter are proportionately represented much more heavily. Moreover, those associations most likely to become involved in defining and solving community problems not only attract the smallest numbers of members, but also recruit much more heavily from the upper than the lower rungs of the socioeconomic ladder.[62] And males and those of higher social standing also tend to be heavily overrepresented among officers and informal leaders in voluntary associations, especially ones likely to have some impact in community affairs.

The most extensively organized segments of the community are the upper and upper-middle classes.[63] From this group come those who comprise the majority in the professional and business associations, who provide most of the leadership for the more prestigeful civic and service clubs, and who normally dominate the boards of private welfare and medical agencies. When their wives also participate in voluntary associations, they are much more likely to hold office or serve in some special task than members from lower strata; and the upper-class women are much more likely to hold top offices or wield real power on an agency board than their middle-class associational counterparts.[64] For most of these upper- and upper-middle-strata associational activists, vocation, civic duty, and maintenance of family social standing are all quite nicely interwoven with their round of organizational contacts and programs.

The case now seems stronger. But what about the people whose au-

[61] Scott, Jr., *op. cit.*, pp. 324–325; Wright and Hyman, *op. cit.*, pp. 288–289; also see Basil G. Zimmer and Amos H. Hawley, "The Significance of Membership in Associations," *American Journal of Sociology*, 65 (September 1959), 198–199.
[62] Bollens and Schmandt, *op. cit.*, pp. 228–229; Presthus, *op. cit.*, pp. 246–253.
[63] Regardless of their disputes over theory, method, and more detailed generalizations, most of those who have inquired systematically into community organization and participation patterns agree on this point—Hunter, Dahl, Form, Miller, Presthus, Freeman, Rossi, and so on.
[64] See Joan W. Moore, "Patterns of Women's Participation in Voluntary Associations," *American Journal of Sociology*, 66 (May 1961), pp. 593, 596–597; and Carol Slater, "Class Differences in Definition of Role and Membership in Voluntary Associations among Urban Married Women," *American Journal of Sociology*, 65 (May 1960), pp. 618–619.

thority and influence most directly shape the community-organizing decisions within the major institutional sectors? [65] By and large they are individuals who combine many of the social characteristics typically valued in an American urban community: most of them are upper-middle- and upper-class, male and married homeowners; they tend, though less clearly, to exclude those who derive from the newer or less "accepted" ethnic groups and who are identified with religious minorities; but they are somewhat less "local," by place of birth and pattern of family residence, than the general public (except in suburbs). This overall pattern varies from one institutional sector to another. Persons from low-status ethnic groups and families appear as leaders only where organized labor dominates. However, upwardly mobile ethnics who come from low-status families in other communities are likely to turn up in technical and professional roles in areas of government such as public housing—indeed, technical experts and professional administrators in such fields as housing, planning, education, and welfare often change cities a number of times while seeking career advancement. On the other hand, where those who make the institutional decisions are in mercantile, legal, or real estate enterprises, or are elected government officials, they are likely to be quite local in origin or background. For the most part, women participate extensively only in decisions concerned with culture, health, or education.

The actual decision makers in the local community, although varied in social background, are clearly a highly selected and very small segment of the total adult population. Those whom the city at present serves best—the well-to-do, the professionals, the highly educated, the suburbanites—predominate. Those for whom life in the city is most difficult and who are often seen as "problem people"—the poor, the still-derogated minorities, many of the youth, those with little formal education, the new arrivals with little means—such people almost never appear among the ranks of the decision makers. Although it is true that some of those who do participate directly in community decision making desire and actually attempt to act as partisans of the deprived and the neglected, it is equally true that *most* local resources allocated by community decision makers without the intervention of the state or federal government have been used to make the life of the

---

[65] The generalizations in this paragraph reflect the findings of Freeman et al., *op. cit.*, pp. 23–24, 27–29; and Linton C. Freeman, T. J. Fararo, W. Bloomberg, Jr., and M. H. Sunshine, *Metropolitan Decision-Making* (Syracuse, N.Y.: University College of Syracuse University, 1962), pp. 10–11. Data from other published research, though often less detailed, are generally supporting.

already "advantaged" members of the community ever more advantageous.[66] Present patterns of community organization fail to bring existing problems effectively to the attention of most citizens, fail to motivate citizens to action even when problems are recognized, and fail to involve in relevant associations and in community decision making those whose needs are met least well by the established uses of community resources.

On Not Organizing the Unorganized

Suppose that we are retained by some enlightened civic group in a large American city to offer plans for major improvements in community organization. We are to find ways to involve a much larger proportion of the citizenry in defining community problems and working toward their solution. These many citizens must become interested in troublesome conditions, informed about the causes of such situations, concerned enough to devote their own time and resources plus whatever can be appropriated by law or voluntary methods, competent enough to carry on the necessary organizational and intellectual tasks and to know when expert help is needed; and they must be supported by whatever associational and institutional arrangements are needed to carry out the programs that will be developed. Confronted by such great tasks our first impulse might well be to seek help from the already organized segments of the local society. What aid might we expect from those who manage the affairs of the formally organized institutional sectors or from the leadership of the voluntary associations?

The Formal Institutional Sectors: Some Exercises in Futility

We would soon discover that the managers of the formal institutional sectors, operating within a traditional and often legally mandated definition of purposes and allocation of resources, rarely take as a goal major changes in how the community is organized. The traditional community organizers do not have this attitude so much because they wish to prevent others from also engaging in the delineation of community problems and the development of solutions. Rather, they see little or nothing to be gained from any important changes in how their respective institutions are organized or in the roles they now play in or-

---

[66] S. M. Miller, "The Public Responsibility of the Voluntary Association," *Proceedings of the Conference on Voluntary Giving for Community Health and Welfare Services, 1964,* and Martin Rein, "The Social Service Crisis," *Trans-Action,* 1, 4 (May–June 1964), pp. 3–6, 31–32.

ganizing the community. Moreover, given prevailing conceptions of their own roles and of what helps and harms organizational efficiency, they almost inevitably view the effort that would be required to promote the participation of large segments of the community as at best wasteful of limited resources, and likely at worst to produce more problems than solutions.

Local government. For example, a facade of participative democracy is maintained by the many meetings of governmental boards and commissions that are "open to the public," at which individuals and groups may present their views with respect to the matters at hand—zoning regulations, operating budgets, proposed statutes, urban redevelopment projects, and so on. If, however, large numbers of genuinely informed and interested citizens appeared at each meeting and participated effectively (and thus at length) in discussions only of the policy implications of the matters at hand, leaving technical concerns to the experts, the wheels of local government would grind to a halt. The prevailing arrangement for developing policy and programs assumes that public meetings, though brief, will dispose of extensive agendas. Those in positions of authority usually make up their minds during the course of the dialogue that goes on between meetings, with fellow officeholders and with those whom they consider important to them in the larger community—either recognized experts or those who might conceivably kick up a politically significant storm, such as top union officials or business leaders. Planners and plotters always ask, "Who should we 'touch base' with?"

In Stackton, for example, the mayor received proposals for solutions to downtown parking and traffic problems from committees of the chamber of commerce and the C.I.O. county council. The mayor-dominated city council passed the plan developed quite independently by his traffic engineer, but the mayor acknowledged his alleged "debt" to each of the two organizations. He had given high priority to the traffic situation because "things were obviously in a mess" and political advantage could be anticipated from almost any action taken.

The whole system is heavily oriented to the rigors and rituals of recurring campaigns for office. Individuals preoccupied with program are seldom found except among such professional staff as the city or county may employ. Between elections the political parties, the voluntary associations of the political-governmental sphere, are not used as vehicles for delineating community problems, motivating and organizing citizens to deal with them, or cultivating a larger cadre of organizers; rather, they serve as a distribution system for whatever patronage is still available and as the means for maintaining a "mothball fleet" of precinct and ward personnel who can be mobilized for the next campaign.

Organized labor has had some impact in local politics, as have some of the well-organized ethnic minorities. In many urban communities the business-professional elite has largely been displaced or has withdrawn, except for a small minority of that elite who enter into local political activity on the basis of strong ideological commitments (whether liberal or conservative) or special personality characteristics.[67] The role of local political activist has come to attract mainly those for whom party position or elective office aids or validates upward social and economic mobility, especially those from groups whose ethnicity is rooted in relatively recent immigration. Those who make it do not seek to cultivate the development of potential successors, and schisms and factions are constantly generated.

Probably no more succinct indictment of contemporary urban government can be made than Robert Wood's charge that "compared to criteria which suggest that government normally possesses qualities of purposefulness, rationality, regularized processes, and the power for the deliberate resolution of issues and conflicts, urban politics is devoid of most of the properties of a manageable enterprise."[68] From this perspective we can understand why the hallelujahs and hosannas with which some politicians and political scientists greeted and promoted proposals for metropolitan government have diminished. Although forms for "metro" that go beyond a mechanical readjustment of boundaries and centralization of functions would undoubtedly be helpful, it hardly comes to the heart of the matter.

Health and Welfare. Public medical and social service agencies have mainly distributed to the most deprived segments of the locality minimum facilities, services, and subsistence sometimes accompanied by more or less custodial supervision. As the refractory character of certain types of poverty and social deprivation have become more evident, the private agencies, normally the source in the United States of

---

[67] C. Wright Mills has argued that this is predominantly a voluntary withdrawal, in *The Power Elite* (New York: Oxford University Press, 1956), pp. 39, 41–42, 44, 46; Peter H. Rossi emphasizes interests and power resources as explanatory variables in "Theory, Research, and Practice in Community Organization," in Charles R. Adrian, ed., *Social Science and Community Action* (East Lansing: Michigan State University Press, 1960), pp. 10–14.

[68] Robert C. Wood, "The Contributions of Political Science to Urban Form," in Werner Z. Hirsch, *Urban Life and Form* (New York: Holt, Rinehart and Winston, 1963), p. 114.

new insight and of experimentation in the welfare field, have been "disengaging" from the poor and providing more and more services to the already advantaged middle strata! Moreover, the proliferation of what Frank Riessman and S. M. Miller have called "the psychiatric world view" has tended to emphasize establishing the problem locus in each individual and providing appropriate therapy rather than making unjust and ineffective institutional arrangements a target of collective efforts through political and social action.[69] There is undoubtedly much unfairness in the derision directed by many Harlem Negroes at the "briefcase boys" whose social work activities take them into the blighted ghetto on a nine-to-five schedule, but it is true that service facilities located in most deprived areas have declined since the heyday of the settlement house, certainly in relation to the need for them.

In most American urban localities today the directors and boards of private agencies decide what the community's medical and social service needs are and how they are to be met. Sometimes the professional personnel who make up the staffs of these private agencies are fully involved in this process; often they are not. The general citizenry are organized only to provide funds, not to help determine goals or to aid in meeting them in nonmonetary ways. Amateurs have been largely eliminated from staff roles except for the nice ladies who tend candy counters or read to children in hospitals or who serve as volunteer receptionists at some poorer agencies. Yet policy is often formulated by another set of amateurs whose wealth and local community prestige qualify them for membership on one or more agency boards. The professionals usually complain about the power thus wielded by people who they allege may lack both technical understanding and a humanistic orientation.

The development of a controlling establishment in private welfare organizations reflects not only the economic dependence on contributions from individual and corporate sources of wealth, but also the use of business-dominated civic and "service" clubs to develop a sizable cadre of individuals motivated and prepared to move onto the boards of community agencies. In many upper-middle- and upper-class associations officers such as president, secretary, and committee chairmen are replaced frequently, sometimes every year. Membership on boards, however, is more stable, consisting mainly of individuals of high prestige and power who, as one of them put it, provide the "continuing management function in community affairs." They watch for bright, energetic members, put them on committees, and then guide and

---

[69] Frank Riessman and S. M. Miller, "Social Change Versus the 'Psychiatric World View,'" *American Journal of Orthopsychiatry*, 34, 1 (January 1964), pp. 29–38.

manipulate those they judge most effective into the lower offices from which, if success continues, they may ascend routinely year by year into the presidency. Of those so elected, a few will then move onto "the board." From these groups the business segment of the community continuously supplies candidates for the boards that manage most of the private health, welfare, and social service agencies. Those who have gone through the civic association and service club system of "office training" thus share experience in this type of leadership as well as many contacts with others in the "nonpolitical" realms of community organization. Although there may be a noticeable minority of business and professional activists who are categorized as "liberals," most of them share to some degree in the solidarity built up within these associations around an ideology of self-proclaimed community service and around the rituals and social pleasantries of meetings and club programs.

Given boards that often have a majority who consider the affairs of the agency a kind of preserve within which they can exercise their own versions of moral rectitude and community responsibility, and given professional directors and staffs who will not use techniques for affecting policy more direct than trying to persuade or manipulate board members, it is little wonder that few effective efforts have been made to involve the rest of the community in delineating the health and welfare problems it faces and seeking the alternatives for meeting them. Those of middling affluence among the public are expected to give their money but keep their opinions to themselves. The clients are expected to accept what is offered, if not with gratitude, then at least with the decency to become less a problem; in such a system it is almost inconceivable that they should help decide what their own problems are and what solutions might work well.

Mass media. Managers of newspapers or of radio and television stations cannot affect the behavior of other citizens as directly as those who manage institutional sectors which deal more immediately with the physical plant and social structure of the city. Though they are often thought to be molders of public opinion and action, V. O. Key suggests their impact on politically relevant patterns of perception and motivation is much exaggerated. The majority of newspaper readers pay little attention to political news even at the more popular national and international level. The majority also tend to skip speeches on radio and television by top government and political figures, even those on major issues during political campaigns. Although there are exceptional cases, television and radio are less likely to structure beliefs and feelings than the printed media.[70] The backing of the mass media for both fund-raising and vote-getting purposes, though avidly sought, has never been demonstrated to be a major determinant of success or failure.

Newspaper editors will, of course, point to their feature series on behalf of one or another civic cause, and television executives emphasize their documentaries. But such efforts are fitful and episodic and seldom are dovetailed with programs to increase citizen participation. If anything, the mass media tend to reinforce the existing forms of community organization. This can be seen quite clearly with the newspapers.[71] Though they "cover" local news and regularly affirm the usual pieties about good citizenship on the editorial page, the news itself portrays a community control structure of notables and quotables. Small efforts by small groups rate little or no space and therefore appear quite unimportant. The letters to the editor column plays as much for sheer stimulus as for serious thinking; among the few who express themselves in this way, fools and hotheads are overrepresented. The letters column itself is usually a jumbled miscellany of unrelated issues and personal concerns. Indeed, the whole newspaper is a vaguely patterned mosaic of local, national, international, human interest, and special interest news items scattered across the pages along with advertisements and amusements. The mass media provide more exhortation than instruction, more distraction than motivation, and in general serve the public relations needs of the already organized.

"Official Reformers": Further Exercises in Futility

Public officeholders, the business-oriented majorities on the boards of social agencies, and the managers of the mass media together constitute a somewhat heterogeneous and far from solidary "local establishment." Whatever conflicts arise among them, they agree that the status quo with respect to community organization needs no basic revision or renovation. They are more likely to devote their political and economic power resources to defending existing arrangements than to overthrowing or even overhauling them. But two types of formal institutions are ideologically committed to the well-being of the lower strata, of the segments of local society rarely directly represented in the ranks of the decision makers; these institutions are the labor unions

[70] Key, Jr., *op. cit.*, pp. 346–355.
[71] During the study of the power structure in Stackton a count of line space and page location was made for individuals and organizations and was supplemented by content analysis. Those who doubt the generalizations stated here should subject their local newspaper (or papers) to a similarly detailed and systematic examination.

and churches. However, their power in the community rests largely on whatever commitment to belief and action they can obtain from memberships that are *formally* voluntary. Indeed, they are sometimes called "voluntary associations," although they are more fully developed as formally organized institutional sectors of the community than most other associations in the "voluntary" category.

In reality, of course, some church groups and some labor unions are at least as conservative with respect to established patterns of community organization as the institutional managers of local politics and government, health and welfare, and the mass media. Indeed, actual efforts to bring about major changes are more likely to be initiated by a minority of would-be reformers within the business and professional segments of the community, who usually form some sort of *ad hoc* association, than by either churches or unions.

Organized labor. Union leaders work hard on any local issues that affect their special areas of concern and will attempt to activate the union members about them. For example, the building trades are interested in laws affecting licensing and inspection in the construction industry. But most local unions avoid involvement as organizations in matters that might divide the membership, such as race relations. Members are urged to participate in campaigns for approved candidates and to vote, but little is done to stimulate, produce, and publicize continuing, serious efforts by members to become involved in community problems between elections. Thus union members trained to serve as volunteer "counselors," guiding fellow workers who need such aid to one or another private or public welfare service, are not also trained to raise fundamental questions about the whole conception and administration of social welfare in the community or to act collectively to correct inefficient or unjust conditions should they be discovered.

Within the labor movement, local leadership rises through the hurly-burly of union politics, grievances and bargaining, and strikes. Once elected, union officers usually make no effort to develop new leadership; they tend to cling to their positions, to discourage challengers, and in larger locals to make paid careers or at least extra part-time jobs out of their union positions. In contrast, the business-professional group, when their associations or the agencies they control require full-time management, tend to hire an executive secretary or director and his staff. Such a job would be a step down for most men at the top of business and professional careers; but for most manual workers the office of local president or treasurer is a step up in prestige and power (and when salaried, in pay), and they are not inclined to diminish such rewards by turning administrative work over to "some college boy."

In spite of the merger of the A.F.L. and the C.I.O., organized labor in most cities is much less unified than business and is often seriously split by schisms, jurisdictional disputes, and political feuds. The relatively few individuals who come onto health and welfare boards or governmental commissions from organized labor tend to be unprepared for the substantive concerns with which they will deal, to have no extensive program of union-developed proposals to advance, to be inexperienced in the subtler forms of political manipulation by which the business and professional majority "get things done." They often suffer from enough status anxiety that they either sit in silence or become unusually aggressive. In general, then, unions have not developed any significant independent programs for organizing those segments of society left out by the network of middle-class associations and agencies, nor have they provided a system for effectively recruiting from their own ranks a sizable number of community leaders and organizers.

Churches. Clergymen have some of the same problems as union leaders in using their organizations for community action and reorganization. Whatever may be the policy at national levels, the local leadership, lay and clerical, must beware of creating schisms and factions within the membership. Moreover, there is a good deal of conflict between some churches, just as there is between some unions, and involvement in community issues tends to exacerbate or compromise these differences. And, of course, the everyday work of maintaining a religious organization and its traditional functions uses up most of the resources, time, and energy that the members of the collectivity will allocate to this area of concern. Both churches and unions often have committees devoted to community affairs and problems, but there is little evidence even of creating citizen concern and action, to say nothing of affecting the course of local events.[72]

The life cycle of bourgeois "civic revolt." As we review the history of various urban reform efforts, we soon discover a repetitive pattern that is either fascinating or dreary, depending on our taste. The basic theme of this civic horse opera involves a few simple episodes. In the

[72] Regardless of the methods used, neither the studies of community power structure cited here nor others which have appeared in various journals have indicated either churchmen or church organizations as playing important roles in community decision making except when the direct interests of their own institution were immediately involved. The only change in this pattern currently appears in the area of race relations in some cities, and the actual impact of churchmen on relevant community decisions in this regard has not yet been systematically assessed.

first act some Good Citizens discover Disturbing Problems in their city; normally these conditions have obtained for several decades just below the sight level and auditory range of the well-to-do activists and their traditional community organizers. In the second act the Good Citizens, full of righteous indignation, have determined the cause of the trouble and its cure, which normally involves "throwing the rascals out," or establishing a "key reform" (such as local civil service or the city manager form of municipal government), or some combination of the two. The climax of the drama comes in the third act when, after great efforts and sometimes bloody battles, some of the Good Citizens have replaced the rascals in office or the key reform has been established. The denouement is provided by a fourth act, which concludes very much as the first act opened; the problems that appear on stage are hardly distinguishable in form or number from those visible when the curtain first went up.

This cycle is in part the result of the limited vision and civic vocabulary of most bourgeois reformers. Since they find life in the city (or suburb) largely satisfactory, it seems unlikely to them that anything basic could be wrong with this local social, political, and economic system. They must therefore conclude either that not-so-good men have somehow gotten into controlling positions within the major institutions or that some specific and limited segment of the machinery needs to be overhauled or replaced. At most, symptomatic relief or temporary remission is obtained for a few of the ills of the community. In a little while they reappear, often in even more virulent form.[73]

The Voluntary Associations: Some Exercises in Triviality

The real home of the Good Citizen, when his involvement in community affairs is avocational rather than vocational, is the voluntary association. Here he serves on committees, listens to notable guest speakers, and exchanges inside information with his counterparts whose local contacts vary but slightly from his own. Together they occasionally endorse or oppose proposed laws; and occasionally they may send a delegation to represent their views to a governmental official or agency administrator or board. Such activities give them a strong feeling of helping shape the character and quality of the community. It never occurs to them that this may be an illusion sustained by

---

[73] My colleague, Kirk Petshek, believes that the civic reformers in Philadelphia during the 1950s managed to institutionalize effectively many of the components of their movement and thus provide a major exception to this pessimistic caricature. He is now engaged in research relevant to that thesis.

group ideology and supported by a deferential local press. Yet examination of their agendas and accomplishments supports this conclusion.

The luncheon clubs often have a "community project," which may range from raising modest amounts for a worthwhile charity to building a pavilion at a youth camp. Rarely does it deal with basic conditions that trouble a community, and even when it does, the resources allocated are seldom consequential. If Rotary, Kiwanis, Lions, and other clubs of this type were all disbanded in the same week, there is little evidence that the life of most communities would undergo significant change—except, of course, that the members would have to start organizing some new associations.

Professional associations remain preoccupied with their traditional functions of protecting and occasionally policing the trade; local chapters generally avoid controversial matters that do not directly and immediately affect them in their professional roles. Local bar associations even tend to avoid or evade problems of law and justice affecting mainly the very poor, the rejected minorities, and the more despised deviants; but they may haggle endlessly over minor changes in the routines of assigning courts and judges. Local medical societies prefer not to consider such problems as racial discrimination, the quality of treatment afforded to charity and relief cases, and the health consequences of slum housing; campaigns against "socialized medicine" are, however, acceptable.

The auxiliaries of formally organized institutions are generally subservient to the established leadership and mainly implement its policies and programs. If any PTA has ever contributed importantly to the recognition of an educational problem or its solution, the event has not received much publicity. They provide, we may assume, at least some boost to school morale, along with minor additions to the equipment of the school and captive audiences for pupil presentations. Church-related groups play similar supportive roles and also provide theologically oriented adult education and in-group recreation and sociability. Some churches have a committee that studies community problems and attempts to inform the congregation and motivate concern; more direct action is seldom taken. Other volunteer groups serve as auxiliaries to hospitals, health clinics, and the like, or conduct fund-raising and propaganda ("educational") campaigns in support of established efforts to deal with mental illness, cancer, heart disease, and so on. Even when they are not merely local arms of national agencies (with hands that exchange brief brochures for loose change and small bills), they do little or nothing to organize others to deal with these concerns as community problems.

Many voluntary associations at one time or another observe, study, and make resolutions about community problems. Such efforts usually have little impact on events. If enough of them occurred concurrently and reached the same or similar positions, they might affect that "climate of opinion" to which some decision makers claim to be sensitive. The League of Women Voters is one of the most effective of the adult education groups that also want to affect the thinking of decision makers. At times it may have effect, but there is little evidence that its impact is either frequent or substantial. Furthermore, it is composed mainly of white, middle- and upper-class women who, like their male counterparts in the civic and service clubs, fail to see any need for basic changes in community organization.

The principal means of recruiting new members in most voluntary associations is through personal contact. Existing members invite friends and acquaintances plus others whom they admire, wish to know, and can contact through "someone who knows someone who. . . ." Since most of the associations which even attempt to affect community affairs are at present essentially middle-class groups, those who recruit new members normally do not know many working-class or lower-class people, nor do they know how to interact comfortably with them in equal-status relationships. Thus the informal processes of recruitment tend to eliminate or restrict the addition of members from lower strata, from the Negro minority, and sometimes from other minority groups as well. Efforts to change this pattern are essentially symbolic: a luncheon club may signify its alleged "devotion to democracy" by adding to its roster several carefully selected, high-status Negroes, or a chamber of commerce may include a few top union leaders. But these are trivial deviations from the prevailing pattern.

Voluntary associations can have an important impact on community affairs if they are *persistently* involved on behalf of a *few* goals to which they devote *substantial* resources. A well-financed private development association, the political arm of a strong union movement, a chamber of commerce with substantial staff and business backing—such groups are likely to affect the specific areas of the community with which they are concerned: promoting industrial growth, securing public office for approved candidates, maintaining a good "climate" and supportive facilities for business. These are not minor matters, but there is little evidence that they lead to any of the major changes in the status quo that in turn might solve some of the community's problems.

Clearly, the voluntary associations do not compensate for the failure of the formally organized institutional sectors to engage in extensive and effective forms of community organization. There may be many other reasons for valuing these groups, but their present impact on community development is usually conservative or trivial.

The Myth of Citizenship

Why don't more citizens simply "organize themselves"? Why is it that growing up in an American family, being educated in a public or parochial school, being guaranteed the rights and opportunities of citizenship all fail to produce adults concerned about their communities and active in the definition and solution of community problems? One answer has been suggested by Dahl after contemplating the low level of participation in politics (taken broadly) in New Haven and noting that this is typical rather than unusual in the United States: "At the focus of most men's lives are primary activities involving food, sex, love, family, work, play, shelter, comfort, friendship, social esteem, and the like. . . . It would clear the air of a good deal of cant if instead of assuming that politics is a normal and natural concern of human beings, one were to make the contrary assumption that whatever lip service citizens may pay to conventional attitudes, politics is a remote, alien, and unrewarding activity." [74] But, as Dahl so well recognizes, the social scientists cannot simply make assumptions that fit the case. Research, however, has done much more to describe the failure to organize American communities than to explain it. Moreover, the minority of citizens involved in establishing what conditions will be considered as problems and what will be done or not done about them are also displaying their "human nature." The concerned, participating American citizen may often be mythical, but so, too, are most popular beliefs about human nature.

We must turn to differences in competence, motivation, and situation among various individuals and groups to explain differences in the way they behave. Such variables may be interrelated: people lacking competence may have less motivation in areas where they have learned they are likely to fail; but those with sufficiently high motivation may go to great lengths to acquire needed competence; and the actions and beliefs of those with whom one associates plus other environmental conditions can have a great deal to do with what is considered either possible or worth pursuing.

Obviously, any explanation will be complex. At this stage of our understanding we must be satisfied if we can assemble what seem to be

[74] Dahl, *op. cit.*, p. 279.

the main components of an adequate explanation, even if we cannot fit them all together into a neat and complete package of theory.

The "urban peasant." A great many people in our society are, as Greer has bluntly put it, "the equivalents and descendants of the illiterates of a hundred years ago" who, like their peasant or town laborer forebearers, have a round of life largely encapsulated by hearth and workplace, reinforced in modern times by television or backyard sociability. Their horizons of action, as contrasted with spectatorship, are barely expanded by their recreation, travel, and other popular uses of leisure. They maintain an essentially "privatized" existence rather than relating to the affairs of the community.[75] They have developed neither a feeling that they ought to be involved nor the skills that would make them effective and gratified participants in organizational activities.

It is not surprising that persons with little education and low income should so often know little about the community, devote few of their meager resources to efforts to change situations whose nature they do not even comprehend, fail to join associations, and display only a middling or low sense of "civic duty" with respect to voting.[76] But what about those who have acquired better jobs, more education, more life chances?

The point is that nothing happens to most upwardly mobile individuals to alter their privatized life style as they move through the broad range of skilled blue-collar and middle white-collar statuses, however much they may be enriched materially and, in certain limited ways, intellectually and culturally. They do not suddenly begin to read the editorial page instead of the sports page, join social service groups instead of fraternal societies or veterans clubs, or start worrying about the tax base of the metropolis instead of the payments on the mortgage. Nor do secondary schools seem to promote active participation and a sense that one's actions count, although they help to inculcate such basic

---

[75] Scott Greer, "Individual Participation in a Mass Society," in Roland Young, ed., *Approaches to the Study of Politics* (Evanston, Ill.: Northwestern University Press, 1958), pp. 329–342. A detailed study of almost 600 individuals in Waterbury, Connecticut, revealed that about 80 percent of leisure time was spent around the house—see Alan M. Voorhees, "Public Opinion and Goals for Planning," *Proceedings of the 1963 Annual Conference* (Washington, D.C.: American Institute of Planners, 1963), p. 197.

[76] For belief in the citizen's duty to vote, see Key, Jr., *op. cit.*, p. 325; with respect to information about the community, see Gresham M. Sykes, "The Differential Distribution of Community Knowledge," *Social Forces*, 29 (May 1951), pp. 376–382—especially his footnotes 7 and 8.

pieties as believing that citizens ought to vote and that elections are important.[77] One careful study revealed that students in high school who took a civics course tended to be more supportive of the democratic creed and less chauvinistic; but willingness for political *participation* was not affected, and seeing politics as a process necessarily involving power and politicians and resolving group conflict was an outcome only in a high-status community where such views were already prevalent among the adults.[78] College students usually have greater freedom and encouragement to become politically active. They also have more effective adult models; few professors are as servile or as anxious to be noncontroversial as are public school teachers.

Class, education, and ethnic social heritage do not, however, shape the behavior of persons as isolated individuals. What sort of life style predominates where each lives is likely to affect the extent to which people who are otherwise similar in income, education, and so on become active in associations, pay attention to local conditions, and become motivated to participate in community affairs. For example, as the number of people in an area likely to be adherents of the "familistic" round of life (home-centered sociability plus some commercial recreation) increases, even those who are (in terms of other social characteristics) the probable participants seem to be drawn away from community involvement and into the life style of the majority of their neighbors. The reverse is also true: where the familistic mode is less likely to prevail—where there are many apartment dwellers, fewer children, and more working wives—individuals with less income and education tend to participate more than we might expect in ways that are closer to the overall statistical patterns.[79] This "multiplier effect," which is sometimes rather mystically called the "ethos" or "spirit of the place," may set in only when one or another type constitutes a visible majority. Deriving from a general inclination among human beings to "drift" toward conformity with perceived patterns of group behav-

---

[77] For correlations between education and the value attached to voting, see Key, Jr., *op. cit.*, p. 325, and Bollens, *op. cit.*, p. 441; for correlations between education and levels of participation, see Key, Jr., *op. cit.*, p. 331, and Bollens and Schmandt, *op. cit.*, pp. 20 and 236.
[78] Edgar Litt, "Civic Education, Community Norms, and Political Indoctrination," *American Journal of Sociology*, 68 (February 1963), pp. 70–73.
[79] Scott Greer, "Urbanism Reconsidered: A Comparative Study of Local Areas in a Metropolis," *American Sociological Review*, 21 (February 1956), pp. 19–25; Wendell Bell and Maryanne T. Force, "Urban Neighborhood Types and Participation in Formal Associations," *American Sociological Review*, 21 (February 1956), pp. 25–34.

ior, this curvilinear cumulation of tendencies to engage in or withdraw from community affairs probably contributes much to the buildup of the distinctive subcultures of some suburbs and small towns.[80]

Alienation and participation. An important and different explanation for involvement in or withdrawal from community problems and actions has received increasing attention in recent years among a variety of social scientists. The term "alienation" denotes one or more states of mind and emotion in which the individual perceives himself as somehow not a meaningful part of the social arrangements which by any objective measures obviously enmesh him.[81] This attitude may reflect (1) a sense of powerlessness, of being at the mercy of a system which controls the individual for purposes other than his own; (2) normlessness, when goals and standards of conduct no longer have that self-evident, convincing quality we usually take for granted but instead appear uncertain, capricious, conflicting; (3) social isolation, which may be objective if the person attempts to withdraw from or is rejected by other members of his group, but which may also be largely subjective if he perceives and feels this separateness from others even though objective measures of interaction do not justify such feelings and perceptions.

Any of these forms of alienation, of estrangement from the social order, can easily lead away from rational concern for community problems. If we perceive ourselves as utterly powerless, such concerns and actions are futile; we can only withdraw from the system or protest blindly and violently against it, as in the riots in several Northern Negro ghettos during the "long, hot summers" of 1964 and 1965. Again, action is unlikely if we cannot ascertain the ends to be sought or the means that may be used or must be avoided. Finally, common cause cannot be made with others if they seem to reject us or seem separated from us by some barrier, however intangible.

On the other hand, there may be a self-confirming circularity to these interrelated perceptions and feelings. Failure to attempt to solve a problem may reinforce a conviction of powerlessness when even a par-

---

[80] For examples of such "subcultures," see Greer, *Governing the Metropolis, op. cit.*, pp. 85–86 and 97–102; Bloomberg and Sunshine, *op. cit.*, pp. 26–42 and 146–155; Irwin T. Sanders and Douglas Ensminger, "Alabama Rural Communities: A Study of Chilton County," *Alabama College Bulletin 136*, 1940.

[81] The use of the term here follows the conceptualization developed and explicated in Melvin Seeman, "On the Meaning of Alienation," *American Sociological Review*, 24 (December 1959), pp. 783–791; and Dwight G. Dean, "Alienation: Its Meaning and Measurement," *American Sociological Review*, 26 (October 1961), pp. 753–758.

tially successful effort would reduce it. Again, if enough people begin to behave in erratic, unpredictable, or conflicting ways because they no longer have clearcut goals or entrenched standards of conduct, such consensus about means and ends as still obtains among the whole group may be further and even fatally disrupted. Finally, when we feel isolated or rejected, we are likely to react with symptoms of anxiety or resentment that many others find objectionable, leading to negative reactions on their part, intensifying the sense of isolation or rejection. It is essential to keep in mind this apparent circularity—that the state of mind and emotional pattern called alienation may through time both result from the pressures of the social environment and contribute to the intensification of them.[82]

It is not surprising, then, to find that alienation increases among segments of the community further down the class ladder.[83] Some areas in modern urban slums seem designed to generate it. Nor is it surprising to find that alienation decreases as participation in voluntary associations increases. Organizational involvement, which is as good a predictor of political participation as class standing, or better, also correlates negatively with alienation. But is an individual who is not drawn into a network of associations less likely to participate in community affairs and, as a result of both of these forms of noninvolvement, more likely to feel powerless and socially isolated, less likely to feel himself an integral and effective part of a well-organized, goal-oriented social order? Or is someone who already feels deeply alienated less likely to be motivated to associate with others in a voluntary organization or to participate in community affairs—indeed, is he motivated to stay out?

The best analysis available at this writing indicates that differing degrees of both alienation and political participation derive largely from the effects of interrelated variations in socioeconomic status and organizational involvement.[84] Certainly, both civil rights organizers and union leaders have found that many of those who appear deeply alien-

---

[82] Dahl, *op. cit.*, pp. 287–292; no adequate longitudinal studies are available that settle the question of temporal and causal priority.
[83] William Erbe, "Social Involvement and Political Activity: A Replication and Elaboration," *American Sociological Review*, 29 (April 1964), p. 207; also see Edward L. McDill and Jeanne Clare Ridley, "Status, Anomia, Political Alienation, and Political Participation," *American Journal of Sociology*, 68 (September 1962), p. 207; and John L. Haer, "Social Stratification in Relation to Attitude Toward Sources of Power in a Community," *Social Forces*, 35 (December 1956).
[84] Erbe, *op. cit.*, pp. 210–215; social mobility also is taken into account in Arthur G. Neal and Melvin Seeman, "Organizations and Powerlessness: A Test of the Mediation Hypothesis," *American Sociological Review*, 29 (April 1964), pp. 216–226.

ated can be drawn into associations that are clearly relevant to their own perceived needs. Moreover, most psychiatric theory suggests that only those who are seriously "neurotic" or "ill" consistently reject opportunities to fulfill their own needs. If a sense of alienation is not mainly a manifestation of a personal psychological condition, the individual should be receptive to opportunities to reduce his feelings of social isolation, to increase his power to cope with his environment, and to gain a greater focus and purpose in life. Of course, such individuals must themselves perceive the opportunity as real and may need help in overcoming habits of withdrawal, servility, and aimless or apocalyptic anticipations of tomorrow.

Those for whom alienation is part of a deep-seated personality disorder can be found in all groups in our society. Undoubtedly there are more of them where the pressures of deprivation, social isolation, and disorganization are greatest and are felt from earliest childhood on. But alienation should not be considered an entrenched component of the personality of most of those who tell interviewers that they feel powerless, neglected, at times isolated from their fellowman, and often without purpose in a world which is confusing and arbitrary. It is more likely that such thoughts and feelings reflect in personalized and internalized caricatures the social, economic, and political realities faced by those below the participative ranks of the well-to-do and outside the comfortable but nonparticipative cultural microcosms of familistic neighborhoods.

Toward Effective Community Organization

Present modes of community organization fail to bring the city's resources to bear upon its problems or to elicit the participation of the citizen. Preserving the status quo has been given the highest priority by most of the managers of the established institutional sectors, and their first response to many urban problems has been to evade them. When troublesome conditions become so pressing that they must be recognized, assurances are made that the existing machinery is adequate to meet the problem if only enough money is provided through taxes or contributions. Failure to deal adequately with problems can then be blamed on the refusal of citizens to provide adequate support, especially when the private sector is overflowing with affluence. Rarely does a community leader ask whether the existing machinery is worth even what it presently costs or suggest any basic reforms of the prevailing patterns of community organization. Efforts are made to contain the problem in the sense of preventing any real "blowup." In large measure the system works to maintain and service community problems at a less-than-crisis level rather than to solve them.

In fairness, we should note that many social scientists do not agree fully with this negative evaluation of prevailing patterns, or at least would demur from the harshness of the judgment. Greer, for example, has argued that the self-selected activists of politics and the voluntary associations are diverse enough to be considered at least somewhat representative of a broad range of the total population. Moreover, he argues that ethnic and lower-class groups most likely to be poorly represented in the community-relevant voluntary associations are important voting blocs to whom elected officials make pointed appeals and for whom they provide many services. And, Greer adds, the ills of the metropolis, though annoying, are not critical. "When 'problems' are potentially lethal, the machinery for problem solving begins its creaky action—developing *ad hoc* solutions, expedients, special districts, or getting federal intervention. The metropolitan community is continuously improvised; its evolution is organic, not rational; change is crescive, not revolutionary; problems are solved by trial and error, not by fiat." [85]

We should not exaggerate the distance between Greer's perspective and the more urgent, critical, and hopeful views of this chapter. The assertion made here is not that the American city is on the verge of collapse, but that it could be much better, and that to make it better we must improve greatly the way in which the community is organized and meets its problems. But formidable obstacles to community development in America's cities have been identified.

1. Some unorganized citizens cannot be drawn into a community effort because they are too profoundly alienated; even if they do participate they may be more disruptive and ineffective than helpful. This group is probably only a small proportion of the total citizenry, but we do not know just how small a proportion they comprise, or exactly how to identify them.

2. More people are alienated as a result of the deprivation they have experienced and their exclusion from any persistent and satisfying associational involvement. If ways can be found to involve them in associations and in action relevant to their needs, this sense of alienation can probably be reduced or eliminated. But it is difficult or impossible to get them involved and participating by means of conventional political and organizational techniques.

[85] Scott Greer, *The Emerging City* (New York: The Free Press of Glencoe, 1962), p. 199; and see the argument developed in Chapters 4, 5, and 6.

3. Persons who are satisfied by privatized pursuit of sociability and recreation after work hours make up an even larger segment of society. When whole neighborhoods or subcommunities are inhabited mainly by this type, they generate something of a familistic subculture reinforcing as a group pattern preferences and predispositions that constitute a social inheritance from their historically not-too-distant peasant and town laborer forebears.

4. Most of those who manage the institutions and lead the voluntary associations have been either uninterested in the task of organizing the great majority of the citizens for participation in community affairs or unable to do so if they wanted to. The voluntary associations that have least to do with community problems and most to do with child rearing, job protection, recreation, and sociability seem to be the most attractive to the broad middle range of citizenry.

Clearly, to organize the unorganized on any substantial scale where community affairs are concerned means challenging established traditions and social arrangements on a broad front. To assume that less is at stake is to misread the findings of research and to mislead the idealist who may be willing to give it a try. The result can only be unrealistic plans and expectations followed by ineffective actions and disillusionment.

How would an effectively organized community differ from contemporary American cities? What conditions and arrangements might produce more citizen participation? How might the amount and disposition of local resources devoted to solving community problems be changed? Each of these questions requires some commentary. We might answer the first in revolutionary and utopian terms, designing for an industrial society a sort of local settlement radically different from anything we have ever known.[86] But in this chapter imagination will be constrained by the obligation to show some possible bridges between present and proposed patterns, and by awareness that increasing participation does not automatically guarantee any better recognition of community problems or use of resources to solve them. Improvement requires that the new participants behave differently from the traditional community organizers and their followers, and that their behavior in turn lead to changes in the behavior of those who are already participants. The problem of resources is so complex and exten-

[86] For examples, see Margaret Mead, "Values for Urban Living," *Annals of the American Academy of Political and Social Science (Metropolis in Ferment)*, 314 (November 1957), pp. 10–14; Percival Goodman and Paul Goodman, *Communitas* (New York: Random House Vintage Books, 1960), pp. 119–224; Erich Fromm, *The Sane Society* (New York: Rinehart, 1955), pp. 299–352.

sive that it must be dealt with in very limited and overly simple ways here. Questions about tax base, grants from extralocal sources (federal, state, foundations), and physical plant and materials will not be considered. The emphasis, following the lead of community development doctrine, will be upon "human resources"—the number of people who can be involved, the competences and motivation they have, and the effectiveness with which they are organized to perform the tasks of recognizing and solving community problems.

The Power to Make a Problem

Meeting community problems begins with "initiators" who identify a condition as troublesome and "get it, in effect, on the city's 'civic agenda'" (page 386). There are various ways this may happen. Though the managers of the formally organized institutions have power to compel a great deal of organized attention or to make it difficult to get such a focus on one or another situation, that power is far from absolute. The routine life of both private and public agencies is subject to a certain amount of disruption by outsiders who become discontented with conditions they believe should be taken care of by one or another of these community institutions.

Whose complaints are taken seriously by whom? Those who can distribute their words widely are more likely to be heard than those who can do little more than make individualized comments to next-door neighbors or low-level clerks in one or another bureaucracy. The mass media are still the megaphone of the metropolis; extensive exposure in the media may help to put a condition on institutional agendas. Money speaks, though not as loudly as some believe, when organizations depend on contributions for their continued operation. Elected officials are appropriately sensitive to the opinions of those who they believe can have some important impact on the voting patterns of particular segments of the electorate—persons they perceive as major "opinion leaders" in various religious and ethnic groups, organized labor, and the like. Certain kinds of prestige sometimes command attention; at least occasionally individuals may be listened to simply because they are accepted as being highly expert or exceedingly wise.

Finally, ordinary people who lack these various sources of power, if they act together vigorously, may get their specific concerns on the agendas of the managers of the major institutions. School integration becomes a high-priority problem in some communities only as a boycott develops. Or funds are somehow found to expedite programs alleviating slum conditions when a riot or two have shaken the complacency of the upper strata. On a much smaller scale, garbage collection in certain areas improves after residents deliver the uncollected material to the doorstep of city hall, and a traffic light that could not be allocated from this year's budget is installed when angry mothers blockade the dangerous intersection. But mass action, whether planned or spontaneous, is fairly rare and so discontinuous that any problem it forces onto the civic agenda may subsequently be subject to only casual and unproductive attention. In any case, a variety of undesirable urban conditions have received much too little attention because so few people have been able to have their discontents designated as community problems.

Clients, dependents, and other "nobodies." The existence of deprived, disadvantaged, dependent, and deviant people within the community may be viewed as a problem, but the nature of that problem is almost always defined by others: social workers, policemen, charitable civic leaders, upper-class reformers, successful practical politicians, union leaders, and so on. A few researchers have obtained accounts of what those who are usually both weak and inarticulate believe their problems to be; these views are sometimes communicated to some of the elite groups in the context of materials to which whatever prestige the expert enjoys has been attached. Occasionally the mass media do the same with a compelling documentary, but brevity here makes some superficiality almost inevitable. In general, however, "down" and "out" people are excluded from community determination of what their problems are or what solutions might be tried. They have little direct access to the community agenda. Enabling them to become more articulate and to gain such access would be one way of improving community organization.

Artists, intellectuals, and moral philosophers. Few of the people most talented and trained in matters of aesthetics, scientific knowledge, and values help in any direct way to establish the generally recognized needs and priorities of the community. (It should be remembered that not all who paint pictures are artists, that not all with graduate degrees are intellectuals, and that many churchmen are neither theologians nor moral philosophers.) Individuals who are preoccupied with the problems of beauty, knowledge, and good conduct constitute a great and almost totally unused resource for delineating community problems—a potential imagination, brain trust, and conscience for the city. Such people are found in every urban center of any size. Some of them are deeply alienated and so not likely to become even minimally involved in the problems of the community; others are oriented so completely to the larger society and their professional fields within it that local events strike them as mainly some sort of distraction to be avoided.[87] But even those who do care about the city where they live go almost entirely unheard. They tend to be poor organizers and are seldom joiners except for associations of their own craft or profession. They usually do not want and most often would retreat from the continuous involvement of the community activists. Yet they often see the community in fresh ways, both in what ought to be considered its problems and what can be done about them. A new approach to community organization would give currency to their ideas and concerns and make them a part of whatever problem-focused dialogue can be generated among the diverse segments of the city's inhabitants, especially among its opinion leaders and decision makers.

The locals: neighbors without neighborhoods. Many parts of cities are inhabited predominantly by "familistic" households generating and sharing in a subculture which, as has been pointed out, tends to detach its adherents from the larger community. But such areas, though characterized by a good deal of neighboring, often turn out to be poorly developed as neighborhoods. They lack boundaries, a common sense of identity, and a capacity to act in concert when confronted by common problems. Many conditions treated as if they were community-wide problems are actually quite localized and could be dealt with by much smaller units of action than the city government or city-wide welfare or service organizations. But means have not been developed for making decisions and taking action at the level of neighborhoods or even multiple-neighborhood sections of the city. Scattered efforts can be found in most cities in the form of neighborhood improvement groups

[87] This follows the local-cosmopolitan concept as developed by Robert K. Merton, "Patterns of Influence: A Study of Interpersonal Influence and of Communications Behavior in a Local Community," in Paul F. Lazarsfeld and Frank N. Stanton, eds., *Communications Research 1948–1949* (New York: Harper and Brothers, 1949), pp. 189–190. Unfortunately, the concept has been drastically oversimplified in operationalizing it as an underlying attitude indicated only by scaled questionnaire responses: see William M. Dobriner, "Local and Cosmopolitan as Contemporary Suburban Character Types," in W. M. Dobriner, ed., *The Suburban Community* (New York: G. P. Putnam's Sons, 1958), pp. 132–143; Thomas R. Dye, "The Local-Cosmopolitan Dimension and the Study of Urban Politics," *Social Forces*, 41 (March 1963), pp. 239–246. Also see the descriptions of alienated and nonalienated intellectuals in Jan Hajda, "Alienation and Integration of Student Intellectuals," *American Sociological Review*, 26 (October 1961), pp. 774–775; but note the organizational activist character of the highbrow media purists identified by Harold L. Wilensky, "Mass Society and Mass Culture: Interdependence of Independence?" *American Sociological Review*, 29 (April 1964), p. 194.

and community councils; they vary greatly in character and effectiveness.[88]

Certainly there is evidence that at least some "familistic" individuals will participate in the processes of recognizing and reacting to common problems if the scale of organization and the horizons of concern are small enough. On the one hand, they need to be able to keep problems that can be handled at a local level from going onto the agenda of some community-wide agency, whether through default because the neighborhoods are organized only to gossip and shuttle soup to the sick, or through the imperialism of the formally organized institutions and their managers' preferences for a highly standardized pattern of action throughout what they assume to be their proper realm. On the other hand, highly localistic citizens need to be able to get onto the proper community-wide agenda a concern for supralocal conditions which, though not viewed as important problems by those with community-wide commitments, have the effect of making the development and maintenance of neighborhoods and subcommunities unnecessarily difficult. A new approach to community organization would give the "locals" of every strata more voice in determining what conditions are problems and *whose* problems they are.

The cosmopolitans: the community as a "cause." Paradoxically, many cosmopolitans are as lacking as the familistic locals in ways and means to express their actual or potential interest in what they see as the problems of the city. These are the people who are inclined to look beyond the locality to the national and international scene in matters of both cultural and political interest. When they do turn their attention to community concerns, they tend to see them in this broader context. They also tend to be insensitive to many of the boundaries that are both guideposts and blinders for the typical community-oriented activists. Political and institutional jurisdictions mean little to them; they are inclined to grasp the metropolitan milieu "as a whole." A small, generally well-educated minority, they are best suited to establish, sustain, and promote an image of a community that is metropolitan in scope. Not committed to any one local government, school system, shopping district, or the like, the cosmopolitan is more prepared than most urban dwellers to see problems of race relations, poverty, education, welfare, and so on in a metropolitan or national context and to emphasize problems (such as conservation and recreational re-

[88] For example, note the contrast between the theoretic model and empirical realities in Frank L. Sweetser, "Organizing Communities for Urban Renewal: A Structural Model and Its Application," in Sussman, *op. cit.*, pp. 196–206.

sources) that those with more limited spatial perspectives often overlook or see but dimly. Most cosmopolitans, however, also lack an effective means of being heard, and their potential as partisans for the community is seldom tapped by others. Linking their voices and points of view into a continuing community colloquy would be another step toward better organization.

The Function of Conflict: Creative Discord in Community Settings

One condition for effective community organization, then, is to have a great many people and more varied people participate in the processes by which conditions are recognized as problems and placed on the agenda for action which develops segmentally among the formally organized institutions and community-relevant voluntary associations. This extension and broadening of participation in community affairs will inevitably involve recognition of neglected needs and revision of the priorities set for allocation of community resources. But there are two related by-products about which some might feel trepidation. The number of conditions stipulated as problems for the community will increase drastically, as will the number of conflicts over goals for the community, priorities for limited resources, and procedures for solving problems. These by-products, however, are highly desirable in spite of some accompanying dangers.

This judgment rests upon the conclusion that the apparent imbalance between many problems to be met and limited resources to be used in solving them is, from a causal point of view, normally not a result of absolute limitations on resources, but the consequence of problem solving on too small a scale and with too little motivating drama. There is, of course, a theoretic saturation point where, in a relatively democratic and voluntaristic society, addition of more problems to the agenda and intensification of interest through the drama of conflict will not yield further voluntary inputs of resources or acquiescence to additional levies through governmental agencies. But until that upper level is approached, increasing the range of concern and the variety of projects underway, and enlivening and illuminating the area of activity by visible clashes will tend to increase the total commitment of resources.[89]

The belief held by so many community leaders and social scientists that the citizen has just about been "mined out" at the local level has

---

[89] See the analysis of the "slack" in a "liberal" political system by Robert A. Dahl, "The Analysis of Influence in Local Communities," in Adrian, ed., *op. cit.*, pp. 35–39.

become a self-confirming hypothesis preventing the very kinds of action that could bring about a fuller release of existing resources and development of new ones. It is something of a political analogue to the "scarcity" orientation that dominated economic theory until so recently. Like traditional economists and entrepreneurs, analysts and practitioners treat established and entrenched patterns of social organization as "givens" and on this basis determine what is possible "in the real world." Because they are so often liberal in their preferences for social legislation and candidates for office, the fundamental conservatism built into their apparently objective theory and research remains hidden even from their own view. At a time when more and more systems of action are rapidly increasing the energy applied to the pursuit of goals, the view is widely held that the local community must remain, in effect, a low-energy system. The alternative view developed here asserts:

1. People generally have a limited and specialized range of concerns and commitments reflecting their beliefs and life situations; slum dwellers do not become exercised about investment opportunities for new industry, and suburbanites (whether living within the city limits or beyond) will seldom become active in behalf of basic reforms for slum schools.

2. The total number of participants in community affairs can therefore be increased substantially only by increasing the total number and variety of problems actually being dealt with.

3. The resultant increase in resources for meeting problems can be more than additive if those who manage problem-solving activities have the skills necessary for bringing related interests and concerns into combination.

4. Citizens in our cultural tradition respond to the drama of clash and crisis much more readily and extensively than to the continuous but low-key pushes and pulls of conventional pieties; conflict is therefore a basic component for motivating the citizenry.

5. The rule of frequency and variety also applies to conflict; commitment of resources to community needs can be increased substantially only by increasing the total number and the heterogeneity of conflict situations arising in the locality.

Conflict can have both functional and dysfunctional consequences.[90] Helpful from the point of view of this chapter are the surfacing of repressed or neglected problems, the involvement of the apathetic and

[90] James S. Coleman, *Community Conflict* (Glencoe, Ill.: The Free Press, 1957) provides an excellent discussion of the dynamics and consequences of conflict.

the alienated, the emergence of new leaders and activist groups, and the re-examination and sometimes the reshuffling of alignments among established groups, the re-examination and sometimes the revision of established programs—all consequences likely to increase citizen participation and the amount of energy directed to meeting community problems. On the negative side are tendencies toward extreme polarization of individuals and groups, severe distortion of issues, and the replacement of a pragmatic concern for redress of grievances by a moralizing focus on the opposition of men and doctrines. The negative consequences become more likely when controversies and conflicts arise one at a time and only from time to time, and when those who become involved are inexperienced in organizational work and conflict situations. Thus the dysfunctional consequences of conflict tend to be limited or eliminated to the extent that a community is characterized by many controversies and conflicts (some of which occur concurrently), by high participation, and by increasing organizational experience among the citizenry.

Americans in the broad middle socioeconomic range share in a vague ideology which rejects controversy and conflict. (Perhaps it derives in part from the small entrepreneur's conviction that good business relations require that "you don't argue about politics or religion.") Jefferson may have asserted that the tree of liberty needs to have its roots bloodied regularly; modern labor and management executives may remind the public that strikes are an inevitable and useful element in free collective bargaining; and Martin Luther King can repeat endlessly and eloquently that love and conflict, in communities as in personal relationships, are not necessarily incompatible. But most middle-class Americans still repress enjoyment of conflict except for the spectator's vicarious involvement in the ritually confined and limited engagements of sports and party politics and in the dramas of the mass media, both fictional and documentary. The development of conflict must therefore depend largely on those who have been excluded or alienated from the ranks of the more conventional community activists —the lower strata, the artists and intellectuals, and familistic individuals. But these people, because they lack organizational experience and sophistication, are most likely to promote the dysfunctional consequences of controversy and conflict.[91] The creation of means for developing organizational competence should therefore have high priority in any program for major improvements in community organization.

[91] *Ibid.*, pp. 19, 21–22.

The Development of Organizational Competence

Several beliefs dominate much of the thinking about what makes a citizen competent as well as involved, beliefs sustained more because they "feel good" than because evidence supports them. One of these beliefs is that formal education and its correlates (such as high income and middle-class manners) are important requisites for effective participation in community affairs. This belief is based on the fact that lower-class people are seldom found among the ranks of community activists. However, we have already seen that this can be explained without any reference to the capacity of these people to become competent. Community organizers who have made the opposite assumption, though few in number, have often been successful. Saul Alinsky is the most publicized but far from the only one who operates effectively with the "down" and the "out." [92] Civil rights groups and unorthodox social workers also have scored many successes with both the rural and urban poor.[93]

A second belief is that effective participants have some special and infrequently encountered psychological qualities. Such an assumption fits the fact that only a small minority of persons whose social characteristics give them easy access to involvement in community decision making actually participate. It is undoubtedly true that there are individuals whose extreme psychological traits would seem to make them unfit for most roles in community action programs: people with unusually low thresholds of anxiety or aggression, with disturbances that make them unable to communicate effectively, with tendencies to withdraw or to suppress drastically normal energy levels. Nevertheless, we would do well to keep in mind the case of an unemployed psychotic with extreme withdrawal tendencies who had been under the unsuccessful care of a psychiatric caseworker for almost three years. Somehow he became involved in an organization started by a social worker experimenting in the creation of social action groups among the poor. He became a block leader and subsequently was interviewed on television! Although he was far from mentally well, a great many of his most extreme symptoms were drastically reduced.

Programs for developing organizational competence would do well to affirm the old saw that "heroes are made, not born." Until strong

---

[92] Saul Alinsky has set forth an ideology and some organizational doctrines in *Reveille for Radicals* (Chicago: University of Chicago Press, 1946), a volume now clearly outdated; a new book by Alinsky is hopefully forthcoming.

[93] Much helpful data on this point has been provided to me by an as yet unpublished description of such groups by Warren Haggstrom, School of Social Work, Syracuse University.

evidence to the contrary is brought forward, the best assumption to make is that most people can develop effective organizational skills if provided with adequate motivation and given training opportunities appropriate to their backgrounds and styles of action.

Education for community organization. For many years institutions that engage in adult education have offered courses and conferences on community problems and organizational leadership. But unless attendance is by invitation, those who enroll are seldom people already deeply involved in community affairs. Nor is there any evidence that those who register for leadership training or for opportunities to contemplate metropolitan problems go from the extension classroom into the ranks of the activists in any greater proportions than they would without such educational experiences. Many workers in union education long ago abandoned efforts to bring education to the rank and file generally and have concentrated on programs for the minority who are activists and officers. They also have found that they are most successful if they build out from a central concern for immediately needed techniques, tying philosophical and theoretical issues to the pragmatic pursuits of organizational activity.

Experimenters in action education among the lower strata have learned an essentially similar lesson. Education must take place within a context of participation and involvement. The educator himself may have to be an organizer; he may have to create a protest group for his classroom and laboratory. Here, also, a teacher encounters an evaluation process that reverses the usual academic pattern (and makes remarkably good sense in certain ways): if the "students" decide they are not learning much that works, they flunk him by the simple expedient of not coming to meetings any more. It is therefore important that education for organizational competence lead to action that is in some degree successful.

There is no reason to believe that these basic precepts must be altered as the personnel to be trained become wealthier and better educated. The content of education for community action must take account of differences in concerns, in already available skills, and in styles of action. For groups from any strata the capacity to move from low-risk efforts usually involving minor matters into problem areas of greater scope and import, thereby increasing the risk of failure, must be assiduously cultivated and reinforced. Surviving failure is a lesson that is inevitably encountered but not always mastered. The time of encounter is not easily predicted in this unique kind of educational endeavor.

Institutionalizing accomplishment. Whatever gains an action group may make through any one project or series of efforts are likely to prove ephemeral unless they are built into the routines of the social organization of the community, especially its formally organized institutional sectors. Failure to understand and accomplish this has a great deal to do with the life cycle of the bourgeois "civic revolt," just as it contributes to the rapid erosion of gains made by the mass protest of slum dwellers. Reformers need to know how to transfer programs and projects into the ongoing machinery of the major community institutions and how to minimize the risk that old bottles will corrupt the new wine.

Associational euthanasia. Organizations that are successful in pressing for solutions to community problems but remain involved in the resulting programs over a period of time tend to become a part of the institutional sector, complete with staff, permanent quarters, and a minimally participative mass membership. Those who once were leaders become executives and administrators, sometimes unhappy ones. The only sure way to prevent this institutional evolution is to keep most community-relevant associations *ad hoc* and situation-specific. I do not mean that new formal organizations and institutional sectors should never evolve. Rather, I suggest that many associations are kept alive after they have lost much of their thrust and function. They are sustained by leaders and a minority of the original cadre of activists who may find it difficult to bear the pain of dissolving their own handiwork, or who may not know how. But failure to accomplish such acts of organizational euthanasia leaves the landscape cluttered with groups that have diminishing relevance for the present problems of the community and have waning, or stable but low, capabilities for improving conditions for the inhabitants of the locality. The time, energy, and resources devoted to such associations could well be used elsewhere on the local scene.

In the Realm of the Possible: Some Slightly Heretical Proposals for Enhancing Urbanity and Community in Urban Settlements

What has been envisioned, when all the conditions stipulated in the preceding argument are taken together, is a city that would seem much like, and yet different from, what we are now familiar with. It would still be a large, sprawling, densely populated, heterogeneous, busy, changing local community. But it would be functioning in part as a deliberate and well-maintained problem-solving system. Such a quality would be difficult to see in physical terms, except as some of the most visible signs of unsolved problems, such as badly deteriorated slums, at last disappeared. We would have to become familiar with the life of the citizens to perceive the change, and even here no great social revolution would be immediately evident.

The mass media would provide the first clue. For anyone interested in the problems and prospects of life in the city there would be much more to read than at present. Many controversies would be reported, patently hard-fought by serious and apparently sophisticated contenders; and they would run the gamut from the state of the public treasury to the beauty of the street furniture. Photographs and interviews would focus attention upon a strangely heterogeneous set of newsworthy residents; governmental officeholders and society leaders would share the first few pages of the paper or the television screen with a committee of the Arts and Crafts League, a mass meeting of residents in an old section of the city called South Valley, the city's official poet, and the board of directors of the Association of Unwed Mothers. A little research at the central library would provide other clues. The reference bureau's listing of permanent clubs and associations would be no larger than now, and might even be smaller; but a whole new reference section would be busy servicing "citizen groups." More systematic fieldwork would reveal that a large number of people in all the strata belonged to some community-relevant association or *ad hoc* organization or had belonged to one during the past few years. Diverse forms of small talk would still dominate the daily round of conversation, but the increase in concern for and comment about various community problems would be noticeable, especially among those middle- and lower-class groups for whom such topics now have no conversational interest.

So much for the vision. It is of a city somewhat more community conscious, involved, concerned, participative, urbane, and humanistic than we now know. This city may be no one's utopia; yet it is separated from the contemporary scene by a very wide gulf of entrenched habits and institutional arrangements. What bridges might we try to build should we wish to get to the other side?

Between Theory and Practice: The Missing Dialogue

Most Americans assume that new knowledge gained by science is brought into use almost as soon as practical applications can be suggested. Although this is frequently true of hardware and hard science, and holds true to a very large degree in medicine's relationship to biology and chemistry, it is unusual in the realm of human organization. This reflects in part the more inexact character of the social sciences and the difficulty of attaining that extensive verification of theory so common in the physical and biological sciences. As the confidence possible in research-based generalizations declines, the inclination increases to rely instead on the accumulated practical wisdom of the craft plus one's own experience and insights.

Yet there are gains to be had from the use of the limited knowledge of human behavior that can now be obtained from scientific inquiry; certainly a good deal of self-defeating action could be avoided. Such use, however, is very rare in efforts to delineate and meet the problems of the urban community. Probably the greatest single reason is the incompatibility between lines of action implied by social research and those that constitute the prevailing convictions and habits of most institutional managers and association activists. Another reason is the lack of circulation of knowledge among those whose efforts are most relevant. Even when they want to, few people now shaping the community's perceptions of its troubles and reactions to them are able to keep up with the relevant knowledge that does accumulate in the social sciences. (If there are partial exceptions to this generalization, they are in the fields of economics, psychology, and, to some degree, education.) The absence of a continuing dialogue between science and practice also is dysfunctional for the researcher, who is deprived of the kind of feedback data received from some practitioners in medicine and various fields of engineering.

Universities have occasionally attempted to bring about a dialogue between social scientists and those who are, whether they like the term or not, the social engineers of the urban community. So have certain foundations. But the usual technique of *ad hoc* conferences and institutes has had very low yield and lacks needed continuity. The creation in each city of a permanent, local, applied social research agency serving both public and private institutions would seem to offer far more hope of eventually reaching mayors, aldermen, and board members along with their professional staffs. Besides consulting with legitimate groups and their leaders, it could publish both special reports and a regular journal focused on local needs and problems for modestly educated laymen.

Urban Extension: Every Little Movement Should Have a Meeting All Its Own

Although the local social research agency could help move those who control the formally organized institutions and major voluntary associations toward more effective patterns of community organization, it would not have any more effect on the chances of the poor to become involved in the processes of recognizing and meeting community problems. Here the challenge is to the various public and private agencies of adult ("continuing") education. The major agencies are in the universities, but in some localities the public school system provides a substantial program also. Unfortunately, as far as developing the skills of citizen participation is concerned, most of those in the field of adult education have matched a great dedication with small imagination and little courage for effective experimentation.

Urban extension needs to borrow from successful innovators in the creation of social action groups. Educators concerned with enabling those who are underpowered and alienated to understand their lot and to develop means for obtaining redress of their grievances must realize that action itself is the best classroom. They themselves must learn to find and recruit into training programs incipient as well as established citizen groups, instead of simply publishing each semester's calendar of courses and programs and waiting for the multitude of undereducated citizenry to descend upon them (for a modest fee).

Perhaps they should consider opening up some "storefront extensions" in areas where the people to be educated live and encounter their problems, both in the slums and in the suburbs—storefronts can be plain or fancy! Perhaps there must be poolhall institutes and tavern seminars. In any case, social action classes should be provided with the minimum equipment for the lab work of such a course or seminar—a mimeograph, tape recorders, a meeting place, and help in doing some minimal, crude amateur research if needed. Advanced classes might well prepare their own documentaries for local television and radio.

Extension units willing to try such radical procedures might find allies among certain private welfare agencies and labor unions that still have some residual commitment to the dream of a grass-roots democracy and that are not too immobilized by institutional gout. Of course, it will be much easier to find critics and opponents in both the community and the university, for the best means for developing effective community organization almost inevitably disturb many established relationships and habits of action. And innovations such as those just mentioned would no doubt further enrage on-campus faculty snobs who already label university extensions "Mickey Mouse outfits."

A Federal Contribution: Planned Parochialism and Selective Demetropolitanization

One of the most persistent myths in American political life is that the intervention of the central government into the affairs of the community weakens the local polity. But the opposite effect is possible if federal intervention both encourages or requires greater responsibility for solving local problems on the part of the resident managers of urban institutions and at the same time provides resources and technical aid in developing and carrying out efforts to solve those problems. Experiments along such lines have not been fully successful by any means, but they still appear to be a hopeful technique.

We may note here the attempt to create citizen advisory committees for uban renewal and redevelopment, the encouragement given to the formation of neighborhood and community councils, and the insistence upon a degree of comprehensive planning. Federal grants to private and public agencies in areas of housing, relocation, compensatory education, juvenile delinquency, and so on have all served to strengthen local agencies and to establish some minimum standards for planning and evaluating the effectiveness of projects. It is true that the advisory citizen committees, potentially an exciting experiment in functional as against spatial representation in government, have almost always proved ineffective and have been easily co-opted or subverted by the established institutional officialdom. It is also true that many federal standards are complied with more on paper than in practice and that positive results of demonstration projects have too often had more of a verbal than a behavioral existence. Nevertheless, federal intervention seems over the long run to be strengthening the organization of communities, pushing local agencies toward more effective and responsible efforts to deal with pressing problems on an adequate scale. The consequences include a growing rather than receding importance for local government and a slow but continuous upgrading of its personnel.

Efforts should be made to build into all federal programs for urban reform—in housing, school, expressway, and other physical redevelopment, race relations, education, delinquency reduction, and so on—provisions encouraging or requiring further development of neighborhood and other subcommunity organizations. These are the only agencies likely to pull some members of the familistic households into activities relevant to the recognition and solution of community problems. There are those who reject "neighborhoodism" as dreadful and even as a distraction from the achievement of the "right" perspective—a cosmopolitan, metropolitan view. Such protestations may be rejected on two grounds. First, in realistic terms the choice is not between a parochial and a metropolitan perspective, but between a parochial involvement in community affairs and no involvement at all. Second, many decisions made at a city or metropolitan level, standardizing behavior for the entire area under that jurisdiction, are both destructive of citizen participation and unnecessarily uniform, detracting from the interest and identity benefits to be gained from sectional heterogeneity. What gains beyond the psychological well-being of certain planners and administrators can be demonstrated for the standardization now obtaining in house setback, traffic patterns (other than those for arterials), and rules likely to affect subcultural behavior such as business hours or use of public property for street fairs and festivals? There is some case for federal encouragement of further metropolitanization in local governance; there is an equally good case for encouraging the development of subcity governance units for certain types of decisions.

Deprivatizing the American Citizen: Neither Sparta nor Zenith

There has been a growing consensus among social scientists and social critics that many of America's urban problems reflect, among other things, a maldistribution of our national wealth between the private and public spheres, affluence being concentrated in the former to the detriment of all efforts to improve the lot of those who are not affluent. What has been said in this chapter amounts to an argument that a better distribution is not likely to be obtained so long as so many citizens lead highly "privatized" lives. The amount of resources devoted to the solution of the problems of our communities and the efficiency with which they are used would both increase if ways could be found to draw a much larger proportion of the citizenry into at least occasional participative roles in community affairs, especially those in the lower strata and in the "out groups" of middle-class life—artists, intellectuals, and adherents to the familistic round of life in ethnic and suburban enclaves.

There will be readers who transform the relatively modest suggestions of this chapter into a utopian vision of a society in which everyone belongs to countless organizations, rushes from meeting to demonstration to hearing to conference, and gabs endlessly about social problems and social science. The artist would seldom get to his canvas except to paint protest posters, and the poet would compose mainly political tracts in rhyme or blank verse. Before long nothing would remain of the lifeways of the ethnic enclave except special foods and voting blocs. No housewife could relax for long in the cozy little world of *kaffeeklatsches* and car pools without suffering all sorts of guilts for neglecting her public trust as a citizen of the community.

Any such fears are, of course, groundless. The hold of the private round of life on American citizens is quite secure. At present the most *active* strata of citizens average only 30 to 50 minutes out of their nine hours of leisure time each day in community work and citizen associations! And for those whose income falls below the 5000-dollar-a-year level, the average is not even measurable in units as small as one-tenth of an hour per day.[94] What is hoped for and expected is that a great many individuals would discover areas of interest and dimensions of their personalities not brought to the fore by the television screen, the aimless car ride, or the vaguely boring amiability of overextended sessions of small talk. It is difficult to see how anything precious could be endangered by the diversion of a few hours each week from the typical privatized round of life in the middle or lower strata of American cities.

Thus we would seek neither Sparta nor Zenith—neither the community compulsively regimented to collective aims in which no life can be private and no goals have primacy over those of the polity, nor the class-ridden social system, the preoccupation with household aggrandizement above all else at all times, and the superficial attachments to banal associations which Sinclair Lewis satirically portrayed in Babbitt's hometown of Zenith. Actual American communities obviously lie between these two hypothetical extremes. But they lie much closer to the end of the continuum labeled Zenith than the end labeled Sparta.

The rights and duties of the amateur citizen. Dahl has called those who manage the formally organized institutional sectors of the community and others whose participation in community decision making is continuous, broad, and intensive "the professionals."[95] Their activities are regulated by custom as well as by law, for there are special political ethics, rituals, and loyalties that help to determine the rights and duties of "the pros." If the reforms proposed in this chapter were successful, a similar body of informal doctrine would in time develop for the amateur citizen whose involvement is specialized, discontinuous, and not always so intense. There would begin to emerge in our urban culture well-defined and strongly held expectations that those who dwell in the city, whatever their social rank, would in certain circumstances take a hand in shaping one or another aspect of community life in much more direct and focused ways than casting a ballot every few years. The rights that would accompany and complement that set of duties would include access to the facilities and the knowledge necessary to make participation easier, more effective, and more meaning-

---

[94] Voorhees, *op. cit.*, p. 200.
[95] Dahl, *Who Governs?*, pp. 300–301.

ful. To facilitate these periods of active citizenship would be one of the major obligations of both private and public community institutions.

Commitment and withdrawal: for all things a season. The term "urbane" has many connotations. Often it is used to designate the suave manners and blasé outlook attributed stereotypically to the "city slicker." Again, "urbanity" frequently designates a commitment to the "high culture" of the city—its facilities for the fine arts, the sophisticated crafts, the performing arts; its centers of higher education, of research; and its counterpoint opportunities for a cultivated spectatorship of the "low culture" of jazz, bohemia, and ethnic eateries. The role of citizen is often oddly absent from images of the urbane urbanite.

In this chapter a good deal of evidence has been offered to the point that "citizen" is indeed a minimal or nonexistent role for many who live in the city. One result, it has been argued, is an ineffective polity, a community which cannot organize itself to recognize and meet its problems effectively. A case has been made for the assertion that there is no substitute for broadening participation in community affairs. Only in this way can many conditions which merit the attention and resources of the community be put on the civic agenda; only in this way can education for the role of citizen proceed effectively among many people in the middle and lower strata.

Beyond all this, however, is another version, or vision, of "urbanity." It is the image of men and women who could and would move selectively and alternatively among at least several of the worlds of the city. Sometimes they would be very much part of a neighborhood and could enjoy the insulated microcosm of backyard sociability. But this would not be the whole compass of their lives after work. At some times and for certain purposes they would move on the level of perception, concern, and association by which we now identify the cosmopolitan. In much the same way they could alternate among privatized and public roles. The mix would vary greatly among individuals, but the variations would reflect more of choice and less of the presently compulsive concomitants of social rank.

For I would argue that the requisites for better community organization are in many ways also the means for establishing in the modern city a kind of life to which we could attach the word "community" in its ideological sense—a human settlement whose inhabitants are not only in it, but also of it and "with it."

9

Poverty, Inequality, and Policy

▼▼▼▼▼▼▼▼▼▼▼▼▼▼▼▼▼▼▼▼▼▼▼▼▼▼▼▼▼▼▼▼▼

S. M. Miller and Martin Rein

> The test of our progress is not whether we add more to the abundance of those who have much; it is whether we provide enough for those who have little.
>
> —Franklin Delano Roosevelt

The Rediscovery of Poverty

"YE have the poor with you always." Darkness and neglect usually mark the struggles of the poor. Yet, in other times, in other places, the poor have become our concern and obligation. After long neglect of the poor in the United States, the enactment of the Economic Opportunity Act of 1964 signified the legislative recognition of poverty and of social responsibility for alleviating and reducing it. How did this happen?

The main historic view is that poverty is the problem of the poor—a condition of the individual pauper and not a characteristic of social organization. It was in the last half of the nineteenth century, while Charles Booth was undertaking his monumental social survey of the

---

* We are indebted to William G. Grigsby, Gabriel Kolko, Jesse Burkhead, Sidney Sufrin, Bertram Gross, and Jerry Miner for critical comments and to Betty L. Saleem and Pamela A. Roby for checking the manuscript. Fern Freel typed the manuscript with care and fortitude, often acting as a translator between an idea and its written expression; our debt to her is enormous. Grants to S. M. Miller from the Stern Family Fund and the Ford Foundation were important in the preparation of this chapter.

Life and Labor of the People of London, that poverty came to be defined as a condition of society. This perspective changed the crucial questions for social policy: Did the state have a moral obligation to help the victims of poverty—the poor and the pauper? If it did, was it necessary to break up the old poor law system that was founded on the concept of "less eligibility" and to replace it with a concept of social justice based on the principle of "social provision"? Only gradually in the nineteenth century did the rising power of the poor, evidenced in the Chartist movement, lead to the extension of suffrage, to the development of the Factory Acts to improve conditions of work, and to new governmental mechanisms for regulating unemployment and mitigating the economic travails of old age. Slowly the rich, industrial nations of western Europe assumed national responsibility for the plight of the poor and began to rely on government intervention rather than on the market economy to improve the conditions of the poor.

In the United States developments were less speedy. The scope of protection for low-income groups remains less today than in industrial western Europe and in many developing nations where a heavy commitment to social legislation is emerging in a relatively early stage of industrialization. In our country the comparatively unregulated market place was thought to provide sufficient opportunity for improvement of the conditions of the poor. The Populist surge of criticism of the late nineteenth century forced some reforms, but these reforms had meager effects. In some areas, including transportation and public utilities, government regulation was instituted, but the enforcement agencies concerned often fell under the influence of the corporations they were supposedly regulating. No major federal social legislation [1] was enacted in the United States until the 1930s when fear of prolonged unemployment and economic stagnation led to Franklin D. Roosevelt's election.

Roosevelt's New Deal lasted only five years, a fact that is often overlooked. The sweeping changes associated with the New Deal occurred between 1934 and 1938, but it ended before it was able to make improvements in American life that might have eliminated the third of the nation described by Roosevelt as "ill-housed, ill-clad, ill-nourished."

Roosevelt's policies had no overall plan; they were efforts to patch up the glaring deficiencies in the economic system made evident by the Great Depression. The thrust of circumstances pushed Roosevelt to be

[1] On the other hand, during this period many states enacted legislation on workmen's compensation and minimum wages and maximum hours.

more radical in his programs than he had originally intended: natural market forces were not reviving the economy, and balanced budgets were unattainable if other objectives were to be met. Social legislation was necessary to win the support of discontented groups responsive to radical redistribution schemes, including the "share the wealth" platform of Senator Huey Long (political boss of Louisiana), Francis Townsend's proliferating old-age Townsend Clubs, and the ideas set forth in Father Coughlin's weekly radio talks, which had a vast audience.

Old-age insurance, unemployment benefits, minimum wages, the Wagner Act spurring management-union bargaining, increased governmental expenditures, and economic pump priming to stimulate the private economy resulted from such pressures. By 1938 the New Deal had died: Roosevelt was unable to win further support in Congress as the conservative strength of farm and small-town America reasserted itself in a long-enduring coalition of Southern Democrats and Midwestern Republicans. The failure of Roosevelt's 1938 "purge" of conservative congressmen left him without adequate support for new legislation, and the growing menace of war in Europe and the resulting domestic alignments became the focus of Roosevelt's attention.

The unions increasingly oriented themselves to the successes they could achieve for their members in collective bargaining and were less interested and less successful in achieving general gains through governmental legislation in the area of social welfare.

The promise of the New Deal ended early. It changed the American economy and society, but it did not produce the transformations many had originally hoped for. True, great and important steps were taken, but much was left untouched. The New Deal did not produce permanent solutions for such problems as unsteady employment for many and unemployment for others, the medical needs of a growing population, inequalities in income distribution, inadequate schooling for the low-income areas, poor housing, the haphazard growth of metropolitan areas, and limited social services.

The slow recovery of the 1930s was finally accelerated by the economic effects of World War II which pulled people into work, drained off young adults into the military, expanded industrial production and personal income, brought many Negroes and other neglected groups into the main economy, virtually eliminated unemployment, and compelled vast expansions of agricultural output. This vast wartime expansion combined with the New Deal measures to produce a social revolution, advancing the conditions of great numbers of people in probably the shortest time in history: it was the economic equivalent of a four-minute mile.

Prosperity continued after the war despite warnings of failure; there were recessions, but the gross national product continued to increase. The "Fair Deal" of Truman was only a slogan; a national coalition was unable to develop to force improvements in social legislation. The Eisenhower Administration was ideologically committed to reliance on the market economy as the vehicle for improving the conditions of all and to reducing the role of the federal government. During these years of the 1950s, complacency prevailed. Despite reports of the Joint Economic Committee of Congress on low-income families and on poverty, it was believed that not only was the economy expanding rapidly but that all were benefiting. Those still recognized as poor, that is, Appalachian whites, migratory laborers, were viewed as isolated groups who would be sucked gradually into the main economy and pulled up from poverty. The poor were written about as an encyclopedia of stigmatized and handicapped persons rather than as a stratum, or series of strata, omitted in the achievement of affluence.[2]

The Kennedy-Johnson years saw the rediscovery of poverty. The first major social legislation (Civil Rights Act, the Economic Opportunity Act, the Manpower Development and Training Act) in a quarter of a century was enacted. A spate of books [3] combined with hard economic and political facts overturned complacency.

Although it is difficult to understand fully the renewed interests in poverty, nine factors seem especially important.

1. The rates of unemployment had not dipped below 5 percent for more than half a dozen years. Hard-core unemployment was a continuing problem despite rising general employment and increasing gross national product. This was especially true for young, low-skilled, Negro, and poorly educated workers. The employment suction power of the wartime economy was no longer evident.

2. During the 1950s the economy in the United States did not expand as rapidly as it did in many other countries. Large military and space expenditures did not buoy up the economy. The possibilities of a détente between the United States and the Soviet Union increased the likelihood that military expenditures might be curbed. Under these conditions unemployment might grow if new employment activities were not undertaken.

3. The changing nature of the demand for labor (a "structural" issue, in labor market terminology) indicated that many persons (perhaps in increasing numbers) were unemployable with their present

[2] Donald Wilson, "The Ideology of the End," a paper written for a graduate sociology seminar on "Poverty and Inequality," Syracuse University, Spring 1964.
[3] For a discussion of these factors, see Frank Riessman and Arlene Hannah, "The Poverty Movement," *Columbia University Forum*, 6, 4 (Fall 1963).

skills. An increasing gross national product was not enough to solve unemployment problems because structural changes as well as insufficient growth generated strains. Compounding these difficulties, some believe, was the threat of labor unemployment caused by the potential for swift increases in productivity (loosely called automation).

4. As the population became more urbanized, poverty startled us by its visibility. Urban renewal programs, designed to offset urban decay, to restore a sounder tax base for the city, and to preserve downtown business interests, made the poor more visible by displacing them. Between 1950 and 1963, some 200 cities forced 100,000 individuals to move because of renewal projects. The problems of uprooting and of locating new homes for the poor, the deprived and the dependent, especially Negroes, increased awareness of the existence of these groups. The squalor of central-city slum life is more apparent than the despair in relatively inaccessible and politically quiescent mountain hollows. Increasing general concern for the state of education has highlighted inadequacies in improving the conditions and prospects of the poor.

5. The Negro revolution focused attention on the plight of the Negro poor. Attempts to do something about poverty among Negroes has led to concern about poverty generally.

6. The increasing concentration of Negroes in large cities, especially in the North, gives them greater political importance. Their vote in large industrial states can swing elections, as did the Negro vote in the Kennedy election of 1960. Fifty-five percent of Negroes continue to live in the South, but as the shift northward continues the potential political power of Negroes becomes more evident. The Supreme Court decisions for legislative reapportionment are likely to increase further the importance of the poor, since the underrepresentation of urban areas in legislatures will be reduced. The urban, low-income vote is growing in importance.

7. The aggressive campaign of John Kennedy against Hubert Humphrey in the 1960 presidential primaries in West Virginia highlighted the poverty and bleak future of that state and of the region called Appalachia. President Kennedy committed himself to aid areas unable to overcome the cutback in the demand for coal mine and farm labor resulting from technological advances and the competition of high-productivity farms. Kennedy's concern led to increased attention (though few programs) to deal with the problems of Appalachia. The migration of many from Appalachia to large cities where they often had employment and housing difficulties underlined the importance of regional dislocations and poverty.

Although the loss of economic base and the absence of economic opportunity for men were not limited to Appalachia (nor did all of Appalachia suffer economically), the concern about Appalachia highlighted the existence of rural poverty and the ineffectiveness of the market place for improving the future of this area and other economic backwaters.

8. The *apparent* growth in rates of juvenile delinquency and crime, illegitimate births, and other indicators of what has been termed "social disorganization" focused attention on the social costs of poverty.[4] The ineffectiveness of punitive institutions such as reform schools in reducing recidivism has led to increased attention to prevention. Although the concern with prevention has led to some emphasis on the intrapsychic origins of delinquency, the reported extent of delinquency in some low-income areas has forced increasing analysis of social and economic forces that might be factors in causing delinquency. Social analysis has been threaded with the themes of alienation, anomie, and the culture of poverty, while economic analysis has stressed blockage of opportunity and the toll of inadequate incomes.[5] The growth of the youth population has accentuated such concerns. In the 1960s, 27 million persons will reach adulthood and one of three is likely not to have finished high school.

9. A number of monographs and books on poverty focused attention on the extent and the burden of poverty. We no longer assumed that poverty was "gracefully succumbing" to the pull of the affluent society and that the effects of economic growth would fairly and equitably filter down to benefit all income groups in society. From seeing the poor as a series of small, isolated groups, each produced by

[4] To a large extent, changes in these rates are social artifacts of community practices of measurement. A repressive attack on all signs of "juvenile indecency" increases the rate of delinquency with no change in the frequency of overt actions; they are now differently evaluated. Similarly, social class differences in rates cannot be taken at face value. For example, a thorough study in a California county of pregnancies conceived out of wedlock concludes that, contrary to common belief, the low-income population does not have a higher rate than does the higher-income population. Based on Clark Vincent, *Unmarried Mothers* (New York: The Free Press of Glencoe, 1961). But the facts may be less significant than the *belief* in a swift incline in rates of "wrongdoing" in a particular population.

In a careful study of self-reported delinquencies, Hardt shows that class differences in delinquency rates are greatly affected by differential treatment by police. Robert Hardt, "Delinquency and Social Class: Studies of Juvenile Deviation or Police Dispositions?," Syracuse University Youth Development Center (mimeographed), December 1964.

[5] The social and economic analyses have been brought together in Albert K. Cohen, *Delinquent Boys* (Glencoe, Ill.: The Free Press, 1955) and in Richard A. Cloward and Lloyd E. Ohlin, *Delinquency and Opportunity* (Glencoe, Ill.: The Free Press, 1960).

special or unique factors, we have come to regard poverty as more intimately related to affluence.[6]

Before we can address ourselves to the question of the policies that are needed, we must travel a long route through the analysis of the concepts of poverty and inequality, the characteristics of the poor—and related subjects. To leap to policy before we have analyzed the contours of change would lead to temporary solutions for what are turning out to be long-term problems. We would also fail to understand the society which creates and maintains poverty—the study of poverty opens doors to knowledge about many important aspects of our society.

The Concept of Income

Income has a dollar and cents sign on it. Variation in one's income over time seems a simple matter to compute, but actually this calculation is a complicated process when we recognize the important changes that have occurred in our economy. If we wish to have a satisfactory view of our command over resources (which is the significance of income), we must attend to a variety of influences. Price level changes affect the purchasing power of each dollar of income; modifications in the level and structure of taxes reduce or expand what is available for personal expenditure; changes in social policy as well as taxation affect how many goods and services are publicly provided rather than individually purchased. Increasingly, nondirect payments are part of our economic well-being and should be added to dollar income. The outlays of an employer on pension benefits, which are a form of deferred income until retirement, or health insurance, which is a form of income in kind, are important. Indeed, in collective bargaining, the role of so-called fringe benefits is clear, since increases in these benefits are often obtained by reducing the size of the direct money increase in wage rates. Fringe benefits have grown enormously. Higher-income groups are receiving greater advantages than the lower-income groups.

[6] Galbraith's earlier discussion of poverty surprisingly emphasized the special character of poverty, not tying it up with "the affluent society" (a term that he coined). He divided poverty into two types, case and insular. The latter referred to those reluctant to leave areas without an industrial base. Case poverty referred to the aged and fatherless families, the mentally and physically handicapped, the poorly educated. His use of a very low standard ($1000 family income) to define the poverty line plus his mode of classification of the poor into residual groups of society tended to downgrade the extent and importance of poverty. John Kenneth Galbraith, *The Affluent Society* (Boston: Houghton Mifflin, 1958). It was not until the mid-1960s that affluence and poverty were recognized as connected.

Although we can put a dollar figure on such job-related benefits as a medical insurance program, an expense account, or even a company-supported country club similar to IBM's, other items are more difficult to assess. For example, what are the differential values of two jobs providing the same income if one offers more long-term security in employment than the other? The provision of security is important but difficult to measure.

If we look at income, then, not only as the direct dollar income available to individuals but also as general command over resources, we have problems of assessment, but our approach is directly related to how individuals fare. Monetary income provides an increasingly inadequate indication of the position of an individual or family. Although simple and often used as an indicator of economic position, it provides only a partial report.[7]

Because of the changes in the manner in which resources are distributed, we need a fuller view of the production of income. Titmuss[8] provides this in his three-part delineation of the sources of income: (1) *occupational benefits*, including not only pay but all job-related benefits such as pensions,[9] company-provided and financed medical protection,[10]

---

[7] The measurement of pure monetary income alone is extraordinarily difficult and can be misleading. Income is often underreported; illegal income, which may be 10 percent of legal gross national product, is ignored; intrafamily transfers of income (e.g., from parents to a newlywed couple) are unestimated; wealth (accumulated assets) is frequently a transfer of income into a new form. In a specific family income during any given year may be atypical because of fluctuations in income. We are indebted to William G. Grigsby for focusing our attention on these and other deficiencies in income measurements.

[8] Richard Titmuss is the leading international social welfare expert; see his seminal essay, "The Social Division of Welfare," in his *Essays on "The Welfare State"* (New Haven, Conn.: Yale University Press, 1958). We have been heavily influenced by the work of Titmuss and his colleagues at the London School of Economics. Their framework provides a more effective point of view than is generally employed in analyzing the distribution of the resources in society. We shall use it in our later discussions, for the Titmuss variables permit viewing the new forms of stratification and cleavage in the affluent society.

Titmuss has attempted to marshal the British data on protected assets and to estimate their influence on income. Richard Titmuss, *Income Distribution and Social Change* (London: Allen and Unwin, 1962).

[9] New York City policemen, who can retire with a substantial pension after 20 years of work by paying a substantial annual pension contribution handsomely matched by the city government, may have a low weekly take-home pay. They are, in effect, shifting part of their potential income to later years (in order to lower tax rates). To assess their economic position, such shifting of income would have to be analyzed.

[10] Macaulay reports that fringe benefits of all types accounted for approximately 15 percent of payroll costs in 1949 and 24 percent in 1957. In examining the impact of some of the fringe benefits on consumption patterns, he offers the startling

nontaxed expense accounts; (2) *fiscal (or tax) benefits*, referring to the differential impact of tax regulations on various types of income groups [11] and (3) *welfare benefits*, the direct distribution of public and private funds in different categories, for example, welfare allotments, veterans' benefits.

To use any scheme to estimate a family's command over resources requires attention to their assets. The effort to reduce taxes on current income has led to practices that attempt to translate (potential) income into assets, for special tax benefits. Corporate profits are less often distributed in the form of current dividends than in the 1920s. Delayed stock dividends are a common form of tax reduction. Gabriel Kolko estimates that retained corporate income is about $20 billion a year. This accumulation increases the capital value of shares held. If this wealth were distributed and taxed as personal income, upper-income groups would have much greater manifest incomes and higher income taxes.

Our problems of analysis are compounded when we aggregate individual income to obtain the national income. Our national income accounting scheme is not always seen realistically, for the concept of national income is actually a series of compromises to facilitate statistical computations. For example, if a bachelor or widower employs a housekeeper and pays her $200 a month, that is part of the national income. If he marries her and continues to give her the $200 as a personal allowance while she performs her customary household duties, gross national product and disposal income have been reduced by $200. Another example is tax manipulation of the rate of amortization of a new plant. A faster rate of amortization reduces what is defined as taxable or profits, increases the cash reserves and swells the value of stock held by an individual. This increase in assets does not immediately show up as income either for tax purposes or in computation of national income, though it has certainly improved a firm's command over resources.

---

estimate that "in large cities like New York, Chicago, and Washington, at any moment over one-half the people in the best hotels, night clubs, and restaurants are paying for the services they receive via the expense account." Hugh H. Macaulay, *Fringe Benefits and Their Federal Tax Treatment* (New York: Columbia University Press, 1959), pp. 8–11, 58. The strong response of elite restaurants to more stringent regulation and limitation of expense accounts by the Internal Revenue Service in 1962 revealed the dependence of these restaurants on customers whose expenditures are subsidized by special tax privileges.

[11] A multitude of devices reduce or eliminate the taxes of individuals and families who are able to utilize them. A lively account of the inequities of tax practices is found in Philip Stern, *The Great Treasury Raid* (New York: Random House, 1963).

The Definition of Poverty

An adequate definition of the economic condition of a family should include (1) current income, including covert as well as manifest forms of income; (2) assets, especially the accumulation of retirement benefits and deferred income claims; and (3) access to public and private services, the quantity and quality of schools, medical services, recreational areas, and the like that are available. This definition, developed by Bertram Gross and S. M. Miller, cannot as yet be made operational. Consequently, we shall have to rely on monetary income data. Even with this limited perspective, the concept of poverty is elusive.

If by poverty we mean subsistence, poverty does not appear too difficult to specify. Subsistence refers to what is necessary to maintain life in a given place at a given time. But when we examine "subsistence," we find that it is not sharply refined: For example, what is the food input needed to sustain life? In Britain it takes 50 percent more calories to provide basic maintenance than in India (at least that is what the British nutritional experts seem to be saying when their statement about nutritional needs in Britain are compared with the estimates for India made by Indian nutritional experts).[12]

We see another illustration of the difficulty in determining a "subsistence level" in the World War II estimate that less than a hundred dollars were required to purchase an adequate diet for one family for the *entire* year. This low sum resulted from estimating the number of calories needed for survival and then pricing the cheapest bulk basket of goods—for example, wheat, potatoes, and such—that would provide these calories. Following this logic, and allowing for price changes since 1944, less than $200 a year would cover the food needs of a family today.

A third difficulty of specifying poverty is the goods owned by those defined as living in poverty in the United States. Of husband-wife primary families living below the poverty level, 57.6 percent have a telephone, 79.2 percent own a television set, and 72.6 percent possess a washing machine.[13] Certainly, these consumption goods set off the

---

[12] Peter Townsend, "The Meaning of Poverty," *British Journal of Sociology*, 13, 3 (September 1962), pp. 210–227.

[13] These data are presented in the *U.S. Census of Population,* 1960, PC(2)–4A, "Families," Table 43. The figures are reproduced in Committee on Education and Labor, House of Representatives, "Poverty in the United States," 88th Congress, 2nd Session, April 1964, p. 287. We feel compelled to add that observations of low-income homes in large cities lead us to believe that at least the washing machine percentage is overstated. The restriction to husband-wife families may

poor of America from those of other nations. But we should guard against overestimating the importance of these impressive materialistic gains; poor education and medical care cannot be balanced by old washing machines and used cars.

Obviously, there is no universal definition of poverty. It is relative to time and place. Those labeled poor today would certainly not be poor by the standards of 1870. To say "relative to time and place" implies that what we define as poverty is related to the conditions and possibilities of the society: the poverty line is "determined by prevailing standards of what is needed for health, efficiency, nurture of children, social participation, and the maintenance of self-respect and the respect of others." [14] As a society changes in the quantity and kind of production and in the "prevailing standards" of life, the definition of poverty changes.

This point is not novel: our practices in estimating the costs of minimum budgets reflect the changing conditions of life. "Postwar costs of 'modest but adequate' budgets for self-supporting families, roughly deflated for price change, range from about 30 to 60 per cent higher than the 'minimum comfort' budgets of the early 20's." [15] This statement means that between the 1920s and the post-World War II period, our nominally acceptable basic standard of living, as measured by governmental agencies, increased by at least 30 percent and possibly by more than a half, depending on which estimates are used. Though we are not always clear about this point today, a century ago it was recognized that "as a society advances, the standard of poverty rises." [16]

To be impoverished implies that a family is falling behind other families in access to the resources of society: "People are poverty stricken when their income, even if adequate for survival, falls markedly behind that of the community . . . they are degraded, for in the literal sense they live outside the grades or categories which the community regards as acceptable." [17]

Viewing poverty as a relative concept rather than as an absolute one leads to confusion about inequality. The absolute concept refers to the comparative distribution of the overall resources of society. In our usage growing inequality means that the bottom 20 percent of

---

inflate the possession of these items among the poor. Nonetheless, the percentages are staggeringly high.

[14] U.S. Bureau of Labor Statistics, *Workers' Budgets in the United States*, Bulletin 927, p. 6.

[15] Helen H. Lamale, "Changes in Concepts of Income Inadequacy over the Last Century," *American Economic Review*, 78 (May 1958), p. 297.

[16] This statement by Theodore Parker is quoted in the Lamale article.

[17] Galbraith, *op. cit.*

income recipients receive a smaller *percentage* of the economic pie in one year than they receive in another. If the number of poor families increases as the poverty line moves up with improving standards of living in society, we cannot speak of increasing inequality. In this situation we are dealing with a growth in the number who are relatively poor, not necessarily in the aggregate income position of the poor relative to better-off groups in society.[18] It is important to keep distinct the differences between poverty as the inability to obtain a specific level of living and inequality as the relative sharing of the economic and social output. The two can be moving in different directions. For example, fewer people may be living in poverty, but they may also receive less of the society's output than a similar number of people did in former years. We believe that the importance of inequality has been neglected in the recent concentration on poverty, and we shall return to this issue later.

The Scope of Poverty

Until we develop more adequate measures of the economic or material conditions of a family, we shall have to rely on income data. How many people are poor depends on what level of income is used as the poverty line and how income is measured. This is both a technical and a value question. The current mélange of estimates has led to a "numbers game" in which everyone can pick the estimate that substantiates his convictions. We devote considerable space to the problems of estimation because they are fundamentally public policy issues, even though technical questions are involved.

The main technical problems are the sources and methods for collection of income data, the consumer unit for which income is ascertained, and variations in need as affected by geographic differences in the cost of living.

Ideas about what constitutes income vary. The calculations of the U.S. Bureau of the Census cover all money income except capital gains. Nonmoney income (in-kind benefits), which may be an important item among poor farm families, is excluded. The Office of Business Economics of the U.S. Department of Commerce includes money income and many forms of income-in-kind. But its exclusion of expense accounts, undistributed profits, and unreported income are especially important in estimating the extent of inequality in income distribution. On the other hand, unreported income may be significant for some

---

[18] Inequalities are not restricted to the distribution of income but occur in the distribution of wealth, services, education, health, and social status.

poor families. The studies of the Survey Research Center of the University of Michigan covered money income alone.

Census data, the most frequently used source, may account for only 75 to 80 percent of all income, according to an estimate made by Selma Goldsmith. Consequently, the use of Census data may lead to an overstatement of the scope of poverty to the extent that underreporting occurs among lower-income units.[19]

The definition and extent of poverty are also affected by the consumer units for which income is estimated. These consumer units include (1) individuals living alone; (2) a husband and wife without children; (3) a husband and wife with a varying number of children; (4) a diversity of other family types, including individuals related to and living with nuclear families (such as a parent living with a married son or daughter). Although we conventionally think in terms of a family with both father and mother present in one living unit with two children under the age of eighteen, the majority of American families do not have all these characteristics.

Obviously, a family's income needs depend on its size and composition. Thus families with four or more children can be poor even if their income is substantial by frequently used poverty line standards. Similarly, for smaller families, changes over the life cycle may affect needed incomes—aged couples may require less income than young couples without children. Consequently, the use of any single income unit will be inadequate, overstating the extent of poverty among units with few individuals and understating the extent of poverty among large units. Unfortunately, much of the public discussion of poverty centers around a single poverty line for all types of families.

Although some variations in the cost of living from one region or community to another reflect differences in the standards of living and the quality of housing, others result from real differences in costs. For example, rural Southerners undoubtedly require less income to match the living level of a family resident in the high-priced San Francisco Bay area; on the other hand, the advantages of climate and view cannot be held constant between the two localities. The importance of price differences among localities in the estimation of income needs is revealed by the finding that there is a 20 percent differential in the cost of living in the most and least expensive of the twenty largest cities in

[19] Gabriel Kolko, *Wealth and Power in America: An Analysis of Social Class and Income Distribution* (New York: Frederick A. Praeger, 1962), pp. 11–13. Assets are used to define well-being in one set of estimates. The study by Morgan and associates does not classify as poor any family unit with assets of more than $5000. The aged are affected by this provision since they are the group most likely to have low incomes and over $5000 in assets. James N. Morgan et al., *Income and Welfare in the United States* (New York: McGraw-Hill, 1962), pp. 188–189.

POVERTY, INEQUALITY, AND POLICY

the United States. The absence of adjustments for cost of living variations leads to overestimates of poverty in low-price areas like the South and other rural sections and to underestimates of poverty in large urban areas, especially outside the South. These needed adjustments are not made in most poverty estimates.

Turning now to the value side—our attitudes and commitments affect the level at which the poverty line is pegged. Do we want to define as poor those living at or below a near-starvation, merest "subsistence" level? Or, at the other extreme, are the poor those who do not receive what is now conceived of as the income necessary for a modest health and comfort standard? Or is our choice somewhere in between? Obviously, the total number of poor will differ depending on what income level is used as the cutting-off point to differentiate poor from nonpoor.

Galbraith resorted to a conservative definition of poverty, using $1000 cash income as the dividing line. At this level only 10 percent of the population in the United States were found to be living in poverty, a conclusion supporting the complacent notion of the 1950s that poverty was rapidly disappearing.[20] This is a level below the welfare allotments of even the poorest states.

Herman Miller contends that poverty is not a line but a band, the lower limits of which are defined by the income level below which a family or person is eligible to receive public assistance. This yardstick obviously varies with community standards and definitions.[21] The average welfare cost standard for basic needs in Arkansas for a family of four receiving aid under the AFDC program is $1326, annually. Actual allotments are lower; over 25 percent of the AFDC families in Arkansas had total incomes that were below the requirements. In the state of Washington the average cost standard is $2213, the highest of all states.[22] Using these standards, Herman Miller concludes that about

---

[20] Galbraith, *op. cit.* Galbraith's book deepened the awareness of the changes in our economy and gave a title to the society. It ushered in a new level of analysis which led to the reappraisal of poverty, even though Galbraith himself underestimated the scope and persistence of the problem. His ambiguous position is further revealed in his sociologically sophisticated definition of the poor as those falling behind the rest of society, contrasted with his utilization of an income line lower than that of any other economist in defining the poor!

[21] Herman P. Miller, "A Minimum Estimate of Poverty in the United States" (mimeograph).

[22] The only available figures for the estimate of welfare standards were for the Aid to Families and Dependent Children, the main welfare assistance source. Miller recognizes the limitations of this measure. He observes that the use of this standard "represents an understatement of need for the general population, for families of a given size not receiving AFDC are likely to include a husband and wife, whereas the AFDC families are typically mother and child groups." *Charac-*

17 percent of all units (that is, families and unrelated individuals), 13 percent of all wage-earning persons, and 10 percent of *all* families had substandard incomes in 1959.

In New York the Community Service Society, a voluntary family agency, estimated that in 1957 a family of four required $4330 to maintain itself without need for public assistance or free medical care. The Survey Research Center of the University of Michigan, in its important national study, defined families with nine-tenths or less of this level, adjusted for family characteristics, as possessing "inadequate incomes." By this measure 20 percent of families and 28 percent of adult spending units were living in poverty in 1960.[23]

Robert Lampman set the poverty line at $2500 income for a family of four. He concluded that 19 per cent were living in poverty in 1957.[24]

Leon Keyserling, in an influential report, used $4000 family income, unadjusted for family characteristics, as the poverty line and estimated that 23 percent of American families were living in poverty in 1960.[25] He concluded that a family income between $4000 and $6000, unadjusted for family characteristics, did not constitute poverty but neither was it full participation in the economy. He regarded this group as living in "deprivation" and concluded that 23 percent of all families were living in this condition. Altogether, he estimated that almost 46 percent of all American families were living in poverty or deprivation in 1960.

Ornati has attempted to clarify the value issue by making clear the varying standards that can be applied. "The minimum subsistence level" for a family of four is $2500 per year; "minimum adequacy" is $3500 and "minimum comfort" is $5500. In 1963, 10 percent of families in the United States were below the minimum subsistence line, 25 percent were below minimum adequacy, and 38 percent were below minimum comfort.[26]

President Johnson's Council of Economic Advisors in the 1964 *Eco-*

---

teristics of Families Receiving Aid to Families with Dependent Children, Bureau of Public Assistance, Report 42 and Preliminary Report, issued April 1963. Requirements in 1958 and 1961 were averaged to produce an estimate for 1959.

[23] Morgan et al., *op. cit.*, Chapter 16.

[24] Robert J. Lampman, *The Low-Income Population and Economic Growth*, U.S. Congress, Joint Economics Committee, Study Paper 12, 86th Congress, 1st Session, December 1959.

[25] Conference on Economic Progress, *Poverty and Deprivation in the United States*, 1961, pp. 19 ff. This document is known as the "Keyserling Report," since the chief author was Leon Keyserling.

[26] Oscar Ornati, "Poverty in America," National Policy Committee on Pockets of Poverty, March 1964. The fuller study, directed by Professor Ornati for The Twentieth Century Fund, is entitled *Poverty in an Affluent Society* (forthcoming).

nomic Report of the President straddled the issue by fixing the poverty line at $3000 family cash income. They justify the use of a $3000 standard by assuming that setting the poverty line higher or lower would affect only the size and not the character of the problem. The report states, "But the analysis of the sources of poverty and the programs needed to cope with it would remain substantially unchanged." We do not agree with this assumption. Thus we find that income levels of $1000, $2500, $3000, $3500, $4000, and $5500 have been used to demarcate the poor.[27] Clearly, the definition of poverty reflects one's view of needs and one's expectations of possibilities.

The Council's $3000 income level has become the official poverty line.[28] Our feeling is that this line is too low and too rigid. We prefer the more flexible analysis of Morgan and his associates which starts with a higher estimate for a family of four and adjusts the estimate for certain family characteristics. The Social Security Administration makes more adjustments for special characteristics, but the estimates are pegged at low levels.[29] The important things to recognize are that poverty is constituted by variable income positions and that poverty no longer refers merely to the inability to survive physically.

But it is the Council's $3000 figure that has been involved in the estimates of the needed scope of the "war on poverty." Therefore it deserves careful attention. Of the 47 million families in the United States in 1962, 9.3 million, or one-fifth, had total money incomes below the $3000 level. Thirty million Americans lived in these poor families; eleven million were children, one-sixth of all our youth. Serious poverty also existed among persons living alone or in nonfamily units such as boarding houses. Forty-five percent of these "unrelated individuals," five million persons in all, had incomes below $1500, the Council's poverty line for unattached persons. Thus 35 million Americans were "living at or below the boundaries of poverty in 1962—nearly one-fifth of our nation."

These calculations may appear high. A more conservative estimate,

---

[27] Most of these estimates focus only on families, not on single individuals who make up about 10 percent of the poor.

[28] An alternate procedure for setting the poverty line is to use a fixed proportion, perhaps 50 percent of prevailing wages or median income in the community. In this way the poverty line would move with income changes in the community.

[29] Mollie Orshansky, "Counting the Poor: Another Look at the Poverty Profile," *Social Security Bulletin*, 28, 1 (January 1965), pp. 3–29. This article is exceedingly important, for it shows that using poverty lines adjusted for family size and other variables leads to different characteristics of the poor than using a single poverty line. In Orshansky's analysis Negroes and urban dwellers are more significant among the poor than they appear to be in simple poverty analyses.

which few would think too high, would use $2000 as the poverty level for families, the $3000 level for large families, and the $1000 level for single individuals. On this basis 5,400,000 families, containing more than seventeen million individuals, were poor or, by our estimate, extremely poor. Another half-million families with four or more children, containing perhaps 2.7 million persons, had incomes between $2000 and $3000. Twenty-nine percent of all "unrelated individuals," three million persons, had incomes of less than $1000. Totaling these three groups gives an estimate of almost 27 million individuals, or about one of seven Americans, living in extreme poverty in 1960.[30]

A surprising aspect of these various ways of estimating the number of poor is the limited variation among them, despite large differences in the level of the poverty line. This convergence is due to the offsetting of the different biases in the estimates. For example, an estimate based on, say, $2000 and restricted to cash income reports low urban poverty and high rural poverty; a higher poverty line on a full income basis reduces the number of rural poor and increases the size of the urban poor. Although the various estimates lead to some disagreement on the number of poor, the greater disagreement is in regard to the characteristics of the poor. (We shall discuss this later.)

The Distribution of Income

We can better appreciate the significance of the poverty line when we study the overall distribution of income. College students, as well as many others, are often unaware of the relatively high income of their families. Herman Miller has described the situation in the title of one of his chapters, "Who, Me? In the Top Income Groups?" in his *Rich Man, Poor Man*.

Table 1 shows that slightly more than a quarter of American families received above $8000 annual income in 1959. One of 25 families had an income above $15,000, and a $25,000 income put a family in the upper one percent of income recipients in the United States. On the other

[30] The information in this and the preceding four pargraphs refers to Chapter 2, "The Problem of Poverty in America," of the *Economic Report of the President*, which includes the Annual Report of the Council of Economic Advisors. This chapter is reproduced with other valuable material in "Poverty in the United States," Committee on Education and Labor, House of Representatives, 88th Congress, 2nd Session, April 1964. The estimate of large families in the $2000–$3000 bracket is computed from Herman P. Miller, *Trends in the Income of Families and Persons in the United States: 1947 to 1960*, Technical Paper No. 8, U.S. Bureau of the Census, 1963, p. 114. Three million children live in families with four or more children and less than $2000 income.

hand, more than one of ten families had an income of $40 a week or less.

Although a high percentage of our population compared to other societies is doing very well indeed, we still have great contrasts in access to the products of our society.

The Hurt of Poverty

A recent flood of books and magazine articles has eloquently etched what it means to live below the poverty line in America. Appalachian whites, Southern rural whites and Negro tenant farmers, Negroes of

Table 1 Families by Income Levels in 1959

Income Level	Number of Families	Percent
All families	45 million	100
Under $2000	6 million	13
Between $2000 and $4000	8 million	18
Between $4000 and $6000	11 million	23
Between $6000 and $8000	9 million	19
Between $8000 and $10,000	5 million	12
Between $10,000 and $15,000	5 million	11
Between $15,000 and $25,000	1.5 million	3
$25,000 and over	.5 million	1
Median income		$5660

SOURCE: U.S. Bureau of the Census, *How Our Income Is Divided*, Graphic Pamphlet 2, 1963.

the Northern large-city slums, migratory workers and the aged Indians on reservations—the once invisible poor who make up "the other America"—do not live lives of genteel poverty, merely missing some of the comforting benefits of the affluent society. They frequently live in great misery.

John Davenport reports of life in Appalachia:

> All that remains of the Famous Blue Grass mine, right across the Kentucky River from Hazard, is a dark hole in the hill's face and a smashed and rusting tipple. Below the mine the Blue Grass mining camp still stands —thirty or more houses in various stages of dilapidation laid out with specious precision on deeply mudded streets. Mining families still live here, some on pensions, and some finding other work. Others have been less fortunate. In the vicinity of Hazard (Kentucky) a small shack clings

to the side of the mountain supported on one side by long stiltlike poles, with an errant mountain stream nearby. The boards on the front porch are rotting, and the glass of one window is broken and papered over. An extraordinarily fine-looking woman opens the door, and ushers the visitor into a bedraggled room with an open coal stove. At one side is a tumbled bed with two children lying on it. There are four more children at school; an older son and daughter have moved away. The father, an unemployed miner, is seeking work "somewhere in Ohio" and can contribute little to the family. How does the woman live? "I get surplus food when they pass it out—flour, corn meal, and the like. I don't eat much myself, sometimes buy a little for the children." She plants a garden in the summer months. She belongs to the Holiness Church, and the meetings mean a great deal to her. "I don't expect to be around too long," she says. "You've got to be ready to go." And again, brooding, "Life ought to be forward—a widening out." Her voice trails off. The door opens and closes, and one is outside again in the harsh snow-banked valley.[31]

In Columbus, Ohio, welfare allotments were cut below state minimums in 1962. "Children sickened from malnutrition; mothers went to pieces and had nervous breakdowns; children were kept from school because their parents had no breakfast or lunch to feed them and would not send them out hungry to school." A mother described those bitter months of 1962:

> When relief went to 40 per cent, we just went down. Our rent was $50 and our checks came to $56. We had $6.00 left for food and utilities after we paid the rent. We paid it, because even to be sick or starve, you need a place to do it in. But the gas and electricity was shut off. I didn't have lights for seven months. Gas wasn't off so long. But when the gas went, I began to cook with coal oil. That was horrible. The fumes almost knocked my eyes out. I couldn't breathe. Then I began not to see. I thought I was blind—but later the clinic said it was the coal oil and nerves. We sat in the back room; shut the rest of the house off and tried to heat just one room. We were in the dark—just coal oil fumes and no light; we ate stuff people give us and commodities. It was a horrible time. When we got our lights turned back on, it was queer. I didn't think the winter would ever end or that we would make it.[32]

The plight of the American Indian is revealed by medical statistics:

[31] John Davenport, "In the Midst of Plenty," *Fortune*, 63 (March 1961), p. 108.
[32] *Settlement News*, South Side Settlement, Columbus, Ohio, II, May 1963; reported in Charles N. Lebeaux, "Life on ADC in Detroit, 1963," *Newsletter*, Metropolitan Detroit Chapter, National Association of Social Workers (10801 Curtis, Detroit 21, Michigan). The Lebeaux study is a very useful compendium of information on the aid-to-dependent-children program at the community level.

The Indian infant death rate declined 36 per cent to 41.8 deaths per 1,000 live births (between 1954 and 1962), but is still 70 per cent higher than the rate for infants in the population as a whole. The death rate among Indian infants 28 days through 11 months of age was 3.8 times the rate for all races.... With virtually all Indian babies now being delivered in hospitals, mortality rates of babies under 1 week of age is actually slightly lower than in the general population. However, this situation is reversed—and sharply—in the subsequent weeks and months of life as the infant is removed from the sanitary conditions of the hospital to the rigorous conditions of his hogan home.[33]

Who Are the Poor?

In the nineteenth century, discussions of the poor chiefly concerned those who were employed but lived under the most dire circumstances. Inadequate wages caused poverty. In the 1930s the discussion of the poor fundamentally concerned the unemployed; large numbers of urban and rural people had no economic support in a society with meager welfare arrangements. Today, the poor are more clearly a mixed group, and it is important to delineate the diversity of the poor if we wish to have effective policies to reduce poverty.

The level at which the poverty line is pegged affects the characteristics of the poor. In general, the lower the poverty line, the more the poor differ from the overall population. This is why Galbraith, with his $1000 poverty line, emphasized the very special nature of the poor. Keyserling, with a $4000 line, has another poor in mind and consequently stresses the general economic forces which impede the eradication of poverty.

The characteristics of the poor can be analyzed in two ways. The failure to recognize these two perspectives has led to much confusion about who are the poor. One way of cutting the data is to study the *incidence* or frequency of poverty—what percentage of persons in a particular category, such as female-headed households, is poor. The second way is to concentrate on the *composition* of poverty—what percentage of all the poor is in a given category. It is possible for a high percentage of female-headed households to be poor (incidence) but to contribute a much lower percentage of all the poor (composition).

In the following analysis of the poor, we attempt to isolate both incidence and compositional effects and to see the importance of various categories at different income levels. The categories we chose to study

[33] "Indian Poverty and Indian Health," in *Poverty and Deprivation in the United States, op. cit.*, p. 113.

are size of community, geographical region, age of household head, race, sex of household head, and labor force status.

Some have taken these characteristics of the poor to represent the causes of poverty, which is an inadequate approach to causation, for it looks at poverty mainly in terms of individual deficiency.[34] Nevertheless, the examination of characteristics does give us a view of who bears the burden of poverty and what course remedial policy should take.

Size of Community [35]

According to an unpublished analysis for 1963 by the Census Bureau for the President's Task Force on the War on Poverty, 70 percent of poverty in America was in rural areas and small cities with populations under 50,000. Only 2.8 million families, or 30 percent of all poor families, were concentrated in large cities. The twelve largest cities in the United States furnished only 11 percent of all poor families.[36] These findings may appear striking to those who have assumed that poverty is largely caused by "the microbes of metropolitan social disorganization," or to those who have recognized the curious inattention to poverty outside of large urbanized areas in the Economic Opportunity Act of 1964.

Even when we look at all urban poverty, not just the large-city poor, we are impressed with the relative importance of rural farm and nonfarm conditions.[37] In 1959, 50 percent of poor families lived in any

---

[34] Leon H. Keyserling, *Progress or Poverty*, Washington Conference on Economic Progress, December 1964, pp. 36–37. We have omitted discussion of the educational characteristics of the poor—frequently cited to show that lack of education induces poverty—because the absence of an age breakdown of educational achievements leads to peculiar results since so many of the poor are elderly and therefore not well educated by present standards.

[35] In this section all references to poverty, unless otherwise stated, involve the $3000 poverty line set by the Council of Economic Advisors using Census data. The analysis is of poor families only, ignoring the unattached individuals who live in poverty. The data are from Herman P. Miller, *Trends in the Income of Families and Persons in the United States: 1947 to 1960, op. cit.* We are indebted to Betty Saleem for the recalculations of these data. Herrington J. Bryce reworked the Keyserling data for us. Generally, the data refer to 1960 and, for comparison, 1947. When figures for 1960 were unavailable, 1959 data were used as indicated. Miller's data were given in constant dollars, using 1959 as the base year; thus changes in cost of living are controlled to some degree.

[36] Morgan et al., *op. cit.*, p. 214

[37] "Urban" refers to a community of 2500 persons or more; thus it includes a wide range of communities. In 1959, 61.3 percent of all families lived in one type or another of urban communities. Rural nonfarm areas—settlements of under 2500—contained 30.3 percent of all families and rural farm areas held 8.4 percent of all families.

kind of urban area, 30 percent in rural nonfarm areas, and 20 percent in farm areas. The importance of the urban and rural nonfarm poor has been growing; they furnished 46 percent and 24 percent of the poor, respectively, in 1947. Rural farm poverty is contributing less than the 30 percent that it was in 1947. On the other hand, the lower the poverty line—$2000 or $1000—the greater the contribution of nonurban areas to poverty.

The incidence figures show the high risk of poverty in farm areas: over half (52.6 percent) of all farm families were below the $3000 poverty line in 1960, compared with a fifth (21.8 percent) of rural nonfarm families and less than a fifth (18.2 percent) of urban families. Our estimate, based on Morgan, is that the incidence of poverty in the twelve largest cities was about 12 percent.

As we lower the poverty line to $2000 and $1000 family income, the economic disadvantage of farm inhabitants grows. Although the proportion of those in poverty is three times that of urban residents at the $3000 level, at the $1000 level the risk grows to six times that of the urbanites (18 percent of farm families and 3.1 percent of urban families).[38] Extreme poverty is much more common among our farm population: "Over a million (farm) families must somehow stretch $80 a month to cover their needs. . . . Nearly half a million of these rural youths between the ages of 14 and 24 have completed no more than the sixth grade. Their horizons stop at the edge of a few acres of exhausted land." [39]

Obviously, leaving a farm area improves one's chances of staying out of or of emerging from poverty. This situation continues to be true, for the prospects of farm areas have not improved markedly in almost a decade and a half. Between 1947 and 1960, the incidence rate dropped in all three areas, but rural areas had the lowest reduction—from 57.1 percent in 1947 to 52.6 percent in 1960. Rural nonfarm localities had the biggest drop in incidence—from 37.2 percent to 21.8 percent—and urban communities reduced their risk of falling into poverty from 25.8 percent to 18.2 percent.

It is rather surprising that we know little about the characteristics of the urban poor and that little of the knowledge we have appears to

[38] The concept of "risk of poverty" is discussed in Ornati, *op. cit.* If one out of three persons in group A lives in poverty and one out of six persons in group B lives in poverty, persons in group A have twice the "poverty risk" of persons in group B.
[39] *The War on Poverty, A Congressional Presentation*, March 17, 1964, pp. 5–6. This document was organized by The President's Task Force on the War on Poverty which developed the legislation which became the Economic Opportunity Act of 1964.

affect social policy. Some poverty-linked characteristics widely associated with urban life may actually be more important in the rural setting. For example, in 1960 the incidence of poverty among female heads of households was less than 50 percent in urban areas but approximately 70 percent in rural farm settings.

Urban and rural poverty intersect because of the rural exodus to large cities. "There is a growing legion of unskilled, uneducated workers who come to the city in search of something they may not find: better opportunities. Often they find they have accomplished nothing but a relocation of their poverty." [40]

If the preceding analysis is accurate in pinpointing three-quarters of American poverty as existing outside of large urbanized areas of 50,000 population or more, and much urban poverty is produced in rural areas, then we may need to re-examine present priorities in our programs of intervention to reduce poverty. Current solutions in the forms of a Job Corps and work training, stressing the importance of inculcating proper work habits, may be inappropriate. Regional programs, such as those to aid the Appalachian area and special aid to maintain small farmers, may be more important. To some extent, we must decide whether we wish to temper criteria of economic efficiency (are small farms sufficiently productive and their output needed?) with those of social well-being (the absence of other possibilities for farmers and ex-coal miners living in depressed areas may indicate the desirability of subsidizing small farms and building up new industries in depressed areas).

Region

In 1960, almost half (45.6 percent) of the under-$3000 poor in the United States lived in the South.[41] A quarter (26 percent) of the under-$3000 poor resided in the North Central States; 17 percent made their homes in the Northeast; and only 11 percent lived in the West. The South (where about 30 percent of the United States population lives) was the only one of the four regions overrepresented by poor families.[42] Between 1953 and 1960 there was little change in the relative importance of the four regions in the composition of poverty.

The significance of the South is especially revealed by these statis-

---

[40] *Ibid.*

[41] The University of Michigan study, with its careful adjustments for family conditions, estimates that the South had 51 percent of all the poor in 1959. Morgan et al., *op. cit.*, p. 213.

[42] The Northeast contains 25 percent of the total population, the North Central States 28 percent, and the Western states 17 percent.

tics: of the aged poor, 41 percent reside in the South, as do 50 percent of the disabled poor, 64 percent of poor one-parent families, 46 percent of the unemployed poor, and 83 percent of the nonwhite poor. The incidence figures similarly show the great risk of poverty in the South: one-third of all Southern families were below the $3000 poverty line in 1960.[43] In the North Central States the incidence was 20.8 percent, and in the Northeast and West it was about 15 percent. The trend in all sections was downward between 1953 and 1960, but the West and the South had the greatest drop in incidence.

Although the economic prospects of the Southern states have improved markedly since the 1930s, when they were known as America's "forgotten lands," these states still play a cardinal role in producing poverty. Antipoverty planning must place special emphasis on our underdeveloped subnation.[44]

The Aged

One in eight American families (13 percent) is headed by an aged (over 65) individual. Yet, depending on the standards used, from 25 to 33 percent of all poor families are aged; no other ten-year age span comprises more than 17 percent of poor families. At the $3000 poverty line, 30.9 percent of all poor families had a head who was at least 65 years old in 1960. Considering the small size of families with older heads, perhaps a quarter of all the poor, whether they live in families or as single individuals, are aged. At the $4000 poverty line, the percentage of aged heads dropped to 27.4 percent of all families, and at the $2000 line, the aged contributed 33.2 percent. Under $1000 the aged dropped to 25.4 percent of the families; this reduction may result from the floor provided by social security payments. To assess the role of the aged, it is also necessary to consider unat-

---

[43] At the $4000 poverty line, 45.7 percent of Southern families are poor. Recomputed from Keyserling, *op. cit.*, p. 42. The figures in this paragraph indicating the percentage of aged poor, disabled poor, etc. who reside in the South are from Morgan et al., *op. cit.*, p. 213.

[44] Southern poverty may be overstated because most of our poverty-estimating procedures do not allow for differences in the cost of living by region and degree of urbanization. Thus a lower income level might be appropriate for measuring poverty in the South. Moreover, consumption of home-produced food and fuel by farmers is important in the South. The extent of Southern poverty, therefore, may be overestimated. Our *guess* is that modifications would reduce the incidence and contribution of poverty in the South, but not by enough to make it especially important to reduce resources for the improvement of conditions there. This is the conclusion of Lampman, *The Low-Income Population and Economic Growth*, *op. cit.*

tached individuals. Of unattached individuals receiving less than $2000, 49 percent were aged.

Looking at the trends in family poverty (under $3000 in 1959 constant dollars), we find that the aged furnished 19.8 percent of the poor in 1947 and 30.9 percent in 1960. Similarly, the trend for unattached individuals shows an increase from 33.1 percent in 1947 to 44.3 percent in 1960. These important facts show why an increasing percentage of the poor exist outside the labor force. The incidence data also show that the aged have by far the highest risk of poverty; more than half (52.5 percent) of all aged families—the bulk of the aged live in families—were below the poverty line in 1960. The only age group in the same incidence range was the 14-to 24-year-old household heads, who had an incidence rate of 32.5 percent. This latter group, however, constituted only 8 percent of all poor families. In 1947 the incidence rate for the aged was 58.5 percent, demonstrating a smaller incidence decline (6 percent) between 1947 and 1960 than any other age group. This was also true for aged single individuals.

The extent of extreme poverty—under $1000 family income—among the aged is startling: one-tenth were below this level in 1960. Despite the growing coverage of social security, two-thirds of the poorest aged—those living alone and earning less than $1000 a year—were not covered by social security.[45]

Increasingly, we are developing an urban aged poor. Slightly more than half (53 percent) lived in rural nonfarm localities and less than an eighth (13 percent) resided in rural farm areas. In 1947, on the other hand, farm areas furnished a fourth of the poor, indicating that the aged are becoming increasingly urbanized. A tenth of the aged poor in 1959 resided in the twelve largest cities; another seventh in other large cities.[46] That there are more aged persons in large cities helps account for the increased demand for social services in large cities.

Demographic factors increase the significance of the aged among the poor: the number of older persons is growing and they are living longer. Between 1947 and 1960, the number of aged families grew by more than 40 percent, the highest growth rate of any age group in the population. Thus the growing importance of the aged among the poor is partly because the proportion of aged in the population at large is expanding. The aged are living longer—a man aged 65 can expect to live until age 79 and a 65-year-old woman to age 81. As they age their ability to support themselves and to receive adequate assistance diminishes. The increased number of years of life in which individuals are

[45] *The War on Poverty, op. cit.*, p. 8.
[46] Morgan et al., *op. cit.*, p. 214.

"old" increases the risk of poverty, especially for women who outlive their mates. They are twice as likely as the aged males to fall below the poverty line. We can no longer treat those over 65 simply as a homogeneous group. We now have two generations of the elderly—those between 65 and 75 and those above 75—with different financial and health problems and prospects.

A social norm also contributes to poverty among the aged. The parent-child two-generation nuclear family is now considered to be "the healthy family." Only in emergencies should parents live with their married children. Filial responsibility, formerly a moral imperative, has withered in an affluent society.[47] The norm of two-generation households rather than of three-generation households has been nurtured by the social security payments that have enabled many older couples to maintain themselves as independent low-income families. Paradoxically, our social welfare programs thus contribute to both independence and poverty.

The inadequacy of social services is shown by the finding that in the early 1960s three-quarters of the aged poor did not have hospitalization insurance of any kind, despite their high hospitalization risk. By contrast, "63 percent of the national population . . . had . . . coverage for the entire spending unit." The inadequacy of their incomes and/or assets required 29 percent of aged poor families to receive public assistance (welfare).[48]

The growing likelihood of the aged living in poverty is also revealed in the sources of their income. The largest single source in 1962 was their own earnings, providing 32 percent of total income according to the findings of the 1963 "Survey of the Aged"; more than one-third of aged men and one in seven of aged women were in the labor force in 1962. The percentage of aged men in the labor force has shown a marked decline from 47 percent in 1957 to 38 percent in 1962, but the proportion of aged women with work experience remained about the same, 14 percent.[49] Finally, employers are reluctant to employ older workers, and it is likely that employment as a source of income will decline even further.

Social insurance provided 30 percent of the total income of the aged. Fewer than half received social security payments, but the coverage is

[47] See Seymour S. Bellin, "Extended Family Relations in Later Years of Life," unpublished Ph.D. thesis in sociology, Columbia University, 1962.
[48] Morgan et al., *op. cit.*, pp. 204, 216.
[49] Erdman Palmore, "Work Experience and Earnings of the Aged in 1962: Findings of the 1963 Survey of the Aged," *Social Security Bulletin*, 27, 6 (June 1964), Table 16.

growing (though not as rapidly among low-income groups as among others) and social security pensions will be of increasing importance in the future as a source of income. Without other income (or reliance on savings) the benefit level of these pensions leads to poverty: in May 1964 the average monthly old-age insurance payment was $78.34, a figure including almost $17 for special payments for medical care.[50] Since benefits are tied to previous income, "These programs are of least help to those whose earnings have never been adequate." [51]

Public assistance furnished 5 percent of the aged's income. Added to the social insurance payments, 35 percent of the aged's income is from "welfare state" measures. About one-third of old-age assistance recipients also get old-age and survivor's insurance benefits, and about 50 percent of persons now entering the old-age assistance rolls are also social security beneficiaries. If social security payments do not improve markedly, assistance will probably increase as a source of income among the aged. Government employee, veteran, private, and union pension plans provide 13 percent of the aged's income. These pensions will undoubtedly grow, but they mainly affect the more privileged employees. This is especially true of private employers' plans which utilize pensions as a way of deferring income to lower personal tax rates. Finally, income from interest, dividends, rents, and cash contributions from children or other relatives contributed 16 percent of the income of the aged.[52]

Many aged poor were always poor. Others have dropped into poverty as their usual sources of income have declined over time and form a "new poor." Social welfare payments provide an economic base for many of the aged, but not at a high enough point to prevent the poverty of many. Increasingly, the level of these payments will determine what proportion of the aged will be poor. Reviewing the assets and hospitalization and pension coverage of the poor, Morgan and his colleagues conclude: "Clearly, short-run cash deficiencies and temporary loss of earning power are not the sole explanation for the economic deficiencies of poor families; their difficulties also develop from inadequate long-term protection against those contingencies which are likely to curtail further their incomes in the future." [53]

[50] *Welfare in Review*, 2, 8 (August 1964), p. 37.
[51] Council of Economic Advisers, *op. cit.*, p. 69.
[52] Data on the sources of income of the aged are taken from Lenore A. Epstein, "Income of the Aged in 1962: First Findings of the 1963 Survey of the Aged," *Social Security Bulletin*, 27, 3 (March 1964), pp. 3–24.
[53] Morgan et al., *op. cit.*, p. 205.

Negroes

No discussion of poverty can fail to note the special plight of the American Negro. The civil rights movement has served as an important cutting edge not only in the rediscovery of poverty, but, even more significantly, in creating a climate of concern that has made it politically feasible to make reduction of poverty a national goal. It may therefore seem paradoxical to assert, as we do, that the Negro does not play an especially prominent or growing role in the overall problem of poverty. The increasingly critical problem for the Negro is inequality, not poverty. The importance of Negroes in the poverty picture has been misconceived. A high percentage of Negroes are poor. As a consequence, many have been led into believing that the majority of poor in the United States are Negro. This is far from the truth. Although Negroes are overrepresented among the poor (they comprise 10 percent of the population of the United States but 20 percent of the poor) poverty is a problem for more white persons.[54]

Almost eight of every ten families living below the $3000 poverty line are white. Twenty-one percent of poor families are Negro. Although at lower income levels the percentage of Negroes is larger, at no income level are Negroes more than a quarter of the poor. *Even in the South more than 70 percent of poor families are white.*[55]

The incidence of poverty does show that Negroes and other nonwhites fare very badly. At the under-$3000 level almost one-half (47.1 percent) of Negroes live in poverty; the incidence for whites is about one in five (19.4 percent). The trend data show a small rise in the importance of Negroes in the under-$3000 strata. In 1947 Negroes constituted 18 percent of the poor families; in 1960 they were 21 percent. At lower poverty lines the relative importance of Negroes is growing more rapidly. At the $2000 level Negroes moved from 21 percent of the poor in 1947 to 23 percent in 1960. The data on the composition of

---

[54] To some extent, the significance of Negroes in poverty depends on the kind of measurement of poverty used. Shortly, we shall use one which shows Negroes as constituting a very large slice of the poor. Similarly, the importance of poverty to Negroes depends on what economic aspect of their life is being analyzed. For example, the unemployment data, which we discuss later, do show an absolute decline in the fortunes of Negroes.

[55] This statistic is calculated on the basis of the $4000 poverty line. Keyserling, *op. cit.*, p. 42. It may be that Negroes are a higher proportion of the large-city poor, but such data are not available. Most data refer to whites and nonwhites; the latter includes not only Negroes but also American Indians, Chinese, Japanese, Filipinos, etc. Negroes constitute 90 percent of the nonwhite category and it is common practice to use nonwhite data as Negro data.

the lowest fifth of families, that is, the 20 percent of families with the lowest incomes, show no change in the relative importance of non-whites (21.5 percent in 1947; 21.4 percent in 1960). Since the Negro population is increasing more rapidly than the white, these trend data suggest that no great change is taking place in the importance of racial factors at the low-income levels.

Despite the growing Negro migration to the North, about 70 percent of the under-$4000 Negro poor lived in the South in 1960.[56] Herman Miller is not optimistic that migration from the South will solve the low-income problems of Negroes. He estimates that 42 percent of all Negroes will still reside in the South in 1980. Although this number is a great decline from the 72 percent in 1940, it is not an enormous 20-year decline from the 1960 figure of 54 percent.[57]

The overall unemployment data show that the risk of unemployment for Negroes is twice that for whites: in 1963 the white unemployment rate was 5.1 percent, the Negro rate 10.9 percent. Additionally, Negro youths, 14 to 19 years old, had twice as much unemployment as their white counterparts. Because of high unemployment among all youth, this meant that a quarter of all Negro youth in the labor force were unemployed. The discrepancy between Negro and white girls of this age was even wider—a third of the Negro girls were unemployed, compared to a ninth of the white girls. The most striking aspect of the unemployment data is that Negro unemployment is growing relative to that of whites. In 1940 the Negro unemployment rate was 20 percent higher than the white.[58] From 1947 to 1963 the average unemployment rate for Negro workers was 71 percent greater than for white workers. Between 1953 and 1963 this average differential rose to 112 percent.[59] The Negro unemployment rate was much higher in the early 1960s than in the 1950s and 1940s. It seems that,

[56] Calculated from Keyserling, *op. cit.*, pp. 42, 59.
[57] Herman P. Miller, *Rich Man, Poor Man* (New York: Thomas Y. Crowell, 1964), pp. 212–214.
[58] Calculated from Philip M. Hauser, "Differential Unemployment and Characteristics of the Unemployed in the United States, 1940–1945," in Universities–National Bureau Committee, National Bureau of Economic Research, *The Measurement and Behavior of Unemployment* (Princeton, N.J.: Princeton University Press, 1957), p. 253.
[59] *Manpower Report of the President and A Report on Manpower Requirements, Resources, Utilization and Training by the United States Department of Labor* (March 1964), pp. 27, 103 ff. This report is a remarkable compendium of data. The disparity between whites and Negroes in the rates of males who are not in the labor force (which is, to some extent, unemployment) is also growing. Thus the differentials are probably greater than the straight unemployment figures reveal.

with respect to unemployment, the Negro decline is genuine, not merely a decline relative to white trends. With regard to other economic aspects, however, *relative* decline seems to be more important.

Not only are Negroes and other minority members "the last to be hired, first to be fired"; they are paid less than their white counterparts in the same job and are concentrated in low-wage occupations. A Council of Economic Advisors report estimated what we are losing because of racial discrimination in employment:

> . . . if the education and training of the Negro population were fully utilized by the elimination of racial barriers in employment, our national product might rise by as much as 2½ per cent each year. In 1961, this would have raised our income as a nation by $13 billion. These wasted skills amounted to one-fourth of the total that was spent for national defense in that year.[60]

Discrimination produces poverty. The University of Michigan study attempted a multivariate analysis of salary differentials between whites and nonwhites, taking into account education, rural background, and skills. This analysis made possible a close assessment of the impact of discriminatory practices on nonwhites. When all these factors were considered, the nonwhites earned almost $900 less than whites.[61] Thus pure discriminatory factors rather than skills and the like operate to reduce Negro income.

As Negroes increasingly become an urban and metropolitan population, their poverty becomes more visible than much of white poverty.[62] Half of white poverty is still nonurban. As a consequence, Negro poverty has gained great attention. The civil rights demonstrations have contributed to this recognition of poverty among large-city Negroes, and we therefore tend to ignore the absolute gains of Negroes. It is important to recognize that great gains have been made: real [63] mean nonwhite family income almost doubled between 1950 and 1960 (from $2128 to $3921).[64]

Growing affluence has touched Negroes, but not as much as it has

[60] Herman P. Miller, *Rich Man, Poor Man*, op. cit., p. 77.
[61] Martin David, "Income and Dependency in the Coming Decades," an address before the National Conference on Social Welfare, May 22, 1963.
[62] Thirty-eight percent of the Negro poor are in large cities, compared with 26 percent of all poor. Morgan et al., *op. cit.*, p. 214.
[63] "Real" refers to adjustments for changes in the cost of living; the gains reported here are substantial improvements in the command over resources.
[64] Herman P. Miller, *Trends in the Income of Families and Persons in the United States: 1947 to 1960*, op. cit., Table 9.

whites. Consequently, the relative position of the Negro has grown worse as the income chasm separating the races has grown wider. The average wage or salary of a nonwhite male worker in 1960 was $3075, or three-fifths of the average income of white male workers. Compared with the wage differentials of 1939, when a nonwhite male worker received only 41 percent of the average white man's wages, this salary is a substantial improvement, but the more recent trend is important. In the years from 1950 to 1962, the earning gap between whites and nonwhites widened: in 1950 nonwhites received 61 percent of white income; in 1962 nonwhite income was 55 percent of white income.[65] The relative gains of nonwhites during the World War II and immediate postwar periods have not continued. This widening gap is not due to the marginal nature of most Negro employment. When experienced, year-round, full-time workers are compared, a similar decline during this period is noted—the income of nonwhite income as a percentage of white income dropped from 67 percent to 63 percent.[66]

Nor does the position of the Negro in relation to the white income recipient improve over the age cycle. According to the 1960 census, the median income of nonwhite men, as a percentage of that of white men, dropped steadily from 57 percent at ages 20 to 24 to 45 percent in the 55 to 64 age bracket. It is only in old age, when the Negro has retired from the labor force, that the nonwhite median income rises to 51 percent of that of the white.[67]

Nor is education a guarantee against discrimination:

> Even more dramatic than the growth of inequalities with respect to age is that increased education for the Negro, instead of reducing inequalities, serves to augment them. When non-white lifetime earnings are compared with that of white, we find that non-whites earn about half as much during their lifetimes as whites. *The lower his school achievement, the less the Negro is disadvantaged when compared with whites.* Elementary school and high school graduates earn approximately two-thirds of white income, but college graduates earn less than half.[68] [Emphasis added.]

These data point not only to inequalities in income but to inequalities in education as well. As Herman Miller points out, "nonwhites

---

[65] *Manpower Report of the President, op. cit.,* Table H-10, p. 275.
[66] Herman P. Miller, *Rich Man, Poor Man, op. cit.,* p. 43.
[67] Lenore A. Epstein, "The Aged: Income and Welfare," in *Poverty and Deprivation in the United States, op. cit.*
[68] Herman P. Miller, *Rich Man, Poor Man, op. cit.,* p. 156. "The Negro college graduate can expect to earn only as much income as the white worker who never went beyond the eighth grade. . . ." *The War on Poverty, op. cit.,* pp. 5–6.

who have completed the same number of years of schooling as whites will not be as well educated, on the average."[69] The poor quality of education for Negroes is now a national issue.

For the Negro the problem of inequality is becoming crucial. The Negro family may live above the poverty line, however defined, but suffer from inequalities because of the gap between its income and the income of white families. Discontent among Negroes is growing because their conditions have improved, but not as rapidly as that of whites nor as swiftly as Negroes now expect. Our recent experience raises the question whether reliance on general advance of the economy or on the rising educational levels of Negroes will satisfactorily reduce inequalities.[70]

Female-Headed Families

It is widely believed that the female-headed family (FHF) is of great importance in describing the poor. The recent literature on the culture and subculture of poverty singles out this social unit as the fulcrum on which the subculture rests, encouraging the transmission of poverty among generations. The emphasis on the FHF may be misplaced: although incidence rates are high and growing, the compositional rates are relatively stable, except for urban, Northern Negroes.

Of all families below the $3000 poverty line in 1960, not quite a fourth (23 percent) were headed by females. At lower income levels the contribution of female-headed families to poverty was greater. But some of the families are aged or disabled and without children. *Restricting our estimate to one-parent families with children reveals that only about a tenth of all poor families were in this category.*[71] If we deal with only the smaller group of the nonaged, nondisabled poor, female-headed families with children furnished 16 percent of the poor.

At lower poverty lines, however, the compositional importance of the FHF grows: at the $2000 poverty line, the FHF contributes

[69] Herman P. Miller, "Income and Education; Does Education Pay Off?" in Selma J. Mushkin, ed., *Economics of Higher Education* (Washington, D.C.: U.S. Department of Health, Education and Welfare, 1962), p. 132.
[70] In this discussion we have ignored other American minority groups who have high incidences of poverty: Puerto Ricans (of whom there are nearly a million living in the United States, mostly in New York City and large Eastern cities); Spanish-name Americans in the Southwest (three and a half millions); and Indians (a half million).
[71] This estimate is based on Morgan et al., *op. cit.*, p. 195. It is not strictly comparable with the 23 percent figure because of the sliding poverty line used by the University of Michigan. We believe it is a reasonable figure. In any case, it is important to recognize that not all households headed by women contain children.

slightly more than a quarter (27 percent) of the poor, at the $1000 line, almost a third (32 percent) of poor families are headed by females; at the $4000 line, the FHF falls in importance to a fifth of the poor.[72]

The data do show that the FHF is of great importance among low-income Negroes, especially in urban areas in the North and West. Among all nonwhite families with incomes below $3000, more than a fourth (27.6 percent) were headed by females.[73] If we exclude families headed by persons over 65 and compute the percentage that female-headed families are of all families headed by persons under 65, this percentage increases sharply. Of families headed by persons under 65, about a third have female heads. Of poor urban families the percentage is 41 percent, and of urban families resident in the North and West it is almost half (48.6 percent). These figures contrast with the one-third of similarly located whites with incomes under $3000 in 1960.[74]

The difference in incidence of poverty between the white and Negro FHF is very striking: almost four of every five Negro female-headed families were in poverty, compared to somewhat more than half of white female-headed families.[75] Although the total number of FHF who were poor grew 22.6 percent between 1947 and 1960, there has been no appreciable change between these years in the percentage of all families that are female-headed. During the entire period, approximately a tenth of American families had a female head. The overall figure marks the great expansion of the female heads among poor families. Between 1949 and 1960, the FHF grew from 14 percent to 23 percent of the under-$3000 poor, from 18 percent to 27 percent of the under-$2000 poor, and from 20 percent to 32 percent of the under-$1000 poor. The lower the poverty line, the greater the growth in the compositional importance of the FHF.

[72] In this paragraph, we are back to the census clarifications utilized in Herman P. Miller, *Trends in the Income of Families and Persons in the United States: 1947 to 1960, op. cit.*, Table 2. Compositional importance is probably overstated because the "female head" in this calculation may not have any young children, unlike the category discussed in the previous paragraph.
[73] The University of Michigan data, which are restricted to single heads of family *with* children, show only 17.2 percent of nonwhite families as having female heads. This finding suggests that the statistics in this paragraph, which include childless families, overstate the importance of female heads of family among Negroes.
[74] Calculated from *Poverty and Deprivation in the United States, op. cit.*, pp. 260–261. More than a third of the poor, single-parent families resided in the largest cities; two-thirds lived in the South. Morgan et al., *op. cit.*, pp. 213, 214.
[75] Computed from Mollie Orshansky, "Children of the Poor," *Social Security Bulletin*, 26, 7 (July 1963), Tables 2–5. Part of the Negro-white poverty variations result from different family sizes.

The incidence of under-$3000 poverty in the FHF was slightly more than half in 1960. This is a small drop from the 1949 figure, but it is still almost three times the incidence rate for families with male heads (18.9 percent).[76]

Female-headed families have not participated, as much as other groups, in the economic advances since World War II. From 1947 to 1960 the real, median income of female-headed families increased by 3 percent; that of families with male heads increased by 43 percent.[77] This is an astonishing difference. The female heads were not being drawn into remunerative employment; welfare assistance payments were too low and not sufficiently available (only 38 percent of female-headed families received some form of public assistance).[78] Special measures are needed to improve the conditions of female-headed families.

Life in a female-headed family is widely believed to be inevitably destructive to children. This view, we suspect, ignores the adaptations in these families that reduce strain and neglect. Although a "complete family" may be desirable for a number of reasons, we do not believe that they are likely to grow in the next years among the poor. Consequently, we must deal with the female-headed family as a fact of our social life, and we must relieve their economic plight. Where our concern is with reducing the production of one-parent families, we suggest—as an *obiter dicta*, for no data exist—that direct social services to improve family functioning may be less important in reducing broken families than increased income and education. Improved economic conditions and social mobility may be most significant in reducing the number of fatherless families.[79]

Labor Force Status

Contrary to the notion of a shiftless poor who will not work, two-thirds of the families that were poor in 1960 (at the $4000 poverty

---

[76] An indication of the growing importance of female labor is that the incidence rate of poverty was 11.3 percent in families with a male head when the wife was in the labor force contrasted with the 21.7 percent in families when the wife did not work.

[77] Herman P. Miller, *Trends in the Income of Families and Persons in the United States: 1947 to 1960, op. cit.,* Table 2.

[78] Morgan et al., *op. cit.,* p. 216.

[79] See S. M. Miller, "Poverty and Inequality in the United States: Implications for the Social Services," *Child Welfare,* 44 (November 1962), pp. 442–445; reprinted in Frank Riessman, Jerome Cohen, and Arthur Pearl, eds., *Mental Health of the Poor* (New York: The Free Press of Glencoe, 1964). Services specifically oriented to aiding low-income children in school may be more powerful than general casework aid to a family.

line) were headed by persons in the civilian labor force.[80] At the $3000 poverty line, 60 percent of the heads of families were working or actively looking for work. Reducing the poverty line to $2000 or $1000 does not affect the extent of labor force participation of heads of families.

To interpret these labor force participation rates, it should be remembered that 35 percent of the families of the poor are headed by aged or disabled persons and an additional 10 percent are headed by single individuals, most of whom are female.[81] The labor force participation rate of 66 percent for heads of family who have incomes under $4000 is high; it is not substantially less than the rate (78 percent) for all heads of American families (which have a smaller proportion of aged, disabled, and broken families than do the poor).[82]

Especially critical is the inability to agree on an appropriate public posture for the female-headed household that receives public assistance—the Aid to Families and Dependent Children (AFDC) recipient. On the one hand, consistent with the original provision of the Social Security Act, we believe that women should be able to stay at home and care for their children. Pressure to re-examine this policy has been mounting, however, now that more than a third of all women are in the labor force. The 1962 amendments of the Social Security Act were directed at the reduction of dependency, a philosophy most clearly aimed at the female-headed household. Despite this step, we have been unwilling to abandon the policy that women have a right to care for their children and to receive public aid when they are unable to provide for themselves. But apparently we have reserved this right for women with very young children. An authentic policy to encourage women to work, of course, must be supported by appropriate services—child care, education, and job placement. Simply hiring

---

[80] The concept of the labor force refers to those who are employed, serving in the armed forces, or unemployed. In the Miller data, however, members of the armed forces are grouped with the out-of-labor-force category. To be classified as "unemployed" requires the individual to have been actively engaged in seeking work in the week previous to the survey. Herman P. Miller, *Trends in in the Income of Families and Persons in the United States: 1947 to 1960, op. cit.,* p. 30.

[81] Morgan et al., *op. cit.,* p. 195. Data on labor force participation are not available by income level and occupation. It is likely that a sizable percentage of the labor force poor are in rural farm and nonfarm areas. Out-of-labor-force status is probably more common in large cities, where not working is more visible.

[82] Contributing to the high participation rate of the poor is the large proportion of farmers and farm laborers among the poor. The rate is deflated, on the other hand, by the out-of-labor-force status of many of the urban poor who seek employment but who do not meet the Census definitions of "unemployed."

more public assistance workers to apply what Alvin Schorr has described as "pressure and prescriptiveness" (the stress on client attitude and motivation) on the poor will not avail.

The trend, however, is clearly toward a sharp decline in labor force participation. In 1948, 63 percent of the heads of families in the lowest-income fifth—that 20 percent of families receiving the lowest incomes—were in the labor force; in 1957 the rate was down to 53 percent.[83] Poor families are increasingly headed by individuals outside of or marginal to the market. They are members of the "economic underworld of the bypassed."[84]

The trend among poor (under $2000) single individuals is similar. In 1947, 55 percent were wage earners, but in 1960 the percentage was 41. This decided decline probably reflects the growing percentage of aged people among single individuals and the importance of old-age pension and assistance payments.

Increasingly, to be out of the labor force means economic privation. Families that include no wage earners are falling further behind families which do have wage earners. The median real income of all families without a wage earner increased 35 percent from 1947 to 1960, while the median real income gain was 43 percent for families with one earner. The redistributive mechanisms of public assistance, social security, and private philanthropy have improved the conditions of the economically disabled, but not as rapidly as the position of the rest of society has improved.

It is curious to observe that in March 1963 the proportion of the poor who were unemployed, as opposed to those out of the labor force and not searching for work, was only slightly higher than the proportion of all families who were unemployed—6 percent as compared to 4 percent. One factor contributing to this situation may be the tendency of the poor to withdraw from the labor force once they lose their jobs, rather than to continue the search for work and thus be classified officially as unemployed. Myrdal estimated that unemployment in the United States was at this time about 9 percent if account were taken of the underemployed, who would work full time if sufficient jobs were available, and the disemployed, who wish to work but were no longer actively searching for jobs because none were available.

Two broad forces are leading to the increasing number of disemployed families among the poor. One factor is demographic—the increasing prominence of females and the aged as heads of households among the poor.

[83] Lampman, *The Low-Income Population and Economic Growth*, op. cit., p. 21.
[84] *The War on Poverty*, op. cit., p. 4.

Shifts in the traditional relationship between economic growth and unemployment may be a second factor in the declining participation of the poor in the labor force. Continued economic growth in recent years has not produced a drop in unemployment rates. Although economic growth increased from 2.5 to 3.5 percent between 1960 and 1962, the rates of unemployment remained the same. Between October 1957 and July 1964, the rate of unemployment dropped below 5 percent only once. The unemployment rate among youth was three times the overall rate. With the prospect in the 1960s of 26 million young workers, of whom eight of ten will not have earned a college degree, of whom three of ten will not have completed high school—10 percent of the latter not even having completed grade school—the unemployment rate for young workers could increase substantially.[85]

Persons qualified for only low-skilled labor will be in trouble. The supply of unskilled jobs is not increasing, and a drop in the rate of economic growth probably will lead to a tighter labor market. The growth of credentialism [86] and testing reinforces the trend toward more selectivity in hiring. The assessment or attesting of skill is becoming less frequent, while the capability of social performance along approved class lines is more often the criterion for employment. Some experts have even argued that the tendency to overdefine the competencies needed to perform tasks has gone so far that a major approach for expanding unskilled jobs would be to downgrade the skill requirement for many professional and technical jobs. The Mayor's Poverty Council in New York City recently recommended, as an important program to reduce poverty, a restructuring of civil service jobs so that "functions requiring lesser skills will be separated from functions requiring higher degrees of professional and technical ability." [87]

The period of full employment during and following World War II provides a sharp contrast with today's conditions. The lower birth rates of the Great Depression, the war demands for many able-bodied men, and the postwar concentration on further education through the G.I. Bill of Rights created a scarce supply of labor and disadvantaged groups were sucked into the labor force.[88] In the 1960s participation

[85] Robert E. Weber, "Education and Employment in the Next Two Decades: Some Perspectives," Office of Juvenile Delinquency and Youth Development, Welfare Administration, U.S. Department of Health, Education and Welfare, June 1964, p. 6. Unemployment rates are especially high among Negro youth.
[86] Credentialism is the reliance on credentials, such as the diploma, as criteria for employment and economic mobility.
[87] *New York Times*, June 28, 1964.
[88] See S. M. Miller and Martin Rein, "Poverty and Social Change," *American Child*, 46, 2 (March 1964), pp. 10–15.

in the labor force for such groups as youth, the aged, nonwhites, and women is more difficult than for other members of society. In short, the normal operation of our economy presents constraints on these groups which affect their poverty. These trends highlight the importance of developing a national policy of income distribution outside of the normal operation of the market, if a solution is to be found for the problem of poverty among that half of the poor who are outside of the labor force.

This discussion of long-range trends toward the disengagement of the poor from the labor force should not lead us to neglect the 60 percent of the under-$3000 poor who are in the labor force—53 percent employed and 7 percent unemployed. In 1960 well over one-half of family heads employed in *occupations such as farm labor and foremen or domestic service lived in under-$3000 poverty* (58.9 percent and 78.9 percent respectively). Slightly more than one-half of farmers and a fifth of self-employed businessmen were below the $3000 poverty line. A twelfth of the families of clerical and sales employees were poor. A total of 15 percent of all civilian workers who were heads of families earned less than the poverty level.[89] These figures serve to remind us that the inability to earn an adequate income, even when employed, is an important contributor to the problem of poverty. Clearly, if we used still higher cutoff points, the number of employed persons in poverty would increase sharply.

Our modern public assistance system, reminiscent of the Speenhamland Act of eighteenth-century England, is called upon in some communities to serve as a public wage supplementation for marginal industries. In New York City public assistance serves as a form of wage supplementation for 51.8 percent of all individuals who are on Home Relief, for 85 percent of all individuals receiving Veterans Assistance, and for 16.2 percent of all persons temporarily receiving Aid to Dependent Children. Despite employment, income was insufficient. In all, of those receiving public assistance in November 1962, 12 percent of all persons and 5.3 percent of all cases were in need of such supplementation.[90]

An Overview

In citing the compositional importance of various categories (women, youth, unemployed, etc.), we have generally ignored the

[89] Calculated from Herman P. Miller, *Trends in the Income of Families and Persons in the United States: 1947 to 1960, op. cit.,* Table 7.
[90] This information is based on personal correspondence with Commissioner James Dumpson of the New York City Department of Welfare.

Table 2 Characteristics of Heads of Poor Families

Proportions and Aggregate Estimates of Heads of Poor Families Having Characteristics Related to Poverty

Likely Causes of Poverty	(1) Aged	(2) Disabled	(3) Single and Has Children	(4) Usually Employed, Unemployed in 1959	(5) Nonwhite	(6) Self-employed Businessman or Farmer	(7) None of These	(8) Percent with Other Indications of Poverty
(1) Aged	100% 2.8 mil.	32% .9 mil.	1% .04 mil.	2% .04 mil.	22% .6 mil.	17% .5 mil.	0%	65%
(2) Disabled (not 1)		100% .8 mil.	15% .1 mil.	4% .03 mil.	26% .2 mil.	26% .2 mil.	0%	62%
(3) Single and has children (not 1–2)			100% 1.1 mil.	14% .1 mil.	43% .5 mil.	4% .03 mil.	0%	60%
(4) Usually employed, worked less than 49 weeks in 1959 (not 1–3)				100% .9 mil.	29% .2 mil.	0%	0%	29%
(5) Nonwhite (not 1–4)					100% 1.4 mil.	14% .2 mil.	0%	14%
(6) Self-employed businessman or farmer						100% .9 mil.	0%	0%
(7) Not 1–6							100% 2.4 mil.	0%
Aggregate	2.8 mil.	1.7 mil.	1.2 mil.	1.1 mil.	2.9 mil.	1.7 mil.	2.4 mil.	

SOURCE: James N. Morgan et al., *Income and Welfare in the United States* (New York: McGraw-Hill, 1962), p. 195. (Personal correspondence with Dr. James N. Morgan has led to recalculation of the figures of column 6, which differ somewhat from those reported in the book.)

fact that these categories overlap. A person can be aged *and* Negro, for example, or engaged in agriculture *and* disabled. The University of Michigan study, summarized in Table 2, permits us to separate out various categories to eliminate overlapping.

The table is not as complicated as it first appears. It attempts to separate out the effects of various poverty-linked characteristics. In column 1, the Aged, 2.8 million heads of poor families are aged; of them, .9 million are disabled as well. The underlined figure of row 2 shows that another .8 million of heads of poor families are disabled but not aged; looking across the disabled row, we see how many of these nonaged, disabled persons have other characteristics. The aggregate row at bottom shows that a total of 1.7 million of the heads of poor families are disabled. Column 3 and row 3, single heads with children, show that 1.1 million of the poor are nonaged, nondisabled, single heads with children. The diagonal, underlined figures show how many heads have only the indicated poverty-linked characteristics and no other. If we want to know the total number of poor family heads who have a given characteristic, whether or not they have any other, we need merely look at the aggregate row. By the criteria of the University of Michigan study, there are 10.4 million families in poverty. The percentage that each column aggregate is of 10.4 million indicates what percentage of all poor heads have this characteristic. The percent figures refer to the row category. Thus 2 percent of the aged were also unemployed poor.

These data show that about a third of all heads of poor families were aged and disabled, that more than a quarter of the nonwhite poor were aged and disabled, and that another sixth headed one-parent families. A tenth of the poor were self-employed businessmen or farmers without any other poverty-inducing characteristics.

Perhaps the most striking thing about the table is that the six categories leave a considerable part of poverty unexplained. Almost a quarter of poverty is *not* due to being aged, disabled, and the like. We still lack a full portrait of the poor.

We shall refer to these demographic characteristics in the final sections when we turn to issues of policy.

Inequality

The rediscovery of poverty in the United States had a sharp impact partly because a comforting myth of an "income revolution" had settled over American intellectual life. The feared post-World War II depression did not occur; the Korean War prevented the possibility of a serious depression and contributed to the end of the 1949 recession. Although recessions occurred throughout the 1950s, the trend was definitely up. The level of gross national product was moving astonishingly high—from $374 billion in 1950 to $585 billion in 1963 (adjusted for price-level changes).

Not only was the economic pie larger, it was believed to be more equitably distributed than previously. Economist Simon Kuznets' analysis of income distribution seemed to reinforce this conclusion.[91] The small group at the top of the income pyramid, the upper one percent, received 13 percent of all 1919 income and 15 percent of 1929 income. The figure dropped to 11.4 percent in 1941 and to 9 percent in 1946. A similar drop occurred among the upper 5 percent, who received 23.1 percent of the 1919 income and 26.7 percent of 1932 income, but only 21.9 percent in 1941 and 18.2 percent in 1946. With the declining numbers of families with incomes under $2000, the income distribution appeared to shift from a pyramid to that of a barrel, bulging at the center but trim at the top and bottom. Only case and insular poverty seemed to remain in what Galbraith termed "the affluent society." Coupled with the figure of seventeen million for persons owning stock in American industry, these data supported the slogan of the peaceful American revolution, the emergence of "people's capitalism." [92]

In truth, a great change had taken place. The general shoring up of incomes in the United States made a high percentage of the American population comparatively affluent.[93] The proportion of the poor had declined from 26 percent of the population in 1947 to 19 percent in 1957 (using $2500 as the poverty line).[94] Economic dips were relatively short; we avoided the massive unemployment of the 1930–1940 variety.

Unfortunately, our confidence that increasing total production and income were also leading to a more equitable distribution of that income was not well founded. The "income revolution" never spread to

[91] Simon Kuznets, *Shares of Upper Income Groups in Income and Savings* (New York: National Bureau of Economic Research, 1953).
[92] Reagan gives a political reason for the stress on the "income revolution": "Because conservatives now fear to admit what they once loudly proclaimed—that political equality cannot exist in the face of substantial economic inequality—an attempt has been made in recent years to proclaim a myth of economic equality belying the evidence of our personal observation." Michael D. Reagan, *The Managed Economy* (New York: Oxford University Press, 1963), p. 34.
[93] At constant 1962 dollars, 5 percent of families received incomes of $10,000 or more in 1929 compared with 9 percent in 1947 and 19 percent in 1962. Jeanette M. Fitzwilliams, "Size Distribution of Income in 1962," *Survey of Current Business* (April 1963), Table 3.
[94] Lampman, *The Low-Income Population and Economic Growth*, op. cit.

the bottom groups of society. The "income revolution" thesis has been attacked on the technical grounds that Kuznets underestimated the income of the upper income groups. The new forms adopted to reduce taxation—trusts, the distribution of income among individual members of the same family, the retention of income in corporations so that wealth accumulates, the utilization of capital gains as a way of reducing taxes, tax-free expense accounts, and so forth—are inadequately reflected in the usual income records which are based on the reports of individuals.[95]

The thesis of increasing equality does not necessarily stand up, even if the modifications in the income of the top 5 percent do not show a decline in the concentration of income. If the upper 5 percent receive a smaller proportion of total income than before, we have to examine who is getting more. A reduction at the top does not mean that an even redistribution to all those below the peak has occurred. The fascination with Kuznets' conclusion about the upper 5 percent turned attention away from the analysis of who benefited from the decline at the top of the economic heap.

When we examine the data more closely, we see that this oversight is significant. The reduction in the slice of income going to the upper income groups has *not* been evenly dispersed over all other strata. It has gone mainly to the middle income groups, especially the upper-middle levels. It has not filtered down to the lowest income level. Kolko has used Census data to show a long-term *decline* in the percentage of income going to the bottom 10 percent and the bottom 20 percent of American families. In 1910 the lowest tenth received 3.4 percent of national personal income before taxes; in 1959 the lowest tenth had only 1.1 percent of personal income. In 1910 the lowest fifth received 8.3 percent of total income; the corresponding figure for 1959 was 4.0 percent. These data, then, show a long-term decline in the percentage of income going to the bottom tenth and fifth families of the United States, despite the decline in the percentage of income going to the top group.[96]

The reliability of Kolko's data has been questioned, for it is highly difficult to construct valid long-term income accounts.[97] Herman Miller's analysis of more recent income data for the lowest 20 percent and

---

[95] For a critical analysis of the imperfections of Kuznets' analysis of the income of the upper 5 percent, see Kolko, *op. cit.*, pp. 16 ff.
[96] *Ibid.*, p. 14.
[97] In response to the criticism, Kolko has pointed out that there is independent corroborating data for 1918, 1929, and 1936. In any event, there is little question about the reliability of the data since 1941.

40 percent shows that during World War II there was a slight increase in the percentage of income going to these groups but that since 1944 the lowest groups have not been improving relative to other groups. The lowest fifth received 5 percent of family income in 1944 and 1961; the second lowest fifth received 11 percent in both years.[98]

Table 3 Percent of Income Received by Each Fifth of Families and Individuals and by Top 5 Percent

Families and individuals ranked from lowest to highest	1929	1935	1941	1944	1961
Lowest fifth	13%	4%	4%	5%	5%
Second fifth		9	10	11	11
Middle fifth	14	14	15	16	16
Fourth fifth	19	21	22	22	23
Highest fifth	54	52	49	46	45
Top 5%	30	27	24	21	20

U.S. Bureau of the Census, *Historical Statistics of the United States, Colonial Times to 1957*, p. 166, and Jeanette M. Fitzwilliams, "Size Distribution of Income in 1962," *Survey of Current Business* (April 1963).

SOURCE: Herman Miller, *Rich Man, Poor Man* (New York: Thomas Y. Crowell, 1964), p. 35.

A cross-sectional view of 1961 shows the extent of inequality in the United States: *40 percent of American families received only 16 percent of family income while the top 5 percent of families received 20 percent of all family income.* This latter figure is much smaller than the 30 percent received by the upper 5 percent in 1929, but it still shows substantial concentration of income.

The most striking thing about the data is that the suction power of the war and immediate postwar prosperity is no longer reducing inequalities. The decline in the percentage of income going to the upper 20 percent and the upper 40 percent had stopped by 1944. Little change, if any, has occurred since then. This process can be seen in the movement of wages and salaries in this century. In 1907 "the median

[98] Herman P. Miller, *Rich Man, Poor Man, op. cit.*, pp. 35–36.

earnings of skilled workers in manufacturing industries was about twice that received by unskilled workers." [99] This gap was gradually reduced so that by the end of World War I skilled workers made 75 percent more than unskilled; by the end of World War II the skilled workers' advantage was reduced to 55 percent. Since then, the movement has been in the other direction. In the 1950–1961 period the skilled had a far greater increase of income than the unskilled, in contrast to preceding periods where the percentage increase was greater for those at the bottom of the occupational pyramid. Herman Miller has summarized the situation: "The narrowing of the income gap between the skilled and the unskilled, the high-paid and the low-paid workers, which was evident up to and including the war years, has stopped during the past decade and the trend seems to be moving in the opposite direction." [100]

The same trend is found within the white-collar sectors. The upper white-collar groups—the professional and managerial occupations—are improving their incomes more rapidly than are those in clerical and sales work at the bottom of the white-collar sector.

The changing relationship between education and earnings also shows a pronounced trend toward inequality. The following comparisons are for mature male workers in their prime earning years, 45 to 54. In 1949 an elementary school graduate earned 79 percent of the income of a high school graduate; by 1958 this figure had dropped to 75 percent. The earnings of the high school graduate were 66 percent of the college graduate's earnings in 1949, but by 1958 this had declined to 59 percent (a drop of 7.5 percent). The income of elementary graduates, as a proportion of the income of college graduates, was 58 percent in 1949 and 49 percent in 1958 (a drop of 9 percent). A high school diploma had only a minor impact on reducing the growing inequality between college graduates and other education groups.[101] Vance Packard's term, "the diploma elite," referring to college graduates, is an eloquent description of the increasingly advantaged situation of this segment of the population.

Education is increasingly becoming the route for social advance. As average educational levels move up in the United States, the point at which education makes a marked difference in occupational and in-

[99] *Ibid.*, p. 44.
[100] *Ibid.*, pp. 46–47.
[101] U.S. Bureau of Census, *Current Population Report*, Series P-60, Nos. 33 and 27, and U.S. Census of Population, 1950 Special Reports P-E, No. 5B, reported by Herbert Bienstock, "Realities of the Job Market for the High School Dropout," in Daniel Schreiber, ed., *Guidance and the School Dropout* (Washington, D. C.: National Education Association, 1964), pp. 84–108.

come opportunities escalates. Our "credential society" is likely to lead to the accentuation of inequality rather than to its diminution. Abramovitz has declared: "If one side of the coin of industrialization is the greater opportunity which is afforded to skill and education, the reverse is the barrier it sets up against the employment and advancement of young people who are deprived of formal training." The extension of training "has aggravated the disabilities imposed on the substantial fractions of our youth who may be deprived of a chance to gain all the formal training from which they are able to benefit." [102]

In the realm of wealth, inequality is also growing. (Income is the annual flow of monetary receipts; wealth refers to accumulated assets.) Lampman's study [103] shows that from 1922 to 1949 there was a downward trend in the concentration of wealth in the upper one percent of wealth-holders: in 1922 the top one percent held 32 percent of the wealth; in 1949, 23 percent. The major drop was during World War II. Since then the trend has been reversed: the upper one percent held 24 percent in 1953,[104] 26 percent in 1956, and 28 percent in 1961.[105] Because of the various ways wealth is disguised and divided, these figures may underestimate the degree of concentration.[106] Since the distinction between wealth and income is increasingly an arbitrary one, these data question the "income revolution" thesis of the postwar years.

[102] Moses Abramovitz, "Growing up in an Affluent Society," in Eli Ginzberg, ed., *The Nation's Children*, Vol. 1: "The Family and Social Change" (New York: Columbia University Press, 1960), pp. 164, 167.
[103] Robert J. Lampman, *The Share of Top Wealth-Holders in National Wealth, 1922–1956* (Princeton, N.J.: Princeton University Press, 1962), p. 24. The 1961 figure is a later estimate by Professor Lampman. For a criticism of Lampman's methods, see Kolko, *op. cit.*, pp. 149–150.
[104] "The top group owned at least 80 percent of the corporate stock, virtually all of the state and local government bonds, and between 10 and 33 per cent of each other type of property in the personal sector in that year." Lampman, *The Share of Top Wealth-Holders in National Wealth, 1922–1956, op. cit.*, pp. 23–24.
[105] The mode of calculation affects the results: "It is probably that the decline (between 1922 and 1953) in inequality among individual wealth-holders is greater than would be found if families were considered as the wealth-holding units, since it is apparent from the data that married women are an increasing part of the top wealth-holder group. Converting to a measure of 'adults less married women' suggests that half of the percentage decline found for individuals between 1922 and 1953 would disappear on a family basis. . . ." *Ibid.*, p. 24.
[106] The inadequacy of the claim that stock ownership is becoming more evenly distributed in the United States is discussed in Kolko, *op. cit.*, pp. 50–54, and Reagan, *op. cit.*, pp. 36–38. The general point is the extent of concentration of ownership: 2 percent of shareholders owned almost 60 percent of total shares.

The most disturbing piece of evidence about inequality is one that we have previously cited: the declining relative income position of Negroes. The trend *may* change with recent civil rights legislation, but there does not appear to be an economic mechanism clearly reducing the income differential so that Negro advances match the gains of whites. Willhelm and Powell have argued that to understand the plight of the Negro today, we must recognize that now he is not so much a victim of economic exploitation as of economic uselessness, resulting from occupational shifts which have thwarted growth of the need for unskilled labor. If this analysis is accurate, we can anticipate a continued growth in inequality for the Negro unless his educational level advances greatly and unless market forces cease to play a central role in determining his place in the American economy.[107]

World War II produced important changes in America. But "our social revolution" did not continue in the postwar period. It may be that inequality grows when production expands and that it declines when production and national income are reduced. The new economics of manipulated and prolonged expansions through governmental intervention may mean that we are in a novel period of important structural changes in the economy, changes which will produce a greater inequality unless there is concerted government policy and action to reduce it.

Why Be Concerned about Inequalities?

Despite the continuation and growth of inequalities, most families are better off than ever before; the number of the under-$3000 poor have declined from 34 percent in 1947 to 22 percent in 1960.[108] Is it not enough to improve the levels of living of families without worrying about whether the income gaps between various groupings have narrowed? Are not substantial improvements in income sufficient to change the conditions and outlooks of individuals?

Undoubtedly there is much in this argument. Substantial material improvements may bring families new security and delight. Some analysts of American life believe that the potential of automation may ne-

[107] Sidney M. Willhelm and Elwin H. Powell, "Who Needs the Negro?" *Trans-Action*, 1, 6 (September–October 1964), pp. 3–6.

[108] These figures are in constant 1962 dollars. They tend to overestimate 1947 poverty and thereby the extent of the decline. If constant 1947 dollars were used, the extent of decline would be smaller. The choice of method in computing data profoundly affects the results. Lampman, for example, shows in *The Low-Income Population and Economic Growth* that the scope of poverty changes depends not only on the year for which the dollar is held constant, but also on whether the unit of measure is the family or the spending unit.

gate the impact of inequality. With a much higher average income level for the great mass of population, and the consequent availability of many new services and prerequisites, satisfying lives can be led, even though inequality is not declining and is perhaps increasing. They argue in favor of keeping the income distribution pattern the same, that is, maintaining the standard deviation from the mean, while raising the level of the mean.

There is a contrasting view. A man's outlook, hopes, and satisfactions are not determined by the absolute level he has attained, but how his position compares with that of other groups. Today, America's poor, as we have said, live in incomparably better conditions than the poor of a generation or two ago, and certainly of a century ago. The Calcutta poor of today are a world apart. But the feeling of poverty —of limited hopes, of deprivation, of powerlessness—still exists among many American poor. In a society with increasing national standards of living, with openness of communication and visibility of style, the reference groups of the poor, in terms of adequacy of income, increasingly lie outside themselves. Material improvement over the past quickly loses its poverty-softening effect when others advance even more. Indeed, revolutions frequently are the actions of the deprived whose conditions have improved, but more slowly than they consider acceptable. Herman Miller has stated well the psychological importance of relative income:

> . . . needs stem not so much from what we lack as from what our neighbors have. . . . Except for those rare souls who have hitched their wagons to thoughts rather than things, there is no end to "needs." So long as there are people who have more, others will "need" more. If this is indeed the basis for human behavior, then obviously the gap between the rich and the poor cannot be ignored, however high the *minimum* levels of living may be raised.[109]

A second argument supporting the stress on inequality is based on a pessimistic view of current prospects of reducing poverty. This view, which we have outlined elsewhere,[110] contends that a reduction in poverty requires, at least to some extent, a reduction in inequalities. If the children of the poor are to obtain jobs in the mainstream of the economy, they will need considerably more education than they now are getting. This means that the inequalities in education must be reduced; a small gain in education for the poor, coinciding with more rapid educational advancement for children of the well-to-do, will

[109] Herman P. Miller, *Rich Man, Poor Man, op. cit.*, pp. 38–39.
[110] Miller and Rein, "Poverty and Social Change," *op. cit.*

have only limited effects upon the prospects of the poor. Thus for the poor to become high school graduates, rather than high school dropouts, is no great advancement, since college and postcollege education is becoming more essential in securing jobs which provide a secure income. (See the earlier data on income by educational levels.)

A third reason for paying attention to inequality is that a small rise in income, by itself, is often insufficient to allow the poor to change the physical and psychological environments in which they live. Slight increases in income, for example, cannot be translated into big improvements in housing and neighborhood; nor would some monetary gain overcome the isolation of many poor from the mainstream of society, or reduce "the hostility and despair which such isolation can breed." As two English observers have commented, "there are reasons to think, in short, that a little bit of clothing, the odd appliance, and a drop more beer do little to change the meaning and significance of poverty." [111] Large-scale improvements in the conditions of the poor will require large reductions in inequalities.

A fourth argument is that the economy would benefit from a vast expansion in the spending power of low-income groups: "the inadequate shares of total consumer income flowing to the poor and the deprived have repressed the total volume of consumer spending." Income shifts to the low-income would spur the economy "because these people spend all or even more than they earn, while higher-income groups do most of the saving." [112]

A final reason for concern about inequality is an ideological one—the concern for "social (or redistributive) justice." Some desire a society with small or no differentials in incomes. Others aim at reductions in differentials without moving to a goal of zero differentials.[113] In both cases the feeling, as Toynbee expressed it, is that "the unequal distribution of the world's goods between a privileged minority and an

---

[111] R. H. Cassen and S. D. Gervasi, "Social Priorities and Economic Policy," *The Political Quarterly*, 35 (April–June 1964), p. 139.

[112] Keyserling, *op. cit.*, p. 92. Gordon has suggested direct income gains by the poor may have limited effects on the total level of expenditures; rather, the effect would be to reduce the rate of dissaving and borrowing by the poor. Margaret Gordon, *The Economics of Welfare Policies* (New York: Columbia University Press, 1963). For a different point of view, see Kolko, *op. cit.*, p. 140.

[113] Cartter suggests a measure of inequality:

> Most persons who favor greater income inequality . . . do not think of precise equality per capita as a desirable norm. They think, instead, of diminishing the gap between the highest and lowest incomes while retaining absolute differential rewards and incentives. In place of perfect equality, therefore, it may be interesting to substitute a narrow range of incomes around the average income as a yardstick. Let it be assumed . . . that the equalitarian's concept of an ideal distribution is one in which the following is true: the

underprivileged majority has been transformed from an unavoidable evil to an intolerable injustice." [114]

How the United States compares with other nations on the issue of inequality depends, as we might expect, on the statistics used. If we use the percentage of income received by the top 5 percent of families as the indicator of inequality, the United States, Sweden, and France are similar at 20 percent, Britain yields 21 percent, and West Germany, India, and Italy provide 24 percent to the top 5 percent. The United States is not distinctively low in inequality. Cartter, employing the indicator discussed in footnote 113, concludes that "The initial distribution of private income in Britain and the United States was of a similar pattern before (World War II), but in the postwar period (1948) there appears to have been a tendency towards greater equality in Britain, while inequality in the United States remained about the same." Further, "the distribution of final consumer income in post-war Britain was considerably less unequal than in the United States. This is true whether one measures inequality against a yardstick of precise equality or against a hypothetical ideal range of income around the average income." [115]

The issue is whether advanced industrial societies and sustained economic growth lead to greater equity in the distribution of advantage and privilege, or, alternatively, whether economic maturity leads to the concentration (or reconcentration) of privilege in the hands of an enlarged but still limited elite, resulting in the growth of an underclass reminiscent of the "two nations" discussed by Disraeli in his analysis of nineteenth-century British society. The direction that social policy should take depends largely on how this question is answered.

Opportunity and Inequality

The growth of equality of opportunity has been one of the great social changes in modern industrial society.[116] The diminution of hered-

---

highest income is not more than ten times greater than the lowest income, and the lowest income is not less than half the average income. Thus, the upper and lower limits of such a semi-equalitarian range would be $.5x$ and $5x$, x being the average income.
Allan Murray Cartter, *The Redistribution of Income in Postwar Britain* (New Haven, Conn.: Yale University Press, 1955), pp. 77–78. This band is narrow, but it does suggest a procedure for thinking about the limits of inequality.
[114] Arnold Toynbee, *Civilization on Trial* (New York: Oxford University Press, 1948), p. 25.
[115] Cartter, *op. cit.*, pp. 91–92.
[116] Equality of opportunity must be distinguished from freedom from want and protection against the contingencies of old age, ill health, unemployment, and the like. Education is now the most significant means of access to equal opportunity; income is the most important protection against want.

itary privilege has often been the essential goal of revolutionary movements. Increasingly, public opinion will not tolerate the blatant expression of hereditary privilege. To the extent that family connections influence job placements (which they still do to some extent), they have been less visible.

Some argue that economic necessity, rather than social or political pressure, has forced these changes. As Parsons has claimed, the pressure of industrialization toward an efficient, rational economic order, has increasingly forced the substitution of criteria of performance, ability, and achievement for that of birth.[117] Broad, universalistic principles of selection supplant choice by birth and family connections.

The growth of universalistic principles is assumed to mean increasing equality of opportunity, but it is important to recognize that equality of opportunity does not necessarily mean equality of conditions. A society can, in theory, provide equal access to educational and employment opportunities and still be highly stratified, with great differentials in prestige and income separating those in various positions. Michael Young has satirized such a society in his *The Meritocracy*,[118] where an aristocracy of intelligence prevails. Increasing opportunity and increasing social mobility should not obscure the plight of those left behind. Being disadvantaged because of lack of educational credentials (and presumably, therefore, because of low intelligence) can be even more disturbing than disadvantage resulting from lowly birth.

Nor are economic gains automatically translated into gains in other important realms of life. Much of the present concern about inequality in England grows out of the discontent of those who have achieved educationally and, to some extent, economically, but are not fully accepted socially. This theme dominated the writings of the "Angry Young Men," the authors and playwrights who seared the English literary world in the 1950s with their accounts of the social barriers against those who had benefited from the growth of opportunity in England.[119] But this situation may be peculiar to England with its special problems of intense class feelings. On the other hand, some have argued that the discontent of newly rising ethic groups in the United States emerges because of the disparity between their newly found comparative affluence and the obstacles to full social acceptance.[120]

[117] Talcott Parsons, *The Social System* (Glencoe, Ill.: The Free Press, 1951). This theme runs through most of Parsons' writings.
[118] Michael Young, *The Rise of the Meritocracy* (Baltimore: Pelican Books, 1964).
[119] These writings include John Osborne's plays, *Look Back in Anger* and *The Epitaph of George Dillon;* Kingsley Amis' comic novel, *Lucky Jim,* and John Braine's *Room at the Top,* later made into a very successful film.
[120] See Daniel Bell, ed., *The Radical Right* (Garden City, N.Y.: Doubleday, 1963).

From an engineering point of view, can a society with a high degree of stratification have equal opportunity? Take equal opportunity in education: Do youths of the rural South or of metropolitan slums have the same opportunity to attend college as do suburban youths of affluence? Even assuming that college is free, and that the education provided through high school is of equal quality in all communities, what about the differences in attitudes among students in schools where a minority go on to college and where the overwhelming majority do not? [121] What about the imprint of community and family values and knowledge about education? *To be born in different positions within society molds the ability to handle access to institutions and the development of levels of aspiration and achievement motivation.*[122] *In this sense, then, equality of opportunity can never be fully present in a society with great social divides within it.*

Open public and private institutions become the resources of the "haves." To the extent that these institutions receive public tax advantages, they reinforce the prevailing distribution of opportunity. A self-conscious public policy may be necessary to reverse maldistribution.[123]

Variations in opportunity among social classes are smaller in the United States than in many other societies. But equality of opportunity to move into the high-level jobs of society does not exist here.[124] Are

---

[121] In an analysis of Berkeley schools, Wilson shows that working-class students going to a middle-class school have higher educational aspirations than do working-class students attending a predominantly working-class school. Unfortunately, selective reasons for going to schools at a higher class level are not controlled in the study. Alan T. Wilson, "Residential Segregation of Social Classes and Aspirations of High School Boys," *American Sociological Review*, 24 (December 1959), pp. 836–845.

For a similar study, see Robert Hardt, "The Impact of School Milieu on Pupils' Educational Plans," Syracuse University Youth Development Center, 1960.
[122] Wilbert E. Moore, *Industrial Relations and the Social Order* (New York: The Macmillan Company, 1946).
[123] Cartter offers a political argument for the stress on the importance of reducing poverty:

> The most necessary prerequisite for a successful long-run policy to diminish the inequality of opportunity (and therefore the inequality of future earned income) is the abolition of poverty. Until this goal has been achieved, political and social pressures make it more expedient for any government to concentrate on immediate, although temporary, relief through current taxation and income transfers.

Cartter, *op. cit.*, pp. 96–97.
[124] The analysis of intergenerational social mobility data (the comparisons of sons' occupations with their fathers') shows that the United States compared to other nations is high on some indicators of equal opportunity and low on

our mechanisms for reducing inequality effective? This issue has been raised most sharply in education, where it is known that gifted low-income youth are less likely to attend college than are less gifted middle-income youth.[125]

A strict reliance on universalistic criteria alone for admission to colleges or for employment, some have argued, may operate to perpetuate inequalities rather than reduce them. Harvard University has been criticized by a few commentators because it selectively admitted Negro students who did not meet the usual Harvard criteria for academic performance in secondary school. The university was recognizing not only that relatively mediocre performance by those in difficult environments may reflect high ability, but that special consideration should be given to those who have been submerged by poverty and discrimination. The National Urban League, under Whitney Young's leadership, has raised a somewhat similar issue in asking for "compensatory" effort to place Negroes in jobs. Such measures are controversial, but at least they focus attention on the issue of how, in practice, to achieve greater equality of conditions. Our historic concern with fostering equality of *formal* opportunity may not be adequate to do the job at the present moment in society.

The new situation of our economy is discussed in the following section in order to highlight the structural changes that affect the goals of social policy and the means for accomplishing them.

Structural Changes

The difficulties of unemployment, poverty, and inequality may be short-run phenomena, but there is a growing belief that they are indicators of longer-term societal and economic change. We seem to be moving into a new kind of economy, and our present difficulties provide blurred markers of the beginnings of these transformations.

The vision of the new period is unclear and consequently much disagreement about it occurs. The population expansion is the least controversial aspect of the changing circumstances of American life. The pre-World War II predictions about the leveling out of population in this country were clearly wrong. In the 1950s, 29 million persons were added; in the present decade of the 1960s, 28 million will be added, bringing the total to about 208 million in 1970. The big increase, how-

---

others. See S. M. Miller, "Comparative Social Mobility," *Current Sociology*, 9, 1 (1960), pp. 1–89.
[125] See Dael Wolfle, *America's Resources of Specialized Talent* (New York: Harper and Brothers, 1954).

ever, will be in the 1970s, for the population may reach 260 million people. This is a doubling of our population in 40 years.

A population of this size will need facilities and goods much beyond our present production. By the end of this decade much additional housing will be needed as new suburbs grow to accommodate the young families of the grown-up, post-World War II, baby boom generation. To accommodate these new families and communities an intricate set of supporting services—what economists call infrastructure—is required: schools, roads, water supply, sewage, recreational facilities, and so forth.

These activities will lead to expansion of the public as well as the private sector. The absolute amount expended in the public sector will undoubtedly increase, but, as in the past, the rate of increase may not be at a faster pace than the overall rate of increase in gross national product, if social service expenditures other than those for education are considered.

The nature of the population expansion will be especially demanding of the public sector in the coming years. We have sizable and increasing numbers at the young and aged ends of the population profile. These are "dependent" groups, considered unavailable for employment or physically unable to work. Both groups are likely to continue increasing, and their upkeep—for the young through schools and social services, and for the aged through money transfer payments and social services—will be expensive.

The level of adequacy with which essential services are provided and the total amount to be spent are political decisions, in which technological requirements are only one element. How money should be spent will probably be an increasingly important issue in the next years. New kinds of relations between the public and private sectors are likely to emerge.

Population expansion in the United States is paralleled by important changes in the content and methods of production. Agriculture, for example, has declined drastically, but service industries have experienced a remarkable increase. Production methods are changing with the introduction of factory and office automation and cybernation, the fount of our latest industrial revolution. Their impact is unclear.

These changes have produced significant shifts in the distribution of the labor force: the demand for unskilled labor is being reduced rapidly; the number of production workers in manufacturing, the center of the blue-collar labor force, is not increasing. The number of white-collar workers of all kinds has decidedly increased, and the professional and technical category is the fastest growing segment of the labor force. The market for unskilled labor is being reduced. Higher education credentials—which may not always be the same as higher skill performance—are demanded, effectively blocking out the low-educated and low-skilled.

While automated processes are widely heralded as demanding high-skill labor, so far the evidence does not warrant the conclusion that their introduction strongly upgrades the labor force. The evidence is mixed, but it is clear that automation is likely to reduce the number of employees needed in a specific work place. Many believe that overall employment will diminish sharply as productivity rapidly spurts ahead of needed production.

A variety of solutions for these anticipated problems have been suggested, including shorter work weeks, longer vacations, sabbaticals from work, and other measures designed to maintain or increase the number of persons employed by reducing the productivity of the worker. The more pessimistic conclude that it is unlikely that enough work can be offered for all who, under previous circumstances, might have entered the labor force. Consequently, working will not provide a major claim to income; the market place will have to be supplemented by the emergence of new standards for judging an individual's contribution to society. It is argued that a basic minimum level of life should be insured all families; this could be done by using the mechanism of a negative income tax which pays out funds when a family's income is below a specified level. In short, a major revamping of our social values will, in time, accompany the great increases in production.[126]

A contrary view holds that demand will increase, new products and industries will emerge, and the productivity of America will give rise to new standards of living. In the conservative variant, minimal government intervention is envisioned as the private sector asserts its adaptability and strength. In the liberal variant, considerable government activity is needed to insure high output, high employment, and high planes of living.

Those fearful of increased productivity have probably underestimated the possibilities of offsetting forces in the economy and have made a long-term projection of contingency as though it were a statement of probability in the short run. But we do suspect—and at this

---

[126] The Ad Hoc Committee on the Triple Revolution issued in 1964 a widely cited document, "The Triple Revolution," which warned of the unemployment potential of automation. This document is rewritten in Michael D. Reagan, "For a Guaranteed Income," *New York Times Magazine*, June 7, 1964, p. 20. This general position is influenced by Robert Theobald, *The Challenge of Abundance* (New York: Robert Potter, 1962).

stage of development analysis can only be highly speculative—that relatively untrammeled market forces may worsen inequalities as the general level of living rises. This possibility emerges because of important changes in the nature of the American economy and polity.

The general tendency, Kalecki and others argued a generation ago, was that in the upswing of the business cycle inequalities in the distribution of income increased, but that in the downturn inequalities were reduced. The movement of equality-inequality was cyclical. Today, as we have suggested earlier, we may be in a situation of new dimensions in which inequality within rising prosperity will be a dominant thrust unless deliberate policies are made to offset this tendency. These trends may *not* accentuate inequalities, but in any event they are likely to shape an economy quite different from textbook accounts.

In summary form, here are some of the important current trends.

1. We operate in what Michael Reagan has termed a "managed economy." The manipulation of tax and monetary policies retards the long-term market forces of adjustment. Inflation is likely to emerge. The result is the growth of monopolistic practices; producers are protected, especially if they are in defense activities; wealthier groups can multiply advantage, and high profits permit investment without resort to the selective controls of the capital market.

2. We are undergoing technological and economic change: the amount of capital required to produce one dollar of output has been reduced from four dollars to two dollars. Thus our technology is capital-saving, demanding less capital investment. At the same time our new technology is labor-saving; huge expansions in production require small increases in the labor force. On the other hand, the increase in gross national product needed to generate one job has increased from $5000 (about the time of World War II) to $10,700 in 1955, $20,000 in 1959, and $40,000 in 1960. New investment, which formerly resulted in tripling total production as a result of accumulative expenditures, now has a multiplier effect of only two. This indicates the role of monopolistic pricing practices as well as the limited *creative* power of defense activity to lead to *additional* personal consumption expenditures.

3. The balkanization of our economy proceeds apace. We always have had declining, sick industries in periods of expansion.[127] Not all industries participate equally in economic change; some are more sensitive to cyclical upturns and downturns than others. Although these conditions occur generally, it seems that the present period is unusual

---

[127] Arthur F. Burns, *Production Trends in the United States* (New York: National Bureau of Economic Research, 1934).

in the unevenness of economic change. Production and employment increase but so does unemployment, because of the large number and relatively low skill of many persons in the labor market. The general level of gross national production goes up and median income increases, but the number of poor is not significantly decreased. Large numbers are outside the labor force or outside the pull of high-wage industry and the economy is increasingly divided between a high-income sector and a low-income, unstable sector, producing the "Two Americas" of affluence and poverty.

4. At present the great economic and social divide in the United States is, as we have suggested, the college diploma. The old divide between manual and nonmanual (blue-collar and white-collar) workers is becoming less significant; many of the lower white-collar workers are no better off than upper blue-collar workers. Within the blue-collar segment there is increasing differentiation between those at the top, the skilled workers in manufacturing, and those at the bottom, the unskilled workers in service industries such as restaurants and hotels.

The upper manual workers and the lower white-collar workers are fusing in terms of income. At the top they are marked off from the managerial and professional groups, rapidly expanding in number and swiftly rising in income; at the bottom they are increasingly better off than the exiles from the main economy, who are in low-wage jobs or out of the labor force. New forms and dimensions of stratification are developing in the United States.

5. The relation between income and work is becoming exceedingly tenuous. It is difficult to provide a rationale for the income differentials which exist in the United States:

> Occupation influences earnings even after adjustment for variation in the age and education of different occupational groups. *Professionals, managers, and self-employed businessmen earn more than one would expect after allowing for their educational advantages.* Farmers earn even less than their generally advanced age and lower education would indicate. [This is also true of blue-collar workers.] Thus, occupation can be interpreted as a supplemental measure of ability or perhaps as an indicator of differing opportunities available to various groups.[128] [Italics and parenthical material added.]

Wage payments are related to skill, training, responsibility, and other characteristics of the worker. The great spread in income for persons in the same occupation suggests that a host of noneconomic

[128] Morgan et al., *op. cit.*, p. 51.

elements, many unclear, may also be involved in income determination. The issue of economic and social equity in present differentials of income will probably emerge in the next few years.

The prospects of increasing productivity, new types of jobs, and decreasing demand for the labor of our expanding population will eventually raise the question of what will provide the claims to income now tendered by the wage relationship.

6. Increasing employment in large organizations is a major trend, with ramifying effects on the quality of life. Many critics have questioned the impact of such employment upon self-realization, independence, conformity, dehumanization, and alienation.[129] The tension between social responsibility and organizational loyalty has been increased by the Eichmann question: To what extent does a subordinate have a responsibility to behave in ways that go counter to his organization when higher moral standards are flouted? Can a personnel officer merely go along with a discriminatory policy in hiring of Negroes and Jews without fighting it, publicizing it, and/or resigning?

With the expansion of industrial welfare programs, what degree of control will these organizations exert over the private lives and beliefs of individuals? This question involves employees of private as well as government establishments. Harrington's *Life in the Crystal Palace* provides us with one portrait of the "world to be."[130] These issues will be of increasing importance.

7. The rights of citizens are more than ever dependent on the role of government. We no longer live in isolated frontier agricultural settlements, or in town hall democracies where the role of government was limited and control of government was immediate. Some believe we can harken back to the days of more limited government;[131] others believe that our present industrial life requires considerable government activity. Increasingly, the issue becomes how to govern government. What limits should be placed on police activity—for example,

[129] Some of the well-known critics have been C. Wright Mills in *White Collar* (New York: Oxford University Press, 1951); David Riesman et al. in *The Lonely Crowd* (New Haven, Conn.: Yale University Press, 1950); and William H. Whyte, Jr. in *The Organization Man* (New York: Simon and Schuster, 1956).
[130] Alan Harrington, *Life in the Crystal Palace* (New York: Alfred A. Knopf, 1963).
[131] It should be noted, however, that American governments have always financed economic growth and development. This was true at the time that railroads and canals were being built; it is also true today. In practice, few really believe in complete laissez-faire. The issue of the extent of government intervention is frequently the mask of the question, government intervention for whose benefit? See Oscar Handlin, "The Myth of Laissez-Faire," *Journal of Economic History* (1943 supplement).

the right of search and the institutionalization of civilian review of police practices through civilian panels to judge public criticism of police behavior? Which kinds of activities does society want to encourage by public subsidies? [132]

8. Government involvement in the economy will undoubtedly expand. At present, federal expenditure is almost 20 percent of total output. Adding the expenditures of the state and local governments, the percentage is raised to almost 30 percent.[133] Indirectly, these government expenditures affect other slices of production and employment in the United States. Public social services are growing rapidly. It may be a surprise to learn that nineteen million persons in the United States received social security payments in 1964. The large number of recipients and the expanded coverage of the population by social security laws mean that the operation of the government will have increased importance in determining the well-being of individuals. Social services are not a casual element in our lives. They are an essential part of urbanized, industrial life.[134] To insure adequacy of these services will require constant surveillance.

We lack a theory of political and social economy that adequately conceptualizes the present situation in the United States. We have presented some fragments of the changes taking place but there is doubt even about them. An overall picture of the direction in which the United States is moving and outlines of the policies that should emerge are lacking.

The ideological alternatives are debated today only in terms of the expansion and contraction of the public sector. This is excessively crude since the public sector can be expanded by offering subsidies and inducements to the private sector to engage in certain kinds of activities, like retraining workers or hiring difficult-to-place workers. The degree of centralization and democratic control that operates in the public sector and the measure of accountability in the private sector are important issues going beyond the dollar amount of expenditures.

Policies to reduce poverty and inequality have to be viewed in the

---

[132] The panoply of governmental activities as forming new bases for wealth and property is brilliantly raised by Charles Reich, "The New Property," *Yale Law Journal*, 73 (April 1964), pp. 733–787.

[133] The recent growth in government employment and expenditures is at the local and state levels, not at the federal. Our estimate for the federal sector is based on total expenditures, which are higher than those reported by the peculiar estimates of the federal budgeting process.

[134] S. M. Miller and Martin Rein, "Change, Ferment and Ideology in the Social Services," *Proceedings*, Council on Social Work Education, 1964.

context of the long-term trends in the economy and society. "Narrow perspectives lead to narrow programs."[135] Short-term solutions to long-run problems breed defeat and disillusion.

Self-Revelation and Criticism

Social policies reflect social values, and social values reveal what is important to a group or a nation. Policies toward the outsiders and the poor are especially revealing of what is important to the dominating group. In this regard Titmuss has noted that "The attitudes that society adapts to its deviants and especially its poor and politically inarticulate deviants, reflects its ultimate values. . . . We must learn to understand the moral presuppositions underlying our action."[136]

In Britain the Speenhamland Law of 1795 humanely provided financial assistance to low-wage workers.[137] It led to lower wages and retarded the economic development of Britain by limiting the emergence of a national labor market. The Poor Laws of 1834 removed the wage supplements, forced the poor to work, and drove the able-bodied paupers into stigmatized, segregated, policed institutions. These "poor houses" furnished the most meager "indoor relief," in contrast to the "outdoor relief" of Speenhamland which permitted the poor to live in the community, did not coerce them into work, and did not segregate and concentrate them into compounds of squalor. Degradation of the poor became acceptable as a way to achieve economic progress; it was the price of creating a mobile labor force and treating labor as a commodity.

Similarly, the British refused to offer much aid to the colony of Ireland during the potato famine of 1848 because aid was seen as interfering with the natural forces of economic law.[138] Economic myth triumphed over disease, malnutrition, and human life. Approximately 25 percent of those seen by the voluntary agencies in England during this period were Irish vagrants. These agencies, it should be noted, defined their poverty as pauperism, a condition of moral defect that inhered in the individual. Even in our sophisticated society, we aim at paying

---

[135] Miller and Rein, "Poverty and Social Change," *op. cit.*
[136] Richard Titmuss in the introduction to A. F. Philip and Noel Timms, *The Problem of 'The Problem Family'* (London: Family Service Units, 1957).
[137] The classic account of Speenhamland is Karl Polanyi, *The Great Transformation* (New York: Rinehart, 1944). For an interesting discussion of Speenhamland, see David Matza, *Delinquency and Drift* (New York: John Wiley and Sons, 1964).
[138] Cecil Woodham-Smith, *The Great Hunger* (New York: Harper and Row, 1962).

minimum rather than adequate levels of support to those who cannot support themselves because we are still fearful of sapping morale and incentive to work.

Views of the Poor

Obviously, the way one views the poor and the sources of their difficulties will affect the kinds of proposals made to improve their conditions and the humanity with which plans are implemented. Ideology and analysis often fuse. Three major views of the poor prevail: the undeserving poor, the self-defeating poor, and the victimized poor.

The undeserving poor. Some believe, as Gladwin has asserted,[139] that only selected segments of the poor are deserving of help. Others, as Alfred Doolittle declares in Shaw's *Pygmalion* and in Lerner and Lowe's *My Fair Lady*, are an "undeserving poor," content in squalor, resistant to work, sponging off society. This view of the poor leads to efforts to reduce payments to the poor and to make them as uncomfortable as possible. The "Newburgh incident" in the Hudson River city in 1961 illustrates the harshness that can prevail when the poor are considered as undeserving. Aged citizens on welfare were "mugged" (photographed) and forced to pick up their checks at the police station as though they were committing an economic crime. Young fathers of growing families were lopped off welfare even though no work was available for them.

Obviously, some poor are undeserving, in the sense that they are not interested in being self-supporting. However, this stricture is irrelevant to the aged and the young children who made up more than 75 percent of the almost eight million welfare cases in this country in May 1964.[140] Only 23 percent of the poor are supported by welfare. Clearly most poor are "deserving." Nonetheless, the view of the poverty-stricken as undeserving is undoubtedly common in the United States, affecting the extent and character of aid to the poor.

Present legislation has been affected by this view of the poor. The 1962 amendments to the Social Security Act, for example, are committed to the reduction of dependency, which is viewed as a personal defect and not a condition which is related to the level of economic organization in the society at large. One writer recently described

---

[139] Thomas Gladwin, "An Anthropologist Looks at Poverty," *Social Welfare Forum, 1961* (New York: Columbia University Press, 1963).
[140] The median age of aged persons receiving OAA is 76.4 years; the median age of children receiving AFDC is 8.6 years, and more than three-quarters of all children are under the age of thirteen years.

these amendments as "social workers responded to Newburgh but . . . they shared a basic premise with the proponents of the Newburgh plan; namely, the assumption that the preferred address to the problem of economic dependency was to intervene in the life of the individual family." [141]

The self-defeating poor. A variant of the "undeserving poor" argument is that many, if not most, of the difficulties of the poor arise from the way in which they deal with their problems. Poverty becomes equated with incompetence.[142] One form of the argument is that since other American poor have risen from poverty to achievement—the Jews, the Irish, and more recently the Italians—the poor can pull themselves out of poverty. But the present poor, especially the minority poor and the Negroes in particular, are seen as preventing themselves from rising. Their cultural values discount saving, it is believed, their family structures encourage male desertion; impetuosity and impulse rule their lives. They cannot govern themselves to defer gratification into a successful future. Their family life, especially the high incidence of fatherless families, is not conducive to educational emphasis, and their cultural values and practices do not lead to the development of the verbal abilities necessary for success in school.

This view emphasizes pathology among the poor and does not recognize strengths of the poor on which to build.[143] It leads to a heavy emphasis on individual rehabilitation rather than social change as a source of improvement for the poor. If the poor are as unrelievedly badly off as these portrayals claim, individual rehabilitation certainly is needed and is extraordinarily difficult to achieve. This attitude, however, fails to explain what appear to be spontaneous positive developments of self-help and social action in some low-income communities.

The view of the poor as incompetents stresses training and retraining the poor (for jobs and for social living) rather than opening up the job structure, providing basic changes in social amenities, and the like. Undoubtedly, some of the poor are self-defeating, and individual counseling and personality probing may be necessary for them. But we do not

[141] "1956 Amendments to the Social Security Act: After the New Look—the First Thought," *Journal of Public Law,* 6 (1957), p. 123.

[142] Rowntree, in his conceptualization of poverty, referred to "secondary poverty" as arising not from inadequate incomes but because "some portion (of income) is absorbed by other expenditures, either useful or wasted." Seebohm Rowntree, *Poverty and Progress* (London: Longmans, Green and Company, 1941), pp. 101–103.

[143] Frank Riessman has consistently raised the question of discovering strengths as a basis for promoting change. See his *The Culturally Deprived Child* (New York: Harper and Row, 1962).

share the assumption that most of the poor suffer from "inadequate personality," a phrase of dubious descriptive value, or that the source of poverty is the poor.

It is extraordinarily difficult, as we have said, to separate cause from consequence. For example, "deficient" education is in part a consequence of poverty as well as a cause of it. The chain of causation twists back upon itself: "At most ages above 9 years, the proportion of the AFDC children retarded in school is somewhat more than twice that for the given age group in the total population." [144]

Nor do we think that the problems of most of the poor arise from family incompetence alone, leading to economic incompetence and requiring "training" and "retraining" to overcome the skill barriers.

Clark has stated well the possibilities of change among the poor:

> . . . individuals and groups modify their behavior only to the degree and in the direction demanded by the external situation as it is perceived. The internal determinants of behavioral changes are themselves the product of past external effects, and are subject to modification by the continuous interaction of the organism in the situation. While to bring about a specified desired change in behavior within a given period of time may require a concern with the internal effects of past influences, the habituation of the verbalized attitudes, and past patterns of behavior, these factors do not operate as a permanent block to future changes but rather determine the strength and duration of the external pressures which are required to effect them. When these are determined and applied, appropriate relearning-demanded changes in behavior occurs and is internalized and reinforced in the same way as the previously learned behavior.[145]

The victimized poor. In this view people are poor because of the ineffective or pernicious working of society. They are poor because of long-time discrimination, economic change destroying economic livelihood, preying of unscrupulous landlords and businessmen in the slums,[146] and the neglect of government in providing adequate services to the poor.[147] They are the casualties of the affluent society.

In this view, improving the conditions of the poor largely depends

---

[144] Robert H. Mugge, "Education and AFDC," *Welfare in Review*, 2, 1 (January 1964), pp. 1–14.

[145] Kenneth Clark, "De-Segregation: An Appraisal of the Evidence," *Journal of Social Issues*, 9, 4 (1953), p. 76.

[146] David Caplovitz, *The Poor Pay More* (New York: The Free Press of Glencoe, 1963), portrays sharp business practices which fleece the poor.

[147] Patricia Sexton has described the comparative disadvantages of educational facilities in low-income areas. *Education and Income* (New York: Viking Press, 1961).

on a commitment to all the poor, not just those likely to improve with little help, and to institutional change to provide more and better paid jobs, to widen and deepen the social security and assistance schemes, and to improve the educational systems, employment services, and other governmental activities. Although some of the poor may need counseling, guidance, and help from social workers to be able to take advantage of opportunity, the stress is on providing opportunity, rather than on preparing individuals to seize opportunity which may not exist. Social change rather than individual rehabilitation is the reference point.

All these subgroups, and others, can be found among the poor. The question is, however, what are the major emphases and tendencies among the poor which might be a basis for the primary (though not exclusive) orientation of policy?

A Typology of the Poor

Obviously, these views of the poor are founded to a large extent on what one thinks their potentials are. Two difficulties intrude in making these estimates: thinking of the poor as an undifferentiated mass with little variation, and conflicting views of the orientation and values of the poor.

S. M. Miller has stressed the importance of both economic and cultural factors in producing the life styles of persons with low incomes.[148] He emphasizes the variations among the poor. Although a great many types of poor should be delineated, at present he is able to depict only four variants: the stable poor, the strained, the copers, and the unstable poor.

"The stable poor" are those whose income is fairly secure, though at a low level, and whose family life is stable—bickerings among the parents are not constant, the children are not neglected. The nonurban and aged poor are most likely to be stable. A number of Negro families are of the stable poor. They have higher social status in the Negro community than their economic counterparts have in the white community because of the general scaling down of incomes and occupational levels of Negroes in the United States. The children of the stable poor families are the most likely to be educationally and occupationally mobile.

[148] S. M. Miller, "The American Lower Classes: A Typological Approach," *Social Research*, 31 (Spring 1964), pp. 1–22. It is also available in the Syracuse University Youth Development Center Reprint Series; in Shostak and Gomberg, eds., *Blue Collar World* (Englewood Cliffs, N.J.: Prentice-Hall, 1964); and in Riessman, Cohen, and Pearl, eds., *op. cit.*

"The strained" have a secure, low-income economic pattern but an unstable family pattern. This might involve a life-cycle problem, for example, "wild" younger workers or alcoholic older workers who disturb family functioning. Or, the pattern could manifest the beginning of a move into the unstable style as a low-income family finds increasing difficulty in maintaining its economic security because of family or personal problems or the economic situation. Many of the offspring of strained families, Dennis Wrong has suggested, may be unable to attain the economic security of their parents and experience intergenerational skidding. The strained situation may not be transitional; many families persist with a low but steady income and a great deal of internal strain.

"The copers" manifest economic insecurity and familial stability; they are families and individuals having a difficult time economically but managing to keep intact. This group undoubtedly increases considerably during periods of extensive unemployment. Probably a large number of Negroes and Appalachian whites are in this group, and their children may be more mobile than those living in strained patterns. Many copers had parents who were in higher occupational positions. Downwardly mobile persons may be more likely to retain a stable family style than others in the same economic predicament. Their children are more likely to rise occupationally than children of families which have been at a low economic level for some generations.

"The unstable poor" have neither economic nor personal stability. It is an extremely varied grouping: partially urbanized Negroes and mountaineer whites new to the north and to cities, remaining slum residents of ethnic groups which have largely moved out of the slums, and long-term (intergenerational) poor white families. Also included are some physically handicapped and aged persons who have dropped through the class structure. Within the unstable groupings there are degrees of instability and strain—not every family is a "hard-core case" or has a "multiple-agency problem." Nor is it certain that an unstable family will always remain unstable.

Only the strained and unstable groupings may be described as having a culture of poverty, and even in these groups not all will fall in this pattern. As we shall see, the "welfare poor" are a minority of all the poor; in turn, the hard-core and multiple-problem families that preoccupy discussions of the poor are only a thin wedge of this small slice. But it is not just that many views of the poor have been undiscriminating, ignoring the wide variations that exist. The most widely popular view itself must be questioned.

A negative view of the poor as self-defeated has emerged from three different sources. Davis and his co-workers, arguing that the lower classes are unable to defer gratification, found that this inability to delay action in order to reap future rewards prevents school or occupational success.[149] Following this work in the middle and late 1950s, a new analysis of delinquency grew up, asserting the existence of a delinquent subculture that developed because of the inability of low-income youth to find legitimate channels to achieve success in American society. Seeing that they "couldn't make it," they repudiated these legitimated routes.[150] Other analyses of delinquency argued that the values of the poor are not contracultural; they do not arise out of opposition to middle-class society but, rather, out of the history and experiences of the poor themselves.[151] The poor do not reject the larger society but they possess a subculture centered around a different set of values.

A third strand developed at the end of the decade with Oscar Lewis' intensive case studies of Mexican families in poverty.[152] In verbatim excerpts from fascinating, evocative interviews, Lewis portrayed what he felt was a "culture of poverty." This pattern of culture cut across societies, merging many of the poor of the world into a life of apathy, failure, discontent, and anguish.

These three images have somehow been blended in the current view of the poor. There is obvious value in seeing the poor not as isolated individuals but as influenced by interaction with other poor as well as with the rest of society. But we do not find the portrait sufficiently realistic. In general, the poor are painted in unrelievedly negative terms. No signs of health are reported; no bases of constructive action exist. The surge of Negroes in the so-called "Negro Revolution" came as a surprise because low-income Negroes were seen, by and large, as living in the culture of poverty, incapable of self-action. Although in-

---

[149] Allison Davis has espoused this position in a number of papers: "Child Rearing in the Class Structure of American Society," in *The Family in a Democratic Society*, Anniversary Papers of the Community Service Society of New York (New York: Columbia University Press, 1949); Ruth Cavan, *The American Family* (New York: Thomas Y. Crowell, 1953), pp. 182–183; Allison Davis, "Socialization and Adolescent Personality," in Swanson, Newcomb, and Hartley, eds., *Readings in Social Psychology* (New York: Henry Holt, 1955).

Schneider and Lysgäard have codified the position in Louis Schneider and Sverre Lysgäard, "The Deferred Gratification Pattern," *American Sociological Review*, 18 (April 1953), pp. 142–149.

[150] Cohen, *op. cit.*

[151] Walter B. Miller, "Lower Class Culture as a Generating Milieu of Gang Delinquency," *Journal of Social Issues*, 14, 3 (1958).

[152] Oscar Lewis, *The Children of Sanchez* (New York: Random House, 1961), and *Five Families* (New York: Basic Books, 1959).

capacitating elements do appear among the poor, nondestructive and nondebilitating features coexist.

If the culture of poverty is more than an interesting metaphor, it implies an intergenerational transmission of values and practices that inhibits constructive action. To some extent this occurs. But we should not neglect the number of times a family attempts to improve its conditions only to fail and finally to give up the struggle. Apathy is often a protection against repeated failure rather than the barrier to initial efforts. As we understand the situation, contemporary experiences and difficulties rather than intergenerational pressures are frequently more important in determining behavior.[153]

We feel that many who utilize the approach of the culture of poverty—though not Oscar Lewis himself—underestimate the impact of the environment on the poor. The problems of the poor are more difficult than those of the better-off. They have fewer resources to deal with their exigencies, and therefore many happenings become transmitted into obstacles. "Lower-class life is crisis-life, constantly trying to 'make do' with string where rope is needed." [154] Many behavioral patterns are not so much normatively prescribed as they are results of weak norms, easily succumbing to outside pressure. We cannot conclude that the results of behavior are always normatively desired.[155]

Consequently, many patterns of the poor are subject to change in new circumstances. A century ago it was argued that to provide the British poor with better housing would result in their putting coal in the bathtubs. They would not know how to use the new homes. This kind of inability to take advantage of new opportunity may exist, but it usually falls away over time for most of the poor.[156] The culture of poverty theme underestimates the changeability of many of the poor in new circumstances.

An essential part of the current view of the poor is the contention that they lack the ability to defer gratification. This statement is com-

---

[153] The data on intergenerational inheritance of poverty usually report only on the children who have inherited their parents' status, neglecting the majority who do not.

[154] S. M. Miller, "The American Lower Classes: A Typological Approach," *op. cit.*, p. 13.

[155] Rodman has raised this point in terms of illegitimacy among the Caribbean poor. Hyman Rodman, "The Lower-Class Value Stretch," *Social Forces*, 42 (December 1963).

[156] Much of what is regarded as new opportunity for the poor disintegrates into form without substance when closely examined. We explore this possibility in training programs in a later section.

parative, with the middle class as the other part of the dyad. There is growing evidence that this analysis is not valid.[157] In addition to this direct empirical questioning of the thesis, there are conceptual problems. To compare two groups' capacity to defer, we have to assume that they equally desire the deferred objective, that they are making equal sacrifices in deferring, and that they have equal opportunity to realize success at the end of the deferment period. These conditions are difficult if not impossible to hold constant in cross-class comparisons.[158]

Although the notion of a psychodynamically based inability to defer gratification is probably not valid, it is true that low-income people have a shorter time span, and that they expect rewards to be visible, concrete, and immediate. In our view, the narrowed time pattern arises from immediate conditions of life and is changeable. This view contrasts with the nondeferred pattern, presumably rooted in early-life experience and impervious to new circumstances. In our perspective, for example, it might be possible to train people to expand their time span by spacing out rewards. In the nondeferred view, this would be difficult because of the deep roots of the life pattern.

Our assessment of the poor—which, it should be said, is not widely accepted—is as follows.

1. Great variation occurs among the poor.
2. There are important differences from many middle-class patterns. Many of the middle-class values, like success, are of less importance or have a changed character. "Getting by" is more important than "getting ahead" for most of the poor. More stress is placed on activity, on toughness. Unemployment is not as stigmatizing an experience among the low-income population as among those better-off. The poor are in economically vulnerable positions and recognize unemployment as a recurring possibility, mostly out of their control.
3. Although many of these patterns and orientations are carried from generation to generation, contemporary influences are important in maintaining them.
4. Some positive elements of strength, of coping, exist as well as negative ones that make it difficult to handle life.

[157] The literature on this subject is analyzed in S. M. Miller, Frank Riessman, and Arthur Seagull, "Poverty and Indulgence: A Critique of The Deferred Gratification Pattern," in Louis Ferman, Joyce Kornbluh, and Allen Haber, eds., *Poverty in America* (Ann Arbor: University of Michigan Press, 1965).

[158] S. M. Miller and Frank Riessman, "The Working-Class Subculture: A New View," *Social Problems*, 9, 1 (Summer 1961), and Miller, Riessman, and Seagull, *op. cit.*

5. Many of the poor are open to change, to taking advantage of new possibilities. But in offering new possibilities, their experiences and orientations must be considered.

Although this assessment is less succinct and less pessimistically glamorous than the culture of poverty thesis, we feel that it is a more reasonable basis for the development of policy.

Policy Choices

A variety of approaches to the reduction of poverty is being followed or suggested in the United States. Two basic issues intertwine in the choice of alternatives. One theme is the relative concern for economic incentive and social justice. The stress on avoiding the diminution of economic motivation leads to low-benefit programs so as not to confirm the work-shy in their ways or encourage others to prefer nonwork to work. The contrasting principle is that of social justice, that, for example, the aged should not end their lives in a condition of economic want. These principles are in conflict, especially in the determination of the benefits paid out by social welfare programs, but they are interwoven in other antipoverty programs as well. When an "economic-productivity value bias" is ascendant, job opportunity becomes the primary emphasis; when it is not, social welfare measures can have greater importance.

The second theme is the role of government. Is that government best which governs least? Should governmental activity—and at what level, federal, state, or local—be extended to meet the problems of the poor? Or, are the long-term gains to the economy, polity, society, and humanity greater if the governmental role is restricted to stimulating the private profit sector of the economy that will advance and carry along the poor in the general upward sweep of society?

We shall see these two tensions in the following analysis of the major programs of poverty reduction: [159]

1. *Increasing the supply of jobs* by stimulating and regulating the private economy and by increasing public employment.

2. *Improving job skills of the poor* by education and by rehabilitation and training.

3. *Providing dollar income* by government payments through grants, insurance, assistance, or taxation.

[159] Our classification has been influenced by that of Robert J. Lampman, "Programs for Poverty," a paper at the meetings of the National Tax Association, Pittsburgh, September 15, 1964. This paper is highly suggestive and technically imaginative.

The Supply of Jobs

For those of the poor who are in low-paid employment, or are unemployed or "employable" in an expanding economy (though "unemployable" in an economy of labor surplus), the need is obviously for an expansion in the total number of jobs. As our earlier discussion of the characteristics of the poor has shown, those who would be aided by economic expansion are more than a majority of all the poor families today.

But our economy had been unable in the late 1950s and earlier 1960s to achieve a rate of growth above 3 percent; in the mid-1960s the rate advanced but was still below that of many of the nations of western Europe, the Soviet Union, or Japan. Especially perturbing is that even during the protracted period of economic expansion following 1961, the unemployment rate seldom fell below 5 percent, in contrast to Sweden's unemployment rate of 2 percent.

The economy can be spurred to create more jobs in several different ways, reflecting different technical means of economic expansion and different social ideologies.

Stimulating the Private Economy

Since power seems to make Keynesians of all of us, even the Republican administration of Eisenhower attempted manipulation of fiscal (tax and budget) and monetary (interest rate) policies to push up levels of production and consequently of employment. Today there seems to be a consensus that fiscal and monetary policies are useful and politically acceptable ways of stimulating the private economy, though there is less consensus about the degree of effectiveness of these policies.

In monetary policy, the interest rate is kept low in order to make investment in new plant and equipment and in commercial and residential construction more attractive. The supply of credit is enlarged by a variety of techniques available to the Federal Reserve System—the lowering of required bank reserves, decreasing the reserve rediscount rate to banks, reserve purchases of securities on the open market.

There are two basic forms of fiscal policy that can be followed singly or in combination. The less-favored approach, because of business attacks on increasing government budget deficits, is to increase government expenditures without increasing taxes so that the economy is stimulated by the additional purchasing power generated by the government budgetary deficit. The government is taking less out of the economy through taxes than it is pumping in through expenditures.

The other fiscal policy involves tax reductions. If government expenditures are not reduced as much, there can be a marked stimulating effect on the economy. The tax cut can occur by reducing either personal or corporation income tax or both.

The reduction of personal income tax increases consumer demand and is often supported by liberal economists as well as conservative ones. A recurring issue in discussions of personal income tax cut is whether high- or low-income taxpayers should benefit primarily from the reductions. Recent tax cuts have cut the burdens of the high-income more than those with low income, and many liberal economists have argued that this type of cut does not spark the economy as much as would a tax cut benefiting the low-income groups. Since the latter are more likely to spend most of their tax gains, rather than to save some proportion as do higher-income families, the net stimulation to the economy would be greater. Another type of argument for differential tax relief to the poor is that they carry an enormous tax load. Lampman concludes that five billion dollars—20 percent of their total income—are paid by the poor in taxes! This amount is greater than the total spent on public assistance in the United States, and Lampman argues that "Even partial relief from these taxes would go far to close the income deficiency of the poor." [160]

The purpose of a corporation tax cut, or of a modification in regulations which lightens the tax burden of a corporation (for example, speeding up the rate of depreciation of capital goods reduces reported and taxable profits), is to make investment more attractive, particularly in heavy-goods industries. Industrial expansion would lead to greater consumer purchasing power, because of new jobs, and the new purchasing power would lead to further increases in demand, resulting in further production and employment.

A further, largely unrecognized policy of stimulating private enterprise lies in the emphasis on special, large-scale government expenditure programs. Road construction is heavily dependent on federal government expenditures. The roads encourage the sale of cars and gasoline and are widely supported as useful activities. Regional programs, like that for development of Appalachia, have heavy highway-building plans. Defense expenditures, about 50 percent of the federal budget, are important bulwarks to several industries and to a number of states, as witnessed by the outcries when a military installation is closed or a contract is terminated. The government housing insurance programs stimulate the construction industry by cheapening the cost

[160] *Ibid.*, p. 12.

of purchasing a home. Direct subsidies to airlines and shipping companies support the transportation industry. Roads, water, housing, transportation, and defense expenditures support and stimulate the private economy, even though other issues may be involved in the formulation of these policies.[161]

The emphasis on stimulating the private sector is basically a funnel-down approach, from the point of view of the low-income population. Improving the position and prospects of the private economy may, in time, lead to additional jobs, drawing into employment those of the poor who are unemployed but able to work and upgrading those receiving low wages. A rapidly expanding economy will also make it easier to achieve political assent to enlarged social welfare expenditures. Objections to these funnel-down policies stress the adequacy of the filtering system, the importance of structural unemployment, and fiscal justice.

To reduce unemployment below 4 percent will require an increase of economic activity of more than $40 billion. The 1964 tax reduction of $11.545 billion was planned to expand total production by $30 billion. An additional expansion through tax reduction was expected to reduce unemployment even more as the economy grew. The tax cut undoubtedly decreased unemployment below what it would have been if this purchasing power had not been added to the economy. (Since many new workers are joining the labor force in the 1960s, the computation of how many new and old workers would have been unemployed is highly conjectural.) The official unemployment rate [162] still hovered around 5 percent after the 1964 tax reduction, and increasing government expenditures or further tax reductions or both would be necessary to drive the unemployment rate to a lower level.

The years 1960 to 1964 were marked by a great increase in economic sophistication, and by growing acceptance of tax reductions, which would augment the already large federal budgetary deficits. But it is still unclear whether the government will be able to produce the economic power necessary to reduce unemployment much below the 5 percent level. In short, monetary and fiscal efforts may not be great enough to push the growth rate to a level that will provide work for all who want it.

---

[161] This discussion neglects state and local governments, which are the most rapidly growing segments of the government field.
[162] The "official" rate, it should be remembered, underestimates total unemployment, neglecting the partially employed and those listed as "out of the labor force," but who are, in actuality, job seekers.

When the labor market expands because times are good, generally the poor are least likely to benefit from these changes. For example, over the past ten-year period from April 1951 to March 1961, the number of mothers in the labor force increased by 3.5 million, accounting for 37 percent of the increase in the total civilian labor force.[163] Who are these women? Although the labor force participation of wives increased for all income fifths during approximately the same period of time (1949 to 1959), the largest increases were in the middle and upper quintiles—10 percent for the lowest quintile as compared with 31 percent for the highest quintile. When the distribution of working wives is examined we find that, in 1957, 16 percent of the lowest income fifth consisted of husband-wife families with the wife in the paid labor force, as compared with somewhat over 40 percent for the highest income fifth. During periods of prosperity we can also expect more moonlighting (the holding of a second and third job). "Among men and unmarried women who were already employed 4.8 percent, or more than 3 million, were moonlighting in 1958 as contrasted with only 2.9 percent in 1950." [164] The nature of labor demand is such that only some of the unskilled poor will be pulled into employment by economic expansion.

A further difficulty is that many of the poor are unlikely to work, nor would many of us wish that they did. The aged, the disabled, and many of the female heads of families with young children should not be drawn into the labor force. A major emphasis on economic expansion would ignore the plight of those poor who can only benefit from direct allocation of money through our social security and welfare apparatus.

A similar kind of argument is that across-the-board increases in labor demand are unlikely to have much impact on those caught in the pockets of poverty—whether in the regional poverty of an Appalachia or in a city undergoing economic decline or change. For example, New York City is undergoing economic change, so that between 1950 and 1960 white-collar employment increased while blue-collar employment

[163] *Research and Statistics: Notes No. 14*, Social Security Administration, Division of Program Research, U.S. Department of Health, Education and Welfare, June 20, 1962.

[164] Kolko, *op. cit.*, p. 104. The increase in overtime may also reduce the impact of expanding need for labor. The effort to increase overtime payments from one-and-a-half to twice base pay is aimed at making it financially wise for employers to hire additional workers rather than to save on fringe labor costs of pensions, medical insurance, and the like by increasing hours of work of the present labor force.

declined absolutely.¹⁶⁵ Expanding national employment may not improve the prospects of the poor in localities suffering from poverty and unemployment.

A final criticism of the "heating up the economy approach" is that it accentuates inequalities in income. The tax reductions have been principally benefiting the higher-income taxpayers. Taxes, as a result, do not redistribute incomes. Indeed, recent tax changes probably will move in the opposite direction as the surtax rates on higher incomes are reduced while tax loopholes remain. The resulting economic expansion is unevenly distributed—those better off gain much more than those at the bottom.

Despite these objections, it is clear that "heating up" the economy does provide more jobs; that it makes more possible, though it does not insure, the employment of low-skill workers by reducing slack in the labor market, and by forcing employers to reconsider their employment requirements; and it probably pushes up wage levels, which is important to the employed, low-paid poor. Most important, possibly, is that swiftly increasing gross national product makes it politically more acceptable to divert some of the additional income to improving the situation of the poor. This may not reduce inequalities, but it does aid the poor. An economy that is not expanding is not likely to divert great resources to those who are not economically productive.

Some of the difficulties in this approach can be overcome if more selective measures are undertaken. Instead of broad, aggregate measures to benefit the economy generally, more pinpointed efforts at affecting the private economy are possible. The Area Redevelopment Administration program has the specific goal of encouraging industry to locate in communities that have suffered economic decline. A variety of benefits and inducements are offered in pursuit of the goal of relocation or expansion of private industry.¹⁶⁶ The Appalachian program is similarly oriented to a specific area, although the connection to private enterprise stimulation seems somewhat indirect in that the emphasis is on highway construction. The increased concern of the Small Business Administration to make loans to Negro businessmen is again an example of selective measures at affecting the private economy. Keyserling has urged large-scale government stimulation of the construction in-

---

[165] *New York Times*, March 2, 1964, 27:1. Two out of three of New York City's employees have white-collar jobs. In 1963 the number of white-collar jobs increased by 35,000 and the number of production or blue-collar jobs decreased by 15,000.

[166] We are not assessing here the level of success of the ARA, which has been criticized from a variety of points of view. See Sar A. Levitan, *Aid to Depressed Areas* (Baltimore: Johns Hopkins Press, 1964).

dustry, not only because this expansion would spur the economy to higher total production and demand, but also because it would provide low-skill employment to many.[167]

It would be possible along these lines to attempt to promote the hiring of unskilled labor. In European nations, companies are encouraged and rewarded for hiring difficult-to-place labor like the physically handicapped. Adaptations of the unemployment compensation rates might induce American employers to hire school dropouts, low-skilled workers, or the handicapped. But in an economy with considerable unemployment, such programs might shift the burden of unemployment from one group to another, and they would have little chance of adoption. This point underlines the contention that high-level economic activity is basic to a wide variety of policies.

The general theme here is that the private economy could be induced to do many things that are socially desirable. There is, perhaps, too much of a residue of mechanical, 1930ish thinking among many liberals that only the expansion of the public sector is a social good. Many social improvements can be attained by making it economically worthwhile for private enterprise to engage in them.[168] Indeed, in the present political climate of the United States, the engaging of the private profit motive in the pursuit of socially important objectives may be the most easily obtainable procedure for purposeful social advance. Other goals may not be achieved in the emphasis on the private sector, but the latter should not be disregarded as an activity that can be steered into better social adaptability.[169]

Regulating the Economy

Two kinds of recent legislation regulate the economy so that it benefits the low-income populations, minimum wage laws and civil rights legislation.

The minimum-wage laws, federal and state,[170] attempt to provide

[167] Keyserling, *Progress or Poverty, op. cit.*
[168] A decline in federal defense expenditures might prompt many firms to rethink their priorities and expectations. Many see the "war on poverty" as taking up the slack of reduced defense activities if some fronts of the Cold War melt.
[169] This paragraph has been stimulated by the writings of Harry Bredemeier and by discussions with Bertram Gross, who has emphasized the importance of the political implementation of blueprinted economic programs. See Harry Bredemeier, "New Strategies for the War on Poverty," *Trans-Action*, 2, 1 (November–December 1964). Bertram Gross is editing a series on comparative national planning, published by Syracuse University Press.
[170] New York City has passed laws to provide a municipal minimum. They have been involved in litigation about the right of a city to have such legislative powers.

an income floor. They obviously benefit those at the unskilled level who are unable to develop enough bargaining power to achieve higher wages by themselves. It is clear that the minimum wage affects only those of the poor who are employed in jobs covered by the law.

Low-paid workers often lack minimum-wage protection, specifically migratory workers and farm laborers who are not covered because agricultural lobbies have been successful in winning specific exemptions from the law. In all, only half the nonagricultural and salaried workers are covered by some form of minimum-wage legislation.

Coupled with this problem is the question of the level of the minimum wage. Frequently, it is so low that it does not afford much income protection. In 1956, when the federal minimum wage was raised to $1.00 an hour, only 2 million of the 24 million in covered occupations actually earned less than the minimum. Many workers earning less than $1.00 per hour were simply not included under the broadened definition of covered employment. In 1961, 3.6 million new workers were added, but again only two-thirds of a million of these newly covered were earning less than one dollar per hour.

Despite increases in coverage in recent years, our minimum-wage legislation still fails to provide protection for persons in our lowest-paid occupations. These people fall foul of the contention that extending coverage or moving up the minimum wage level would eliminate jobs for the low-skilled. Employers might be bankrupted by a higher wage bill or might resort to labor-saving technology to reduce wage costs. For these and other reasons, some have argued for an assurance of a minimum income level rather than a minimum hourly wage.[171]

Antidiscrimination employment laws and regulations at the federal, state, and local levels seek to improve the chances of the minority poor—the Negroes, the Spanish-Americans, the Puerto Ricans—so that they may move out of poverty by moving up to higher-level jobs. Because of the difficulty of proving discrimination and the reluctance of many governments to use power to insure fair employment, these laws and regulations have not produced significant improvements as yet.

These two types of measures designed to regulate the economy are not likely to have great immediate effects. Raising the overtime penalty to increase the number of jobs might be more effective. As employers need more labor, they often increase the overtime employment of those already employed, since this practice is cheaper than hir-

---

[171] Cf. Lampman, "Programs for Poverty," *op. cit.*, p. 14; Milton Friedman, *Capitalism and Freedom* (Chicago: University of Chicago Press, 1962), pp. 192–193; Edward E. Schwartz, "A Way to End the Means Test," *Social Work*, 9 (July 1964).

ing a new worker whose "fringe benefits" costs of pension contribution, hospital insurance, etc., would be greater than the increased costs of overtime and fringe benefits of current employees. By raising the penalty rate for overtime from the present rate of one-and-a-half times base rate, overtime could become more expensive than hiring new labor. It has been argued that a great many *new* jobs could be generated in this way. The counterargument is that it is costly and might lead to cost-price inflation and to reduced production and employment. Although new jobs would be created, we do not know whether there would be more jobs for low-skilled workers.

The Kennedy administration was against the idea of a reduced regular workweek, but the workweek has been reduced drastically over the decades, and a 40-hour "normal" workweek has only the sanction of custom behind it. Indeed, in many offices the workweek is no more than 35 hours. Increased agitation for reducing the workweek as an employment stimulator is likely to occur in the 1960s.

The expansion of the federally supported, state-administered employment services is also suggested as a means of improving job opportunities by more effectively linking individuals with jobs. In recent years the state employment services expanded their activities in the field of placement of professionals, but the impact of the Economic Opportunity Act is likely to move them toward concern with low-skilled workers, especially youth. One way of improving their usefulness is to make it mandatory for firms with government contracts, especially those in the defense industries, to place their openings with the services, though they would be free to recruit wherever they wished. This expansion of the services would be in the right direction. At present, our public employment services play a very limited role in the job placement field, compared to the role played by public bureaus in other nations, because of the lobbying of private employment agencies in the United States.

Public Creation of Jobs

The private sector has been able to produce relatively few jobs in recent years. Between 1950 and 1960, "nine out of ten of the net new jobs added to the American economy were added outside of the private sector." [172] The main source of new employment was the public sector, the nonprofit agencies, and government contracts with private industry (as in the defense field). The unemployment of Negroes would have been much greater than it was if it had not been for the

---
[172] Eli Ginzberg, "Needed: A New Perspective," *American Child*, 47, 1 (January 1965), pp. 22–23.

availability of jobs outside the profit sector: in 1958 to 1962, 85 percent of the new jobs for Negroes were in the public and nonprofit sectors.[173] Nor is the demand in the private sector likely to absorb a large number of those with limited skills. Consequently, many like Bayard Rustin, a civil rights leader, have argued for more direct public creation of jobs.

The nature of the jobs that we wish to create or expand depends, in part, on the assessment of the structural changes which have contributed to the problems of unemployment, poverty, and inequality. From one position the problem is viewed as temporary; consequently, only one-shot measures are needed until the economy recovers from its lethargy and economic expansion resumes at the pace needed to provide jobs and opportunity for all. So defined, a program of road building, public works, and such can serve as useful pump priming for economic expansion, and also as a device for the provision of temporary jobs for people who are temporarily disadvantaged.

An alternate view defines the task as expansion of the public sector on *a permanent basis*. Long-term employment to compensate for the declining availability of unskilled employment in the private sector must be found. In order to achieve such a redistribution of job opportunities, it is necessary to seek out and to develop labor-intensive rather than labor-saving industries. The new frontier, the new job-creating industry of the future, the new consumer market, is believed to lie in accommodation to the unsatisfied demand for social services—health, education, recreation, and housing for the poor. This new consumer market is best satisfied (some would argue that it can only be satisfied) by the public sector, since service, not profit, and jobs, not efficiency, are the major underlying motives for the expansion of social and physical amenities.

Already there have been sustained efforts by both public and voluntary sectors to cope with the demand for housing, medical care, and educational and recreational services. The amount expended annually for the purchase of these services lies between 30 and 90 billion dollars, depending on the definition of the social services. But a problem arises in using social services as a source of employment for the unskilled, since many of these services appear to require a high level of training and skill. If the expansion of services is to reduce unemployment, it will be necessary to redefine the tasks of the professionals who man the social service industry. This can be achieved by delineating the profes-

---

[173] This figure was obtained from the Ornati–Twentieth Century Fund study of poverty in an affluent society.

sional tasks that can be delegated to lower-skilled persons.[174] Such a move would, in effect, reverse the tendency of the helping industries that have sought to raise standards and increase the quality of services by expanding the employment of professionals.

The nonprofessional proposal, of course, poses many troublesome issues: the career line for these subprofessionals, the opportunity for advancement, the role of performance and skill achievement, experience rather than education as the sources of credentials, the possibility of stigma for those working in the programs. There is the more disturbing problem of getting professionals to accept a division of function, especially when limited previous experience in the use of subprofessionals has demonstrated that they can be effective helping persons and can sometimes succeed where professionals, because of trained incapacities, fail. The threat to professionals can be great. In the absence of effective career lines for moving to higher-level, better-paying jobs, nonprofessional positions will be dead-end; since there is no place for the incumbents to go, unskilled labor will pile up, requiring constant increases in the number of such jobs. Consequently, the employment of subprofessionals may, in the end, only prove to be a gimmick, an inauthentic response, if we cannot solve the political problems of entrenched professional interests. But it does offer possibilities of wholly new job opportunities of great benefit to those serviced (and to the former poor providing the services).

At the present time, the number of proposals for augmenting public employment is overwhelming. Most are valid and better than the programs we now have. The overriding question is the political context of the discussion: to what extent are these reforms possible? Strong political support for the direct creation of public and nonprofit employment is lacking. This is, after all, the heart of the matter. If we do educate and train many people, the question of where they will be employed may lead to increased emphasis on assuring employment for those who maneuver through the educational and training maze.

Education

Increasingly, education is suggested as the route out of poverty.[175] This makes much sense for the one-third of the poor under the age of

---

[174] See Frank Riessman and Arthur Pearl, *New Careers for the Poor* (New York: The Free Press of Glencoe, 1965).

[175] The link between education and poverty, as we indicated earlier, is not as pronounced as is frequently asserted. The incidence of poverty among those with eight years or less of education is 37 percent; for those with nine to eleven

eighteen, especially the youngest. Unfortunately, however, this solution is sometimes offered as a substitute for other programs, neglecting the needs of other poor, especially the aged.

Galbraith has suggested that each year we make massive educational investments in the 100 poorest areas until we are able to serve all the localities suffering from educational neglect. This program would require much more money than is presently spent on education or in poverty programs. Few communities can afford additional outlays, especially Appalachia, and federal aid would have to be greatly extended.

The Negro Revolution has forced political concern for slum schools. In the early 1960s, the President's Committee on Juvenile Delinquency, the Ford Foundation, and other agencies provided financial fuel for schools in the low-income areas of large cities. The expenditure on vocational education rose to much higher levels as a result of the Vocational Education Act of 1964. High-prestige universities are now providing summer tutelage to low-income high school students to strengthen their interest in going to college and to improve their possibilities of entrance to and success in college. But much more has to be done if education is to be the vehicle for social mobility of the poor.

Increased expenditures on education must be disproportionately spent on the poor, as is the intent of President Johnson's educational proposal of 1965. The recent increases in the total amount spent on education have benefited students from poverty homes, but probably not as much as they have benefited the better-off students. As we pointed out earlier in the discussion of inequality, universalistic measures may not benefit the poor as much as other groups.

The education solution assumes that there will be sufficient high-level employment for all who have education. Will this be true of those who do not go on to college or technical school? The rate of unemployment among high school graduates is lower than that of dropouts, but it is still high. The prospect with the shift in labor force demand is that a great increase in high school graduates might result in higher unemployment rates among these groups.

The occupational prospects of the next years suggest that high school graduation will not be sufficient to guarantee decent, secure employment, especially if the quality of education offered by our

---

years, it drops to 20 percent. Council of Economic Advisors, *op. cit.*, p. 66. Since the aged, the nonwhites, and farmers—groups with a high incidence of poverty—are likely to be a large part of the poorly educated family heads, the independent role of education in "causing" poverty is reduced. It may be that poverty is linked to these other characteristics, rather than to lack of education per se.

schools is not substantially improved. The current emphasis on the occupational effectiveness of the high school diploma is probably exaggerated. For education to be a real help for poor children, they must finish college or technical school.[176] Thus the needed educational programs are more costly and difficult than many of our statements about education imply.[177]

In education, as in other matters, we must not overlook the difficulty of obtaining true equality of opportunity. To enable the poor to take advantage of educational opportunity will require that many influences that at present retard their educational achievement be overcome. There must be better teachers and schools, signs of economic advance among those who have had higher education (which frequently has not been true of Negroes), and financial assistance that can give reasonable hope of attending college. These advances will require sweeping changes in teacher preparation, reshaping schools for greater flexibility, the development of a positive school climate, and the provision of scholarships, fellowships, and financial aid. Some youths will have to be recognized as late bloomers or as talented despite their low grades. We are making important gains along these lines, but much more has to be done.

For those who do not go on to college, vocational preparation must be vastly improved. Frequently we train for obsolescence, since agricultural education and home economics are the major recipients of funds. We do not know which occupations to train for or how to train difficult youth. Our vocational schools are in need of drastic changes —they lack the status, funds, modern equipment, adequate staff, and tradition that make training relevant to career choice. Often they are ill-equipped to provide vocational training and to upgrade skills so as to enhance an individual's capacity to participate effectively in the economy.

The economic effectiveness of education requires that jobs be available. Education and vocational training cannot assure a payoff at the end of the line; the new skills of youth must be in demand. The education of one generation cannot be considered apart from its employment. Nor should older persons and those who do not become high school or college graduates be neglected. "Education" can become a slogan to escape from the wider responsibility of aiding the poor.

[176] Rising education levels do not seem to be solving the economic difficulties of the Negro. The median income of a Negro who is a college graduate is at the level of a white who has had no more than eight years of schooling. Discrimination is not fully overcome by education.
[177] Peter Marris, "Synopsis for an Analysis of Poverty Programs," Public Affairs Program, Ford Foundation (mimeograph), April 1964, p. 22.

Rehabilitation and Training

A popular approach to the reduction of poverty is that of rehabilitation and training. The rehabilitation emphasis assumes that many, if not most, of the poor are the unstable poor, a hard core in great need of various kinds of social work services in order to be able to function more effectively. The hard core is seen as resistant to the progress of the economy; their children are maimed psychologically by growing up in a fatherless family, and they inherit a welfare status in their adulthood. Consequently, the general orientation is to rehabilitate to economic self-support, so that dependency is reduced.

The theory of the poverty cycle is the basis for these programs. Inadequate family life is believed to create a poor milieu; children are not motivated to an early interest in learning and consequently do badly in school. School failures lead to limited jobs with inadequate pay, high unemployment, and vulnerability to occupational obsolescence. Marginal participation in the economy is simply another way of describing marginal capacity to adjust to the urban environment, accompanied by unstable family life. Thus childhood deprivation presages poverty in adulthood and, as the new adults procreate, a new cycle of poverty ensues. This theory directs attention to the importance of personal inadequacy. Early intervention to strengthen family life, with programs of education and youth retraining, becomes the strategy to reverse the cycle. Sometimes a saturation theory is proposed whereby interventions at many different points in the cycle are attempted.

Theories that focus on the deficiencies and limitations in individual personality are in vogue because, as Wooton has observed, they "enjoy a considerable practical advantage": it is easier to put up a clinic than to rebuild a slum.[178] Certainly a good part of the appeal of rehabilitation and training is that they emphasize changing individual characteristics rather than modifying the institutions which impinge on the poor.

There *are* roles for rehabilitation and training. But they are not magic forces in a war on poverty. Surely, some of the emphasis on rehabilitation is primarily a way of reducing welfare rolls with little concern for those who need financial aid. Sometimes the theme is punitive —"Rehabilitate or else be cut off from welfare!"

Some of the poor do suffer from the inability to handle their problems. Providing fresh opportunity may not be effective since they cannot take hold and grow with opportunity: "in some families where

---

[178] Barbara Wooton, *Social Science and Social Pathology* (New York: Humanities Press, 1959).

economic conditions have improved after a long period of economic deprivation (or) family difficulties, withdrawing the stress of economic insecurity may be insufficient. The toll of the stress frequently must be overcome. Special help may be necessary to bring about familial changes of great importance." [179]

To say this is not to assert confidence that we have professions that know how to deal effectively with the problems of the poor. Over the years the social work profession disengaged itself from the poor; [180] now it is beginning to reorient itself to them. Many goals and techniques of rehabilitation will have to be adapted to the needs and perspectives of poor families. It is not clear whether the social work profession is willing to do this.

In the emphasis on professionalized help to the poor, needed institutional changes may be neglected. For example, a frequent strategy is to upgrade the educational level of the professionals who deal with the poor. The Welfare Act of 1962 concentrated on making it possible to have smaller case loads and more highly trained personnel in local welfare departments. The evidence is scanty that professionalizing of services greatly increases effective service. More important, perhaps, is the continued debilitating stigma which is frequently attached to the recipient of welfare. Investigative and rehabilitative functions are still not clearly separated in many welfare departments.[181] Frequently welfare recipients are subject to humiliating scrutiny and policing.[182]

The community action programs under the Economic Opportunity Act of 1964 emphasize rehabilitation and training. In so doing, they may find institutions which have failed with the poor without exacting important changes from these institutions.[183] These institutions need additional funds, but they also require new perspectives, programs, technology, and commitments.

Today the major approach to the reduction of poverty is preparation of youth for work. (By contrast, efforts to overcome poverty in England have focused on the realization of income and the provision of

[179] S. M. Miller, "The American Lower Classes," *op. cit.*, p. 16.
[180] For a masterful account of this disengagement, see Richard Cloward and Irwin Epstein, "Private Social Welfare's Disengagement from the Poor: The Case of Family Adjustment Agencies," *Proceedings of Annual Social Work Day Conference* (Buffalo, N.Y.: University of Buffalo, 1965).
[181] Eveline Burns, "What's Wrong with Public Welfare," *Social Service Review*, 36 (1962), pp. 113–114.
[182] Charles Reich, "Midnight Welfare Searches and the Social Security Act," *Yale Law Journal*, 72 (June 1963), pp. 1347–1360.
[183] Martin Rein and S. M. Miller, "Social Action on the Installment Plan," *Trans-Action*, 3, 2 (January–February 1966).

physical and social amenities for the aged.) This theme is most prominent in the Job Corps of the Office of Economic Opportunity (OEO), but undoubtedly it will also be strongly represented in the OEO projects financed by the Community Action Program. This emphasis on retraining is an exceedingly important thrust in social policy in the United States. Its importance can readily be noted in programs to reduce unemployment by job retraining (Manpower Development and Training Act), to attack the scourge of depressed areas (Area Redevelopment Act), to meet the dislocations of those who are affected by our trade agreements with other countries (Trade Expansion Act), and to reduce dependency (1962 amendments to the Social Security Act).[184] The emphasis on training and education is also found in the Grey Area Projects, sponsored by the Ford Foundation, and in the delinquency prevention programs, sponsored by the President's Committee on Delinquency and Youth Crime.

Many of the training programs for youth presently supported by MDTA funds are increasingly emphasizing prevocational training, "motivation for work," personal grooming, the development of aspirations, and the development of "appropriate work habits." It is likely that the Job Corps and the projects financed by the Community Action Program will follow this pattern. These are remedial programs which take as their major assumption that if unemployed youth have a new outlook, their employment opportunities will improve considerably. Often, too, the programs rely on work as a device for correcting individual defects, rather than as an employment-inducing venture. The assumption is that the children of the poor are immersed in a "culture of poverty" and that their poor work habits and deficient motivation must be sponged off. Although this may be true of many candidates for "retraining," it is certainly not true of all.

One danger of the training programs is that "creaming" may occur; only high-level risks may be included in the programs.[185] The experiences under the U.S. Manpower Development and Training Act are instructive here. The Act is aimed at rooting out the hard-core, poverty-stricken workers who are marginally employed, unemployed, or underemployed, and providing them with skills and jobs. Preliminary reports issued by the Labor Department indicate that the retraining program has favored those with the greatest amount of education —perhaps those who are most able to secure jobs on their own initiative. Nearly 63 percent of all the nation's unemployed have not

[184] *Ibid.*
[185] We must also consider those who drop out of the training programs, out of school, and out of retraining. What next for them?

completed high school, and 40 percent have never passed the eighth grade. Yet, after the first year of operation, 60 percent of those who participated in the new federal training program were high school graduates, and only 3 percent had not gone beyond elementary school. Similarly, only 10 percent of enrolled trainees were 45 years of age and over, although this age group accounts for about 30 percent of the unemployed.[186]

Programs which make youth more employable are the easiest to initiate because they are least disturbing to the operation of established institutions. In the main, they remain peripheral to vocational training, job placement, and job creation.[187] The effectiveness of these programs depends on their success in integrating education, training, and the world of work, but the task of coordinating the work of governmental departments and agencies, which are jealously independent of one another, is extraordinarily difficult. If the efforts to win cooperation fail, while the prevocational program succeeds, there is danger that the youth who are motivated to continue training or to secure work may find themselves unable to satisfy their expanded aspirations. To avoid this danger, effective mechanisms for reabsorbing graduates into the educational and occupational systems must be provided.

To achieve successful integration of autonomous programs designed to motivate, to train, and to place in jobs, the theory of the poverty cycle must be extended to embrace a theory of institutional change. On the one hand, there is the formidable task of coordinating different functional tasks administered by and responsible to different levels of government. On the other hand, there is the equally formidable task of creating vitally needed reforms in our vocational and job placement systems.

Retraining programs are not adequately conceived in the setting of a broader framework for a step toward a national labor policy, that is, a strategy for promoting institutional reforms in vocational training, job placement, and job definition.[188] They are likely, consequently, to be-

[186] Seymour L. Wolfbein, "The First Year of the Manpower Act," in Arthur M. Ross, ed., *Unemployment and the American Economy* (New York: John Wiley and Sons, 1964), pp. 65, 66.

[187] In this discussion we have underplayed the significance of job retraining for adults because the "war on poverty" is more specifically linked to youth and because many of the issues are similar.

[188] An important exception is the report of Senator Joseph Clark's Subcommittee on Employment and Manpower Committee on Labor and Public Welfare, United States Senate, *Towards Full Employment: Proposals for a Comprehensive Employment and Manpower Policy in the United States*, 88th Congress, 2nd Session, 1964.

come "aging vats," controlling youth and keeping them out of the labor market for a while, with the hope that increased age will make them more "employable." Training is a dangerous course if we cannot assure employment at the end of the sequence.

Income-Maintenance Programs

Another strategy is to employ economic measures that directly redistribute funds to the poor, raising them to higher levels of income. Transfer payments, or income-maintenance programs, as these government disbursements of income (e.g., social security, welfare assistance, veterans' benefits, etc.) are called, provide an economic floor for recipients. Obviously, transfer payments are crucial for those poor families in which the head is unemployed or out of the labor force. In some situations welfare payments go to families with an employed wage earner whose income is insufficient.

The redistributive emphasis is supported by those of a liberal persuasion in economics and politics. Shifting funds to the poor through transfer payments, lowered taxes, and public consumption is seen as stimulating the economy by expanding consumption. In contrast to the first approach of stimulating the private sector to expand economic activity, this approach directly benefits the consumer. In spending his increased income on various goods, he furnishes increased demand for products, leading to increased sales, production, investment, and employment. The underconsumptionist bias reverses the funnel-down orientation of the private sector approach.

Tied in with this underconsumptionist orientation is the emphasis on the need to expand public consumption. Galbraith has eloquently described the crisis of private affluence confronting public squalor in analyzing the inadequate expenditures on recreational facilities, hospitals, schools, and mass transportation. Increased government expenditures are needed on those things that cannot be purchased by individuals. Such increases in the public sector are primarily aimed at benefiting individuals as consumers and not as producers. As such, ideological lines are drawn between those who wish to stimulate business directly and those who seek to improve the conditions of consumers directly.

The increase in the public sector expenditures may not benefit the poor as much as other groups, but it does provide greater opportunity to utilize certain kinds of resources than do the approaches involving primary stimulation of the private economy. We lump the expansion of the public sector with other measures of redistribution, because it attempts to provide services that would be missing if these expenditures were not provided. The extent to which these expenditures are redistributive depends on the nature of the tax system and the utilization of the services—do lower-income taxpayers receive increasingly more, or less, in service than they pay in taxes?

The general emphasis on increasing redistributive measures or the public sector is under attack. To some, the welfare state symbolizes man's humanity to man, but for others it suggests the loss of individual responsibility and control and the substitution of a flabby, ineffectual, and misplaced do-goodism.

Social security payments relative to the average income level in the United States are lower today than a generation go. In the short run, benefits have failed to maintain a constant purchasing power and have not provided the aged with a share in rising productivity. "The worker who retired in 1954 with the average benefit of $66.60 on the one hand, not only lost out in relationship to working neighbors, but his $71.00 benefit check at the end of 1962 brought 7 percent less goods and services than his first benefit." [189]

Social security is largely self-financing. Its base assumption would have to be altered if the present form of financing is to be progressive and if the program is to be redistributive. If the wage base were raised to $15,000 or $20,000 with a progressive tax, the social security program could prove to be a major instrument of redistribution. As of now, it probably redistributes some income from those slightly above the poverty line to those below. Higher-income groups do not contribute to the reshuffling because of the structure of the system. Unemployment compensation has a similar history of inadequate levels: average payments relative to wage levels are lower today than in 1939. Furthermore, persons in the poorer states receive lower unemployment payments than persons in wealthier states. Many exhaust their benefits before they are able to secure new employment. As periods of unemployment become longer, this is an increasing problem.

The most surprising fact is that only slightly more than half (55 percent) of the poor receive any form of public transfer payment such as social security, unemployment compensation, or public assistance. Contrary to much writing about the exploitation of public welfare by the poor, only 23 percent of all the poor receive any form of public assistance.[190] Those most economically disprivileged receive limited help from our social welfare machinery.

Myrdal has pointed out the inadequacy of protection from vicissitudes: various social security schemes, as well as many minimum wage

[189] Lenore Epstein, "Income Security Standards in Old Age," Research Report 3, Social Security Administration, U.S. Department of Health, Education and Welfare, 1963, p. 23.
[190] Morgan et al., *op. cit.*, pp. 215–216.

regulations, stop just above the neediest groups of people. Voluntary health insurance schemes are much too expensive for the poorest, who show the highest incidence of illness and ill health, both mentally and physically. The introduction of Medicare should greatly improve the economics of health for the aged. In the same way, agricultural policy has mainly aided the big and progressive farmers and has done little if anything for small farmers, small tenants and agricultural workers.[191]

Indeed, we have quite a different picture of the so-called welfare state when we examine all sorts of overt and hidden transfers and subsidies. It is surprising to learn that as much money is spent on agricultural subsidies, which go largely to higher-income farmers, as is spent on public welfare by all forms of expenditure. Airlines and shipping firms receive sizable subsidies. Tariffs are a form of a subsidy which we all pay as consumers. A huge subsidy goes to oil companies through a special depletion allowance permitted them on their tax returns.

As one studies the tax situation, one learns of all kinds of hidden and unrecognized subsidies and inequities. For example, the tax deduction for dependents has the result of reducing the tax burden of higher-income recipients much more than that of lower-income recipients. It is a form of subsidy to large, high-income families, although it is not recognized as such.[192] The minor changes in the distribution of income before and after taxes suggest that our tax structure is not redistributing income as is commonly thought.

Whether the public sector expenditure actually benefits the poor depends, in part, on how public consumption is financed. Low-income groups can be taxed to pay the bill. This raises what we believe to be one of the most fundamental policy issues: who pays and who benefits? Data already available in this country and abroad suggest that the poor are heavily taxed, and public benefits tend to reach the middle- rather than the lowest-income groupings. The ineffective protection to the poor and the variety of subsidies to industry have led Michael Harrington to conclude that our policy is "free enterprise for the poor, socialism for the rich." [193] In his view, the poor are relatively unprotected, subject to market forces, whereas industry is in privileged enclaves, protected from the vicissitudes of market forces.

In this country we have not begun a systematic analysis of the distribution of social benefits. In Britain, Titmuss [194] and his colleagues

---

[191] Gunnar Myrdal, *Challenge to Affluence* (New York: Pantheon Books, 1963).
[192] See Stern, *op. cit.*
[193] Harrington, *op. cit.*
[194] Richard M. Titmuss, "The Social Division of Welfare," in *Essays on The Welfare State* (New Haven, Conn.: Yale University Press, 1958), and *Income Distribution and Social Change* (Toronto: University of Toronto Press, 1962).

have attempted to assess the overall distribution of the benefits of their welfare state—a program presumed to be far more advanced than the American service state. The conclusion reached is "that the major beneficiaries . . . have been the middle classes, that the middling income groups get more from the State than the lower income groups, that taxation often hits the poor harder than the well-to-do, and in general that the middle classes receive good standards of welfare while working people receive a Spartan minimum." [195]

In a probing analysis of America's social services, Hacker challenges the rhetoric that assumes social services are distributed as a matter of political right and not charity, that the quality of services is as adequate as those open to individuals who are able to draw on their private resources, and that collective protections are available to care for the individual unable to provide for himself. His searching analysis supports the conclusions reached by Abel-Smith. He notes: "Urban renewal programs tear down slums but they have not been notable for raising low-rent housing after the bulldozers have left the scene. And price supports go chiefly to upper-income farmers rather than to those at the marginal level. Activities such as these tend to benefit well-organized interest groups or at best the middle class as a whole." [196]

Stigma attaches to those who receive transfer payments for consumption; subsidies for business are exempt from shame. "Outdoor relief" for farmers, which encourages individuals to stay in an industry no longer requiring their labor, is seen as a transfer to a business and is not stigmatized as are welfare payments. In contrast, special social services for the poor tend to be inadequate in quality; frequently they are demeaning in their eligibility requirements, utilizing a "means test" and demanding a behavior which evidences a "deserving poor." Nonetheless, the recipients are stigmatized as incompetents or worse.

On the other hand, universalistic services tend to be more effectively utilized by the middle- and upper-income groupings. The British National Health Service is not redistributive; in fact, it appears to work the other way. It enhances the disparity between classes. The main reason for this is that payment for the health service is by a flat rate, a poll tax which, by taxing all income groupings equally, is regressive. Thus the burden falls disproportionately on the low-income groups. This disproportion in payments is reinforced by the inequality of utilization. The working classes continue to define the doctor as a superior,

---

[195] Brian Abel-Smith, "Whose Welfare State?," in Norman MacKenzie, ed., *Conviction* (London: MacGibbon and Kee, 1958), p. 55.
[196] Andrew Hacker, "Again the Issue of the Welfare State," *New York Times Magazine*, March 22, 1964.

higher-class person to whom one must assume an attitude of deference. The doctor should not be bothered with minor ailments. Doctors, by their very demeanor, reinforce rather than weaken such attitudes. The working classes in general have a more stoic attitude toward pain and disease and are not as likely to seek remedies at the first signs of discomfort. The middle classes have a different attitude toward pain and discomfort; they have a broader range of illnesses—flatfeet, orthodontures, etc.—about which they are concerned. The doctor is more likely to be seen as a public servant. They view the service as something to which they are entitled; and, finally, they are better informed about their privileges and more capable of negotiating obstacles when they are encountered.

Perhaps the most dramatic inequity of entitlement is the National Assistance scheme (public relief in this country), in which the poor are entitled to dentures, glasses, and other medical benefits without an additional cost which recipients of the Health Insurance programs are required to pay. But those entitled to this free service often do not know about their privileges, and little is done to bring them to their attention. There appears to be a conspiracy of silence against the poor; by keeping their rights quiet, they will not use them and expenditures will be less.

In the United States it is claimed that the poor have access to the finest medical services in outpatient departments of hospitals and inpatient hospital ward services. Yet the more typical pattern in the clinic is fragmented, discontinuous services, where the same physician seldom sees the same patient twice. Ward services are likely to be inferior in any but a teaching hospital, and even in a teaching hospital the uninteresting (from a teaching point of view) medical histories of the poor are likely to work against their receiving quality service.

The provision of high-quality, unstigmatized services to the poor is a crucial issue in our society where welfare is frequently employed as a measure of social control over the poor. Often our concern is not to eliminate poverty but to reduce the financial burdens of dependency on public support.

We still have a residue of feeling that social services are a temporary, fringe element in society. In truth, they are a necessary and permanent ingredient of a mobile, urbanized, industrial society.[197] Our concern with maintaining incentive to work and limiting public expenditures often leads us to provide only minimal subsistence levels rather than adequate levels of maintenance. We adhere to this concern for uphold-

[197] See Miller and Rein, "Change, Ferment and Ideology in the Social Services," *op. cit.*

ing the incentive to work, even with those whose labor is unwanted—the aged and the handicapped.

The issue of how to distribute social service will become increasingly critical in the 1960s and 1970s. In this period the emphasis in America's welfare state will probably shift away from individual security and price stabilization to the expansion of opportunity and economic growth. With this change attention will have to focus on the machinery employed to distribute services more effectively and equitably. The most biting criticism of many of our present services is that they fail to reach those in greatest need. The allocative mechanisms will become important political as well as technical issues. We will need to rely on new measures of distribution if we are to be successful in reaching the poor, the disadvantaged, and those with little access to opportunity, if we are to gain for them a greater share of the rewards of our society. The aim is not only to reduce poverty in the affluent society, but also to attentuate some inequalities—and to do so without stigma for those who are benefiting from the new and reshaped mechanisms of redistribution.

Conclusion

Our analysis has emphasized that poverty is part of the basic character of our society and economy; it is the other face of the affluent society. Poverty is an outgrowth of the inequalities in treatment accorded to the Negro; it is the plight of the employed poor; it is the neglect of marginal groups who cannot compete in a selective, market-oriented economy and are pressed out of the labor force; it is the unsettledness of those who were left behind in the great migration from a rural to an urban America. We believe that most of the poor are not the slothful and work-shy that nineteenth-century public policy so dreaded. Their poverty can best be understood in the setting of the organization of our economic and value systems which disfavor these groups. But there is danger that present policies to reduce poverty will continue to be wedded to the view that poverty is largely a reflection of individual pathology. There is danger that we will continue to respond to today's problems with nineteenth-century ideas of causation and treatment.

Conservative definitions of these problems imply that the poor are morally, socially, and psychologically disorganized, that inhabitants of slums are fundamentally unsocialized. Thus we disregard theories of change and respond with individual solutions. The solutions we advance to social problems are typically those in which professionals who work with *individuals* play the most prominent roles. Our response to the problem of insufficient or inadequate medical care is to train more doctors—not to reorganize the distribution of medical services. Our response to delinquency has been to favor more police, more probation officers, more judges, more caseworkers, and reduced case loads. Our response to poverty is to rely on expanding the motivation of vulnerable groups. We have not been trained to respond in terms of intervening more directly at strategic points in the social structure; indeed, we have probably been socialized against such an approach.

To change "the tangled roots of poverty" requires a widely ranging and well-financed set of programs. But we also need an *authenticity* in our commitment to help the poor, so that our programs are flexibly adaptive, the climate of our helping agencies is receptive to the poor, and personnel are decent in their behavior. Also needed is a strengthened societal *commitment* to improve the condition of the poor—and we believe that to reduce poverty today requires the reduction of some inequalities.

Some of the poor, especially Negroes, are finding a political and public voice. We think it likely that more and more of the poor will become politically aware. And in so becoming they will learn to bring attention to their problems; at the same time, they will overcome the debilitating feelings of powerlessness. We have tried to express our anguish that poverty exists in an economy of our plenitude and our conviction that the solution to poverty does not lie in blaming the poor and avoiding institutional change. In our society the manner of dealing with poverty will show our values and our style.

10

Problems of Housing and the Renewal of the City

Scott Greer

W<small>HY</small> is housing a problem? This may seem a foolish question, but it is by no means apparent that housing constitutes a "social problem." To be sure, houses are unevenly distributed, the poor getting poor houses, the rich getting better ones. Still, that is true also of automobiles, and we do not speak of an "automobile problem." Why should housing be a social problem or a problem of policy? In order to understand this, it is useful to consider some of the history of housing conceived as socially problematic.

The Middle-Class View: Housing as a Social Anchor

One useful hint comes from a study of the origins of modern town planning. In talking about the slums of the early nineteenth century in Great Britain, Ashworth states:

> Their inhabitants were in no position to obtain the constitution of any additional governing body, and for the time no one from outside felt much interest in discovering what their problems were or, indeed, that they had any special problems at all. But the societies of the new congested districts were not discrete entities and more and more people outside them gradually became aware of the pressure of their novel, powerful, and alarming qualities. Even if he were not his brother's keeper, every man of property was affected by the multiplication of thieves; every one who valued his life felt it desirable not to have a mass of carriers of virulent diseases too close at hand. . . . It was morality (or, more exactly, criminality) and disease that were causing concern. Overcrowding and con-

gestion, poverty, crime, ill health and heavy mortality were shown to be conditions found altogether.[1]

Such a situation led some citizens to become concerned with crowded housing as a source of social evil. Their concern did not disappear as time went on. When, 150 years later, I asked people in one American city after another, "Why did you ever get urban renewal going here?" they answered, "There's one reason. People looked at a certain part of this town and they said, 'It's a slum. Something should be done about it.' "

The belief that housing and neighborhoods are "social problems" is largely based on the notion that problems arising in areas filled with people are in some sense contagious. This contagion is largely confined to such "diseases" as criminality, poverty, illiteracy, and physical breakdowns. Some people, however, are concerned with the slums because of their suspicion that those living inside the slums are likely to have anarchistic effects upon the society as a whole. Thus a recent interview in one of the new nations:

> QUESTION: "How do you see urban redevelopment—as a tool or as an end?"
> ANSWER: "This area could be the nucleus of an epidemic—because a lot of the domestic help of all this city lives here. Then, there's the social anchor concept—the notion that you produce illegitimacy and early sex by eight or nine people living in one room. They grow up in the wrong moral atmosphere. Segregation of the sexes after the age of ten is what we want to achieve."
> QUESTION: "Do you really think this is true?"
> ANSWER: "I really don't know." [2]

Often we see that people are trying to cure a wide variety of ills in the society by applying the poultices of housing policy.

In the same vein, urban redevelopers in the new nations have said that housing is their country's *number one* problem. Asked why they think this, they say, "We believe that the people who are have-nots, who are concentrated in these areas, are going to create massive civil disturbances in this society." (Social scientists, studying such societies, often find such disturbances unlikely.) In old and new nations alike, the old fear of the have-nots crowded into certain areas of the city is still powerful. The "haves" see the slums as the bailiwicks of disease, organized crime, and revolution.

This belief has been largely due to rapid urbanization and the devel-

---

[1] Williams Ashworth, *The Genesis of Modern British Town Planning* (London: Routledge and Kegan Paul, 1954), pp. 47–48.
[2] Interview, official of the Ministry of Housing, Jamaica, 1962.

opment of "noncitizens" within the urban society as a whole. One origin of the notion that housing is a social problem is the assumption that we *create* outsiders by housing them together in segregated parts of the city. Culturally different and differently rewarded, the successful do not find it comfortable to deal with such people. Therefore the interest in abolishing the slums; it is thought that improved housing increases the outsider's stake in the society, in law and order. The outsider is tied to a house as to a "social anchor." (Others, of course, prefer to build walls around slums.)

The Argument for Equity

Housing is an important reward of an urban society. It can be a "problem" if many people think it *unfairly* distributed. This is the argument for equity; the person who evaluates his housing evaluates his reward; if he finds that as a "decent and honest person," working hard and gaining recognition in other areas, he still does not have "decent housing," he feels cheated. The United States Housing Act has a deceptively simple purpose: it proposes to provide "a decent home and a suitable living environment for every American family." Fairly well-defined consumer norms indicate what a "decent" and "average" household should expect from the society.[3] (This has nothing to do with the larger question: What kinds of housing are needed by what kinds of people in a society?)

The Confusion of Norms: A Problem of Definition

Housing norms vary enormously. The palace of Louis XIV at Versailles was an elaborate and beautiful building with no plumbing. By contemporary American housing codes, which place great emphasis on plumbing, the palace of the Sun King would be substandard. In this respect it would resemble two-thirds of the substandard dwelling units in the United States. Furthermore, so various are consumer norms that the United States, as measured by the norms of some of the poorer nations, has hardly any substandard housing units. In contrast, some of these nations, as measured by American standards, have few standard dwellings. Thus we should carefully ask ourselves: What are the accepted norms for housing? What are the ideal norms for housing? What are the *administrative* norms of housing, as they vary between societies? We must know what we are talking about.[4]

[3] See, for empirical evidence of such norms, Janet Abu-Lughod and Mary Mix Foley in Nelson W. Foote, ed., *Housing Choices and Constraints* (New York: McGraw-Hill, 1960).
[4] For the importance of plumbing alone in creating the substandard, see William G. Grigsby, *Housing Markets and Public Policy* (Philadelphia: University of Pennsylvania Press, 1964).

Housing in the United States is distributed according to two qualifications: ability to pay and race. An individual can pay only up to a limit, within the bounds of race, for housing that may or may not be what he thinks he deserves. The type of housing people think they deserve is not necessarily what others think they deserve, nor is it necessarily what they get. When we look at the United States as a whole, we find great variation in the discrepancies between the norms defined by housing codes and the kinds of houses in which people live. We find that, judging by the housing codes, some 27 percent of the population lives in substandard housing. Percentages vary from one metropolitan area to another. In Chicago, one of the richest cities in the United States, about 16 percent of the population lives in "substandard" housing.

Different groups of people have different housing norms. On a large scale, the percentage of household income invested in housing has been going down for the entire population for several decades. Among certain social categories the percentage of income invested in housing is consistently lower than the percentage of income invested by others. Renters pay less for housing than owners. There is differential *access* to housing by social type. Some people may not get as much for their housing dollar as others do. In short, there is a lack of consensus on what should be adequate and normal housing for American citizens. The variation in the norms for ordinary housing greatly complicates the question of who is getting adequate housing in the United States.

Social Change and Housing Norms

The question is further complicated by the increase in average income in the United States over the past seven decades. This increase is both the result of, and the cause of, expanded higher education and more demanding and better paying occupations. One general consequence has been a consistent increase in the amount of social choice. Thus the neighborhoods of American cities have become increasingly differentiated by "urbanism" or "familism," since the majority of our urban population now has the choice between the apartment house neighborhood and the horizontal tract development. But there are also important political and financial restraints. Those who define the bases for financing housing, the Federal Housing Authority and the Federal National Mortgage Assurance Agency, have much to do with the kind of housing that is available. Furthermore, those who frame the housing codes have much to do with defining what is a decent and suitable kind of house and neighborhood for American citizens.

The importance of rules is obvious in a large, growing society. But by imposing standardization we may force people to acquiesce to unacceptable, arbitrary norms. Housing codes in the United States are handed down by experts; these experts often cannot justify the requirements of the housing codes by anything except average, middle-class taste. But taste renders all arguments possible. Yet codes based on the preferences of "experts" are made the law of the land, the legal definition of the humanly habitable dwelling.[5]

We have been talking as though the significance, the social *meaning*, of housing were apparent. This is to be expected, for in everyday discourse we assume a complex set of beliefs and values about such ordinary matters as housing. Yet in exploring the kind of social problem found in housing, it is useful to look at those beliefs and values. In so doing we will keep in mind such questions as (1) What social processes result in housing being distributed in a given way among a population? (2) What are the social consequences, if any, of such distributions? (3) What is the effect of the latter on the former? Does housing cause a kind of behavior that results in a particular kind of housing? Is there a vicious circle (or social structure) here?

The Social Significance of Housing

Most societies have developed permanent shelter structures. These shelter structures provide protection, help conserve body heat, and give some privacy to members of the household. Not only are they useful, but they are symbols of the values cherished in the society. They usually tell us something about the prestige structure as well as the definition of an "attractive location." The man's house in the Kerakai village of New Guinea stands central to the village and soars above the huts of the women, just as the luxury hotel rises far above the roofs of the tenements.[6]

Housing reflects, however, more than the prestige system. It rests on the technology and resources of the society. Although the imperial Romans built houses of several stories, these were typically tenements rather than luxury hotels, and Roman heating systems and engineering skills were such that hardly a day passed without several serious fires,

[5] The vague and uncertain grounds for American housing codes are evident in the discussion by a person in charge of the American Public Health Association's work in forming them. Allen A. Twichell discusses his thinking on the subject in "Measuring the Quality of Housing," in Coleman Woodbury, ed., *Urban Redevelopment; Problems and Practices* (Chicago: University of Chicago Press, 1953).

[6] For a cross-cultural discussion see E. Adamson Hoebel, "Housing" in *Man and the Primitive World* (New York: McGraw-Hill, 1949.)

and the collapse of tenements was common.[7] Technology severely limited the height of safe buildings; the wealthy lived in villas. Variation in available resources are also important, as in the adobe mud "apartment houses" of the Southwestern Pueblo Indians, the wooden houses of the northwest coast tribes and, at an extreme, the usual shelter of the Tierra del Fuegan—a scooped hole where the inhabitant huddles, covering his naked body with the hide of a beast.

Within the limits of resources and technology, however, sedentary societies invest heavily in their houses. Much of their wealth is spent on shelter. Thus the "home" is typically the most valuable possession of the American family, and building construction is one of the biggest industries in the United States. Since housing is a reward, it varies with the reward-distributing system of the society; in the United States for the overwhelming majority of the population, the salary earned by the head of the household is the distributing system.

Housing Distribution and Social Choice

Thus patterns of housing distribution result from a range of available housing and a range of choosers—and the choosers vary by the freedom of choice they have. Those with ten dollars a week to spend have little choice in a contemporary city, while those with a thousand dollars a week have almost the entire range of available housing to choose from. Because of this variation and the tendency to build houses of similar price together in "developments," the early social ecologists explained the patterns of people in houses as a result of competition, with "the survival of the fittest to survive" in a given area of the city. Ecological "forces" sorted the people by income and ethnic background and a balance resulted. McKenzie defines the slum as "the area of minimal choice," for here the "losers" congregate. As such, they have in common only their poverty.[8]

Such an approach makes sense if there are rigid limits to most people's choices. A hierarchy of housing advantages coincides with a hierarchy of income. If, further, jobs are inherited, people and their descendants tend to stay in the same neighborhoods. However, as technology and wealth increase our control and choice, the pattern becomes fluid. Modern technology has radically lowered the time needed to travel in the city, and the average real income in the United States

---

[7] Jerome Carcopino, *Daily Life in Ancient Rome* (New Haven, Conn.: Yale University Press, 1940).
[8] R. D. McKenzie, "The Scope of Human Ecology," reprinted in George A. Theodorson, ed., *Studies in Human Ecology* (Evanston, Ill.: Row, Peterson, 1961), p. 35.

has more than doubled during the twentieth century.[9] At the same time, as more demanding and rewarding occupations increase, relative to the total, many people move to higher levels of income, occupation, and education than those of their parents.

The pattern of people in houses now reflects a wider range of choice for the average American. He was once tied to the neighborhood near his place of work (the horsecar was slow and relatively costly), living in a tenement or a three-decker flat building (space was precious when the cost of moving was high). He has been liberated by his rising income and the automobile. Now he can choose the tract development in the suburbs, the older single-family house in the outer city, or the apartments toward the center. There are still limits, of course, and not only at the extremes. Income is not elastic for the average householder, and there are many objects other than houses that he desires. But he is not chained by the friction of space to a "mill-workers' neighborhood" or "the garment district." [10]

Consequences I: Ways of Life

The pattern of people in houses reflects, then, the reward structure of the society. It is a modest clue to that structure, but one increasingly blurred by the widening limits of choice. Aside from this, what importance does it have? What are the *consequences* of differences in housing and housing patterns?

The shape and size of the dwelling unit may affect the kind of social life carried on in it. Walls are social fact; they limit and direct interaction. Thus in the Southwestern Indian pueblos, the first multiple-family dwelling units of North America, the primitive floor plans forced people who lived in the back rooms to walk through all the rooms between the front and back to reach their bedrooms. This resulted in a lack of privacy; the inescapable impingement of one person's actions on another contributed, in turn, to the pacific and courteous behavior found among these nonaggressive and Apollonian people. Without rules of "see no evil, hear no evil, speak no evil," they could not have accommodated. (However, scholars have speculated that the taboo on open violence and hostility might have been one reason for

---

[9] Scott Greer, "Traffic, Transportation, and Problems of the Metropolis," in Robert K. Merton and Robert A. Nisbet, eds., *Contemporary Social Problems* (New York: Harcourt, Brace and World, 1961).
[10] For the pattern of neighborhoods see Chapter 3 in Scott Greer, *The Emerging City: Myth and Reality* (New York: The Free Press of Glencoe, 1962).

their extensive fear and practice of witchcraft—their hostility was expressed in secrecy.)[11]

In contemporary American cities apartment house dwellers are significantly *less* likely to know their neighbors, even though they have easy spatial access to them.[12] The good neighbors in the apartment house are pre-eminently "decent, quiet people who leave you alone." Forced proximity of *actions* does not result in meaningful *interactions* or a strong friendship circle within the apartment house; the privacy of the household is preserved through the use of doors and distant politeness. In the single-family neighborhoods of suburbia, where much activity takes place out of doors, it is more difficult to avoid meaningful interactions with "the neighbors." Furthermore, the single-family house is more useful for the family preoccupied with raising children, since they can be outside the house and still within the surveillance of the parents; thus the single-family neighborhoods are overwhelmingly chosen by family-centered households. The children, in turn, serve to knit the social fabric of the neighborhoods together. They increase interaction among adults, carrying information and presenting problems whose solutions force agreements among households. In other words, the inevitability of interaction in the single-family neighborhoods tends to produce a *normative* structure, a loose understanding of rights and duties, reinforced by familiarity and common interests.

Thus the dwelling unit facilitates or hampers the carrying on of a specific round of life. At one extreme, it makes child rearing a matter of danger and anxiety, as with families of many children who live high up in public housing towers. Here adults must either live in the midst of their children or delegate their safety to someone else. At another extreme, housing can simply fail to provide either health, safety, or comfort.

Consequences II: Differential Association

The clustering of similar housing, resulting in the stocking of neighborhoods with similar people, has further consequences for social behavior. We have mentioned differences in relations with the neighbors. The assignment to a type of house in a type of neighborhood also affects one's access to a local neighborhood within the metropolis. These neighborhoods, whether they are incorporated suburban municipalities or simply "named places" centered on schools and shopping centers within the great city, allow for some collective action on mat-

---

[11] Cf. Hoebel, *op. cit.*
[12] Scott Greer and Peter Orleans, "The Mass Society and the Parapolitical Structure," *American Sociological Review*, 27 (October 1962), pp. 634–646.

ters of common concern. Across the array, from apartment house neighborhoods in the center to the single-family tract developments farther out, there is great variation in the social strength of such neighborhoods. Where neighborhoods are socially strong, chiefly in the single-family areas, they encourage community actions through voluntary organizations. These organizations are concerned with maintaining public order, carrying out community tasks, and representing the community before governmental agencies. In some areas of the metropolis we find a dense network of voluntary community organizations (the Rotary Club, PTA, Boy Scouts, and so on) caring for many needs of the household as a unit.

We have discussed the effect of the dwelling and the neighborhood on the daily round of activities that characterize the household. It is important to emphasize another social consequence of housing—the social meaning of *address*.[13] It has been said that after obtaining an answer to "What do you do for a living?" the most revealing fact about an American can be learned by asking "Where do you live?" Neighborhoods have many consequences for their residents. Obviously, the prestige value is important, whether for the house in "Elmwood's most exclusive district" or the house in a "decent neighborhood of homeowners." The former is a claim to high social prestige, the latter at least a demonstration of virtue. Similarly, the confession that one lives in what is commonly defined as a shabby neighborhood, or one that is "going downhill," may affect interaction in many kinds of social situations.

The neighborhood affects life chances. As the place where children are raised, it may provide them with many of their peers, mentors, adult models, friends, and often spouses. (Urban ecologists have found that half the population tends to marry someone living within a short distance of home.) Or the neighborhood may provide little beauty or friendship, but a great threat to person and property. (One woman told an interviewer, "I don't live in this *neighborhood;* I live in this house." The quality of her area led her to shut the door against the surrounding world.)[14] There are attributes of a neighborhood that last for many years. One area in Chicago had high juvenile delinquency rates for decades, even while the whole array of ethnic groups passed through it.

Then too, many of our public goods and services are administered

[13] For a discussion of the "address," see James Beshers, *Urban Social Structure* (New York: The Free Press of Glencoe, 1962).
[14] Personal communication from Irwin Deutscher, Youth Development Agency, Syracuse University, 1961.

by neighborhood areas. Education, street cleaning, garbage disposal, police and fire protection are all broken down into small administrative units, and all vary in quality by the kind of neighborhood served. Politics tends to be organized similarly, and whether a person lives in the "mattress wards" where the political workers "vote the graveyard," or in the "silk stocking wards" where the mayor and the president of the chamber of commerce live, has a measurable effect on the schools his children attend and the protection and service given him by local government.

Finally, the address is often meaningful because it informs us that the person lives in an ethnic enclave: Little Italy, Chinatown, or Spanish Harlem; among "hillbillies" or Swedes, German Jews, or Southern Negroes. Where concentration is *voluntary*, it may produce the protective community, the "urban villagers." Most American ethnic enclaves outside the South are a mixture of ghetto and community. The spatial concentration of persons with the same ethnic background tends to promote greater association within the areas and less association outside the areas. Such differential association may then limit the scope of the person's social world, his knowledge of the larger society, and his access to that society.[15]

Causes, Consequences, and Further Causes: The Vicious Circles

When a cause produces a condition whose further consequences reinforce the original cause, we call it "positive feedback." Social structures may usually be conceptualized in this manner. The "vicious circle" is the typical base for stability in a society. There are at least two such feedback phenomena relevant to housing.

First, as we have noted, housing is a *reward* in our society. If the rewards doled out to one generation are useful in preparing the next generation to achieve goals that will be honored by the society, the first loop of the circuit is established. If these goals are achieved and the son is rewarded by, among other things, the same quality of housing as his father had, and if this improves his chances in life, the circuit is closed (neighborhood = opportunity = achievement = reward = neighborhood). Whether poverty leads to life in a tenant farmer's shack and resulting ill health, low energy level, and poverty, or wealth leads to life in a wealthy suburb and a wide range of advantages, a wealthy career, and back to a wealthy suburb, the patterns are similar.

Again, we can note vicious circles in the biographies of given neigh-

[15] Herbert J. Gans, *The Urban Villagers* (New York: The Free Press of Glencoe, 1962).

borhoods. If a neighborhood is not well maintained as it grows older, for whatever reason (perhaps the shortages of material in wartime, or the excess of demand over supply in housing during a crisis), it tends to lose its *relative* value for those seeking new homes. As it loses value, prices decline and the neighborhood attracts people who cannot afford to maintain or upgrade the houses. Since older houses are more expensive to maintain anyway, the gap between what the houses were and what they are now widens. The housing goes from declining "input" of energy to declining "output" of profit, to a further decline of input.

Socially too the process works itself out. As the neighborhood becomes shabby, the residents who are most prosperous and able to invest in it leave. Those who are most self-confident and able to organize the neighborhood as a community also leave. Those who remain are likely to be demoralized and uninterested in collective action. As this happens, people turn inward to their dwelling and family, trying to evade their social surroundings. Then the neighborhood is defined by the city government agencies as one that is "skidding"; public services are slighted for these blocks, and police prefer to avoid them. Then those who *seek* anonymity arrive. Parallel chain reactions occur in the public schools, parks, and other facilities. This is an example of a downward spiral, a negative "feedback." The community unwinds into anarchy. Human values have been lost; what was desired by many, separately, has been collectively destroyed.

Summary: Social Significance and the Social Problem

The significance of housing distribution lies in its essentially social causes and consequences. Differential distribution is caused by the reward system of the society; and the consequences are great variation in the style of the individual's life and in his opportunities to associate with others. These variations, in turn, can limit such activities as child rearing (when the dwelling unit is unsuited to the care of the young) and economic achievement (when the neighborhood marks a person a failure and allows association only with other failures).

Recalling the two major themes in the definition of housing as a social problem, the "social anchor" and the problem of equity, we see that each has its roots in the social significance of housing distribution. Adequate housing is desired as a means of integrating adults into the social structure—a way of minimizing the powerful evidence of alienation, the slums. Through a change in the physical structure it is hoped that the neighborhood's career will be reversed, spiraling upward into order instead of downward into anarchy. At the same time, the argument for equity is invoked, emphasizing some *minimal* level of decency, below which no family should have to live. This argument is powerfully buttressed by considering the fate of children in the slums; however appropriate the "rewards" of substandard housing and neighborhood may be to their parents, they are unfair to the children.

Political Definitions of the Problem

Given the aims of those who see housing as a social problem, a number of strategies could be used. If it is the *concentration* of substandard housing that is deplored, the concentration can be broken up by subsidizing the rental or purchase of housing scattered throughout the city. If *adult poverty* is the target, it can best be attacked through a direct focus on increasing education, jobs, and income—with the increase of income as the major goal. If, however, we are primarily concerned with the *environment within which a new generation of the poor is coming of age*, it might be necessary to move them, not only out of their neighborhood but out of their families. The major handicap they suffer may be simply "family traditions," the culture of their parents.

None of these programs was ever seriously proposed as governmental policy in the years when the American political response to the "slums" was being formulated. Instead, the complex of interlocking social conditions that had produced concentrations of poor people in poor housing was *reified*—the causes were confused with the concrete existence of areas in the city where, as Ashworth says, "Overcrowding and congestion, poverty, crime, ill health and heavy mortality were . . . found together." Men were bemused with the physical structures and their associated statistics. From this it was a short step to the belief that the physical structures alone accounted for the associated ills— that substandard buildings "bred" substandard social behavior.

Such thinking, obsessed with the metaphor of the map, allowed us to collapse two different policy goals. One was the provision of housing, at some minimum level of adequacy, for all American households. The other was the integration of the underprivileged, the second-class citizens of poverty and race, into the larger society through an improvement of their housing, but also through improvement of their income and changes in their style of life. As these two goals were collapsed into one, the former goal, that of housing, became the dominant fixation.

Now, a commitment to minimum housing standards for the society seems perfectly defensible given the arguments we have considered.

PROBLEMS OF HOUSING AND RENEWAL OF THE CITY

Adequate housing, however, should not be viewed as capable of radically changing the behavior of parents, children, households, and neighborhoods—much less underprivileged ethnic groups or the broad social category called "the poor." Nor should we assume that "self-help" can greatly improve housing, if the basic causes of poor housing are simply low incomes, the disbarment of Negroes from most of the housing market, and a short supply of cheap housing. Those who live in substandard housing are typically so limited in resources as to be passive victims of the market in cheap housing; with little bargaining power, they take what they can get.

These propositions are so simple they may seem self-evident. Yet our housing policy for the past 20 years has denied them. I accept both the goal of minimum housing standards and the goal of increasing *internal inclusiveness* of the society (so that first-class economic and intellectual citizenship are available to all), but it seems to me that these two goals should be clearly separated in our thinking. Empirically they are sometimes related, sometimes not; the connections are certainly complex. Few serious reformers would try to improve education, occupation, and income through housing alone, or try to improve housing through long-range efforts at upgrading the jobs and incomes of the Negroes and other poor.

The quality of housing can best be improved through increasing the amount of standard housing that can be rented or sold cheaply. This means increasing the cheap housing built for the private market, so that dwellings may be vacated by the not-so-poor and occupied by the poor. It does *not* mean destroying cheap dwellings because they look deplorable to more fortunate citizens and then claiming "slum clearance" as the achievement. It also means providing heavily subsidized housing, public housing, for the extremely poor—those who could not maintain a standard dwelling even if it were given to them. Finally, it means allowing Negroes to buy housing on the open market, as the remainder of the citizenry does, cashing in on the "democracy of the buck" and thus escaping from a politically restricted and unfree market. Whoever limits the purchasing power of Negroes to "Negro districts," whoever subsidizes expensive housing while destroying cheap housing, is simply "pegging the price" for the substandard, overpriced housing of the poor.

In the remainder of this chapter we shall examine the American adventure with housing policy, the American response to housing as a social problem. We will sketch in a history of the housing program, noting its origins in the Great Depression of the 1930s, the declining support for public housing and disillusionment with slum clearance, the rise of the urban renewal program as a substitute, and the fate of that program as it encountered the hard realities of the American political system. The account may seem disillusioned. We should bear in mind, however, how recently the American society has decided that such social problems as housing are a public responsibility. Remembering, then, the late development of social science and the absence of a scientific focus on policy problems, we may understand how the best of intentions may produce results 180 degrees away from their aim.

The story is not of evil men doing evil deeds, or even of stupid men acting stupidly. It is the story of public servants working within an intellectual tradition no better than it should be, responding to the pressures of a political system remarkable in its proliferation of veto groups, and attempting to carry out novel public purposes under these handicaps. The wonder is not that they often failed, but that the impulse survived and that we still speak seriously of a housing policy aimed at solving a housing problem.

The First Housing Act: Depression Baby

The National Housing Act of 1937 was the first major American attack on housing as a social problem. A part of the government's response to the Great Depression, it had several goals: to get lenders to lending and builders to building, to increase the supply of housing, and to clear slums and replace them with better housing. The two means for achieving these goals were federal mortgage insurance, for those who could afford to buy housing if they could only borrow the money, and public housing for those who could not afford standard housing in any circumstances.[16]

Slum clearance under this program consisted of grants and loans to local housing authorities. These, in turn, used the power of eminent domain to raze the offending neighborhoods, building on them public housing units equal to the number of units destroyed. Public housing increasingly tended to become "projects" of huge "high-rise" buildings housing thousands and tens of thousands of the poor. The reasons for these buildings were originally, perhaps, principles of design or concern with economies. As time went on and the depression gave way to prosperity, the chief reason became the shortage of suitable sites.

Public housing was unpopular with those who did not use it, and projects were seen as stigmas by the surrounding residents. Thus it be-

[16] Ashley A. Foard and Hilbert Fefferman, "Federal Urban Renewal Legislation," *Law and Contemporary Problems*, 25, 4 (Fall 1960), pp. 635–684.

came increasingly difficult to locate public housing anywhere except in the small spaces vacated by slum destruction; thus if the destroyed units were to be replaced by the same number of new units, surrounded by "open space," it was necessary to build upward. The political squeeze resulted in the physical squeeze and the construction of skyscraper apartments. So public housing agencies provided dwellings that were the diametrical opposite of those chosen by the more affluent—the horizontal house surrounded by its own yard in the suburbs.[17] Public housing, the reward of the poor, was stringently limited in its spatial distribution. Space, as we have noted, reveals the prestige system of the society.

Meanwhile, public housing was increasingly inhabited by segregated populations. As the postwar society continued in a state of almost full employment, the economic constraints of the Depression that had led many "poor but respectable" whites to live in public housing vanished. Those who remained in the projects were, increasingly, the "problem families" of white society—the broken families, the older people who had survived their families, the unemployed and unemployables. Even these declined proportionately, however, and their places were taken by those whose constraints were racial as well as economic. Here the lower income of Negroes gave them, for once, an advantage; if housing was available only to those with low incomes on a first-come-first-served basis, then over time the projects would probably become increasingly Negro-occupied. This is indeed what happened. That part of the population with the generally lowest rewards was allocated the stigmatized housing, increasing the stigma in the process. The vicious circle was complete.

The unpopularity of the public housing program has many causes. Certainly it has been fought bitterly by private housing enterprisers, even though it is meant to provide only minimal charity for those who (in the late Senator Robert Taft's phrase) cannot be housed by the private market. The high-rise projects have been vigorously condemned as inappropriate to the family and community life of most of the people who live in them; one critic speaks of them as simply "immuring the slums." Yet public housing authorities seldom have vacancies—in the large cities there are tens of thousands of households on the waiting list. Bad as it may look to the middle-class critic, public housing seems highly preferable to what is otherwise available for the poor householder in most of our great cities. For this reason the de-

[17] Martin Meyerson and Edward Banfield, *Politics, Planning, and the Public Interest* (Glencoe, Ill.: The Free Press, 1955).

mand for public housing is much larger than the present supply and in 1964, 27 years after the Public Housing Act was passed, less than 2 percent of the housing in the country was low-cost public housing.[18]

The fact that more public housing is not provided indicates another aspect of the "affluent society." The truth is that those who want public housing are politically weak and have little leverage on the political reward system. Segregated in a few areas of the city, they are unable to exercise much political force on city government; increasingly occupied by Negroes, the "slums" are seen in racial terms by the dominant whites who control the civic purse strings. And, as public housing is increasingly occupied by the underdogs of the society, it is accused of ills that could more sensibly be accounted for by poverty, rural backgrounds, racial segregation, ill health, and old age. The amount of personal and family disorganization in new and sanitary public housing projects does clearly indicate that much of what worries people about "the slums" is not a housing problem at all; the vicious circles are not so easily broken as that. Nevertheless, the stain of poverty has rubbed off. A general disillusion with public housing has resulted in a slowdown of new construction. The slums grow faster than the slum clearance operations.

The Mythical "Decline of the City"

The growth of slums is often used to "prove" that our cities are in a state of massive decline. But this reasoning ignores the two-thirds population increase in less than 50 years; our urban population has increased at an even greater rate, from 60 to 140 millions, or over *130 percent*. The truth is that everything in the metropolis has been growing at a brisk rate, including the slums. The feeble effort to eliminate the latter through redevelopment and public housing has simply been inadequate to the magnitude of the task.

Paradoxically, one reason for this inadequacy has been the rapid growth of new housing. Subsidized by Federal Mortgage Insurance (originally intended to get the housing industry out of its depression), new housing on the periphery of the cities and in the suburbs has solved the housing problem for the great majority of Americans. The Federal Housing Authority (FHA) together with the housing privileges of World War II veterans did much to facilitate and channel the new housing built after 1945. Working through private lending agencies, however, these programs have perpetuated existing conventions, for private mortgage lenders have definite preferences about housing. The

---

[18] C. E. Elias, Jr., James Gillies, and Svend Riemer, Chapter 7, "Housing," in *Metropolis: Values in Conflict* (Belmont, Calif.: Wadsworth, 1964), pp. 172–202.

new house is preferred to the old, the single-family dwelling unit to the apartment; segregated housing is preferred to integrated housing; white owners are preferred to colored owners; young families with long futures are preferred to older ones; privately owned units are preferred to cooperatively owned units.[19]

The result has been a heavy loading of the dice in favor of suburban housing—single-family detached units, expensive in land and of necessity built on the outskirts of the metropolis. The suburbs have been, of course, precisely the location of the great housing booms of the 1940s, 1950s, and 1960s. Many argue that this is only an indication of the control exercised by the real estate market upon the homeseekers, reinforced by a federal subsidy which works through existing market channels. They see the Federal Housing Authority as creating a "self-fulfilling prophecy," a variety of the vicious circle. Others, however, point out that every study we have of the preferences of American homeseekers points to this housing as the desired kind. Overwhelmingly, Americans want the detached house surrounded by its crop of grass and children playing; overwhelmingly, they believe it is morally right for people to want such houses. Ninety percent of one sample indicated that a person should own his own home; in another study home ownership was an ideal norm for a majority of every income class above relief recipients.[20]

In short, it seems unlikely that the effect of the FHA and VA (Veterans Administration) mortgage insurance schemes was to turn the majority from what was preferred. Instead, the provision of help for *only* the average homeseeker had the effect of making life more difficult for those with unusual preferences. The range of choice was, to this degree, narrowed. Those who wanted older houses or apartment living, in older neighborhoods, were unable to obtain government insurance for their mortgages. Those who needed exceptional help—the poor, the colored, and the aged—received *less* help than those with fewer handicaps. Since the federal programs were subsidies, we may question the justice of such limits, for at best the programs tended to perpetuate the given distribution of housing by age, race, and income.

America's stock of housing has improved since World War II. Over 4.5 million substandard units were eliminated in six years, and our production of new housing has been adequate for most "average" citizens.[21] This housing has been, preponderantly, on the outskirts of the

---

[19] Charles M. Haar, *Federal Credit and Private Housing, The Mass Financing Dilemma* (New York: McGraw-Hill, 1960).
[20] See, for example, Abu-Lughod and Foley, *op. cit.*
[21] Grigsby, *op. cit.*

cities. Suburbia has been the area of major investment, and neighborhoods of the central cities have declined in relative value. Young families, finding what they want in the suburbs, leave the old neighborhoods. Then, as their parents grow old, property is poorly maintained; when their parents die, property moves into another market, and the house is occupied by poorer people, by darker people, or by more people.

The Persistence of Slums: A Metropolitan Problem

Despite the overall improvement in housing, many aspects still elicit expressions of concern. At the most general level, there is concern for the dwelling unit, its shape, size, and condition. The widespread incidence of substandard housing is seen as an inequity, since the housing codes express ideal consumption norms. Yet the worst housing has actually been increasing in price faster than standard housing. There is concern for poor housing because it is seen as multiplying evils, producing a vicious circle, and encapsulating Negroes and other poor in the slums. Furthermore, the concentration of substandard housing within the boundaries of the old central cities creates a social problem at another level: the suburbs grow at a great rate, attracting young families and new housing, while the center of the city simply grows older. As it does so, its neighborhoods spiral downward, the cost of services rises, and the tax base shrinks. Looking at the central city and suburbs together, some people see the problem as one for the metropolitan area as a whole. Although slightly over half the metropolitan population now lives in the suburbs, the metropolitan area is still *one* housing market, *one* transportation grid—in short, its parts are interdependent. The housing problems of the central city are, in this view, inseparable from the processes taking place in the suburbs. Despite the political separation of the latter, housing is a metropolitan-wide problem.

In these broader perspectives, one substandard house cannot singly be replaced with a new house. The quality of the neighborhood may be so low that the new house simply attracts the same kind of use as the old one and rapidly declines to the level of its surroundings. Nor can a slum neighborhood singly be replaced by a housing project; outside the boundaries of the project the endless neighborhoods continue to decline, creating new slums faster than old ones are bulldozed out. Thus the key problem must be formulated: How can the amount of energy that is invested in the older neighborhoods be increased, reversing the vicious circle so that neighborhoods improve rather than decline? At any given time, 97 percent of the housing is the "standing stock," the already existing structures. If that stock could be maintained and upgraded, there would be little need for slum clearance.

An American Solution: "There Ought To Be a Law . . ."

Influential persons decided that substandard housing resulted from substandard behavior. The typical American answer to this kind of problem is of a moral nature: people *should* maintain their houses and improve them. The typical instrument is legal: there ought to be a law against anybody living in substandard housing. The prescription is for rigorous enforcement of housing codes, with poor housing either repaired ("brought up to code levels") or condemned and destroyed. Housing codes are, however, as we have already noted, radical innovations. Prescribing the amount of space per person, the amount and kinds of light and sanitation, the type and condition of structure, they force a whole new normative structure upon an American population used to the permissiveness of boomtowns and frontier shacks. As late as the 1930s, only 15 percent of America's farmhouses had electricity, yet in three decades we have ruled it morally and legally wrong in most American cities, to live in housing without electricity, hot and cold running water, and other conveniences absent from the vast majority of houses on earth, and unknown in many places.

Furthermore, the naive belief that slums occur because good housing simply gets "run down" by the immoral behavior of its residents is blatantly false. The majority of substandard housing is so termed, not because the housing has changed but because standards have. It was built substandard because it was built to other and less luxurious standards. (Quite a bit of substandard housing is being built today in the open country, in the small towns, and in the "boondocks"—the areas of the metropolis without effective local government in the matter.) Rigorous enforcement of the housing codes amounts to ordering the citizen to improve his housing beyond the quality it had when he bought it.[22]

Such action is not popular with those who cannot afford the improvements; it is not popular with the inspectors who are asked to assist in the judging of the homes and the decision to "dehouse" them; nor is it popular with the elected officials who can see the political backfire, even if they are blind to the economic consequences of destroying low-cost housing without offering an adequate replacement. Since that replacement, with standard housing, can only be public

[22] *Ibid.*

housing, the unpopularity of the latter tends to sign, seal, and deliver the "rigorous enforcement of the housing code" to speedy oblivion. In truth, only a handful of American cities make an honest effort to enforce their housing code across the board.

Meanwhile, large areas within the cities are obsolete by our present middle-class standards. As these areas accept the poor and the increasing numbers of nonwhite citizens who, because of discrimination, have nowhere else to go, they are overcrowded and undermaintained. The central business district of the city is encircled by them, since these were the earliest neighborhoods built and therefore the oldest. In the circumstances, public-spirited citizens speak not only of the slums but also of the "decay of the center," the "sprawl of the suburbs" (sometimes called "slurbs"), and the loss of urban form. They speak of our cities as sick, and they prescribe cures.[23]

One of the major cures provided was the redevelopment of land by private enterprise. Miles Colean urged the use of the right of eminent domain to condemn large areas of the city and sell it to redevelopers.[24] He thought that the dispersed ownership of property in a given neighborhood was a key block to its redevelopment; wholesale replacements were necessary because the environment made small areas undesirable for private capital, and wholesale replacement required the use of governmental power. (Otherwise, "holdouts" could demand outrageous prices, knowing that their parcel of land was necessary to the larger enterprise.) Colean, then, suggested that slums were less important than the changing shape of the city, and he urged that governmental powers be used to control that shape. His book, significantly, was called *Renewing Our Cities*. It became the title of the whole enterprise, the improvement of housing, neighborhoods, cities, and the metropolis.

The New Start: Renewing Our Cities

The term was new and pointed toward a public conception of the city that was novel in American government. The piecemeal and welfare-oriented efforts to improve housing were to be transformed into an organized attack on the city and its problems, of which housing was now only one among many. In 1949 the Congress passed an act

---

[23] See, for example, the Editors of *Fortune*, *The Exploding Metropolis* (Garden City, N.Y.: Doubleday, 1958); Hal Burton, *The City Fights Back* (New York: The Citadel Press, 1954); E. A. Gutkind, *The Twilight of Cities* (New York: The Free Press of Glencoe, 1962).

[24] Miles L. Colean, *Renewing Our Cities* (New York: The Twentieth Century Fund, 1953).

emphasizing slum clearance, largely growing from the Housing Act of 1937. Title I of the act, however, allowed for slum clearance when the land was *not* residential; "rebuilding our cities" could then be seen as rebuilding the commercial and industrial center. Under Title I the slums and "blighted areas" could be bought by a local public authority (by negotiation or condemnation), cleared at public expense, and resold to new developers (by auction or negotiation). Since the cost of clearing the land was more than its "fair market value," there remained a loss. One-third of this was to be paid for by the local public authority, two-thirds by the Federal Urban Renewal Program.[25]

The major battles on the bill were concerned with its public housing aspect, and that aspect "ran interference" for Title I. The latter was not seriously attacked except by Senator Taft, Republican from Ohio. That conservative gentleman was all for public housing, but opposed to a bill whose purpose was "the improvement of cities in general." He was opposed by the liberals, the planners, and those with central-city interests, business or political. This controversy dramatized a conflict that runs throughout the history of the urban renewal movement; on one side are the welfare-oriented people (the "Housers," for want of a better term), concerned with the inadequacy of housing. On the other side are the Planners, whose chief concern is for the overall pattern of the city and for whom slums are only symptoms of poor land use. The planners aim at the proper use of the land, that is, the economically most productive use. The Housers, however, focus on the "inhuman use of human beings." The two approaches are not contradictory. But a Houser, like Taft, need not care about improving cities in general, and a Planner need not care about slums as long as they are in the right place. Indeed, the planning emphasis led to the accusation that slums meant, for the urban renewal approach, that *"that* land is too good for *those* people."

Senator Taft lost the battle. In 1954 the program was revised with an emphasis on broad-scale, planned redevelopment of American cities. The resources for nonresidential renewal were increased, and general land-use planning was encouraged by several provisions of the law. Since, however, this legislation was enacted under a Republican administration committed to free enterprise, the effort was made to shift responsibility and costs to the local community and to private enterprise. Thus code enforcement was underlined, and much of the language of the bill specifies the use of loans to encourage private redevelopment. Of great importance, a consistent and interlocking set of requirements

[25] The Housing Act of 1949, As Amended Through June, 1961 (Public Law 171, 81st Congress, Section 2).

was written into the law: failing compliance with these requirements, no city could gain federal support for its urban renewal activities. This code is known as the Workable Program, and its requirements are as follows.

1. Adequate codes and ordinances for structure and use, adequately enforced.
2. A comprehensive community plan for land use and public capital development.
3. Neighborhood analysis for the determination of blight.
4. Administrative organization adequate to an all-out attack on slums and blight.
5. A responsible program for relocation of displaced families.
6. Citizen participation in the entire program.
7. Adequate financial resources for carrying out the program.

These requirements are the responsibility of the local community, and that community's political leaders must sign a contract binding them to their performance. Altogether, the Workable Program amounts to an extremely strenuous set of demands upon American civic government. Why were they made?

The Assumptions Underlying the Urban Renewal Program [26]

The urban renewal program has always been conceived within two narrow limits. First, it is distinctly federal, a cooperative venture of national and local governments. Programs are initiated by the local community, not by the national government; the latter accepts or rejects them. Second, urban renewal programs can condemn, clear, and sell land; they cannot build on the cleared land. Thus the private market is protected from governmental enterprise (except for schools, city halls, low-rent public-housing, and other conventional public structures). Almost all building, then, is by private enterprises.

Neither of these limits is inherent in the nature of man or government. In Britain half the housing built in a given year is public housing, and the local municipal corporation has little veto power over the national government.[27] Similarly, in Sweden all buildings must be approved by public planning bodies—the free market operates within

---

[26] Scott Greer, *Urban Renewal and American Cities* (Indianapolis: Bobbs-Merrill, 1966).
[27] For an indication of the differences see Hilda Jennings, *Societies in the Making, A Study of Development and Redevelopment Within a County Borough* (New York: Humanities Press, 1962).

strict public limits. In the United States, however, the political norms with respect to the local community prescribe a large degree of autonomy; norms concerning the activities of government jealously protect private enterprise.

Underlying the urban renewal program are a number of assumptions about the possibility of redeveloping our cities within the limits just stated. It is an effort at *social control*. Requiring that local communities initiate programs, help finance them, and—through their political leadership—agree to carry them out to specification is assumed to provide a guarantee of local concern and commitment. This concern should, in turn, protect the program against a simple waste of money in unneeded public works; the local agencies are assumed to have a stake in determining what places will be rebuilt by the private construction market once the land is cleared. Most importantly, it is assumed that the land desirable for the private market will be the same land that the local public authority will want to redevelop.

The Workable Program is, then, the concrete tool for spelling out the specifications of an urban renewal program that makes sense in any given city. It is meant to be a technique of control and assumes the following.

1. If you punish those guilty of owning substandard buildings, they will bring them up to standards; it is assumed you can punish them.

2. If the buildings are beyond repair, it is assumed that this can be determined by "neighborhood analysis"; it is assumed they can be razed.

3. It is assumed that the private market (plus some public housing) will then be able to redevelop the land with substitute structures.

4. It is assumed that the latter will make up for the loss in structures incurred in item 2.

5. It is assumed that local government can see to it that those who are unhoused are relocated in standard housing.

6. It is assumed that citizen participation will develop support for the program among the interested citizens.

7. It is assumed that the future state of the city is protected by

(*a*) New growth in redeveloped areas and areas that are brought up to standard.

(*b*) A comprehensive plan for the city that protects new development against blight and destructive landuse patterns.

Questioning the Assumptions

As we have noted, one major assumption is questionable indeed. The enforcement of housing codes requires either a massive shift in norms, brought about by adult education, or a major police action. The difficulty with the first is that those who live in substandard houses that they own are very resistant to changing norms, either because they do not share the norms or because they do not have the money. Those who rent substandard housing do so because their poverty or their race give them little choice. Yet housing codes are supposed to apply equally to the homeowner and the tenement dweller. On the other hand, massive police enforcement creates the political backfire and corruption of enforcement common to all efforts to shift norms by force.

Another questionable assumption is the belief that any district so deteriorated that it can be condemned can also be renewed by private enterprise. This belief rests on the notion that it is the deterioration of structures that has produced the low market value of the district, and this deterioration is thought to result from a situation that has been called "the prisoner's dilemma." [28] The essential condition for the prisoner's dilemma is lack of communication and, hence, lack of trust. Applying this situation to the urban district, we could say that if a man's house is deteriorating he can either maintain it at a given level or let it deteriorate. If he and his neighbors all maintain their houses, he will be a winner; if he maintains his house while others let theirs decay, he will be a loser, since it will have only the value commensurate with the quality of the neighborhood; finally, should he let his house decay while the neighborhood remains stable, he may be ahead of the game. (This analogy also applies to the situation of white homeowners when nonwhites move into a residential neighborhood.) Each separately is safest if he invests little in his house—with general decay the result. The prisoner's dilemma indicates how, through lack of organization, we can all vigorously cooperate in producing something nobody wants.

Certainly some areas of a city can spiral downward in this fashion. It is important, however, to see whether the major cause is not the declin-

[28] In the prisoner's dilemma, two men are arrested for a crime and placed in separate cells. The prosecuting attorney does not have enough evidence to convict them, but they do not know this. Each is told (separately) that he can plead guilty or innocent; if he pleads guilty, he will be let off with a light sentence; if he and his partner *both* plead innocent, they will be set free; if he pleads innocent and his partner pleads guilty he will be put so far back in jail that he will never see daylight again. The strategy that minimizes the maximal loss here ("minimax" as it is called) is, of course, to plead guilty whether you are guilty or not—since you cannot tell what your opposite number will do when exposed to the temptation, nor can he tell what you will do. I am indebted to Otis A. Davis and Andrew B. Whinston for this neat application to neighborhood spirals. See their article, "The Economics of Urban Renewal" in *Law and Contemporary Problems*, 26, 1 (Winter 1961), pp. 105–117.

ing value of the neighborhood but other reasons, obsolescence of the structures, for example, or the changing values of the location. Then the declining investment is a *result* of declining value, not the cause, and clearing the land for redevelopment may be an exercise in futility, leaving vacant lots in the place of buildings which, whatever their quality, were being put to human uses and therefore had some human value.[29]

But the urban renewal program planners assume a permanent potential value for land in the older parts of the city. This assumption seems to rest on a static conception of the city borrowed from the urban sociology of another day, a picture of the city as a highly centralized structure with concentric rings spreading outward from the commercial center, that center, in turn, increasing use value and market value by spreading outward into the older residential areas near it. It is assumed that, within the fixed boundaries of the central city, the older areas have an intrinsic value because of their centrality, and they are called, significantly, "zones of *transition*." It only remains to supplement the private market, using the power of eminent domain to solve the prisoner's dilemma and clear the land of objectionable structures. In some central cities, the planners believe, only a few houses need be destroyed ("spot clearance") and most can be brought "up to code." This is called rehabilitation. In others complete redevelopment would seem necessary to allow commercial use, generated by the expanding central business district.

How the Program Works Out

At the time I completed a study of the program, in 1962, over 600 cities had urban renewal programs in some stage of development.[30] Today the figure is closer to 1000. The program has been in effect since 1949, the year Title I was added to the housing bill, so perhaps it is not too early to assay some of the results. These may be considered from the point of view of three goals: (1) the housing goal, to put every family in a "decent house and a suitable living environment"; (2) the city redevelopment goal, the renewal of the central business district; and (3) the planning goal, the development and use of a comprehensive renewal plan for the city as a whole.

The housing goal. The effect of the urban renewal program has been, thus far, a substantial net loss of low-cost housing.[31] Of the

---

[29] This argument is powerfully presented by Jane Jacobs, in *The Death and Life of Great American Cities* (New York: Random House, 1961).
[30] Greer, *Urban Renewal and American Cities, op. cit.*
[31] Jerome Rothenberg, *Cost-Benefit Analysis of Urban Renewal* (Washington, D.C.: The Brookings Institution, 1964).

work now in progress, four dwelling units are destroyed for every one replaced; of the projects completed, it is still two-for-one for destruction over replacement. Little of the new housing built on cleared land is cheap; it ranges from middle-class to luxury apartments; after all, the fair market price for the land is high and builders have the freedom to make a profit. This net destruction has been especially true of low-cost housing available to Negroes; between 70 and 80 percent of the houses in cleared areas were once occupied by Negroes. Although Negroes occupy only about 35 percent of all substandard housing in the country, their settlement near city centers has resulted in a disproportionate loss of cheap housing available to them. No wonder urban renewal is called "Negro removal."

Relocation of the displaced persons has varied enormously by community. Where there is a surplus of standard low-cost housing available to Negroes, cities have been able to fulfill their commitments to the Workable Program. This has been a rare situation however, made rarer by the Federal Highway Program's demolition of similar housing. The Highway Program's motto seems to be "the shortest line through the cheapest land," and the Highway Program is under no obligation whatever to provide relocation housing. The combined results of the *two* programs of destruction often make the relocation task of the urban renewal agency impossible. The only compensation would be an increased supply of low-cost housing, but even a staunch free enterpriser like Taft accepted the obvious: there is no profit in building low-cost standard housing for the poor, and many large cities already have tens of thousands of applicants on their public housing waiting lists. Giving urban renewal displacees priority in the waiting lists simply means increasing the years that others must live in existing slums.

The chief result of decreasing the number of low-cost housing units is the relocation of the slums. We cannot force people to pay a considerably higher rental if cheaper quarters can be found in the tolerated substandard tenements. Thus the common pattern is movement from the clearance area to the immediately adjacent low-cost housing neighborhoods, thereby increasing rents and crowding. Then, since landlords of substandard housing have a "seller's market," they feel less pressure than ever to maintain and upgrade their properties.[32]

The excess of demand over supply for low-cost housing is the basic reason why urban renewal has not fulfilled its housing goals. Standard housing is far beyond the ability of many to pay, and most standard housing cannot be rented by Negroes, even if they can afford it. The obvious answer to the first condition is public housing; that to the sec-

[32] Grigsby, *op. cit.*

ond, desegregation of the housing market. Neither is politically easy. But to many proponents of urban renewal it does not matter anyway, for they have ceased to be concerned with the goal of a "decent home and a suitable living environment for every American family." Instead, they dismiss the residential slums as the inevitable result of poverty and turn to a program which *can* create enthusiasm and political support in the local community, the rebuilding of downtown.

Central business district redevelopment. The central business districts of our large cities are experiencing a proportionate (and often absolute) decline in retail trade. Though the number of autos entering these districts increases daily, the number of people decreases. Meanwhile, new industrial plants are built out in the far suburbs, where the tract developments and shopping centers flourish. The "zone of transition" is really a "zone of stagnation"; there is no demand for new commercial sites in the older neighborhoods near the center. This situation is often described as "decay at the center and growth at the peripheries."

This development is seen as a problem by a wide assortment of people. The government of the central city is concerned with declining property value which results in a lowering of the tax base, at the same time that the cost of services is rising with the increase in the city's poor. Under these conditions either tax rates must rise or services must decline. Either way, business enterprises committed to the downtown are also concerned. The metropolitan daily newspapers, the banks (especially in states that do not allow branch banking), the big department stores, the public utilities—all those who could not easily transfer their activities elsewhere—are concerned with the steady decline in the prosperity of business firms and neighborhoods in the older central city. They want to redevelop the downtown, to make it an economic hub and symbolic center of the city again. In the process they hope to lure the white middle class back from the suburbs through construction of expensive apartment complexes in the center of the city.

And, indeed, there are shining new towers on urban renewal land at the heart of our cities. Frequently, however, they are surrounded by older buildings that cannot compete, have increasingly high vacancy rates, and become obsolescent. The bold new start may easily produce blight in its wake if there is no net increase in economic value for the location; water is poured from one pitcher to another without increasing the amount of water. Where such decline in surrounding blocks does not occur, we may ask whether the new development would not have come about anyway, without urban renewal. The economist, Morton Shussheim, has put it succinctly:

> Indeed, the most impressive renewal program of all has occurred in . . . a district without writedown of land costs, without uses of eminent domain, without any other important public bounties. I have reference, of course, to the reconstruction in the postwar period of the East Side of Manhattan with office buildings and luxury housing. More than a billion dollars worth of private construction has been poured into this area since 1947.[33]

This redevelopment came about when there was a real demand for the space. And if there is no such demand? Shussheim goes on: "The warning flags are up: Vernon, Weimer and others have cautioned us that only a few regional centers can realistically hope for a heavy and sustaining demand for new office space in their core districts." [34]

As for the goal of "bringing the middle class back into the city," we have already noted the overwhelming preference of middle-class (and just about any other class) Americans for single-family dwellings. With high land costs, they can be built in the center only at unbelievable prices. The alternative is, of course, apartment houses. But all the studies of middle-class apartment house dwellers in the center of the city show them to be a specific type of household: they are exceptionally prosperous; they do not have school-age children; they work in the central business district. Looking at the expected growth of this population in the Philadelphia metropolitan area, Rapkin and Grigsby project a demand for 8000 central-city apartments over twelve years, and this for a metropolitan area of some four million inhabitants. It is, at best, a token victory.[35]

The planning goal. Through time the scope of urban renewal planning activities has steadily expanded. First it was the project, then general neighborhood renewal, and now the goal is the comprehensive renewal program. The comprehensive program would schedule growth and redevelopment for the entire city over long periods. The aim is the renewal and maintenance of the whole, minimizing what we lose individually and collectively through piecemeal and accidental efforts. This is a grandiose undertaking subject to all the limitations on public planning in the United States.

The planning function in the United States is severely limited by our insistence on maximum freedom for private enterprise. The "problems" that the planners see today in the metropolis are the results of

[33] Morton J. Shussheim, "Urban Renewal and Local Economic Development," a paper given before the New York Chapter, American Institute of Planners, December 9, 1960.
[34] *Ibid.*
[35] Chester Rapkin and William G. Grigsby, *Residential Renewal at the Urban Core* (Philadelphia: University of Pennsylvania Press, 1960).

past decisions of entrepreneurs in a free market. And the problems of tomorrow can easily be imagined when we survey the endless seas of subdivisions surrounding our greatest cities, where billions of dollars are invested in housing for millions of families, with little restraint on the actions of designers and builders who are little interested in the metropolis as a whole.

Furthermore, even at its best, urban renewal is a central-city program. The federal agency can contract only with a local agency, and that agency is the municipal corporation. But today over 51 percent of the metropolitan population lives outside the central city. Ironically, comprehensive renewal programs leave out of their scope the most vital and rapidly growing parts of the metropolitan area. When they do this, they ignore the interdependencies within that area, ignore that it *is* one housing market, one labor force, one transport grid. Demolition in one part affects others, and new construction on the peripheries decisively affects the attractiveness of redevelopment in the central city.

Furthermore, even if planners had the power and the jurisdiction to control development over the metropolis as a whole, it is doubtful that they could achieve their aims. The task is gigantic and the great city is moving and changing rapidly. A comprehensive renewal plan would require a degree of knowledge and an application of that knowledge to the ideals of a given city in specific terms. But planning does not really provide rigorous criteria for development; it has been used, instead, as a critique of what exists—and on such a basis the remedy is designed. (What matter if one is applying a Band-Aid to a fracture? The situation is defined by the planner as being so bad it could hardly be worse.) Thus comprehensive planning is based on a truncated portion of the metropolitan area; it is static in its general conceptions and vague and general where precise rules are badly needed.[36]

Urban renewal, the brave new start, seems to be accomplishing the following. First, it is applying the cosmetic of slum clearance to certain areas of the central cities, substituting high-rise luxury apartments and banks for the substandard housing of the poor. Second, it is increasing the supply of expensive central-city housing, inaccessible to the poor Negroes, and decreasing the supply of housing available to them. Third, it is having some effect on new building in the central business district, subsidizing it through land clearance operations—at the expense of other sites in the metropolitan area where it could have been

---

[36] Several eminent planners seem to agree. See, for example, Lloyd Rodwin, *The British New Towns Policy* (Cambridge, Mass.: Harvard University Press, 1956), p. 187: "The fact is that the town planners' intellectual lines have been overextended. . . ."

built. Fourth, it is promoting a dangerous myth—that a comprehensive renewal program can be planned for 49 percent of the metropolis without regard for the other 51 percent.

The Tremendous Act and the Trivial Consequence: The American Polity

The constraints within which any local urban renewal project is planned and carried out are a function of the local situation, not the federal program.[37] The director of the local public authority must retain political support from the local government; he needs ordinances, condemnations, public works, code inspections, and so on. He must also retain the support of some of the economic entrepreneurs; they must be willing to bid for his land (or more often, negotiate for it) within the broad limits set by the federal agency. So intricate are the negotiations, and so time consuming the process, that the entrepreneurs will have to expect several years to pass before a project is completed. Finally, the director also needs support from the federal agency and its regional offices, for he needs expeditious, authoritative decisions.

In consequence, the local director becomes what has been called a "public entrepreneur." The local public authority is not really an organization, in the sociological sense. It is not bounded, centralized by authority, rationally controlled. Instead, it is a loose collection of organizations which the director has to pull together by threat, cajolery, and other tactics, to gain any object. In short, it is an "enterprise" among organized groups.[38] Since the director is dependent on these other groups but has no coercive power over them, he tends to shape the program to the specific constellation of groups whose support he needs.

Confined by his mode of operation, the director will not insist on rigorous code enforcement when he knows that it will encounter widespread public opposition. Such resistance can lead to second thoughts about renewal in the government and to the loss of bond issue support among the citizens. Nor is he likely to insist on relocation in "decent, safe and sanitary housing" for Negroes when the only available housing of this quality is in white neighborhoods; the Negroes "make do" within their given limits. His respect for the comprehensive plan will

[37] For extensive quotations of interviews with Directors of LPA's see Greer, *Urban Renewal and American Cities, op. cit.*
[38] George S. Duggar, "The Federal Concept in Urban Renewal: The Local Renewal Enterprise," in *Community Development in the Western Hemisphere* (San Diego, Calif.: Public Affairs Research Institute of San Diego College, August 1961).

be tempered by the knowledge that its vague generalities would be difficult to defend, and by the knowledge that planners have only advisory powers anyway. If his only customers for a given plot of land violate future plans for the city, the plans will have to be changed. The city, the federal government, and the director of the authority have too much at stake.

In short, the set of opportunities within which the local public authority operates is also a cage of pressures. And the greatest pressure is the generalized one—to get something off the drawing board and into construction, to get that vacant land built up. So urban renewal projects vary immensely in their purposes and outcomes. The projects seldom flow from a careful analysis of demand; "need," that amorphous term, is used instead. And after projects are completed, no one is subject to a strict accounting of costs and benefits. Indeed, there are reasons why persons committed to the programs would not appreciate such analysis; their plans are not conceived in these terms. As I have said elsewhere, "In the absence of more knowledge, the program rains on the just and unjust alike, and whatever lies in the soil—rocks, flowers, tares, will probably flourish each in its kind."

The Changing Program

Thus the drive to provide better housing and eliminate slums has turned into a program to save the competitive position of the central business district. The comprehensive renewal program functions, in these circumstances, as a fig leaf representing civic virtue. The program seems to have no other future alternative than a simple extrapolation of projects that renew given areas, central business districts, medical centers, university neighborhoods, huge redevelopment firms, at the behest of powerful political and economic interests.

Yet the limitations of power are not the only, or even the major, limits on urban renewal. More important is our lack of a clear theory of what the city is and, equally important, what we want it to be. These are the two requirements for sensible intervention in the ongoing process of urban society. They are interdependent, for our knowledge of what is can act as an editor of what we aspire to; and what we want to accomplish should help us focus on the aspects of things that are critical for our effort. Neither the empirical theory of urban renewal nor its normative theory, has ever been clearly set forth.

The program has, however, been in a constant process of evolution since 1937. It is, willy-nilly, a "natural experiment." We are finding out more about our problems through our efforts to solve them; they turn out to be complicated by our uncertainty about ourselves and our goals. The three aims of urban renewal—improved housing for those Americans who need it, improved central cities for those who want them, and improved overall planning for our cities, seem admirable to some people when considered separately. When they are combined, the political process suffers from indigestion, and goals fall by the wayside. The housing goal is forgotten as central-city redevelopment flourishes at its expense. The planning goal is a will-o'-the-wisp, in the light of massive trends toward decentralization of the city. Even the goals of downtown renewal are capable of only limited attainment.

It is a radical effort, after all, to intervene in the typically unplanned growth of American cities. It will probably be a partial success and a partial failure. Because this is true, nothing is more important than a careful evaluation of what has failed and what succeeded, and how things came about. Public policy can be experimental *only* if we assay its results in terms of clear standards. And public policies must be experimental—we know so little about our collective fate, and it is so important that we learn. Therefore the changing nature of the urban renewal program may be its most valuable characteristic, especially if change is in the direction of growth, emergence, and bold new approaches to age-old human problems.

11

Popular Culture in America: Social Problem in a Mass Society or Social Asset in a Pluralist Society?

▼▼▼▼▼▼▼▼▼▼▼▼▼▼▼▼▼▼▼▼▼▼▼▼▼▼▼▼▼▼▼▼▼▼▼▼▼▼▼

Herbert J. Gans

In a small, relatively homogeneous society such as an African tribe, there is almost universal agreement about how people ought to live, if only because of the few opportunities for choice. In a huge, heterogeneous society like ours, however, disagreement is rife, especially when a choice of life styles is available.

This chapter is about the criteria of choice, primarily in the conduct of life outside the workplace.[1] Advocates of high culture believe that people ought to spend their free hours in self-realization and self-expression through the pursuit of the fine arts. They reject people's

---

[1] This chapter was written as part of the author's research project on "The Shaping of Mass Media Content: An Analysis of the Creation and Decision-Making Processes in the Mass Media," supported by the Bullitt Foundation. Earlier formulations of portions of the chapter were developed in two unpublished papers, "The Metaphysics of Popular Culture" (1950) and "The Social Structure of Popular Culture" (1959). A brief summary of some of the ideas appears in "Pluralist Aesthetics and Subcultural Programming: A Proposal for Cultural Democracy in the Mass Media," in *Studies in Public Communication*, No. 3 (1961), pp. 27–35.

I am indebted to Peter Marris, Rolf Meyersohn, Ned Polsky, and David Riesman for comments on an earlier draft of this chapter.

preferences for mass culture—mass-produced art, entertainment, and related consumer goods—because they believe this preference to harm both the society as a whole and people as individuals. For this reason, mass culture is thought of as a social problem.

This chapter will consider the critics' argument. I should warn the reader that I do not approach my task from a disinterested or neutral perspective. Although many intellectuals and critics view mass culture as a social problem that requires urgent public action, I believe that mass culture is, rather, another manifestation of pluralism and democracy in American society. The institutions that provide mass culture can be improved, but unlike those causing poverty or racial discrimination, for example, they need not be eliminated to create a healthy society. This initial bias colors what I write, although as a sociologist, I have tried to maintain some detachment in my empirical discussion.

The chapter first analyzes the charges against mass culture and its users, and evaluates their accuracy. Not only is there little evidence to support the charges, but the perspective of the critics results in a distorted view of mass culture (Part I). An attempt to correct this view is made by a sociological analysis of the varieties of mass culture, the characteristics of their users, and the relationship between users and their cultural choices (Part II). The addition of some value judgments to this analysis makes it possible to develop an evaluation of mass culture and some policy proposals for its improvement (Part III). A brief conclusion reviews the issue of mass culture as a social problem (Part IV).

What Is Mass Culture?

The term "mass culture" is a combination of two European concepts: mass and *Kultur* (the German word for high culture). The mass is or was the nonaristocratic, uneducated portion of European society, especially the people who today might be described as lower-middle class, working class, and lower class. *Kultur* refers not only to the art, music, literature, and other symbolic products that were and are preferred by the well-educated elite of that society but also to the styles of thought and feelings of those who choose these products—those who are "cultured." Mass culture, on the other hand, refers to the symbolic products used by the "uncultured" majority.

The term "mass culture" has undesirable connotations. It is obviously pejorative; "mass" suggests an undifferentiated collectivity, even a mob, rather than people as individuals or members of a group, and "mass culture" implies more homogeneity and mass production than in fact exists. This can be counteracted by the use of more positive terms like "popular culture" or "popular arts," and I shall use them instead.[2] But even these terms assume the existence of two kinds of culture, high and popular, that are qualitatively so different they cannot be compared, forcing the analysis into an a priori dichotomy that hides more than it reveals.

In reality, there are a number of popular cultures, and they as well as high culture are all examples of *taste subcultures* (or *taste cultures* for short) whose values are standards of taste or aesthetics. When these subcultures are compared, high culture turns out to be similar in many ways to the others. Popular culture includes several subcultures but not high culture: it will be used in this sense here. All the taste subcultures taken together make up the national taste culture: the total array of art, entertainment, leisure, and related consumer products available in the society.

A taste culture consists of the painting and sculpture, music, literature, drama, and poetry; the books, magazines, films, television programs; and even the furnishings, architecture, foods, automobiles, and so on, that reflect similar aesthetic standards and are chosen by people partly for this reason. People who make similar choices among these products, and for the same aesthetic reasons, will be described as a *taste public*.

A brief listing of other terms is necessary. I will describe taste cultures as composed of *content* or *products* that are created or produced by *creators*. They are used or consumed by *users, consumers, audiences*, and the aggregations of users whom I have called taste publics. By content I may mean a film, or only themes within a film. By creators I mean both the so-called serious artist and the writer, director, or producer who is employed in the mass media. In the choice of content, people apply *aesthetic standards*, and I use the term aesthetic broadly and loosely to refer not only to standards of beauty and of taste, but also to a variety of other emotional and intellectual values that people satisfy when they choose content from a culture. Moreover, I assume that people apply aesthetic standards not only in the

[2] Dwight MacDonald rejects the term popular culture because a work of high culture is sometimes also popular, and argues for the term mass culture because "its distinctive mark is that it is solely and directly an article for mass consumption." Dwight MacDonald, "A Theory of Mass Culture," in Bernard Rosenberg and David M. White, eds., *Mass Culture: The Popular Arts in America* (Glencoe, Ill.: The Free Press, 1957), pp. 59–73, quote at p. 59. As I will argue in later pages, that popular culture is created for a larger audience does not mean either it is mass-produced in the same way as an automobile, or the audience is a mass.

choice of high culture but in all taste cultures.³ Some of the terms are borrowed from marketing, and although they may lack stylistic appeal, they facilitate the comparative analysis of taste cultures. The assumption that taste cultures can be compared is of course central to my argument and forms the basis for both the analysis and the evaluation that follow.

I The Critique of Mass Culture

The charges against mass or popular culture have been repeated so frequently and consistently—indeed, many of them can be traced back to the eighteenth century—that it is possible to view them as part of an established ideology or critique.⁴ In its contemporary form, that critique has four major themes:

1. *The negative character of popular-culture creation.* Popular culture is undesirable because, unlike high culture, it is mass-produced by profit-minded entrepreneurs solely for the gratification of a paying audience.

2. *The negative effects on high culture.* Popular culture borrows from high culture, thus debasing it, and also lures away many potential creators of high culture, thus depleting its reservoir of talent.

3. *The negative effects on the popular-culture audience.* The consumption of popular-culture content at best produces spurious gratifications, and at worst is emotionally harmful to the audience.

4. *The negative effects on the society.* The wide distribution of popular culture not only reduces the level of cultural quality—or civilization—of the society, but also encourages totalitarianism by creating a passive audience peculiarly responsive to the techniques of mass persuasion used by demagogues bent on dictatorship.

Each of these charges will be discussed in detail, although I should note at the outset that I cannot describe all the separate arguments that go into these charges, and I cannot properly indicate differences of opinion among individual critics.⁵ To do either would require a book-

---

³ This assumption, like the others referred to here, is spelled out in greater detail in Part II.
⁴ Leo Lowenthal and Marjorie Fiske, "The Debate over Art and Popular Culture in Eighteenth Century England," in Mirra Komarovsky, ed., *Common Frontiers of the Social Sciences* (Glencoe, Ill.: The Free Press, 1957), pp. 33-96.
⁵ The principal contemporary statements of the critique are presented in two books: Rosenberg and White, eds., *op. cit.*, particularly in articles by Bernard Rosenberg, José Ortega y Gasset, Leo Lowenthal, Dwight MacDonald, Clement Greenberg, T. W. Adorno, Marshall McLuhan, Irving Howe, Ernest van den Haag, Leslie Fiedler, and Melvin Tumin; and Norman Jacobs, ed., *Culture for the Millions*

length study. Once the charges are summarily presented, however, evidence about them will be discussed. Unfortunately, little empirical research is available to test the factual statements in these charges, and I will sometimes have to rely on personal observations, impressions, and even speculation.[6] More important, many of the charges rest on value premises which cannot be studied empirically, and in this case I shall discuss these premises and analyze the assumptions implicit in them, questioning those that seem to me undesirable.[7]

The negative character of popular-culture creation. The criticism of the process of popular-culture creation breaks down into three charges: that mass culture is an industry organized for profit; that in order for this industry to be profitable, it must create a homogeneous and standardized product that appeals to a mass audience; and that this requires a process in which the industry transforms the creator into a worker on a mass production assembly line, where he gives up the individual expression of his own skills and values.

For example, Lowenthal writes:

> The decline of the individual in the mechanized working processes of modern civilization brings about the emergence of mass culture, which replaces folk or "high" art. A product of popular culture has none of the features of genuine art, but in all its media popular culture proves to have its own genuine characteristics: standardization, stereotypy, conservatism, mendacity, manipulated consumer goods.[8]

Dwight MacDonald puts it more sharply:

> Mass Culture is imposed from above. It is fabricated by technicians hired by businessmen; its audience are passive consumers; their participation

(Princeton, N.J.: Van Nostrand, 1961), particularly the articles by Hannah Arendt, Ernest van den Haag, Oscar Handlin, Randall Jarrell, and Stanley Edgar Hyman. See also T. S. Eliot, *Notes Towards the Definition of Culture* (New York: Harcourt, Brace, 1949), and the works of F. R. Leavis, e.g., F. R. Leavis and Denys Thompson, *Culture and Environment* (London: Chatto and Windus, 1937).

[6] The best empirically based evaluation of the charges against mass culture may be found in Raymond A. Bauer and Alice H. Bauer, "American Mass Society and Mass Media," *Journal of Social Issues*, 16, 3 (1960), pp. 3–66. See also Joseph Klapper, *The Effects of Mass Communication* (New York: The Free Press of Glencoe, 1960), Wilbur Schramm, ed., *The Science of Communication* (New York: Basic Books, 1963), and Edward Shils, "The Mass Society and Its Culture," in Jacobs, ed., *op. cit.*, pp. 1–27, and the sources cited in these references.

[7] On this problem, see Paul Lazarsfeld, "Afterword," in Gary Steiner, *The People Look at Television* (New York: Alfred A. Knopf, 1963), pp. 409–422.

[8] Leo Lowenthal, "Historical Perspectives of Popular Culture," in Rosenberg and White, eds., *op. cit.*, pp. 46–57, quote at p. 55.

limited to the choice between buying and not buying. The Lords of *Kitsch*, in short, exploit the cultural need of the masses in order to make a profit and/or to maintain their class rule.[9]

And Ernest van den Haag describes the creators of popular culture as

> ... salesmen; they sell entertainment and produce with sales in mind. ... Today's movie producer, singer or writer is less dependent on the taste of an individual customer, or village, or court, than was the artist of yore; but he does depend far more on the average of tastes and he can influence it far less. He need not cater to any individual taste—not even his own. ... He is like a speaker addressing a mass meeting and attempting to curry its favor.[10]

Implicit in these charges is a comparison with high culture, which is portrayed as noncommercial, producing a heterogeneous and nonstandardized product, and encouraging a creative process whereby an individual creator works to achieve his personal ends more than those of an audience.

Systematic evidence to evaluate the charge is scarce, but the differences between popular and high culture as economic institutions are smaller than suggested. To be sure, popular culture is distributed by profit-seeking firms that try to maximize the audience, but then so is much of high culture, at least in America, where lack of state subsidy and the absence of patrons give it no other choice. Both popular and high culture distribute content chosen on the basis of taste standards, and thus resemble each other and all organizations selling "taste products." For example, although much has been written about the intense competitiveness and cynical marketing ethos of Hollywood and Madison Avenue, a study of art galleries, magazines, and book publishers appealing to a high-culture public would show similar features. Indeed, pressures to deceive the customer and to cut corners in relationships with competitors may be even more marked in high-culture firms, if only because there are fewer customers and a less profitable and more unpredictable market, making it necessary to struggle harder to get business. This similarity must not be exaggerated, for much of high culture is distributed by nonprofit agencies, people with independent incomes, and firms willing to accept lower profits to provide what they consider to be a desirable product.

Perhaps the major difference between popular culture and high cul-

---

[9] MacDonald, *op. cit.*, p. 60.
[10] Ernest van den Haag, "Of Happiness and Despair We Have No Measure," in Rosenberg and White, eds., *op. cit.*, pp. 504–536, quote at pp. 519–520.

ture is the size of the total audience.[11] High culture appeals to a relatively small number of people, probably less than a million, whereas the audience for a popular television program may be as large as 40 million. As a result, high culture must often be provided under nonprofit auspices or by firms that set a high markup on what they sell, while popular culture is almost always profitable, but must create a product that will appeal to many millions of people, or a set of products that responds to the variety within a huge audience.

The second claim, that the popular-culture product is homogeneous and standardized but the high-culture one is not, is also questionable. Popular culture is more often mass-produced, because it must be distributed to a much larger audience, but not all its products are either standardized or homogeneous. Some media firms create for a market that they view as an undifferentiated mass, but others create for specialized audiences. Television is an example of the former although even it seeks increasingly to appeal to different segments of its large audience; magazine publishing is an example of the latter, for over 8000 different magazines are published in America today. Moreover, formerly standardized mass media, such as the movies, are less so today because Hollywood no longer has a loyal audience of habitual moviegoers.

Of course, there are numerous similarities and only minor differences in many commercial popular-culture products, but this is often also true of high culture, although we tend to be less sensitive to it. For example, all rock-and-roll music sounds similar to the uninitiated listener, but then so does baroque music; only those who are familiar with each notice variations within the genre. Similarly, there are many formal and substantive differences in popular art, although they are not as visible as those in high-culture art, where they are emphasized and ennobled by academic classification into "schools of art."

Since each taste culture is sensitive only to its own diversity and judges the others to be more uniform than itself, a careful comparative study would be needed to say whether there is more diversity in high culture than in popular culture. The same observation applies to the amount of originality, innovation, and conscious experimentation. Both cultures encourage innovation and experiment, although in high culture experiments that are rejected by audiences in the creator's lifetime may become classics in another era, whereas in popular culture they

---

[11] The implications of audience size are discussed more fully in Rolf Meyersohn, "A Critical Examination of Commercial Entertainment," in Robert W. Kleemeier, ed., *Aging and Leisure* (New York: Oxford University Press, 1961), pp. 243–272, especially pp. 254 ff.

are forgotten if not immediately successful. Even so, in both cultures innovation is rare, although in high culture it is celebrated and in popular culture it is taken for granted.

Finally, the differences between the motives, methods, and roles of the creators are also fewer than has been suggested. My observations in American and English film, television, and publishing companies suggest that many popular-culture creators want to express their personal values and tastes in much the same way as the high-culture creator and want to be free from control by the audience or by mass-media executives.[12] Conversely, the so-called "serious" artist also wants to obtain positive responses from his peers and audiences. Like the mass-media creator, his work is also a compromise between his own values and those of an intended audience, although the compromise is of different priority, for his own values come first and he is willing to accept a smaller audience.

Actually, the significant difference between creators in the two cultures is not so much in what they want to do but in what they can do. For one thing, the high-culture creator works in an economy of scarcity; there is often less demand for his art than he can supply, and so he does not expect to earn a living by it. For the popular-culture creator, demand frequently outruns supply, and he can expect to earn a living from his work. If he is commercially successful, he is under greater pressure to produce something similar that will repeat the original success, although even the high-culture creator, with a much smaller audience, experiences this pressure.

Moreover, and more important, in popular culture the compromise between creator and audience values is institutionalized and taken out of the creator's hands, for his work is often changed by editors, directors, and producers before it is distributed. In high culture the compromise more often takes place within the creator, for even he is sometimes under pressure to change his work. For example, some years ago the producers of the avant-garde Living Theater of New York required the author of an experimental play to change it in order to make his work intelligible to the audience. The resulting conflict between playwright and producer was no different from that constantly going on in popular culture.[13]

---

[12] Herbert J. Gans, "The Creator-Audience Relationship in the Mass Media: An Analysis of Movie-making," in Rosenberg and White, eds., *op. cit.*, pp. 315–324. See also Joan Moore, "The Writer Views the Viewer," unpublished paper delivered at the 1963 meeting of the American Sociological Association.

[13] For a poignant example in an industry that is middle rather than highbrow, but where the process is not institutionalized, see William Gibson's autobiographical

Differences in the motives and roles of creators attributed to differences between high and popular culture are often a function of the creator's position and power in the culture. In both cultures the famous creator can insist on the freedom to do what he wants, and the unknown cannot. Thus Herman Wouk is probably as free from editorial interferences as was William Faulkner, but their less powerful peers in both cultures must choose between rejection of or tampering with their work.

In summary, the conditions in which culture is created and within which creators work in the two cultures differ in degree largely because of audience size. As long as the audience for high culture is smaller than that for popular culture, the high-culture creator finds it easier to work as an individual; he is freer to reject producer and audience demands than the popular-culture creator. Even so, to think of the former as concerned primarily with individual self-expression and the creation of culture, and the latter as an opportunistic hack out only to give the audience what it wants is to surrender to stereotypes.

Negative effects on high culture. The second theme in the popular-culture critique consists of two charges: that popular culture borrows content from high culture with the consequence of debasing it, and that by economic and prestige incentives popular culture is able to lure away potential high-culture creators, thus impairing the quality of high culture. As van den Haag puts it, "The greatly increased lure of mass markets for both producers and consumers diverts potential talent from the creation of art." [14]

Clement Greenberg describes the process of borrowing by mass culture as "using for raw material the debased and academicized simulacra of genuine culture." [15] MacDonald argues that

> There seems to be a Gresham's law in cultural as well as monetary circulation; bad stuff drives out the good. . . . It threatens High Culture by its sheer pervasiveness, its brutal overwhelming *quantity*. The upper classes, who begin by using (mass culture) to make money from the crude tastes of the masses and to dominate them politically, end by finding their own culture attacked and even threatened with destruction by the instrument they have thoughtlessly employed.[16]

description of how he had to change his play, *Two for the Seesaw*: William Gibson, *Seesaw Log* (New York: Alfred A. Knopf, 1959).

[14] Ernest van den Haag, "A Dissent from the Consensual Society," in Jacobs, ed., *op. cit.*, pp. 53–62, quote at p. 59. See also van den Haag in Rosenberg and White, eds., *op. cit.*, pp. 520–522.

[15] Clement Greenberg, "Avant Garde and Kitsch," in Rosenberg and White, eds., *op. cit.*, pp. 98–107, quote at p. 102.

[16] MacDonald, *op. cit.*, p. 61.

Van den Haag describes the process:

> Corruption of past high culture by popular culture takes numerous forms, starting with direct adulteration. Bach candied by Stokowski, Bizet coarsened by Rodgers and Hammerstein . . . Freud vulgarized into columns of newspaper correspondence advice (how to be happy though well-adjusted). Corruption also takes the form of mutilation and condensation. . . . works are cut, condensed, simplified and rewritten until all possibilities of unfamiliar or esthetic experience are strained out . . .
>
> What eagerness for high culture there is in popular culture has abetted the invasion of high culture, with unfortunate effect on the invaded territory. Often the effect on the invaders is unhappy too. In biting into strange fruits they are not equipped to digest, they are in danger of spoiling their appetite for what might actually nourish them. . . . Doubtless they are eager for intellectual and esthetic experience. Yet their quest is not likely to succeed . . . it takes far more than training and formal preparation fully to experience a work of art as meaningful. It takes an environment and a life experience which do not easily grow on the soil of our society.[17]

While both borrowing and the luring away of creators occur, the consequences attributed to both processes strike me as questionable. It is true that popular culture borrows from high culture, but the reverse is also true, for jazz and folk music have been borrowed by high-culture composers. In the past, high culture borrowed only from folk art, especially after the folk had taken up newer versions of it, but as folk art becomes extinct, high culture must borrow from its successor, commercial popular culture. For example, today comic-book illustration has been transformed into pop art. Of course, popular culture borrows much more from high culture than vice versa, but if the high-culture audience were larger, this might not be the case.

When a high-culture product, style, or method is taken over by popular culture, it is altered, but this also happens when popular arts are taken up by the high culture. When something is borrowed from high culture, however, it can no longer be used by high-culture artists because borrowing, having lowered its cultural prestige, would cause it to be rejected by the status-conscious audience for high culture. Popular-culture audiences, on the other hand, are probably pleased by content borrowed from a source of higher status.

To understand properly the charge of debasement, we must distinguish between effects on the creator and effects on the culture as a whole. Undoubtedly, high-culture creators suffer when they see their

[17] Van den Haag, in Rosenberg and White, eds., *op. cit.*, pp. 524–525, 528.

work changed, but so do popular-culture creators, even though only the former call it debasement. There is no evidence, however, that borrowing has led to a debasement of high culture per se, or of its vitality. The creation of high culture continues even when it is borrowed and changed, and I do not know of any high-culture creator who has stopped working because his previous creations were taken over by popular culture.

The charge that popular culture lures away potential high-culture creators is undoubtedly accurate, at least in some of the arts, where outlets are scarce and working conditions are poor. Young poets must become teachers or jingle writers; concert violinists have to earn their living playing popular music; and currently, fewer young people are preparing themselves for careers as performers of high-culture music than in the past, because opportunities for playing are so few. The performer who cannot play undoubtedly suffers, but it still has not been proved that the high-culture creator who earns his living in popular culture is therefore less creative in his high-culture work. This charge can only be tested, however, if he is given a chance to spend all his time on the latter. More important, it is not at all clear that there would be more high culture if the pay scale of popular culture were not so tempting. And not every kind of high-culture creator can work in popular culture. For example, high-culture writers often cannot write for popular audiences, as the failure of famous novelists in Hollywood has repeatedly demonstrated.

Even if popular culture did not lure away potential recruits to high culture, the vitality of high culture would not necessarily be increased. Given the present size of the audience for high-culture music, concert violinists would still have no more opportunity to play, even if popular music did not exist; indeed, they would have to earn a living in nonmusical activities. The genuine issue is not the profitability of popular culture, but the unprofitability of high culture because of the smallness of its audience, so that its creators must be supported by public or private subsidy. This support is already available to many painters and novelists, but it must be extended to poets, musicians, sculptors, and to all creators of high culture who cannot support themselves by their creative work, or who cannot find a place to perform it.

If one looks at high culture from a strictly economic perspective, it may be described as a low-wage industry that loses some of its workers to high-wage competitors and hopes that the rest will be satisfied with the spiritual benefits of low-wage employment. Given the affluence of the rest of society, the spiritual benefits that were once attractive no longer suffice, resulting in a shortage of high-culture creators. This shortage can be reduced only by raising wages, not by reducing the wages of popular culture. Indeed, the effective solution is to tax highly profitable cultural enterprises to subsidize the ones that are unprofitable but socially necessary. Although the television networks now make occasional grants to educational television stations, and book publishers use the profits from best-sellers to subsidize the publication of high-culture books, these efforts, now voluntary, should be made compulsory through legislation.

Negative effects on the popular-culture audience. By far the most serious charge against popular culture is the alleged negative effects it has on its audience. A number of such effects have been postulated: that popular culture is emotionally destructive because it provides spurious gratification, and that it is brutalizing in its emphasis on violence; that it is intellectually destructive because it offers meretricious and escapist content that inhibits ability to cope with reality; and that it is culturally destructive, impairing ability to partake of high culture. For example, MacDonald describes popular culture as "a debased, trivial culture that voids both the deep realities (sex, death, failure, tragedy) and also the simple spontaneous pleasures . . . The masses, debauched by several generations of this sort of thing, in turn come to demand trivial and comfortable cultural products." [18] Irving Howe argues:

> Mass culture is . . . orientated toward a central aspect of industrial society: the depersonalization of the individual . . . It reinforces those emotional attitudes that seem inseparable from existence in modern society—passivity and boredom . . . What is supposed to deflect us from the reduction of our personalities actually reinforces it.[19]

And van den Haag puts it similarly:

> All mass media in the end alienate people from personal experience and though appearing to offset it, intensify their moral isolation from each other, from reality and from themselves. One may turn to the mass media when lonely or bored. But mass media, once they become a habit, impair the capacity for meaningful experience. . . . The habit feeds on itself, establishing a vicious circle as addictions do. . . . Even the most profound of experiences, articulated too often on the same level (by the media), is reduced to a cliché. . . . They lessen people's capacity to experience life itself.[20]

[18] MacDonald, *op. cit.*, p. 72.
[19] Irving Howe, "Notes on Mass Culture," in Rosenberg and White, eds., *op. cit.*, pp. 496–503, quote at p. 497.
[20] Van den Haag in Rosenberg and White, eds., *op. cit.*, p. 529.

Of these charges, the most important is emotional destructiveness, and much of my discussion will be devoted to it.[21]

Implied in this part of the critique are three assumptions: that the behavior for which popular culture is held responsible actually exists and is widespread; that the content of popular culture contains models of such behavior; and that therefore popular culture is the main cause of it. These assumptions are not supported by the available evidence.[22]

To begin with, there is no evidence that the American people can be justly described as brutalized, narcotized, atomized, escapist, or unable to cope with reality. These descriptions are difficult to translate into empirical measures, which is why they can be bandied about effortlessly, but the available community studies and some recent research on the epidemiology of mental illness suggest that the vast majority of people are not isolates but members of familial, peer, and community groups.[23] The great amount of mental illness in both urban and rural areas is mostly neuroses and mild character disorders; only a minority suffer from psychoses, the serious mental illnesses implied in the popular culture critique. Serious mental illness does seem to be especially high among the poverty-stricken.[24] This group uses the mass media intensively, but it has been suffering from social and emotional problems caused by poverty for many centuries, long before popular culture was invented, and indeed while the folk art considered healthy by the critics flourished around it.

Although one could therefore reject the charge of negative effects at the outset by showing that the picture of the popular-culture audience

---

[21] Complaints about the effects of popular culture content, particularly about violence, have also come from sources quite unrelated to the critics cited here, including especially church and PTA groups. The existence of "too much violence" is also noted by 13 percent of a random sample of viewers studied by Steiner and reported in Steiner, *op. cit.*, p. 141. See also Ira O. Glick and Sidney J. Levy, *Living with Television* (Chicago: Aldine Publishing Company, 1962), Chapter 4.

[22] See the summary of existing studies by Bauer and Bauer, *op. cit.*, especially pp. 31–35.

[23] For reviews of the major community studies, see Maurice Stein, *The Eclipse of Community* (Princeton, N.J.: Princeton University Press, 1960), and Harold Wilensky and Charles N. Lebeaux, *Industrial Society and Social Welfare* (New York: Russell Sage Foundation, 1958), Part I. See also Harold Wilensky, "Mass Society and Mass Culture," *American Sociological Review*, 29 (April 1964), pp. 173–197, at p. 177. The major mental health studies are: Leo Srole et al., *Mental Health in the Metropolis* (New York: McGraw-Hill, 1962), Thomas S. Langner and Stanley T. Michael, *Life Stress and Mental Health* (New York: The Free Press of Glencoe, 1963), Dorothea C. Leighton et al., *The Character of Danger* (New York: Basic Books, 1963).

[24] August B. Hollingshead and Frederick C. Redlich, *Social Class and Mental Illness* (New York: John Wiley and Sons, 1958), Srole, *op. cit.*, and Langner and Michael, *op. cit.*

is drawn not from reality but from the fantasies and even wishes of the critics, it may still be that the existing mental illness and other negative qualities implied by the charges can be traced to the effects of popular culture. The evidence from a generation of studies on the effects of the mass media suggest that this is not so. The media do not have the simple Pavlovian impact attributed to them, and it is thus impossible to deduce effects from content. Instead, media content is just one of many cultural stimuli people choose, to which they respond, and, more important, that they help to create through the feedback they exert on the popular-culture industries.

Several studies have shown that people choose media content to fit individual and group requirements, rather than adapting their life to what the media prescribe or glorify. They are not isolated individuals hungering for and therefore slavishly accepting what the media offer them, but families, couples, and peer groups who use the media when and if the content is relevant to group goals and needs.[25] Thus the audience cannot be considered a mass.[26] Moreover, people pay much less attention to the media and are much less swayed by its content than the critics, who are highly sensitive to verbal and other symbolic materials, believe. They use the media for diversion and would not think of applying its content to their own lives.[27] Even adolescents, some of whom are loyal fans of teen-age performers during the period just before puberty, do not model themselves or their choice of dates and spouses on these performers, press agent claims notwithstanding. Finally, content choice is strongly affected by *selective perception,* so that people not only choose content that agrees with their own values but also interpret conflicting content so as to support these values. Thus the prime function of the media is to reinforce already existing behavior and attitudes, rather than to create new ones.[28]

There are, of course, exceptions to such a general finding. People copy dress and other fashions from the media, although those who do so are a tiny percentage of the total audience. People are also known to accept unquestioningly media content on subject matter of little interest to them. Moreover, children are more impressionable than adults

[25] Among the principal studies are Matilda Riley and John W. Riley, "A Sociological Approach to Communications Research," *Public Opinion Quarterly,* 15 (Fall 1951), pp. 445–460, and Elihu Katz and Paul Lazarsfeld, *Personal Influence* (Glencoe, Ill.: The Free Press, 1955).

[26] Eliot Freidson, "Communications Research and the Concept of the Mass," *American Sociological Review,* 18 (June 1953), pp. 313–317.

[27] For one illustration, see Herbert J. Gans, *The Urban Villagers* (New York: The Free Press of Glencoe, 1962), Chapter 9

[28] Klapper, *op. cit., passim.* See also Rolf Meyersohn, "Social Research in Television," in Rosenberg and White, eds., *op. cit.,* pp. 245–257.

and will accept content at face value, although even they become trained in what Freidson calls "adult discount" before they are ten.[29] In addition, some recent experimental studies have shown that mass-media content may have an immediate impact that disappears soon afterward.[30] For example, in the laboratory, movies with aggressive content stimulate the acting out of aggressive impulses among the subjects, but then romantic movies have encouraged balcony necking parties for generations without apparent ill effect. More important, socially marginal and psychopathic personalities may be affected by media content more easily than others.[31] Most important, the mass media may add to the difficulties of the deprived who must watch as outsiders in their own society. Thus a recent community study made in a New York slum concluded that "public communication media and advertising tend to aggravate the effects of poverty. Television, automobiles, holidays such as Christmas, and advertising in general create more serious alienation and psychological damage than is generally assumed." [32]

Finally, all the studies measure conscious effects, and say little or nothing about possible unconscious consequences. Moreover, they deal with short-range impact occurring weeks or months after media exposure, and do not report on the long-range effects of living in a society where media use takes up so much time. There are thus significant omissions in the available evidence, mainly because subconscious and long-range effects are difficult to study empirically.[33] Nevertheless, if these effects existed—and in the alarming proportions suggested by the mass-culture critique—they should make themselves visible in the society. There is no evidence, however, of a rising tide of violence, crime, or mental illness.[34]

This brief survey of the effects studies permits some evaluation of

[29] Eliot Freidson, "Adult Discount; An Aspect of Childen's Changing Taste," *Child Development*, 24, 1 (March 1953), pp. 39–49.
[30] L. Berkowitz, R. Corwin, and M. Heironimus, "Film Violence and Subsequent Aggressive Tendencies," *Public Opinion Quarterly*, 27 (Summer 1963), pp. 217–229.
[31] Wilensky, "Mass Society and Mass Culture," *op. cit.*, p. 183.
[32] Sherman Barr, "Poverty on the Lower East Side" (New York: Mobilization for Youth, mimeographed, May 1964). The quotation reflects the preliminary nature of the data and is cited here mainly to note a possible effect that deserves systematic study.
[33] For a good discussion of subconscious effects and their empirical identification, see Arthur J. Brodbeck, "The Popular Arts as a Socializing Agency," paper presented at the 1955 meetings of the American Psychological Association.
[34] On crime, see Daniel Bell, Chapter 8, "The Myth of Crime Waves," in his *End of Ideology* (Glencoe, Ill.: The Free Press, 1960); on mental illness, see Herbert Goldhamer and Andrew M. Marshall, *Psychosis and Civilization* (Glencoe, Ill.: The Free Press, 1953).

the charges about mass culture's impact on the audience. As to emotional destructiveness, the only evidence brought forth by the critics is a deduction from content: that since the media content is often violent, it must encourage violence and brutalization in the audience. Of course, the depiction of violence is a frequent theme in the popular arts, but this proves nothing about audience behavior. Undoubtedly violence reinforces pathology among pathological audience members and frightens some children, although an English study showed that the latter were less fearful of the fictional violence that is most often condemned than of more realistic violence in newsreels and naturalistic drama.[35] Moreover, some psychiatrists argue that the vicarious consumption of violence may reduce its expression in behavior. More violence in the popular arts may thus mean less violence among people, although recent experiments that encourage children to be aggressive after having seen a film in which aggressive behavior is prominent suggest that this is not true, at least not in the laboratory.[36] My own feeling is that only when other, more real provocations toward violence are present can mass-media violence affect behavior, and even then the media only influence children and pathological individuals. Further research is unfortunately necessary before it can be determined whether media violence ought to be reduced.

A perhaps more serious charge, with more widespread consequences, is that popular culture provides overly facile, spurious, and misleading gratification of emotional needs, notably through happy endings, false heroics, the appearance of a *deus ex machina* to solve insoluble problems, and stereotypical characterization, whereas high culture offers genuine gratifications through its honest and reality-oriented treatment of individual and social themes. Thus van den Haag has argued that the entire pattern of vicarious emotional release in popular culture is false, that needs for aggression and sexuality are not properly gratified, and that the media offer "substitute gratifications . . . which strengthen internalized hindrance to real and gratifying experience

---

[35] H. Himmelweit, A. Oppenheim, and P. Vance, *Television and the Child* (London: Oxford University Press, 1958). The principal American studies of the effects of the mass media on children are Lotte Bailyn, "Mass Media and Children: A Study of Exposure Habits and Cognitive Effects," *Psychological Monographs*, 73 (1959), pp. 1–48; and W. Schramm, J. Lyle, and E. Parker, *Television in the Lives of Our Children* (Stanford, Calif.: Stanford University Press, 1961). An up-to-date review of all studies of the effects of television on children is to be found in Wilbur Schramm, ed., "The Effects of Television on Children and Adolescents" (Paris: UNESCO, Reports and Papers on Mass Communications, No. 43, 1964).
[36] These studies are summarized in Schramm, "The Effects of Television on Children and Adolescents," *op. cit.*, pp. 14–15.

... that we are diverted temporarily and in the end perhaps drained —but not gratified." [37] This theory can be discussed as part of a more general charge, that popular culture distorts reality through escapist fiction, meretricious advertising, and superficial news reporting.

Undoubtedly, the content of popular culture can be described and evaluated in this way, but it still permits no conclusion about effects. Van den Haag offers no evidence, for example, that people are drained rather than gratified, or that high culture has the reverse effect, and if so, how. Certainly there are people who fit the mass critique model, living their entire emotional life within and through the mass media, but such people are emotionally disturbed and their use of the media is only a symptom, not a cause, of their difficulties. Conversely, there are also people whose emotional existence is limited to high culture and devoid of human relationships. Although their pathology is no different, it is not considered such and is valued as a testimonial to the desirability of high culture.

Similarly, there are people who use the mass media as guides to problem solving, and who suffer from the false version of reality presented in their entertainment and informational content. Although there are no adequate studies of where people get information used in problem solving, the effects described previously indicate that most people do not take media content at face value; that they use it to provide temporary respite from everyday life, rather than as a guide to it; and that they take material that supports their prior values and predispositions rather than new solutions.[38]

There are also people who are taken in by the puffery and dishonesty of advertising, especially among the most poorly educated, although studies of advertising impact and the complaints of advertising executives show that most people retain little of the ads they see or hear, and misinterpret much of the message. This does not justify dishonest advertising but does cast doubt on the intensity of the effect of advertising on people. Repetitive, hard-sell commercials are equally unjustifiable, especially since they do seem to have a Pavlovian effect on some audience members, at least judging by their effectiveness in raising sales of the products so advertised.

Finally, there is no doubt that popular culture's coverage of national and world events is quantitatively and qualitatively poor; "human interest," sensationalism and the evasion of controversy are major faults.

[37] Van den Haag, *op. cit.*, pp. 533–534.
[38] Herta Herzog, "Motivations and Gratifications of Daily Serial Listeners," in Wilbur Schramm, ed., *The Process and Effects of Mass Communications* (Urbana: University of Illinois Press, 1955), pp. 50–55.

Even so, all the evidence suggests that the mass media provide more news and controversy than the majority of the audience is willing to accept.[39]

More important, voting studies show that people do not make up their minds about their vote on the basis of mass-media content—or campaign speeches—and that they generally seem to know how to vote their interests, without what intellectuals would consider adequate information.[40] When an issue does not affect them, however, people may accept and vote on the basis of the version that is provided by the mass media. This recourse is especially undesirable when the competing points of view have unequal resources, and the well-financed group is able to obtain publicity for its point of view while the poorly financed group is unable to do so. Here the fault lies less with the mass media than with economic inequities in the society that can be used for political advantage. In fact, the national media usually try to present a "balanced" view of controversial issues by including all points of view in their content and, on television at least, by letting both sides purchase advertising. There is considerably less balance in the content of local media, however. This is also true at the national level of points of view held by small minorities. Nevertheless, the problem is not an effect of popular culture, but a public failure to protect the goals of political democracy in profit-seeking institutions with political communication functions.

Thus, although the content of popular culture may have many of the defects charged to it, and the economic factors in the distribution of content may too often disregard political consequences, the effects logically inferred from the content do not take place. This raises the question: Why do the critics of mass culture make such an inference? The answer is not difficult to find. The critics come to popular culture with the aesthetic standards of high culture and are shocked aesthetically by its content. Since they assume that the entire audience shares —or ought to share—their standards, especially the well-educated, they naturally project their own reactions on the audience. But the same process occurs when people who prefer popular culture come into contact with high culture; they are shocked, for example, by the explicit sexual content and condoning of social deviance often found in it, and they condemn it in terms not altogether different from those

---

[39] Bauer and Bauer, *op. cit.*, p. 53. See also Bernard Cohen, *The Press and Foreign Policy* (Princeton, N.J.: Princeton University Press, 1963).

[40] Paul Lazarsfeld, B. Berelson, and H. Gaudet, *The People's Choice* (New York: Columbia University Press, 1948), and B. Berelson, P. Lazarsfeld, and W. McPhee, *Voting* (Chicago: University of Chicago Press, 1954).

found in the mass-culture critique. They label the social satire of high culture as "sick" comedy, and they harass, censor, and even prosecute creators such as Edward Albee or Lenny Bruce for violating the standards of those who choose popular culture. Whereas high culture expresses its disapproval in books and literary journals, popular culture uses the police, the courts, the pulpit, and the political arena for this purpose.

In both instances, however, the process is the same. Advocates of one culture come to the other with different standards, disapproving of what they find, and they express their disapproval by alleging deleterious effects on the audience. Why they do this, why their standards differ, which standards are the right ones, and how this affects the evaluation of high and popular culture will be discussed in detail in later parts of this chapter.

Negative effects on the society. The critique of popular culture's effects on society contain two charges: that popular culture lowers the level of taste of the society as a whole, and that through such effects as narcotization and atomization it renders people susceptible to techniques of mass persuasion that in the hands of skilled demagogues can lead to the abrogation of democracy.[41] As Rosenberg puts it, "At its worst, mass culture threatens not merely to cretinize our taste but to brutalize our senses while paving the way to totalitarianism. And the interlocking media all conspire to that end." [42]

The evidence suggests that the first charge is inaccurate, and the second is not an effect of popular culture. The argument for the decline of taste levels is based on a skewed comparison, with the best features of past society compared to the worst contemporary ones.[43] Writers such as Oswald Spengler, for example, call attention only to the high culture of the past and some romanticized remnants of folk culture, but they ignore the elements in the latter that are more brutal and vulgar than anything in today's popular arts. By any comparison that takes into account the majority of people, however, there has been a steady rise in the level of taste, especially so in the last generation, when the

---

[41] The principal statement of this part of the critique is probably in José Ortega y Gasset, *Revolt of the Masses* (New York: Norton, 1932). See also his "The Coming of the Masses" in Rosenberg and White, eds., *op. cit.*, pp. 41–45.

[42] Bernard Rosenberg, "Mass Culture in America," in Rosenberg and White, eds., *op. cit.*, pp. 3–12, quote at p. 9.

[43] Paul F. Lazarsfeld and Robert K. Merton, "Mass Communication, Popular Taste and Organized Social Action," in Rosenberg and White, eds., *op. cit.*, pp. 457–473, especially at p. 467. See also the excellent critique of the declining taste-level charge in Bauer and Bauer, *op. cit.*, pp. 42 ff.

proportion of people going to college increased sharply. Although statistics about the number of symphony orchestras and book club members may not prove that Americans are becoming cultured, they do suggest a significant change in taste from the days when even semiclassical music was considered highbrow.

The charge that popular culture can lead to totalitarianism is based on the argument that with the increasing centralization of society, and what Karl Mannheim calls its "functional rationalization," the primary and secondary groups as well as local institutions that stand between individual and state are losing strength, leaving the individual as a powerless atom vis-à-vis the state. If a demagogue can take over the mass media, he can use techniques of mass persuasion like those allegedly now employed by the media to persuade individuals to accept dictatorship.[44] This argument is supported by the effectiveness with which Hitler and Stalin used their control over the mass media to maintain their totalitarian rule.

This analysis needs to be broken into constituent elements. It is true that the state can take over the society's mass media for its own goals; it may happen in wartime even in democratic societies. It is doubtful, however, that popular culture has the power to destroy the small institutions and other sources of opposition. As I suggested in the previous section, the media have not impaired the family or the peer group, and voluntary organizations in America have grown in number and in strength even during the most rapid growth of the mass media, not because of the influence of the media but because of the expansion of the middle class that is active in such groups.[45]

Even so, the power of the state is increasing, and under conditions of crisis it is possible that people will become fearful and panicky, or so threatened by social change that they are willing to give power to a strong leader who can promise to solve their problems. This is the case among John Birch Society members, and among Southern whites who have encouraged the establishment of near-totalitarian state political machines to save white supremacy. Such a leader might gain control of the mass media, especially if he promised economic or social relief to those who own them, or to their audiences. But here, too, the role of the media would be no different from its present one, the reinforcement of existing social trends. Thus, if the audience were in favor of dictatorship, it could easily force the media to provide content in its support. But the inability of the mass media to significantly influence

[44] *Ibid.*, pp. 56 ff.
[45] On the question of voluntary associations in the mass society, see William Kornhauser, *The Politics of Mass Society* (Glencoe, Ill.: The Free Press, 1959).

voting behavior suggests that the media could not persuade their audiences to accept dictatorship. In short, popular culture can become a tool of dictatorship, but it cannot and does not by itself encourage the establishment of a totalitarian society.

Popular Culture and Mass Society

The critics of popular culture respond to the analysis questioning the negative effects of popular culture in two ways. One approach is to suggest the irrelevance of the analysis, as Lewis Coser has done in commenting on the previously cited article by the Bauers. He writes: "I have no quarrel with most of the findings which are so ably but also so selectively reported by the Bauers. I only believe that most of them are of no relevance to a problem which, to me at least, is paramount; the problem of the quality of life in mass society . . . the loneliness of people who are not hermits but rather so highly attuned to the need to adjust themselves to the responses of others that they lose the ability . . . to act autonomously. . . ."[46] The other is to charge popular culture's destructiveness: that people have been trained by generations of exposure to popular culture to want what it provides, and to protect themselves against its dangers, but that in this process they have learned to accept only substitute gratifications, and have thus become dehumanized, brutalized, and impaired. If earlier generations had been given the opportunity to share in high culture, or to retain the folk culture of the past, this would not have happened.[47]

Both reactions express the humanist idealism that suffuses the popular-culture critique, suggesting that society ought to be judged by the standards of humanist philosophers and critics, who place a high value on personal autonomy, individual creativity, and rejection of group norms. In comparison with these standards, the quality of life in today's society is indeed low. The cause, as Coser sees it, is mass society and those who provide it with popular culture.

Coser cites a number of studies on the low quality of life in today's society, but these do not prove his thesis that the majority of people are being held back in practicing humanist values.[48] The sad fact is

---

[46] Lewis Coser, "Comments on Bauer and Bauer," *Journal of Social Issues*, 16, 3 (1960), pp. 78–84, quote from pp. 82–83.

[47] *Ibid.*, especially at p. 82. See also MacDonald, *op. cit.*, p. 72 and van den Haag in Rosenberg and White, eds., *op. cit.*, p. 529.

[48] Coser, *op. cit.*, p. 82. Among the empirical studies he cites are Merton's *Mass Persuasion*, Seeley's *Crestwood Heights*, Vidich and Bensman's *Small Town in Mass Society*, and Stein's analysis of a number of community studies, *Eclipse of Community*, as well as two more impressionistic works, Whyte's *Organization Man* and Hoggart's *Uses of Literacy*. Despite the high quality of all these books, they

that there are no adequate empirical studies of how people feel about these values and about high-culture standards, whether they want them, and if so, what prevents people from living by them at present. There is, however, no evidence that the majority of people share or want to share these standards.

As Coser rightly notes, whether people want to share these standards is not the same question as whether they should share them. This issue will be discussed in considerable detail in Part III, but it should be noted that these are standards that guide the life of high-culture creators and intellectuals, and as such are specifically suited to their environment and the creation of high culture. Whether they are suited to other styles of life is, however, open to question—and research. This question of suitability is reflected in the antagonism to high culture found among people from other taste subcultures. Thus Coser's charge is only a restatement of the essence of the popular-culture critique: that all people ought to live by high-culture standards, and that these are the only ones possible for the good life.

The second argument is essentially historical and hypothesizes a continuing decline of the quality of life, tracing it to the replacement of the small, cohesive community and folk culture by the urban industrial society and popular culture. This argument contains much romantic nostalgia about the happy peasantry and ignores the many people who lived under subhuman conditions, exploited by feudal landlords and employers, and who endured hunger, pestilence, rampant violence, and crime on public streets. As their lives deteriorated further with the beginnings of urban industrial society, one response was a leisure diet containing more violence and brutality than is even imaginable today. Edward Shils shows in a brilliant attack on this romantic nostalgia that such things as bearbaiting, visits to the lunatic asylum to taunt the mentally ill, attendance at public executions, and frequent drunkenness were staple items in that diet.[49]

Indeed, studies of people in transition from so-called folk culture to modern society suggest that many of the charges laid against today's industrial society actually apply to preindustrial and early industrial societies but become inapplicable when these have achieved an adequate level of affluence. The romantic nostalgia about the solidarity and "com-

provide little evidence that the people studied want what Coser wants for them. Nor do they provide the historical data to sustain his hypothesis that "mass culture . . . emerges when community, that is, groups of individuals linked to each other by concrete values and interests, is eroded and mass culture, in turn, further undermines community" (*ibid.*).

[49] Edward Shils, "Daydreams and Nightmares: Reflections on the Criticism of Mass Culture," *Sewanee Review*, 65 (1957), pp. 587–608.

munity" of folk culture notwithstanding, people in such cultures were apathetic and submissive automatons who were not considered capable of holding opinions about their society. Lacking this right, the power to defend themselves, and the vote, they were subject to restrictive group pressures and domination by feudal and religious elites.[50]

Only in a modern industrial society have ordinary people been liberated from these oppressions. They have become, in Lerner's phrase, members of a participant society in which they can hold opinions and, if the society is democratic, begin to affect their own destinies. Moreover, thanks to the availability of education, they have been enabled to begin to think of themselves as individuals, to develop themselves as such, and to want the values of autonomy and individual creativity which the humanists seek for them.

Popular culture has also played a role in this process, by permitting people to express their new, increasingly diverse interests. Although the critics of popular culture consider painting-by-the-numbers or the use of home and garden magazines as instances of spurious gratification and mass-media manipulation, these can also be interpreted as the beginnings of individual creativity and the striving for aesthetic satisfaction among people whose ancestors did not think themselves capable or worthy of painting a picture, and lacked the funds and aesthetic skills to "decorate" their homes.

This interpretation neither denies the value of the humanist ideal or suggests that society today is perfect. Considerable improvement is still necessary and possible, but any interpretation of present conditions must take into account the past. Moreover, if the critics of mass culture resort to a historical argument, they must consider the real past, not a nostalgic construct developed to justify their analysis of the present.

Edward Shils has put the issue well:

> A new order of society has taken form since the end of World War I in the United States. . . . This new order of society, despite all its internal conflicts, discloses in the individual a greater sense of attachment to the society as a whole, and of affinity with his fellows. . . .
>
> The new society is a mass society precisely in the sense that the mass of the population has become incorporated into society. The center of society—the central institutions and the central value systems . . . has extended its boundaries. Most of the population now stands in a closer relationship to the center than has been the case either in premodern so-

---

[50] Daniel Lerner, *The Passing of Traditional Society* (Glencoe, Ill.: The Free Press, 1958).

cieties or in the earlier phases of modern society. In previous societies, a substantial proportion, often the majority, were born and forever remained "outsiders." [51]

The term "mass society" is not appropriate to describe this social order, however, precisely because people are no longer bound by the social and psychological restrictions that are implied in the term "mass." Lerner's term "participant society" would be more apt.

It could be argued that at the time people were shedding the restrictive patterns of folk culture and feudalism, they could have been encouraged to participate in high culture, thus doing away with the need for popular culture. However, high culture was inaccessible to them. The social and political elite that supported high culture not only rejected popular participation in elite activities generally, but made no effort to provide the rest of society with the educational and other prerequisites needed to share in high culture. Until the last century upper income groups were strenuously opposed to educating lower ones, for they were fearful that literacy would only lead to revolution and the loss of their privileges.

Even today, data on the socioeconomic and educational backgrounds of high-culture publics make it clear that it is not popular culture that prevents people from participating in high culture but the lack of opportunities to obtain the prerequisite background. This point will be considered again in the evaluation of high and popular culture in Part III.

The Sources and Biases of the Popular-Culture Critique

Given the available evidence, the popular-culture critique does not stand up well. Not only are there similarities in how popular and high culture are created, but the former poses no genuine threat to high culture or its creators. Moreover, its content does not have the effects attributed to it, except perhaps on a minority of people who consume it in other than the accepted ways. Because of this lack of overall effect, it cannot be considered a major source of imminent danger to the society or to a democratic form of government.

Consequently, the critique boils down to a statement of aesthetic dissatisfaction with popular-culture content, justified by an incorrect estimate of negative effects, based on a false conception of the use and function of popular culture. Before embarking on a sociological analy-

---

[51] Edward Shils, "Mass Society and Its Culture," in Jacobs, ed., *op. cit.*, pp. 1–27, quote at p. 1.

sis of both high and popular culture, it is worth discussing why the critique exists and the major biases that render it inappropriate.

At one level, the critique is a plea for an ideal way of life guided by the humanist dictates of high culture. If this were its sole function, a policy-oriented analysis of the kind I am undertaking would seek to discover obstacles to the implementation of the ideal and suggest ways to removing them. At another level, however, the critique is a plea for power. Specifically it is a plea for the maintenance or restoration of an elitist order by the creators of high culture, the literary critics and essayists who support them, and a number of social critics—including some sociologists—who are unhappy with the social, economic, and political tendencies of modern society. The analysis of the political function of the critique requires a brief exploration of the history of popular culture and its critique.

During the preindustrial era, European societies were divided culturally into high and folk culture. The latter was sparse, homemade, and because peasants lived in isolated villages, largely invisible. The former was supported by the city-dwelling elites—the court, the nobility, the priesthood, and merchants who had the time, education, and resources for entertainment and art, and were able to subsidize a small number of creative people to produce these things for them. Both artists and intellectuals were close to the sources of power and shared to some extent the prestige and privileges of their employers and patrons. Because of the low social status and geographical isolation of folk culture, they also had a virtual monopoly on public and visible culture.

When economic and technological changes forced the peasants into the cities and gave them the free time and disposable income for their own art and entertainment, they shed the rural-based folk culture and became customers for a commercial popular culture that soon outnumbered in quantity the products and creators of high culture, and that eventually destroyed the old monopoly of public and visible culture. As the economic resources and powers of the patrons decreased, the creators of high culture were forced to leave the court society and look for support and audiences elsewhere. Eventually, they had to compete with popular culture in what might be called the culture market.

These changes could only seem undesirable and threatening to many of the creators of what was now explicitly described as high culture. The decline of the elite reduced their prestige, their source of support, and their privileges. The rise of a huge market for the popular arts meant for them not only a severe reduction of cultural standards but also a loss of control over the setting of standards to publics of lower status and less education. In this process the artist forgot the subordination and humiliation that he had often suffered at the hands of his patrons. He did not appreciate the freedom and dignity that he acquired, even as he lost his guaranteed audience and its economic support. He solved the problem of his audience by denying that he needed one; he created only for himself and his peers who could understand his unique genius. Consequently, he had only contempt for the new, bourgeois publics on whom he depended for economic support, even though they offered him greater rewards and more freedom than he had had before. The cult of the artist as genius, later transformed into the romantic image of the artist, provided culture with the prestige it lost when it was no longer associated with the aristocracy.[52]

The creators of culture thus experienced a considerable and rapid change of status and power; some were faced with drastic downward social and economic mobility. Among the elite patrons, this downward mobility led to the development of reactionary political and social movements, but among the artists and intellectuals it produced an ideology of discontent, expressed not only in novels and other content that bemoaned the passing of the old order, but also in the formulation of what has now become the popular-culture critique.[53]

Some of the writers who propagate this critique today are themselves descended from old European elites, or from equivalent groups in American society who opposed the nineteenth-century European immigration that helped to transform American into a non-Puritan, urbanized society. Others are descendants of the European immigrants and have become influential in today's literary and intellectual elite. Many are apolitical, but some, like the late José Ortega y Gasset and T. S. Eliot, were identified with conservative political groups. Russell Kirk and Ernest van den Haag are active in American right-wing political circles today. Alongside them is a group of socialist critics, notably Clement Greenberg, Irving Howe, Dwight MacDonald, Bernard Rosenberg, and Harold Rosenberg, whose criticism of popular culture is in many ways similar to that of the conservatives, although in no case are they—unlike some of the conservatives—hostile to political democracy or to political, social, and economic equality.[54]

The socialist critics also diverge from the conservative in their analysis of the causes of the problem of culture. The conservatives explain the existence of popular culture by the inadequacy of its audiences; the

---

[52] I am indebted to Peter Marris for many of the ideas in this paragraph.
[53] The origins of this critique are described in Lowenthal and Fiske, *op. cit.*
[54] Greenberg, *op. cit.*, Howe, *op. cit.*, MacDonald, *op. cit.*, Bernard Rosenberg, *op. cit.*, and Harold Rosenberg, "Pop Culture and Kitsch Criticism," *Dissent*, 5 (Winter 1958), pp. 14–19.

socialists point out that mass society and the use of the market mechanism to provide culture are at fault, and that these have led to the destruction of folk culture, while failing to provide people either with a better culture or with the economic and educational opportunities needed to participate in it. The conservatives attack popular culture because they resent the rising political, economic, and cultural power of the so-called masses; the socialists, because they are disappointed that these masses, once liberated from proletarianism, did not accept high culture or support socialist advocacy of it.

Despite their differing explanations of the rise of popular culture, the two groups are in virtual agreement about the present. They are both fearful of the power of popular culture, reject the desirability of cultural democracy or cultural pluralism, and feel impelled to defend high culture against what they deem to be a serious threat from popular culture, the industries that provide it, and its publics.[55] The socialists continue to view popular culture as stemming from cultural and economic inequities in American society, but they fail to accept the fact that people who have become affluent are not thereby willing to embrace high culture. Yet while these critics defend the right of people to choose their ways of living and their ideas, and support those who still choose folk culture, they are not ready to defend people who choose commercial popular culture. In the cultural realm, they are artists and intellectuals first, and libertarians second, giving priority to the defense of high culture, although unlike the conservatives, they do not advocate the restoration of cultural power to an elite of artists and intellectuals, at least not explicitly. What Peter Marris has written about the English socialist critics of popular culture, that "they are trying to resolve a personal conflict of loyalties between the working-class culture into which they were born and the elite culture by which they earn their living," also applies to the American socialists, although most of them are of middle-class origin, and have resolved the conflict in favor of their occupational role.[56]

[55] The ambivalence about cultural democracy is expressed in a panel discussion in Jacobs, ed., *op. cit.*, pp. 155 ff.
[56] Personal communication to the author. An interesting example of the conflict between the socialist identification with high culture and the working class can be found in England, where the Labour party initially opposed the introduction of commercial television because its leaders, middle-class intellectuals, wanted their working-class constituents to accept high culture. When these constituents made it clear that they liked commercial television much better than the middle-class programing provided by the British Broadcasting Corporation, the party was forced to tone down its cultural criticism of commercial television, and in recent years its attacks have stressed the high profits being made by the distributors of television programing.

The same conditions that led to the development of the popular-culture critique also produced its major biases. The first of these is the previously noted pessimistic view of history that sees high culture and the quality of life in the entire society as being in a steady and continuing state of decline following the development of popular culture. Such pessimism is not unusual among downwardly mobile groups, for they exaggerate their own loss of influence into a theory of overall social deterioration. Since this point of view is unsupported by evidence, however, it is a historical fallacy.

Although statistical evidence is scarce and although it is difficult to agree on criteria to measure viability and quality in high culture, it seems to me that even with the rapid growth of popular culture, high culture today is stronger, more viable, and more creative than it has often been in the past. Not only are more creators working and finding outlets for their work, but the quality of both creative and critical content is high. The critics argue that if popular culture did not exist, it would be even higher, but there is no evidence for this argument. In fact, the attempts of socialist governments, inside and outside the Soviet bloc, to discourage popular culture and to promote high culture have created adequate economic support for high culture, but have not significantly increased its vitality or its popularity. The Russian government initially supported the spread of high culture, but when it was not accepted by the citizenry, the government had to resort to an official popular culture called "socialist realism" and, to assure its creation, had to discourage artists from concentrating on the creation of high culture. Even so, the government has found it impossible to halt a lively black market in imported Western popular culture.

The critics find it difficult to accept an optimistic assessment of the state of high culture in Western societies today because they compare what has survived from past high culture—which is usually the best or classic portion—with the mixture of good, bad, and indifferent high culture of the moment. They remember only the Shakespeares and Beethovens of the past and forget their imitators and inferior colleagues whose work is lost or ignored. Their forgetfulness is only partly accidental, for there is an urgent need to prove that things are getting worse, especially among the conservative critics.

A similar bias pervades high culture's conception of society and of popular culture. As I noted earlier, only in the past century has the average person achieved the opportunity for individuality and self-development along with the right to leisure, art, and entertainment. This change stimulated the rapid expansion of the popular arts and encouraged the invention of the popular daily newspaper, the movies, and radio. In the short time since, there has been a substantial improvement in the quality of the popular arts. If we compare the newspapers, films, popular novels, art, or music of today with those of only the past generation, the present products are better if "better" is measured by criteria such as complexity, subtlety, sophistication, and the departure from simple stereotypes and formulas. Only by the use of a skewed comparison, which usually compares the life and culture of the nineteenth-century middle class with those of today's working class, can the critics find evidence for the cultural and social decline they wish to see.[57]

The historical fallacy shores up two other biases. One is a marked disdain for ordinary people and their aesthetic capacities, illustrated by the previously noted belief that the media have a Pavlovian hold on their audience and can persuade it to accept any emotion or idea they wish. The critics' low opinion of the popular-culture audience and the role it plays in their critique has been tellingly noted by Shils in a statement that summarizes in two paragraphs the essential fault of the popular-culture critique:

> The contention has been made frequently that mass culture is bad because it serves as a narcotic, because it affects our political democracy, because it corrupts our high culture. I don't think there is any empirical evidence for these contentions and what impressionistic evidence there is does not support them either. I think we are not confronting the real problem: Why we don't like mass culture. . . . It is repulsive to us. Is it partly because we don't like the working classes and the middle classes?
>
> Some people dislike the working classes more than the middle classes, depending on their political backgrounds. But the real fact is that from an esthetic and moral standpoint, the objects of mass culture are repulsive to us. This ought to be admitted. To do so would help us select an esthetic viewpoint, a system of moral judgments which would be applicable to the products of mass culture; but I think it would also relieve our minds from the necessity of making up fictions about the empirical consequences of mass culture.[58]

A second bias that stems from the historical fallacy is the assumption that the entire output of today's high culture must compare favorably with what has survived of past high culture, and that it must come up to the standards of what are today interpreted as golden ages of high

---

[57] The skewed comparison is at the heart of Ortega y Gasset's critique, *op. cit.* See also MacDonald, *op. cit.*, and Oscar Handlin's argument that late nineteenth-century popular culture was superior to today's, in "Comments on Mass and Popular Culture," in Jacobs, ed., *op. cit.*, pp. 63–70, especially at pp. 66–67.
[58] Edward Shils, "Panel Discussion," in Jacobs, ed., *op. cit.*, pp. 198–199.

culture, such as Periclean Athens, Elizabethan England, and the Renaissance. Such comparisons forget, of course, that most of the ordinary people of these societies lived in poverty or even slavery, and that directly or indirectly they contributed to the support of an elite that could in turn support high culture. Since this comparison judges the quality of society by the quality of its (surviving) high culture, the critics are implying that the major goal of society is to assure the creation of the best high culture possible, and that all other goals, such as the general welfare, are secondary.[59]

The final bias of the popular-culture critique follows directly from the preceding—what I call its *creator* or *producer orientation*. Any item of culture may be analyzed and evaluated from two perspectives —that of the creator and that of the consumer. The former views culture as existing for the people who create it, rejecting any attempt to satisfy an audience; the latter looks at culture from the point of view of the consumer, and asks to what extent culture is meeting its wishes and needs.

High culture is creator-oriented, and as I will show in Part II, its aesthetics and its principles of criticism are based on this orientation.[60] The belief that the creator's intentions are crucial and the values of the audience almost irrelevant functions to protect the creator from the audience, making it easier for him to create, although it ignores the reality that every creator must respond to some extent to an audience.

The popular arts are, on the whole, *consumer-oriented*, and exist to satisfy audience values and wishes. This is perhaps the major reason for the antagonism of high culture toward the popular arts and the tone of the mass-culture critique. High culture needs an audience as much as popular culture, but it is fearful that the audience will be wooed away by a consumer-oriented culture or that it will demand what might be called its cultural right to be considered in the creative process of high culture.

As a result, high culture needs to attack popular culture, and especially its borrowing of high-culture content, because it transforms that content into a consumer-oriented form. Moreover, high culture needs to think of popular culture as of low quality, of its creators as hacks, and its audience as culturally oppressed people without aesthetic standards. If high culture is to maintain its creator orientation, it must be

---

[59] See Lyman Bryson, *The Next America* (New York: Harper and Brothers, 1952), especially Chapter 17.
[60] Wilensky's definition of high culture includes as one characteristic that "critical standards independent of the consumer of the product are systematically applied to it." Wilensky, "Mass Society and Mass Culture," *op. cit.*, p. 176.

able to show that only *it* is guided by aesthetic standards, and that only *its* creators and audiences are complete human beings, and that for these reasons it has a right to maintain its cultural status and power. The irony is that to defend its creator orientation it requires status, and to claim such status it must compare itself to something lower. This is one reason why the popular-culture critique continues to exist and to put forth the charges it does despite the lack of supporting evidence.

In short, the popular-culture critique is partly an ideology of defense, constructed to protect the cultural and political privileges of high culture. Like all such ideologies, it exaggerates the power of its opposition and the harmful consequences that would follow from permitting this opposition to exist. Yet even if high culture has lost its monopoly on culture, and has had to give up some of its privileges and power in the cultural marketplace, its continuing and increasing vitality in an age when the popular arts are also flowering suggests that the defensive portions of the ideology are not as necessary for high culture as the critics believe. This portion of the ideology is also undesirable, for it seeks to protect high culture and its creators at the expense of the rest of culture and society. In this process it conjures up false dangers and spurious social problems, making it impossible to understand the popular arts or to evaluate them properly.

In the remaining parts of this chapter, I will develop an alternative way of looking at high culture and popular culture that accepts both, and makes it possible to arrive at a more desirable and effective evaluation of the popular arts.

II A Sociological Analysis of High and Popular Culture

A sociological analysis of high and popular cultures must begin not with judgments about their quality but with a perspective that sees each of them as social facts that exist because they satisfy the needs and wishes of some people, even if they dissatisfy those of other people. Moreover, it is useful to begin with a perspective that goes beyond American society and asks whether similar needs exist in other societies and how they are satisfied there.

The basic assumption of a sociological perspective—or at least of mine—is that every human being has aesthetic urges;[61] a receptivity to symbolic expressions of his wishes and fears; a demand for both knowledge and what might be called anti-knowledge (or wish fulfill-

---

[61] The Selznicks describe this as "the strain toward the esthetic." Gertrude and Philip Selznick, "A Normative Theory of Culture," *American Sociological Review*, 29 (October 1964), pp. 653–669, quote at p. 664.

ment) about his society; and a desire to spend free time, if such exists, in ways that diverge from his work routine. Therefore, every society must provide art, entertainment, and information for its members. All societies have some form of what I earlier called a national taste culture, as well as audiences or taste publics and creators who serve these. The audiences may be their own creators, or they may simply recruit someone to function temporarily as a creator, or they may turn, as in American society, to trained creators who spend all their time in this way.

Moreover, the content of the taste culture does not develop in a vacuum; it must meet standards of form and substance which grow out of the values of the society and the needs and characteristics of its members. Thus the aesthetic standards of every society can be related to other of its features, and one can expect a tribe of hunters to have concepts of beauty, and of art and leisure that are different from those of a group of factory workers or intellectuals. Homogeneous societies offer little cultural diversity; they generally develop only a single concept of beauty, one style of religious art, and one way of home furnishing. American society, with its pervasive division of labor and heterogeneity, includes varieties of art ranging from pinups to abstract expressionism, types of music ranging from the latest song hit to electronic chamber music, and most important, an equally large number of aesthetic standards to determine the choices people make from the available content.

These choices are not made randomly. Research into consumer behavior, leisure-time activities, and cultural choices indicates that all of them are related: people who subscribe to a specific magazine, say *Harper's*, are also likely to choose the so-called art films, attend concerts of classical music, play tennis, prefer Danish modern furnishings, and eat gourmet foods; and conversely, they will not read *Popular Confessions*, see Elvis Presley films, listen to rock and roll, attend boxing matches, like overstuffed furniture, or eat pigs' knuckles for dinner.[62]

The diversity of information, art, and entertainment, and the diverse standards by which people choose from them, are organized into taste subcultures, which I will hereafter call *taste cultures*. Each taste culture serves its own *taste public*, people who consider the content of that culture desirable. Although there is some agreement about the na-

---

[62] The pioneer study is W. Lloyd Warner and Paul S. Lunt, *The Social Life of a Modern Community* (New Haven, Conn.: Yale University Press, 1941), especially Chapter 19. See also Hollingshead and Redlich, *op. cit.*, Appendix 3 (Social Stratification and Mass Communication), pp. 398–407.

ture of beauty among taste publics, and thus some consensus on aesthetic standards, there is also much dissensus, reflected in the bitterness of the popular-culture critique and the resentment toward high culture among the lower taste publics. For example, there is probably consensus about the desirability of perceptual order in the cultural product, but there is also dissensus about how order is to be defined, what constitutes order and disorder in different items of culture. The perceptual order of a de Kooning painting would be interpreted as disorder by lower taste cultures, and the perceptual order of calendar art would be considered outside the proper sphere of art by high culture. Similarly, all taste cultures value sincerity in the cultural product, but in high culture the determination of sincerity or its absence is made by an inquiry into the motives or feelings of the creator, whereas in the lower taste cultures people are satisfied if the cultural product strikes *them* as sincere; they do not care whether its creator meant what he wrote or painted. What appears to high-culture publics as a cynically created mass-produced item may thus express feelings of sincerity experienced by other taste publics.

At a high level of abstraction, a comparative analysis of formal aesthetic principles would probably reveal substantial consensus among the taste cultures, but when it comes to choosing culture, differences in the application of these formal principles bring out the dissensus, so that in practice each public has somewhat different aesthetic standards than every other. This variation of standards is reflected in the cultures incorporating them. Every major taste culture has its own art, music, fiction, nonfiction, poetry, films, television programs, architecture, and favored foods, to mention only a few items; and each culture has its own writers, artists, performers, and critics.

Each culture also has its own institutions for meeting its aesthetic needs. For example, though all Americans consume art, high-culture publics select their art from original oils and "quality reproductions," often in galleries, whereas other publics choose mass-produced ones, bought in museums or at department store art counters; and still others may rely only on magazine pictures which they tear out and hang on their walls. Similarly, the universal demand for drama is satisfied for some publics mainly by the legitimate theater, for others by movies and television, and for yet others by baseball games and wrestling matches.

The sociological approach thus rejects the dichotomy of high and popular culture and the idea that the former maintains aesthetic standards while the latter exists for nonaesthetic reasons. Instead of assuming a single popular culture, the sociological approach proposes that the number of cultures is an empirical problem, to be determined by studies of who chooses what content, and what relationships exist among content choices. Until such studies are available, the hypothesis is that several taste cultures and publics coexist in the society and even share some creators and media. This idea is not new; it has been described in literary and popular writings by the conception of cultures and publics as being highbrow, middlebrow, or lowbrow.[63] I call this idea *aesthetic pluralism*.

The Major Taste Cultures and Publics

Taste publics and cultures are not official bodies or organized groups but aggregates of similar people making similar choices, and aggregates of similar content chosen by the same people who can be identified through sociological research. Several factors probably determine a person's identification with a taste public and his choice among taste cultures. For the purpose of this analysis, which is primarily to illustrate the diversity of taste publics and cultures, it is possible to oversimplify and stress one factor, *class*. As I noted earlier, aesthetic standards and leisure choices reflect people's backgrounds and in American society, where ethnic, religious, and regional differences are rapidly disappearing, the major source of subcultural variety is increasingly that of age and class, especially the latter.[64]

Perhaps the most important criterion for cultural choice is education, for two reasons. First, every item of cultural content carries with it a built-in educational requirement—little for the comic strip, much for the poetry of T. S. Eliot. Second, aesthetic standards and taste are taught in our society both by the home and the school. Thus a person's educational achievement and the kind of school he attended will probably predict better than any other single index that person's cultural choices. Since both of these are closely related to an individual's (and his parents') socioeconomic level, the range of taste cultures and publics follows closely the range of classes in American society.

The following descriptions of publics and cultures have the limitations of thumbnail sketches; I shall describe only American cultures and will even leave out ethnic, religious, and regional variants within them. Moreover, although each taste public culture is stratified by age, containing children, adolescent, young adult, and adult subgroupings, I will deal only with adult publics and their cultures. (Incidentally, this

---

[63] Van Wyck Brooks, *America's Coming of Age* (Garden City, N.Y.: Anchor Books, Doubleday, 1958), and Russell Lynes, "Highbrow, Middlebrow, Lowbrow," in *The Tastemakers* (New York: Harper and Brothers, 1954), Chapter 13.
[64] Herbert J. Gans, "Diversity Is Not Dead: A Report on Our Widening Range of Choice," *The New Republic*, 144 (April 3, 1961), pp. 11–15.

theory questions the existence of a single American "youth culture" and suggests instead the existence of several, with some common elements that reflect the position of adolescents in contemporary society.)

Publics and cultures will be treated as relatively homogeneous and static wholes, even though in reality each has factions that might be called traditional, contemporary, and progressive (or academic, establishment, and avant-garde, as they are referred to in high culture). Undoubtedly age correlates strongly with these factions; the progressives are younger than the traditionalists. Ethnic and religious backgrounds may also be relevant, and I suspect that in each taste public Catholics and Jews are likely to be more progressive, Protestants more traditional. Finally, the descriptions identify tendencies and cannot be used to classify individuals or even individual cultural items.

I will identify six major taste publics and their cultures. For other purposes, such as the formulation of public policy, more specificity would be necessary, and one might identify twenty or more publics and cultures, including the age, ethnic, and other subgroupings just referred to. The decision to describe publics and their cultures rather than the reverse was made because the characteristics and standards of publics are better known and are fairly stable, whereas the cultures shift somewhat over the years as new fashions and ideas replace old ones.

Because taste is a function of class, the six publics are labeled with class terms. Although stylistically poor, these terms have the advantage of being neutral.[65] The six publics and cultures to be described are called creator high culture, consumer high culture, upper-middle culture, lower-middle culture, lower-culture, and lower-lower culture.[66] The distinction between the two high-culture publics is based on the previously made distinction between creator orientation and consumer orientation. A creator-oriented public or culture is one whose aesthetic standards have to do with what the creator intended to do, how he did it, what methods he used, and how they relate to the content. Such an evaluation asks the audience to take the creator's role, to look over his shoulder in using the cultural product. The aesthetic standards of a consumer-oriented public or culture stress the content's effect on the audience. Thus the evaluation of the product asks first whether the

---

[65] Edward Shils, who maintains the tripartite division used by Brooks and Lynes, used the terms refined, mediocre, and brutal, which are hardly neutral. See Shils, "Mass Society and Its Culture," *op. cit.*

[66] Another alternative would be to use the model educational level of each public, thus calling them university, collegiate, high school, tenth grade and grade school.

audience thought it good or bad; whether they liked it or not; and what kind of an impact it had on them, with the creator's aims being secondary.

Since all cultures include both creators and consumers, everyone has creator- and consumer-oriented aesthetic standards. These standards and the people who hold them are often in conflict. In each of the cultures one could therefore describe creator and consumer factions, but I will do so only for high culture, partly because there the conflict is most visible. In the other cultures the conflict is muted, largely because commercially supplied culture is consumer-oriented. Although its creators have their own aesthetics and may oppose the consumer orientation privately, they usually give first priority to satisfying their publics while trying to include content that meets their creator standards as well.[67] When it comes to activities in which the publics themselves function as creators, however, they will have standards different from those of consumers. For example, people who build their own hot rods reject the standards of people who buy Detroit's high-powered sports cars, just as those who own sailboats are at odds with their neighbors who prefer to be driven through the water by a motor.

Creator-oriented high culture. This is the taste culture of the "serious" artist, the critic, and the scholar who select and judge cultural content on the basis of creator standards. It is thus principally the culture of a creator public, and also of a noncreator public of highly educated predominantly upper-middle-class people who work largely in academic and professional jobs. The latter is subdivided into a creator-oriented public and a consumer-oriented public.

Although it is difficult to summarize the aesthetic standards of high culture in a few paragraphs, it is fair to say that they stress the relationship between method and content (or form and substance) and the higher priority of the former. These standards, which are formulated by creators and critics rather than by the culture's public, also place high value on subtlety in content and on the careful depiction of mood and feeling. Analysis and abstraction are desirable as long as there is also a final synthesis in which the personal values of the creator are indicated explicitly or implicitly.

In the culture's dramatic content the emphasis is away from plot and

[67] This content is usually described as "technical effects" and is often not visible to the consumers. For a good illustration of creator and consumer differences and conflicts, see Howard S. Becker, "The Professional Dance Musician and His Audience," *American Journal of Sociology*, 57 (September 1951), pp. 136–144, and also Moore, *op. cit.*

toward the emotional and logical developments of the character and his relationships with others. Fictional content stresses basic philosophical and psychological themes, with the heroes often modeled on the creators themselves, emphasizing, for example, the conflict between individual and society and the problems of familial and other relationships (for example, the ability to love) that reflect the marginal role of the high-culture creator in contemporary society.

Because high culture is creator-oriented and dominated, there is much discussion about aesthetic standards, and differences of opinion become major sources of disagreement. These disagreements are often institutionalized, leading to the explicit formation of factions, representing not only academic, establishment, and avant-garde divisions, but also more specialized ones. For instance, at present there are many schools of film making and film criticism, reflecting differences of opinion about appropriate content, techniques of filming, and the role of the director.

Since the culture serves a small public that prides itself on exclusiveness, its products are not intended for distribution by the major media. Its art takes the form of originals distributed through galleries; its books are published by subsidized presses or commercial publishers willing to take a loss for prestige reasons; its journals are the so-called "little magazines," its theater is concentrated largely in New York's Off-Broadway and occasional university repertory companies, although it may share a few Broadway plays with the upper-middle public. Its movies are either European and shared with upper-middle culture, or American "underground cinema" productions made on a shoestring, which are not so shared; its radio is limited to a handful of urban or collegiate FM stations; and what little high-culture television exists is shown on big-city and university educational channels.

The desire for exclusiveness is not necessarily shared by the creators, some of whom want larger audiences, and high culture is constantly attacked by other taste publics. Magazines like *Time*, which appeal to upper-middle-culture publics, provide up-to-date coverage of new trends and fashions in high culture, partly to let their readers in on the ways of the "cultural upper classes," and judging by the disparaging tone of much of the coverage, to show that high culture and its public are also given to fads and other normal human foibles. In this manner they seek to debunk the exclusiveness of high culture and its claim to aesthetic and moral superiority.

The creator orientation of high culture means that more status is awarded to creators, such as writers, painters, and directors, than to performers. For example, actors are not viewed as stars but as tools of the director and writer. Critics have almost as high a status as creators, since they determine whether a given item of content deserves to be considered high culture, or whether it is only an example of middle-brow culture.

Consumer-oriented high culture. The consumer-oriented high-culture public draws on the same content but selects what satisfies it without placing itself in the creator role, or to put it another way, without doing the "work" that high-culture creators demand from their audiences. As a result, conflict develops between this public and the creators, with the latter accusing the former of not being genuinely interested in culture.

The consumer-oriented public is somewhat more concerned with the status and fashionableness of the content, partly because it perceives the content differently from the creators and partly because it seeks to maintain the boundary between itself and upper-middle culture, which is constantly threatening it by borrowing and by debunking press coverage of high-culture fashions. Yet like the upper-middle-culture public, the consumer-oriented high-culture public sometimes relates to creators as fans, in the process making "stars" out of the better-known ones. Most recently, for example, this method of romanticizing the artist has been applied to James Baldwin and Norman Mailer. Partly for this reason, the consumer-oriented public gives higher status to performers than does the creator-oriented.

Although the consumer-oriented public must accept prevailing high-culture content if it is to remain within the culture, and must therefore go along with the creator-oriented, its size and affluence are tempting to the commercial distributors of high culture. As a result, they try to find content that will be acceptable to them and advertise it in consumer-oriented ways. For example, Grove Press, a publisher of avant-garde high-culture literature, has recently begun to advertise its novels by their effect on the reader—sometimes quite luridly so—and seems to be transforming its magazine, *Evergreen Review,* into a high-culture version of *Playboy*. Similarly, Susan Sontag's advocacy of "camp" as a proper taste for high-culture creators has been taken up by the consumer-oriented high-culture public to justify its use of high culture for enjoyment.[68]

[68] Susan Sontag, "Notes on 'Camp,'" *Partisan Review,* 31 (Fall 1964), pp. 515–531. Miss Sontag defines camp as a "disengaged, purely esthetic and unserious vision," "a mode of enjoyment, of appreciation, not judgment," which emphasizes style and "blocks out content" (*passim*). It has a natural appeal to the consumer-oriented public because it values frivolity, rejects the "work" involved in creator-oriented high culture, approves of the ostentatious and the shocking, and provides

As the consumer-oriented public tries to transform creator-oriented culture, the creators and their public escape to new outlets and even new forms of content, for example, by founding new art galleries and magazines, such as the *New York Review of Books*. As abstract expressionism became popular with consumers, some painters began to develop new interest in the human figure, and now that pop art and op art, both of which create an easy effect on museum and gallery visitors, have been taken up by the consumer-oriented public, the creator-oriented art world is seriously concerned about how to maintain some distance between itself and the demands of the audience.[69]

These issues are on the whole limited to avant-garde high culture, and since it, as well as the majority of the creator-oriented and the consumer-oriented high-culture publics are located in New York City, the conflicts between them take place there. Indeed, the consumer-oriented public could be described as "hanging around" the major social and cultural centers of creator-oriented high culture in that city. The news magazines report the latest events on the New York cultural scene to the rest of the country, but in what New York high-culture publics call the hinterland, high culture exists on a minute scale, is usually traditional or contemporary in form, and is almost entirely consumer-oriented. Avant-garde high culture can also be found at some of the major universities around the country, although it is usually a pale duplication of what is being done and argued in New York.

---

another source of content which can be used to maintain the boundary with upper-middle culture. Camp also justifies the borrowing from lower taste cultures and, indeed, these are a major source of what Sontag calls naive or pure camp, that is, content which is unintendedly in accord with the aesthetic standards of camp. Interestingly enough, one of the first subclassifications of camp was into high, middle, and low camp, not because the lower taste cultures were also interested in it, but to permit high-culture publics to borrow from these cultures without impairing their own cultural status. For a description of the consumption of camp and an example of how new high-culture trends are reported for upper-middle-class publics, see Thomas Meehan, "Not Good Taste, Not Bad Taste; It's Camp," *New York Times Magazine*, March 21, 1965, pp. 30–31, 113–115. In my analytic scheme, camp is a new subfaction—and fashion—in avant-garde high culture, and especially among its sizable and influential homosexual public.

[69] I do not mean to suggest that painters change their styles and methods either to satisfy or to escape from the consumers, but that those who are experimenting with new approaches are brought to the attention of other painters and they are then encouraged to experiment also. There are, however, many high-culture creators whose work imitates that of their leading peers, and there are also those who want to do something different when a current fashion becomes popular with consumers. As a result, high culture goes through the same process that is called a "cycle" in popular culture, for example, the monster situation comedy cycle in television, or the war movie cycle that took hold in Hollywood in 1964.

Upper-middle culture. This is the taste culture of America's upper-middle class, the professionals, executives, and managers, people who have attended the better colleges and universities. Although well-educated, they were not trained as creators, intellectuals, or even humanists, and therefore they neither see themselves in these roles nor share the interests associated with them. Like the consumer-oriented public of high culture, they shy away from the critical analysis of ideas and feelings, but unlike this public, they do not wish to participate in a creator-oriented milieu. They are consumers of culture, and for them substance is more important than method. As a result, the culture's dramatic content places more stress on plot than on character and mood. This public wants content that contains the ideas and feelings relevant to their own endeavors, for example, their active social and civic life. Since they are economically and politically influential, their dramatic heroes are more concerned with power and the ability to achieve their goals vis-à-vis other power blocs than with problems of relating to the larger society; more interested in the conflict of familial and occupational responsibilities than in the ability to love.

Because this public values being "cultured," it makes selective use of high-culture content, for example, the less subtle films of Bergman or Fellini. Its affluence and its rapid growth as a result of the boom in college attendance encourage distributors of high culture to seek it out to increase their audience. Moreover, distributors of upper-middle content look over high culture to see what can be borrowed, thus incurring the wrath of that culture's creators and critics. In fact, some of high culture's opposition to popular culture represents displeasure and disappointment over the failure of well-educated people to choose high culture.

Despite the borrowing, most of this culture's content is from its own creators, and they have little contact with high culture or high-culture creators, except perhaps at publishers' parties. Upper-middle-culture creators have attained added prominence in recent years by being invited to the White House for cultural ceremonies and performances.

Upper-middle culture is distributed through the so-called quality mass media. Its public reads magazines such as *Harper's,* the *New Yorker,* and the *Saturday Review;* it purchases most of the new books and determines which are to be best-sellers; it supports the Broadway theater, goes to see foreign film comedies, and provides the major audience for television documentaries and Sunday afternoon "cultural ghetto" programming. It finds its art in museums and is responsible for the popularity of modern furniture and architecture, although its conservative faction fights to preserve eighteenth- and nineteenth-century architectural landmarks.

This public pays considerable attention to creators as "stars." It relies extensively on critics, especially those of the *New York Times*, to differentiate between high- and upper-middle culture content when both are served by the same media.[70] They carry out this function by disapproving of content which is too philosophical, pessimistic, difficult, enthusiastic about sexual and political deviance, or critical of upper-middle-culture values.

Lower-middle culture. This is America's dominant taste culture and public today. It attracts middle- and lower-middle-class people in the lower-status professions, such as accountancy and public school teaching, and all but the lowest-level white-collar jobs. Although older members of this public have only a high school diploma, many of its younger ones have attended and graduated from state universities, community colleges, and the many small private schools that dot the American landscape.

This public is not interested in what it calls "culture," by which it means both high and upper-middle culture and standards, although some of its women have long been interested in being "cultured." The culture it seeks is traditional, often adopted from the upper-middle culture of the late nineteenth and early twentieth centuries, and it rejects the intellectual and the cosmopolitan sophistication of today's upper-middle culture. For example, it dislikes abstract art and condemns satire as "sick" comedy.[71] This public obtains some of its content from high and upper-middle culture, but accepts it only in simplified and bowdlerized form as in the altered film versions of Broadway dramas and best-selling novels.[72]

The aesthetics of lower-middle culture emphasize substance; form must serve to make substance more intelligible or gratifying. Dramatic materials express and reinforce the culture's own ideas and feelings, and although some questioning is permitted, doubts must be resolved at the conclusion of the drama. Its heroes are ordinary people, or extraor-

---

[70] The *New York Times* Sunday edition is probably the major organ of upper-middle culture in the United States, especially its book review, entertainment section, and magazine.

[71] For an example of this rejection, see David E. Scherman, "Alienated Hero, Please Go Home," *Life*, 57 (July 24, 1964), pp. 8-9.

[72] Lester Asheim, "From Book to Film," *Quarterly of Film, Radio and Television*, 5 (1950), pp. 289–304, 334–349; 6 (1951), pp. 54–68, 258–273. See also George Bluestone, *Novels into Film* (Baltimore: Johns Hopkins Press, 1957).

dinary ones who turn out to be ordinary in that they accept the validity of traditional virtues, such as wholesomeness, and traditional institutions, such as the church. For example, familial dramas deal primarily with the problem of upholding tradition and maintaining order against sexual impulses and other upsetting influences. Unlike high culture, lower-middle culture never makes unresolvable conflicts explicit.

The lower-middle-culture public provides the major audience for today's most popular mass media; it is the group for which these media program most of their content. This public reads *Life*, *Look*, the *Reader's Digest*, the *Saturday Evening Post*, and *McCall's*. It also supplies the book buyers who make the big best-sellers. It attends Hollywood's "spectaculars" and watches the situation comedies, popular dramas, and adult westerns that constitute the staple of television. It finds his art in *Life* and buys reproductions of representational paintings at department store art counters. Its architectural and furniture tastes are conservative, as reflected in the prevalence of "colonial" styles in the suburban single-family houses where this public lives. Given its consumer orientation, this culture's public pays little attention to writers or directors, concentrating on performers. It prefers the word-of-mouth judgment of friends and neighbors to the views of published critics.

Aside from high culture, where factional differences are sharp and highly visible, this culture displays perhaps the greatest internal differentiation between its "traditional" and "progressive" wings. For example, although Norman Rockwell and Grandma Moses are the favored artists of the former, the latter has begun to buy reproductions of nineteenth-century Impressionists, such as Cézanne and Van Gogh, and is much more receptive to the discussion of resolvable social problems and the depiction of erotic encounters (as in the novels of Irving Wallace) than the conservative, and probably older, members of this culture.[73] The current search for new formats and types of content by the *Saturday Evening Post* and *Life* is a reflection of the growing importance of the progressive faction in lower-middle culture, and in the case of *Life*, of its incipient interest in some forms of upper-middle culture.

Lower culture. Lower culture was America's dominant taste culture until the end of World War II, when it was replaced by lower-middle culture. It probably still has the largest public of all, even though the size of the public has been shrinking steadily, partly because of longer

---

[73] Herbert J. Gans, "The Rise of the Problem Film," *Social Problems*, 11, 4 (Spring 1964), pp. 327–336.

school attendance. This is the culture of the older lower-middle class, especially the working class: the people with low-status white-collar jobs and skilled or semiskilled blue-collar and service jobs, those who obtained their education at working-class high schools and often dropped out after the tenth grade.

Like the lower-middle culture public, this one also rejects "culture," but it does so with more hostility. It finds culture not only dull but also effeminate, immoral, and sacrilegious; it supports vigorously church and police efforts at censorship.

The aesthetic standards of lower culture stress substance, form being totally subservient. There is no concern with ideas per se. Thus there is almost no contact with high- or upper-middle-culture content, even in bowdlerized versions. The standards emphasize dramatization of values; much of the culture's content consists of modern forms of the morality play, in which traditional values win out over temptation, conflicting behavior, and impulses. The culture's dominant values are not only expressed, as in lower-middle culture, but also dramatized and sensationalized, with strong emphasis on demarcating good and evil. The drama is melodramatic, and its world is divided clearly into heroes and villains, with the former always winning out eventually over the latter.

Working-class society practices sexual segregation in social life: male and female roles are sharply differentiated, and there is relatively little social contact between men and women, even within the family.[74] These patterns are reflected in lower culture. There are male and female types of content, rarely shared by both sexes. Sexual segregation and working-class values are well expressed in the Hollywood "action" film and television program, and in the confession magazine, the staples of male and female lower culture respectively. The action film insists on a rigid distinction between hero and villain; the only social problems that are explicitly considered are crime and related violations of the moral order. These are dealt with by an ostensibly classless hero with such working-class characteristics as masculinity and shyness toward women in all nonsexual relationships. He works either alone or with peers of the same sex, depends partly on luck and fate for success, and is distrustful of government and all institutionalized authority. Clark Gable and Gary Cooper were the prototypes of this hero, and that they have not been replaced is indicative of low culture's loss of dominance. Conversely, the confession magazine features the working-class girl's conflict between being sexually responsive to be popular

[74] Gans, *Urban Villagers, op. cit.,* Chapters 3 and 11.

with men and remaining virginal until marriage. Familial drama that deals sympathetically with the problems of both sexes at once is rare.

In this culture the performer is not only paramount but is revered as a "star," and contact is sought with him, for example, through the fan clubs that are peopled by younger members of the lower-culture public. Moreover, this public does not distinguish between performers and the characters they play; it wants its stars to play "themselves," that is, their public images. Writers and other creators receive little attention.

Lower culture is provided through the mass media, but despite the size of this public, it must share much of its content with lower-middle culture. Often it does so by questioning lower-middle-class content, or by reinterpreting it to fit working-class values. For example, in a working-class population that I studied, people watching a detective serial questioned the integrity of the policeman-hero and identified instead with the working-class characters who helped him catch the criminal. They also protested or made fun of the lower-middle-class heroes and values they saw depicted in other programs and commercials.[75]

Exclusively lower-culture content exists as well, but has little status on Madison Avenue.[76] For one thing, this public reads very little because of its low educational level. It buys tabloid newspapers that stress dramatic happenings among ordinary people and entertainers; the men also read sports and adventure magazines, the women fan and confession magazines.

Most Hollywood films once were made for this taste public, but this is no longer true. Lower-culture people now watch television. Although they share this medium with lower-middle publics, they probably constitute the major audience for westerns, mysteries, comic action such as Red Skelton's, the acrobatic vaudeville of the Ed Sullivan show, and situation comedies such as "Beverly Hillbillies" and "McHale's Navy" (which describe how working-class people outwit the more sophisticated and powerful middle class). Much of this public's need for dramatic content is also met by women's soap operas and televised sports programs. It is served by independent radio stations, especially in the major cities, which feature rock and roll as well as country music and brief news broadcasts that use various sound effects to duplicate the attention-getting device of the tabloid newspaper headlines.

[75] *Ibid.*, Chapter 9.
[76] One indication of this is the frequent appearance of advertisements by the MacFadden Publications, a major publisher of lower-culture magazines, reminding manufacturers to advertise to their large, if low-status, audience.

Lower-culture art reflects the sexual segregation of its public. The men choose pinup pictures (more overtly erotic than those featured in the upper-middle-culture *Playboy*), which they hang in factories and garage workshops at home. The women like religious art and secular representational pictures with vivid colors. Home furnishings reflect the same aesthetic; they must be solid, overstuffed, with bright floral or "colorful" slipcovers. While high- and upper-middle-culture publics value starkness and simplicity, lower-culture publics prefer ornateness —either in traditional, almost rococo, forms, or in the contemporary style often described as "Hollywood modern."

Lower-lower culture. This taste culture serves the lower-class public, people who work in unskilled blue-collar and service jobs, and whose education ended in grade school. Today, much of this public is rural or nonwhite. Although large, its low status and low purchasing power mean that its cultural needs receive little attention from the mass media; by and large, it must get along with the content aimed at lower culture.

Data about lower-lower culture are scarce, but it seems primarily a simpler version of lower culture, with the same sexual segregation, with the same stress on morality, and with almost the total content emphasis on melodrama and morality play. This public's reading matter is probably tabloids and comic books; its films are old westerns and adventure stories now shown only in side-street movie houses in the slums, and for Spanish-speaking audiences the simple action films and soap operas made in Mexico. Television and radio fare is that of lower culture. Because its culture is almost entirely ignored by the mass media, this public probably has retained more elements of folk culture than any other. This culture is re-created at church festivals and other social gatherings.

The Social Structure of Taste Cultures

Despite the preceding categorization, taste cultures and publics are not entirely separate or independent groupings. To begin with, there is multicultural choice. Although most people restrict their content choices to one culture or to two "adjacent" ones, there is some wider spread, as when members of high-culture publics choose detective stories for their light reading and follow a major league baseball team. People who are creator-oriented in one field of high culture may be consumer-oriented in another, and will even prefer middle-culture choices outside their specialty. As Susan Sontag points out, "one of the facts to be reckoned with is that taste tends to develop unevenly. It's rare that the same person has good visual taste and good taste in people and good taste in ideas." [77] Finally, higher-culture publics sometimes take up popular culture that has been dropped by its audience, currently, for example, the Hollywood musicals of the 1930s and the films of Humphrey Bogart. Although cultural straddling of various kinds takes place among all publics, it is most prevalent in the higher ones.

In addition, there is mobility of choice, for some people are upwardly mobile culturally as well as socially and economically. Usually, this mobility occurs during the school years, with college a major agent of the shift to upper-middle culture. It generally ceases with parenthood, when reading and "going out" are cut drastically. In old age there may even be downward mobility, as the content that people found gratifying in their youth becomes too difficult or upsetting.

Content also moves between cultures. They borrow from one another, often transforming the content to make it acceptable to different publics. Content may also be shared. Thus a book written for a high-culture public may be made available to the upper-middle one through an article in *Harper's*, which is then cut and edited to appear in the *Reader's Digest*. Eventually, the central thesis of the book might even receive passing mention in a lower-culture publication.

Occasionally, a specific cultural product or a performer may appeal to several cultures and publics at once and thus become extraordinarily successful; for example, the comic strips "Li'l Abner" and "Pogo," or performers such as Charlie Chaplin, Frank Sinatra, and Marilyn Monroe. Generally speaking, the multicultural appeal is possible because the content is complex enough to allow every culture to see something in it to meet its needs. Thus Charlie Chaplin was seen as a slapstick comic and clown by the lower cultures, and the higher ones perceived him as a satirical critic of society. Once in a while, a product is accepted by all cultures because it conforms to aesthetic standards that are shared by all of them, but this is rare because there is so little agreement about what is beautiful or desirable.

Finally, and in some ways most important, content is shared because several of the taste cultures are served by the same medium. For example, television fare, which is provided by three networks, must serve all cultures. In practice, it serves primarily lower-middle- and lower-culture publics, offering higher-culture content mainly to meet the public service requirements of the Federal Communications Commission. Much of the effort and anxiety of television programing executives stems from their attempt to find content that will be acceptable

[77] Sontag, *op. cit.*, p. 516. I am indebted to David Riesman for calling my attention to this quotation.

to the major taste cultures and their age groupings, and much of the conflict between executives and creators follows from the need to alter content so that this will happen. Similarly, when Hollywood makes high-budget films, it plans for content that will appeal to several publics, for example, by including characters that can be played by stars who appeal to diverse cultures and age groups.

Taste cultures and publics, especially those served by the mass media, may also be seen as participants in a societal taste structure, where the creators and industries providing content attempt to obtain the attention of as many publics as possible, and the publics use what veto power they have as ticket buyers or purchasers of sponsored goods to try to get the content they want. The overall structure is not unlike that of party politics, in that it consists of executives and creators who, like politicians, offer alternatives, and of audiences who, like voters, choose among them. Networks compete with each other like political parties, and the careers of network executives, like those of politicians, ride on their ability to guess what the public will accept. They are aided by the fact that taste, like party preference, is related to socioeconomic background and is therefore relatively stable, so that Ed Sullivan and Art Linkletter have been "in office" longer than most senators from one-party states. Even so, the media's need to appeal to several taste publics at once forces them to act like political parties whose constituencies cut across class lines and include opposing interest groups.

The publics themselves can be conceived as interest groups, for they are competing with others to make sure that the content they want is created. When resources are scarce, as with television channels, or when values are contradictory, as with high culture's espousal of sexual or political deviance and low culture's hostility to it, there is likely to be conflict among publics. Since these do not exist as organized groups, however, the conflict usually takes place among creators and decision makers. Since mass-media creation is a group process, it can be shown that group members often function as self-appointed representatives of conflicting taste publics.[78]

Like all structures that deal with profits and power, the taste structure is hierarchical. Economic dominance is today located in the lower-middle public since it has the largest purchasing power. This dominance is naturally accompanied by some political power, as may be seen by the failure of the Federal Communications Commission to enforce the legislative requirement for public service programing of interest primarily to upper-middle publics. Upper-middle culture has

[78] Gans, "Creator-Audience Relationships in the Mass Media," *op. cit.*

political power over public allocations for culture, because the civic leaders who plan and support national or local art centers such as New York's Lincoln Center for the Performing Arts are usually drawn from the upper-middle public, much to the chagrin of high culture. They tend to emphasize the performing arts at the expense of such nonperforming ones as musical composition; and when they support high-culture ventures, they prefer traditional or establishment ones, shunning the avant-garde. The latter are supported by private foundations or individual sponsors, if they are subsidized at all.

When it comes to prestige, however, the cultural hierarchy follows the stratification pattern, with high culture at the top and lower-lower culture at the bottom, thus reflecting the social statuses of their publics. Consequently, when a culture of lower status borrows the content of a higher one, the latter usually drops this content from its repertoire. For example, when Ingmar Bergman's films became popular with upper-middle-culture moviegoers, he lost much of his standing among high-culture "film buffs," and when prints of Picasso's Impressionist paintings began to be sold in department stores, the high-culture public and its galleries turned to other of his paintings that had not yet become popular.

There is an important difference between the conflict that exists among taste publics and the conflict among socioeconomic strata. Although poor people would like to have the income and power that is available to the upper income groups, low taste publics do not feel deprived by their inability to participate in high culture. The antagonism and public conflict between taste publics are therefore much milder than those between socioeconomic strata.

The prestige of high culture derives not only from the status of its public but also from its historical alignment with the elite and its occasional alliance with "Society" in America. This culture, like all others, insists that its standards are universally valid and that the standards of other cultures are inferior. But because of the influence and occupational roles of its public, this insistence makes high-culture standards more overt and powerful. They are constantly applied in the literary journals, discussed by scholars and critics, and taught in the most prestigeful universities. The standards of the other cultures are more covert and less publicized. As a result, high culture has more influence than the relative size of its public suggests.

This influence is even felt in the mass media, because most of the critics of film, theater, and television are conscious of high-culture standards, although in their evaluations they tend to apply upper-middle-culture standards. Moreover, even when the publications in which they appear are circulated primarily among lower-middle-culture publics, their criticism is concentrated on high- and upper-middle-culture content, so that, for example, the critics of the *New York Daily News*, which has a principally low-culture readership, regularly review the plays and the serious foreign films that their readers probably never see.[79] On the other hand, the content seen by most people—the weekly installments of popular television series—receives no public criticism at all.

For this reason publics in the lower taste cultures become their own critics, developing their criticism in conversation among family members, friends, and fellow workers. This criticism is called "word of mouth" in the mass media and is more influential than that of the published critics in determining which popular novels, films, and even television programs become hits.[80]

Nevertheless, the public dominance of high- and upper-middle-culture criticism encourages obeisance to the aesthetic standards of these two cultures, especially among people who place some value on being "cultured" or who are upwardly mobile in the class structure. Such obeisance is also encouraged by the status implications of cultural choice, so that people in all cultures are loath to admit they use content popular among people of lower status than their own. Consequently, they often make distinctions between what they publicly think is good and what they privately choose. The advocates of high culture interpret the existence of this distinction as evidence of the universality of their standards and conclude either that people want more high culture than they actually get, or that they prefer to choose what they think is bad rather than what they say is good. Both interpretations are inaccurate, however, and reflect the invisibility of the aesthetic standards of the other taste cultures.

The invisibility of the standards has other implications. For one thing, it hides the fact that these standards, like those of high culture, include criteria for bad content as well as good. Although some critics of popular culture have argued that only high culture can choose between good and bad content, the publics in other cultures make similar qualitative judgments. The people whose favorite type of drama is the western can and do distinguish between good and bad ones in the same way as theatergoers distinguish between good and bad plays. The

---

[79] However, when critics review the offerings of a higher taste culture not shared by their readers, they are often negative and use their reviews to demonstrate the cultural inferiority and the moral deviancy of the higher culture.

[80] The popular evaluation of popular culture content has been studied tangentially by sociologists interested in the flow of influence. See Katz and Lazarsfeld, *op. cit.*

theatergoer's judgment may be more sophisticated, and more explicitly related to his standards, but this is only because his standards are public and explicit, because he has been trained in making judgments based on these standards, and because his judgments are supported by professional critics. The viewer of television westerns lacks the explicit standards, and therefore the training to apply them, and he cannot resort to published criticism to test and sharpen his own views.

The difference between the two publics is in the amount of aesthetic training, but this does not justify assuming a difference in aesthetic concern. Thus low-culture publics may think calendar art and overstuffed furniture as beautiful as upper-culture publics consider abstract expressionist paintings and Danish modern furniture; the difference between them is in their ability to put their feelings into the proper aesthetic vocabulary. High-culture housewives may have learned interior design in school or may be able to hire professional decorators, but every housewife of every taste culture who can afford to buy furniture seeks to make her rooms into a work of beauty expressing her standards. In this process she chooses form, color, and relationships between individual pieces, as does the trained decorator. Differences among housewives are in the amount of training in their standards, in the skill with which they can put their standards into action, perhaps, as well as in verbal fluency with which they justify their choices and, of course, in what they think is beautiful.

Aesthetic Pluralism and the Popular-Culture Critique

The sociological analysis of popular culture makes it possible to look at the popular-culture critique in a different light. Such an analysis suggests that popular culture is composed of varying taste cultures and publics that in both structure and function resemble high culture and its public. All of them have aesthetic standards that reflect their cultural backgrounds and needs, and all of them seek to express these standards in their cultures. They differ only because differing backgrounds have caused them to develop different aesthetic standards.

Most high-culture charges against popular culture reflect their different aesthetic standards. For example, the borrowing that high culture views as "debasing" or "watering down" can be understood as the transformation of content to fit other aesthetic standards. Of course, high culture still *feels* itself debased; but this feeling of debasement can now be seen as a way of maintaining taste culture boundaries between high and upper-middle cultures and publics, rather than as a sign of the imminent destruction of high culture. Similarly, what the critique calls the "spurious gratifications" of popular culture reflects differing values and standards on the part of other cultures and publics. In the absence of evidence that these gratifications are emotionally spurious or destructive, it is fair to conclude that "spurious" is only a negatively loaded word for "different."

Many other reinterpretations of the critique can be developed from a sociological analysis. For instance, what the critique calls mass-media "manipulation" of the audience is really publics with standards differing from those of high culture exerting feedback control over the media and thus being able to obtain content meeting their own standards, however imperfectly. Popular-culture creators characterized as "cynical hacks" by the critique are so described because they are employees of commercial firms, rather than the individual entrepeneurs who predominate among high-culture creators. If they are more cynical than high-culture creators, it is because the media for which they work must serve several taste publics at once. Faced with conflicting demands and imperfect feedback, the creators must engage in the difficult and wearing task of creating content that satisfies both themselves and their diverse audience. Needless to say, if that audience were the homogeneous and passive mass pictured in the critique, the creators would not have to behave in this fashion.

Moreover, the sociological analysis indicates that the hostility of the critics toward popular culture is based not only on differences in aesthetic standards but also on the class differences that create conflict in so many other institutions and, of course, on the disproportion of power and influence between high culture and its politically or numerically dominant competition.

Finally, the comparative approach inherent in sociological analysis makes it possible to sort out both similarities and differences between the taste cultures, and thus to show that the one crucial and qualitative difference between high culture and the others—aside from conflicting aesthetic standards—is the creator orientation of the former and the consumer orientation of the latter. Although the creators of all taste cultures have and pursue a creator orientation, only high-culture creators give a significantly lower priority to their audiences, even if they too unconsciously adapt content to get a favorable response. This is why they are called "serious" artists.

Moreover, the preservation of the creator orientation is high culture's most urgent priority if it is to maintain itself. This culture needs audiences as much as the others, but finds it difficult to persuade them to take a creator-oriented position when they become aware of their opportunity to insist on a consumer-oriented one. Thus high culture must continually insist on the virtues of the creator orientation, which helps to explain the intensity of feeling toward popular culture. Nevertheless, only one of the charges of the popular-culture critique—the negative character of popular-culture creation—speaks explicitly to the defense of the creator orientation, and does it poorly at that, for it offers no evidence that popular culture is a threat. But the comparative analysis of all taste cultures makes it possible to see how important the maintenance of the creator orientation is to high culture.

III The Evaluation of Taste Cultures

Like any other sociological analysis, my description of the taste culture has normative implications and can be developed into an evaluation by the addition of explicit value judgments.[81] Such an evaluation is not itself sociological, for value judgments cannot be justified empirically, although some of the consequences of such judgments can be tested.

Evaluations may be both private and public. The former is an individual's private choice for his own life; the latter deals with the welfare of society and is ultimately aimed at formulating public policy. Although every person makes both private and public evaluations, the two are not necessarily equivalent. For example, no one who decides to be a sociologist would therefore demand public policy to make all Americans into sociologists. The same principle is applicable to the evaluation of taste cultures. In his nonprofessional role and in his leisure hours, the sociologist, like everyone else, belongs to a taste public and makes private content choices. As such he may even criticize the standards and content of other taste publics and cultures. This is his right and privilege.

The critics of popular culture have translated their private evaluation into a public one, however, arguing that their own antipathy to popular culture justifies a public policy for eliminating it. This translation assumes that everyone should live by the norms embodied in the private evaluations of the critics of popular culture and embrace high-culture standards, but such an assumption is not justified in a democratic and pluralistic society, any more than the similar claims of other taste publics that their standards alone are desirable. The assumption of the universality of high culture would perhaps be justified if the critics could prove that popular culture harmed the society, interfered

[81] I do not claim that the evaluation proceeds from the analytic scheme, for the two are interrelated. Although I have refrained from explicit value judgments in the sociological analysis of taste cultures, implicit ones run through it, and the analysis itself is strongly influenced by my views about high and popular culture.

with the achievement of the goals of the majority of individual citizens, or seriously endangered the goals of a minority. Since the critics have not provided such proof and their norms are not shared by a majority of the population, it is necessary to develop a public evaluation that takes other norms into account.

Two Value Judgments about Taste Cultures and Publics

The public evaluation is based on two value judgments, one about the taste cultures, and the other about the taste publics.

If one compared the taste cultures alone, without taking into account the taste publics who choose them, it would be fair to say that the higher cultures are better than the lower ones, and that high culture is better than all the rest. This is my first value judgment. The higher cultures are superior to the lower ones because they can provide greater, more intense, and perhaps even more lasting aesthetic gratification, and this I believe may one day be determined empirically. Moreover, the higher cultures are broader; they can include some of the content and standards of the lower ones, whereas the reverse is not true. Thus high-culture publics can choose lower culture content more easily than low-culture publics can choose higher content. Finally, the higher cultures provide much more adequate information for the citizenship role, for solving personal and social problems, and for reality testing. This is of course the credo of the advocates of high culture, but as it stands, it leaves out the people who choose culture.

Taste cultures are chosen by people and cannot exist without them. Therefore the cultures cannot be evaluated without taking their publics into consideration. The amount of education required for the understanding and appreciation of cultural content and the amount of education possessed by the intended public can be related. Since every item of cultural content requires a certain amount of education from the person choosing it, his educational background is of prime relevance to the evaluation. Specifically, people cannot be expected to choose content that is incongruent with their education and, more generally, with their socioeconomic level. Although the elementary school graduate who has educated himself to choose high culture deserves praise, to expect this from everyone would be a demand for heroic behavior. Such cultural heroism may be commendable, but any public policy that requires people to act heroically would be unenforceable, except perhaps in wartime, even if it were desirable.

The choice of high culture requires a quality university education with strong emphasis on the humanities. Such a choice could therefore not be expected from a high school graduate, or for that matter from a college graduate not trained in the arts. For this reason the belief of popular-culture critics that all college-educated people should choose high culture is not justified. Both the high school graduate and the college graduate should be expected to choose content that fit their educational levels and aesthetic standards; and both should be judged negatively only if they consistently choose below these levels. A college graduate should not read mainly detective stories and watch television regularly, nor should a high school graduate devote himself to comic books. And while it would be praiseworthy if both read Proust, it should not be expected from them, at least not in evaluations that result in public policy.

These examples assume that all people seek aesthetic gratification and that if their choices accord with those of their taste public, they are equally valid and desirable whether the culture is high or low. A person from a high-culture public may choose abstract expressionist paintings, whereas one from a low-culture public selects calendar art, but both choose from content related to their standards and educational level. Moreover, both derive emotional and intellectual rewards from their choices, and both may add new ideas, feelings, and insights to their lives as a result. *The rewards may differ because their educational backgrounds and previous experiences differ, but the choice of both individuals results in addition to that experience.* The former's choice of a de Kooning painting does not necessarily provide him with greater rewards in relation to his previous experience than the latter's choice of a Norman Rockwell magazine cover. The evaluation of their choices cannot depend only on content but must compare what might be called the *incremental aesthetic reward* that results from their choice: the extent to which each person's choice adds something to his previous experience and his effort toward self-realization.[82] This incremental reward can be as great for a member of a low-culture public as for a high-culture one, for the reward has nothing to do with the quality of the cultural content; it takes into account only the person's progress from his own past experience.[83] Someday, behavioral science

---

[82] In the same vein, David Riesman and Christopher Jencks have been arguing that colleges should be judged by "value added" rather than as at present by the intellectual skills and status of the students they admit. See also Riesman's judgment of personal autonomy as incremental to a person's own situation and what can be expected of him, in David Riesman, with Nathan Glazer, *Faces in the Crowd* (New Haven, Conn.: Yale University Press, 1952), Chapter 6.

[83] If only the content of the reward is measured, and the person's background and experience is left out, it is of course true that the individual from a high-culture public derives more reward from his content choice than a person from a lower-

research methods may be sufficiently refined to measure such incremental rewards.

My second value judgment argues, therefore, *that the evaluation of taste culture must also take the taste public into account, that the evaluation of any item of cultural content must be related to the aesthetic standards and background characteristics of the relevant public, and that because all taste cultures are functions of the characteristics and standards of their publics, they are for that reason equal in value.*

This judgment may seem to contradict the initial one, which argues the superiority of higher taste cultures. The two can easily be reconciled, however, if an accompanying qualification takes into account the differences in taste publics. Specifically, the higher taste cultures *are* more desirable in the abstract; but if this desirability is to be translated into social reality and public policy, the educational and socioeconomic backgrounds of lower taste publics must be changed so that they can obtain the prerequisites for choosing from the higher taste cultures. The higher taste cultures are better, and people ought to have the opportunities that would enable them to choose their content. What is wrong with the argument of popular-culture critics, especially the conservative ones, is that they demand allegiance to high culture from people who lack the prerequisites they themselves possess; many of them ask for a society of high culture without at the same time concerning themselves with ways of enabling people to become members of high-culture publics. This is an elitist position that has no place in a democracy.[84]

The two judgments may now be combined. *American society should pursue policies that would maximize educational opportunities for all so as to permit everyone to choose from higher taste cultures. Until such opportunities are available, however, it would be wrong to expect a society with a median level of education still below high*

culture public. The difference stems, however, not from the content but from the training the former has received in the aesthetic standards of his culture. As a result, he sees more and is able to relate what he sees to many other facets of his emotional and intellectual life. This extra benefit derives not from his being a member of the high-culture public, however, but from his training in aesthetics. If the members of other taste publics were given the same amount and quality of aesthetic training cued to their own standards, and if they had the benefit of the scholarship and criticism in their taste culture that is available in high culture, they would benefit in the same way as the former.

[84] The conservatives want public policy to maximize the resources, freedom, and power of high-culture creators but do not mention social and economic policies that would increase the size of the high-culture public. In other words, they want society to support high culture without permitting universal participation in it, a position that bears some resemblance to taxation without representation.

school graduation to choose from the higher taste cultures, or for that matter, to support through public policies the welfare of the higher ones at the expense of the lower ones. Moreover, it would be wrong to criticize people for holding and applying aesthetic standards that are related to their educational background, and for participating in taste cultures reflecting this background.

This value judgment might be called *aesthetic relationism;* it is a normative restatement of the concept of aesthetic pluralism used to describe the existence of diverse taste cultures.

Two alternatives for public policy are implied by this statement. Either society must find ways of implementing the cultural mobility that would allow people to have the educational and socioeconomic background prerequisite to choice in the higher taste cultures, or if these ways are not provided, it must permit the creation of cultural content which will meet the needs and standards of the existing taste publics.

Cultural Mobility

The policy of cultural mobility assumes that if every American had access to the income, education, and other background characteristics of what is now known as the upper-middle class, many although not all would choose either upper-middle- or even high-culture content. In all likelihood most people would choose the former. Few are likely to choose creator-oriented high culture, for it requires an extraordinary amount of emotional involvement with ideas and symbols that does not come by being recruited into the upper-middle class.[85]

Even the attainment of majority participation in upper-middle culture would result in a sharp increase in the overall taste level of society, not to mention a dramatic flowering of creativity and diversity within this taste culture, leaving the country with probably more cultural diversity than now exists.

But implementing such a policy requires drastic changes in American society and economy, especially in the distribution of income, educational opportunity, and power. Although it is possible to program policies to bring about these changes, they are difficult to implement. If it could be done, it would take a generation or two. Even if such a policy could be implemented, it might not be desirable. The policy has much to recommend it, if the resources and the power of the society to alter itself are unlimited. In the real world, however, where resources

[85] See here Wilensky's finding that in Detroit college-educated people do not choose high-culture material. Wilensky, "Mass Society and Mass Culture," *op. cit.*, p. 191.

are not unlimited, there are many more urgent social problems, including poverty, unemployment, racial discrimination, functional illiteracy, mental illness, alcoholism, and similar social and physical illnesses. Until these are done away with, policies aimed solely at the raising of taste levels are of lesser importance. Such policies need not be rejected entirely, but they deserve a much lower allocation of public resources than the others mentioned.

This priority determination is based on two judgments, that a good life can be lived at all levels of taste, and that the taste level of a society is not as significant a criterion for the goodness of that society as the welfare of its members. These judgments are supported by the available empirical evidence that the mass media do not have a significant impact on people's lives. To put the matter bluntly, neither high culture nor any other is at present so essential to life and welfare to give programs for cultural mobility a high priority in public policy, at least not until there is evidence that low culture hurts some people.[86] Whatever the deficiencies of this taste culture and of any other, I do not believe that they are harmful for their publics.

I do not mean hereby to reject cultural improvement per se, but to concentrate on what I consider the basic functions of culture: to encourage human self-realization and to enhance leisure time. Neither requires a high taste level. If people are able to strive for their own aesthetic standards and find cultural content that meets them, self-realization and a satisfying leisure life—that is, one marked by the absence of boredom—are possible at all levels.

Moreover, as I noted earlier, rising incomes and the improvement of education are already producing a considerable amount of cultural mobility, and within less than a generation the dominant taste culture in America has moved from low to lower-middle. Although public policies for further cultural mobility may become more desirable in some future generation, when changes in the economy and technology have reduced the length of the workday or workweek, the increase in leisure time expected in the next generation is not likely to exhaust the existing supply of leisure activity aspirations. Despite frequent expert

[86] Interestingly enough, here one of the major critics of popular culture agrees; he writes "One can live happily and well without high culture. Socrates' plea that the unexamined life is not worth living after all came from a professional examiner of life, an intellectual and perhaps platonic lover of it, a man with an axe to grind. For him, perhaps, the unexamined life was not worth living. For most people it is." Van den Haag, in Rosenberg and White, eds., *op. cit.*, p. 528. Van den Haag's identification of self-examination with high culture is gratuitous, however, and reflects his own feelings about people who do not share high culture. There is self-examination outside high culture as well.

pronouncements that most Americans cannot cope with more leisure time, my own observations convince me that most people now lack the blocks of leisure time to do all the things they want to do. The real threat is not more leisure but feelings of social uselessness brought about by unemployment; and these feelings cannot be dealt with by leisure education, for leisure cannot really help people feel useful.

Unemployment, the lack of social functions, and the resulting feelings of uselessness already exist among many members of the lower-class population, and especially among youth and old people. These are also the people who have the least access to the popular arts, the fewest friends, and the most impoverished leisure life.[87] Their first needs are for larger incomes, jobs, higher-quality education, and freedom from racial discrimination. Once they obtain these, they can begin to think about their leisure time, but the same opportunities that would help them escape from poverty would also remove many of the obstacles to more gratifying leisure and provide opportunities for self-realization.

The Pros and Cons of Aesthetic Relationism

If cultural mobility is not an urgent public policy, the other alternative is aesthetic relationism and the provision of content for existing taste cultures. Before spelling out ways by which such a policy can be implemented, let me discuss the general principle.

First, aesthetic relationism proposes content to satisfy the aesthetic standards of taste publics, rather than what is now offered these publics by the mass media. Although spokesmen for the media often argue that they are giving people what they *want*, aesthetic relationism suggests that these industries ought to supply what people think is *good*.

The media have so far not provided any evidence that they are pursuing such a policy. Nor have they even been able to prove that they are giving their audiences what they want, for the feedback that they now obtain from the audience is incomplete and poor. For example, the programming decisions of network television are heavily influenced by the results of Nielsen ratings, drawn from a sample of the operation of 1200 television sets. Not only is this method deficient for measuring viewer evaluations, but the sample is much too small to take account of the cultural diversity of the total television audience. To be sure, a better rating system might not result in radically different evaluations of current programs, but it would probably indicate the need for more

---

[87] Genevieve Knupfer, "Portrait of the Underdog," in Reinhard Bendix and Seymour M. Lipset, eds., *Class, Status and Power* (Glencoe, Ill.: The Free Press, 1953), pp. 255–263. See also Marie Jahoda, P. Lazarsfeld, and H. Zeisel, *Die Arbeitslosen von Marienthal* (Allensbach, Germany: Verlag fuer Demoskopie, 1960).

content diversity to meet the requirements of different taste publics. As such, it would question the present media policy of seeking to attract the largest possible audience for every program or the evening schedule of programs. The movies use box office figures to measure feedback, but these only reflect a decision to see a film, not a reaction to a seen film. Magazine readership studies do provide reactions to published content, but these are conducted by advertising departments, and on most magazines they are not used for making editorial decisions, except when readership is declining precipitously. Moreover, television, magazines, and even newspapers are often organized, not to provide content that meets either the wants or aesthetic standards of their audience, but to tempt them into purchasing the goods of the advertisers. This has little to do with meeting aesthetic standards.

Second, aesthetic relationism condemns content that is socially undesirable, that is, harmful to universally shared goals—the public interest —or harmful to the goals of individual consumers, as long as there is *evidence of the existence of harm*. For example, if horror films were proved dangerous to the emotional development of children, the public interest, the goals of most parents, and the yet unrecognized goals of the children themselves would justify that such films be altered or banned.

The effects studies made so far, and discussed in Part I of the chapter, indicate that the impact of any item or even type of cultural content is negligible. Although much more research is needed, the present evidence suggests that censorship of any kind is more harmful than the effects it purports to eliminate. Of course, people who feel that they or their children should not be exposed to violence, erotica, or other content which conflicts with their own values have a perfect right to practice private censorship, but they cannot rightly demand that society do it for them and thus deprive others of such content.

Third, in accepting the right of taste publics to make aesthetic choices, aesthetic relationism also accepts what I earlier called a consumer orientation, and thus rejects the priority of creator orientation claimed by high culture. Although a consumer orientation should not endanger high culture, it is otherwise justified simply because the consumers of culture have as much right to satisfy their demands as do creators. Both are human beings with legitimate wants.

The critics who oppose consumer-oriented culture do so for several reasons. They believe it is wrong to give people what they want, partly because people have poor taste or because, if left alone, they would satisfy their so-called lower needs rather than their higher ones. This argument is a remnant of Puritanism; it assumes that entertainment is evil and education good, and that if only education is offered, people will be forced to choose it. Such Puritanism is not only undesirable but impossible to implement.

The critics also argue that popular culture gives people what they want and only high culture gives them what is good. This argument reflects the critics' belief that high-culture standards are universal, and that the other taste cultures do not have aesthetic standards. However, it is clear that all taste publics seek both what they want and what they think is good, and that the existing taste cultures reflect a diversity of aesthetic standards. The solution, then, is not to make people choose what high culture thinks is good but what they as members of their taste cultures think is good. Undoubtedly people frequently choose what they think is bad, because they find it entertaining or cathartic, but this is as true among high-culture publics as among all others. There is no evidence that people in the lower taste publics choose what they think is trashy any more often than people in the higher ones. Moreover, there is no reason to outlaw such choices, for leisure time is supposed to be devoted to recreation and catharsis. What is wrong is immoderate use of content considered inferior.

The critics argue further that a creator orientation is more desirable than a consumer one, for the former puts the consumer into the role of the creator and thus encourages him to be one. Their argument assumes that consumption is a passive act, and therefore undesirable, whereas creation alone is active and therefore desirable. This too is an overly Puritanical judgment and neglects the response that reading or watching movies evokes in the consumer, which may be a creative act even if it does not result in a visible product.

Actually, the argument of high-culture advocates against a consumer orientation is to save maximum resources and freedom for high-culture creators. For one thing, they want to raise the taste level of the society, or to restore it to some past level when only the elite counted. They also want to maximize the quantity and quality of high culture to make a better cultural record for our society in a contrast of past and present civilizations. The concern with societal taste levels and with intersocietal competitions strikes me as deserving low priority in the making of public policy. The welfare and satisfaction of people—people now living—are more important than a cultural record compiled for an unknown recordkeeper in an irrelevant competition.

In addition, the argument for a creator orientation is that it is necessary to protect the vitality of high culture. If it could be proved that consumer orientation endangers high culture, it would be desirable to protect it, but there is no such proof. Indeed, the creators most affected by a consumer orientation are not those in high culture, who are well protected by their aesthetic standards, but the creators of the popular arts, whose artistic privileges and liberties are now limited by the structure of the mass-media industries. They need support to guarantee their freedom to create as they wish. High-culture creators, on the other hand, need the economic security they now lack because of the smallness of their audience, and it ought to be provided by public policy or private sources. The sum involved is not large and, as I suggested earlier, it could be obtained partially from taxes on the cultural industries that have large audiences.

The best solution is therefore neither a consumer orientation nor a creator orientation but both. In the ideal situation creators are free to do what they want and to create for the publics they wish to reach, and consumers are free to choose from the available content. Some suggestions for achieving this ideal will be discussed.

Fourth, aesthetic relationism can be attacked on the grounds that superficial and distorted information provided by the lower taste cultures make it difficult for their publics to function properly as citizens of a democratic society or to solve social and individual problems. There is no doubt that present media content is deficient on these counts. We could argue that insofar as aesthetic relationism is guided by what people think is good, not by what they now accept, these deficiencies could be eliminated. Such an argument would not, however, solve the difficulties. It is likely that the provision of more adequate information would not alter the way most people act most of the time, for as the effects data showed, they are not significantly influenced in their actions by the mass media now. Thus to propose better news coverage, which really means supplying all taste cultures with high- or upper-middle-culture news content, is not a solution.

People tend to act only on matters that concern them directly and immediately, and they select the kind of information they think is relevant. Although they are then prey to distorted information, especially if they are poorly educated, much of the time they seem to welcome such distortion. If people hear only what they want to hear, alternate content will not reach them however loudly it is shouted. While this should not discourage shouting, it should also not inspire false confidence that the shouting will be effective.

Moreover, the extent to which people's predilections for distorted information impairs democracy deserves to be treated with less a priori panic and more thought. Much anxiety about this issue reflects the fact that our theory of democracy was formulated in a society in which the only citizens who counted were the educated elite and which still assumes that all citizens must be educated on all issues. Nevertheless, democracies must and do function even when citizens are not educated. When people's interests are at stake, they generally act rationally despite being poorly educated and unable or unwilling to obtain proper information. Often, opposition to the uneducated voter is an expression of the conflict of interest that exists between him and the educated, a conflict the latter wrongly believes would disappear with better information. For example, the uneducated voter's lack of interest in civil liberties would not be altered significantly if television were saturated with news and commentary on civil liberties. In a close election such saturation might swing enough votes to make a difference, but it would not alter the low interest in the subject among most working- or lower-middle-class citizens. Ironically, the group that is politically least effective and perhaps most irrational is the lower class, the poverty-stricken population that makes least use of mass-media news content.

The solution is not so much a change in media news coverage as in re-evaluation of the information requirements of democratic theory, to determine what kinds of information, in what amounts, and at what levels of analytic complexity are essential for democracy and are effective in maintaining it. Better civic education and a new approach to mass-media news coverage, one that combined the analytic method of the higher taste cultures with a style to attract the lower ones, would help but would not solve the problem. It can only be solved if and when people find it useful to participate more actively in politics and are motivated to demand more accurate information.

The problem of content used to solve individual and social problems is even more complex. People come to the arts not only for insight but also for catharsis, escape, and entertainment. This is true of all taste publics. High-culture ones are supposedly more ready to confront reality, yet content that deals specifically with the problems and the dilemmas of these publics is about as rare as in other taste cultures. Creators of a radical political persuasion have developed a viable tradition of naturalism and social protest in high culture, some of which has been taken over by other taste cultures as well. They have informed high-culture and high-income publics about the inequity and injustice still prevalent in American society, especially about minorities and the poverty-stricken, but they have been less active in portraying the society and the problems of their own audience. They are not solely responsible for this deficiency, for high-culture publics seem to prefer cultural content about the poor, just as poor people like to see films about the rich.

In recent years a new form of theater, popularly labeled the Theater of the Absurd, has emerged to speak to the problems of the high-culture audience. The plays of Genet, Beckett, Ionesco, and others deal with philosophical, social, and psychological issues relevant for this audience, but they do so symbolically, which may remove the immediacy of these issues for the audience. Such writers contribute to high culture by their innovations, and their symbolic method of expression offers a new way of looking at old issues, but one would have to study the audience to find out whether the plays actually have this effect. Do theatergoers actually develop new insight through the experience of symbolic reformulations, or do these plays only allow people to feel that the writer's concerns are irrelevant for them? Doubtless, Albee's *Who's Afraid of Virginia Woolf?* evoked some second thoughts among high- and upper-middle-culture audiences about their own marriages, but it is questionable whether Beckett's *Waiting for Godot* made them realize their reliance on false hope in their own lives.

Plays like these are needed and valued cultural contributions even if they do not evoke the intended effects on their audiences. These observations suggest, however, that high culture evades depicting the effective reality of its audience almost as much as the other taste cultures. In high culture the evasion takes the form of undue abstraction and use of symbolism, whereas in the popular taste cultures, it is done through oversimplification, exaggeration, pseudo-realism, and comedy.

Because people do not use culture—high or low—primarily to find solutions to their own and society's problems, they are not upset by the evasions and distortions of content. So little is known about how and where people obtain information about problems, and to what extent they use informational or fictional content from their taste culture for this purpose, that it is impossible to suggest standards for cultural policy.

One thing is clear; if present popular-culture content lacks or distorts political and problem-solving information, this fault stems less from the inability of existing creators than from the unwillingness of consumers to want to accept such information, at least in current forms. Providing "better" content, that is, content meeting the standards of higher taste cultures, is thus not likely to attract the intended audience from the lower taste publics. Lacking the prerequisite background, they will not accept it. When the popular arts are provided by profit-seeking agencies, the lower taste publics can discourage high-culture content because it is unprofitable. When government controls content, it can restrict audience *choice*, but it cannot bring about audience *use*.

The previously noted failure of the Russian government to persuade its citizens to accept the official culture or the inability of the British Broadcasting Corporation to convert English television viewers to the virtues of educational programing while it was the sole source of television fare would suggest that public policy cannot easily alter audience preferences. When audiences have some influence over content, it will reflect the preferences of dominant taste publics. Although this fact does not justify the principle of aesthetic relationism, it points to the difficulty of gaining acceptance for unpopular alternative types of content.

Implementing Aesthetic Relationism

Aesthetic relationism requires policies that create content for specific taste cultures and their publics in line with the aesthetic standards of these cultures and publics. Such policies can be called *subcultural programing*.[88]

Subcultural programing involves three major steps.

1. Identifying significant taste cultures, publics, and their aesthetic standards. A systematic effort to do this would go far beyond the simple analysis presented in Part II; it would identify many more such cultures, especially subgroupings and age grades, resulting in perhaps twenty or more significant cultures and publics.

2. Creating content aimed at one or at most two to three of these cultures at a time.

3. Creating content to satisfy aesthetic standards; what various taste publics think is good, not only what they will accept.

Subcultural programing would enable audiences to find content best suited to their needs, thus increasing their aesthetic and other satisfactions. In addition, it would increase diversity of content. It would also improve working conditions for creators in the taste cultures served by the mass media, since they would be freed of the present need to satisfy several taste cultures at once or to have their work revised in line with this requirement. They could then create material to fit the aesthetic standards of their own taste culture, much as high-culture creators do now.

Finally, subcultural programing would make it easier to create controversial content, especially that considered undesirable by one taste public but not by another. For example, a television sponsor now unwilling to associate his product with controversial issues like birth con-

[88] The term "subcultural" refers to my initial concept of taste cultures as subcultures.

trol or the recognition of Communist China could advertise on channels or in programs that appeal to the publics more willing to accept controversy, and with less fear of condemnation from those who oppose debate on these issues.

Research requirements. Subcultural programing would, of course, require a number of changes in the institutions and industries now supplying cultural content. The first step would be an intensive research program to identify the significant taste cultures, the characteristics of their publics, and their aesthetic standards. Such a research program would involve qualitative and quantitative studies of audience choices in all media and art forms to determine clustering of choices and the relationship between choices and audience backgrounds. In addition, studies of audience reactions to specific products and items of content should be made to determine what different people think is good and bad, content analyses of both the content and the reactions to isolate implicit aesthetic standards, and intensive interviews to get at the standards in yet other ways.

These studies would result in at least a preliminary picture of significant taste publics and could be used to alter present content and develop new types for unserved publics and unmet aesthetic standards.

If such research were added to the intuitive skill of the creator to appeal to an audience, it might allow him to get closer to that audience and create content that would touch it more, both emotionally and intellectually, than at present. The research would also remove some of his, and his superiors', fears of what an audience will and will not accept. Under ideal conditions, it would bring the creator into a modern form of the relationship alleged to have existed between folk artist and folk audience, and it would also enable him to escape from the onerous and difficult role of having to create for an audience he does not understand.

One problem would be to persuade creators to take such research into consideration. At present, most of them strenuously resist exposure not only to the primitive forms of audience research extant in the mass media, but to any feedback, arguing that what pleases them will also please their eventual audience, and that any involvement with the audience would interfere with the creative process. This argument neglects the fact that much of the conflict between media writers and producers is over questions about what the audience will accept, questions that could be answered less arbitrarily if proper research was available.

Care would, of course, have to be taken that such research did not stifle creativity. This danger is small, however, partly because even the most comprehensive research program cannot uncover what Larrabee calls the "hidden, half-formed and yet unsatisfied . . . public wants." [89] Moreover, surprise and novelty are essential qualities of all art and entertainment. Thus data on past wants and choices are never directly applicable to the creation of new content.

The research program suggested here is not likely to be initiated by the mass media until the present content is no longer acceptable to its audiences and sales figures begin to decline. If expected increases in the sophistication of the audiences develop and content changes are required, particularly in television, some audience research may be stimulated.[90] Nor is research commonly a precursor to governmental action. Subcultural programing policies could, however, proceed without research, on the basis of what is now known about taste cultures and publics. If my analysis is correct, audiences would be attracted by content that took account of their backgrounds and standards, and some would reject present forms of content. Successes and failures in providing the new content could be measured by more effective versions of current feedback techniques, leading to further content change until eventually a trial and error approach would create subcultural programing for all significant taste publics.

Another less ambitious and less systematic substitute for research would be the stimulation of formal criticism in the middle and lower taste cultures. At present, criticism is largely written for and by high and upper-middle cultures, forcing the others to generate their own amateur criticism, most of which never reaches the creators and decision makers in the mass media. If trained critics reflecting the standards of the lower taste cultures could be developed, they would not only attract a large number of readers, but their evaluations would have impact on the mass media and might gradually move these in the direction of subcultural programing.

Requirements for content change. Subcultural programing also requires departing from the present practice of many media to create content that seeks to reach the largest possible audience. Although this solution simplifies the task of the national media and is profitable at

---

[89] Eric Larrabee, "Journalism: Toward the Definition of a Profession," *Studies in Public Communication*, No. 3 (1961), pp. 23–26. Although the title does not indicate it, this article is a thoughtful analysis of the feedback problem as viewed by the professional writer.

[90] Herbert J. Gans, "Some Changes in American Taste and Their Implications for the Future of Television," in Stanley T. Donner, ed., *The Future of Commercial Television, 1965–1975* (Stanford, Calif.: Department of Communications, Stanford University, 1965), pp. 35–50.

present, it often results in content that cuts across and compromises the standards of several taste cultures, providing no intense satisfaction to any of them. Subcultural programing would develop content appealing to a smaller audience, including perhaps only one taste public or only its avant-garde sector, or only its adolescent age group.

Some subcultural programing already exists today, notably in book publishing; in the magazine field, where periodicals aimed at specific interests and age groups are rapidly supplanting such general magazines as *Life* and the *Saturday Evening Post* or forcing them to specialize too; and in the movie industry, which now distinguishes between commercial and art films and also makes many films exclusively for teenagers. The traditional Hollywood practice of trying to attract the largest possible audience for every film is obsolescent, hanging on only in the production of costly "spectaculars."

The opposite pattern exists in the two numerically most important media, the newspaper and television. The number of newspapers has been declining rapidly, leaving many cities with only a single daily paper for all publics. In television all evening programs seek to attract the largest possible number of viewers, so that often every program competes with every other simultaneously for the same audience.

Yet, even in television there are tendencies toward diversity as advertisers learn that they can best sell their products not by amassing the largest number of viewers but by attracting the largest number of potential buyers. The pattern of subordinating content to commercials is not reduced, however; it is subcultural advertising rather than subcultural programing. Proper subcultural programing would go much further; it would systematically attempt to reach every one of the twenty or more taste publics that I suggested can be uncovered and provide each with content fitting their cultural standards and needs.

One prime consequence of such a policy would be to identify the taste publics that are poorly served today. Since it is unfortunately true in our society that those who need the most get the least, the major deficiencies probably exist among the lower, and especially the lower-lower taste cultures; the aged, and even the middle-aged; and more generally, among all publics who are either low in purchasing power, or who do not need the kinds of products whose advertising supports the mass media today.

For example, if it is true that present mass-media programing aggravates the effects of poverty and adds to the psychological problems of coping with middle-class society among the poor, subcultural programing for the poverty-stricken lower-lower taste publics would be desirable. Such programing would differ from what is presently available by focusing on topics of interest to this public and by emphasizing stories and characters which treat poor people as just that, and not as misfits, comic figures, or even as unfortunates damaged by personal or social and economic problems. Although the poor may be unfortunate victims of our social system, content which is aimed primarily at the guilt and pity of more affluent audiences can only be patronizing to the poor who are exposed to it as well. Subcultural programing does not mean content that would encourage acquiescence with their living conditions—no content could produce that reaction—but information and entertainment that would speak to their own experiences, standards, and values.

Similarly, subcultural programing would mean more content for the Negro, Puerto Rican, and other nonwhite populations. Although the civil rights movement has persuaded the media to produce more content *about* Negroes, and to use more Negro actors, there is still too little television, radio, and even print *for* the majority of Negroes that meets their cultural needs.

Finally, the high-culture public could also be included in the list of poorly served minorities, although this is true only with respect to daily newspapers, television, and American movies, all of which need larger audiences than can be recruited among this public. Since high culture is already so well supplied by other outlets, however, its complaints about lack of proper television programing strike me as of lower priority than those of other taste cultures.

As these examples indicate, subcultural programing would introduce new forms of segregation and stratification in the mass media. Although this would happen in the creation and distribution of cultural content, it would not need to develop among the consumers, for they would be as free as they are now to choose whatever content they want. In some ways they would be freer, since there would be greater diversity of content, and although most people would choose from material intended for their own taste public, everyone would be able to select whatever content pleased him.

Subcultural programing would also reduce the cohesive function of the mass media, that is, their present ability to focus the attention of the entire country on the same content at the same time. If there was ever a need for that function, the erosion of regional, ethnic, and other cultural diversities in American society has reduced it. Conversely, the tendency of the media to create for the largest possible audience fails to recognize the new diversities of education, taste, and cultural interests that are more important today.

The most crucial question about subcultural programing, however, is its feasibility, whether it would be profitable enough for the existing media industries, or whether there is enough demand for it among present taste publics to encourage governmental action in the face of media opposition. Subcultural programing would probably be more expensive than present programing, for it would require more content creation and more decentralized distribution. For example, since subcultural programing for television would have to reach more publics than are now reached by the three networks, more television channels, programs, and creators would be necessary. Additionally, the audiences for every product would necessarily be smaller. Both changes would raise the cost of creating and distributing content, at least at the start. In the long run, subcultural programing might increase the size of the total audience, and if the content does a better job of meeting audience needs, it might also increase the sales potential of the advertisers' commercials. Although the cost of reaching a thousand viewers would rise, the thousand viewers might be more satisfied with the content and thus more prepared to support the sponsor. Ultimately, then, subcultural programing may be more profitable than the present kind. Before this stage is reached, however, it might be necessary to subsidize media and creators to develop new television channels and new content, as well as to attract audiences to them.

The other alternative would be for government to encourage or demand subcultural programing from the media, or to compete with them by providing it through government-owned media. The latter is most desirable, for two reasons. First, competition for audiences is always healthy; and if the government competed it could provide programing for publics too small or too poor to be served adequately by the mass media. Second, having the government supply content would be more desirable than increasing the dependence of programing on advertising. Although there are some drawbacks to governmental participation in culture, especially with respect to news and other politically sensitive content, these would be minimized if government was a competing supplier rather than a controller of content.

The likelihood of any of these proposals being implemented is obviously small. Since most mass-media enterprises are profitable, they have little incentive to change. Nor is the government likely to act, for the belief in laissez-faire in the demand and supply of the arts has traditionally discouraged subsidies to high culture and any attempt by the Federal Communications Commission to interfere significantly in the mass media. Government would act if audiences demanded it, but since people do not seem to be especially dissatisfied with the content they are now receiving, they are not likely to press for major change.

Subcultural programing may, however, become more feasible in the future. The opening of ultrahigh-frequency channels for television;

continuing technological improvements that make filming, printing, and other methods of communications cheaper, faster, and simpler; and the beginning tendencies toward subcultural programing in magazines, films, and even in television all suggest that its prerequisites are already on the scene. All that is needed now is demand for more and more diverse content from the consumers. The rising affluence of at least part of the public, its growing diversity of taste and interests with increasing years of schooling, and the availability of more leisure time with the expected reduction in working hours indicate that in the years to come such demand may be forthcoming. At that time, subcultural programing will not only be financially rewarding but politically feasible as well.

Requirements for satisfying aesthetic standards. The creation of content that satisfies the aesthetic standards of the various taste publics is probably the most difficult to bring about, since little is now known about the aesthetic standards of anyone except those of the creators of high culture. Until research identifies these standards among the taste publics, and determines how far these publics want to implement them, it is not possible to be more specific about policy. Such research may even show that the important aesthetic standards are already being met, or that people do not want to choose what they think is good. There are, however, indications that this is not the case. For example, the annual amount of turnover in television programs suggests that the viewing audience is not opposed to change, and the increasing educational level of that audience will probably be accompanied by greater aesthetic awareness. Most important, the empirical evidence indicating the lack of impact of current mass-media content certainly makes it clear that if it is desirable for content to affect the audience, there is considerable room for content change.

Whether or not it would be desirable for the mass media to have more significant impact on the audience is another question. If the argument of popular-culture critics that good culture should have an impact on people is taken seriously, however, research on people's aesthetic standards and the implementation of the findings in subcultural programming deserve to be undertaken.[91]

[91] The outcome might be the replacement of what Hall and Whannel (in a book published after this article was written) call mass art by popular art. They define mass art as mass-produced popular culture, popular art as a more vital and individuated—or perhaps more creator-orientated—popular culture. Stuart Hall and Paddy Whannel, *The Popular Arts* (New York: Pantheon Books, 1965), Chapter 6.

IV Conclusion: Mass Culture as a Social Problem

It is now possible to give a more adequate answer to the original question of this chapter: To what extent is mass culture a social problem? The answer is in five parts.

First, the conclusions of all present studies of effects and other data cited suggest that popular culture is not a social problem either for the majority of its audience or for high culture. Further research is needed, however, to determine to what extent violent content, meretricious advertising, superficial or distorted informational content, and public censorship of controversial sexual, political, and religious content may affect the entire audience, and especially children, the emotionally disturbed, especially in terms of long-range effects.

Although no firm conclusions can be reached until such research is conducted, the present evidence convinces me that however much of the content of today's popular culture deviates from the aesthetic standards of high culture, and from the universal standards of truth and honesty, the effects of that content are not socially dangerous except to the minority who for reasons of age or emotional and social marginality cannot cope with the content distortion. I am further convinced that they would be helped more by policies that do away with the causes of their problem than by even the most drastic alterations of popular-culture content. The protection of children from adult content can be handled by more content that appeals to children and by the kind of consumer and citizen education that teaches people to cope with exaggeration and dishonesty, whether in the mass media or the encounters of everyday life, and that encourages them to exert social and political pressure for truth and honesty everywhere.

Second, popular culture is socially deficient not because its content fails to meet high-culture standards, but because it does not adequately respond to the aesthetic pluralism of American society. What is needed is more content and more diverse content that meets the needs and standards of all taste publics. This could be achieved through subcultural programing. Such a policy should also guarantee and enhance the vitality of high culture, maintain the ability of high-culture creators to work by creator-oriented standards, and increase their economic security so that they can devote themselves more effectively to high-culture creation.

Third, a policy of national cultural mobility to raise the country's taste level to that of present upper-middle publics is possible in theory but difficult in practice. Such a policy would not satisfy the critics of popular culture, however, for they object to upper-middle culture more than to the others.

Fourth, the genuine need is not for cultural mobility but for economic and social mobility by the poverty-stricken and others. The people now most inadequately served with leisure time, leisure-time activities, and cultural content are probably the poor, and especially the adolescents, the aged, and the nonwhite among them. Although policies to enlarge their leisure and cultural choices are desirable, their most urgent priorities are for an improvement in their nonleisure existence: an end to poverty, unemployment, discrimination, and social deprivation. If these ills can be removed, and the populations affected can share the affluence of the rest of the society, they will be able to meet their leisure and cultural needs on their own.

Finally, whatever the deficiencies of America's popular culture and mass media, these cannot be understood or dealt with through the approach of the critics of popular culture. Although their critique offers no clear policy proposals, they seem to ask for either a universal acceptance of high culture by all publics, or the elimination of the popular arts without concern about the consequences. Neither solution takes cognizance of the aesthetic standards and cultural needs of publics outside high culture, and thus neither is adequate as a guide for public policy.

I do not mean thereby to negate the need for high culture, and especially for creator-oriented high culture, in American society. Although it is not as distinctive a culture as its advocates claim and shares some common elements with other taste cultures, high culture serves vital functions not only for its own publics but also in providing ideas and criticism for all others. Consequently, its welfare must be considered, but this does not require the rejection of other taste cultures.

Social criticism is always in short supply, and for this reason the critics of popular culture have played a useful role even if their critique has been concerned primarily with the welfare of high culture. What is needed now, however, is criticism that accepts the existence of the other taste cultures, stimulates research to increase our now primitive understanding of their standards, and results in policies that will lead to their achievement through the encouragement of maximal cultural diversity. Such diversity provides the best guarantee for the vitality of a pluralist society.

Part Four

World Problems

Question: —

What population problems will we have ○ ○ ○ ○?

We want to not only look at growth of population, but also changes in distribution and composition.

● "Every significant change in population — whether growth or decline, change in distribution, or in composition — generates a range of problems."

p 625

∴ the different problems may be classified under changes in ~~growth numbers~~, growth, distribution, or composition.

Dobrev, Chavdar Atanasov.
  Живот и сцена. София, Наука и изкуство (Враца, печ. В. Александров) 1971.
  251 p. 21 cm. 1.60 lv   Bu 72112
  At head of title: Чавдар Добрев.

  1. Bulgarian drama—Addresses, essays, lectures. 2. Theater—Bulgaria—Addresses, essays, lectures. I. Title.
  Title romanized: Zhivot i stsena.

PG1011.D6   72–317486

Library of Congress   72 [2]

1. maintaing standard of living
2. provision of education
3. of opportenities for useful work
4. of recreation
✗ 5. opportunites for self-realization

Zakhoder, Boris Vladimirovich.
  Волчья песня. [По мотивам нар. сказок. Для старш. дошкольного и младш. школьного возраста. Илл.: В. Чижиков. Москва,] "Малыш," [1970].

  [25] p. with illus. 28 cm. 0.24rub   USSR 70-VKP

  Cover title.
  At head of title: Борис Заходер.

                                            Title romanized: Volch'ia pesnía.

  I. Chizhikov, Viktor, illus. II. Title.

PZ68.Z23   72 [2]   72–319396

Library of Congress

12

Population Problems in Perspective

▼▼▼▼▼▼▼▼▼▼▼▼▼▼▼▼▼▼▼▼▼▼▼▼▼

Leo F. Schnore

POPULATION problems are among the most ubiquitous social problem in the modern world. They are being experienced, for example, by rich and poor nations alike; within many nations they are being experienced in different ways. Nations typically encounter the problem engendered by rapid growth, but at the same time regions and local areas may be faced with problems of population "stagnation" or decline.

Population problems have a kind of "invisibility." They are not so dramatic as those posed by crime, delinquency, or racial unrest. There is a massive character to shifts in population and, in some instances, a kind of glacial inevitability that makes them less subject to dramatic treatment in the headlines. It is true that certain population problems, notably the rapid growth of world population, are receiving more attention in the mass media. But many others are underrated or overlooked altogether. World population growth is only the most obvious and dramatic of a whole series of population problems confronting us. Every significant change in population—whether growth or decline, change in distribution, or in composition—generates a range of problems.

What Is a Population Problem?

Population problems, unlike so many other social problems that concern us, stem from the most "normal" kind of human behavior, such as having children or moving from one place to another. In the aggregate, repeated many times, these mundane individual actions may add up to serious problems.

Just what do we mean by a "population problem"? The study of population, of course, deals with quantities, and so we usually think of a population problem as involving "too many" people in relation to some standard. If people were asked to name the first population problem that occurred to them, we can be reasonably confident that it would be "the problem of world population," that is, the tremendous increase in human numbers that is going on today, especially in the less developed parts of the world. If they were asked, however, to specify just what problems arise with this increase, we would receive a range of answers. Perhaps most answers would focus on maintaining the standard of living. The simple provision of food, clothing, and shelter at some minimum level would certainly have to be mentioned. After that, some might mention the provision of education, of opportunities for useful work, for recreation, for self-realization, and so forth— provision of all the things they might like to include in their conception of a meaningful human way of life, at something above the brute level of survival.

No matter how long or how short the list of things might be, we would at least be making an implicit quantitative comparison—the number of people to be provided with these "things" *versus* the number of these things available or potentially available, whether calories, dwellings, jobs, or schoolrooms. In other words, we would be making normative judgments, and as a consequence there might be substantial disagreement on the extent of the population problem facing the world. If the list of *desiderata* were relatively short and appeared to be easy to attain, the problem would be seen as minor; if it were long and difficult of attainment, the problem would be seen as very serious. In short, our *reference points* make the difference in our judgments.

Our conception of the seriousness of any population problem— world, national, or local—is heavily influenced by our views about the probable ease or difficulty involved in providing those things thought to be in short supply at present or in the future. Concerning the world population problem, for example, there is a wide range of opinion about the feasibility of simply *feeding* many more than our present 3.3 billion fellow human beings. This example of food supply—the simplest and most fundamental in that it bears most directly upon the sheer survival of the human species—also illustrates how complex the analysis can be. How much food will be available? The statements of experts vary widely; the relevant variables are hard to identify, let alone to manipulate in some purposive fashion; and projections into future time are difficult.

It is not easy to determine just what is a population problem. Is human survival as a species a "population" problem? Certainly it is when it is posed in its simplest terms—what some writers have characterized as the Malthusian "heads-bushels" dilemma. But what about the role of "population pressure" in international relations? Do population imbalances around the world pose a threat to peace? In the nuclear age the species is certainly jeopardized if they do. Is the current "urban explosion" a population problem? It is not easy to draw the line, for some things that are commonly called population problems could just as easily be recast under different headings. In some respects, the world population problem could just as readily be rewritten as a problem of world poverty since more poor people are alive today than at any time in history. Similarly, other problems that are *not* commonly thought of as population problems have that aspect; for example, the current crisis in race relations in this country involves radical changes in population distribution. To take another example, the number of "juvenile delinquents" will probably increase by about 45 percent between 1965 and 1975, even if the rate of delinquency remains constant, simply because the age group between 15 and 19 will grow by that much.

The Demographer's Sphere of Interest

One way to have a firmer grasp of population problems is to identify those facets of human population that specifically interest the scientists who study population, the demographers. Once we have identified these demographic factors, we are in a better position to talk about the causes and effects of population change.

The demographer is essentially concerned with three things: population size, population distribution, and population composition. He wants to know how many people there are—whether in the world as a whole, or in some part of it, such as a continent, a country, or a city. He also wants to know how people are distributed in space; evenly or unevenly, bunched in clumps and clusters called cities, or spread over the landscape. Finally, the demographer wants to know the composition or "makeup" of these populations. How many young people and how many old people are there? What is the balance between the sexes? What are the proportions in various racial or ethnic categories? How many are in the labor force? How many are employed in different occupations and industries? [1]

---

[1] The most comprehensive introduction to demography as a discipline is Philip M. Hauser and Otis Dudley Duncan, eds., *The Study of Population* (Chicago: University of Chicago Press, 1959).

All three features—size, distribution, and composition—can be determined at any specific point in time, even though they are constantly changing. They are "static" aspects of population, since they can be determined by a *census*—an enumeration of the numbers, locations, and characteristics of people at a given point in time.

But there is a "dynamic" as well as a "static" side to population analysis. The demographer is interested not only in population size but also in *changes* in population size. Is the population under study growing, remaining stable, or declining? He is interested not only in distribution but also in *re*-distribution. Is the world's population becoming more urbanized, and if so, at what rate? In other words, what *changes* in spatial distribution are occurring? The demographer is interested, too, in *changes* in the composition of population. Is the population getting older? Are there changes in the "sex ratio," or the balance between the sexes? Are some racial or ethnic groups growing more rapidly than others? Which are the growing occupations and industries, and which are stabilizing or declining?

Such questions lead the demographer to an interest in certain classes of events commonly called "the demographic processes." Chief among these are the so-called "vital processes," fertility and mortality. (Fertility in demographic terminology applies to the actual frequency of births and does not relate to the ability to have children.) They are given the greatest attention in discussions of population for good reason. Changes in the population of the world as a whole are entirely dependent on these two processes. As long as the number of births exceeds the number of deaths, the world population will increase. But as soon as the demographer begins to consider any specific part of that world, a new factor, *migration*, has to be taken into account.

Changes in the population size of a country or a city between any two points in time must be examined from the standpoint of four quantities: (1) the number of births occurring there during the time interval in question; (2) the number of deaths occurring there during the same period; (3) the number of people who moved into the country or the city in question (the "immigrants"); and (4) the number of people who moved out of the country or the city under study (the "emigrants"). The balance between births and deaths is called "natural increase." The figure, of course, may be positive or negative, since the number of deaths may exceed the number of births, as happened in France during the early 1930s. The balance between immigration and emigration is called "net migration." It too can be positive or negative: a country can increase through net migration (as the United States has done through most of its history), or it can decrease by sending out more migrants than it receives in return (as with Ireland, which has been losing population through migration for over a century).

Interest in population composition requires demographers to look at another kind of population "movement," not through space but from one social status to another. The process of aging—moving from one age group to another—is one kind of "mobility" that demographers work with. For one thing, age has a vital bearing on fertility and mortality, as well as on migration. Another kind of status change that has long interested demographers is change in marital status—from single to married, from married to widowed, separated, or divorced. The reason for this special interest in marital status is its obvious influence on fertility. Other things equal, a population that has a higher married proportion will experience higher fertility.

There are other kinds of status change, or "mobility," that demographers study. The process of acquiring an education, for example, can be regarded as an experience in social mobility, a progressive movement from one educational status to another. Similarly, movement into and out of the labor force and movement from one job to another are subject to mobility analysis. A person can remain *spatially* immobile, in other words, and be *socially* mobile in a significant way, and these "moves" are of great interest to the demographer.[2]

Selected Population Problems in the United States

Most attention today is properly focused on the problems of world population, for the magnitude of the problem is immense. We live in one world, and the birth rates in India and China must be of interest to us. It is a matter of importance that we be aware of the demographic situation around the world. But we must also be aware of population problems facing the United States.

At first glance, the United States has no severe "population problems." We are the wealthiest nation in the world. We occupy a wide continent, rich in natural resources. Far from having a food problem, we are faced with an embarrassment of riches—agricultural surpluses that cost millions of dollars to store. This is not to say that some of our citizens do not go to bed hungry; recent discussions have made clear that in the midst of our affluence there are "pockets of poverty" that will be difficult and costly to eliminate. But most of us are not aware of pressing population problems, and for good reason: compared to the problems of, say, our Latin-American neighbors, our problems seem insignificant. The Latin-American countries make up the most rapidly

[2] See Leo F. Schnore, "Social Mobility in Demographic Perspective," *American Sociological Review*, 26 (June 1961), pp. 407–423.

growing region in the world, many of them growing at 3 percent annually, while our rate of growth is less than the annual world average of 2 percent.

These rates may seem low. We must remember, however, that population grows by multiplication and can compound rapidly. This compounding can be shown by considering the number of years required for a population to double its numbers at given rates of increase.

Annual Average Percentage Increase	Number of Years Required to Double Population
1	69.3
2	34.7
3	23.1
4	17.3
5	13.9

The United States now has about 200 million people, which is an enormous increase over the last two generations. (Our population was only a little over 76 million in 1900.) Despite this tremendous increase, our population density is only about 50 persons per square mile. This is a moderate "man-land" ratio compared to that of most major nations. (India has about 300 people per square mile, China about 150 per square mile, and Japan well over 600 per square mile.) We seem to be in no immediate danger of "standing room only." In fact, nearly half our counties *lost* population between 1950 and 1960 (the dates of our two most recent censuses). There is, too, an increasing unevenness of population distribution in the United States. Some regions and states are losing population while others are growing rapidly. To take the outstanding example, California gained over five million people between 1950 and 1960, an increase that more than exceeds the current total population of Wisconsin. These figures testify to the dynamism characteristic of the American population.

The physical mobility of the population is such that one out of every five of our citizens changes his place of residence every year. One result of this high rate of internal migration is that we have become an increasingly urban nation. Until the census of 1920, just after World War I, the United States continued to register rural majorities; such has been the force of urbanization, however, that by 1960 over 70 percent of our people were urbanites. One out of every four Americans now lives in our twelve largest metropolitan areas.

The point of these statistics is that some of the most significant changes in population are changes in population *composition* and *dis-*

tribution. The very fact of change brings problems. Every change in population distribution, for example, means that new facilities have to be provided in the areas that are growing, and that existing facilities in areas of out-migration are likely to be underused. This holds for housing, schools, roads, and all other things that people need and use.

What are some pressing problems? Consider urbanization. The rural-to-urban population shift is far from complete. Many areas, especially in the South, still contain surplus numbers of farmers engaged in subsistence production. Most of their meager output does not find its way into commercial market channels so they are not contributing to the food surplus that gives much trouble. What they have to export is themselves. We may reasonably assume that this "marginal" farm population will ultimately be drawn into other sectors of the economy. Trends in recent years indicate that the elimination of this relatively unproductive group is well under way. Nevertheless, a key policy problem persists beneath the surface, a problem that is not ordinarily taken up in the continuing political debates over parity, price supports, and the proper disposition of farm surplus. The hidden issue has to do with the role the government should play in aiding the adjustment of displaced farmers, many of whom become rural-to-urban migrants. The available evidence indicates that under laissez-faire conditions the farm-reared migrant typically enters the urban labor force at or near the bottom of the occupational scale, taking the jobs requiring the least training and receiving the smallest rewards.[3]

The problem faced by the migrant is worse, of course, if he is not white. One of the most striking population statistics concerning the United States is that in 1910 over 70 percent of all Negro Americans were rural dwellers. Most of them lived in the South; but in 1960 over 70 percent of Negro Americans were urbanites, increasingly concentrated in Northern cities. Almost 30 percent of the nonwhites in this country now live in the twelve largest metropolitan areas—New York, Los Angeles, Chicago, Philadelphia, Detroit, San Francisco, Boston, Pittsburgh, St. Louis, Washington, Cleveland, and Baltimore. It is not just the handful of large cities that is undergoing this specific change in population composition. Outside of the South, nine out of ten metropolitan areas experienced gains in the proportion of nonwhites between 1950 and 1960.[4] Thus our great cities are generally faced with the problem of absorbing massive numbers of people who are often— through no fault of their own—totally unprepared for life in the

[3] See Ronald Freedman and Deborah Freedman, "Farm-Reared Elements in the Nonfarm Population," *Rural Sociology*, 21 (March 1956), pp. 50–61.
[4] See Leo F. Schnore and Harry Sharp, "Racial Changes in Metropolitan Areas, 1950–1960," *Social Forces*, 41 (March 1963), pp. 247–253.

metropolis. They have neither the training nor skills to allow them to be readily assimilated into the social and economic life of the great city.

Urbanization, the continuing concentration of our population, has been going on for a long time, though the pace has quickened in recent decades. In one sense, the increased tempo of urbanization has simply meant that old solutions have had to be applied more quickly. Other population changes, however, have not had this character. This is especially true of changes in the age composition of our population over the past 30 years. We have had our attention repeatedly called to the so-called "baby boom" that followed the low fertility years of the Depression in the 1930s and World War II. From a compositional standpoint, the result is a series of indentations and bulges in the "population pyramid," the graphic device that demographers use to portray the age-sex structure of the population.

Stated simply, we are confronted with the problem of age groups of radically different size, passing through various age-graded institutions and services. In the 1950s, as a result of the limited number of births in the Depression and war years, small numbers of people were going into high schools and colleges of this country, and subsequently into the labor market. Over the past several years primary and secondary schools have been feeling the impact of the tremendous revival of the birthrate. Today these large numbers are beginning to reach our colleges, and shortly thereafter they will burst on our labor and housing markets and enter the "marriage market." At that time the small number of Depression cohorts (people born in a given year) will be having children, and in such reduced numbers as to lower the birthrate and the absolute number of births to a certain extent. This is, in fact, already happening; the American birthrate has been falling since 1957.

Only a few years will pass, however, before we will witness the reassertion of higher birthrates when the postwar cohorts themselves marry and have children. The overall prospect, then, is for a more or less rhythmic series of "delayed reactions" to the fluctuations in fertility that marked the period between the early 1930s and the late 1950s. The influences on the housing market, educational facilities, and industries oriented to the needs of infants and children are obvious. To the extent that population size determines levels of output in an economy closely geared to the mass market, we may thus anticipate a long-term alternating sequence of expansion and "stagnation" in at least some industries.[5]

[5] For a very lucid account of this matter, see Norman B. Ryder, "Variability and Convergence in the American Population," *Phi Delta Kappan,* 41 (June 1960), pp. 379–383.

The amplitude of these fluctuations is probably narrow enough to permit adjustment on the part of the American economy as a whole. The real problems appear when we consider the *localized* manifestations of these trends, especially when we give simultaneous attention to both population distribution *and* composition. Any resident of a mushrooming suburb will testify to the high costs of providing school facilities for a rapidly expanding child population. One disturbing possiblity not considered by many local authorities is that an equally sudden shrinkage in the demand for educational services may eventually follow the completion of suburban families. Newer suburbs with heavy concentrations in a narrow parental age range are especially vulnerable. In short, some of our most pressing population problems will stem from peculiarities in age composition, peculiarities now "built into" our population structure.

Population Growth in World Perspective

We now return to the question of population change in the larger world setting, and focus specifically on some of the connections between population growth and economic development. This has been a topic of interest at least since 1798 when Thomas Robert Malthus published *An Essay on Population*.[6]

One need not adopt a Malthusian position, of course, to assert that total population growth is of the greatest relevance to the level of welfare in a nation. Economists and sociologists of a wide variety of theoretical persuasions have placed sheer growth in human numbers in the forefront of their analyses.

---

[6] "In his *Essay on Population* (1798, revised in 1803) Malthus introduced his 'natural law'—that living creatures multiply faster than the food supply. He pointed out that population had a tendency to increase in a geometrical progression (2:4:8:16: 32), whereas agricultural production could increase at most in an arithmetical progression (2:4:6:8:10). And the ways in which the rate of population growth might be checked were either ineffective or bad. The desire to maintain or improve their status by having fewer mouths to feed prompted some men to use 'moral restraint' in sexual relations with their wives, but Malthus had no faith in its effect on population statistics. As an Anglican clergyman Malthus also considered contraception immoral. To avoid impregnating their wives, men sometimes frequented prostitutes; this was bad because it encouraged vice. The 'positive checks' on population enumerated by Malthus were also bad because they shortened the duration of human life: unwholesome occupations, severe labor and exposure to the seasons, extreme poverty, bad nursing of children—and, of course, war, pestilence, and famine. By saying that nothing more 'positive' than these abominations could check the population explosion, Malthus was in effect formulating a law of increasing misery." Edward R. Tannenbaum, *European Civilization: Since the Middle Ages* (New York: John Wiley and Sons, 1965), p. 382.

The real significance of population growth for economic development arises from a simple fact: man is a consumer as well as a producer. Overly rapid increase may thus wipe out any gains in productivity achieved by dint of technological or organizational change, because a sharp increase in the numbers of people may "eat up" the newly won surplus. A drop in the average level of living may ensue.

The extent to which real gains in productivity are difficult to achieve in the face of uncontrolled growth may be dramatized by an historical example. It is commonly agreed that the economy of the United States developed in what must surely be one of the most promising settings mankind has ever known. Even discounting chauvinistic claims about the role of superior national character, or the impetus provided by favorable political institutions, the advantages were enormous: environmentally, a thinly settled land rich in a wide variety of natural resources; technologically, the possibility of drawing upon Europe's material-cultural base, consisting of highly efficient systems of energy conversion and transportation; organizationally, an emergent social structure unencumbered by the heavy yoke of feudalism. Yet even given these rare advantages, it is reliably estimated that until recently the gross national product of the United States improved at an annual average rate of only 3 percent.

In contrast, consider the possibilities of human increase. A growth rate of 3 percent annually is the difference between a birthrate of 40 per thousand and a death rate of 10 per thousand. A glance at any recent international series of fertility and mortality data will show how frequently rates such as these are juxtaposed in today's world. Moreover, the coincidence of high fertility and low mortality appears most often in just those underdeveloped areas where the prospects of rapid gains in productivity are most remote. Small wonder, then, that people concerned with economic development have given high priority to the population growth factor in both their practical and theoretical deliberations.

Malthus Reconsidered

All that had been said up to this point may give the appearance of a Malthusian interpretation. However, contemporary thinking deliberately avoids some of the more obvious errors of a purely Malthusian analysis. In the first place, man does not face his environment naked and alone; on the contrary, he is a "social animal" and a tool-using creature. Thus human populations confront their environments in ways that are effectively mediated by their forms of social and economic organization and by their technological repertoires. In the original

Malthusian argument, these latter variables—technology and organization, constituting what Malthus called the "state of the arts"—were deliberately "held constant" for purposes of analysis. This procedure was analytically proper, of course; the deficiency in the Malthusian account was that these terms were never permitted to vary. The resulting "principle of population" was a truism at best, merely restating the assumed propensity of organic life to multiply beyond the capacity of the supporting environment. At worst, the result was a prematurely closed analysis, yielding no possibility of deriving further propositions.

An even greater deficiency was Malthus' tendency to reason in what may be called a "local context." On close examination, it becomes evident that Malthus implicitly adopted a variant of "Robinson Crusoe economics"; that is, he assumed that populations work out their salvations with the resources locally and immediately available in space and time. Given the perspective afforded by a modern urban-industrial society, nothing could be further from the truth. A society like the United States literally draws on the resources of the entire world, and it is more than a metaphor to say that we live on the bounty of the past, for we select from a cultural accumulation unequaled in history.

One route to a better understanding of the population question can be provided by showing the basis of the Malthusian model's frequently cited failure to "predict" the course of Western demographic experience that was unfolding at the beginning of the nineteenth century. First, his apparent reluctance to give full play to technological and organizational variation makes it impossible for Malthus' model to accommodate the most salient features of Western history over the past two centuries. The radical innovations in technology and social organization displayed in this period were absolutely without historical precedent, at least on the scale at which they developed. As a consequence, rapid population growth was so readily absorbed that many areas were actually *underpopulated,* in the sense that the demand for labor could not be filled. The Western world in modern times has seen the greatest population upsurge ever known at precisely the same time that it experienced the most massive upgrading of living levels.

This period brought unprecedentedly rapid and sustained advances in the efficiency of energy conversion, in the ease of transportation and communication, in the release of men from beast-like toil on the land, in the intensity and scope of external trade, in the levels of income, health, and literacy, and in concentration of population in immense urban agglomerations. As a result of some of these technological and organizational changes, the friction of space was reduced and the movement of people, commodities, and information was facilitated, so that man appears to have broken out of the narrow constraints of a limited, localized environment once and for all.

In matters of economic development, however, we may consider the role of recent population growth from a slightly different perspective. It is perhaps an historical anomaly that the same nations that could "afford" population growth on a grand scale have displayed some of the lowest rates of growth. In short, the wealthy nations of the Western world—the "developed" countries—have already passed through the "demographic transition," in which falling death rates were followed by declining birthrates, yielding what amounted to a new vital equilibrium at a low level of overall increase. Until recent years the underdeveloped areas of the world presented the traditional Malthusian picture; both vital rates seemed fixed at high levels, and heavy mortality offset fertility that came close to the biological maximum in many instances. In the last few years, however, mortality rates have plummeted in the less-developed areas, in response to massive public health programs. It took Sweden 140 years to cut her mortality from 25 to 10 deaths per thousand population per year. It has taken Ceylon only 30 years to do the same thing. Exporting the technology and organization of "death control" has worked only too well. The years since World War II especially have seen a drop in mortality in these poverty-stricken regions that is more startling than the recovery of the birthrate in Western nations, the "baby boom." Such changes in vital rates prevent a completely unambiguous interpretation of recent growth rates around the world.

National Income and Population Growth

Before World War II there was a rough inverse correlation between population growth rates and national income, with the wealthier nations showing low rates of population growth. In fact, in these rich countries population experts became concerned with the prospect of imminent absolute losses of population. This concern had the effect of producing a "demography of decline," in which technical statistical measures (such as the "net reproduction rate") were developed to demonstrate the population losses implied by the low schedules of fertility then current. The recovery of the birthrate after World War II (the "baby boom") in some industrialized nations has reduced the pre-World War II negative correlation between population growth and economic development by pushing their rates of population increase upward. On a worldwide basis, however, the negative correlation has been maintained by the unprecedented mortality experience of the underdeveloped areas since World War II. In these areas the headlong plunge of mortality rates has occurred along with essentially unchanged patterns of fertility. In some areas, indeed, health improvements appear to have raised already high birthrates. The results are shown in Table 1.

The underdeveloped areas of the world now appear to have entered the initial phases of the "demographic transition" already accomplished by the West. The Western nations cut their mortality slowly, over a span of decades stretching from the early part of the 1800s into the

Table 1 Estimated Population and Population Increases, by Continent, 1900 to 2000

Continent	Population (in millions)					Average Annual Percent Increase			
	1900	1925	1950	1975	2000	1900–1925	1925–1950	1950–1975	1975–2000
Africa	120	147	199	303	517	0.9	1.4	2.1	2.8
North America	81	126	168	240	312	2.2	1.3	1.7	1.2
Latin America	63	99	163	303	592	2.3	2.6	3.4	3.8
Asia (excluding U.S.S.R.)	857	1020	1380	2210	3870	0.8	1.4	2.4	3.0
Europe (including U.S.S.R.)	423	505	574	751	947	0.8	0.6	1.2	1.0
Oceania	6	10	13	21	29	2.3	1.4	2.4	1.6
World total	1550	1907	2497	3828	6267	0.9	1.2	2.1	2.6

SOURCE: United Nations, *The Future Growth of World Population* (New York: United Nations, 1958).

present century. Fertility declines typically occurred much later; with a few exceptions like France and the United States, most countries embarked on this course of declining fertility only after the 1870s. In the intervening years rapid increase ensued, and the high-growth phase was "telescoped." In other words, the later a country entered the entire cycle, the more quickly it completed the shift to low levels of fertility and mortality, with consequent slow growth. The numerous repetitions of this pattern have led some writers to adopt an optimistic interpretation that verges on accepting this transition as some kind of inevitable and automatic sequence. The case of Japan has been used to buttress this argument; even in that country, so culturally dissimilar from the West at the outset, the demographic transition was repeated (and, in comparison with earlier transitions, very quickly) with all essential details intact. Other writers, of course, have understandably urged caution, arguing that we should await the accumulation of more evidence from other areas.

Let us briefly summarize the relevance of population growth for the analysis of economic development. (1) Population growth, if it proceeds faster than productivity, impedes and may even stop economic development. This has been widely appreciated since Malthus. (2) The Malthusian interpretation, however, fails to include all the relevant variables *as variables*. It also has the defect of posing the whole population-resource problem in a strictly local context. A more realistic perspective avoids these pitfalls and seems to yield more testable propositions; that is, it comes closer to being a "scientific" theory of population. (3) The main empirical fact to be considered is the continuing negative association between rates of population growth and levels of economic development around the world today. The underdeveloped areas are growing most rapidly, and the key question is whether or not they can pass through the demographic transition in time to avoid cataclysmic misfortunes—misfortunes which, in an increasingly interdependent world, will affect all of us.

The "Causes" of the Historic Pattern

In a naive fashion, some writers have interpreted the demographic history of the West as the result of a calculated "choice," that is, the desire to substitute a higher level of living for a larger population. These writers argue that individual families choose between children on the one hand and consumer goods on the other. This is an intellectually seductive mode of reasoning, but it has one grave defect: all the variables are inferred from the same behavior. To be more specific, the procedure used is as follows: it is observed that the historic decline of population growth rates has been accompanied by a more-or-less steady rise in the average level of living. "Choice" is then invoked to supply the links between these two observable trends. But the critical variables—the individual attitudes and values that are assumed to generate changing patterns of choice—are never directly observed or measured. Without some kind of *independent* measurement of the causal variables, the hypothesis is untestable, and the "choice" interpretation becomes, upon close examination, far less compelling. In some respects, it seems more reasonable to interpret higher levels of living and lower rates of population growth as the common product of some third factor, or some combination of factors that operate to bring about both of these changes. Certainly urbanization and industrialization have to be considered, for they seem to involve concomitant alterations in both variables.

Since the immediate demographic cause of falling rates of Western growth was a decline in the birthrate, it would be well to concentrate attention on this demographic variable. Although there is no immediately apparent reason for modern urban-industrial systems to *require* low levels of fertility, there is ample cause for believing that primitive and "mass peasant" societies will necessarily exhibit high birthrates. In a subsistence economy based on village agriculture, there are a number of factors favoring high fertility. First, birthrates must remain high to offset the decimating effects of high mortality rates, especially the high rates of infant mortality. Second, subsistence agriculture is a "man-consuming" operation, typically carried on within the family unit; a larger family may be of considerable economic value because it provides the manpower needed at periods of peak labor demand, such as planting and harvesting times. We could add a whole array of institutional practices favoring high fertility that seem to be indigenous to the society existing at a low technological level. It is enough to say that such a peasant agricultural regime offers more than a single "motivation" for the maintenance of high fertility. A high birthrate seems to be built into the system.

Some writers have emphasized how rapidly sustained population growth can act as a barrier to modernization. The concentration of heavy densities on rural land, for example, can only serve to impede the transition to modern agriculture, especially when the lack of opportunities elsewhere prohibits the surplus farmers from turning to other useful work, such as manufacturing. Most writers have come to regard programs of fertility control as essential parts of any plan for economic modernization. The suspicion has grown that we may hurt the underdeveloped areas when we help them to check mortality without, at the same time, introducing techniques and inducements for fertility control.

The whole role of population growth in economic development is complicated, however, by other historical considerations. We cannot conceive growth as inevitably deleterious. We must be aware of some of the *positive* economic forces that are likely to be set in motion by population growth. Such growth seems to spur economic development, under certain conditions, by increasing the demand that generates technological improvement, plant expansion, and the like. One need only observe our own economy during the marriage and baby booms after World War II to see these consequences of growth. It is apparent, however, that rapid population growth can only be accommodated by an economic system that has already reached a high level of productivity. Growth in a country without the capacity of absorption that we possess may only mean that low levels of living will be further reduced.

Viewing growth in broader perspective reveals its possibly stimulating influence upon an economy in a different light. Effective "growth" of demand need not be achieved by higher natural increase. Rather, substantial additions to the level of demand are preferably to be gained by higher levels of real income per capita, or by more intense and sustained trade contacts with other populations. These means yield what may be called "effective population increase," in contrast to the "natural increase" resulting from a surplus of births over deaths. The establishment of trade relationships with other areas, for example, has the immediate effect of widening the market without the burdensome costs of rapid natural increase.

Thus the relationship between growth and economic development acquires a different meaning in different settings. Under certain conditions growth may yield "positive" results. Under other circumstances —and these seem to characterize most of the world today—the desirable kind of effective population increase is better achieved by technological and organizational changes that yield a wider network of interdependence than by a simple increase in human numbers.

Sociological Factors Encouraging Population Growth

What are the more prominent sociological factors that encourage population growth? We have mentioned some features of the social and economic organization of village peasantry that seem to stimulate high fertility. The familistic basis of production and consumption is especially worthy of emphasis. In such circumstances, where the birthrate is seemingly frozen at a high level, it only requires some slight reduction in mortality for rapid growth to occur. As we have noted, the progressive worldwide diffusion of medical technology and public health organization has established the perfect conditions for sustained growth at a high level. A society geared to high fertility may multiply with astounding speed once mortality has been brought under a minimum of control; a population may double within a single generation (about 23 years) at an annual growth rate of only 3 percent—the difference between a birthrate of 40 per thousand and a death rate of 10 per thousand annually. In the modern nation, advanced technology and urban-industrial organization combine to press mortality downward and to keep it low.

At the same time, however, these organizational features apparently have had such profound implications for the parallel reduction of fertility that extremely rapid growth on a sustained basis is almost out of the question. Although we are still ignorant of the precise mechanisms by which organizational imperatives operate to lower fertility, we can point to certain salient structural features as among the most powerful inhibitors of fertility. Most of these organizational factors work through the family, the key unit of procreation.

Sociologists and demographers have joined to compile a long list of qualities of the modern family that make it a small unit. First, the changing economic significance of children is cited; far from representing a positive value, either in terms of youthful labor or support in later years, the child in the urban-industrial setting is almost a pure consumer. The lengthening period of expensive dependency, including costly education, is not offset by later returns to the parents in a familial system in which a new household is established independently in each generation. These facts combine with a labor force and a welfare system organized along nonfamilial lines to alter completely the economic significance of children. There are also increased possibilities for women of wage labor outside the home. Household duties have been lightened by domestic labor-saving devices and a host of domestic services. Thus a married woman now has time to work outside the home on at least a temporary basis. In addition, the different types of jobs available in an economy making use of mechanized industry and increasingly devoted to the provision of services yields opportunities for female labor that do not exist under other circumstances. The combination of such factors produces the most striking long-term trend in the American labor force: the markedly increased participation of married women in remunerative work. Despite the fact that much of this activity is on a part-time or short-run basis (as between marriage and the birth of a first child), and despite the recent impact of "automation," the consequences for fertility are almost self-evident.

There are other organizational sources of low fertility in the modern world. The requirements for physical and social mobility in a constantly changing urban-industrial regime have been widely discussed as bearing directly upon the birthrate. A modern society is in constant flux, and writers have observed that a large number of children constitute a real burden to mobile parents. Other writers have pointed to various aspects of urbanization—from observable physical features like the limited availability of housing in growing cities to such qualities as a "rational-utilitarian psychological milieu"—which depress fertility well below the biological maximum. In truth, the list of organizational factors that have been brought forward as explanations of low fertility is very long.

In addition to these organizational attributes of modern society, the Western world has long possessed an important technological advantage: fertility control methods of unparalleled reliability and efficiency. The various social classes and residence groups have lowered their birthrates at different times, apparently according to the progressive diffusion of contraceptive devices and techniques, downward from the higher social strata and outward from cities.

The wealthier the nation, of course, the more easily it can accommodate rapid increase with no consequent ill effect upon the level of living. The wealthy countries, however, have tended to exhibit the lowest rates of growth in recent decades. Having already passed through the rapid stages of growth during their demographic transitions in the nineteenth and early twentieth centuries, these nations appear to have reached an equilibrium between fertility and mortality that results in relatively slow growth. The underdeveloped areas, despite being least able to afford the luxury of unimpeded growth, continue to expand most rapidly. In many such areas the problem is rendered even more serious by the pre-existing huge populations that are the product of long decades and even centuries of tortuously slow increments, in which periods of numerical gains somehow offset catastrophic losses over a long span of time. The problem posed by large size is one of the "demographic multiplier," for even a modest *rate* of growth applied to such immense populations produces absolute increases beyond the apparent capacity of most of the impoverished nations to absorb. Thus the hope of escape from poverty is imperiled by the "population specter," and it is small wonder that prophets of demographic disaster have repeatedly appeared on the scene, painting a picture of a future so dire as to make Malthus seem an optimist.

The general relationship between wealth and population growth seen today seems to be the very one that struck Malthus as the only hope for mankind. Malthus perceived that the wealthier classes seemed to be growing only slowly, exercising "prudential restraint," but the poor—least able to feed extra mouths—showed an unbridled propensity to procreate. Would it not be possible, he reasoned, to encourage restraint on the part of the benighted masses? His answer to his own rhetorical question was by no means unequivocal, for his faith in the efficacy of education was offset by his feeling that population increase itself posed an almost insuperable obstacle to genuine progress. From this came the reluctant conclusions that gave Malthus' work its pall.

It may strike a contemporary today that Malthus, examining his beloved England at the beginning of the nineteenth century, was only seeing today's problem in microcosm, observing a miniature replica of the situation that would finally emerge from the swiftly changing world of the 1800s. It is the classic Malthusian problem on a grand scale that we see today: unrestrained growth in the face of abject squalor, with population increase itself apparently preventing the elimination of poverty. It would almost seem that poverty, in and of itself, contains the seeds of unrestricted growth.

To take such a view, however, is to be more than simply pessimistic in the face of discouraging evidence; it is to miss the true significance of the observable association between income and growth. As we have seen, wealth is the product of specific technological and organizational situations, and is not to be regarded as some kind of automatic yield, given a population of a certain size in an environment of fixed resources. Nor is growth to be regarded as a mystical natural phenomenon beyond the range of human understanding and control. Rather, we have attempted to display the rich variety of ways in which population numbers are responsive to variations in technology and organization. This responsiveness is the lesson of the nineteenth century that Malthus could not read from even a short distance, for his preconceptions about the power of population growth blinded him to the emerging realities of his own time.

Perhaps we are overly harsh in finding fault with Malthus for his lack of vision; it may be only from our present vantage point that the main facts become reasonably clear. Be that as it may, the errors that Malthus committed should make our own analyses more realistic. Specifically, our demographic models should avoid the postulate of some unlimited growth potential, and we should give full play to variables that count. First and foremost, we must regard growth as the product of a dynamic interplay between a population and its entire environment, with the relationship effectively mediated through technology and organization. These two variables are, to use Wilbert E. Moore's striking phrase, the "dynamic middle terms" that link population and resources.

Population Problems in Underdeveloped Areas [7]

Some social scientists have suggested that population growth is *the* problem in underdeveloped areas, and that it arose out of the simple

[7] This section is adapted from Leo F. Schnore, "Social Problems in the Underdeveloped Areas: An Ecological View," *Social Problems*, 8, 3 (Winter 1960–1961), pp. 182–201.

application of some of our modern machinery of lifesaving (DDT, antibiotics, vaccines, and such) to other parts of the world. These borrowed elements of material culture have brought the death rate to low levels with unprecedented speed in many backward areas; growth rates far in excess of anything previously realized are now in evidence, simply because birthrates have remained essentially unchanged in the interim. One of the main questions for policy makers contemplating the current "population explosion" thus is whether or not the technology of birth control is to be widely disseminated, in an effort to offset the impact of the exported technology of "death control."

Social scientists have been intrigued by the different reactions of backward societies to various elements of technology, and they agree that elements affecting *mortality* are more likely to be adopted than those influencing *fertility;* the dissimilar behavior of the two "vital rates" themselves is usually taken as *prima facie* evidence for this view. On the basis of these observations an elaborate but loosely integrated theory has gained widespread currency. It attempts to explain the sequence and timing of the well-known historical trends in vital rates. This formulation can be briefly summarized. All societies, it is pointed out, have confronted more or less difficult habitats that are no more than indifferent to human welfare; in the process of adaptation to such forbidding environments, certain fundamental "values" concerning life and death have become firmly established in tradition, with most of them favoring life over death. Life is positively evaluated and death is negatively conceived by most peoples of the world, both past and present. So powerful are these values, it is said, that societies lacking a strong negative orientation to death have disappeared from the face of the earth. The same thing is said of societies that somehow failed to develop value systems favoring high fertility, for large numbers of births have been required to offset the heavy toll of human mortality until very recent times. How does one explain the continuation of high fertility after the decline of mortality? It is argued that the birthrate fell later only in response to new "value systems" based on a kind of calculus in which children came to be weighed against consumption goods.

This theory seems quite plausible at first glance. It appears to explain the divergent behavior of the two vital series in all the areas that have undergone the so-called "demographic transition," wherein mortality has inevitably fallen first to be followed by a lesser decline in fertility. It also seems to square with experience, in the sense that it is consistent with the opinions regarding life and death held by most of us. Of course, the "survival value" facet of the argument cannot be readily tested; we can only assume that a society which was indifferent to these matters might have had difficulty in maintaining itself. However, there are graver flaws in this theory than the mere fact that it rests on an untestable assumption. The major weakness lies in a lapse in logic. Although other factors are recognized as being operative, "values" are assumed to be of pre-eminent importance. If values are so critical, however, we may inquire why societies with such strong negative orientations to death actually suffered such high mortality losses for so many generations. It would appear that other factors have more important implications for mortality than the usual interpretation would grant them. At best, the theory may require modification to give greater weight to factors other than values; as it is ordinarily stated, the theory suffers because it attributes *variations over time* (in mortality) to precisely those factors (values) that the theory itself assumes to be *constant in time*. Indeed, we could argue with some plausibility that "values" are better conceived as *responses*—whether rational or not—to objective situations, and are thus subject to change when external circumstances are altered. (We might even hypothesize that the historical emergence of "Western" values regarding death actually *followed* and did not precede the achievement of some appreciable control over mortality, and that there are varying demographic contexts in which "individualism" versus a blind acceptance of one's sorry fate might be expected to appear.)

What "other factors" deserve greater stress? Unfortunately, we have few empirically verified propositions. Generally, of course, *any* factor that increases the average life chances in a population will lower the death rate accordingly. Such a statement, however, opens the door to an infinite number of factors, namely anything that increases or at least stabilizes the food supply, anything that reduces war, banditry, and civil strife, anything that influences the virulence or scope of infectious disease, and so on. Two general classes of factors seem to have been historically instrumental in bringing down the Western death rate: certain critical *technological* innovations and certain *organizational* changes.

Historically, there has been a long and gradual development of an expanded area of interdependence; during the process formerly isolated localities established exchange relations, permitting an area of shortages to draw upon the surpluses of other territories. In this *organizational* process, improvements in transportation *technology* were vital. Similarly, the development of effective means of storage permitted the transportation of surpluses through time. Thus, we might argue, certain Western populations were enabled to break out of the

Malthusian dilemma posed by isolated existence in a strictly local context. The annihilation of space and the conquest of time destroyed man's utter dependence upon the here and now. In contrast, the fall of mortality in areas that are now underdeveloped has been primarily a response to the introduction of *nonindigenous technological and organizational elements*. The "other factors" have thus had different weights in these two situations; where transportation once played the critical role, medical technology and organization now have primacy.

The point is this: the different rates of change seen in the usual sequence—a mortality decline followed by falling fertility—suggest that *the successful introduction of a technological element will depend primarily on organizational factors*. Wherever an element can be introduced without seriously affecting the established routines that constitute the structure of daily activities within a population, it will have an immediate impact upon mortality without affecting fertility. An illustration to which writers have referred may be found in the postwar health programs aimed at the elimination of malaria in underdeveloped areas like Ceylon: organized and directed from nearby cities by foreign specialists, and using modern aircraft in spraying swamps, these programs have required no organizational changes in the village, and mortality rates have dropped sharply while fertility remains persistently high.

Whatever the village "value system" might be, then, the introduction of imported modern technology has a tremendous demographic impact. In Western history the organizational changes accompanying the rise of territorial interdependence seem to have played an analogous role. No matter what the orientations toward birth and death held by the population of an area, involvement in an expanded geographic division of labor tended to bring the death rate down. In addition, fertility declined when the family system had been fully exposed to accompanying structural alterations. The same changes may be required before fertility can be expected to fall in the backward areas, but, as we shall see, there are special reasons for believing that these organizational changes will be delayed in the underdeveloped areas.

The historical behavior of these two vital rates in response to variations in certain other factors throws some light specifically on the technological factor. *Any element of technology that is being considered for export to backward areas should be evaluated for its potential bearing on social structure.* Where it is evident that an item may have an immediate and profound impact on the whole organizational framework and the population balance of the area, a strategy of introducing the item by calculated stages is probably needed. In contrast, a "neutral" item may be disseminated widely and rapidly with little threat of violent reaction.

It is also evident that any modern nation that employs the gadgetry of modern medicine as an instrument of policy in backward areas—thereby inducing rapid population growth—must at the same time consider the technology of production. We cannot bestow upon other peoples the "gift" of increased numbers without also giving them the means of accommodating those numbers, at least at the same low level of living. If population is to grow at a rate of, say, 2 percent per year, output must be increased by at least that much if living levels are not to fall.

Some of the new leaders of the underdeveloped world are well aware of the obvious demographic difficulties confronting their countries. Population pressure to them is "a clear and present danger." (In fact, a kind of exaggerated fear of this pressure might even propel a new nationalistic regime into expansionist adventures.) Instead of displaying an appreciation of their population and production problems, however, we often give the impression that we are only concerned with increasing output via "free enterprise." We fail to understand that the loudest champions of free enterprise in many underdeveloped areas are members of hereditary elites, who are disposed to translate its underlying philosophy into another rationale for continued exploitation of increasingly restive masses. The latter, in turn, are easily persuaded that our policy is only further evidence that we are more interested in preserving the status quo than in helping to improve their unhappy lot.

There are increasing signs that the traditional elite cannot be trusted to lead the way to technological modernization. For one thing, it is difficult to demonstrate the supposed advantages of costly mechanization in an economic setting where human labor power is in practically limitless supply at a low price. The major resistances to technological change may thus stem from the oligarchy at the top of the social structure, rather than from those laborers at the bottom threatened with displacement by machines.

A number of considerations seem to point to the same conclusion. The *ancien régime* cannot be expected voluntarily to place enormous sums in investments that promise returns for their inferiors in the distant future. Accustomed to quick and substantial returns on their investments, the members of the hereditary elite can hardly be expected to embrace a broad program built around the hope of small and modest gains for someone else. The payoff is far in the future, and the major benefits of schools, roads, and hospitals will go to an ignorant and servile public for whom the elite tends to have disdain. If these needed facilities are to be built, it appears that a radical break with tradition may be required, with the initiative in the hands of a revolutionary and strongly nationalistic government that is not subservient to the dictates of the old ruling families. Our policy makers, however, seem to deplore such changes where they do occur, or accept them with something less than enthusiasm. Granted, every policy maker concerned with large and persistent social problems yearns for simple predictability. However, predictability need not mean a rigid insistence upon stability. We might do better to expect and even welcome change in backward areas, and to seek some measure of predictability by attempting to determine the probable directions of that change. A policy built around inducing technological modernization, then, must reckon with contextual factors, organizational and demographic, that will probably shape the direction of any technological change.

If we turn to more narrowly *demographic* considerations, we can state a number of related problems under the three headings—size, composition, and spatial distribution. We will see that the policy implications are intricately intertwined. As far as size and composition are concerned, the major problems are those stemming from continued high fertility in the face of falling mortality. Social scientists have carefully described the kind of explosive growth that follows from mortality declines unaccompanied by a diminution of fertility. Not only do total numbers increase, but the largest numerical gains are initially registered in the younger and economically dependent age range. The familiar result is that the portion of the population in the productive years is obliged to assume an even heavier burden of dependency. At the same time, restive masses of unemployed youths stand ready to heed the call of the demagogue. (One must be struck by the youthfulness of street mobs everywhere.)

The keen awareness of the population problem displayed by the emerging leaders of the underdeveloped areas can be seen in the policies adopted by the governments of India and China—two countries with a combined population in excess of one billion, or roughly two-fifths of the world's people. In India, the population question has been a major focus of the Five-Year Plans, and the government is distributing birth control information and devices. Following Marxist doctrine, the Chinese Communists long held that population problems were products of certain defects inherent in bourgeois capitalism, and that such problems had no place in the well-ordered socialist state. This ideologically based position, however, was at least temporarily shaken by the facts in the Chinese census of 1953. Not long after, the party line shifted radically and contraceptive information suddenly became available and was, for a time, prominently advertised in the mass media. Although the population panic has apparently passed in China, there are some implications of both the Indian and Chinese birth control programs that deserve examination.

The governments of underdeveloped areas that have launched such programs seem to have fallen into the "technological fallacy" which has long marked Western thinking in this area. They have adopted a kind of blind faith in the gadgetry of contraception without fully appreciating the possibility that crucial *organizational* changes may be required before birth control techniques can have any significant impact. It is widely understood, of course, that the particular chemical and mechanical devices that have proved to be so effective in the West may not be entirely appropriate to a village situation in which families live in squalor, without running water and electrical lighting. But experiments with the intra-uterine coil and the persistently hopeful discussions concerning a "foolproof" contraceptive pill suggest that many population experts are still inclined toward a narrowly technical interpretation of the fertility problem.

The demographic history of certain Western nations reveals that technology is not the sole factor in fertility control, or *even the most important*. The French peasants cut their own fertility sharply long before the advent of "modern" means of birth control. A full century's experience in Ireland presents an even more dramatic example, for the Irish countryman has limited fertility by using the exact social device that was advocated by Malthus, the one that has led so many modern demographers to reject his programmatic ideas as naive and pious. That device is "moral restraint," the term Malthus used for the deferral of marriage. These two historical instances strongly suggest that the lack of contraceptive gadgets is no insuperable barrier to cutting fertility when the social situation otherwise encourages reduction of the birthrate.

More important, widespread availability of chemical and mechanical means of preventing conception is no guarantee that fertility will fall automatically. Here some appreciation of the physiology of reproduction is helpful, for there are a number of points at which fertility may be blocked. Since reproduction occurs in an organizational setting of some complexity, different cultural practices and varying structural arrangements impinge at many points. A systematic review of the many factors that may combine to yield high or low fertility has already been carefully set forth by Davis and Blake.[8] Of course, there is no simple, easy way to assign weights to the various factors they identify, though it is clear that some of them (such as marriage patterns) are of greater importance than others. Still, the Davis-Blake analysis summarized in Table 2 is enormously useful in its attempt to provide exhaustive coverage and balanced consideration of the forces affecting fertility.

Table 2 Intermediate Variables Through Which Cultural Conditions Can Affect Fertility, as Identified by Kingsley Davis and Judith Blake

---

I. *Factors Affecting Exposure to Intercourse:*
  A. Those governing the formation and dissolution of unions in the reproductive period.
    1. Age of entry into sexual unions.
    2. Permanent celibacy: proportion of women never entering sexual unions.
    3. Amount of reproductive period spent after or between unions.
       (*a*) When unions are broken by divorce, separation, or desertion.
       (*b*) When unions are broken by death of husband.
  B. Those governing the exposure to intercourse within unions.
    4. Voluntary abstinence.
    5. Involuntary abstinence (from impotence, illness, unavoidable but temporary separations).
    6. Coital frequency (excluding periods of abstinence).
II. *Factors Affecting Exposure to Conception:*
    7. Fecundity or infecundity, as affected by involuntary causes.
    8. Use or nonuse of contraception.
       (*a*) By mechanical and chemical means.
       (*b*) By other means (including the "rhythm" method, withdrawal, various "perversions," etc.).
    9. Fecundity or infecundity, as affected by voluntary causes (sterilization, subincision, medical treatment, etc.).
III. *Factors Affecting Gestation and Successful Parturition:*
    10. Foetal mortality from involuntary causes.
    11. Foetal mortality from voluntary causes.

SOURCE: Kingsley Davis and Judith Blake, "Social Structure and Fertility: An Analytic Framework," *Economic Development and Cultural Change*, 4 (April 1956), p. 212.

[8] Kingsley Davis and Judith Blake, "Social Structure and Fertility: An Analytic Framework," *Economic Development and Cultural Change*, 4 (April 1956), pp. 211–235.

These diverse factors do not vary at random; rather, they tend to polarize in accordance with the overall structure of the family and the community. Family structure in the type of community exemplified by the agricultural villages of Asia often tends toward the form labeled "extended" or "joint" by anthropologists, in which families are compounded over two, three, or more generations by matrilocal or patrilocal residence practices. In contrast, the modern urban community is more frequently characterized by the independent "nuclear" and "neolocal" family, formed at marriage when the partners establish a new residence apart from their respective parental families.

These structural variations are well known to social scientists. Less widely appreciated, however, are some of their implications for fertility. We should remind ourselves that primitive areas are largely made up of semi-isolated and quasi-independent village communities, mainly engaged in unmechanized agriculture. Such a situation generates pressures leading to a "pronatalist policy" on the part of individual families. Manpower is important. The family is the critical production unit, and large numbers of hands are needed in peak periods of labor demand such as planting and harvesting seasons, when the diverse skills of both sexes and all ages can be employed. There is also the need for replacement because of the constant attrition of death; in other words, the high mortality of a semi-isolated village may also function to keep fertility rather high.

The contrasting situation facing the nuclear family in the urban setting is too familiar to require detailed elaboration. Obliged to be "on its own" to a greater degree, required to be somewhat mobile, and forced to assume substantial burdens of dependency with each added child, the nuclear neolocal family is typically smaller than its village counterpart. The urban family is not a significant production unit, and there is no marginal return on an increment in size; indeed, an increase in size may provoke serious problems. Finally, low infant mortality schedules mean that the "replacement effect" is probably not operative; since more children survive, fewer need to be born. All in all, the size requirements of the two types of family in the two types of community context are radically dissimilar, and their bearing upon fertility levels in the larger society can be readily inferred.

Family structure is itself an organizational response to a wider setting. Profound structural changes in the family are called forth by major alterations in the social fabric of the larger community and society. At the same time, the surplus manpower created in the rural hinterland tends to alter that fabric by playing such a large role in the growth of cities and nonagricultural industries. On the basis of these assumptions about the interrelations of different organizational units, it seems reasonable to interpret fertility trends in the West as ultimately traceable to changes in the larger social structure—changes that are mediated through the family, the agent of reproduction. At the same time, the *lack* of change in non-Western patterns of fertility may be attributed to the fact that there have been no profound structural alterations in community and society. *We may then anticipate no significant change in family structure until a different pattern is demanded by a new form of community and a new type of society.*

There is obviously nothing novel in this listing of elements; the high fertility, the large extended family, the quasi-independent village of the agrarian society are quite often contrasted with the low fertility, the small nuclear family, the dependent urban community of the urban-industrial society. Equally familiar is the idea that smaller structures (family forms) represent organizational responses to the wider social framework in which they are imbedded. The implications of this view are far-reaching, however. For one thing, the observer should first examine changes in the more macroscopic forms (community and society) and then attempt to read from them the general course of change to be expected in the more microscopic parts (families), because the larger organizational context seems to have a major part in determining family structure and functions, including the function of reproduction.

Toward a New Population Policy

There are also implications for policy to be derived from this view. It should be clear that we would not advocate a program built around the mass shipments of contraceptive devices to a backward country without close examination of the structural setting in which the majority of its population is found. Without careful study, the easy assumption that simple availability of the technology of birth control will be effective could lead only to wasteful expenditures, and our efforts might be repaid only by new suspicions and hostilities. Neither would we be prepared to endorse an "educational" program aimed at diffusing knowledge of family planning without first determining the extent to which such information is appropriate to the structural situation. We must be aware that many peoples of the world are only a few years removed from social and economic settings in which the most rational family "plan" was no plan at all, or simply a continued effort to maximize fertility.

We should certainly not ignore the pleas of governments that actively desire fertility control and that seek our aid by demonstrating the readiness of the general population to make use of modern contraceptive knowledge and techniques. Moreover, we must resist the efforts of pressure groups in our own country to prevent our agencies and representatives overseas from taking any effective action in these areas. (A modest but promising program of research on fertility control undertaken during the early years of the Japanese occupation was eliminated because of the insistent demands of special interest groups in the United States. The gravity of the Japanese situation was clearly revealed when abortion rates in Japan subsequently reached the highest levels to be found anywhere in the world.)

A policy that results in cutting mortality drastically must also include some heroic measures aimed at reducing birthrates. In line with the essentially structural interpretation just outlined, we are pessimistic about the possibilities of such governmental programs in the absence of profound organizational changes at the communal and societal levels. Although there is little firm evidence about the "best" means of cutting fertility, and alternatives are still matters for philosophical and ethical debate, the gravity of the current demographic situation indicates that fertility cannot be ignored much longer. A policy, however motivated, that succeeds only in condemning increased numbers to slow starvation can hardly lay claim to moral approval. Any general policy regarding demographic matters will also be weakened if it is wholly concerned with fertility and mortality, growth and composition, to the exclusion of migration and spatial distribution. One route to a realistic appreciation of the major problems facing underdeveloped areas is to begin with the question of the distribution of human numbers through space. The rapidly mounting agricultural densities found in thousands of backward villages constitute a formidable barrier to modernization. Migration must be considered, both international and internal. Estimates of the actual prospects for redistribution on a sufficiently large scale lead most experts to conclusions that are far from optimistic.

The considerable stretches of "open land" in underdeveloped areas have led some observers to view government-sponsored migration as a possible way out of the dilemma posed by too many numbers in too little space. It is striking that many primitive areas show an overall pattern of distribution that is as patchy and uneven as any found in the industrialized countries, where huge urban agglomerations occupy small portions of national territory, much of which is virtually empty. However, closer examination reveals that much of the "open" space in the underdeveloped world is unfit for human habitation, especially in tropical areas. Moreover, the few attempts at planned migrations have so far proved to be tremendously expensive, and the results have been generally disappointing. Wholesale transfers of agricultural populations, even with extensive land clearance programs, have been notable failures except where coercion has been employed; the only remaining signs of some of these efforts are to be found in scattered and shrinking clearings. There are strong arguments against sponsoring any further agricultural undertakings along these lines. Enormous sums must be gambled, with the odds heavily against success. Even if such a program is successful, in the sense that new rural settlements become firmly established, we may question the wisdom of populating even more territory up to the limits of a traditional agricultural regime. The genuine alternative that migration may present to underdeveloped areas hinges on quite another kind of population shift—from country to city—and not upon large-scale movements to new agricultural colonies at home or abroad. The problem of encouraging rural-to-urban migration reduces to the problem of providing new nonagricultural opportunities. Questions of population distribution deserve fully as much attention as problems of demographic composition and growth, whether our interests in underdeveloped areas are primarily practical or purely analytical.[9]

[9] For two excellent book-length introductions to the full range of population problems, see Philip M. Hauser, *Population Perspectives* (New Brunswick, N.J.: Rutgers University Press, 1960), and Ronald Freedman, ed., *Population: The Vital Revolution* (Garden City, N.Y.: Anchor Books, Doubleday, 1964).

13

New Nations: The Problems of Change

Arnold S. Feldman

Problems and Problematics

ONE of the most important contributions made by students of social problems to the development of sociology is the recognition that behavior is not intrinsically deviant.[1] The classification of behavior as deviant or conforming is itself an intricate social process. The *processes* whereby certain behavior or acts are assigned the label "deviant" or "pathological" is therefore a central focus for the student of social problems. "Social problems" are in part the consequences of the labeling processes and therefore as much a function of the classification scheme as of the actual behavior being classified. The same holds true for the study of nations as social problems.

Put another way, the criteria employed to distinguish new nations from old, that is, the bases upon which nations are classified, define how one or another of the classes of nations are thought to be problems. In this chapter we are concerned with nations that are attempting to transform their social, political, and economic systems. The special concern is with the problems generated by such changes. Thus new nations are *defined* as attempting to become industrial societies. The nature of the transformations and processes that together constitute

---

[1] This is made starkly evident by Aaron V. Cicourel and John I. Kitsuse in their study, *The Educational Decision-Makers* (Indianapolis and New York: Bobbs-Merrill, 1963). The introduction to this book by Howard S. Becker discusses this point in greater detail.

industrialization is viewed as the source of problems. For this reason we have subtitled this chapter "The Problems of Change."

Value and problem. Of course, there are alternative ways of defining new nations and different ways of viewing the problems of new nations. Assertions that a specific class of nations is a problem, and corollary assertions that this or that class of nations is encountering great problems, are value-laden. The social scientist can hardly avoid the use of such value judgments; but he can make them explicit. Moreover, by careful use of terms social science can avoid the more common value judgments and the errors such judgments may generate.

The label "social problem" is often used pejoratively. As the various chapters of this book have shown, most students believe that it is better to be rich than poor; to be sane than insane; to be law-abiding than criminal; to be tolerant and fair-minded than bigoted and cruelly unjust.

Moreover, the types of characteristics labeled as "problems" are thought to represent a departure from, at the least, an ideal state of affairs, and often a departure from a state of affairs that is "natural" and capable of being achieved. The characteristics labeled "problems" are considered pathological rather than inevitable.

In this sense the term "social problem" is hortatory, for the common property of all problems is that they require solutions. It is generally assumed that the purpose of studying social problems is to discover how they may be removed or resolved; and the nature of the "solution" to social problems is often thought to be akin to a cure.

In sum, the language of social problems is too often the language of the clinic. The value judgments involved in both the definition of a set of behaviors as a problem and in the notion of possible solutions are especially troublesome when nations, indeed classes of nations, are examined as social problems.

Nations as problems. It is not uncommon for the citizens of one nation to consider another nation a problem. In the United States, for example, Russia (perhaps decreasingly) and China (certainly increasingly) are thought to be serious problems. But what the term "problem" connotes in this instance is that one or more nations are perceived as hostile and threatening.

Nations are also labeled "problems" according to the degree and kind of national differences that exist between them and those who are doing the labeling. Such expressions as "the Mysterious Orient" and "the Dark Continent" refer to a class of nations often believed to be problems. Ignorance and ethnocentrism are involved in this method of classifying nations as problems. It is assumed that one kind of cultural organization is both natural and superior. Yet often "other countries" are consigned to unnatural and inferior categories through ignorance. Neither national hostility nor assumptions of national superiority are adequate bases for the social scientist to label nations as social problems. Such criteria of classification and their associated "problems" are excessively pejorative. In this sense, to many people almost *nothing* about new nations is not a problem. They are thought to be corrupt, barbaric, economically backward, and politically unstable. Thus, at a meeting held in Chicago, it was possible to hear some trained social scientists talk about the great corruption in Liberia. Scholars from Alabama and Mississippi vigorously abhor the totalitarian regimes in Paraguay and Ghana.

We do not mean that all the differences among nations are relative, culturally or socially. We can be aware of the value biases of such classifications without denying the relevance of the values upon which the judgments rest. Corruption, poverty, and disease are durable characteristics of many new nations—they exist to an unparalleled degree. Nevertheless, it is not the fact of corruption or the existence of poverty that distinguishes new nations from old. There is no greater commitment to ill health or poverty, per se, in new nations. Just as in old and economically developed nations, poverty, disease, and other "problems" are generated by social contexts. Corruption and political instability, for example, are both embedded in, as well as being manifestations of, a specific social environment. It is the nature of the surroundings, of the social fabric in which corruption, poverty, disease, and their like are interwoven, that concerns sociologists.

Problems and solutions. One consequence of attending to a specific thread (or threads) rather than the nature of the fabric is that proposed solutions become simplistic. As just mentioned, one characteristic common to all social problems is that they are considered to require solutions; and solutions are often assumed to be curative or therapeutic. Thus if nations are classified by their level of wealth, and poverty, per se, is considered the "social problem," there is a tendency to conceive of the rich nation as problem-free, or as "cured."

This line of reasoning classifies nations by the number of problems they have. It assumes that national problems are finite and that they can be "cured" in the same sense that individuals can be cured. This point of view has the concept of a problem-free society as a terminus. Presumably, the old nations are closer than the new to this problem-free condition.

Two incorrect corollaries stem from this point of view. One associates the solution of a set of problems with the presence of a specific kind of social and cultural system. As pointed out, the term "social problem" is hortatory, and in this case the argument is typically "become as we are." This kind of problem solving for nations ignores the primary fact that similar threads can be parts of dissimilar weaves.

The fact of poverty *does not define* the processes whereby it can be eradicated. To the contrary, the processes required to raise levels of living are partly determined by the social processes that breed exceedingly low standards of living. What may have been an efficient way of raising income levels in one kind of society may be inappropriate in another. An excellent example is the use of contraceptive techniques to reduce family size. In many new nations excessive fertility levels impede most efforts to raise the standards of living.[2] In the United States contraception has permitted families to control and plan their size. Such success, however, is not automatically or easily transferred, because the efficient use of mechanical and chemical contraceptive practices depends on family structure, the status and role of women, and the values placed on childbearing. Additionally, these techniques require certain knowledge. Even Japan, an advanced society, has found abortion and sterilization more appropriate than contraceptive devices for lowering fertility.[3]

The second error in viewing new nations by the number of their problems is the assumption that such problems are permanently soluble. Put another way, this point of view more or less asserts that societies are capable of becoming and remaining relatively problem-free, and that rich nations are close to this utopian condition. Given the preceding chapters of this book, perhaps the error of this type of thinking needs no further discussion. History does not cease with the completion of an industrial revolution. Profound social problems are constantly being generated as well as being solved.

The problematics of nations. In what sense, then, are we to consider new nations as problems? And what are the problems of new nations?

---

[2] Two major studies of consequences of high fertility rates in new nations are Kingsley Davis, *The Population of India and Pakistan* (Princeton, N.J.: Princeton University Press, 1951) and Paul K. Hatt, *Backgrounds of Human Fertility in Puerto Rico* (Princeton, N.J.: Princeton University Press, 1952). For general readings on this topic see Frank Lorimer, ed., *Culture and Human Fertility* (Paris: United Nations Educational and Cultural Organization, 1954).

[3] See William Peterson, *Population* (New York: The Macmillan Company, 1961), pp. 486–490. The classic study of Japanese population is Irene B. Taeuber, *The Population of Japan* (Princeton, N.J.: Princeton University Press, 1958).

NEW NATIONS: THE PROBLEMS OF CHANGE

Every society has certain essential tasks to perform if it is to exist, let alone flourish. Thus reproduction, socialization, provision of economic goods and services, the maintenance of order are all characteristics of the societal condition. The performance of these "functions" or the provision for these services is problematic for every society.

The societal condition is always subject to uncertainty. For example, socialization—the inculcation of appropriate norms in new members of the society—always presents a problem. Although a great deal of contemporary sociology assumes what Wrong has called "over-socialization," [4] socialization is typically incomplete. Freud defined childhood socialization as "like a garrison in a conquered city." [5] The student-reader has only to examine his own feelings about the norms of his college or university to understand the incomplete nature of adult socialization.

The genesis, maintenance, and continuing change of nation-societies are all problematic. The societal condition is at best uncertain and at worst subject to threats of destruction. The ubiquity of both uncertainty and threat are fundamental problems that any nation-society faces. It is in this sense that societal problematics are also societal problems. Such problems are not fruitfully conceived of as instances of deviant behavior; nor are they amenable to total or permanent solutions. The content of such a total solution would be a static utopia.[6]

A list of societal problematics. Societies are never static. Certain factors incessantly make for social instability and volatility. Often such factors are external, for example, the behavior of other societies. The social environment in which a nation exists poses permanent challenges to that nation, whether it be powerful or weak. The attempts of a nation to cope with these challenges represent powerful sources of social change. The external challenge may be military, economic, ideological—among others. Thus the behavior of India versus China, England versus the Common Market, and Yugoslavia versus Russia are all examples of one society changing to cope with the threats or challenges of another.

Problems of societal existence are also internally generated; the internal organization of a society is never complete or perfect but exhib-

---

[4] Dennis H. Wrong, "The Oversocialized Conception of Man in Modern Society," *American Sociological Review*, 26 (April 1961), pp. 183–193.

[5] Sigmund Freud, *Civilization and Its Discontents*, trans. by James Strachey (New York: Norton, 1961), pp. 70–71.

[6] The utopian tone in modern sociological thought is the subject of a controversial and exciting essay. Ralf Dahrendorf, "Out of Utopia," *American Journal of Sociology*, 64 (September 1958), pp. 115–127.

its its own set of internal strains or tensions. It is possible to construct a general list of such strains.

Authority, the right to give orders and the willingness of subordinates to carry out or submit to orders, is always problematic. Some sociologists assume that one reason for the development of ideologies is the justification of authority. Thus Bendix argues that much of the ideological development in nineteenth-century England was a response to the need for new industrial entrepreneurs to bolster their right to authority.[7] Loyalty is always scarce; authority is always subject to competition.

The distribution of rewards is also problematic. Alongside the problem of authority we may place the problem of equity. Although every society contains inequality, the basis of such inequality, that is, the beliefs and values that define who is to be rewarded and who is to be punished, is always subject to question.

Another source of strain is the physical environment in which social life takes place. The physical world is at best indifferent and at worst hostile to the societal condition. Because of this, the management of the environment is always problematic. Toynbee argues that this source of uncertainty is a major stimulus for civilizations.

A final source of strain lies in the competing demands all societies impose on their members. At bottom, this is the problematic nature of "social time"; the manner by which different societies segregate roles, allow room for one to "bargain with time," represents an attempt to manage the scarcity of time.

Problematics and change. Taken together, these factors constitute the problematics of a society. We have also used the word "strain" to characterize these factors. Thus we can refer to the strain of authority, of equity, and so forth. The word "strain" carries with it a problem-like meaning. Each factor presents a challenge to the continued existence of the society. Such challenges become visible in the form of societal problems. In many new nations the strain of authority may become manifest as tribal or regional loyalties and the resulting problems of achieving political integration. (Nigeria illustrates this condition.) The strain of equity often becomes overt in many new nations in the form of labor union demands for an immediate wage increase when rapid capital accumulation is being attempted, thereby challenging government policy on allocation of income.

The problematics or strains of a society and the specific societal

[7] Reinhard Bendix, *Work and Authority in Industry* (New York: John Wiley and Sons, 1956).

problems they produce are important sources of social change. In other words, societal strains provide social areas that are receptive to change. The one thing all problems share is that they are thought to require solution. Although the types of problems we are concerned with in this chapter have no unique or permanent solution, they nevertheless elicit problem-solving attempts.

These problems take the form of tensions that require management; what is meant by a "solution" to these problems is a device to manage tension. Since the strains, whether external or internal, are never fully dissolved, tension management is never fully efficient. New nations may thus satisfy the demands of labor unions, but, as a consequence, may encounter severe capital shortages; these shortages will in turn require new devices to manage tension.

In summary, the external challenges and internal strains present in every society engender sets of problems; the problems, in turn, stimulate social devices that attempt to reduce those tensions; the social techniques by which these tensions are managed partially determine what changes a society will experience. The "solutions" to societal problems, or the changing composition of tension management devices, constitute the trajectory that a society will describe in time. We are concerned, in the remainder of the chapter, with the lines of development that new nations either have or will have developed in an effort to manage their societal problems.

Problematics of new nations. Although we have emphasized how the problematics of a society influence social change, the direction is also reversible. The relationship between societal problems and social change is truly interactive. Attempts to engineer large-scale changes will stimulate societal problems. The effort to bring about social transformations is itself a great challenge to any social system.

New nations experience the problems associated with the basic strains or problematics of social life. What distinguishes new nations is that they are also attempting to transform themselves. The strains or challenges are multiplied in depth and scope as a consequence of the effort to bring about societal transformations. New nations are thus subject to a kind of double jeopardy.

New nations have before them a period of unparalleled change. Industrialization will necessarily require profound economic transformations. In addition, because these are new nations in a social sense as well as a political, many have not as yet achieved internal social cohesion. Often new nations are little more than political artifacts, whose arbitrarily drawn boundary lines reflect the power of their former colonial masters, for example, the comparative power of European societies during the nineteenth and early twentieth centuries. As a result of these now capricious boundary lines, new nations include culturally dissimilar and even warring groups.

The special problems of new nations, then, are seen as (1) achieving economic development, primarily through industrialization, and (2) achieving the required levels of social solidarity for continued national existence and development. Both of these primordial national transformations are regarded as the generators of the immediate problems of new nations.

Nations and Societies

The concept of society, though used as a basic sociological tool, does not refer to one specific or concrete social entity. Sociologists are usually careful to define society analytically rather than concretely.[8] Thus the concept of society is defined as a set of structures or a list of functions, not as a concrete group, organization, or nation. The concept is useful for studying a college fraternity, a factory, a political party, or a nation.

Nevertheless, the concrete thing, the empirical substance that most often serves as the referent for the concept of society, is the nation-state, especially the nation-state as it emerged during the nineteenth century in Europe and Europe overseas.[9] When societies are studied, the data most often concern nations; the study of society in an American university is commonly the study of the United States.

The use of nations as the main empirical referent for the concept of

[8] Kimball Young and Raymond W. Mack in *Sociology and Social Life* (New York: American Book Company, 1959), p. 28, conceptualize a society as "a number of persons with a locus, . . . some permanence and a history. . . . The broadest grouping of people who share a common set of habits, ideas and attitudes, live in a definite territory and consider themselves a social unit."

Even more abstract and analytic is the definition given by Kingsley Davis, *Human Society* (New York: The Macmillan Company, 1958), p. 52. After defining societies as a characteristic common to many species of animal life, Davis asserts "The unique trait in human society—the thing which transforms the primate grouping into a new emergent reality—is the system of symbolic communication."

[9] See, for example, the role that the concept of the European nation-state as a social organism has in the analyses of this critical social change in the works of George Herbert Mead, *Movements of Thought in the Nineteenth Century* (Chicago: University of Chicago Press, 1936) and Reinhard Bendix, *Nation-Building and Citizenship* (New York: John Wiley and Sons, 1964). The phrase "Europe and Europe overseas" refers to the highly developed societies of western Europe and non-European societies that are very much like them, i.e., the United States, Canada, Australia, New Zealand, etc.

society assumes that the concrete entity has most of the essential characteristics of the concept. The United States, according to this line of reasoning, concretely displays the analytic elements summed up in the society concept. It has the appropriate component structures, such as family, economy, polity, and so forth; it performs the appropriate functions, including reproduction, socialization, provision of material necessities, and maintenance of order and solidarity. The connection between concept and phenomenon is happily, in this instance, close.

This close relationship between the concept of society and the phenomenon of a nation is also employed in the comparative study of societies, or what is called comparative sociology. The data studied in comparative sociology are "national," that is, the data are about nations. For example, a comparison of economic systems usually consists of analysis of per capita incomes or rates of economic growth of nations.[10] This type of comparative sociology assumes that the nations involved are comparable in that they all more or less satisfy the requirements of the concept society. Although there are many problems with such reasoning, it nonetheless seems useful for much of comparative sociology.[11]

For the most part, then, when sociologists study societies, they observe nations; when sociologists compare societies, they often compare nations. The extent of congruency between concept and phenomenon, between society and nation, is often an important issue.

Nation and Variation

The assumption that nations are societies implies that nations are *essentially comparable*. Put another way, it is accepted that nations are

[10] See, for example, the long series of studies undertaken by Simon Kuznets and published as special issues of the journal, *Economic Development and Social Change*, University of Chicago Press. There are nine such publications by Kuznets. The most relevant for the reader of this chapter are "I. Levels and Variability of Rates of Growth," Vol. 5, No. 1, October 1956; "II. Industrial Distribution of National Product and Labor Force," Vol. 5, No. 4, July 1957; "V. Capital Formation Proportions: International Comparisons for Recent Years," Vol. 8, No. 4, Part II, July 1960; the last issue was "IX. Level and Structure of Foreign Trade: Comparisons of Recent Years," Vol. 13, No. 1, Part II, October 1964.

[11] Some important examples of the ways in which comparative analyses of nations can be put to good use which are also relevant to the subject of this chapter are S. M. Lipset and R. Bendix, *Social Mobility in Industrial Society* (Berkeley and Los Angeles: University of California Press, 1959); A. Inkeles and P. H. Rossi, "National Comparisons of Occupational Prestige," *American Journal of Sociology*, 61 (January 1956), pp. 329–339; W. J. Goode, *World Changes in Family Patterns* (New York: The Free Press of Glencoe, 1963); John H. Kautsky, ed., *Political Change in Underdeveloped Countries* (New York: John Wiley and Sons, 1962).

members of the *same class of things*. This assumption is, of course, not limited to social science. The essential similarity of nations is currently a tenet that underlies a great many international organizations. It is most clearly exemplified by the General Assembly of the United Nations and its one-nation–one-vote principle of organization. The existence of such an organization, especially its great visibility, in turn reinforces the belief of essential similarity.

Nevertheless, nations differ in almost all characteristics. Even among members of the United Nations, nations vary widely in size, wealth, power, and age. Such variation suggests that the degree of congruence between concept and matter, between society and nation, also differs widely. Indeed this is the case. There is good reason to suppose that the concept of society is culture-bound and time-bound. The concept originated with the emergence of the European nations within the past two centuries. These nations do fit the concept more or less closely.[12]

Critical to the emergence of the congruence between the idea of society and its embodiment in specific nations was the agreement between political artifact and cultural system. In the political sphere, this was represented by the transition from subject to citizen.[13] Government became more than a locus of power, a source of constraint or domination. It also became a basis of identification and participation, a focus of social solidarity. Sociologically, this transition from subject to citizen was summed up in the concept of "collective representation." [14] This term means that the essence of any social group—if it is to be appropriately called a group—is a shared consciousness. In other words, societies all have as a minimum condition a subjective or symbolic existence in the minds of their members. With citizenship, national membership could be conceived of as societal membership, and the congruence between society and nation could then be said to exist. For many years changes in national boundaries, whether brought about by conquest, conference, or both, were rationalized as a superior

[12] For descriptions of this process in Europe, see Henri Pirenne, *Economic and Social History of Medieval Europe* (New York: Harcourt, Brace and Company, 1937), pp. 216–219; H. Stuart Hughes, *Consciousness and Society* (New York: Vintage Books, 1961); and a brilliant book by Raymond Williams, *Culture and Society* (New York: Torchbooks, 1966), especially Chapter 1, pp. 3–32.

[13] This transition, critical for the development of the modern nation-society, is best described in Alexis de Tocqueville, *Democracy in America* (New York: The Colonial Press, 1899) and T. H. Marshall *Citizenship and Social Class* (Cambridge: Cambridge University Press, 1950).

[14] The transformation from one form of "collective representation" to another through the process of the division of labor is the center of Durkheim's theory of social order and change. Emile Durkheim, *The Division of Labor in Society*, trans. by George Simpson (Glencoe, Ill.: The Free Press, 1960).

balance between political creation and cultural system, a greater congruence between nation and society. Unfortunately, when we leave the historic and cultural homeland of Europe and the West, such congruence becomes at best problematic and at worst absurd. As the variation among nations becomes extreme, the correspondence between concept and phenomenon becomes partial and limited.

Classes of Nations

One way both social scientists and statesmen attempt to control or encompass this extreme variation among nations is to categorize. The United Nations Security Council, for example, distinguishes between great and small powers. In other areas the United Nations recognizes the legitimacy and priority on certain political issues of regional organizations of nations, such as the Organization of American States, which involves the United States and the Latin-American nations. Still other international groupings are based on ideological criteria, such as the Atlantic Community and the "Eastern Bloc." Most of these specially constituted groups of nations are more limited in scope than the United Nations and manifestly are not intended as alternative international bodies. It is assumed, rather, that such organizations maximize the homogeneity of members and, concomitantly, their common interests or problems, or both.

For statesmen the assertion of greater commonness on the basis of region, ideology, and so forth, is a pragmatic issue. And although the idea of a common culture is often invoked by Latin Americans or Afro-Asians, it is not closely examined as either a criterion for a nation to be so classified or as a prerequisite of membership. Put another way, the classification systems employed by statesmen may invoke ideological rationalization but are rarely if ever *conceptually* based. Such lack of congruence between concept and phenomenon is an unlikely concern for these politically inspired classifications of nations.

For the social scientist, on the other hand, the *concept* is the issue. The social scientist also attempts to cope with extreme variation in nations by categorizing them into smaller classes. But the purpose of such classification is not to decrease size but rather to increase homogeneity and, therefore, comparability. For the social scientist the criteria of homogeneity are empirical and conceptual rather than political and pragmatic.

In contemporary social science almost all classifications distinguish between new nations and old, between nations that are part of Europe or Europe overseas, and all others. It is, however, the criteria employed for such classifications, the differences between the classes of nations so conceived and the consequences of these differences, that concern us. The criteria of classification are both empirically and conceptually problematic. The differences between the classes of nations—no matter how conceived—are extreme and stark. The consequences generated by these differences constitute problems of an unprecedented order for all nations.

The Condition of New Nations

Up to now we have used the label "new nations" loosely and have included under this rubric various kinds of societies and nations. The label "new nations" has current popularity because it is less onerous or negative in its connotations than previous labels. Thus, included in the general class of new nations are poor and nonindustrial nations; nations that are little more than temporary political artifacts; nations that are outside the "culture of the West"; and nations that have only recently achieved political independence. Some new nations are most or all of these things. The Republic of Niger is poor, nonindustrial, little more than a political artifact, outside the Western world, and politically new.[15] Other nations included in this catch-all category have only some of these characteristics. The societies of Asia are not all new, for example, China; not all are political artifacts, for example, Thailand; not all are poor, for example, Japan. Yet they are all outside Western culture and tradition.

As we attempt to characterize and describe the condition of new nations, we must remember that our label is a euphemism for various societal conditions. Some of what is written will not apply to all new nations. Nevertheless, there is enough commonality, especially when we compare new nations with "old," to make the general descriptions worthwhile.

The Content of Change: Goals

The two most common terms applied to the class of nations we are attempting to understand in this chapter are *new* and *poor*. The special appropriateness of these designations is due to their close relationship with what these nations are now and what they are trying to become. These designations define the content of the societal transformations that this class of nations is trying to accomplish. The so-called new nations of the world, the nations of Latin America, Africa, Asia, and

[15] Leo F. Van Hoey, "Social Organization and Emerging Cities in West Africa," unpublished Ph.D. dissertation, Northwestern University, June 1964, is the only sociological analysis of the Republic of Niger I know.

perhaps eastern Europe, are attempting to become politically autonomous, nationally integrated, and economically comfortable—if not affluent.

Each of these major goals is genuinely transformational, for most of these nations are latecomers to political autonomy, with many bonds to their previous colonial rulers. Although formally independent, many of these nations receive only the most tenuous allegiance from their populations, and even when they are both free and relatively stable, they tend to be the poorest nations.

In summary, the goals of new nations involve political, social, and economic transformations. As a class, these nations have fragile governments; they have few if any bases of social solidarity; and they are not only poor but lack the means to achieve national wealth.

We shall concentrate on two of these transformations—the attempt to gain social solidarity and the effort to achieve economic well-being. Although many new nations continue to depend on their past colonial rulers, they are politically and legally independent. They are, as the chapter title indicates, new nations. The fact of nationhood, however, does not determine their societal existence: for many new nations the attempted change is from a nation to a society, from a fragmented political artifact to an integrated social system.

Although many of these nations have only recently achieved political independence, and although their boundaries may encompass quite different and mutually hostile populations, many have in the past been the seats of ancient civilizations and rich cultures. Thus if we call Egypt a new nation and classify her with Nigeria and Indonesia, we must be especially sensitive to the specific connotation of the adjective "new." For all three of these societies have at one time or another contained complex civilizations, and all three still contain elements of culture from great traditions.[16]

Although sociopolitical integration is often desired in its own right, an effort to become a society is typically paired with an attempt to become an economically richer society. New nations want to become what may be called "industrial societies." Yet there are many features of currently industrialized societies that new nations do not desire.

---

[16] This point is well stated by B. F. Hoselitz, "Main Concepts in the Analysis of the Social Implications of Technical Change," Chapter 1, in B. F. Hoselitz and W. E. Moore, eds., *Industrialization and Society* (Paris: UNESCO-Mouton, 1963), pp. 11–31. This collection of essays is one of the very best books on the various aspects of developing nations. For a description of the ancient cultures see Ralph E. Turner, *The Great Cultural Traditions* (New York and London: McGraw-Hill, 1941).

Given the economic condition of most new nations, however, their desire for economic development *cannot* be accomplished through increased efficiency in their predevelopment patterns of economic production and distribution. Economic development is not, nor can it be, a process of doing even better what these underdeveloped nations are now doing. Conversely, economic development for these nations is a process of transforming their economic system, especially the aims and modes of production, and the processes by which the results and rewards of production are distributed. As a matter of convenience, we will group these profound economic changes under the label of "industrialism." The desired changes that characterize the new nations are from nation to society and from preindustrial to industrial economy. Thus the problems of new nations are all related to their endeavors to become *industrial societies*.

The goal of industrialism. When the nations of the world are arrayed along almost any measure of social or economic achievement or both, industrial societies invariably occupy the highest rank. By analogy, we may think of the nations of the world as constituting a stratification system, a set of individual units organized into ranks or strata. The strata are then evaluated according to whether they have more or less of any given reward; that is, they are ranked invidiously. If we think of nations as individual units within this stratification system, the following characteristics are most salient.

1. *The industrial societies form an elite stratum.* As with most elites, the number of industrial societies is small. With one exception, industrialism is still limited to its historic homelands in Europe and Europe overseas. Moreover, again as with more elites, economic dominance is translated into social and political dominance. Thus this elite stratum of nations occupies the first rank on most other indices of social well-being. Not only are the populations of industrial societies wealthier than those in nonindustrial societies, but they also live longer and are healthier. In addition, they receive more education and produce more art per capita.

The quality of life within industrial societies might be challenged on many bases, as documented by the different chapters in this book. Nonetheless, the existence of poverty, delinquency, crime, and other kinds of "pathology" within industrial societies should not obscure the enormous differences between industrial and nonindustrial societies.

2. *The difference between industrial and nonindustrial societies is increasing.* Although most nonindustrial societies—or what have been here termed new nations—are vigorously striving for economic devel-

opment and growth, industrial societies are experiencing economic development and growth at a much more rapid rate. Consequently, the gap or distance in economic units between industrial and nonindustrial societies is increasing, and the rate of increase seems to be accelerating.[17] It appears that even when nations are the units of observation for the study of inequality, it remains true that the rich get richer and the poor get poorer; industrial societies continue to obtain a disproportionately high share of the world's wealth.

3. *On the basis of previous history, the elite stratum of industrial societies is almost completely closed to outsiders.* There are only a few cases on record of "upward mobility" of nonindustrial nations into the industrial elite during the postindustrial era, that is, during the nineteenth and twentieth centuries. Moreover, almost no nation outside of Europe and Europe overseas has managed such a rise. The two most commonly cited examples of nations who "have made it" are Russia and Japan. Both have had illuminating experiences. Russia started the process of industrialization quite early—during the mid-nineteenth century. By the outbreak of World War I, Russia already had many of the characteristics of an industrial society. And the nature of Russian industrialization before the Revolution was mostly European. Russian industrialism *does not* represent an exotic variation; it was not nurtured in a cultural system highly dissimilar to that of the rest of Europe. The communication between Russia and European industrialism was intense and continuous, from as early at least as the time of Peter the Great at the beginning of the eighteenth century.

Moreover, early Russian industrialization was advanced in its structure, although relatively backward in pervasiveness. Because of a unique organization of enterprise, Russian industrialization was highly bureaucratic at its inception.[18] Factories tended to be rather large and technologically sophisticated; industrialization was urban. In any case, it is more accurate to describe the Russian experience in the twentieth century as the rebuilding of an industrialism shattered by the Revolution and two world wars than as the initiation of industrialism. The past two decades have of course witnessed the rapid expansion of Russian industrial power.

Japan represents perhaps the only case of successful, non-European

---

[17] Gunnar Myrdal, *An International Economy: Problems and Prospects* (New York: Harper and Brothers, 1956).

[18] Bendix, *Work and Authority in Industry, op. cit.,* pp. 190–197 and 236–244. See also Leon Trotsky, Vol. 1, "The Overthrow of Tzarism," *The History of the Russian Revolution,* trans. by Max Eastman (New York: Simon and Schuster, 1934), pp. 7–15, especially p. 9.

industrialization. The reasons for Japan's success and especially the conditions under which it occurred are still a matter of considerable debate and conjecture. However, many students of Japanese industrialization argue that one important factor was the high level of social solidarity that Japan enjoyed.[19] Perhaps it can be argued that of the double transformation faced by most new nations—nation into society and nonindustrial state into industrial state—Japan had only the latter to accomplish.

Two conclusions may be drawn from assertions about the difference industrialism makes in national well-being. First, historical facts do not allow us to make optimistic predictions about the ability of new nations to achieve industrialization successfully. This pessimistic position is supported by a comparison of the relative levels of industrial development of new nations and industrial societies. A majority of the industrial societies were among the richest nations on earth even before their period of industrialization. These nations even then had pools of accumulated wealth available as sources of capital. Most important, these countries had already undergone what might be called an "agricultural revolution" and had more or less successfully transcended the Malthusian dilemma. (*But*, even though these were the mightiest and wealthiest of nations, and even though they could feed large industrial labor forces, their period of industrialization was still characterized by brutal exploitation, incredible poverty, child labor, sweatshops, and so on. In other words, the costs of industrialization were high.)

The second conclusion is that where industrialization exists, it is cherished; where industrialism has as yet failed to develop, it is avidly sought. Most new nations are deeply committed to economic betterment. As previously pointed out, economic betterment—especially the great amount desired—requires the transformation of economic activity for new nations. Given the low economic status of new nations, both absolutely and relatively, and given the problems associated with industrial revolutions even under the best of circumstances, new nations face incredible problems in their current efforts to achieve industrial development.

Industrialism: alternatives and variations. From some of the foregoing it appears that the problem of new nations attendant to the achievement of high levels of industrial development may well be insurmountable. It must be stated categorically that not all problems have solutions. Indeed, some problems are such that stating them in

[19] See Marion J. Levy, Jr., "Contrasting Factors in the Modernization of China and Japan," *Economic Revolution and Cultural Change*, 2 (October 1953), pp. 161–197.

terms of suggested or projected solutions may be most unreal. Even where this obtains, there is still good reason to study and understand unsolvable problems, for such problems may not be permanently so.

More to the point, problems, whether solvable in the immediate or even foreseeable future, *do have consequences*. These consequences affect many people in the new nations. The failure of the Congo to achieve anything resembling political stability does not mean that what is going on there is to be ignored. Nor does it mean that the kind of political volatility the Congo seems doomed to experience for some time is itself unchanging. The extent to which such volatility is stimulated by bordering societies, as compared with internally generated political instability, obviously is an important factor producing different consequences for the Congolese, their neighbors, and almost all other nations as well. Put another way, even unsolvable problems change; thus the consequences of these problems for all nations also change.

Specifically, where industrialism seems unattainable for many new nations, is it the only way these nations can achieve significant economic betterment? Are there alternative means to economic development that will bypass the high and apparently durable barriers to industrialism? Or is the European experience with industrialization and industrialism all that binding? Can some of the difficulties and barriers described be avoided, perhaps by learning from currently industrialized societies? Or is it necessary for new nations to repeat the sequential paths followed by the old?

Agriculture into services. There are no sure or certain answers to these questions. Social science does not know the future of industrial societies, much less of those attempting industrialization. We do know, however, that new nations must do new things if they are to improve significantly their standards of living. Certainly variations that may ease the process are possible. For example, European industrialization has been viewed as a shift of labor from one activity to another. One aspect of industrialization has thus been a shift of labor from agriculture to manufacturing. Most industrial societies have experienced an additional shift in the labor force from secondary or manufacturing industries into tertiary or service industries. Indeed, the largest portion of the labor force of the most advanced industrial societies is now engaged in tertiary or service industries, such as personal services and education.

One possible variation for new nations might lie in achieving the move from primary or agricultural labor directly to tertiary or service labor. This would reduce one of the highest-cost "items" in the industrialization bill—the establishment of factories, with the necessity for large-scale capital investments in plant machinery and attendant requirements. It might also be argued that the occupational environment of service industries is more pleasant than that of secondary industries. Therefore the shift from primary to tertiary industry might be more easily accomplished by new nations than a move from primary to secondary industry.

Many have argued that the sequence of primary to secondary to tertiary is inevitable.[20] Essentially this reasoning is based on the fact that the production of new wealth in secondary industries is a necessary prerequisite for widespread service industries. However, a number of studies cast doubt on the necessity of secondary industry for the expansion of service industries.[21] For example, many new nations might develop tourism as a tertiary industry. In this way it becomes possible for a developing society to achieve significant economic development by combining agriculture and specific service industries. For some new nations, at least, the combination of agriculture and tourism seems to provide significant increments in levels of living.

The shift to tertiary industry, bypassing secondary industry, would necessarily pull labor from agricultural occupations. The change in occupational environment as experienced by those making this shift can therefore be as radical as the shift from agriculture to manufacturing. The continuity of many occupational norms between manufacturing and service occupations in industrial societies in great measure stems from a previous large-scale development of secondary or manufacturing industry. In industrial societies the shift from manufacturing to service occupations does not tend to be radical by the norms or rules of occupational conduct and rewards and punishments. Indeed, many who make this shift find service occupations more pleasurable and desirable.

This desirability of service occupations is partly a consequence of the nature of tertiary industry in industrial societies. The recent growth of these occupations has been disproportionately concentrated in the higher levels of the status and prestige hierarchy, including communication, education, and similar fields. Those service industries that have developed demand a relatively affluent population. Thus the growth of tertiary occupations in industrial societies did not require

---

[20] See Colin Clark, *The Conditions of Economic Progress* (London: Macmillan, third edition, 1957).

[21] See P. T. Baver and B. S. Yamey, "Economic Progress and Occupational Distribution," *Economic Journal*, 61 (December 1951), pp. 741–755.

the radical transformation of occupational norms and added, in the main, desirable, prestigeful jobs.

Neither of these conditions obtains for the growth of service industries in the new, developing nations of the world. The shift of labor from primary to tertiary, from agricultural to service occupations, involves many of the identical problems of learning and adapting to new occupational environments as would a shift from agriculture to manufacturing. The norms or rules of punctuality, working under close and intensive supervision, adapting to a complex and detailed division of labor, are as highly developed in a resort hotel as they are in a factory. The amount and kind of learning necessary to shift from farm to hotel is as great as that required for the shift from farm to factory.

In addition, only a small part of the expansion of tertiary industries in new nations is of the resort hotel type. Most of the service labor currently found in new nations is employed in either exceedingly small businesses or in direct personal service; the service portion of the labor force tends to be either "pushcart" or household. In many new nations the urban labor force is actually more heavily concentrated in such service industries than in manufacturing. What happened was an intense specialization of personal services, including separate household servants for sweeping, marketing, children tending, cooking, and cleaning. Matching this proliferation of household workers is the multiplication of small businesses to the point where in many African cities one has the impression that most small commercial establishments specialize in selling soft drinks, beer, and cigarettes to each other.

It therefore appears that agriculture and service industries are not efficient enough or adequate as a basis for significant economic growth, except in rare cases. For example, Puerto Rico is undergoing a high rate of economic growth—approximately 10 percent per year during the last decade. Although tourism is booming, and agriculture remains important, increases in manufacturing income represent the single largest component of Puerto Rican economic growth. To expect that all the societies of the Caribbean could duplicate Puerto Rican experience without the manufacturing component is obviously unreal. Even to consider the possibility that nations like India, Nigeria, or Algeria could achieve high rates of economic growth on such a foundation is absurd.

Agriculture alone. Economic development based on agriculture is often suggested as an additional alternative. It is true that agriculture in many new nations is inefficiently organized. The value of land is often an important aspect of preindustrial cultures; and owning land is a significant source of prestige. Land ownership thus becomes an important cultural goal in its own right rather than merely a means to the goal of increased and more efficient agricultural production.

The cultural pattern of land and kin in the new nations presents itself in a variety of social forms unreceptive to economic organization of agriculture. Some component elements found in various new nations are geographic and social immobility; unwillingness to trade in land; withdrawal from wider product markets; maintenance of small holdings (and often, because of inheritance norms, the further fragmentation of these holdings); unwillingness to enter or use the labor market, with concomitant large-scale agricultural overemployment or wastage of the supply of labor. A typical phenomenon is the impoverished small landholder dispossessed from even tiny holdings. Haiti, Indonesia, and Egypt all represent this social structure in one or another of its forms.

Even where landholdings have become larger, many are owned or controlled by feudal-like absentee owners. In this social context relationships between owner and labor are caste-like and exploitable. It becomes apparent that radical changes in the form and technique of agriculture for such nations should represent a basis for significant economic growth. There are some exceedingly wealthy nations whose primary sources of wealth are agriculture and agricultural exports, Denmark and New Zealand, for example.

An increased rationalization of agricultural production necessarily involves a transformation in the organization of agricultural enterprise. One salient characteristic of such a reorganization is the change from labor-intensive to labor-extensive modes of production. This change necessitates the early creation of relatively large-scale agricultural units and a resultant shift of labor away from agricultural occupations. Efficiency in agricultural production is also to be measured in terms of increasing yields per unit of labor. Both increasing the scale and expanding labor-extensive production, therefore, would necessarily bring about radical changes in the social structure of many new nations.

Increasing the scale and size of agricultural units has been most apparent in the collectivization of eastern European agriculture. These experiences, however, show that such reorganization tends to encounter stubborn and lasting resistance from the agricultural population, especially in a peasant social system where landholdings are small. It is noteworthy that in most nations of eastern Europe collectivization of agriculture has not been very successful as a means of increasing the agricultural yield nor in raising the standard of living of rural populations. Urban-rural differentials in levels of living within the Soviet Union, for example, remain the sharpest of social cleavages. Predictably, therefore, resistance to collectivization remains throughout eastern Europe.

Collectivization of agriculture, whether sponsored by private entrepreneurs as in England, or by state agencies as in China, inevitably involves political coercion. In many new nations the evolution of larger, more efficiently organized holdings was associated with the worst kind of colonial law and oppressive labor practices. Such collectivization often took the form of expropriation of the peasantry and their consequent transformation into agricultural wage labor. Another pattern of change was enclosure and expropriation of tribal lands, as in the highlands of Kenya. Both these changes have generated extreme political movements that continue as legacies of anticolonialism. It is interesting to note that the reverse movement, the splitting up of large-scale holdings into small family farms, has also been a source of social and political upheaval and economic disintegration. Haitian agriculture is a classic example. In Haiti inheritance laws that demanded equal shares for all brothers fragmented holdings to the extent that agriculture was completely disorganized and impoverished. The *ejido* movement in Mexico—an attempt at the fair redistribution of appropriated land to the peasantry—has also proved unsuccessful for the same reasons, uneconomical size and consequent shortage of capital.

The proper organization of agricultural production remains problematic for most new nations. No matter how altruistically inspired, most innovations are vigorously resisted and consistently sabotaged by the rural population. Land reform, whether centrifugal or centripetal in content, whether privately or publicly initiated, whether locally or nationally administered, has rarely been successful. Realistically, the reorganization of agriculture remains a poor basis for an immediate increase in national wealth.

An additional set of problems is associated with the transformation from labor-intensive to labor-extensive agriculture. In many new nations, particularly those of Asia, exceedingly large and dense populations live on and are supported by the land. Agricultural employment in these nations is frequently underemployment, that is, part-time, seasonal, or wasteful, so that much of this labor could be dispensed with without any decrease in productivity. It might, to the contrary, result in increased production.

In a rural economy such as this, any change toward a more labor-extensive mode of agricultural production through mechanization or other technological improvements would of necessity result in high and rapidly increasing levels of rural unemployment. It is most unlikely that agriculture, no matter how greatly expanded, could ever again absorb this labor. Presumably this newly created class of unemployed labor would have to find jobs in manufacturing or service industries or both; it must be assumed that these people would be given interim aid to prevent starvation. This pool of displaced agricultural labor would therefore represent a considerable drain on welfare programs and the national economy until such time as they could be gainfully re-employed.

To sum up, economic rationalization of agriculture in many new nations would yield fewer jobs and therefore higher levels of unemployment. The successful consummation of an agricultural revolution would therefore apparently require either an expansion of poverty or an increase in the number of jobs available in other sectors of the economy. Agricultural production alone is not an adequate realistic base for sustained economic growth, and Denmark appears to be a poor model for either Egypt or India to emulate.

The Social Desire for Industrialization

In this section we have discussed some of the major obstacles to the industrialization of new nations. We have also described and analyzed some possible alternate sources of economic development and suggested that each of these alternatives either duplicated the problems associated with industrialization or initiated other and often equally serious problems. We have concentrated on economic and general technical difficulties, such as the heightened unemployment created by a rationalization of agriculture in many new nations. In addition to these economic and technical barriers, we have explained the cultural resistance to change characteristic of rural and especially peasant societies. This emphasis on the barriers to change must, however, be balanced by the recognition that there is nevertheless a great desire for change; this simultaneous existence of great desire and high barriers is true of new nations in general.

The urge for another environment, often called "the revolution of rising expectations," is frequently unrealistic and contentious. Nevertheless, desire is an important propellant for change. Moreover, the nature of the need influences the context of the attempted transformation. To the extent that the populations of new nations associate industrialism with the fulfillment of their aspirations and expectations, the economic or technical arguments *against* industrialization are not likely to convince.

Attempts by new nations to industrialize are motivated by more than economic factors. Such attempts have their source in the *rejection* of the social and economic status quo. The desire for change is also, in part, the unequivocal drive to imitate and duplicate the wealth, if not the social structure, of industrial societies. Both rejection of the old and desire for the new are so intensely felt by segments of the population of new nations that politicalization of the populations occurs. Political parties and movements consequently tend to be organized around such value commitments as antifeudalism, pro-industrialism, pro-change. It can therefore be stated that industrialization is socially and politically, as well as economically, stimulated.

Routes to Industrialization

The problems of new nations are in large measure associated with and created by industrialization. They are the concomitants of transition, social and political as well as economic. Understanding the problems of new nations consequently means understanding the nature of the changes that together comprise industrialization and the social upheavals generated by these changes.

The close connection between industrialization and the inception of major social problems is a basic fact for much of social science, with specific application in the study of social change. A majority of classic studies and theories of social evolution were actually studies of and theories concerning the processes and consequences of industrialization in European societies.

The researches of Marx and Engels, of Tonnies, Durkheim, and Weber—the classic studies of social change—have as a shared central concern those alterations brought about through the industrial revolution, the expansion of community size and participation, the new bases of social solidarity and value commitments, and the development of new organization forms. Almost all analyses of social change generated by industrialization share an awareness of the social problems associated with or attributed to industrialization: abysmal poverty and exploitation of the working class; the erosion of previously existing bases of social and moral integration; the alienation of workers caused by separation of work and home, plus the detailed specialization of factory work; and the general personal and social disorganization assumed to be typical of slum and factory life. All these social problems were indeed germinated by the industrial revolution and, as various chapters in this book indicate, most of them still persist in industrial societies. Some have become less severe, for example, exploitation; some have changed in their effects, for example, poverty; and others have apparently been regenerated, for example, alienation.

A basic question, then, pertaining to the experiences which new nations must expect to confront as a consequence of industrialization, is: Will their problems be roughly identical to those associated with European industrialization? This assumes a prior question: To what degree will industrialization in emergent nations parallel the industrialization of European societies?

Industrialization and Societal Similarity

Earlier it was noted that the status of European societies during the period of their industrialization was different from that current in the new nations; preindustrial European societies were economically advanced and rich and had been in existence as nations with more cohesive social organizations for longer periods of time. Moreover, except in Japan, industrial societies of the world shared a more common culture in that preindustrial period than do the new nations currently. Thus, despite their long history of political conflict, France and Germany shared many more cultural traits than do Brazil and China today. As a category, the new nations seem, socially and culturally, to be more variable than the "old nations," that is, the already industrialized societies. Stated more precisely, new nations are not to be thought of as the societal equivalent of preindustrial Europe. Indeed, the significant differences among new nations and the equally striking dissimilarities between new nations and old would tend to make any *general* analysis of contemporary industrialization inexact.

At issue are both the extent and type of similarities attributable to industrialization as a process and industrialism as a societal state. These, however, are matters of concern not only to the new nations, for many of the issues that engross a social science also focus on the role of industrialism as a creator of societal similarities. For example, the internal and external political changes that apparently are taking place in the Soviet Union are of great interest and involve judgments of the consequences of advanced industrialism for political liberty.

Industrial societies share some common social structures. In the aggregate, these structures constitute an empirical description of industrialism. They include formally organized and spatially segregated production, such as the factory or its commercial equivalent; a complex and extensive hierarchy of skills, such as a highly specialized division of labor, a system of rewards and punishments that fits such a division of labor and an equally complex and extensive stratification system; and an educational system capable of filling the various positions, given such a division of labor.

These institutions exist in all industrial societies, and in that respect it may be said that all industrial societies are similar. One widespread assumption is that these characteristics must be generated and developed in all industrial societies. Having this requirement in common, it is fair to extrapolate that these societies will become more alike. Yet even with respect to these institutions, considerable variation can be noted. Factories differ in size, degree of bureaucratization, and extent of automation. Stratification may vary, depending on how rewards are distributed, that is, the extent of inequality, and on which positions are placed in the most elite rank. Education varies in its accessibility to the masses, in its differentiation by occupational category, and in how selectively it operates. Despite many such differences, these societal characteristics apparently tend toward greater homogeneity among industrial nations.

Much of the irresolution over the degree of similarity among industrial societies is related to other major social institutions, such as family, polity, and religion. The uncertainty is not merely a matter of how similar or dissimilar these institutions are among industrial societies; it also includes the extent to which technical and economic structures constrain or determine the content of other social structures. On the one hand, certain scholars argue for a high level of influence of factory on family, of education on religion, of division of labor on politics. Unfortunately for scientific neatness, other scholars find a low level of such influence. They have found complicated productive systems closely intertwined with extended family systems and identical production systems extant in highly dissimilar political systems.

The uncertainty is repeated in emerging nations. Some scholars view industrialization as a source of societal similarity; others believe that the differences among these societies will endure despite industrialization. Often this single issue is a most important aspect of the political debate in new nations. In India, for example, Ghandi championed economic change of a more or less nonindustrial character, such as small or cottage industry; Nehru was equated with a humane industrialization involving economic changes that would avoid the exploitation and alienation experienced by industrial societies; the Communist party has advocated full-scale industrialization under political leadership. Adherents of each of these positions are to be found in most new industrialized nations.[22]

Different points of origin. Much of the preceding discussion concerns the terminus of industrialization. The direction of a changing

[22] For a discussion of this debate with citation of relevant literature see Neil J. Smelser, "Mechanisms of Change and Adjustment to Change," Chapter 2 in Hoselitz and Moore, eds., *op. cit.*, pp. 32–58.

society is additionally determined by its social condition at the inception of its industrialization, however.

Much of the social and cultural adversity confronting new nations has been discussed. Some of the differences stressed were the extent to which new nations are the heirs of great cultural traditions, for example China and India; the extent of internal social solidarity and political organization, for example Egypt contrasted with the Congo; the preindustrial level and rate of economic growth, for example oil-rich Venezuela as compared to Afghanistan; population size, composition, and rate of growth, for example overpopulated India and relatively sparsely settled Nigeria; and the kind and degree of involvement with European societies, for example independent Ethiopia and colonial Algeria. These factors as well as others define for new nations the starting place for their efforts to achieve industrialization. Despite some shared factors (a history of colonialism and excessively high rates of population growth), the diversity in social, cultural, and political arenas is most salient.

How does this diversity influence the development of industrialization? Most obviously, to the extent that the social structures of new nations are either contradictory or at least neutral toward industrial social structures, they constitute barriers to industrialization. These initial structures often both complement and supplement each other, presenting what may be loosely termed an obstructive "united cultural front" to any efforts to effect profound social change.

More specifically, these preindustrial structures tend to increase the amount of change required for industrialization. Large and rapidly increasing population is the most frequently cited factor. The image evoked is of a person on a treadmill who has to run ever faster to remain in the same place. As population increases, commensurate amounts of food, clothing, and other commodities must be produced to maintain the existing standards of living.

Other problems are imposed by population factors. It is not merely the *rate* of population increase that affects economic growth, but also the *kind* of population increase. Thus, if India were to acquire only skilled labor and aggressive, well-trained entrepreneurs, the assumption is that her rapidly expanding population would be welcome because the rate of her economic growth would increase more rapidly. This, however, is not what happens. Most of the population growth in societies such as India results from a decreased mortality. Fertility rates are typically elevated in new nations and are not subject to much fluctuation. The reduction in mortality is the result of the introduction of

Western sanitation techniques and medical technology, which have the effect especially of reducing infant mortality. Thus the *kind* of population increase in this situation is economically parasitic, consisting of consumers who will not be producers in the immediate future. Such additions constitute a drain on the economy.

The population factor may also illustrate the "united cultural front" effect. If population growth is to decline, reductions in fertility rates must be effected. Such a process obviously involves profound changes in sex roles, family structure, sources of prestige for males, and other allied social habits. Efficient fertility control involves, in addition, either mastery of a complicated counting system with "the pill," or the relatively high economic costs of mechanical-chemical means of contraception. Thus, as with other preindustrial factors, any given change is complex, broad in both its essential prerequisites and consequences, and often expensive.

The route of new nations. As set forth here, the process of industrialization is likely to be a shift from relatively dissimilar points of origin to relatively similar social systems. In this limited sense, industrialization of new nations is most likely to yield greater amounts of societal similarity, which means that economic and technological institutions will change from considerable diversity to greatly increased homogeneity.

It should be emphasized that the comparison made here between new nations and old is a comparison between a set of nations with varied economic systems and another set of industrial societies, all of which have developed a similar economic system. Therefore the assertion that new nations are in their preindustrial state more varied than industrial societies is not entirely true. If we subdivided the broad, loose category of new nations into smaller groupings of those that have hunting and gathering economies, those that have peasant agricultural economies, and those with plantation economies, each subcategory would display at least an equivalent level of societal similarity. For this specific characteristic of industrial societies, the similarity component may be as much a function of economic systems as of the preindustrial-industrial comparison.

We may restate this: the industrialization of new nations involves a line of development from different to relatively similar economic institutions, especially in the social organization of production and division of labor. Moreover, the line of change is described by two points only: a preindustrial beginning and an assumed industrial end. As yet our discussion of the direction of this industrialization has not taken cognizance of the context within which it occurs, or of what actually happens during industrialization.

The historical era that gives rise to industrialization is an important source for both the specific features of the goal and the specific means to achieve it. As Schumpeter points out, the ethos of contemporary enterprise is managerial rather than entrepreneurial.[23] The "Spirit of Capitalism" has been supplanted in the West by the "Organization Man" and in the East by the "Spirit of Communism." However, these available models of industrialization are equally bureaucratic. The distinction between capitalistic and communistic industrialism resides currently in the extent to which bureaucracies are privately or publicly controlled. Thus both industrial models available to new nations include bureaucratic organization as a most salient feature.

The Communist version has, in addition, special appeal to many new nations. The industrialization of Russia *appears* to be historically a much more recent phenomenon and its preindustrial condition to have been parallel to the condition of new nations today. Both of these factors tend occasionally to be interpreted by new nations as making the Communist experience especially relevant.

In Africa, Latin America, and parts of the Far East, Russia has no colonial history as does England, for example. Since the leadership of many new nations developed during a period of struggle primarily against Western colonialism and imperialism, often these leaders feel that Communist societies are more sympathetic ideologically to their aspirations for industrialization. Because of these factors, unique to this historical era, contemporary industrialization tends to be politically managed, bureaucratically organized, and vaguely socialistic in ideology. Administrative planning rather than the interplay of markets is therefore a most significant feature of the industrialization of new nations. Changes are deliberate and often centrally planned. The route of industrialization is generally premapped; but the widespread tendency to plan such a route does not necessarily mean it will be successfully traversed; planned changes may also have unanticipated consequences.

The historical era also provides new nations with the specific content of their goal, industrialism. The nature of this goal is currently represented by features common to vastly different industrial societies. One advantage accruing to new nations in the process of their development is the possibility of using the experiences of already industrialized

[23] Joseph Schumpeter, *The Theory of Economic Development* (Cambridge, Mass.: Harvard University Press, 1934).

societies for their own benefit. In this way the political elites of most new nations might be able to avoid some of the problems associated with European industrialization, such as worker exploitation and alienation. So too, the managerial class may be able to profit from innovation and more sophisticated additions to knowledge and technology, as these are developed in industrial societies, among them efficient and relatively inexpensive sources of energy.

New nations are usually economically undeveloped and technologically primitive; their social systems may be reminiscent of preindustrial Europe or even pre-Roman Europe. They are, nevertheless, an integral part of the *contemporary world;* they exist now, in the latter half of the twentieth century, created in and a part of this century and not the eighteenth or nineteenth centuries. Their populations are *today*. Their students are educated in twentieth-century universities, many of them being sent to the institutions of industrial societies for their education. Their engineers—no matter how few—are trained in modern technology; the science of new nations is modern science; their plans for industrialization are modern plans.

Routes and Problems

We have mainly been concerned with the problems of achieving industrialism. We have described these in narrow terms, including the difficulties of capital formation, agricultural development, and labor force shifts. Many of the problems discussed are related to the destruction of preindustrial social and economic structures since, both singly and collectively, preindustrial structures may be obstacles or barriers to change. To the extent that preindustrial social systems differ in new nations, so also will the barriers to change differ. Consequently, industrialization as a process will everywhere follow different routes. For example, some new nations have dense rural populations. Industrialization in such countries requires a high level of agricultural production to permit urbanization and the formation of an industrial labor force. Other new nations are relatively underpopulated. In these nations the major barrier to industrialization may be an absolute labor force shortage. Whereas one set of new nations may find population control an essential part of their route to industrialism, others may find it necessary to encourage population growth to prevent an anticipated labor force shortage.

In any case, each new nation has to face its own unique obstacles to change. The programs and policies whereby such obstacles are surmounted constitute individual routes to industrialism. As the obstacles differ, so must the programs and policies; as the programs and policies differ, so must the routes of change.

Although barriers and obstacles to modern development may be "problems" for nations attempting the "forced march" to industrialism, social, political, and economic programs can also constitute problems. Earlier chapters of this book show how attempts to solve one set of problems in American society inevitably gives rise to others. The turbulence attending racial integration today is the result of one way of handling yesterday's labor shortage. Today's increasing urban congestion and decay is the result of yesterday's solution to the problem of transportation and concentration of the labor force.

Sometimes solutions to initial problems themselves become problematically durable and progressively more serious to the nation going through industrial transformation. This regression from solution to problem is a more potent deterrent than that the original barrier structures remain unchanged and thus continue to impede efforts to industrialize. Rural tribesmen do migrate in large numbers to cities. Wealth is actively sought by peasants. But "solutions" to the initial problems may indeed cause deep strains and tensions within a nation. Cities of new nations are always accompanied by slums and shacktowns, with their incredible poverty, disease, and disorganization. The search for wealth often involves extensive exploitation.

Thus the route to industrial development, the very process of achieving national goals, produces problems. Assessment of social changes is always a "double-entry" bookkeeping process. Change always subverts the status quo, always destroys the existing social fabric.

The Problem of National Integration

In an earlier section we discussed the relationship between the nation as a phenomenon and society as a concept. We stated that many new nations lack both the historical and cultural prerequisites of the societal condition and that the very act of national birth generates the problem of social solidarity.

Almost all nations contain what are euphemistically called minority groups. These segments of the population participate, at best differently and at worst less than equally, in the national life. Independence for the United States of America did not also mean citizenship for Negroes any more than the achievement of independence for Ghana meant automatic citizenship for tribal or bush peoples. The British are still quick to describe and categorize each other in regional-ethnic terms, such as Scot and Welsh. Cultural differences at national birth leave a residue of intergroup tensions, strains, and problems of discrimination and inequality.

The characteristics relevant to ethnic distinctions are varied. Briefly, the following are some likely bases for such distinctions:

1. *Physical properties.* Among others, physical size (pygmies, Watusis); skin color; complexion.

2. *Historical properties.* Time of settlement or inclusion in the area; cultural tradition (from a more or less complex civilization); historical rule (conqueror or conquered).

3. *Sociocultural properties.* Language or dialect; family and kinship system (matriarchy or patriarchy); religious system; type of economic system (tribal-nomadic, peasant).

4. *Sociogeographic properties.* Regional isolation; urban or rural; occupant of dominant center or region.

A nation, then, can include minorities who look very different; who came to or were included in a system at different times, either as conquerors or as conquered; who have very different values and traditions; and who are geographically isolated or distinctively urban. Almost every nation is differentiated in one or several of these characteristics, and therefore the meaning of national homogeneity is always relative. Nor is national solidarity and its presumed consequences of political stability and durability necessarily correlated with the degree of ethnic homogeneity. The nations of the world include the stable, durable Swiss who display an extreme amount of ethnic heterogeneity, as well as the relatively unstable Egyptians who, despite a Coptic minority, are as a nation quite homogeneous. The value and consequences of ethnic homogeneity may be moot, being countered at the value level by the theme of cultural pluralism and the "melting pot" ideology, and it is in fact rare, and perhaps even nonexistent.

Within the new nations the strains of heterogeneity as a process may be classified as either separatist or amalgamist, depending on the conditions of national birth. This may be interpreted as the geographic inclusion in a single nation of quite different populations as, for example, the various tribes in the Congo, the Kurds in Iraq, or the Chinese in Malaya. In these countries the strains will be *centrifugal* in that the distinctive and differentiated populations will tend toward *separation*. The political and social cost of maintaining national unity and achieving political integration will be correspondingly high. Such cost may include coercion and constraint, denial of full political rights to "minority" groups, or special treatment of certain groups in an effort to induce integration. The independence of India and Pakistan was accompanied by costly religious and regional conflicts, the migration (often either forced or escapist) of large populations, and the continued problems of linguistic integration.

The contrasting condition of national birth involves the "artificial" division of relatively homogeneous populations by new national boundary lines, so that previously unitary groups find themselves members of different although contiguous nations. In Europe, this situation was and is represented by the Polish, Austrian-German, and Sudeten-German speaking groups. Sukarno claims that Malaya includes an essentially Indonesian population. The border between the Congo and Rhodesia divides a tribal community to which Tshombe belongs, although his father-in-law, the tribal chief, resides in Rhodesia. The strains and tensions produced by this situation are *centripetal,* and the political force tends to be *amalgamist* and often *expansionist* in tone. Political action and movements are likely to be organized to achieve reinclusion or rejoining of the group. These political movements are national in source; some observers felt that Tshombe's power in Katanga rested in part on the benevolence of his Rhodesian father-in-law.

Often the magnitude and importance of these strains depends on how many and which of the factors making for differences exist within a given minority. It would be reasonable to expect that those who are physically distinctive and had been included through earlier conquest, had a different culture pattern and language, and were geographically isolated, would be most separatist and thus most subject to discriminatory and inequitable treatment by the majority group. The conflict between the exceedingly tall, aristocratic Watusi and their erstwhile serfs, the Burundi, is an example.

Lack of integration, however, is not perfectly correlated with the number of factors determining differentiation. Under certain circumstances a single axis of differentiation can create intense feeling and activity. Language differences, necessarily accompanied by cultural differences, often assume special importance; witness the recent riots in India over an attempt to make English the single common language.

The special salience of a given differentiating factor is related to the propensity of the specific factor to create greater differences or to erode existing ties between the groups. For example, geographic isolation in many new nations necessarily brings with it diminished communications, since the technology of communication between regions of these nations is primitive at best. Such regionally isolated groups are more likely to develop distinctive cultural patterns. At the least, geographic isolation of populations encourages autonomous activity and political militancy. The inclusion of different groups or the separation of unitary groups through the birth of new nations or both has a continuing power. The problems are not only those that result from the initial arrangement; they may also be augmented by the generation of new or more thorough group cleavages.

There is an additional possible consequence of either the continuation or increase of the problems associated with ethnic or regional differentiation, especially where it involves the arbitrary fragmentation of previous unitary groups. Nationalism as an ideological force and as the dominating basis of political activity *is not limited* to the drive for independence of currently emerging nations. Instead there is reason to believe that nationalistic movements will continue and perhaps become more xenophobic following independence. This development would partly be the reaction of an emerging or new government to disintegrative forces. Independence may also encourage antistate, nationalistic (that is, separatistic) political movements. Independence is not likely to bring about the termination of nationalism as a powerful propellant of further political and social change. New nations are more likely than not to experience extended political instability, if not chaos.

The Problem of Social Solidarity

The problem of political unity is mirrored in the social structure of new nations. The ethnic and cultural divisions just discussed are accompanied by more exclusively social structural divisions that are principally socioeconomic. New nations tend to have systems of stratification or inequality that are subdivided into a relatively small number of quite distinctive strata. The relationship between top and bottom levels in such systems is determined to a great extent by differences between the ranks. The result is that, in many new nations, the various socioeconomic strata often appear to be different worlds rather than different ranks of the same system.

The appalling nature of the differences between top and bottom strata in many new nations is manifest in several ways. First, there is in these systems almost no middle class. The absence of a middle class means that there are few if any social links between top and bottom. There is typically little mobility between strata. Sons are born into their statuses and the assignment to status is consequently permanent.

All these aggregate characteristics—the extreme disparity of status, the lack of intervening ranks, and the absence of any mobility between them—discourage any effective or continuing communication. Hence there is almost no dialogue between the various strata of such a social system, and each level tends to develop disparate cultural patterns. These varying customs might include such behavioral mores as style of dress, housing, child rearing and socialization, and family organization and interaction, all of which make for significant and contentious differences.

Perhaps even more important, however, the nature of such highly diversified stratification also causes value differences. Each separate level has its own beliefs and unique sets of values. For example, in many Latin-American societies, not merely manual labor but all work is generally considered degrading by some members of the upper class. Variations in dialect develop between classes as do differences in physical stature; both may represent stigma.

To sum up, many new nations have systems of stratification that are caste-like. Each class not only varies in socioeconomic status but also has its unique beliefs and values; each level has its own individual speech and characteristic appearance. There is little or no mobility between classes, an absence of middle or intervening status, and consequently no effective social communication between strata. They are different subcultures.

Historically, the intrusion of European societies into what we currently designate new nations often magnified such differences as existed. This intervention, typically colonial in structure and imperialistic in function, added a new dimension to pre-existing variations. Frequently, a new elite stratum was superimposed. The Dutch in Indonesia, the Spanish in Latin America, the English, French, and Belgians in Africa—all established a new closed elite. As a consequence, socioeconomic inequalities became more closely equated with ethnic differences. In Latin America stratification reached the extreme of a Spanish aristocracy ruling an Indian peasantry. The Dutch attained a similar status in Indonesia, and the Belgians in what is now the Congo Republic. Where the "native" populations died off rapidly—as in some areas of the Caribbean—Negroes and lower-class Spaniards, mostly from southern Spain, took their place.

These artificially established elites were, however, oriented toward world markets, and through exports they participated in a world money economy. Because of this, modes of production were drastically altered. Emphasis on cash crops for export led to the establishment of large-scale units such as the plantation, the latifundia, and the labor-extensive mining operation. In this way the stringent stratification differences became an integral part of the labor system. Though these stages may be thought of as the beginnings of social change and economic development, their effect was to increase and solidify social stratification. As a result, the system evolved into a world-market-oriented, cosmopolitan elite ruling a native and coerced labor force, tribally or locally oriented, and often ethnically distinct.

This social structure is so rigidly divided that in general usage it has been named the "dual" society; many students of new nations refer to it also as a "dual stratification" system. Contemporary economic development theories frequently emphasize the duality of such societies and their systems of stratification. With independence, the distinction between the elite and all other classes becomes less ethnic as colonials are either expelled or stripped of their positions. The differences are then manifest in the inability or the unwillingness of the nonmarket, locally oriented labor force to participate in efforts to foster further development.

The presumption of dual stratification systems or of a dual society entails two major postulates. The first, and most easily comprehended, is that, objectively, the variations between strata are significant in size, broad in scope, and almost impossible to change. We refer to the disparity in the distribution of rewards such as income, social honor, and political power. Plantation labor, whether it is ruled by the Portuguese in Angola or the Negro elite in Liberia, is poverty-stricken, lacking the means to accomplish personal change and the power to change the system. This is presumably true as well of the Peruvian Indian, the South African miner, and the Egyptian peasant.

The second premise of the concept of a dual society applies primarily to the values and beliefs of the various segments of the population. The distinction here within both societies is not simply a division into high and low; it is the more cogent matter of the values upon which socioeconomic action depends, dictating not only the kinds of behavior considered worthy of reward, but also the kinds of positions considered desirable. Of the two stratification systems, one is disposed to value and reward occupational skills, market-oriented behavior such as use of land for economic profit, and behavior patterns that tend to elevate economic position, such as education, migration, and mobility. The second stratification system inclines toward valuing and rewarding acceptance of the status quo, that is, of a given position in life, family and kinship orientation, ownership of land as a cultural good in itself, and the affirmation of tradition and rejection of change. It is in this aspect of duality, adherence to traditional status stratification, that industrialization in the new nations meets resistance. Furthermore, this resistance is typical of a traditional, aristocratic elite as well as of a locality-, tribal-, and/or kinship-oriented lower class.

There is some basis for rejecting at least part of the concept of dual society in new nations. Although it is clear that unbelievable extremes in the distribution of rewards are tolerated in many new nations, it is not clear that these disparities are accepted and justified in all strata of the society. New nations do contain unequal value systems, but it is rare to find two distinctively arrayed sets of strata that are differentiated on the basis of two separate value systems. The relationship between strata and value systems is uneven.

Occasionally one stratum of the society will acquiesce to practices that contain elements of both value systems, as does the traditional Mexican peasant whose children attend a teachers' college. The distinctions of strata relative to these value orientations are more likely to be true for upper socioeconomic levels than for lower. In many new nations it therefore becomes possible to contrast a traditional with a modern elite. Indeed, economic development, as it introduces new sources of prestige, wealth, and power, *generates* distinctive elites. The differentiation of the lower stratum, however, never keeps pace. Thus the two value systems may have a parallel coexistence at the top of the socioeconomic hierarchy but are more likely to be jumbled together at lower levels, so that there may exist what appears to be a contradictory or ambivalent behavior and reaction within the lower stratum.

In Puerto Rico, for example, the rural lower classes are linked economically to a traditional plantation form of labor. It may be said that their values include the acceptance of certain labor practices almost feudal in form, such as low mobility between employers. Politically, however, these same sugar plantation workers give overwhelming support to a party that vigorously encourages economic development. These workers are unlikely to violate the tenets of the Catholic Church on artificial contraception and therefore tend to have large numbers of children and the traditional family structure. Yet they support the political party that has sponsored many birth control clinics and openly fought the Catholic hierarchy on this issue.

Economic development proceeds unevenly. Individual socioeconomic levels are affected at different times and participate in the change in varying ways. Changes in the division of labor caused by economic development are also uneven in rate and extent. Much of what is called multiple or dual stratification in new nations may be accounted for by the combination of exceedingly large inequalities in the distribution of social rewards and the uneven involvement of a population in flux. Since these two factors are themselves correlated—the lower segments are affected more slowly and farther along in the process—value commitment to preindustrial forms tends to be exaggerated.

In the West, in both Europe and Europe overseas, the divergence between social classes was *greatest* during the initial phase of industrialization. As industrialism flourished in these societies, these differences gradually diminished. The middle class as a societal entity expanded more rapidly than the upper or lower classes. It follows, therefore, that the course of industrialization changed from explicit and highly differentiated class systems to a large number of strata with the greatest concentration of people in the middle levels. Even where ethnicity was a factor, as in the United States, these diverse groups were assimilated.

In general, the more pronounced the differences between classes, the more problematic the achievement of societal membership. In the United States, even though the Negro in both North and South may be making great strides toward internal political cohesion, there is relatively little progress in the attainment of integration with the dominant white society. In Russia, though the *urban* lower classes apparently receive somewhat greater rewards, *rural-urban* distinctions are of an order that match racial distinctions in the United States.

In societal development, the new nations appear to be following a course roughly parallel to the progress of the Negro in the United States and the rural peasant in Russia. Individuation of status levels is at least as marked as those characteristic of preindustrial Europe. Industrialization apparently does not erase these diversities with its inception, and indications are that new nations will continue to be highly differentiated systems. Therefore social solidarity will in all likelihood continue to be fragile, dependent on coercion and constraint.

The Problem of Recruitment and Training

The stratification system just described will undoubtedly generate continuing problems of social cohesion and integration as it evolves toward industrialization. Nevertheless, the prognosis is that it too will change. Some of the predicted changes are described by the more modern of the two stratification systems discussed, the one that encourages a valuation of occupational skills, market orientation, achievement. Many new jobs are created in the course of industrialization.

One characteristic shared by these new positions is occupational specificity. Industrialization separates labor from previous cultural contexts; work is no longer a characteristic concomitant of family and community. The skills required for occupational performance are distinct from those of the general family or community. Skills become more specific to given generations; sons no longer automatically succeed to their fathers' occupations, and required performances no longer can be learned exclusively through imitation of or exposure to the performance capability of other members of the family.

Socialization for work is thus separated from other aspects of socialization, and specific training structures are needed. Whatever the socioeconomic level of the new positions, literacy is likely to be an almost universally required skill. The general demand for literacy as well as the more specific needs of both manufacturing and service occupations have resulted in the evolution of the school as the most important agency for occupational training or socialization.

Many newly created occupations require a high degree of training. Industrialization creates many middle-class positions that must be filled by white-collar labor, skilled blue-collar labor, semiprofessional and professional engineers and managers. Such highly skilled occupations are not limited solely to new industries, for the initiation and maintenance of these—whether manufacturing or service in nature—also depend on and bring into being other secondary or service occupations and businesses. These ancillary industries are called *infrastructures*. Engineers and scientists depend on suppliers and maintenance personnel to keep equipment in good repair. Industry requires transportation and communication service workers and specialists. Economic development thus disproportionately adds occupations high in socioeconomic status, and these are especially visible at the elite levels of the system. New nations require new elite strata.

All these changes increase the need for training facilities. We have discussed two sources of this need. First, the new positions are of a kind that require lengthy and complicated education. Second, the existence of nonfamilial work in itself produces new needs for training facilities, as occupational inheritance and consequent inheritance of skills diminishes sharply. There is a third source of the demand for training facilities. Despite the cultural resistances prevalent in the lower classes, desire for social betterment is strong. Although this striving for better jobs and higher standards of living is often restricted by ignorance of the conditions required for upward mobility, most new nations recognize the utility of and need for formal education. The desire for more education, whether for self or children, is widespread in the populations of many new nations. Political leaders often are faced with a great demand for more and better educational facilities with which to service those segments of the population that previously had not participated in or demanded formal extrafamilial training.

The number of positions which require relatively high levels of educational achievement increases rapidly with the initiation of development programs. Scarcity of personnel capable of filling these positions is, typically, great. For reasons noted earlier, the number of positions increases much more rapidly than the existing institutions can provide appropriate manpower. In addition, the pressure on existing training facilities far outstrips the abilities of these institutions to keep up. Training requirements in new nations therefore frequently suffer from a triple scarcity: a shortage of trained personnel, a shortage of training facilities, and a shortage of personnel capable of expanding training facilities.

The process of development occasionally may mean the dilution of the quality of existing training facilities. Since these institutions are in their predevelopment state, they are likely to be geared solely to the education of a small elite. Frequently new nations contain only a few high-quality educational facilities, and this same situation is likely to exist in government agencies and health facilities. Industrialization generally brings about the expansion of these facilities, though the quality of service may have to be diluted. The initial experience of training facilities in new nations may thus include a precipitous decline in quality as a correlate of an incredibly rapid expansion of quantity. As a result of this effect there is likely to be an increase in resistance to industrialization by the conservative elites.

One approach to a solution of the problems inherent in the training and recruitment of labor is to dilute the criteria for job qualification, encouraging the participation of anyone who can satisfy even the most minimal requirements. Any such recruitment policy will necessarily entail great waste as a progressively greater proportion of workers to be educated fails to complete current requirements. The standards may be lowered to the most minimal criteria: visibility to the recruiting agent and at least lack of resistance to being recruited.

The consequences of such a policy are often most visible in the failures. A common, negative assertion about subsidized education in new nations is that many recipients of financial aid are either poor or disinterested students—an almost essential concomitant of the need to expand education levels rapidly. These failures, however, must be evaluated in terms of the potential consequences of a more rigid recruitment policy which frequently wastes potential talent and ability in previously untapped segments of the population. There is reason to argue that the shortage of talented and able recruits is greater and more disabling than the shortage of available scholarship aid. An "open-door" policy with minimal requirements for aid may be the most economically efficient solution. Such a policy would consequently maximize participation in national efforts to bring about industrialization, and it might also decrease political instability and social apathy. Labor force participation in this situation may depart significantly from merit considerations, and labor recruitment may involve such nonmarket criteria as nepotism and geographic particularism.

New nations are undergoing rapid economic development. Such attempts imply an equally rapid and radical shift in labor market recruitment patterns, including the practice of allocating labor through a market mechanism. During this phase of development, barriers to entry may be considerable in that the search for work, as well as the use of market criteria as the basis for such a search, are novel experiences. Any possible route toward such employment may represent an acceptable basis for extensive recruitment of labor. Since the conditions of employment will also represent radical departures from preindustrial labor activities, other bases for the employer-employee relationship may be equally efficient.

This pattern of recruitment does not necessarily imply the carryover of village or other preindustrial patterns of work activity. The issue here is all possible routes of access to newly formed and forming structures and organizations. In this context, nonmarket recruitment patterns may have special advantages for both employers and employees. In any specific recruitment pattern the employer can depend upon a type and level of commitment somewhat independent of job and skill conditions. In addition, it is possible for the employer to make certain demands of potential employees that he is unlikely to be able to do otherwise.

The use of family or tribal members, for example, may maximize such labor characteristics as fiduciary honesty, trust, and identification with employer interests and may account for high levels of nepotism in small firms, especially in consumer sales. On the basis of kinship identification, employers may also be able to demand longer hours. These conditions may compensate for whatever loss in skill or competence specific labor practices involve.

14

The Conflict Society: War as a Social Problem

Irving Louis Horowitz

The Distinction Between Conventional War and Nuclear Conflict

THE title of this chapter might well read "Annihilation as a Social Problem Versus War as a Social Fact." The great issue of the moment is indiscriminate and unrestricted annihilation rather than selective and restricted war. Warfare, an occupational hazard of human existence, has been with us always. It is part of history. Nuclear annihilation is the very antithesis of warfare. It is nonselective in its destruction; it offers little chance of victory (or defeat); it is the negation of human history.

The vision of a world at peace, a warless world, a federated world, is not our concern here. Indeed, it might be said that in the past, peace, since it was often purchased at the price of social mobility and economic growth, was no less a "social problem" than warfare. What qualitatively transforms the situation, what gives the present period an urgent note, is that conventional war, and not only conventional peace, is a minor social problem involving, it is true, death, destruction, and agonies of all sorts, but for relatively tiny segments of the human race. In a nuclear conflict the "payoff" is so different that we call all non-

---

* I should like to register my thanks to Robert L. Hamblin, Murray L. Weidenbaum, Stewart Meacham, Morton Deutsch, Anatol Rapoport, and Gordon Christiansen for their aid, at various times and stages, in the completion of this study. Needless to say, they are absolved from any and all remaining errors of fact or fancy.

nuclear situations "conventional." Let us first note some of the more fundamental distinctions between warfare and nuclear conflict.

1. In war there is a victor and a vanquished, whereas in annihilatory nuclear conflict there is either mutual destruction or such a high degree of destruction, even of the "victorious" nation, that it is not absurd to maintain that the "living will envy the dead."

2. In war there is a trained cadre of men, organized and uniformed, comprising a fighting force called an army. In nuclear conflict the army gives way to a scientific-technological unit. The distinction between military and civilian citizens is diminished if not dissolved.

3. War is an undertaking of some duration, which permits rallying new armies, new alliances, and changes in strategies and personnel. In nuclear conflict time is compressed. Military battles are resolved in minutes; surprise, gamble, and higher gamesmanship replace courage, fortitude, and strength, separating the conventional from the nuclear era.

4. Conventional war maximizes *socialization*, especially in insurgency actions. Conscription creates renewed faith in collectivity. A well-defined enemy provides long-range national purposes. War also broadens popular interest in such worldly activities as military science, technology, and, recently, the behavioral sciences. Nuclear conflict, on the other hand, maximizes *privatization*. The shelter society, living underground for a prolonged period, snaps the bonds of association by reducing people to their primitive survival impulses.[1] The ambiguous nature of enemies in such conflicts confuses a populace about the true character and purposes of friend and foe alike. The impotence of the person when confronted by large-scale nuclear activities effectively destroys impulses to bravery, courage, and personal valor, replacing them with fear and retreatism.[2]

[1] This refers only to shelter living in a prolonged state, that is, two- or three-week periods. Brief moments in a shelter, as during the bombing of London in World War II, may actually result in increasing socialization and minimizing of class barriers. For a study in thermonuclear shelter morale, see Arthur I. Waskow and Stanley L. Newman, *America in Hiding* (New York: Ballantine Books, 1962). This might be contrasted with shelter morale in a conventional air attack; see Hilton P. Goss, *Civilian Morale Under Aerial Bombardment* (Maxwell Air Force Base, Ala.: Documentary Research Division, Air University, 1948); and for data on the World War II situation, see Fred Charles Ikle, *The Social Impact of Bomb Destruction* (Norman: University of Oklahoma Press, 1958).

[2] The most concrete expression of this double process of socialization and privatization is contained in Walter Millis, *Arms and Men: A Study in American Military History* (New York: G. P. Putnam's Sons, 1956); also see his earlier and equally worthwhile study, *Road to War: America 1914–1917* (Boston: Houghton Mifflin, 1935).

THE CONFLICT SOCIETY: WAR AS A SOCIAL PROBLEM

The very massiveness of nuclear conflict indicates a large-scale social problem. In the congressional "nuclear war" hearings of 1959, testimony was presented on the casualties that would result from a 3000-megaton attack on the United States. It was assumed that each of the

Table 1 Casualties in a Nuclear Attack on United States Urban Areas

Target Area and Weapons	Population	Number Killed First Day	Fatally Injured	Nonfatally Injured
Two 10-megaton weapons each				
Boston	2,875,000	1,052,000	1,084,000	467,000
Chicago	5,498,000	545,000	447,000	648,000
Detroit	3,017,000	820,000	593,000	557,000
Los Angeles	4,367,000	698,000	2,136,000	814,000
New York	12,904,000	3,464,000	2,634,000	2,278,000
Philadelphia	3,671,000	1,309,000	989,000	777,000
One 10- and one 8-megaton weapon each				
Baltimore	1,338,000	591,000	466,000	174,000
Cleveland	1,466,000	394,000	298,000	316,000
Pittsburgh	2,214,000	597,000	659,000	43,000
St. Louis	1,292,000	563,000	370,000	161,000
San Francisco	2,241,000	734,000	769,000	301,000
Washington, D.C.	1,465,000	579,000	433,000	228,000
One 10-megaton weapon each				
Atlanta	672,000	155,000	206,000	160,000
Buffalo	1,089,000	253,000	140,000	158,000
Cincinnati	904,000	461,000	261,000	93,000
Dallas	614,000	130,000	314,000	124,000
Houston	807,000	81,000	57,000	114,000
Kansas City	814,000	265,000	230,000	144,000
Milwaukee	872,000	151,000	112,000	189,000
Minneapolis	1,117,000	201,000	92,000	97,000
New Orleans	685,000	319,000	226,000	74,000
Portland	705,000	156,000	103,000	131,000
Providence	682,000	210,000	263,000	144,000
Seattle	732,000	168,000	99,000	126,000

SOURCE: John M. Fowler, ed., *Fallout: A Study of Superbombs, Strontium 90 and Survival* (New York: Basic Books, 1960), pp. 211–213; also see Robert A. Dentler and Phillips Cutright, *Hostage America: Human Aspects of a Nuclear Attack* (Boston: Beacon Press, 1963).

largest urban areas would be hit by two ten-megaton bombs, and the smaller centers by correspondingly smaller weapons. In Table 1 the estimated casualties in the attack areas are given for only the 24 leading city clusters (the location in each case including the entire metropolitan area). It must be remembered that in the interval since 1959 improvements have been made both in the size and destructiveness of the weapon delivery systems and also in the weapon defense systems.

Opinion, however, is divided on the sharpness of the distinction between conventional and nuclear conflict. The "strategists of deterrence" maintain that although the destructiveness of the nuclear age is unprecedented, it is not in or of itself catastrophic. Opposing this, the "advocates of disarmament" (unilateralists, bilateralists, and multilateralists) hold that nuclear conflict is absolutely and qualitatively different from anything in past history. Put in an abbreviated way, the deterrence group are optimists—experts who have begun to design scenarios about how World Wars IV, V, and VI can be fought and won. The disarmament group are pessimists—experts who have the view that unless World War III can be prevented, life on earth will either come to a halt or the "living will envy the dead."

The Controversy about War as a Social Problem: Deterrence Theory and Its Shortcomings

We shall begin with an inventory of deterrence strategies for peace and survival, followed by a series of criticisms of these policies. The assumption made is that disarmament is the only legitimate alternative to the various types of deterrent strategies, although it is also plain that disarmament itself is a vague concept which has to be studied with respect to its types, phases, and purposes.

Familiar to those concerned with the dialogue between the advocates of deterrence and the advocates of disarmament are the men who project certain concepts of strategy and tactics, now strongly influential in military and political thinking about United States arms policy. Responsible to no political group, themselves not directly involved in the actions they propose or foresee, they have developed their views into what may be considered a "game policy," the conversion of the mathematical theory of games into the political strategies involving "imaginary" enemies.[3]

---

[3] For an introduction to the nature and uses of game theory for the social sciences, see John von Neumann and Oskar Morgenstern, *Theory of Games and Economic Behavior* (Princeton, N.J.: Princeton University Press, 1944), and R. Duncan Luce and Howard Raiffa, *Games and Decisions: Introduction and Critical Survey* (New York: John Wiley and Sons, 1957).

This line of thought originated, in part, in the correct assumption that the new role of the Soviet Union as a thermonuclear power at least as strong as ourselves required a re-evaluation of the strategy and tactics of war making, no less than of the goals and consequences of foreign policy. It was after the sputnik launchings that most of this new thinking about our arms control was undertaken. Academic strategists in the United States who were previously tolerated as purveyors of mathematical paradoxes became respected, necessary adjutants in policy decisions.

The deterrence strategists recommend, briefly, the following set of proposals to satisfy the demands for national security, and at the same time to point up the shortcomings in conventional doctrines of disarmament.[4]

1. A policy of disarmament should be made contingent upon the aims of national policy and national security and not the other way around. All stages in arms control, therefore, should be tactical representations of national self-interests. The escalation (the growth of a small conflict into a broader and more violent one by successive but generally nondeliberative steps) or de-escalation of the arms race or the feasibility of disarmament are not to be decided as central principles of foreign policy but rather on the basis of deterrence strategy.

2. The United States and the Soviet Union are in a delicate balance of terror, which reduces itself to a bipolar arms race. This balance can be thought of as a kind of two-player game. Other "players" tend to form partnerships or alliances with one of the sides. As of now, "players" contribute to the symmetry of the terror balance because two nations hold the overwhelming majority of the blue chips—in this case thermonuclear warheads. But this terror balance is a delicate one, threatening to become more delicate with the passage of time, since initial strikes and retaliations are programmed to occur within minutes and even seconds of each other, opening the possibility of mistakes in calculations. An additional unstable element is the "player" (such as Communist China or France) who may have independent geopolitical

---

[4] Among the sources consulted in the formulation of this section of the paper are the following: Bernard Brodie, *Strategy in the Missile Age* (Princeton, N.J.: Princeton University Press, 1959); Arthur T. Hadley, *The Nation's Safety and Arms Control* (New York: Viking Press, 1961); William W. Kaufmann, *The Requirements of Deterrence* (Princeton, N.J.: Center of International Studies, 1954); Henry A. Kissinger, *Nuclear Weapons and Foreign Policy* (New York: Harper and Brothers, 1957); Klaus Knorr, *The War Potential of Nations* (Princeton, N.J.: Princeton University Press, 1956); Thomas C. Schelling and Morton H. Halperin, *Strategy and Arms Control* (New York: The Twentieth Century Fund, 1961).

interests. Hence a central purpose of deterrence is to establish ground rules for military armament and action.

3. In the thermonuclear age the aggressor has the advantage because of the destructive power of modern weapons. According to the game-theory principles of von Neumann and Morgenstern, a player who starts the game can score a gain of predictable dimensions irrespective of what the other player does. This increases the rate and tempo of thermonuclear arms buildup and also of counterinsurgency weapons. This places an enormous premium on cheating, bluffing, blitzkrieg tactics, and the "game of chicken," and it is precisely these "irrational" factors which disarmament approaches fail to control.

4. In view of this situation, disarmament cannot lead to a final resolution of outstanding world problems, for maintenance of the delicate balance of terror rests on the relative strength of the conflicting powers, an equilibrium that cannot be shown to obtain at any given moment. Thus arms control, defined as the maintenance of symmetry between conflicting players, is the only fruitful line of political discourse.

5. Popular thinking, including that of most disarmament strategists, rests on the false premise that present-day weapons would destroy mankind if used. "Doomsday" weapons can be programmed in the near future, but the likelihood that they will be is slim, since it is a tactical absurdity to program self-annihilation as a means of victory. Anywhere from ten to one hundred million people might perish in a hydrogen exchange, but it would not be a total disaster, not be an "overkill" (the actual population count in the world divided by the approximate number of aggressors who can be killed by the full utilization of current nuclear stockpiles), since man and his cultural institutions would still survive, however mutilated.

6. Given such a set of conditions, discussions between the United States and the Soviet Union ought to be held to provide us with the answers to the following questions: How can local or regional wars be prevented from spreading? How rapid a thermonuclear retaliation should be planned? Under what conditions ought we to make the first strike? How rapid would be the recovery rate from such a war? What are the prospects for a re-establishment of social and political hegemony after a nuclear conflict? All these questions assume that a thermonuclear war, although it would represent an *unprecedented* catastrophe, would by no means be the *unlimited* one that the disarmament experts maintain.

7. We ought to prepare now for the eventuality of a thermonuclear war, rather than to assume its impossibility. In addition to providing

clearcut psychological advantages in mobilizing the population, such planning would see to it that radiation meters for evaluating the extent of somatic damage are developed, that area evacuation programs are formulated, and that experiments in evolving chemical and biological counteragents to nuclear damage are carried out. An advantage for military policy is also involved, since victory might well be determined by which population is able to recover most quickly.

8. Finally, the problems for the period following a thermonuclear conflict are those of survival and reconstruction, problems that do not exist for a disarmament stance, which fatalistically assumes that all forms of human life would perish. Plans to meet postwar problems should be made; these would include ways to prevent violation of agreements arising from negotiated settlement.

These policy assumptions and observations of the deterrence advocates have created a stir in political circles, military agencies, civilian defense organizations, and academic institutions. Contrast the views of historian H. Stuart Hughes and mathematician James R. Newman, both committed to disarmament rather than arms control. Hughes describes Herman Kahn, an advocate of game theory among the deterrence group, as "the master strategist of the mid-twentieth century," and says, "What Kahn tries to do is to look thermonuclear war in the eye and to treat it as a reality rather than a bad dream." [5] Newman, for his part, doubts the very reality of Kahn's work, *On Thermonuclear War*, and asks, "Is there really a Herman Kahn? It is hard to believe. Doubts cross one's mind almost from the first page of this deplorable book: no one could write like this; no one could think like this. Perhaps the whole thing is a staff hoax in bad taste . . . this evil and tenebrous book with its loose-lipped pieties and its hayfoot-strawfoot logic, is permeated with a bloodthirsty irrationality." [6]

We cannot afford the luxury of uncritical praise for those who define the military realities of the present world; neither can we afford cries of outrage. The fact that so expert an authority on nuclear weapons as Jerome Weisner can act as sponsor to the deterrence policy of the NCM (New Civilian Militarists, nonmilitary advisors to the executive branch of government, the Defense Department) and persuasively argue their case for world peace should make it plain that it is not the morality of Kahn, Wohlstetter, Kissinger, Schelling, and Brodie that needs scrutinizing, but the scientific adequacy of their claims.

[5] H. Stuart Hughes, "The Strategy of Deterrence," *Commentary*, 31, 3 (March 1961), pp. 185–192.
[6] James R. Newman, *The Rule of Folly* (New York: Simon and Schuster, 1962).

In order to assess these views on deterrence (and the rival disarmament solutions), let us now look at a series of logical paradoxes in which such strategic solutions are involved.

1. The deterrence advocates insist that their arms control program is tough-minded and practical, yet they also claim prophetic powers that go into "thinking about the unthinkable." Often they do not consider basic "thinkable" factors which exist: psychological factors such as different attitudes toward war, different ways of deciding what is rational, different ideas of right and wrong, different approaches to reality and truth. Structural distinctions between revolution and counter-revolution, and between wars of colonialist initiation and those of nationalist liberation, are badly blurred. These considerations upset the symmetry of a game-theory approach. The actual social and political problems of the moment belong to a historical period designated "post-World War II." But the deterrence group (NCM) carries on analysis in a "post-World War III" universe. Theirs is a hygienic methodology that fails to tabulate the social, political, and economic factors which may create asymmetry in any given set of forecasts about behavior under stress.

The purpose of scientific statements is to make accurate forecasts. To assume a universe of two players displaying symmetry in everything from morals to weapons is to start out divorced from reality. Such essential factors and variables as the mediating function of the United Nations, the role of "third force" nations (those with an independent foreign policy) such as England and France, and "third world" nations (the Afro-Asian bloc) such as India and Communist China are discussed, notably by war-game theorists, as if all must necessarily be partners in one or the other of two coalitions engaged in a simple two-player game, and not independent variables possessing unique interests and ambitions.

For the purposes of analysis, assumptions of two-player contests in which perfect information, rationality, and utilities obtains is understandable. But most decisions at the political level are made, first without the foreknowledge of perfect parity, second without any desire to maintain symmetry even where it may already prevail, and finally without an appreciation of how a concept of public interest can be made consonant with game advantages. Thus the relevance of game theory to matters of logical symmetry is nontransferable to matters of imperfect competition.[7]

---

[7] For a social scientific critique of game theory, see David W. Miller, "The Relevance of Game Theory," in Alfred R. Oxenfeld, ed., *Models of Markets* (New York: Columbia University Press, 1963), especially pp. 265–306. Although this

Even if the social universe is considered to be militarily symmetrical, there is the matter of rifts within each side. These may take the form of a schism over policy questions. For example, should the United States intervene directly in Laos, the Congo, or Cuba? If so, what are the ground rules of such intervention? What are to be the relations between legal sovereignty and political objectives? The rules of a game are, after all, enshrined in custom and tradition. In addition, such games are programmed for a conditional victory permitting the further playing of games. The same cannot be said of intentional political relations when the final answer is annihilation.

2. The deterrence advocates often use language ambiguously. They sometimes talk of disarmament problems when they mean arms control. Often they talk of arms control when they mean deterrence through arms escalation. The difficulty seems to inhere in war-game-theory proposals as such. The concept of deterrence, for example, is sometimes employed as the strategy of the "first strike" (the ability of a nation to deliver the initial nuclear blast and prevent a counterattack) and at other times as the strategy of retaliation to a "first strike." In the work of Kahn and Schelling the notion of deterrence enters the analysis only as a response to a strike, whereas in the work of Kissinger and Wohlstetter deterrence means literally the prevention of hostilities through a policy based on the capacity and the will to originate military action. The deterrence critique of old-line army officers, who note that "if these buttons are ever pressed they have failed in their purpose," is in fact a criticism of the conventional idea of weaponry as a system of defense rather than as a set of blue chips in reserve. Deterrence may work to check military spending by discouraging any unilateral buildup in arms, but more usually it results in a mutual arms buildup.

The deterrence group have redefined deterrence to mean willingness to fight thermonuclear war. Thus the issue which game theory raises is not deterrence as such. If the retaliatory capacity of both players is the measure of deterrence, it is the key in the game of war. The theory of the first strike rests on the belief that large-scale advantages accrue to that nation-player which first uses thermonuclear weapons. The NCM thus do not rule out the possibility that our side may be the first to strike, since such a decision would upset the delicate balance of terror. They also suggest programming our thermonuclear effort in terms of split-second retaliation to any strike, the size of the retaliation to be determined by the extent of the original strike as well as the military

---

article is primarily concerned with the limits of game theory for and upon business behavior, its general relevance can be easily derived.

and political objectives sought. At the same time they advocate invulnerable (Polaris-type) launching sites which would permit a delayed retaliation and thereby provide flexibility of response.

Here the dilemma hinges on an interpretation of the concept of deterrence. Is it aggression, prevention of aggression, or retaliation to aggression? Until the logical status of this concept is made plain, war-game theory can only heighten tensions by casting serious doubt on the worth of disarmament negotiations, or even on any serious effort to limit conflict through retaliatory programming.

3. Classic definitions of warfare imply that there will be victory and defeat. The deterrence advocates, however, have redefined warfare in terms of equilibrium so that any specific gains from thermonuclear conflict seem to be liquidated. They envision the "phasing in" (the gradual changeover from conventional to nuclear weapons) of a brief war, after which both sides would suspend hostilities, at least temporarily, and arrive at some settlement. They define war as a minimum-maximum affair; that is, it is defined in terms of the number of people who can be sacrificed in a thermonuclear holocaust without disrupting the possibility of playing out the game at a later stage. Thus they think of limiting thermonuclear war, but at the same time they so confuse the concepts of deterrence as to make limitation extremely unlikely.

4. This approach involves psychological factors that have not been examined by most war-game theorists. The measuring of economic recovery rates may be quite meaningless when employees or employers suffer radiation injuries or loss of kin. The rate of economic growth is in part contingent upon psychological factors: on the capacity for delayed gratifications, on the desire to expend energies in certain directions with a minimum of returns, or, in short, on the very factors likely to be absent during and after a nuclear exchange.

This brings us to two points of even greater substance. If we assume that men cannot rationally settle affairs except within the spectrum of terror, how can we presume that "doomsday machines" will never be programmed? Conversely, if we believe that man has sufficient reason to stop short of doing violence to self-interest, why not assume that bilateral disarmament could take place before any thermonuclear strike? If, as the deterrent theorists claim, man can distinguish between warfare and annihilation, the need for a terror balance to maintain peace seems nonexistent. If, on the other hand, national interest is the basic motivating force, applicable without assurance of reason, the only alternative to annihilation is disarmament. In either case, arms control seems an unstable halfway house between war and peace.

5. Too many deterrence theorists still take a utilitarian view of hu-

man behavior, assuming that self-interest mysteriously and automatically adds up to the general interest—that what one nation defines as good for itself must also be good for the other nation. Yet game theory permits a definition of common interest only in the context of an explicit contractual agreement, a coalition. It fails to prescribe for those situations in which a coalition is not effected, such as secret and unilateral renewal of tests. It ignores the entire question of bluffing and cheating. Thus, from the *strategic* point of view, any firm decision not to renew thermonuclear weapons testing is irrational, a violation of self-interest. Yet from a *policy-making* point of view, such a decision is necessary.

If we define interest and reason as equivalents, we conclude that any lessening of the arms race injures one or the other "players." But if we define reason apart from simple utility, that is, if we view society as something apart from the modification and adjudication of the claims of self-interests, we are out of the realm of game theory as such and into social science. The aims of retaliatory equilibrium clearly are not the same as those of rational equilibrium. Retaliatory equilibrium must simplify the terms of the game and establish strategic notions of friend and foe. It must project symmetrical models into an asymmetrical political climate, and rules-of-the-game comprehension into a context of social disorganization and political disequilibrium. There is a peculiar resurrection of the classical economy of Adam Smith, in which the forceful pursuits of self-interest somehow, through the operation of the hidden laws of the market, serve the general interest. Thus in this "strategy of conflict" the "principle of static equilibrium" is made primary.

6. The NCM develop a theory of strategies based on a consideration of the mutual strengths and weaknesses of the players. For their theory to be made operational they must assume the morality of the players involved. The problem of cheating heavily clouds the worth of wargame theory. Calculations of mathematical probabilities necessarily assume that all players are fully aware of the rules and scrupulously abide by them. In contrast to this, military-game theorists plan United States foreign policy on the known or assumed military capacity of the Soviet Union, while expecting the Soviets to base their policies on the morality of the United States. How can we safely assume that the Soviets have no immediate war aims, or vice versa? In other words, how can one plan policy—contingency plans included—without a clear idea of what the "rules" are, or how they are to be enforced?

Even if it impartially considers the interests of both sides, strategic thinking is limited to considering the interests of one side at a time, and so, as in the "prisoner's dilemma," may unavoidably come to a conclusion that may be mutually disadvantageous from a strictly military position. Would such a conclusion take into account a morally valid perspective in public policy and decision making? Even if it made good military sense to base policy considerations exclusively on Soviet warmaking potentials, and to ask the Soviet Union to base its policies on the United States' moral fiber, it is asking more of the other side than we have thus far been willing to grant them. Nor does Schelling's view of establishing mutually agreed upon rules of behavior solve the dilemma. Such a consensus transcends the realm of self-interest for either side. It assumes precisely what needs to be worked toward.

7. The deterrence advocates make forecasts that have pessimistic, even fatalistic, premises. Such efforts may generate the conditions they assume and thus bring about the results they prophesy. Such prophecy takes on the power of self-fulfillment, as Robert K. Merton and, before him, W. I. Thomas have pointed out, because when "men define situations as real, they are real in their consequences." The danger of the self-fulfilling prophecy has frightening dimensions when applied to the assumption that nuclear war may take place, on however limited a scale.

Deterrence theorists claim that open consideration of post-World War III conditions can alert the public to the dangers of such a war. But since every effort of the deterrence advocates is based on the possibility, if not the inevitability, of such a war, thoughts are focused on postwar survival, not deterrence. Indeed, deterrence takes on the meaning of combat readiness, if not actual combat. Without institutionalized efforts at peacemaking, the prophecies of the NCM may become real, not because they are based on accurate predictions but because people have unknowingly accepted as fact the assumptions provided by the strategists of deterrence.

These strategists offer the consolation of superstition in place of science. "That will happen which will happen, and what is to be, we know not. God alone knows." Such a thoroughly unscientific theory of determinism surrenders a priori the possibilities for working out alternative models for peaceful relationships. Indeed, the work of Teller indicates that from an NCM point of view the very attempt to reach an international accord itself would put "our" side at a gaming disadvantage—since part of the game of war is not to belie to the "other" side knowledge of the basic orientations of "our" side.[8]

[8] Edward Teller and Albert L. Latter, *Our Nuclear Future: Facts and Opportunities* (New York: Criterion Press, 1958).

8. Deterrence thinking assumes perfect rationality and communication even in times of extreme duress. What if one power should overestimate the signs of belligerence of another power and wrongfully prepare to launch a preventative first strike? By preparing its own strike, this power might cause the rival power to instigate a crucial pre-emptive attack before the first power pressed the "panic button." Even if the military is "rational" in starting a war (because the intelligence services checked all available data on "victory" possibilities), it is vital to the NCM position that the opponent be equally "rational" and have an equally perfect communication network (also in terms of his "victory" possibilities) in graduating the level of his response. The possibility that in times of emergency breakdowns in rationality will occur is rarely considered. When it is, as in the "hot-line" agreement between the Soviets and the United States, the attention is focused on the problem of communication in isolation from the problem of rationality. Thus the "hot-line" may be useful in avoiding an emergency, but it is of dubious merit once a conflict gets under way.

Equally open to doubt is the deterrence assumption that miscalculated decisions to start a war could be eliminated, that a halt could be called before the ultimate gambit of an exchange of cities, and that both sides could then apologize and retire for a period into a "post-attack recuperation," during which time future plans for warfare could be calculated. In nuclear war it is useless to regret errors, since it is impossible to retract them before their consequences are realized in massive destruction. There is no ambiguity, no slender margin for error, no standoff time connected with an atomic bomb.

The deterrence advocates assume that even under stress conditions militarists can perceive the difference between the long-range and the short-term interests of the enemy accurately enough to calculate the exact type of attack to be expected and the power response to be tendered. However, little in the history of warfare or in the nature of men in times of ultimate challenge permits so optimistic a reading of events.

9. Although deterrence advocates claim they are neutral with respect to the values of war and peace, they do place a premium on the side payments of the conflict to society if not on destruction as such. A main argument advanced by some of the game theorists is that preparation for war is necessary for the human quest for knowledge. The assumption is that society does not accept radically new knowledge unless it is somehow connected to crisis. As evidence of this, the educational buildup which followed the launching of the Soviet sputnik is

cited.⁹ But in fact scientific discovery may or may not be connected with warfare. It has always been a variable, unpredictable calculation. The abstract concept of game theory itself developed as a branch of pure mathematics, long before the current war-game theories were stimulated by military questions. Probability theory does not depend on warfare for its existence. The use of a theory ought not to be confounded with its origins.

10. A contrast of Soviet military policy with deterrence proposals reveals several important lines of similarity and dissimilarity.¹⁰ For the Soviets, military action is subordinate to and answerable to overall political aims. According to deterrence theory, military action creates its own aims and fosters its own responses. For the Soviets, in the thermonuclear era as before, the primary objective of military operations is the destruction of hostile military forces, not the annihilation of the economic or population resources of the enemy. Deterrence theory has pioneered in the total war with total weapons. Yet, Soviet technology has refused even to entertain the concept of a "clean bomb," as the United States has.

United States deterrence experts envision a short, brief war, with several strikes, and have little or nothing to say about military operations beyond this thermonuclear phase. This is in contradiction to the Soviet theory of the protracted war. In Soviet policy a long war using conventional methods of destruction would necessarily follow nuclear strikes. Deterrence policy seems geared either to an unconditional surrender or to a conditional surrender based on a restoration of the *status quo ante*. While the deterrence group considers arms escalation a negotiable matter between the contending parties, Soviet policy flatly rejects escalation. The prospect of a conflict in which low-yield atomic weapons could be employed without either combatant rushing for its most powerful weapons is held to be unrealistic by most Soviet militarists, although there are clear indications that this inflexible strategy is shifting under the pressure of new innovations in "limited" warfare.

⁹ For a presentation of this point of view see Edward Teller with Allen Brown, *The Legacy of Hiroshima* (London: Macmillan, 1962); this same view was first introduced by Teller in an earlier volume, *Our Nuclear Future* (New York: Criterion Press, 1958).

¹⁰ See V. D. Sokolovskii, ed., *Soviet Military Strategy* (Englewood Cliffs, N.J.: Prentice-Hall, 1963). For a summary of new Soviet attitudes toward nuclear war see Raymond L. Garthoff, "A Manual of Soviet Strategy," *The Reporter*, 28, 4 (February 14, 1963); and for a slightly older but still useful pair of studies, see H. S. Dinerstein, *War and the Soviet Union* (New York: Frederick A. Praeger, 1959); and Raymond L. Garthoff, *Soviet Strategy in the Nuclear Age* (New York: Frederick A. Praeger, revised edition, 1962).

In general, recent trends in Soviet military theory have drawn closer to deterrence thinking in the United States on a number of subsidiary points, such as the mutual advantages of instantaneous communications and the relative upgrading of nuclear strikes at the expense of conventional military delivery systems. Nonetheless, there remain fundamental differences in the definition of the present military-political situation.

Whether they want to or not, the contrasting pressures on the United States and on the Soviets compel them to operate with considerably different rule books. Without stipulating the actual, empirical state of affairs, game theory applied to war may sow the seeds for the most dangerous sort of miscalculation. Each side is led to overlook the major differences in the options, directives, and goals of the other side. It is precisely the absence of agreement on rules, no less than the absence of long-range goals, that frustrates disarmament negotiations. The question of strategic moment then becomes whether we should attempt to evoke a military settlement on the basis of far-ranging social commonalities or try for a settlement on the basis of an appeal to immediate survival impulses. Raising the issue in such a way may have the effect of moving beyond the war hawk and peace dove dilemma.[11]

That the deterrence position has gained such a wide hearing may be more a consequence of the limited gains in disarmament negotiations between the great powers than a reflection of any intrinsic merit in its proposals. In different ways the United States and the Soviet Union are both witnessing what C. Wright Mills described as "the rise of the cheerful robot and the technological idiot."[12] If war-game theory does nothing else, it can alert us to the dangers of mathematical techniques ignorant of the social sciences and humanities. This separation of rational thinking from human reason and experience, so clearly embodied in the NCM approach, has several and diverse roots, perhaps the most important being the isolation of "is" questions from "ought" problems. What began as science's proud declaration of independence from political or theological edicts has, through the mechanism of *expertise*, spilled over into the totally different assumption that indifference to value issues, indeed even stupidity in the face of them, is the proper image of the true scientific mind. The deterrence group claims this attitude without due regard for its nihilistic content. They provide

---

[11] A recent effort in this direction has been made by Stuart C. Dodd and Stefan C. Christopher. See their "A Far Goals Strategy Toward Resolving Deadlocks and Reducing Conflict," *Journal of Human Relations*, 13, 3 (1965), pp. 320–331.

[12] See C. Wright Mills, *The Causes of World War Three* (New York: Simon and Schuster, 1958), especially pp. 158–167.

policy makers with carefully sifted information, comparative analyses of data, and the likely consequences of taking or not taking an indicated line of action. What the policy makers do with such information is their own business. Division of responsibility is absolute.

Who, then, is responsible? Surely there is a moral undercurrent in the method that sees the military theorist as diagnostician and society as his patient. But no single group of experts can stand totally outside society. They are part of it and are affected by the total situation, even as they attempt solutions. "It is one thing to urge the need for expert consultation at every stage in making policy; it is another and a very different thing to insist that the experts' judgment must be final. For special knowledge and the highly trained mind produce their own limitations which, in the realms of statesmanship, are of decisive importance. Expertise, it may be argued, sacrifices the insight of common sense to intensity of experience. It breeds an inability to accept new views from the very depth of its preoccupation with its own conclusions. It too often fails to see around its subject. It sees its results out of perspective by making them the center of relevance to which all other results must be related." [13]

That the overwhelming majority of men are capable of seeing beyond immediate personal and national gratifications into the wider consequences of a course of action indicates that the use of reason is possible in relation to problems of war. The change in scientific and industrial conditions and the creation of powerful weapons of annihilation have served to minimize self-interest arguments for war, which are at the center of both deterrence and disarmament proposals. Before we can accept the approach of the game theorists, we must accept their assumption that life is a game, and that players will accept the rules set up for them by others. The quality of such reasoning has to be tested against actual experience.

Historical Factors in the Game of War

Today men may hold the power to prevent history from exercising its vagaries by the device of programming doomsday.[14] But as long as

---

[13] Harold J. Laski, "The Limitations of the Expert," in George B. de Huszar, ed., *The Intellectuals* (Glencoe, Ill.: The Free Press, 1960).

[14] This should not be confused with a "doomsday machine," a hypothetical device to destroy the earth under prearranged conditions. Connected to a computer, the thus far *imaginary* machine would be triggered automatically as a countermeasure to a sizable attack on a country. According to RAND Corporation theorists, such a machine could be built within a decade. But doomsday in its more generic meaning as "overkill" is already upon us.

anything short of total annihilation is contemplated, or acted upon, the historical muse will be with us. In the following discussion I shall try to show how this is true, and why historical judgment largely invalidates policies derived exclusively from military gamesmanship.

Much deterrence analysis is based on a disguised appeal to historical pessimism. "Thinking about the unthinkable," the designing of scenarios predicated on negative events, and the simulation, under various control situations, of post-World War III conditions, while clearly postulating future contingencies, are done in a style that prohibits the serious scientific study of political events.[15] To define how men will behave under conditions of maximum tension and strain is not to take seriously the capacity of men to adjust to such conditions.

In the early 1960s we have seen pessimistic literature and films concerned with accidental war (*Fail-Safe, Dr. Strangelove,* and so forth). They tend to show the world in apocalyptic terms of a technological apparatus run wild and generals gone mad. But they do not provide awareness of the political and historical conditions in which the use of such military hardware is contemplated. The problem of World War III has little to do with accidental wars; it has a great deal to do with designed and perhaps even desired wars.

The likelihood of technological "accidents" leading to all-out Armageddon is slim, not simply because padlocking devices are constantly improving (which is so), and not simply because generals are much more knowing and rational than the outsider sometimes imagines, but because the traditional problems confronting mankind are being dealt with more seriously than ever before. The political world is undergoing a steady redefinition of "reality": old "enemies" are becoming new "friends"; the definition of political and social systems is undergoing a process of sophistication thought unlikely a decade ago; modalities of trust, cooperation, and agreement are being entered into now, precisely because both sides to the Cold War see themselves as potential long-range victors. To the degree that the United States and the Soviet Union continue to define the future in optimistic terms, the possibility of "accidental war" diminishes, and the technological means of destruction become subject to mutual agreement. Without an explicit agreement, however, the nuclear standoff creates the basis for increased small-scale wars.

What permits an analysis of the military situation in terms of a two-sided relationship is not simply the conventions of a non-zero-sum

---

[15] This is the chief difficulty in Herman Kahn's *On Thermonuclear War* (Princeton, N.J.: Princeton University Press, 1960) and *Thinking about the Unthinkable* (New York: Horizon Press, 1962).

Table 2 Total Mobilized Armed Forces, July 1963, in Thousands

	Nato Powers					East European Powers				
Country	Army	Navy	Air Force	Total	Country		Army	Navy	Air Force	Total
United States	950	850	885	2685	U.S.S.R.		2300	500	500	3300
France	500	68	137	705	Poland		200	12	45	257
Italy	360	40	60	460	Romania		200	7	20	227
Turkey	400	35	20	455	Czechoslovakia		150	0	35	185
United Kingdom	170	100	145	415	Bulgaria		110	5	20	135
Germany	270	25	83	378	E. Germany		80	11	15	106
Greece	160	17	22	199	Hungary		90	0	9	99
Netherlands	98	23	20	141	Albania		25	3	7	35
Canada	50	22	52	124						
Belgium	85	5	20	110						
Portugal	58	10	12	80						
Denmark	29	7	7	43						
Norway	18	6	10	34						
Luxembourg	5	—	—	5						
Total	3153	1208	1473	5834	Total		3155	538	651	4344

SOURCE: The Institute for Strategic Studies, *Disarmament and European Security: The Effect of Implementing the First Stage of the Soviet Draft Treaty and the United States Proposals*, Vol. II (Tables) (London: Institute for Strategic Studies, 1963).

THE CONFLICT SOCIETY: WAR AS A SOCIAL PROBLEM   713

game, but the actual symmetry in nuclear power between the Western and Soviet bloc nations. This can most easily be seen in a comparison of the total mobilized armed forces (Table 2). Of course, this comparison of *men* does not exhaust the symmetry. An immense amount of *hardware*, enough to "overkill" total populations from 100 to 1000 times, is in the possession of both blocs.[16]

We spoke earlier of the delicate balance of terror, but the present situation is better defined by mutual expectation of long-range victory. There are several powerful reasons for asserting that human survival can never rest on a terror balance. First, any sort of small-scale military action can quickly "escalate" into a general conflict. A serious deterioration of the situation in Southeast Asia could bring into play major nuclear powers on both sides. Second, the absence of a satisfactory nuclear control system, and the heavy emphasis on big-power control in the face of a widening nuclear spread, signifies that even if there is a symmetry in weapons systems, there is no corresponding symmetry in control or dispersion systems. Third, the more we emphasize a peace based on mutual deterrence, the more we must expect a mutual hardening of positions and postures, even when mitigating political factors are present. Fourth, as long as deterrence through maximum weapons systems remains the basis of peace, there is the steady danger of war, either through technical accident or political miscalculation. Thus the model of the world derived from and built upon war-game analogies is bound to run afoul of an essentially asymmetrical world situation.

Both "sides" in the Cold War must perceive the situation in optimistic terms to make survivability worthwhile and inexpensive.[17] If either major force in the Cold War perceived the situation otherwise, thought that "things were going badly," and continued in the same negative direction, the restraints against an all-out military confrontation would be sharply lessened, and the present sluggish arms race would be intensified tenfold.

The Soviet Union, operating as it does within the Marxian doctrine of the historical inevitability of socialism, has optimism built into its calculations irrespective of short-run defeats. It can always translate objective defeats into temporary setbacks. The United States, lacking a State ideology, cannot proceed with quite the same degree of historical assurance. Indeed, the constant assaults on infallible philosophies of his-

---

[16] See Herman Kahn, "The Arms Race and Some of Its Hazards," in D. G. Brennan, ed., *Arms Control, Disarmament, and National Security* (New York: George Braziller, 1961), pp. 89–121.

[17] See T. C. O'Sullivan, "Weapons and Technology, 1964," *Current History*, 47, 275 (July 1964), pp. 6–11.

tory have made the direct appeal to historical optimism not only politically risky but intellectually disreputable. Yet the underpinnings of "the new frontier" or "the war on poverty" do rest on an optimistic reading of the future, including an image of Soviet behavior permitting survival.[18]

However, perceptions of the situation have to be based on "real" indices of victory. These are present in increasing abundance. The United States can claim that the cultural exchange program with the Soviet Union has proved the superiority of the "American way" by the tremendous positive responses of Soviet audiences to everything Western—from Leonard Bernstein to Benny Goodman. Thus, from the official American point of view, continued cultural contacts work to its advantage in the long run. The Soviets, for their part, can perceive the same sorts of cultural contacts as a victory of socialist culture over decadence. The favorable receptions of the Moisseyev Dancers or the Bolshoi Ballet can be interpreted by the Soviets as a hunger on the part of Americans for something different and better than commercialized culture—which ostensibly only a socialist society can provide.

The same sort of "peaceful competition" can be seen at work in the achievements of science and technology in the United States and the Soviet Union. The frequent resort to phrases such as "Soviet science" and "American ingenuity" are strong indications that there is a convergent optimism regarding the future of everything from space technology to experimental psychology. In answer to the question what kind of man is the American man (or Soviet man), the responses have become increasingly similar: free thinking, unrestrained in the uses of imagination, cooperative in the style of work, dedicated to the victory of abundance over poverty, and so forth. Both sides have made powerful claims that the organization of science and technology in their respective countries proves, beyond a shadow of a doubt, the superiority of one system over another. The Soviets may emphasize different features: the rational planning of industrial activities, the absence of waste in factory production, and the coordination of managerial functions. The Americans may emphasize with equal sincerity its distinctive features: high rates of pay for scientific and technological work, experimental attitudes of scientific workers, organizational innovation in factory management, and the self-imposed dedication to hard work of the American scientist.

Whether or not there is an actual conveyance of living styles and

---

[18] See, for example, William A. Gamson and Andrea Modigliani, "Competing Images of Soviet Behavior," International Conflict Study, Working Document 9, University of Michigan, mimeographed, August 1964.

work styles between the United States and the Soviet Union, there is a convergence of historical perception; both sides claim to have produced a superior social system no less than a superior scientific technology.

This kind of historical optimism is not restricted to areas of survival perspectives but extends into areas of military confrontation. The Cuban missile crisis of October 1962 witnessed the astonishing fact of both the United States and the Soviet Union claiming undiluted victory. Nor ought we to imagine that these claimed victories are conjurors' tricks, devices ordered by propaganda chiefs who know better. Both sides could perceive real victory, simply by the relative weighting given to various factors in the Cuban crisis. More importantly, what this shows is that historical optimism is not the special preserve of any one side or any single ideological posture.

We do mean that such optimism is a unique variable. It may be that optimism about future victory in the Cold War through nonmilitary means is a function of faith in education. It may also be that such optimism is conditioned by the high stakes of different social elements. Thus the young generation may be much more disposed to negotiated settlement than older generations, because they have more to risk. It may also be that those generally disposed to political action will be less apocalyptic in crisis situations, and less prone to seek quick military solutions. The optimism of one power may also be generated by a common fear of yet a third power. But these sociological variables, although significant as indices of public opinion, must be considered secondary in the light of the formation of social and political policy. In public surveys numbers count. But these same numbers are weighted differently on a scale of class and power. Thus we may dispense with the argument that historical optimism is simply a consequence of public sentiment at any given point in time.

Historical optimism is quite possible within a realistic political perspective. Thus the late President Kennedy could stimulate optimism despite his blanket acknowledgment of the Bay of Pigs disaster. This point might be generalized as follows: charisma is the capacity of leadership to snatch victory out of defeat by candidly admitting failures and shortcomings, while at the same time generating the sort of optimistic vision of the future which prevents any major internal catastrophe. Put in more conventional terms, "realism" is consonant with either an optimistic or pessimistic reading of social events. Because this is the case, the function of optimism (or pessimism) as a guide to policy is not necessarily impaired by the actual direction of any event.

Where, then, does the immediate threat of war come from? In great part the answer seems to lie in a negative attitude, in the perception of the world as going "bad for us" when something drastic is not achieved. Stalinism carried the disease of the conspiratorial theory to new heights by perceiving the Soviet Union as surrounded by a ring of enemy bases poised to strike at Soviet soil the minute Soviet military vigilance was minimized. On this basis all sorts of internal repression was justified and rationalized, and the Soviet Union accelerated its arms production far beyond the comparable buildup of the Western powers during the period from 1945 to 1955. McCarthyism rested in part on defining the world exactly in terms of the Soviet image of things. Every national liberation effort in Africa, Asia, or Latin America came to be interpreted via historical pessimism as a defeat for the United States and its interests. The policies of "roll-back" (in the late 1940s), of "brinkmanship" (in the 1950s), and now of "fortress America" all rest on a pessimistic perception of historical events, more specifically, on a universe which can be manipulated by any one nation. Things are going badly for us, and therefore "something must be done." The risks of war are higher when this pessimistic reading of events is present.[19]

When the Soviet Union launched the first earth satellite, Americans responded on a large scale—not simply because of the shock of recognition involved, that Soviet science and Soviet society were open enough and resilient enough to permit such advances, but because they looked pessimistically at the event. The similar advances of the United States in manned fighter-bombers has also provoked a dangerous pessimism on the part of the Soviet Union. But thus far the upsetting of the balance of nuclear terror has led one side to reinforce its optimism and the other to become pessimistic. Where pessimism seems mutual, as in the Berlin crisis, with both sides absolutely determined to maintain their respective positions at all costs—the Soviets insistent on their dominion over Berlin and the access ways to the city, and the Americans equally insistent over the free status of the city and the rights of unimpeded access to it—any deterioration of the status quo would cause anxiety and, in turn, more pessimism. It is this, rather than any imaginary nuclear advantage, which could easily trigger World War III. The optimism generated over even a temporary edge in military hardware or delivery systems has not, and probably will not, of itself generate any military adventurism. But given an intractable polit-

---

[19] The appreciation of this is what underlies the position of the late Leo Szilard. See his "Minimal Deterrent vs. Saturation Parity," *Bulletin of the Atomic Scientists*, 20, 3 (March 1964), pp. 11–12.

ical context, such as Berlin, even the power having less "overkill" can easily be provoked into a precipitous military action. What this points to is the continuing relevance of politics based on historical judgment in the study of the Cold War.

Mutual pessimism may generate peace through an inverse process of mutual fear. There may, for example, be an increasing and shared fear on the part of the United States and the Soviet Union that a military threat equal to that of the contracting partners may actually be imminent, for example, the French *force de frappe* (their nuclear "striking force") and the Chinese drive for an independent nuclear weapons system, and hence this fear will generate a spirit of cooperation between the major powers not possible at an earlier historical stage. But such a mutual pessimism about the nuclear power problem, or an increasing fear of unacceptable forms of mass destruction (such as bacteriological or chemical warfare, or use of thermonuclear devices beyond a certain megatonnage), although offering the possibilities of freezing present military postures, or even of a limited arms agreement, cannot be effectively pursued until and unless the United States and the Soviet Union can perceive the definite advantages to themselves by so doing. In turn, the problem again becomes one of historical judgment, beyond the range of deterrence theory.

History no longer exists as the mischievous thief operating behind the backs of men, for the simple reason that men can stop history in its tracks by massive nuclear detonations. Insofar as such ultimate recourse is not relied upon, history is still an operational factor in the lives of men and in the judgment of nations. Historical optimism could become a viable instrument in transforming sentiments of mutual fear into those of shared victory. Historical pessimism can, in the meantime, witness such mutual fears only degenerating into devil-take-the-hindmost attitudes, which can have no logic other than that of total decimation of self as well as others.

It is difficult to deny that the sort of mechanical and contrived strategic thinking we have grown accustomed to has led us into grotesque decisions of major importance. For example, decisions continue to be made as if the Chinese Communists were rapacious beasts intent upon swallowing up enemy shores, as if the second largest land mass on this earth were thirsting for more land. Conveniently forgotten is Chinese Communist military caution in the face of all sorts of opportunities—from Vietnam to Formosa. The India border disputes never became more than that, despite the overwhelming superiority of Chinese arms and manpower. Is it not an entertainable hypothesis that the traditional

Chinese virtue of patience combined with the Communist Chinese faith in ultimate historical success forestalls any precipitous behavior —whether or not they have a nuclear deterrent?

Might not the French posture of the 1960s also be grounded in something considerably more substantive than the dreams of a gallant old soldier? Is it not possible that the French position too is based on an optimistic reading of the immediate future? The great speed with which France has become the leader of the European Economic Community, the speedy revitalization of trade with former colonial nations such as Algeria, the reopening of the Southeast Asia trade market to French business interests, the development of a potent, if minimal, nuclear striking force—are not these objective signs of historical optimism? [20]

Whether historical optimism is warrantable or not, its very presence in the policy-making apparatus of the great powers is a cause for cautious optimism. It has a profound effect on the organizational-bureaucratic apparatus of the contending societies. There is no doubt that the "thaw" in the Soviet Union is directly linked to the relative easing of war hysteria over United States intentions. In American society there has also been a constant, if slow, diminishing of political repression and tests of loyalty.[21]

It is not being suggested that historical optimism can continue to affect policy decisions without some corresponding set of objective circumstances. But given the common denominator of superordinate goals which are shared by the contracting powers, there is sufficient elasticity in historical judgment for each side to claim long-run victories. The very ambiguity in the concept of "long run" is itself a central feature enabling both sides in the Cold War to claim victory as inevitable. Unlike a game of chance, the game of war contains such a wide-ranging latitude of choices—in defining the situation no less than in defining the consequences of a conflict—that both sides can be "right." [22]

The danger of an accidental war arising from a misreading of the maneuvering of one party decreases in proportion to a nation's judg-

---

[20] To be sure, it might well be that this optimism about the future is triggered by some powerful memories of failure in the past. See Alphonse Juin, *Trois siècles d'obéissance militaire: 1650–1963* (Paris: Librairie Plon, 1964). But this does not alter the position herein taken.

[21] See on this Harold P. Green, "Q-Clearance: The Development of a Personnel Security Program," *Bulletin of the Atomic Scientists*, 20, 5 (May 1964), pp. 9–15.

[22] See, for example, the long checklist in Annex II—Civil Defense and Arms Control Objectives in Raymond D. Gastil, *Arms Control and Civil Defense* (New York: Hudson Institute, Inc., August 20, 1963) (HI-216-RR/11).

ment that a nonmilitary solution is to its advantage. High-stakes gambling, in contrast, is stimulated by a belief that the gamble, or the bluff, is all that is left, and that win or lose, it is better to play than not to play. When such a pattern of behavior is manifested by an individual, we tend to term it pathological. The gambler prepared to risk everything on one throw of the dice is a potential suicide (or homicide). His reading of objective events has compelled him, probably erroneously, to conclude that no other alternatives for survival exist than an all-out, all-or-nothing approach.

Politics and Militarism in American Society

Expressions of antiwar sentiment are intrinsically neither more nor less "rational" than pro-war sentiments. Both are often shrouded in the vagaries of superpatriotism, jingoism, chauvinism, national salvation, and personal redemption. We do not mean to equate the objective consequences of "tactical" pacifism and "strategic" war maneuvers. The nature of each past war requires specific examination. It is true that the "rightness" or "wrongness" of a war is not necessarily and invariably linked to the sentiments of people or the decisions of policymakers. The 1916 slogan, "Keep our boys out of Europe," is no more rational or scientifically grounded than the 1917 slogan, "The Yanks are coming." It is necessary to remember that the making of foreign policy does not rest on self-evident principles of perpetual peace or of perpetual war.

Critical junctures in modern international history are invariably accompanied by "panic button" national response. A powerful frustration syndrome is characteristic of Americans whose self-image of greatness is not universally appreciated. What this leads to is harsh words and soft action, followed by a protracted effort to "make good" the words without battle. Interestingly enough, only at the rarest and most severe points in American history have policy statements and policy actions gone together. One clue to policy decisions is that when these decisions are envisoned in *political* terms, the tendency is to eschew military solutions. On the other hand, when identical decisions are framed in *military* terms, the tendency is to eschew, or at least look askance at, political solutions. Thus in 1965 United States troops were in combat readiness in Laos (a military strategy), and no troops were in Cuba (a political problem).

In America the military has functioned as an apolitical, professional caste. It was, from the time of George Washington to Woodrow Wilson, an instrument of a foreign policy initiated and enacted by civilian political administrators. The genius of the American system has been to separate explicitly political from military functions. However, the twentieth-century tendency toward bureaucratization and centralization in government, toward what in effect has amounted to the adoption of military procedures (e.g., "chain of command," "line and staff," "graduated promotions," etc.), has given impetus to the transformation of the military caste into a potent, independent part of the political elite. It has slowly become a decision-making body in its own right, over and above civilian control. It is a legitimate (or at least legitimized) decision-making unit, whose function is identified with other political agencies within the political power apparatus. This historical shift in function and status of the military can be considered in various ways. The question comes down to this: Is the American military responsible for the survival of political power, or is it essentially still responsive to the demands of government? Through a long process of specialization and division of labor, the answer seems sure to be increased power and autonomy for the military, acting in concert with other agencies of government or as a separate agency.[23]

The extent of this transformation of the military from professionalism to politicalization can be measured by the steady increase in the importance of the Secretary of Defense. The struggle between politics and policy, between an overall set of federal principles and an immediate strategic response to specific situations, is reflected in the "competition" now taking place between the Department of State, representing politics and the political tradition of foreign policy, and the Department of Defense, representing policies and the military tradition of effecting foreign policy. A self-consciousness of a new role for the military is evident, a role as policy formulator and not simply as executor of civilian policies.

Whether the United States military is a "power elite" as C. Wright Mills held, or whether the whole country is a "warfare state," as Fred J. Cook recently described it, or a nation in which civilian "veto groups" still supply countervailing political force, as David Riesman maintained in *The Lonely Crowd*, it is clear that the gap between military and civilian functions has been progressively narrowing. In a recent statement to this effect, Riesman and Nathan Glazer pointed out that "the Strategic Air Command has considerably greater power than

---

[23] This chapter confines itself to the United States military. For a study of the Soviet military apparatus, see my *The War Game: Studies of the New Civilian Militarists* (New York: Ballantine Books, 1963); and for an authoritative account of the Soviet view, see V. D. Sokolovskii, *Soviet Military Strategy* (Englewood Cliffs, N.J.: Prentice-Hall, 1963).

any single agency possessed in 1948. It has brought the Navy around to its side (by sharing nuclear 'capability'), and reduced the Army to a role of minor irritant and sometime veto group. In alliance with the AEC (Atomic Energy Commission), it forced the Oppenheimer hearings and temporarily silenced the opponents of Teller and an H-bomb foreign policy. In alliance with the big and little contractors, their unions and workers, and 'their' senators, it has made the war economy so central to our whole economy that the stock market rises when the Summit breaks down." [24]

This process of militarization is an unanticipated consequence of technological developments in armaments which have made traditional diplomatic counterwar safeguards "obsolete" if not entirely useless. The possibility of "the fifteen-minute war" has fed the pacifist argument for unilateralism and/or bilateral disarmament. At the same time, within the Establishment, it has also given impetus and justification to greater concentration of power than has hitherto been the case—a concentration which is rationalized in the name of nuclear feasibility and justified in terms of diplomatic stalemates and provocations both real and imagined.

Earlier public attitudes toward militarism were largely shaped by a general esteem for civilian government. Such attitudes have been considerably reshaped by the bureaucratization of political organisms. Centralization guarantees the rapid formation of policy recommendations, a fact which is of decisive importance in the technology-oriented politics of the present. Hence antimilitarism was formerly a direct expression of the American native animus toward all things related to war. This has steadily moved over into a critique of bigness in government as such, of which the military may be considered one essential part. For example, the criticism of militarism made by Robert La Follette in World War I was a critique of military-mindedness as a war ideology, unsuited to democratic government, but the critique of militarism made by Dwight D. Eisenhower on his last day as President of the United States was in effect a critique of big-scale government. Although in the earlier years of the twentieth century there was a legitimate antiwar attitude, antimilitarism since 1933 has in the main been a traditionalist critique of bigness. The difficulty with the military, according to congressmen, relates to how much they spend, rather than

[24] David Riesman and Nathan Glazer, "The Lonely Crowd: A Reconsideration in 1960," in Seymour M. Lipset and Leo Lowenthal, eds., *Cultural and Social Character* (New York: The Free Press of Glencoe, 1961), pp. 449–450. Also see C. Wright Mills, *The Power Elite* (New York: Oxford University Press, 1956); and Fred J. Cook, *The Warfare State* (New York: The Macmillan Company, 1962).

to any essential features of the military ideology. (This is, however, far less the case in the Senate than in the House of Representatives. Apart from differences in the caliber of the personnel involved, there is a House consensus that peace and war is not an issue—at least not one that can be taken to the electorate every two years. The Senate term, being six years, largely vitiates this pragmatic argument.)

When great tension between powers has eased, American foreign policy veers sharply in an antimilitarist direction. This is rationalized as "trusting the enemy," by which is really meant assuming a moral as well as a military parity. Thus the tendency at present is to consider Soviet "rationality" and "self-control" equal to our own.

A central characteristic of American foreign policy is this: the more protracted the political conflict, the greater the chances for negotiated resolution; and the more immediate and intense the conflict, the greater the chances for precipitous military hostilities. This characteristic was demonstrated by the Korean conflict, and more recently by the Cuban crisis, both of which broke upon the American public suddenly; each conflict received equally sudden policy-making reaction. (The same sort of equation cannot easily be made with respect to European diplomatic and military traditions, e.g., the long wait and buildup before the opening of hostilities between Nazi Germany and England between 1933 and 1939.) In "protracted conflict" of a nonmilitary variety, the possibilities of "controlled conflict," or conflict resolution, qualitatively increase. The relationship between the United States and the Soviet Union since the conclusion of World War II in 1945 reinforce such an estimate. The tendency is to establish a parity at the policy-making level between the Soviet Union and the United States, in which military force is a negative *symbol* rather than the positive instrument of negotiation.[25]

Another special quality of American foreign policy is that, unlike that of most major European powers of the past or present, it is based on considerations of rigid morality to a much greater extent than can be politically warranted. Politics requires room for maneuver, for retreats and advances, for settlement as well as fighting, for partial solutions no less than total solutions. Morality requires a different and, one must say, almost a contrary posture: steadfastness to principles, firmness of action and ideology, willingness to make sacrifices. Morality is a long-range affair, while politics moves toward short-range solutions based on a somewhat circumscribed set of problems.

It is not that politics and morality are mutually exclusive, nor is it

[25] On this Soviet-American phase in "controlled conflict" see D. F. Fleming, *The Cold War and Its Origins, 1917–1960,* 2 vols. (Garden City, N.Y.: Doubleday, 1961).

worth arguing that they even ought to be. It is, however, the case that the problem of "posture," what we condescendingly call "saving face" when the Communist Chinese act the same way, is something which occupies the attention of all nations and peoples. It is one thing to delineate the areas of politics and morality, the negotiable and the non-negotiable. It is quite another thing to insist upon a politics of morality. Such a politics can lead either to hypocrisy (as in the U-2 spy plane incident, when our highest political officials declared it absurd that the "good guys" could ever stoop to spying), or to adventurism (as in the aiding and abetting of the ludicrous and abortive landing of Cuban exiles from American shores on the soil of another sovereign state).[26] The position taken by Robert Gordis that the "breach between politics and ethics can be closed," although argued from the noblest of sentiments, ignores the grounds upon which the separation was made in the first place—namely to make politics into a useful science, a goal which remains distant.[27]

The ambiguity of American foreign policy might be summed up thus: even though the military might of the United States has increased enormously since 1954, there have been no corresponding victories over the enemy. Indeed, nuclear military hardware was impotent to prevent the formation of the newly emergent nation-states of Asia and Africa that came about either through wars of national liberation or through parliamentary mandate.

The position of the "forward strategy" group reveals the classic moral basis for military intervention.[28] For example, as in World War I, Americans were urged to repudiate any government which failed to adhere to the Monroe Doctrine, despite the fact that this doctrine had neither the binding force of international law to support it nor the support of the United States, which was itself unwilling to abide by the isolationist aspect of the doctrine. Since the "forward strategists" or "rollback" group call for a policy of intervention, anything short of "eliminating the Communist menace" is viewed as an American loss. Yet, in the event the challenge is accepted, this "forward strategy" would have to choose between total escalation or total surrender.

[26] See on this David Wise and Thomas B. Ross, *The U-2 Affair* (London: The Cresset Press, 1962) and Haynes Bonner Johnson, *The Bay of Pigs* (New York: Norton, 1964).
[27] Cf. Robert Gordis, *Politics and Ethics* (Santa Barbara, Calif.: Center for the Study of American Institutions, 1961).
[28] Cf. Robert Strausz-Hupé, William R. Kintner, and Stefan T. Possony, *A Forward Strategy for America* (New York: Harper and Brothers, 1961). See also Stefan T. Possony, *A Century of Conflict* (Chicago: Henry Regnery Company, 1953).

The insistence on a moral posture based on "unconditional surrender" wreaked havoc with Woodrow Wilson's desire to keep the United States out of World War I, made possible the major inroads achieved by the Soviet Union during and after World War II, converted a victory into a fiasco in the Korean conflict, and has made the Berlin crisis a literal and figurative wall preventing political accord between East and West. What assurances are offered for those urging the invasion of Cuba (missile sites and launching pads there or otherwise) that the "unconditional surrender" of Castro and the present Cuban regime would, in fact, result in the anticipated consequences, namely the decommunization of the Western hemisphere? Indeed, in the American strategy of blockade rather than any direct invasion or bomber attack upon Cuban soil, it was precisely the historic failure of unconditional-surrender postures that cautioned, prudently, against an adventurist course.[29]

The outcry for an interventionist foreign policy is made in terms of moral postures *abstracted* from politics, for example, destroying or at least "rolling back" the Bolsheviks, preserving the hegemony of the hemisphere, or turning out the bearded monsters of the Sierra Maestra. Military decisions are often projected not on the basis of military consideration, such as a clear and present danger to the population of the United States, or to any other population cluster in the hemisphere, but rather on the basis that the only way of preserving our "superior" democratic way of life is to crush an "inferior" way of life.

The ethics of preservation through military attack are not shared by wide sectors of the American public.[30] Hence strident military solutions are very often coupled with attacks on the United Nations, on universities, and on political leaders in responsible positions, since such extremism must not only justify limited warfare but explain why public sentiments do not support it.

Given "irrationality" as a fact of policy making, and given further evidence that politics is increasingly coming to rest on the heightened need for rationality in public decisions, and since "history" is increasingly man-made, the only legitimate options to both isolationism and

---

[29] The authentic choice between the new civilian militarism and traditional democratic politics is not between morality and immorality in politics, but simply between prudent investors and reckless gamblers, between those who appreciate the existence of unintended consequences and those who do not. Seen in such a light, the call for a morally centered politics is a disguised form of fanaticism and recklessness. We clearly expect the Soviet planners to rise above it. Have we a right to expect less from our own government?

[30] See Allen Barton, "A Survey of Suburban Residents on What to Do about the Danger of War," and Paul Ekman, "Divergent Reactions to the Threat of War," *Council for Correspondence Newsletter*, 24 (March 1963), pp. 3–25.

interventionism are arms buildup or bilateral, or even multilateral, disarmament. The policy of military deterrence, of arms escalation, incorporates both the dangers of isolationism and interventionism. Hence it has become axiomatic in our generation to base foreign policy on the need for, and the possibilities of, arriving at a settlement—one that will have disarmament as its first order of business—if we are not to have an arms race as our very last order of business.[31]

Sociological Factors in the Institutionalization of a Conflict Society

The problem of converting an armaments industry into peacetime production is being seriously posed for the second time since the outbreak of World War II. The first time the Korean War aborted efforts in this direction; and in the mid-1960s the war in Vietnam dampened enthusiasm for such a conversion process. Thus far, the center of concern has been the economic feasibility of the process. There are also sociological factors which have produced a lag between technical know-how for the reconversion process and the implementation of steps toward industrial reconversion. Five major noneconomic deterrents have been singled out: (1) little consciousness on the part of large sectors of the public about the problem of conversion; (2) a rise in new industries dependent on arms spending for their survival; (3) a belief in armaments as a bulwark of social solidarity; (4) acculturation to patterns of secrecy, suppression of information, and even coercion as social norms; and (5) the fear that industrial reconversion would lead to the destruction or deterioration of the Western alliance. Under critical examination these factors, based as they are on a military determinism, prove to be insubstantial.

Knowledgeable economists have indicated that the 10 percent of the

[31] The theory of unilateral initiatives offers the following propositions: (1) A shift from a policy based on the morality of anti-Communism to one based on common survival and the popular right of choice in matters of the social system. (2) A recognition that the policy of deterrence is a halfway house to a policy of disarmament, and at worse a halfway house moving in the direction of a fiercely competitive arms race. (3) An attempt to restructure the political dialogue in terms of social and economic development, and away from the present military determinism. (4) The development of a machinery of *showdown postponement* to replace the present obsolete policy of *instant retaliation*. (5) Greater circulation of elite groups to insure a responsiveness of policy making to the sentiments of the public. (6) The expansion of a system of "checks and balances" or "veto groups" within the decision-making apparatus. See on this Charles Osgood, "Questioning Some Unquestioned Assumptions about National Security," *Social Problems*, 11, 1 (Summer 1963), pp. 6–12; and also his paper, "A Case for Graduated Unilateral Disengagement," *Bulletin of the Atomic Scientists*, 15, 5 (May 1960).

Table 3 Defense-Space Orders to 34 Major Contractors (1962)

Company	Defense Contracts (millions)	NASA Contracts (millions)	Totals (first 2 columns)	Company Sales (millions) (a)	Ratio of Defense and Space Orders to Total Sales
75–100%					
Republic Aviation	$ 332.8	$ 6.9	$ 339.7	$ 295.8	100.00%
McDonnell Aircraft	310.9	68.5	379.4	390.7	97.11
Grumman Aircraft Engr.	303.6	24.6	328.2	357.1	91.91
Lockheed Aircraft	1,419.5	5.0	1,424.5	1,753.1	81.27
AVCO	323.3	1.4	324.7	414.3	78.37
North American Aviation	1,032.5	199.1	1,231.6	1,633.7	75.39
Hughes Aircraft	234.2	9.2	243.4	(b)	(c)
50–74%					
Collins Radio	150.1	3.7	153.8	207.8	74.01
Thiokol Chemical	178.3	0.8	179.1	255.8	70.02
Raytheon	406.6	—	406.6	580.7	70.02
Newport News Shipbuilding and Dry Dock	185.0	—	185.0	267.3	69.21
Martin Marietta	802.7	1.8	804.5	1,195.3	67.31
Boeing	1,132.8	15.6	1,148.4	1,768.5	64.94
General Dynamics	1,196.6	27.9	1,224.5	1,898.4	64.50
Curtiss-Wright	144.6	—	144.6	228.7	63.23
United Aircraft	662.7	34.1	696.8	1,162.1	59.96
Douglas Aircraft	365.6	68.4	434.0	749.9	57.87
25–49%					
American Machine and Foundry	187.3	—	187.3	415.4	45.09

General Tire and Rubber	366.1	66.4	432.5	959.8	45.06
Northrop	152.5	1.3	153.8	347.5	44.26
Hercules Powder	181.6	—	181.6	454.8	39.93
Sperry Rand	465.6	2.2	467.8	1,182.6	39.56
Bendix	285.9	19.4	305.3	788.1	38.74
FMC	160.4	—	160.4	506.5	31.67
Pan American World Airways	146.7	—	146.7	503.9	29.11
0–24%					
International Telephone and Telegraph	243.6	2.2	245.8	995.5	24.69
General Electric	975.9	23.0	998.9	4,792.7	20.84
Radio Corp. of America	339.6	20.2	359.8	1,742.7	20.65
Westinghouse Electric	246.0	3.4	249.4	1,954.5	12.76
International Business Machines	155.5	12.6	168.1	1,925.2	8.73
American Telephone and Telegraph	467.7	10.8	478.5	11,742.4	4.07
Ford Motor	269.1	—	269.1	8,089.6	3.33
General Motors	449.0	1.4	450.4	14,640.2	3.08
Standard Oil (New Jersey)	180.1	—	180.1	9,537.3	1.89

(*a*) Net sales for fiscal year ending during 1962.
(*b*) Not available.
(*c*) Estimated from other sources to be in excess of 75 percent.

SOURCE: Murray L. Weidenbaum, "The Transferability of Defense Industries Resources to Civilian Uses," in *United States Senate Committee on Labor and Public Welfare, Convertibility of Space and Defense Industry Resources to Civilian Needs* (Washington, D.C.: U.S. Government Printing Office, 1964), pp. 848–855; see also his report on the "Industrial Impact of Disarmament," *The American Journal of Economics and Sociology*, 22, 4 (October 1963), pp. 513–526.

national budget directly allocated to arms production is not an economic necessity.[32] The social problem begins with an appreciation that this 10 percent is variously distributed, so that some major industrial enterprises are largely dependent on the continuation of military production (Table 3).

Why, in the midst of abundant intellectual know-how, is so little time spent solving the problem of a peacetime economy? This is an extremely difficult question which can only be answered tentatively. What follows is predicated on two premises: (1) that the chief task confronting Americans is disarmament and not deterrence, that is, a peace based on the institutionalization of world law and juridical limits to sovereignty as well as weaponry, and not a peace grounded on a presumed "delicate balance of terror";[33] and (2) that bilateral settlement between East and West, specifically between the United States and the Soviet Union, is now very possible, and even imminent.[34]

The first point is the failure to recognize that an economy on a permanent war footing carries with it menacing possibilities. Many Americans receive the economic benefits of the arms race in the form of steady work, good living and working conditions, high wages, and often professional standing, without manifesting any real interest in world conflict.[35] Such benefits drown out the overall need to reduce social tension through a reduction in arms production.

The arms industries present high growth combined with minimum sales risk—which makes resistance to change quite understandable. The following statement reveals the pattern of this growth: "Expenditures of the Department of Defense have risen from 19.8 billion dollars in

---

[32] See, for example, Emile Benoit, "Alternatives to Defense Production," in Emile Benoit and Kenneth Boulding, eds., *Disarmament and the Economy* (New York: Harper and Row, 1963), pp. 203–220; Emile Benoit, "Economic Adjustments to Disarmament," in *Economic Factors Bearing upon the Maintenance of Peace* (New York: The Institute for International Order, 1960); William S. Royce, "Economics of Disarmament," *The Nation*, 195, 6 (September 1962), pp. 105–109; and Emile Benoit, "The Economics of Disarmament and Coexistence," in Bert F. Hoselitz, ed., *Economics and the Idea of Mankind* (New York and London: Columbia University Press, 1965), pp. 233–277.

[33] Irving Louis Horowitz, *The War Game: Studies of the New Civilian Militarists*, *op. cit.*, and *Games, Strategies and Peace* (Philadelphia: American Friends Service Committee, 1963).

[34] Irving Louis Horowitz, "Political Morality and Immoral Politics," *Council for Correspondence Newsletter*, 25 (April 1963); and Irving Louis Horowitz, "On the Morality of Detente," *The Correspondent*, 28 (July–August 1963).

[35] See Peter I. Rose, "The Public and the Threat of War," and William A. Gamson and Andrea Modigliani, "Tensions and Concessions: The Empirical Confirmation of Belief Systems about Soviet Behavior," *Social Problems*, 2, 1 (Summer 1963).

fiscal year 1951 to 43 billion dollars in 1961, or by over 100 percent, a growth rate far in excess of that of any other major areas of the American economy. At the present time, Defense Department purchases of goods and services are equal to almost nine-tenths of the gross national product. The proportion reached peaks of 48 percent during World War II and 12 percent during the Korean War, but was, of course, lower during the interwar period of the cold war. An abrupt change in the nature of the external threat would probably cause another major shift in the proportion of the country's resources devoted to armaments." [36] Most business enterprises now engaged in direct or subsidiary forms of arms production simply have given no thought to remobilization of the economy in a nonmilitary direction. Peaceful production is not a felt need because high wages and solid profits have remained essentially unbroken in the American economy ever since 1939, when the nation first went on a partial defense mobilization. And when "recessions" did take place, as in 1949, the Korean War and the rise in some military spending mitigated its economic effects.

In a major survey of defense industry planning for the future, Philip Shabecoff and Joseph Lelyveld found that most defense contractors "have no idea at present of how to plan for a sharp reduction in defense spending. A few companies are confident they would be able to make a smooth transition to civilian business. Fewer still report that they have actually done some long-range planning in this area." [37] The consensus among military producers and contractors is that no arms reduction will take place and that, if it does, the problem can be met through still more government help. There is, in short, a profound inability on the part of defense contractors such as Lockheed Aircraft, General Dynamics, Boeing Company, North American Aviation, to mention only a few, to take seriously their own faith in the private-enterprise system. What they have become used to is government subsidization of private profits—something radically different from the confrontation of buyers and sellers in a symbolic marketplace. Thus the unawareness of the need to disarm is reinforced by the absence of competitive capitalism.[38]

A major reason for this inertia about disarmament is that the conver-

[36] Murray L. Weidenbaum, "Problems of Adjustment for Defense Industries," in *Disarmament and Economy, op. cit.*, p. 67; for data on this see David Allison, "Defense Cutbacks," *International Science and Technology* (October 1964), pp. 20–31.

[37] Philip Shabecoff and Joseph Lelyveld, "Defense Industry Shuns Plans for Possible Arms Ban," *New York Times*, August 16, 1963, pp. 31, 37.

[38] On this whole range of complex issues, see Thomas G. Miller, Jr., *Strategies for Survival in the Aerospace Industry* (New York: Arthur D. Little, 1964).

sion problem, from military to civilian enterprises, is different from the problem that existed after World War II. At that time the issue was reconversion. Industrial firms could once again resume manufacturing the same goods they had made before the war. Indeed, they even drew upon old blueprints and old tools to fulfill the civilian backlog. Two decades later the bulk of military production is concentrated in industries specialized for military production. Few of them have a history of civilian production. The current social problem is one of economic conversion—redesigning the operation of military production plants for civilian needs. The feasibility of such conversion requires political decisions and marketing decisions—something foreign to industries geared to technical efficiency and engineering problems.

In these circumstances the only effective way in which a policy of industrial conversion might be forthcoming—international tensions being held at a constant but minimal level—would be for nonindustrial establishments to take steps to initiate blueprinting for conversion to a civilian economy. State and local agencies should be encouraged to initiate and facilitate regional planning for conversion, including ideological preparation. An agenda of major capital outlays that would show how military plants might contribute to schools, hospitals, highway construction, and so forth should be prepared by a federal planning commission. The government must serve as a clearing house for skilled and technical personnel who are displaced or who require relocation because of defense cutbacks. The federal administration must also fuse older civilian industries with newer military industries—or at least establish a greater rapport between them than now exists.[39]

The difficulty is that "ought" and "is" are too far apart. The situation is such that military allocations are often made by military bureaus and boards, directly and without either the inconvenience or the obstacles posed by civilian authorities. A function of secrecy is to insist that certain funds are necessary and explanations superfluous, since the purpose of the funds is secret. Thus conventional checks against excessive militarization of industry have dissolved in a sea of secrecy.[40] In addition, the military have effectively dominated foreign policy in critical tension areas, and have served as checks against general disarmament proposals. Thus, at the same time a concerted effort at converting from

---

[39] There have been a considerable number of publications issued on this subject; perhaps the most useful is that by the United States Arms Control and Disarmament Agency: *Economic Impact of Disarmament* (Washington, D.C.: U.S. Government Printing Office, 1962).

[40] For an excellent summary of this whole issue, see John M. Swomley, Jr., *The Military Establishment* (Boston: Beacon Press, 1964).

arms production to civilian production is being made by the Atomic Energy Commission, there is a contrasting effort at militarization of the civilian population by no less powerful government sources.

A five-billion-dollar cutback in arms spending was proposed in legislative session in 1964. But, more important, ways in which the effects of this cutback could be mitigated and overcome were also outlined. First, it was proposed that all industries having more than 25 percent of their production in defense contracts be required to establish an "operating conversion committee" to prepare for possible alternatives in the event of a loss in military contracts. Second, it was proposed that a government board be established and have as its main task assisting businesses in the process of considering reconversion. The concentration of defense contracts in the huge corporations and in engineering firms which perform specialized services means that we could convert to a peacetime economy without overall disruption to the social fabric. One economist has seen the problem as a short-run effort to shift 22 billion dollars now allocated for defense purposes to the larger civilian economy.[41]

One contribution of deterrence theory to the present unconscious state of industrialists has been the often-repeated statement that "arms control will not cut defense cost."[42] What is neglected, however, is the fact that a policy of *disarmament* would indeed cut such costs. This fact reinforces the position of decision makers in the war industries who view any policy other than arms control as dangerous to their continued welfare. Coupled with a fear that marketing commercial products would be unprofitable, fear of cuts in arms production has made defense contractors perhaps a conservative force in American society. What is needed to unfreeze these attitudes is first a clearcut federal policy indicating that arms control is only the first phase of arms reduction. This done, the federal administration must assist in the opening up of certain highly monopolistic peacetime enterprises, such as the automobile and communications industries. There is a need for new capital investment in old industries no less than for the creation of new types of commercial production.

One argument employed in defense of high military budgets is that such spending stimulates discovery and the application of discovery.

---

[41] William Vickrey, "Fiscal Strategies for Shifting $22 Billions to the Civilian Economy," in Seymour Melman, ed., *A Strategy for American Security* (New York: Lee Offset-Distributors, 1963), pp. 21–25.

[42] Thomas C. Schelling and Morton H. Halperin, "Arms Control Will Not Cut Defense Cost," in E. W. Lefever, ed., *Arms and Arms Control* (New York: Frederick A. Praeger, 1962), pp. 287–297.

True, the initial application of scientific invention is often an unprofitable venture, which cannot be maintained without heavy federal subsidization. But the conclusion drawn, that peacetime production would involve a cutback not only in military production but in scientific technology as well, simply does not follow. There would not be a withdrawal or retrenchment in federal spending per se but simply the reallocation of funds for nonmilitary purposes.[43]

It must be made clear that the argument for peacetime uses of industry does not imply a nineteenth-century high-tariff, protectionist view of balancing the budget. Indeed, it might conceivably be that a real adjustment of the economy may entail higher rather than lower federal outlays, and an increase rather than a decrease in deficit spending. Highway construction, foreign assistance, space exploration, and civilian uses of energy sources may be applied for war or peace. The application in one direction or another is something quite apart from the quantity of federal expenditures or even taxation.

The problem is ideological in character. Americans are accustomed to government spending being paired with military requisitions, because they view the military establishment as intrinsically national in character. If any conversion is likely to be successful, an entirely novel concept—in American ideology at least—must be institutionalized, namely the introduction of government planning in commercial and industrial enterprises. Without becoming tendentious, it is plain that the Tennessee Valley Authority (TVA) and the Missouri Valley Authority (MVA) are just as legitimate allocations of federal funds as aircraft or rocket production.

Another major obstacle to conversion and reconversion is the directly ideological notion of having a "national purpose." The manifest function of such a search is to define the goals for Americans at mid-twentieth century: to determine the American posture toward the Communist bloc nations, toward newly emerging nation-states, and, above all, toward our own future aims and ambitions. The latent function of such a search, doomed to failure by the nature of a pluralistic society, is to provide what Durkheim called "the total society" with a sense of cohesion. It has become clear even to the rhetoricians of the Cold War that anti-Communism is itself a negative response with built-in boomerang effects. Without a positive program, Americans entered the 1960s immunized to a considerable degree from Cold War policies, and this led to a fractionalized public opinion. A feeling that every-

---

[43] For an analysis of the ways in which the federal government has underwritten the "risk-taking" functions of business, see Murray L. Weidenbaum, "The Defense-Space Complex: Impact on Whom?," *Challenge*, 13, 4 (April 1965), pp. 43–46.

thing was done from the top down and that the "little man" counted for naught translated itself into negative attitudes toward armed service, civil defense, and other civilian activities. Instead of making adjustments, policy making tended to become increasingly strident, reinforcing the rhetoric of oversimplification.

Both as participants and as leaders, members of the corporate structure adhered to policies calculated to retain a Cold War consensus, rather than alter the character of this consensus. The Cold War, which has functioned as the exclusive mode of expression of American political leadership in the postwar period, has succeeded in institutionalizing itself. To dislodge the Cold War from its gray eminence requires the sort of broad-scale political reorientation that defense contractors are least suited to carry forth; those best suited, such as labor organizations and voluntary associations, were the least able to carry it forth. The concept of anti-Communism, negative and frustrating though it may be, is at least a political cement. The Communist menace serves to justify resistance to all kinds of social innovation. As one anthropologist has recently observed, "The view of the Soviet Union as a deadly adversary that at any moment may destroy us also makes real disarmament unlikely; and suggests that instead of getting rid of our arms we will merely rest on them." [44]

David Riesman has noted, "There is something oddly regressive in the spectacle of the United States reducing itself to the size of a new nation that needs a manifest destiny. . . . Affluence ought to mean abundance of purposes, and intense exploration and discovery of new ones, both individual and collective. It might mean a stronger concern for the purposes of others who have not yet reached the dilemmas of abundance." [45] This reducing process, this search for ideological uniformity disguised as a social consensus, is indicative of widespread fear that only a monolith can overcome a monolith, that only a bureaucratized state can defeat another bureaucratized state. The strength of our conservatism stems from the same psychological sources as the strength of communism in the developing regions: a fear that democratic consensus structures are indeed weaker than totalitarian command structures. The war engineers turned strategists thus underwrite this fear—since they have moved policy making out of the public political arena and imitate elitist modes of operating on the body politic. The only problem is that this procedure produces a boomerang effect.

[44] Jules Henry, *Culture Against Man* (New York: Random House, 1963), p. 110.
[45] David Riesman, "The Concept of National Purpose," *Council for Correspondence Newsletter*, 27 (June 1963), p. 11.

Dulling the sense of mass participation in political life has led to a form of "privatization" that locates gratification in a personal and egoistic fashion, not only without regard to the consequences of such behavior for an anticipated "enemy" but, more profoundly, without due regard to the human consequences for family, community, or nation. The reconversion of industry to peacetime uses should have as its essential by-product a corresponding rise in public participation in social affairs. It is precisely the relative deterioration of "peace movements" in recent years that characterizes American political life. It might, of course, be that the emergence once again of politically conscious and irritated teen-agers and the rapid growth of the civil rights movement may result in an increased appreciation of war as a social problem to be *resolved*, and not something to be *lived*. This remains to be seen.

Another problem to be faced is our internal system of secrecy and coercion which has become legitimated. If we assume—and I daresay that it is more than an assumption—that any society tooled up for "spontaneous" outbreak of thermonuclear warfare requires a significant amount of coercion and the institutionalization of this coercion in the form of police, federal investigators, congressional investigators, and the like, then it can be seen that the maintenance of a high military budget directly affects the lives of many people who are described as dissidents in relation to the Cold War. The element of coercion, although more sharply limited in the United States by countervailing and juridical limitations than in the Soviet Union, is nonetheless present.[46]

The armaments industry, with its emphasis on clearance, surveillance, and security, makes coercive intervention in the lives of private citizens legitimate. Since the "next war" will be between arms and arms, rather than men and men, this stress on secrecy generates a growth in the command mechanism. This growth is still more apparent in the Soviet Union, where munitions production is the responsibility not of the military establishment but of economic agencies. Since the mid-1930s planning agencies have specialized to this end.[47] Thus such policing agencies, East and West, have a vested interest in maintaining a huge armaments industry.

This matter cuts both ways. It is a relatively stable law of organizational behavior that a bureaucracy attempts to maximize and retain its

---

[46] Pitirim A. Sorokin, "Mutual Convergence of the United States and the U.S.S.R. to the Mixed Sociocultural Type," *International Journal of Comparative Sociology*, 2 (September 1960), pp. 143–176.

[47] Abram Bergson, *The Real National Income of Soviet Russia Since 1928* (Cambridge: Harvard University Press, 1961), p. 362.

power beyond the point of external necessity. Organizations do not vanish because their need has been obviated; they simply search out new rationalizations for their perpetuation. Thus a number of press reports indicated a frantic interaction between corporation lobbies and the military establishment to sway senatorial sentiment away from the nuclear test-ban treaty.[48] It may be gathered, in view of the limited nature of that treaty, that far more powerful forces would be mobilized in the event of any bilateral treaty which included actual arms reductions in its provisions.

An extremely powerful element preventing maximum demobilization is the customs and mores engendered by military styles of behavior. Military organization has been extended to the social structure, not only ideologically but institutionally in the form of semimilitary associations and superpatriotic clubs. The norms of secrecy, chain of command, and undeviating follow-through on plans, have become generalized patterns of industrial and governmental behavior. Thus "conversion" would not be completed even if all nuclear weapons production were stopped. The dissonance of living in a society politically committed to finding a path to survival, while at the same time adopting military methods of organization, would leave a considerable sociological residue.[49]

There are three substantive arguments against an excess of coercion in a cold-war atmosphere. First, it is difficult to differentiate or to limit coercion so that it does not become terroristic. Second, the secret society inhibits traditional American rights of communication and transportation. Third, coercion inhibits the growth of science—which requires the widest access to information and verification of data. (It is now clear that the Cold War, far from stimulating scientific progress, actually serves to inhibit it by creating an atmosphere of closure about information and the exchange of ideas.) The overall consequences of the reduction in arms spending would be a general liberation from the world of secrecy.

It is not a simplistic question of America's "will" to fight for freedom, or the Soviet Union's "will" to fight for Communism. Suicidal impulses of nations are neither novel nor heroic. It is a question of a will to survive despite differences. Once the threads of the Cold War start coming apart, the entire garment is subject to discard.[50] The

---

[48] Marquis Childs, *St. Louis Post-Dispatch*, September 18, 1963.
[49] See on these problems Stanislaw Andrzejewski, *Military Organization and Society* (London: Routledge and Kegan Paul, 1954); and Morris Janowitz, *The Professional Soldier: A Social and Political Portrait* (Glencoe, Ill.: The Free Press, 1960).
[50] Charles E. Osgood, "Questioning Some Unquestioned Assumptions about National Defense," *Journal of Arms Control*, 1, 1 (January 1963), p. 11. See also Sorokin, *op. cit.*

struggle now is between those desiring to patch up traditional alliances and those seeking a *détente* with the Soviet Union. Political decisions will ultimately determine the rate at which the Cold War will be converted to a peaceful competition of social systems. One significant feature of the Kennedy Administration was the belief within its higher echelons that such a peaceful struggle could be won; the assumption was that time was on the side of capitalist America, rather than on the side of Communist Russia. Whether this optimism was warranted or not, its permeation of administrative policy bodies served to increase the possibilities that conversion and reconversion of the industrial base were in the offing.

Another matter that requires attention is the relationship between what Kenneth Boulding has termed "the world war industry" and foreign affairs. In some measure (although to what extent it is difficult to say) the world war industry inhibits social change. Armaments reinforce regimes with which the United States and the Soviet Union respectively have working relations and thus draw the nations of the world into the bipolarization which has existed since the close of World War II. This monopolization of military hardware serves to make the world dependent on the leading powers to an unhealthy degree. The argument adduced by some to the effect that we have "allies," while the Soviets have "captives,"[51] ignores the fact that military establishments in Latin America, no less than in Eastern Europe, function to maintain a status quo that can hardly be said to embody the popular will.

One argument holds that to reduce investment in armaments is to invite chaos around the world, especially in developing areas. This argument is strictly political in character. From an economic standpoint, according to the General Agreement on Trade and Tariffs (GATT) report on *Measures for the Economic Development of Under-Developed Countries*, the developing regions have needs of such enormous proportions that they alone could absorb the 10 percent of the gross national product siphoned off for military spending.[52] But the purely economic standpoint is inoperative while such political considerations as the character of the social structure and political agencies in these countries are subject to constant scrutiny and veto by Washington or

---

[51] Henry A. Kissinger, "The Unsolved Problems of European Defense," *Foreign Affairs*, 40, 4 (July 1962), pp. 515–541; and see also his essay, "NATO's Nuclear Dilemma," *The Reporter*, 20, 7 (March 28, 1963).
[52] Thomas C. Schelling, "American Aid and Economic Development: Some Critical Issues," in *International Stability and Progress* (New York: Columbia University Press, 1957), pp. 127 ff.

by Moscow. Thus the external aspects of the heavy armaments industry operate to keep change at a minimum.

The world war industry prevents any dramatic shifts in the social structure, yet the "backwardness" of foreign areas is used as an argument to prove that a political crisis would flow from any release of production from armaments to consumption. The statement by Roger Hagan on the reasons for the polarizing simplicity of the Cold War helps to explain why such an undue faith in military hardware continues to block broad-scale reform programs based on principles of relative equality.[53] So much has the political career of much of Congress come to depend on anti-Communist sloganeering that the fight against subtlety seems to have become a matter for survival for vast elements of our society. Behind the congressmen are millions of Americans whose style of life, whose sense of meaning, and whose manner of economic endeavor and personal encounter have come to depend on being publicly patriotic and firm. In a society outdistancing its roots and values and trying to fill the gap with the public virtues of boosterism, the Cold War has become Babbittry gone mad, and it is impossible to be optimistic about the chances for altering the image of Soviet aggressiveness sufficiently to erode the argument against nuclear parity.

Nuclear war is a social problem which profoundly affects all other social problems because the funds and energies allocated for the war machine are precisely the same funds and energies that would be shifted over to peaceful production. It is not simply, or even primarily, that the American *economy* cannot spend for both military and public welfare purposes; rather it is not *socially* possible.[54] The forces most strongly in favor of military spending tend to be most hostile to government action on either social welfare or civil rights. Thus it is not that 55 percent of the American tax dollar is spent for military purposes, and hence minimizes budget allocation for health, education, and welfare measures to 0.07 percent. Rather, it is precisely the faith in military solutions to national ailments that *leads to* such budgetary imbalances between defense spending and welfare spending. Clearly, alternative definitions of social security are entailed.

One knotty problem is that the bulk of Americans remain "economic determinists." They are likely to see only the advantages of large arms budgets. Public awareness of the broad psychosocial consequences of the large output for armaments is needed. A modest begin-

[53] Roger Hagan, "Reciprocal Hardening," *Council for Correspondence Newsletter*, 26 (May 1963), p. 7.
[54] See Martin Oppenheimer, *Disarmament and the War on Poverty* (Philadelphia: American Friends Service Committee, 1964).

ning has been made by the United Nations, which has emphasized a number of basic sociological advantages in a conversion of the international economy to peacetime production. First, the general level of living would rise, since federal agencies would begin to devote far more attention to matters of social welfare, health, and education. Second, a reduction in the armaments industry would accelerate the tendency toward the shorter work week and increase experimentation in types of work habitats and new forms of automation that avoid social disruption. Third, a conversion to peacetime production would decrease the sort of tensions that lead to privatization and general fear for the future. Personal planning would take on more meaning. Fourth, distinctions between have and have-not nations would be fewer, at least in military terms. A by-product would be less spending for nonprofitable and rapidly obsolete military hardware and more spending for commodity production. Fifth, the value system itself would undergo transformation. The faith in raw power could be expected to give way to negotiation and easing of tensions through rational and juridical means. Sixth, cultural contacts would increase as would the possibility of opening yet newer horizons for settlements through deeper understanding.[55]

Given the fears of many Americans about the personal sacrifices involved in a program of disarmament, it is necessary to conduct reconversion and conversion in certain ways. First, the quicker the conversion the less likely that wrong decisions will be made as a result of procrastination. Second, people are more likely to be convinced of the value of a reconversion policy if it is connected with a general policy of arms reduction or disarmament of a specific type. Third, the development of a "crash program" for retraining personnel while retooling factories for peacetime enterprise would reassure the involved publics that conversion does not axiomatically entail unemployment or lower income.[56]

Resources now allocated to the military can be released to civilian production without a boom or bust. This process could create the basis for beneficent social uses of natural and human resources.[57] The

[55] See *Economic and Social Consequences of Disarmament: Report of the Secretary General Transmitting the Study of His Consultative Group* (New York: United Nations Department of Economic and Social Affairs, 1962), pp. 45–46.
[56] See "The Economist Intelligence Unit," *The Economic Effects of Disarmament* (Toronto: University of Toronto Press, 1963).
[57] U.S. Arms Control and Disarmament Agency, *The Economic and Social Consequences of Disarmament* (Washington, D.C.: United States Arms Control and Disarmament Agency, March 1962), p. 35.

breakup of the Communist bloc as a monolithic unit has moved with surprising speed—especially when it is considered that the hegemony of the capitalist democracies was maintained for a far longer time. New forms of social behavior and political organization are being released. In this way, the fear of totalitarian *coups d'état* can be mitigated. It is highly questionable that any amount of military buildup can successfully cope with world Communism in a frontal assault. Direct military confrontations are now, in the nuclear era, ambitious and inconclusive. But it is quite possible that a new *Realpolitik* of mutual existence will involve arms reduction and arms elimination, and in this form institutionalize free choice and democratic norms on both sides of the Iron Curtain.

The age of "winning" a global conflict, after the spread of nuclear weaponry to more than one country, has ended. Logically, the age of complete defeat has also ended. Hence, if all future military actions must be restrictive in size and scope, rarely getting beyond the insurgency versus counterinsurgency stage, it seems eminently reasonable to suggest that agencies for settlement can be institutionalized without recourse to the symbolic, and now largely vacuous, threat of extermination.

There is no day of peace. Public safety comes closer to being realized as sensitivity to the needs of social development increases. There is no perfect planning for World War III because all rungs on the "ladder" to destruction cannot be accounted for. There is also no perfect plan for "phasing in" industrial conversion to nonmilitary production. On the other hand, the prima-facie priority which planning for peace has over planning for war is that war in our age, like peace, is largely a matter of impetus and impulse. Either reconversion of industrial production on one side or continued military production on the other may well prove decisive in pushing us toward the stars, cooperatively, or toward the abyss, collectively. The element of risk cannot be eliminated—no more by exponents of disarmament than by those urging continued arms spending. The real question is not *how much* but just *what* are the United States and the Soviet Union willing to risk?

Social Change and Political Cooperation: Conclusions

The velocity of social development, carrying as it must the destruction of traditional power relations and power matrices, necessarily raises with renewed acuteness the question of conflict and its resolution. Although there is broad recognition that international peace is a basic requirement of social development, it is less well understood that one is sometimes purchased at the cost of the other.[58]

Pax Romana, the peace of the Caesars, was achieved by creating an international hegemony which seriously stifled the growth of the captive states within the Roman Empire. The Congress of Vienna was successful only until the 1848 revolution, that is, only as long as the bourgeois-aristocrat equilibrium could be maintained. The present "delicate balance of terror" is operative only to the degree that a bilateral system of power exists between the American and Soviet bloc nations. On the other side, rapid social development has in the past been accompanied by widespread economic and political upheaval, not to mention wars affecting large numbers of people. The demand for social change on a wide front has been materially assisted by international conflict between the periphery and the center of military power. The fact that power now "cancels out" is a stimulant to further extensive social change.[59]

The great dilemma is that with social development more necessary than ever before, warfare has become a less viable instrument for producing desired changes than ever before.[60] In its most fundamental meaning war has become obsolescent, since the possibility of one side emerging victorious has now been obviated by the power of massive retaliation, by the capacity of both sides to annihilate each other. In this period of possible annihilation, then, the problem of social development urgently requires a reconsideration of the basic forms of human cooperation, or in the language of military analysts, human bargaining.[61] It takes little imagination to construct a utopia in which war could be eliminated. All that is required is a picture of the world in which there are no "sides" at all. The really complicated problem is how to live in a world of "sides," and in a world which witnesses the constant imbalancing of an inherited power equilibrium by the creation of yet new "sides."

In the broadest sense, the problem can be stated as follows: (1) when there is little or no social development, and if a single power can impose a universal dominion, then some kind of Caesaristic consensus obtains; (2) when there is rapid social development, and if no single power can assert a universal dominion, then some kind of conflict

---

[58] See Thomas C. Schelling, *The Strategy of Conflict* (Cambridge: Harvard University Press, 1960).
[59] See Horowitz, *Games, Strategies and Peace, op. cit.*
[60] See Kenneth E. Boulding, *Conflict and Defense: A General Theory* (New York: Harper and Row, 1962).
[61] See Hannah Arendt, *On Revolution* (New York: Viking Press, 1963).

d this shifting about, the agencies for international settlement will
e. In brief, bilateral cooperation will be made possible, if not in-
ble, precisely because of the rise of new nations to power. This
eration may not be altruistic in character; that is, it may be stimu-
 by a common fear that the failure to institutionalize norms of
eration soon, while the power "players" are few in number, will
 it only that much harder to do the same thing later, when the
ber of players in the world power struggle multiply.
at cooperation offers some viable paths to survival and the resolu-
of conflict does not mean that social development will not be ad-
ly affected. Cooperation is itself an ambiguous notion; it can refer
 "balance of power" scheme or to a "balance of number" scheme.
developing regions already outnumber the traditional centers of
er, yet it is clear that ultimate decisions affecting the fate of the
d still reside in the holders of nuclear power. Under such condi-
 the best that developing nations can hope to achieve is the ar-
ement of "nuclear free" zones, in the hope that a wider basis of
eration between the power blocs can be effected. Even if a maxi-
 degree of cooperation is maintained regarding procedural matters
adequate definition of the conflicts, maximization of factual infor-
on regarding potential conflicts, and testing proposals against past
ience), the overriding conflict of interests may forestall any basic
ment. It must be noted that only when interests coincide, as in the
ited use of nuclear weapons, can a *general* theory of cooperation
aintained. Beyond that point, interests come to the foreground.
 the developing regions are considered very much a part of these
ests of major powers. Therefore a basic stumbling block to coop-
on is the limited feasibility of maintaining the "rules of the game"
r conditions where "sides" do indeed have something to lose and
thing to gain.
is real difficulty in maintaining parity raises the generic problem
cooperation is negatively induced. The likelihood of cooperation
r conditions of one side winning and the other losing is a very
herous plausibility—perhaps the best available, yet quite subject to
tion. Therefore the growth of a Third World has a dangerous side
 the abandonment of cooperation, even in establishing the rules for
ramming future conflicts. There are advantages as well as risks. If
r more area clusters gained great power, a two-player game would
restalled. For such an event to occur, the developing areas would
selves have to develop independent nuclear deterrents—and hence
d the size and scale of arms races.
ere is a circularity to the problem of cooperation because there is

obtains—usually stabilizing itself at the insurgency level; and (3) when there is rapid social development, and if the major powers can agree on the rules for the conduct of international affairs, then some kind of cooperation obtains.[62] That another *Pax Romana* (in this case a *Pax Americana* or *Pax Sovietica*) may come into existence is highly unlikely. Therefore consensus, or the internal agreement in principle on the forms of social action, is also improbable in its present form. We know that any further social development through nuclear struggles is no less unlikely, since conflict on any large scale will prove mutually untenable. This leaves us with the problem of how we are to cooperate or bargain with each other in a world which insists on the absolute primacy of social change *even at the expense of life* itself. Neither conflict nor consensus has been able to explain the impulse toward development—for both are total concepts. And what is needed are explanations for insurgency-guerrilla warfare—of systems explaining a partial world of partial commitments.

The idea that world hegemony can be achieved, through either pacific or military means, through either a consensus blanket or outright military conflict, must reckon with the uneven nature of development. Even if the world were thoroughly capitalist in character, peace would not be assured; we have the amazingly warlike behavior of capitalist nations for the last three hundred years to substantiate this. The burden of proof is clearly on the shoulders of those who think that any *Pax Americana* would achieve peace and development. And even if the world were thoroughly socialist in nature, peace would not be assured, because, as has become clearly evident, the problem of nationalism remains.[63] A classic claim of socialist theorists has been snapped decisively by the rise of various forms of communism. The competition between Communist China and the Soviet Union is clearly quite as intense as anything witnessed in the Western capitalist world. The fact that a basic claim of socialism is its ability to forge a new and tolerable world hegemony makes the conflict within the Soviet bloc nations more serious and potentially more violent than anything hitherto seen in the West. The West, after all, allowed for many divergencies, if for no other reason than that the ideology of capitalism has bred competition and freedom in spheres of trade, commerce, and even political forms.

[62] See Irving L. Horowitz, "A Formalization of the Sociology of Knowledge," *Behavioral Science*, 9, 1 (January 1964), especially pp. 52–54.
[63] See on this Hans Kohn, *The Idea of Nationalism: A Study of Its Origins and Background* (New York: The Macmillan Company, 1944); also by Kohn, "A New Look at Nationalism," *The Virginia Quarterly Review*, 32 (Summer 1956), pp. 321–332.

If consensus and conflict have canceled one another out, the possibilities for planned cooperation are immense. The right to be different has become as much a national need as it was formerly held to be an individual need. This right to be different, once institutionalized in world law, in world agreements covering contact situations (such as travel in outer space, zone restrictions, etc.), makes possible the kind of unimpeded social development which emerging societies require, and which the past concentration on consensus and/or conflict seriously blunted.

The issue of human cooperation, although related to consensus and conflict, has a quite unique dimension and operational range. A decision in favor of consensus theory is not automatically a decision on behalf of cooperation. It is simply a decision to examine social structure to the partial or total exclusion of social dynamics, a decision to act as if breaks with tradition, shifts in the culture complex, and disruption of moral patterns can be described as unimportant. There is a kind of safety in the continuing, the prolonged, the enduring. But this safety ignores social change, and hence abandons problems confronting those most directly concerned with achieving human cooperation at group, regional, national, or international levels.

The functional successes of any given social structure should not define the limits of sociological discourse. For we may find ourselves celebrating our social order one day, and another the next—and in precisely the same "functional-structural" terms. The central task of sociology is explanation and prediction, each in terms of the other, and no theory which identifies consensus with the social order as such can fail to come upon hard times: where there is a social consensus there are no social problems. Such a state of affairs hardly exists today.

What, then, is the difference between conflict and consensus on one side and cooperation on the other? There seem to be three distinguishable factors. First, conflict-consensus stands for agreement internally, that is, by shared perspectives, agreement only on the form of behavior. We speak of consensus if all members of the Women's Christian Temperance Union agree to abstain from drinking alcoholic beverages. But cooperation is agreement on the forms allowed for drinking and the forms allowed for curbing the consumption of liquor. As the Prohibition era dramatically showed, the substitution of consensus for cooperation did not lead to a new morality but to chaos.

Second, there is similarly the danger that too heavy an emphasis on consensus in the African states will result in further racial warfare as a mode of settling conflicts. The multiplicity of nations in Africa encourages belief that cooperative forms of polity will prevail. Interest-a circularity to the facts involved. To expand the bargaining power of the Third World entails an expansion of the risks of war by enlarging the possibilities of aggression and conflict. And yet to curtail or limit this bargaining power is to jeopardize the Third World entirely, to make it subject to precisely the forms of big-power bilateral settlement that is so abhorred by the emergent nations.

The assumption of the major powers is that cooperation is possible because development presupposes life. The Third World may be willing to sacrifice life to preserve the principle of development. Formulas cannot break this dichotomy—only the general recognition that anything, either life or development, pushed to its ultimate may prove to be self-defeating will do so.

Cooperation may prove a slender reed upon which to hang our hopes for both the resolution of conflict and social development. Any return to consensus theory, however, would mark a step backward in the toleration of social differences, and any return to conflict theory would mark a step backward from the realities of that amount of "internationalization" of life thus far registered. Human reason has posed the problems in this ultimate way by virtue of the scientific and technological achievements it has thus far gained. It is not too much to hope that this same sort of reason will prove to be the basic variable needed in social and political life.[64]

That something is drastically wrong with the contemporary world scene, and that this something is directly connected to our failure to establish machinery for the preservation of life and limb will come as a shock to no one. What is shocking, however, is the fact that the historical effort to secure international peace through the arts of compromise has been progressively discredited.[65] Conventional diplomacy, big-power chauvinism, and the military-industrial machines have replaced settlement with repression. We are living in an age of military determinism.

If we are not to surrender to the pure utilitarianism of deterrence theory, or the nihilistic cynicism of doomsday "solutions," an alternative to this military determinism must be located.[66] Basically, any appeal for survival has to be aimed at a less ambitious and, perhaps, less

---

[64] For an excellent summary of these issues, see Jessie Bernard, "Some Current Conceptualizations in the Field of Conflict," *American Journal of Sociology*, 70 (January 1965), pp. 442–454.

[65] See Charles Moraze, "The Settlement of Conflicts in Western Cultures," *International Social Science Journal*, 15, 2 (1963), pp. 248–249.

[66] For a discussion of "doomsday machines," see Kahn, *On Thermonuclear War*, *op. cit.*, especially pp. 144–160.

noble level than the levels that characterized our intellectual ancestors. Our position takes for granted the need of men to engage in conflict—whether such conflict is caused by an "innate propensity to violence" (which I doubt) or is a consequence of imperfect social equilibrium (which I consider more likely). We have insisted on "either/or" solutions for too long: either conflict or consensus, either compromise or victory. But when we examine the social infrastructure, what becomes most apparent is that conflict can be programmed no less than consensus. We are in a position not only to tolerate conflict with a low yield of violence but to induce such conflict for the purpose of avoiding all-out conflict that is unstructured. Political parties, voluntary social organizations, and athletic events are examples of the safety-valve factor in such forms of conflict. By taking conflict as a social constant rather than as a social problem, it may yet be possible to avoid the consequences of maximum conflict, that is, a militarized society. Low-yield violence is at least as plausible within a world of programmed conflict as it is in either the demands of consensus or the diplomatic faith in compromise. There is little experimental evidence that such an approach to the pacification of the world will actually work. But there is considerable evidence that the thundering totalisms now proliferating in the press, the pulpit, and the professions can do no better and, indeed, have done much worse.

The foregoing materials can hardly be considered as more than a preface to war as a social problem. We know more about the effects of radiation and postattack conversion problems than we do about the effects of the existence of thermonuclear weapons on adolescent behavior. Put more directly, we know more about *post*-World War III than we do about *pre*-World War II. Little wonder that the feeling of disaster should finally give way to a clinical anticipation of what Leslie Fiedler calls "waiting for the end." Loathing has given way to longing. Efforts to find a solution to war as a *social* problem have given way to efforts to find a solution to war as a *private* problem. To be sure, there are few "hard data" correlating such matters as juvenile rates of crime with expectancies of death, or early marriages with expectancies of short lifetimes. There is even some indication that the proximity of conflict may bring on a condition of mass hysteria in the form of an euphoric response to patriotic symbols and ego identification with the destructive leader-father.

The thermonuclear age in America has presented us with some difficult issues. The quality of conventional thinking about deviance and disorganization is outmoded. The quality of conventional thinking about the place of the United States in a world context is outrageous. Men have become antisocial and antipolitical, in retaliation for the humiliations and the sufferings caused by the development of total weaponry in an age of partial solutions. How ironic it is that the scientific frame of mind should counsel caution and circumspection in judgment and prediction at the very moment when these same scientific habits are producing instruments of military annihilation. Man has learned to live with many paradoxes. It remains to be seen whether he can coexist with this supreme contradiction between *cautious habits* of thought and *criminal products* of thought.

Bibliography

Those wishing to pursue the literature systematically would do well to go through the files of such journals as *World Politics, Annals, International Conciliation,* and *Foreign Affairs.* In addition, the reader's attention is drawn to several journals that have come into existence as a direct consequence of the thermonuclear epoch: the *Bulletin of the Atomic Scientists,* the *Journal of Conflict Resolution, Survival: The Institute for Strategic Studies, War Peace Report,* and the newsletter, *The Correspondent.* The entrance into the field of *Current Thought on Peace and War* fills a huge void in systematizing bibliographical materials. In addition, the various governmental agencies concerned with nuclear conflict have issued bibliographical materials at various times. For the lay reader, the best of these is the one prepared by S. L. Harrison, *Selected Bibliography on Arms Control* (Washington: Institute for Defense Analysis, 1962). Those who wish to consult the field of war and peace research more thoroughly might do well to start with the various readers and anthologies presently available. They, rather than any single book, can provide an appreciation of the spectrum of opinion and information in this strange area.

Benoit, Emile et al., *Economic Adjustments to Disarmament* (New York: Institute for International Order, 1960).
Benoit, Emile and Kenneth E. Boulding, eds., *Disarmament and the Economy* (New York: Harper and Row, 1963).
Bernard, Jessie et al., *The Nature of Conflict: Studies on the Sociological Aspects of International Tensions* (Paris: UNESCO, 1957).
Bramson, Leon and George W. Goethals, eds., *War: Studies from Psychology, Sociology and Anthropology* (New York: Basic Books, 1964).
Brennan, Donald G., ed., *Arms Control, Disarmament, and National Security* (New York: George Braziller, 1961).
Cleveland, Harlan, ed., *The Promise of World Tensions* (New York: The Macmillan Company, 1961).

Fairchild, Johnson and David Landman, eds., *America Faces the Nuclear Age* (New York: Sheridan House, 1961).

Falk, Richard A. and Richard J. Barnet, eds., *Security in Disarmament* (Princeton, N.J.: Princeton University Press, 1965).

Feld, Bernard T. et al., *Technical Problems of Arms Control* (New York: Institute for International Order, 1960).

Fisher, Roger, ed., *International Conflict and Behavioral Science* (New York: Basic Books, 1964).

Fleming, D. F., ed., "The Changing Cold War," *The Annals of the American Academy of Political and Social Science*, 351 (1964).

Fowler, John M., ed., *Fallout: A Study of Superbombs, Strontium 90 and Survival* (New York: Basic Books, 1960).

Frisch, D. F., ed., *Arms Reduction: Program and Issues* (New York: The Twentieth Century Fund, 1961).

Furnis, Edgar S., ed., *American Military Policy: Strategic Aspects of World Political Geography* (New York: Rinehart, 1957).

Glasstone, Samuel, ed., *The Effects of Nuclear Weapons* (Washington, D.C.: U.S. Government Printing Office, revised edition, 1962).

Goldwin, Robert A., ed., *America Armed: Essays on United States Military Policy* (Chicago: Rand McNally, 1963).

Guetzkow, Harold et al., *Simulation in International Relations: Developments for Research and Teaching* (Englewood Cliffs, N.J.: Prentice-Hall, Inc. 1963).

Henkin, Louis, ed., *Arms Control: Issues for the Public* (Englewood Cliffs, N.J.: Prentice-Hall, 1961).

Holton, Gerald, ed., "Arms Control" issue of *Daedalus*, 89, 4 (1960).

Horowitz, Irving L., ed., *Conference on Conflict, Consensus and Cooperation*, Proceedings of the New York State Sociological Association (Geneva, N.Y.: Hobart and William Smith Colleges, 1962).

Kaufmann, William W., ed., *Military Policy and National Security* (Princeton, N.J.: Princeton University Press, 1956).

Kelman, Herbert C., ed., *International Behavior: A Social Psychological Analysis* (New York: Holt, Rinehart and Winston, 1965).

Knorr, Klaus, ed., *NATO and American Security* (Princeton, N.J.: Princeton University Press, 1959).

Lefever, Ernest W., ed., *Arms and Arms Control* (New York: Frederick A. Praeger, 1962).

McClelland, Charles A., ed., *Nuclear Weapons, Missiles, and Future War* (San Francisco: Chandler Publishing Company, 1960).

McNeil, Elton B., ed., *The Nature of Human Conflict* (Englewood Cliffs, N.J.: Prentice-Hall, 1965).

Melman, Seymour, ed., *Disarmament: Its Politics and Economics* (Boston: The American Academy of Arts and Sciences, 1962).

Melman, Seymour, ed., *Inspection for Disarmament* (New York: Columbia University Press, 1958).

Miller, Michael M. and Jacob R. Fishman, eds., *Proceedings of the Emergency Conference on Hostility, Aggression and War*, publication of the *Journal of the American Association for Social Psychiatry*, November 1961.

Nagle, William J., ed., *Morality and Modern Warfare: The State of the Question* (Baltimore: Helicon Press, 1960).

Pear, Tom H., ed., *Psychological Factors in Peace and War* (London: Hutchinson, 1950).

Rosenau, James N., ed., *International Aspects of Civil Strife* (Princeton, N.J.: Princeton University Press, 1964).
Stein, Walter, ed., *Nuclear Weapons and Christian Conscience* (London: Merlin Press, 1961).
Strausz-Hupé, Robert et al., *Protracted Conflict* (New York: Harper and Brothers, 1959).
Thompson, Charles S., ed., *Morals and Missiles: Catholic Essays on the Problem of War Today* (London: James Clarke, 1959).
Wallace, V. H., ed., *Paths to Peace* (Melbourne, Australia: Melbourne University Press, 1957).
Zawodny, J. K., ed., "Unconventional Warfare," *The Annals of the American Academy of Political and Social Science*, 341 (1962).

Name Index

Abegglen, James C., 194n
Abel-Smith, Brian, 513
Abramovitz, Moses, 470n
Abu-Lughod, Janet, 519n, 533n
Adenaes, Johs, 237n, 266n
Adorno, T. W., 552n
Adrian, Charles R., 392n, 413n
Aichhorn, August, 247
Akers, Ronald L., 213
Albee, Edward, 567
Albee, George W., 308n
Albrecht, Ruth, 187n
Aldridge, Gordon J., 192n
Alexander, Franz, 247
Alinsky, Saul, 416
Allen, Francis A., 258n, 263n
Allen, Frederick L., 171n
Allinsmith, Wesley, 289n, 309n
Allport, Gordon W., 356
Amis, Kingsley, 475n
Anderson, C. A., 86n
Anderson, Nels, 367n
Andrzejewski, Stanislaw, 735n
Angle, Paul M., 224n
Arendt, Hannah, 120, 138, 553n, 740n
Aristophanes, 46
Arond, Henry, 334n
Asheim, Lester, 113n, 589n
Ashworth, Williams, 517, 518n

Ausubel, David P., 92, 93
Ausubel, Pearl, 92, 93

Babchuk, Nicholas, 379n
Bailyn, Lotte, 564n
Bakke, E. W., 130n, 136n
Baldwin, James, 586
Bandura, Albert, 227, 231
Banfield, Edward, 531n
Banton, Michael, 252, 356
Barnet, Richard J., 748
Barr, Sherman, 563n
Barringer, Herbert B., 187n
Barth, Ernest A., 386n
Barton, Allen H., 93n, 724n
Bauer, Alice H., 553n, 561n, 566n, 569
Bauer, Raymond A., 553n, 561n, 566n, 569
Baum, Martha, 244n, 273n, 275n
Baver, P. T., 672n
Bazelan, David, 261
Becker, Howard S., 13n, 18n, 20n, 27n, 30n, 86, 204n, 584n, 655n
Bell, Daniel, 138, 475n, 563n
Bell, Wendell, 403n
Bellin, Seymour S., 451n
Bendix, Reinhard, 19, 222n, 375n, 606n, 660, 662n, 663n, 669n
Benedict, Ruth, 172n
Bennett, E. H., 359

751

Benoit, Emile, 728n, 747
Bensman, Joseph, 569n
Berelson, Bernard, 566n
Beresford, John C., 186n
Berger, Bennett, 173n
Berger, Bennett S., 39n
Bergson, Abram, 734n
Berkowitz, L., 563n
Bernard, Jessie, 367n, 745n, 747
Bernstein, Basil, 91
Beshers, James, 525n
Bettelheim, Bruno, 40, 49, 173n, 289n
Beverly, Robert F., 275n
Biddle, Bruce J., 96n
Biddle, William W., 371n
Bienstock, Herbert, 469n
Birren, James E., 167n
Blake, Judith, 650
Blau, Peter M., 18n
Blauner, R., 131n
Bloom, Benjamin S., 80n
Bloomberg, Warner, Jr., 22, 30, 361n, 374n, 384n, 389n, 404n
Bluestone, George, 589n
Blumer, Herbert, 11n
Bogart, Leo, 156n
Bogue, Donald J., 99n, 127n, 128n
Bollens, John C., 383n, 384n, 386n, 387n, 403n
Bond, Horace Mann, 94, 95
Booth, Charles, 426
Borgatta, Edgar F., 228n
Borrowman, Merla L., 98
Boskoff, Alvin, 367n
Boulding, Kenneth E., 728n, 736, 740n, 747
Braine, John, 475n
Bramson, Leon, 474
Bredemeier, Harry, 499n
Brennan, Donald G., 713n, 747
Briar, Scott, 255n
Brink, William, 328, 356
Brim, Orville G., Jr., 269n
Brodbeck, Arthur J., 563n
Brodie, Bernard, 699n, 701
Bromberg, Walter, 25n
Bronner, Augusta F., 227, 228
Brooks, Van Wyck, 582n, 583n
Broom, Leonard, 357
Brown, Allen, 708n
Brown, Bert, 93n

Brown, K. E., 102n
Bruce, Lenny, 567
Bruner, Jerome S., 112
Bryce, Herrington J., 446n
Bryson, Lyman, 578n
Buchanan, William, 195n
Burgess, Ernest W., 16n, 167n, 193n
Burkhead, Jesse, 426n
Burnham, D. H., 359
Burns, Arthur F., 480n
Burns, Eveline, 507n
Burton, Hal, 536n

Callahan, Raymond E., 108n
Cameron, Mary Owen, 240n
Campbell, Angus, 194n
Caplan, Gerald, 299n
Caplovitz, David, 487n
Caplow, Theodore, 317, 318n
Carcopino, Jerome, 522n
Carnegie, Andrew, 123
Carter, Richard F., 384n
Cartter, Allan Murray, 473n, 474n, 476n
Cassen, R. H., 473n
Caudill, William A., 293
Cavan, Ruth, 490n
Chandler, B. J., 107
Charlesworth, James C., 183n
Chauncy, Henry, 103n
Chein, Isidor, 26n
Childs, Marquis, 735n
Christiansen, Gordon, 695n
Christie, Nils, 262n
Christopher, Stephan C., 709n
Cicourel, Aaron V., 54n, 73n, 655n
Clark, Colin, 672n
Clark, Joseph, 509n
Clark, Kenneth B., 87n, 357, 487
Clausen, John A., 286, 303
Clayton, Horace R., 357
Clemmer, Donald, 271, 272
Cleveland, Harlan, 747
Clinard, Marshall B., 248n
Cloward, Richard A., 24n, 69n, 70, 220, 222, 233–234, 270n, 273n, 431n, 507n
Cohen, Albert K., 20n, 216n, 217, 220, 232–233, 431n
Cohen, Bernard, 566n
Cohen, Jerome, 300n, 301n, 459n, 488n
Colean, Miles, 536
Coleman, James S., 39, 41, 73n, 414n

NAME INDEX

Comings, Carolyn, 74n
Commager, Henry S., 171n
Conant, James B., 100n
Cook, Fred J., 720, 721n
Cooley, C. H., 140
Corwin, R., 563n
Coser, Lewis, 569–570
Cremin, Lawrence A., 82n
Cressey, Donald R., 218n, 229n, 230n, 241n, 245n, 271n
Crook, Guy Hamilton, 182n
Crosland, Anthony, 80n
Cumming, Elaine, 252n
Cumming, Ian M., 252n
Cutright, Phillips, 361n, 697
Cutter, Henry S. G., 24n

Dahl, Robert A., 384n, 387, 388n, 401, 405n, 413n, 424
Dahrendorf, Ralf, 376n, 377n, 659n
Davenport, John, 443, 444n
David, Martin, 455n
Davis, Allison, 20n, 91, 489, 490n
Davis, Kingsley, 172n, 650, 658n, 662n
Davis, Louis E., 162n
Davis, Otis A., 540n
Dean, Dwight G., 404n
De Kooning, Willem, 581
DeMarche, David F., 309n
Denney, Reuel, 40
Dentler, Robert A., 697
Deutsch, Martin, 93n, 301n
Deutsch, Morton, 695n
Dewey, John, 82
Diebold, N. W. J., 157n
Dinerstein, H. S., 708n
Dinitz, Simon, 230n
Disraeli, Benjamin, 474
Dobriner, William M., 411n
Dodd, Stuart C., 709n
Donahue, Wilma, 194n, 195n
Donnelly, Richard C., 261n
Douglas, J. W. B., 93n
Drake, St. Clair, 357
Dubin, Robert, 132n, 136
Dublin, Louis I., 168n
Dubos, René, 305
Duggar, George S., 446n
Duhl, Leonard J., 17, 30, 295n, 305n
Dumpson, James, 463n
Duncan, Otis Dudley, 365n, 627n

Dunham, Arthur, 368n
Durkheim, Emile, 41, 216n, 220, 267n, 664n, 677, 732
Dye, Thomas R., 411n

Eastman, Max, 669n
Edell, Laura, 252n
Eells, K., 90n, 91
Eisenberg, P., 130n
Eisenhower, Dwight, 195, 429, 494, 721
Eisenstadt, S. N., 131n, 173n
Ekman, Paul, 724n
Elias, C. E., 532n
Eliot, T. S., 44n, 553n, 574, 582
Elkins, Stanley M., 83n, 357
Elliott, Mabel A., 223n
Ellison, Ralph, 351
Engel-Lang, Gladys, 12n
Engels, Friedrich, 123, 677
Ensminger, Douglas, 404n
Epstein, Irwin, 507n
Epstein, Lenore A., 185n, 456n, 511n
Erbe, William, 405n
Erikson, Erik H., 40, 48, 174n, 285n, 289n
Eulau, Heinz, 195n
Evans, William M., 379n
Evenden, E. S., 97n

Fairchild, Johnson, 747
Falk, Jacqueline M., 167n
Falk, Richard A., 748
Fararo, T. J., 389n
Faris, Robert E., 217n
Faulkner, William, 557
Faunce, William A., 159n
Fefferman, Hilbert, 530n
Fein, Rashi, 308n
Feld, Bernard T., 748
Feld, Sheila, 308n
Feldman, Arnold S., 20, 31
Ferguson, Leroy C., 195n
Ferman, Louis, 492n
Festinger, Leon, 5n
Fiedler, Leslie, 552n
Fisher, Roger, 748
Fishman, Jacob R., 43, 748
Fishman, Joshua A., 377n
Fiske, Marjorie, 552n, 574n
Fitzwilliams, Jeanette M., 466n
Fleming, D. F., 722n, 748
Floud, J., 86n

Foard, Ashley A., 530n
Foley, Mary Mix, 519n, 533n
Foote, Nelson, 519n
Force, Maryanne T., 403n
Ford, Henry, 123
Fowler, John M., 697, 748
Frazier, Benjamin W., 97n
Frazier, E. Franklin, 357
Freedman, Deborah, 631n
Freedman, Ronald, 631n, 654n
Freeman, Howard E., 27n
Freeman, Linton C., 386n, 388n, 389n
Freed, Daniel J., 265n
Freel, Fern, 426n
Freidson, Eliot, 562n, 563
Freud, Sigmund, 247, 281, 289, 659n
Fried, Marc, 305n
Friedenberg, Edgar Z., 18, 20, 28, 111n
Friedman, Milton, 500n
Friedmann, Eugene A., 175n, 182n, 188n
Friedmann, Georges, 132n, 161n
Frisch, D. F., 748
Fritz, John, 113n
Fromm, Erich, 40, 138, 289n, 408n
Frymier, Jack R., 101n
Fuller, Richard C., 2, 3, 5, 6, 11
Furnis, Edgar S., 748

Galbraith, John Kenneth, 432n, 436n, 439n, 445, 466, 510
Galerson, W., 131n
Gallup, George, 375n
Gamson, William A., 714n, 728n
Gandhi, Mahatma, 679
Gandhi, Mohandas K., 319
Gans, Herbert J., 20, 30, 305n, 363, 526n, 556n, 562n, 582n, 590n, 591n, 595n
Garfinkel, Harold, 9n, 243n, 248n
Garofalo, Raffaele, 259
Garrity, Donald L., 244
Garthoff, Raymond L., 708n
Gastil, Raymond D., 718n
Gaudet, Helen, 566n
Geer, Blanche, 27n, 30
Geertz, Hildred, 24n
Gennep, Arnold van, 29n, 172n
Gerard, Donald L., 26n
Gerth, Hans, 140
Gervasi, S. D., 473n
Gibbons, Don C., 239n, 244

Gibson, William, 556n
Gillies, James, 532n
Ginzberg, Eli, 470n, 501n
Gladwin, Thomas, 485
Glaser, Daniel, 242, 274n
Glasstone, Samuel, 748
Glazer, Nathan, 602n
Glenn, Norval D., 357
Glick, Ira O., 561n
Glick, Paul C., 186n
Goethals, George W., 289n, 309n, 747
Goffman, Erving, 18n, 27n, 47, 140, 268, 269n, 292
Goldhamer, Herbert, 25n, 379n, 563n
Goldman, Nathan, 251
Goldman, Richard Franko, 112n
Goldsmith, Selma, 438
Goldstein, Joseph, 256n, 261n
Goldwin, Robert A., 357, 748
Gompers, Samuel, 148
Goode, W. J., 663n
Goodman, Paul, 39, 73n, 155, 408n
Goodman, Percival, 408n
Gordis, Robert, 723
Gordon, C. Wayne, 379n
Gordon, John E., 309n
Gordon, Margaret S., 127n, 128n, 182n, 473n
Gordon, Milton M., 357
Green, Edward, 266n
Green, Harold P., 718n
Greenberg, Clement, 552n, 557, 574
Greer, Scott, 20, 22n, 362, 372n, 402n, 403n, 404n, 407, 523n, 524n, 538n, 541n, 546n
Gregory, Francis W., 194n
Grier, Eunice, 357
Grier, George, 357
Grigg, Charles, 23n
Grigsby, William G., 357, 426n, 433n, 519n, 533n, 544n
Gross, Bertram, 426n, 435, 499n
Gross, Hilton P., 696n
Gross, Neal, 134
Grosser, George, 218
Gruenberg, Ernest M., 300n
Grusky, Oscar, 272
Guest, Robert H., 136n, 159n
Guetzkow, Harold, 748
Gurin, Gerald, 308n
Gurwell, John K., 195n

NAME INDEX

Gusfield, Joseph R., 10n
Gutkind, E. A., 536n
Gyman, Harry, 238n

Haag, Ernest van den, 552n, 553n, 554, 557, 558, 560, 564–565, 569n, 574, 605n
Haar, Charles M., 533n
Habakkuk, H. J., 113n
Haber, Allen, 492n
Haber, William, 151n
Hacker, Andrew, 513
Hadley, Arthur T., 699n
Haer, John L., 405n
Hagan, Roger, 737
Hagen, Elizabeth, 103
Haggerstrom, Warren, 416n
Hajda, Jan, 411n
Hall, Jerome, 206n
Hall, Stuart, 618n
Halperin, Morton, 699n, 731n
Halsey, A. H., 86n
Hamblin, Robert L., 695n
Handlin, Oscar, 372n, 379n, 482n, 553n, 577n
Hansen, Robert C., 373n
Hardt, Robert, 431n, 476n
Harlan, William H., 173n
Harper, Ernest B., 368n
Harrington, Alan, 482
Harrington, Michael, 184n, 512
Harris, Louis, 328, 356
Hart, H. L. A., 202n
Hart, Henry M., 202n
Hartley, E. L., 490n
Hatt, Paul K., 379n, 658n
Haubrich, Vernon F., 86n, 89
Hauser, Philip M., 350, 454n, 627n, 654n
Havighurst, Robert J., 182n
Hawley, Amos H., 388n
Healy, William, 227, 228, 247
Hechinger, Fred, 101
Heer, David M., 186n
Hegel, F., 138
Heinstein, Martin, 182n
Heironimus, M., 563n
Henkin, Louis, 748
Henry, Jules, 35, 45n, 47, 733n
Herzberg, F., 131n, 132n
Herzog, Herta, 565n
Hewitt, Lester E., 231

Hillery, George A., Jr., 365n
Himmelweit, H., 564n
Hirsch, Werner Z., 392n
Hitler, Adolf, 329, 342, 568
Hodges, Harold M., Jr., 20n
Hoebel, E. Adamson, 521n, 524n
Hofstadter, Richard, 82n
Hoggart, Richard, 569
Hoiberg, Otto C., 368n
Hollingshead, August B., 39, 300n, 302, 561n, 580n
Holton, Gerald, 748
Homans, George C., 375n
Hoos, Ida R., 163n
Horowitz, Eugene L., 337
Horowitz, Irving Louis, 22, 31, 728n, 740n, 741n, 748
Hoselitz, Bert F., 667n, 679n, 728n
Howe, Irving, 552n, 560, 574
Howe, John, 25n
Hughes, Everett C., 29n, 356n, 357
Hughes, H. Stuart, 664n, 701
Hughes, Helen M., 357
Humphrey, Hubert H., 357, 430
Hunter, Floyd G., 369, 388n
Husén, Torsten, 90
Huszar, George B. de, 710n
Hyman, Herbert H., 222n, 385n, 388n
Hyman, Stanley Edgar, 553n

Ianni, Francis A. J., 364n
Ikle, Fred Charles, 696n
Inkeles, Alex, 132n, 663n
Irwin, John, 271n

Jacobowitz, Ellen, 275n
Jacobs, Jane, 541n
Jacobs, Norman, 552n, 557n, 572n, 575n, 577n
Jacobs, Paul, 128n, 151n
Jacobson, H. B., 159n
Jahoda, Marie, 283, 606n
Janowitz, Morris, 735n
Jarrell, Randall, 553n
Jefferson, Thomas, 359, 415
Jellinek, E. M., 10n
Jencks, Christopher, 602n
Jenkins, Richard L., 231, 241n
Jennings, Hilda, 538n
Johnson, Guy B., 214n

Johnson, Lyndon B., 355, 429, 440
Johnson, Stuart D., 386n
Johnston, Denis F., 99n
Johnston, Norman, 214n, 219n, 266n
Jones, Wyatt C., 228n
Juin, Alphonse, 718n
Kahn, Herman, 701, 703, 711n, 713n, 745n
Kahn, R. L., 135
Kalecki, Michael, 480
Kaplan, Jerome, 192n
Kaplan, Max, 182n
Kassalow, E. M., 157n
Katz, Elihu, 562n, 597n
Kaufman, Herbert, 387n
Kaufmann, William W., 699n, 748
Kautsky, John H., 663n
Keller, Suzanne, 92, 93
Kelman, Herbert C., 748
Keniston, Kenneth, 40
Kennedy, John F., 195, 309, 311, 355, 429, 430, 501, 715, 736
Keppel Francis, 105–107
Kershaw, J. A., 102n
Key, Barbara, 230n
Key, V. O., Jr., 385n, 395n, 402n, 403n
Keyserling, Leon, 440, 445, 446n, 449n, 453n, 454n, 473n, 499n
Killian, Lewis M., 12n, 23n
King, Martin Luther, 415
Kintner, William R., 723n
Kirk, Russell, 574
Kissinger, Henry A., 699n, 701, 703, 736n
Kitsuse, John I., 54n, 73n, 655n
Klapp, Orrin, E., 156n
Klapper, Joseph, 553n, 562n
Kleemeier, Robert W., 127n, 130n, 182n, 555n
Knorr, Klaus, 699n, 748
Knowles, John, 44
Knupfer, Genevieve, 606n
Koerner, James D., 100n
Kohn, Hans, 741n
Kolko, Gabriel, 426n, 434, 438n, 467, 470n, 473n, 497n
Komarovsky, Mirra, 131n, 552n
Kornbluh, Joyce, 492n
Kornhauser, Arthur, 137
Kornhauser, William, 131, 568n
Krebs, Juanita M., 182n
Krogman, Wilton, 331

Kuhn, Dorothy S., 277
Kuper, Leo, 357
Kurtz, Russell H., 369
Kuznets, Simon, 466, 467, 663n

La Follette, Robert, 721
Lamale, Helen H., 436n
Lampman, Robert J., 440, 449n, 461n, 466n, 470, 493n, 495, 500n
Landman, David, 747
Lane, Robert E., 194n
Lane, Robert P., 368
Lang, Kurt, 12n
Langner, Thomas S., 35n, 561n
Larsen, Otto N., 378n
Laski, Harold J., 710n
Lasswell, Harold D., 17n
Lattner, Albert L., 706n
Laurenti, Luigi, 25n
Lazarsfeld, Paul, 130n, 136n, 411n, 553n, 562n, 566n, 567n, 597n, 606n
Leavis, F. R., 553n
Lebeaux, Charles N., 444n, 561n
Lee, Alfred M., 11n
Lee, Robert S., 26n
Lefever, Ernest W., 731n, 748
Lehman, Harvey C., 195n
Leighton, Dorothea C., 561n
Lelyveld, Joseph, 729
Lemert, Edwin, 30n, 248n
Leopold, Robert L., 17, 30, 295n
Lerner, Allan Jay, 485
Lerner, Daniel, 17n, 571n, 572
LeVine, Robert A., 173n
Levine, Sol, 27n
Levinson, Harold M., 151n
Levitan, Sar A., 498n
Levy, Marion J., Jr., 670n
Levy, Sidney J., 561n
Lewis, Oscar, 20n, 490, 491
Lichfield, Nathaniel, 363n
Lieberson, Stanley, 364n
Lifton, Robert Jay, 40
Lincoln, Abraham, 339
Lindesmith, Alfred R., 8n, 10n
Linton, Ralph, 172n, 331
Lipset, Seymour M., 19, 131n, 194n, 222n, 375n, 616n, 663n, 721n
Litt, Edgar, 403n
Litwak, Eugene, 190n
Livingston, David T., 386n

NAME INDEX

Long, C. D., 127n
Long, Huey, 428
Long, Norton E., 21n, 374n
Lorge, Irving D., 90
Lorimer, Frank, 658n
Lortie, Dan C., 109, 112
Lotka, A. J., 168n
Lowe, Frederick, 485
Lowe, John C., 173n
Lowenthal, Leo, 552n, 553, 574n, 721n
Lowie, Robert H., 172n
Luce, R. Duncan, 698n
Lundberg, George A., 378n
Lunt, Paul S., 580n
Lyle, J., 564n
Lyman, Elizabeth, 132
Lynes, Russell, 375n, 582n, 583n
Lysgäard, Sverre, 490n

McCann, Richard V., 309n
McClelland, Charles A., 748
McCord, Joan, 247n
McCord, William, 247n
McDill, Edward L., 405n
MacDonald, Dwight, 551n, 552n, 553, 554n, 557, 560, 569n, 574, 577n
McEntire, Davis, 357
McGee, Reece J., 318n
McGinnis, Robert, 187n
McKay, Henry, 229
McKean, Roland M., 102n
MacKenzie, Norman, 513n
McKenzie, R. D., 522
McMurrin, Sterling M., 106n
McNamara, Robert, 153n
McNeil, Elton B., 748
McPhee, W., 566n
Macaulay, Hugh H., 433n, 434n
Maccoby, Eleanor, 250
Machlup, Fritz, 155n
Mack, Raymond W., 30, 317n, 329n, 334n, 358, 662n
Maher, Brendan, 275n
Mailer, Norman, 586
Malthus, Thomas Robert, 633, 634–636, 642–643
Mannheim, Karl, 132n, 172, 568
Manor, Stella P., 104n
Manuel, Frank, 124
Marburger, Carl L., 87, 89n
Marris, Peter, 549, 574n, 575

Marshall, Andrew M., 25n, 563n
Marshall, T. H., 664n
Martin, Roscoe C., 387n
Marx, Karl, 123, 124, 138, 677
Mathieson, Thomas, 262n
Matza, David, 217n, 236n, 246, 484n
May, Rollo, 40
Mayer, Kurt B., 375n
Mayer, Martin, 41, 112
Meacham, Stewart, 695n
Mead, George Herbert, 140, 662n
Mead, Margaret, 408n
Meehan, Thomas, 587n
Melman, Seymour, 731n, 748
Merton, Robert K., 2, 16n, 22n, 220, 233, 411, 523n, 567n, 569n, 706
Meuss, Rolf E., 40
Meyer, Henry J., 228n
Meyersohn, Rolf, 549, 555n, 562n
Meyerson, Martin, 531n
Michael, Donald N., 157n, 174n, 179n
Michael, Stanley T., 35n, 561n
Miles, Matthew B., 93n
Miller, David W., 702n
Miller, Delbert C., 373n, 388n
Miller, Herman P., 439n, 442, 446n, 454n, 455n, 456, 457n, 459n, 460n, 463n, 467, 468n, 472
Miller, Michael M., 748
Miller, S. M., 19, 30, 74n, 300n, 390n, 393, 435, 459n, 462n, 472n, 477n, 483n, 484n, 488n, 491n, 492n, 507n, 514n
Miller, Thomas G., Jr., 729n
Miller, Walter B., 24, 213n, 218, 219, 490n
Millis, Walter, 696n
Mills, C. Wright, 4n, 14–15, 138n, 139n, 140, 329n, 482n, 709, 720, 721n
Miner, Jerry, 426n
Mischlev, E., 300n
Modigliani, Andrea, 714n, 728n
Moore, Joan W., 155n, 173n, 388n, 556n
Moore, Wilbert E., 476n, 643, 667n, 679n
Moraze, Charles, 745n
More, Sir Thomas, 124
Morgan, James N., 145n, 438n, 440n, 446n, 447, 449n, 450n, 451n, 452n, 457n, 458n, 459n, 460n, 464, 481n, 511n
Morgenstern, Oskar, 698n, 700
Morris, Terence, 214n
Morris, William, 150

Morse, N. E., 135
Mowitz, Robert J. 387n
Moynihan, Daniel P., 364n
Mugge, Robert H., 487n
Murdock, George, 365
Mushkin, Selma J., 457n
Myers, Jerome K., 300n
Myers, Richard R., 2, 3, 5, 6, 11
Myrdal, Gunnar, 8–9, 25n, 350, 358, 461, 511, 512n, 669n

Nagle, William J., 748
Nasser, Gamal Abdel, 328
Neal, Arthur G., 405n
Nehru, Jawaharlal, 679
Neu, Irene D., 194n
Neugarten, Bernice L., 18, 20, 23, 173n, 187n
Newcomb, G. E., 490n
Newman, Donald, 266n
Newman, James R., 701
Newman, Stanley L., 696n
Newmann, John von, 698n, 700
Nisbet, Robert A., 2, 22n, 139, 523n
North, Robert D., 103n., 335n
Nye, F. Ivan, 207, 213

Ohlin, Lloyd E., 24n, 69n, 70, 220, 233–234, 273n, 431n
Ohrbach, Harold L., 184n
Olsen, V. J., 213n
O'Neal, Patricia, 238n
Opler, Marvin K., 35n
Oppenheim, A., 564n
Oppenheimer, J. Robert, 721
Oppenheimer, Martin, 737n
Ornati, Oscar, 440, 447n
Orshansky, Mollie, 441n, 458n
Ortega y Gasset, José, 552n, 567n, 574, 577n
Osborne, John, 475n
Osbourne, E. S., 102n
Osgood, Charles E., 725n, 735n
O'Sullivan, T. C., 713n
Oxenfeld, Alfred R., 702n

Packard, Vance, 375n, 469
Palmore, Erdman, 25n, 451n
Park, Robert E., 1, 16n, 21n, 22, 31n
Parker, E., 564n
Parker, Theodore, 436n

Parsons, Talcott, 17n, 122n, 172n, 376n, 475
Passnow, A. Harry, 74n, 86n, 87n, 89n, 93n
Pear, Tom H., 748
Pearl, Arthur, 300n, 301n, 459n, 488n, 503n
Peterson, William, 658n
Petshek, Kirk, 398n
Pettigrew, Thomas, 93n, 219n, 225n
Pfautz, H. W., 234n
Philip, A. F., 484n
Philipson, M., 157n
Phillips, Wayne, 224n
Piliavin, Irving, 255n
Pinner, F. A., 128n
Pirenne, Henri, 664n
Plunkett, Richard J., 309n
Polsby, Nelson W., 369n
Polsky, Ned, 549
Pope, H., 131n
Possony, Stefan T., 723n
Potter, David M., 376n
Powell, Elwin H., 354, 471
Powers, Edwin, 228n
Pray, Kenneth L. M., 370n
Presthus, Robert, 384n, 387n, 388n
Prins, A. H. J., 172n
Pugin, August Welby, 150

Raiffa, Howard, 698n
Rapkin, Chester, 357, 544n
Rapoport, Anatol, 695n
Ravitz, Mel, 87n, 88n, 90
Reagan, Michael D., 466n, 470n, 479n, 480
Reckless, Walter, 230n
Redl, Fritz, 231n
Redlich, Frederick C., 300n, 302, 561n, 580n
Reeder, Leo G., 27n
Reich, Charles, 483n, 507n
Rein, Martin, 30, 390n, 462n, 472n, 483n, 484n, 507n, 514n
Reiss, Albert J., Jr., 230n, 379n
Remmers, H. H., 41
Rennie, Thomas A. C., 35n
Reynolds, Harry W., Jr., 363n
Rhodes, A. Lewis, 230n
Ridley, Jeanne Clare, 405n
Riecken, Henry W., 5n

# NAME INDEX

Riemer, Svend, 532n
Riesman, David, 161n, 171n, 482n, 549, 594n, 602n, 720, 721n, 733
Riessman, Frank, 73n, 88, 300n, 301n, 393, 459n, 486n, 488, 492n, 503n
Riley, John W., 562n
Riley, Matilda, 562n
Roberts, Bertram H., 300n
Robertson, H. M., 122n
Robins, Lee N., 238n
Robinson, Reginald, 309n
Roby, Pamela A., 426n
Rockefeller, John D., 123
Rodgers, Terry C., 25n
Rodman, Hyman, 490n
Rodwin, Lloyd, 545n
Roosevelt, Franklin Delano, 195, 426, 427–428
Roper, Elmo, 375n
Rose, Arnold, 174n, 377n
Rose, Peter I., 358, 728n
Rosenau, James N., 748
Rosenberg, Bernard, 551n, 552n, 553n, 554n, 556n, 557n, 558n, 560n, 562n, 567, 569n, 574, 605n
Rosenberg, Harold, 574
Rosenfeld, Eva, 26n
Ross, Arthur M., 152n, 153, 509n
Ross, Murray G., 370
Ross, Thomas B., 723n
Rossi, Peter H., 84, 96n, 361n, 388n, 392n, 663n
Roth, Julius, 27–28
Rothenberg, Jerome, 541n
Roucek, J. S., 159n
Rowntree, Seebohm, 486n
Roy, Donald, 132n
Royce, William S., 728n
Rufeisen, Oswald, 343
Ruskin, John, 150
Russell, James E., 73n
Rustin, Bayard, 502
Ryan, Edward J., 305n
Ryder, Norman B., 22n, 632n

St. Augustine, 120
St. Thomas Aquinas, 121
Saleem, Betty L., 74n, 426n, 446n
Samuelsson, Kurt, 122n
Sanders, Irwin T., 367n, 404n

Sarapata, A., 135n
Savard, William G., 384n
Savitz, Leonard, 214n, 219n, 266n
Sayles, Leonard R., 163
Sayre, Wallace S., 387n
Scanlon, John, 106n
Schachter, Stanley, 5n
Schaffer, Ruth Conner, 369
Schelling, Thomas C., 699n, 701, 703, 731n, 736n, 740n
Scherman, David C., 589n
Schiff, Lawrence F., 66
Schmandt, Henry J., 383n, 384n, 385n, 386n, 387n, 403n
Schmidhauser, John R., 195n
Schneider, Louis, 490n
Schnore, Leo F., 22, 31, 365n, 629n, 631n, 643n
Schorr, Alvin L., 191n, 461
Schrag, Clarence C., 272, 378n
Schramm, Wilbur, 553n, 564n, 565n
Schreiber, Daniel, 74n, 469n
Schuessler, Karl, 267n
Schumpeter, Joseph, 682
Schur, Edwin M., 8n, 256n
Schwartz, Edward, 500n
Schwartz, Morris, 293
Schwartz, Richard D., 261n
Scott, J. C., Jr., 385, 388n
Scott, W. Richard, 18n
Seagull, Arthur, 492n
Seeley, J. R., 569n
Seeman, Melvin, 139n, 404n, 405n
Sellin, Thorsten, 208n
Selznick, Gertrude, 579
Selznick, Philip, 128n, 579
Sexton, Patricia C., 73n, 93n, 487n
Shabecoff, Philip, 729
Shaeffer, Robert J., 88n, 89
Shanas, Ethel, 173n, 190n
Shaplin, Judson T., 107n, 113n
Sharp, Harry, 631n
Shaw, Clifford R., 229
Shaw, George Bernard, 485
Sheldon, Henry D., 169
Shenfield, Barbara E., 192n
Sheps, Cecil G., 369n
Shils, Edward A., 17, 553n, 570, 571, 572n, 577, 583n
Short, James F., Jr., 207, 208n, 213, 230n, 234n

NAME INDEX

Shussheim, Morton, 543, 544n
Simmons, J. L., 5n
Simmons, Leo W., 173n
Simon, Herbert A., 157n
Simpson, George, 216n, 267n, 664n
Skolnick, Jerome, 256n
Slater, Carol, 388n
Smelser, Neil J., 12n, 679n
Smigel, Erwin O., 243n
Smith, Adam, 705
Smith, Ernest A., 174n
Sokolovskii, V. D., 708n
Sontag, Susan, 586, 587n, 593, 594n
Sorokin, Pitirim A., 734n, 735n
Spaulding, John A., 216n
Spencer, Herbert, 123
Spengler, Oswald, 567
Spiegelman, M., 168n
Spier, Rosemary, 219n, 225n
Sprott, W. J. H., 375n
Srole, Leo, 35, 561n
Stalin, Joseph, 568
Stanfield, Robert E., 238n
Stanton, Alfred H., 293
Stanton, Frank N., 411n
Starkey, Marion L., 5n
Staub, Hugo, 247
Stein, Maurice, 561n, 569n
Stein, Walter, 749
Steiner, Gary, 553n
Steiner, Jesse F., 368n
Stern, Philip, 434n
Stiles, Lindley J., 107
Stinchcombe, Arthur L., 22n
Strachey, James, 659n
Strausz-Hupé, Robert, 723n, 749
Street, David, 272n
Streib, Gordon F., 136n, 173n, 182n, 190n
Strodtbeck, Fred L., 208n, 234n
Sudnow, David, 266n
Sufrin, Sidney, 426n
Sullivan, Harry Stack, 40, 140
Sumner, William Graham, 123
Sunshine, Morris H., 374n, 384n, 386n, 389n, 404n
Sussman, Marvin B., 189n, 190n, 368n, 371n
Sutherland, Edwin H., 203n, 218n, 229n, 232, 239n
Swanson, G. E., 490n
Sweetser, Dorrian Apple, 187n

Sweetser, Frank L., 412n
Swomley, John M., Jr., 730n
Sykes, Gresham M., 246, 271, 402n
Szasz, Thomas, 54n
Szilard, Leo, 716n

Taeuber, Alma F., 358, 377n
Taeuber, Irene B., 658n
Taeuber, Karl E., 358, 377n
Taft, Robert, 531, 537
Tannenbaum, Edward R., 633n
Tappan, Paul W., 263n
Tawney, R. H., 122n
Taylor, Carl C., 371n
Teller, Edward, 706, 708n, 721
Theobald, Robert, 479n
Theodorson, George A., 522n
Thomas, W. I., 706
Thompson, Charles S., 749
Thompson, Denys, 553n
Thompson, Wayne E., 136n, 182n
Thorndike, R. L., 103
Thrasher, Edwin W., 229
Tibbitts, Clark, 167n, 169, 175n, 183n, 184n, 188n, 194n, 195n
Tilgher, Adriano, 119
Timms, Noel, 484n
Titmuss, Richard, 433, 484n, 512
Tocqueville, Alexis de, 664n
Tönnies, Ferdinand, 677
Townsend, Peter, 187n, 192n, 435n
Toynbee, Arnold J., 473, 474n
Trillin, Calvin, 36n, 193n
Trotsky, Leon, 669n
Trow, Martin, 18, 23, 97n
Tumin, Melvin M., 349, 358, 552n
Turner, Ralph E., 667n
Turner, Ralph H., 12n, 216n
Twichell, Allan A., 521n
Tyler, Gus W., 212n

Urick, Ronald, 101n

Vaizez, John, 113n
Van Hoey, Leo F., 666n
Vance, P., 564n
Vander Zander, James W., 358
Vernon, P. E., 90n, 91
Veroff, Joseph, 308n
Vickrey, William, 731n
Vidich, Arthur, 569n

NAME INDEX

Vincent, Clark, 431n
Voorhees, Alan M., 402n, 424n

Wagle, Mildred K., 309n
Wahlke, John C., 195n
Wald, Patricia M., 265n
Walker, Charles R., 136n, 159n
Wallace, V. H., 749
Walters, Richard H., 227, 231
Warner, W. Lloyd, 194n, 580n
Warren, Roland, 367n
Washington, George, 719
Waskow, Arthur I., 696n
Wax, Murray L., 53n
Wax, Rosalie, 53n
Weber, Max, 121–122, 138n, 677
Weber, Robert E., 462n
Weidenbaum, Murray L., 695n, 727, 729n, 732n
Weinberg, S. Kirson, 334n
Weinstein, Karol K., 187n
Weisner, Jerome, 701
Weiss, R. S., 135
Werling, Richard, 162n
Wertham, Frederic, 6n
Wesolowski, W., 135n
Westie, Frank R., 345n
Whannel, Paddy, 618n
Wheeler, Stanton, 22, 30, 215n, 210n, 244n, 261n, 269n, 272, 273n, 275n
Whinston, Andrew B., 540n
White, David M., 551n, 552n, 553n, 554n, 556n, 557n, 558n, 560n, 562n, 567n, 569n, 605n
Whitney, Eli, 338
Whyte, William F., 20n
Whyte, William H., Jr., 482n, 569n
Wiener, Norbert, 157n
Wilder, David E., 93n
Wilensky, Harold L., 20, 125n, 130n, 131n, 134n, 141n, 411n, 561n, 563n, 578n, 604n

Wiles, P. F. D., 154
Willhelm, Sidney M., 354, 471
Williams, Raymond, 150n, 664n
Williams, Richard H., 175n
Williams, Robin M., Jr., 358
Wilner, Daniel M., 26n
Wilson, Alan T., 476n
Wilson, James Q., 254
Wilson, O. W., 253n
Wilson, Woodrow, 719, 724
Winch, Robert F., 187n
Wineman, David, 231n
Wirtz, W. W., 73n
Wise, Thomas, 723n
Witmer, Helen, 228n
Wolf, Eleanor P., 377n
Wolfbein, Seymour L., 509n
Wolff, Kurt, 17n
Wolfgang, Marvin E., 208n, 214n, 219n, 266n
Wolfle, Dael, 103n, 477n
Wood, Robert, 392
Wohlstetter, Albert, 701, 703
Woodbury, Coleman, 521n
Woodham-Smith, Cecil, 484n
Woodring, Paul, 98, 106n
Wooton, Barbara, 506
Wouk, Herman, 557
Wright, Charles R., 385n, 388n
Wright, Deil S., 387n
Wrong, Dennis H., 489, 659

Yablonsky, Lewis, 24n, 234n
Yamey, B. S., 672n
Yarrow, Marian Radke, 286n
Young, Kimball, 662n
Young, Michael, 475
Young, Roland, 402n
Young, Whitney M., Jr., 358, 477

Zawodny, J. K., 749
Zawodski, B., 130n
Zeisel, Hans, 606n
Zimmer, Basil G., 388n

Subject Index

Action for Mental Health, 308, 310
Adolescence, and crime, 213, 216–217
  future of, 74–75
  minority status of, 50–56
  and problems of sex, 45–50
  and pro-social youth, 64–67
  psychology of, 40–41
  and role of teenager, 56–64
  and school dropouts, 71–74
  socialization of, 41–45
  views of, 36–41
  see also Juvenile delinquency
Adolescent Society, 39
Aesthetic pluralism, defined, 581–582
  and popular-culture critique, 598–600
Aesthetic relationism, implementing, 612–618
  pros and cons, 606–612
Affluence, and job discontent, 150–157
  relationship to poverty, 432, 466–468
A.F.L.–C.I.O., 391, 397
Age-status system, 172–175
Aged, economic status of, 175–186
  and economics of health, 175–178
  in family setting, 186–192
  index of aging, 169(t)
  and intergenerational relations, 188–189

Aged, living arrangements of, 190–192
  position in United States society, 170–175
  and poverty, 449–452
  problems of, 35–36
  prospects for, 192–196
  as social problem, 167–170
Agriculture, collectivization of, 675
  role in economic development of new nations, 671–676
Alcoholism, 10–11
Alienation, and effective community organization, 404–406, 407
  implications of, 147–148
  incidence and sources of, 142–146
  measure of, 140–142
  and problem of work, 137–140
"Angry Young Men," 475
Antimilitarism, 721–722
Appalachia, poverty in, 430–431, 443–444
Armed forces, Nato versus East European, 712(t)
Association, differential, 524–526
Atomic Energy Commission, 721, 731
Authority, as problematic of new nations, 660
Automation, and job discontent, 157–166
  see also Cybernation

763

Bail system, 265–266
Bay of Pigs, 715, 723
Berlin, 716–717
Brinkmanship, 716

"Camp," 586
Caste system, 319–320
Catcher in the Rye, 41, 44
Children Who Hate, 231
Chinese communists, 717–718
Churches, and community organization, 397
City, mythical decline of, 532–534
  renewal of, 536–548
  urbanity and community in, 418–425
  see also Community development, Urban renewal
Civil liberties, and police efficiency, 256–257
Civil rights, legislation, 429, 499–501
  of Negroes, 339–341
Community, communities within, 363–364
  concept of, 20–22, 360–361
  decision making in, 389–390
  defined, 365–366
  myths and realities of, 361–363
  and national problems, 30–35
  theories of, 366–367
  see also Community organization
Community action programs, 507–508
Community organization, areas of futility and triviality, 390–406
  defined, 359–360, 364–365
  and development of organizational competence, 416–418
  and formal social organization, 372–374, 381
  and function of conflict, 413–415
  goals, 418–425
  grass roots, 401–406
  ideology of professional, 368–371
  and informal social organization, 374–380, 381
  patterns, participation, and performance, 381–390
  and role of federal government, 421–423
  toward effective, 406–418
Cold War, 711–719, 732–736
Community Power Structure, 369

Conflict, function of, 413–415
  See also War
Congo, political instability in, 671
Correctional systems, effects of, 273–275
  and external community, 273
  inmate culture and social structure, 271–273
  prison as social system, 268–270
Courts, 262–263
Crime, and administration of justice, 257–268
  adult careers in, 239–242, 243–249
  and correctional systems, 268–275
  and criminal law, 201–206
  and criminal responsibility, 260–262
  and data of criminology, 206–210
  and disruption of social relations, 216–217
  organized, 212
  patterns of adult, 238–243
  and police, 249–257
  and poverty, 431
  and psychopathology, 246–247
  and rehabilitation, 264
  social psychology of, 225–238
  and struggle for success, 219–223
  tradition of, 223–225
  in United States social structure, 210–225
Crime rates, by sex, age, and socioeconomic class, 213–214
Cuba, missile crisis, 715, 724
Cultural exchanges, 714
Cultural mobility, 604–606
Culture of poverty, 490–491
Cybernation, effects on aged, 178–180
  see also Automation

Defense industry, 726–727(t), 729
Delinquency, group-supported, 228–232
  and organized gangs, 212–213, 224, 232–235
  patterns of individual, 226–228
  situational, 235–238
  see also Crime, Juvenile delinquency
Democracy, and mass culture, 567–569
Demography, sphere of interest of, 627–629
  and underdeveloped areas, 648–652
  and Western growth pattern, 638–640
Denmark, delinquency in, 237

SUBJECT INDEX

Department of Defense, 720, 728–729
Department of State, 720
Desegregation, 347–356
Deterrence, nuclear, and historical pessimism, 711–719
  paradoxes in theory of, 702–710
  theory of, 698–701
Deviance, problems of, 29–30
Disarmament, 698, 699, 700, 701
  economics of, 725–739
Dr. Strangelove, 711
"Doomsday" weapons, 700, 704

Ecology, and definitions of community, 365–366
Economic development, and new nations, 668–676
  and population growth, 638
  routes to, 677–683
Economic growth, and job discontent, 148–150
Economic Opportunity Act, 426, 429, 446, 507
Economy, United States, and conversion to peace, 725–739
  current trends in, 480–484
  and major contractors of defense-space, 726–727(t), 729
  and poverty reduction, 494–503
Education, college preparatory, 78–79, 96–108
  crisis in secondary, 99–108
  demands for reform of, 77–78, 83–84, 114–116
  and development of potentials, 79–80
  equality in, 80–85
  and growing income inequalities, 469–471
  history of secondary, 96–99
  impact of new modes of, 109–114
  and lifetime income, 353(t)
  and reducing poverty, 503–505
  and slum schools, 85–95
  state expenditures for, 348(t)
  see also Schools
Electronic data processing, 157–158, 163
Elmtown's Youth, 39–40
Emancipation Proclamation, 339
Emotional marginality, of teen-agers, 59–60

Employment, *see* Labor force, Unemployment, Work
Equality of opportunity, 474–477
Essay on Population, An, 633
Ethnic minorities, *see* Minorities, Race relations

Fail-Safe, 711
Fair Deal, 429
Families, characteristics of heads of poor, 457–459, 464(t)
  and delinquency patterns, 227–228
  intergenerational relations of, 188–189
Farm areas, poverty in, 446–448
Federal Bureau of Investigation, 208, 211, 212
Federal Housing Authority, 532–533
Federal Narcotics Bureau, 8, 12
Federal Urban Renewal Program, 537
Fertility, and poverty, 658
  variables through which culture affects, 650(t)
Foreign policy, United States, 722–725

Game theory, 698, 700, 702, 703
Geriatrics, *see* Aged
Gerontology, *see* Aged
Government, local, and community organization, 391–392
  United States, and economy, 482–483
  and foreign policy, 722–725
  and reduction of poverty, 493–517
Growing Up Absurd, 39

Health, population having chronic conditions, 177(t)
  and problems of aged, 175–178
High culture, audience of, 555
  debased by mass culture, 552, 557–560
  sociological analysis of, 579–600
Historical fallacy, and criticism of mass culture, 576–579
Hostility, and minorities, 51–52, 58
Housing, basis of pattern distribution of, 520, 522–523
  and beginnings of urban renewal, 536–548
  codes, 521, 539–540
  and confusion of norms, 519–521
  middle-class view of, 517–519

Housing, political definitions of problem of, 528–536
  social significance of, 521–528
  see also Slums, Urban renewal
Humanitarianism, and criminal justice, 258–259, 263–264

Identity, and alienation, 138–139
Income, of aged, 451–452
  distribution of, 442–463
  levels of, by families, 443(t)
  national, and population growth, 636–638
  percent distribution by color, 352(t)
  percent received by ranked families, 468(t)
  and poverty, 432–434
  by race and education, 353(t)
  and reducing poverty, 510–515
Indians, American, plight of, 444–445
Industrialization, and aged, 168–169
  as goal of new nations, 667–671
  problems in, 683–694
  social problems accompanying, 668, 677–678
  and societal similarity, 678–683
Invisible Man, The, 351
IQ tests, 334
  and lower-class children, 90–93

Japan, economic development of, 669
Jews, 318, 328–329, 333, 343
Job Corps, 508
John Birch Society, 568
Justice, administration of, 257–268
  changing conceptions of, 258–259
  and changing institutional structures, 259–264
  and crime prevention, 266–268
  quality of, 264–266
Juvenile delinquency, 12
  aspects of, 67–71
  and poverty, 431
  as synonym for youth problems, 38
  and youth gangs, 24, 212–213, 224, 232–235
  see also Adolescence

Labor force, shifts in distribution of, 478–479
  status in, and poverty, 459–463

Labor force, withdrawals of segments from, 126–131
Labor unions, 428
  and community organization, 396–397
  and featherbedding, 150–157
Leisure, and cultural mobility, 604–606
  uses of, 549–550
Life and Labor of the People of London, 427
Life in the Crystal Palace, 482
Life cycle, aspects of, viewed as social problems, 29
Lonely Crowd, The, 720
Lysistrata, 46

McCarthyism, 716
McNaghten rule, 261
Magazines, and taste cultures, 580, 585, 586, 587, 588, 590, 593, 594
Manhattan Bail Project, 265–266
Manpower Development and Training Act, 429, 508
Mass culture, defined, 550–552
  effects on audience, 552, 560–567
  effects on high culture, 552, 557–560
  and mass society, 569–572
  negative character of, 552, 553–557
  reinterpretations of critique of, 598–600
  as social problem, 619–620
  sources and biases of critique of, 572–579
  see also Mass media, Popular culture, Taste cultures
Mass media, and community organization, 373, 394–395, 419
  creators of, 551, 555–557
  influence of high culture on, 596–597
  and information, 609–610
  and lower-middle culture, 590
  and media content, 562–563, 566
  standardization of, 555
  and subcultural programming, 612–618
  see also Mass culture, Popular culture, *specific media*
Medicare, 512
Mental health, and job satisfaction, 137
  see also Mental illness
Mental Health Study Act, 308
Mental illness, and criminal responsibility, 260–262

SUBJECT INDEX

Mental illness, historical perspective of, 279–283
magnitude of, 277–279
and mass media, 561
and mental hospitals, 291–295
and mental retardation, 287–288
national trends in, 307–313
new treatment trends in, 293–295
and preventive psychiatry, 295–300
psychiatric view of, 283–287
relations to other social problems, 300–307
and role of psychiatrist, 289–291
and social reform, 307
see also Mental health
Meritocracy, The, 475
Migration, internal, problems of, 631–632
Militarism, and politics, 719–725
Minimum-wage laws, 499–501
Minorities, attitudes toward, 50–54
and crime, 214
defined, 320
European, in United States, 320–323, 325
Negroes, 324–329, 337–341, 344–347, 351–356
Puerto Ricans in United States, 323, 326
social definitions of, 341–347
Southern white mountaineer, 323–324, 325–326
see also Jews, Negroes
Mirage of Health, 305
Mobilization for Youth, 235
Monroe Doctrine, 723
Movies, 485, 711
and taste cultures, 551, 555, 580, 585, 588, 591–592, 593, 594
Music, and taste cultures, 558
My Fair Lady, 485

Narcotics, 8, 10, 14
and law, 204
and social disorganization, 25–26
National Housing Act of 1937, 530, 537
National Institute of Mental Health, 308
National Mental Health Act, 307
National Urban League, 477
Nationalism, and new nations, 687
Nations, basis of comparison of, 663–665
classes of, 665–666

Nations, versus societies, 662–665
see also New nations
Negroes, 8, 51, 52, 58, 324–329, 471
and crime, 214
development of attitudes toward, 337–341
educational opportunities of, 76–79, 83–85, 93–95
and female-headed families, 458
and growing income inequality, 471
and integration goals, 24–25
and intelligence, 334–335, 347–349
and low-cost housing, 529, 531, 542
and migration problems, 631
and poverty, 453–457
social definitions of, 344–347
social revolution of, 351–356
urbanization of, and political power, 430
white stereotypes about, 328(t)
see also Minorities, Race relations
Neighborhoods, and differential association, 524–526
New Civilian Militarists, 701, 702, 703, 705–707, 709
New Deal, 427–428
New nations, compared with preindustrial Europe, 678
defined, 655–656
defining problems of, 656–660
and economic development goals, 666–683
and national integration, 684–687
problematics and change in, 660–662
recruitment and training in, 691–694
route to industrialization for, 681–683
social solidarity in, 687–691
See also Underdeveloped areas
Nuclear conflict, casualties in, 697(t)
versus conventional war, 695–698
and strategy of deterrence, 698–710

Occupational groups, and alienation, 143, 146(t)
and job satisfaction, 134(t)
see also Careers
Office of Economic Opportunity, 508
Oliver Twist, 71
On Thermonuclear War, 701
Organization, concept of, 17–19
see also Community organization

SUBJECT INDEX

Peace Corps, and preventive psychiatry, 295–300, 310
Penal codes, 205–206
Penal reform, 258–260, 263–264
Police, and civil liberties, 256–257
 and crime rates, 250–251
 interaction with offenders, 255
 organization of systems, 253–255
 and public, 251–253
Politics, and militarism, 719–725
Polls, 131, 134–135, 224–225
Poor Laws of 1834, 484
Popular culture, sociological analysis of, 579–600
 see also Mass culture, Mass media, Taste cultures
Population, concept of, 22–23
 defining problems of, 625–629
 estimated world increases, 637(t)
 expansion and structural changes, 477–484
 growth and national income, 636–638
 growth in world perspective, 633–638
 and problems of underdeveloped areas, 643–652
 selected United States problems of, 629–633
 and sociological factors of growth, 640–643
 toward new policy on, 652–654
Poverty, and aged, 184–186
 characteristics and analysis of poor, 445–465
 characteristics of family heads, 464(t)
 defined, 435–437
 in farm areas, 446–448
 and high fertility rates, 658
 historical view of, 426–429
 and income, 432–434
 and individual rehabilitation, 486–487
 and inequality, 465–484
 and mental illness, 302–303, 309
 and plight of poor, 443–445
 policy choices to reduce, 493–517
 and public housing, 530–532
 rediscovery of, 429–432
 regional breakdown of, 448–449
 relationship to affluence, 432
 scope of, 437–442
 societal views of, 484–488
 typology of poor, 488–492

Preventive psychiatry, and crisis theory, 296–300
 and role of psychiatrists, 295–296
Primary group, defined, 17
Prison Community, The, 271
Prisons, see Correctional systems
Privatization, and war, 696, 734
Protestant Ethic, 119, 121–123, 182
Psychiatry, see Mental illness, Preventive psychiatry
Psychoanalysis, see Mental illness
Psychopathology, 246–247
Puberty, social challenge of, 45–50
Public housing, history of, 530–532
Public welfare, 383, 511–512
 and aged, 181, 451–452
 and community organization, 392–394
 and female-headed families, 460
 and poverty levels, 439–440
 and public opinion, 485–487
 reducing payments of, 444
 and unemployed, 129–130
 and wage supplementation, 463
Puerto Ricans, as United States minority, 323, 326
Pygmalion, 485

Race, anthropological view of, 330–333, 336
 biological view of, 329–333, 336
 and housing, 520
 and physical characteristics, 331(t)
 and social structure, 333–337
 sociology of, 337–347
 as subculture, 341–344
 see also Minorities, Negroes, Race relations
Race relations, and desegregation, 347–356
 as instance of ethnocentrism, 317–320
 as social problem, 7, 326–329
 and United States minorities, 320–326
 see also Negroes
Reformers, and community organization, 395–396, 397–398
Rehabilitation, of criminals, 264
 individual, 486–487
 and reducing poverty, 506–510
Relocation, 542
Renewing Our Cities, 536
Retirement, 127–129, 180–186

SUBJECT INDEX

"Revolution of rising expectations," 676–677
Rhodesia, and problem of national integration, 688
Role structure, and crime, 217–219
Russia, economic development of, 669, 682
  see also Soviet Union

Schools, and adolescent problems, 39, 41, 49–50, 54–55
  and dropouts, 71–74
  in slums, 85–95
  see also Education
Separate Peace, A, 44
Sex offenders, 203–204, 205–206, 261–262
Sex ratio, 3, 5
Sexual relationships, of adolescents, 45–50
Slavery, 337–339, 341
Slums, and culture of defeat, 85–95
  clearance of, 536–537
  and mental illness, 305–306
  and educational opportunities, 77–79, 83–85
  persistence of, 534–536
  see also Urban renewal
Social Darwinism, 123
Social mobility, 377–378
  defined, 19
Social organization, *see* Community organization
Social pathology, 4
Social problems, classification of, 28–31
  and contribution of social science, 23–28
  defined, 1–11
  development of, 11–14
  social context of, 14–23
Social psychology, of crime, 225–238
Social relations, disruption of, and crime, 216–217
Social security, 181, 185, 511–512
Social stratification, 375–377
  inequality and opportunity within, 474–477
Social structure, of new nations, 687–691
Social system, concept of, 16–17
  of prisons, 268–273
Socialists, as critics of mass culture, 574–577

Socialization, and conventional war, 696
  social function of, 41–45
Society, concept of, 16–17
  versus nation, 662–665
Society of Captives, The, 271
Sociological theory, 15–16
Sociology, perspectives of, 1
Soviet Union, and Cold War tactics, 713–719
  and strategy of deterrence, 699, 708–709
  and useless work, 154
  see also Russia
Speenhamland Law of 1795, 463, 484
Stalinism, 716
Status, and alienation, 143, 144–145 (t)
  structure and crime, 217–219
Strategic Air Command, 317, 720
Stratification system, concept of, 19–20
Success, and crime, 219–223

Taste cultures, consumer-oriented high, 586–587
  creator-oriented high, 584–586
  defined, 551, 582–584
  evaluation of, 600–619
  lower, 590–593
  lower-lower, 593
  lower-middle, 589–590
  social structure of, 593–598
  upper-middle, 588–589
Taxation, and income redistribution, 498
  and reducing poverty, 495
Technological revolution, and teaching, 109–114
Television and radio, and taste cultures, 555, 585, 592, 593, 595
Theater, and taste cultures, 556, 588, 597–598, 611
Theories of Adolescence, 40
Thermonuclear age, *see* Nuclear conflict, War
Title I, 537, 541
Totalitarianism, and mass culture, 567–569

Underdeveloped areas, demographic transition of, 637
  population problems in, 643–652
  see also New nations

Unemployment, 15
  creating jobs to reduce poverty, 501–503
  and educational and occupational obsolescence, 127–128
  Negro, 454–455
  see also Work
Unions, labor, *see* Labor unions
Urban renewal, assumptions behind, 538–541
  of business districts, 543–544, 547
  effect on low-cost housing, 541–543
  failure of, 546–548
  initial congressional action on, 536–538
  and mental illness, 305–306
  and planning, 544–546
Urbanization, and crime, 214
  as population problem, 631–633

Vocational Education Act of 1964, 504
Voluntary associations, 378–380, 385, 388
  and meaningful community organization, 398–401
Voting, 384–385
  studies, 566

War, and antiwar sentiment, 719
  conventional versus nuclear, 695–698
  and conversion to peace, 725–739
  historical factors in game of, 710–719
  limited, 708
  and need for political cooperation, 739–747
  see also Cold War, Nuclear conflict
Welfare Act of 1962, 507
West Side Story, 70
Wolfenden report, 202*n*, 205
Work, and alienation, 137–148
  economic growth and job discontent, 148–150
  history of meaning of, 119–125
  and involuntarily retired and unemployed, 126–131
  and job satisfaction, 131–137
  modern propensity to, 125–126
  as social problem, 118–119
  solutions to problems of, 160–164
  useless, 150–157
World problems, 31

Youth, and employment, 508–509